Religion and Public Reasons

Works of John Finnis available from
Oxford University Press

Reason in Action
Collected Essays: Volume I

Intention and Identity
Collected Essays: Volume II

Human Rights and Common Good
Collected Essays: Volume III

Philosophy of Law
Collected Essays: Volume IV

Religion and Public Reasons
Collected Essays: Volume V

Natural Law and Natural Rights
Second Edition

Aquinas
Moral, Political, and Legal Theory

Nuclear Deterrence, Morality and Realism
with Joseph Boyle and Germain Grisez

RELIGION AND PUBLIC REASONS

Collected Essays: Volume V

John Finnis

OXFORD
UNIVERSITY PRESS

Great Clarendon Street, Oxford, OX2 6DP,
United Kingdom

Oxford University Press is a department of the University of Oxford.
It furthers the University's objective of excellence in research, scholarship,
and education by publishing worldwide. Oxford is a registered trade mark of
Oxford University Press in the UK and in certain other countries

First published 2011
First published in paperback 2013

Impression: 1

Published in the United States of America by Oxford University Press
198 Madison Avenue, New York, NY 10016, United States of America

British Library Cataloguing in Publication Data
Data available

ISBN 978–0–19–958009–5
ISBN 978–0–19–968998–9 (pbk.)
ISBN 978–0–19–968993–4 (set)

Printed in Great Britain by
CPI Group (UK) Ltd, Croydon, CR0 4YY

PREFACE

The earliest of the essays collected in these five volumes dates from 1967, the latest from 2010. The chronological Bibliography of my publications, near the end of each volume, shows how the collected essays are distributed across the volumes. But each volume also contains some essays previously unpublished.

Many of the essays appear with new titles. When the change is substantial, the original published title is noted at the beginning of the essay; the original can of course always also be found in the Bibliography.

Revision of previously published work has been restricted to clarification. Where there seems need for substantive qualification or retractation, I have said so in an endnote to the essay or, occasionally, in a bracketed footnote. Unless the context otherwise indicates, square brackets signify an insertion made for this Collection. Endnotes to particular essays have also been used for some updating, especially of relevant law. In general, each essay speaks from the time of its writing, though the dates given in the Table of Contents are dates of publication (where applicable) not composition—which sometimes was one or two years earlier.

I have tried to group the selected essays by theme, both across and within the volumes. But there is a good deal of overlapping, and something of each volume's theme will be found in each of the other volumes. The Index, which like the Bibliography (but not the 'Other Works Cited') is common to all volumes, gives some further indication of this, though it aspires to completeness only as to names of persons. Each volume's own Introduction serves to amplify and explain that volume's title, and the bearing of its essays on that theme.

For the paperback edition the Index common to all volumes has been significantly enhanced in its coverage of subjects.

CONTENTS

LIST OF ABBREVIATIONS

AAS	Acta Apostolicae Sedis
AG	Vatican II, *Ad Gentes* (Decree on Missionary Activity, 1965)
AJJ	American Journal of Jurisprudence
Aquinas	1998d: John Finnis, *Aquinas: Moral, Political and Legal Theory* (OUP)
CAP	E.R. Norman, 'Christianity in Politics', in Maurice Cowling (ed.). *Conservative Essays* (London: Cassell)
CCC	*Catechism of the Catholic Church* ([1997], London: Geoffrey Chapman, 1999)
CDF	Congregation for the Doctrine of the Faith
CL	H.L.A. Hart, *The Concept of Law* (OUP, 1961)
CMP	Germain Grisez, *The Way of the Lord Jesus* vol. 1 *Christian Moral Principles* (Chicago: Franciscan Herald Press, 1983)
CSE	E.R. Norman, *Church and Society in England 1770–1970* (OUP, 1976)
CTS	Catholic Truth Society
CUP	Cambridge: Cambridge University Press
CWO	E.R. Norman, *Christianity and the World Order* (OUP, 1978)
DH	Vatican II, *Dignitatis Humanae* (Declaration on Religious Liberty, 1965)
DMQ	Germain Grisez, *The Way of the Lord Jesus* vol. 3 *Difficult Moral Questions* (Chicago: Franciscan Herald Press, 1997)
D-S	Henricus Denzinger, *Enchiridion Symbolorum Definitionum et Declarationum de Rebus Fidei et Morum* (ed. Adolfus Schönmetzer) (34th edn, Barcelona and New York: Herder, 1967)
DV	Vatican II, *Dei Verbum* (Dogmatic Constitution on Divine Revelation) (1965)
FHG	Mary Geach and Luke Gormally (eds), *Faith in a Hard Ground: Essays on Religion, Philosophy and Ethics by G.E.M. Anscombe* (Exeter, UK, and Charlottesville, VA: Imprint Academic, 2008)

FoE	1983a: John Finnis, *Fundamentals of Ethics* (OUP; Washington, DC: Georgetown University Press)
GS	Vatican II, *Gaudium et Spes* (Pastoral Constitution on the Church in the Modern World) (1965)
Hermeneias	Aquinas, *Commentarium in libros Perihermeneias expositio* [Commentary on Aristotle's *De Interpretatione* (1269–72)]
HUP	Cambridge, Mass: Harvard University Press
In Anima	Aquinas, *In libros De Anima Expositio* [Commentary on Aristotle, *De Anima*] (c. 1268)
LCL	Germain Grisez, *The Way of the Lord Jesus* vol. 2 *Living a Christian Life* (Quincy: Franciscan Press, 1993)
LE	Ronald Dworkin, *Law's Empire* (HUP; London: Fontana, 1986)
LQR	Law Quarterly Review
NE	Aristotle, *Nicomachean Ethics*
NLNR	1980a: John Finnis, *Natural Law and Natural Rights* (2nd edn, OUP, 2011)
NDMR	1987g: John Finnis, Joseph Boyle, and Germain Grisez, *Nuclear Deterrence, Morality and Realism* (OUP, 1987)
OUP	Oxford: Oxford University Press (including Clarendon Press)
Sent.	Aquinas, *Scriptum super Libros Sententiarum Petri Lombardiensis* [Commentary on the Sentences [Opinions or Positions of the Church Fathers] of Peter Lombard] (c. 1255)
ScG	Aquinas, *Summa contra Gentiles* [A Summary against the Pagans] (c. 1259–65?)
ST	Aquinas, *Summa Theologiae* [A Summary of Theology] (c. 1265–73)

THE COVER PICTURE

View of Lake Torrens, 22 August by S.T. Gill (Adelaide, 1846).

This water colour depicts John Horrocks with, on his right, the artist, gazing out over the dry salt-bed of vast Lake Torrens from its southern shore, on a late-winter morning. Horrocks stands six foot two inches tall, a man of initiative, action, and vision. Educated in England and France; he emigrated in 1839 to South Australia from Vienna, where his restless English family had lately settled. He established a farm, a township, an Anglican church, and a vineyard in the Clare Valley, eighty miles north of Adelaide. Now, in August 1846, he is leading a six-man expedition 125 miles further north, in search of new agricultural lands. The two men have set off in early dawn from the expedition's new base camp, established under the western slopes of the Flinders Ranges the previous day. After riding about twelve miles west-north-west, they are not far from the mouth where water flows from the immense lake in those very rare years when it fills.

Gill is sketching; looking ahead, he sees the scene from behind them. When he did the painting itself later in the same year, he knew the aftermath. At the end of August, Horrocks, Gill, and another had mounted another small foray, further west across even more inhospitable country to a smaller lake-bed which Horrocks named Lake Gill (now Lake Dutton). There the expedition's camel, the first to be used in Australian exploration, knocked Horrocks's gun, which went off and wounded him. Gill and the rest struggled back with him to his farm at Clare, where he died in late September of gangrene, aged 28.

INTRODUCTION

'The causes of atheism', said Francis Bacon, who knew quite a few atheists, 'are: divisions in religion...[and] scandal of priests...[and] lastly, learned times, specially with peace and prosperity'.[1] The essay on the subject by this prodigiously learned man begins, genially,

I had rather believe all the fables in the Legend and the Alcoran than that this universal frame is without a mind. And therefore God never wrought a miracle to [refute] atheism, because his ordinary works [refute] it. It is true, that a little philosophy inclineth man's mind to atheism; but depth in philosophy bringeth men's minds about to religion.[2]

In removing his account of atheism's causes from his essay 'On Superstition' to his companion essay 'On Atheism', Bacon added to the former a closing sentence: 'There is a superstition in avoiding superstition, when men think to do best if they go furthest from the superstition formerly received...'.[3]

Essay 1 sec. II says something (in the context of a later and more famous scientist) to make explicit, and amplify, Bacon's implied argument for affirming a divine creator and providential sustaining of the universe. Moreover, the final chapter both in *Natural Law and Natural Rights* and in *Aquinas* offers direct, explicit argumentation for the same conclusion. So I will not reiterate that argumentation here. Nor does it seem necessary to discuss here the scandals of priests, or the relevance of widespread but uncritical and undisciplined learning amid the complacency of wealth and peace. More important is the doubt that arises from 'divisions in religion'. For this thought may occur to anyone: Isn't it unreasonable to suppose that,

---

[1] Arber (ed.), 346; the passage's first appearance is in the 1612 edn of Bacon's *Essays* in the essay 'On Superstition'; for his 1625 edn, Bacon transferred it to the essay 'On Atheism'. During and since the eighteenth-century Enlightenment, but never before then, some have said that Bacon was a covert atheist; against this hypothesis, see e.g. Matthews, *Theology and Science in the Thought of Francis Bacon*, and McKnight, *The Religious Foundations of Francis Bacon's Thought*.

[2] Arber (ed.), 330, the opening of 'On Atheism' in the 1612 edn; the 1625 edn adds another example of fables. Bacon's word for 'refute' is 'convince'. The 'Legend' is the *Legenda [Aurea] Sanctorum*, the wholly uncritical, indeed myth-ridden set of hagiographies put out c. 1260 by the Archbishop of Genoa.

[3] Arber (ed.), 349.

of all the thousands of forms of religious belief, one and only one is true?
How can it be reasonable to suppose that the form of religion in which one
was raised, or which one's society cultivates, is true (while all others are
false)? In the face of myriad religious claims, isn't the *simple* solution, or at
least *presumption*, that they all are false?

As a matter of logic the doubt is unimpressive. For the same can be
said of all true scientific, logical, mathematical, and historical positions:
each position is true while countless alternative beliefs that have been or
might be held are not true. But there is more to be said. *Atheism is true* just
to the extent that it denies that the divine nature and activity proposed in
each of the countless mistaken religions exist precisely as those religions
respectively propose. That affirmation of atheism's truth is compatible
with saying that all those *mistaken religions are sound* and correct insofar as
they deny atheism's assertion that beyond the world knowable by natural
science's methods there is no transcendent reality on which that world is
radically dependent. Again, many think: given the probable non-existence
of any transcendent reality whose wisdom and creative intention could be
a source and objective correlate of moral truth, there can be no truth or
objectivity in claims of moral obligation. We can and should reply: every
religion which affirms that there can be and are some true judgments of
moral obligation and responsibility affirms a position more coherent (than
atheism's or strong agnosticism's position) with the importance of getting
some right answer to the philosophical, anthropological, moral, and legal
questions discussed in the previous four volumes.

Desire to *simplify* the issues with which philosophy, history, culture, and
one's own individual experience and learning present one in confronting
the most basic religious questions, and to simplify them by a single,
sweepingly exclusory presumption, is a temptation not a truth-finding
guide. If succumbed to, it is by Bacon's standard a kind of superstition.

I. RELIGION IN PUBLIC REASON AND LAW

'Religion' is shorthand for judgments about what explains not only the
existence and intelligibility of the entire universe but also the real possibility,
worth, and responsibility of seeking answers to one's questions about
existence, intelligibility, and worth (and worthlessness); and for practices
judged appropriately responsive to the transcendent explanatory realities
affirmed, however darkly, in those judgments. Religion is fundamentally
an operation of reason, 'theoretical' and 'practical' (and practical because
directed towards choosing and acting). To be sure, reason operating at its
limits—but reasonably confident that doing so is more reasonable than any

simplifying declaration that approaching the limits is out of bounds. And since it is a matter of reason, religion shares in reason's radically public character. For: reason is about truth (and avoiding falsity and nonsense), and a primary mark (though not criterion) of a true judgment is that under ideal conditions (of freedom from distraction, prejudice, confusion, and want of data) *everyone* would concur in it. Actual epistemic conditions being far from ideal, the diversity of religious beliefs, almost all of which must (because conflicting) have some measure of falsity, is a readily explicable, 'predictable' diversity.

Bacon ends his essay on atheism with Cicero's reflection that the Romans had prevailed over every other nation and people because of their understanding of this one truth: that everything is ruled and governed by the mysterious divine power (*numine*) of the immortal gods—and, besides their understanding, their fitting response to it: reverence, and 'religion'.[4] We should perhaps translate 'religion', a word still fresh in Cicero's time, as signifying a kind of gratitude that human existence has a meaning that is not ours to invent. And the Romans, above all others, had greatness of spirit ('Magnanimitye'), Bacon reflects. His reader knows that not too long after Cicero the Roman spirit, despite many hesitations and resistances, began its opening out to the larger greatness of spirit made possible by the mysterious but earthy and public self-disclosure of the *Numen* as, not the many immortal gods, but the one triune God conversing and covenanting, through human persons, first with Israel and then with all peoples willing to hear and respond. A millennium further on, Thomas Aquinas states the fundamental relation between reason and this public divine revelation: if you are discoursing or debating with persons who accept the testimony to divine revelation, you can appeal to the record of that testimony in all its detail; but if you are discoursing or debating with persons who do not, you must appeal solely to natural reason.

Reason is at its most obviously public insofar as it uses data, concepts, and forms of argumentation that are available to all without regard to testimony about the one-off interventions in history by the universe's transcendent source of nature (including our natural capacity for reason). That is what Aquinas called 'natural reason'. But reason does not run out, or become non-public, when reasons appear for accepting the testimony of witnesses to the one-off, and the divine-human communication it testifies to. Much of the message ('public revelation') simply confirms what is accessible (with more or less difficulty) to natural reason; other parts of

---

[4] '…pietate ac religione, atque hac una sapientia, quod deorum immortalium numine omnia regi gubernarique perspeximus…': *De haruspicum responsis* [prob. 56 BC], ix, 19; Arber (ed.), 340.

revelation are more or less 'counter-intuitive' (to use a modern jargon), though they would be unworthy of acceptance if they were internally inconsistent or contradicted anything that natural reason can know with certainty. To be fit to be believed, everything must be exposed to the best investigation one can muster; where conditions allow, this investigation should proceed in the light of unfettered inquiry and debate in institutions specially designed to foster consideration of objections. So the fact and content of revelation, like natural reason's contribution to philosophy, sciences, and history, should be matters of fully public access (no secret evidence or doctrines), scholarship, and discourse.

Since reason is in all these respects inherently public, there is no real need for the phrase 'public reason'. As the first endnote to essay I.16 sets out (in words taken largely from 2005e), the phrase has a curious history. Hobbes uses it to signify one aspect of the totalitarian state control he envisages as appropriate in relation to religious claims. Milton puts the phrase on the lips of Satan at his most cynical. Nearly a century later, Rousseau uses it as a synonym for the state law that binds a judge; a generation later, Kant says that the public use of one's reason (as a learned person addressing the public) must always be free; and at the dawn of the nineteenth century Jefferson envisages public knowledge and opinion about the actions of government as a 'bar of public reason'. None of these usages—each in any case fleeting—approaches the notion ambitiously elaborated and promoted by Rawls. The essence of Rawls's project is restrictive; certain kinds of *true* and philosophically *warranted* propositions must be excluded from the processes of public deliberation and decision on the ground that they are not sufficiently widely accepted. The equivocations and arbitrariness of Rawls's argument are detailed in essay I.16 and need not be repeated here.

But the problem to which Rawls offers so oversimplified a solution is certainly real: the standing possibility that political community and its underlying civil society will be torn apart by civil strife between adherents of different religions or religious creeds. Bacon's essay on superstition, as revised in 1625, hints at the problem; an adherent of the Protestant (Anglican) state religion, he suggests, albeit mildly, that the nation's old religion is superstitious and then, by his final addition about superstitiously excessive and populist reactions against superstition, he indirectly condemns the ever more powerful Puritans. In fact, within twenty years, the English state would be wracked by a sequence of civil wars, its constitution overthrown, and Bacon's form of Christianity dissolved at Puritan hands. The new order was itself soon widely judged excessive, and church and constitution were restored in a lightly modified form consolidated a generation later with the help of a foreign invading force. And in all this, England escaped more lightly than many other nations before and since.

The problem of (in short) religion's place in public and political order, has achieved a provisional but widespread and attractive resolution. This resolution, as it exists at the time and places addressed in these essays, rejects the Anglican doctrine that the state's law and government should directly rule the nation's religion, and the Puritan doctrine that the nation's religious assemblies of right-believing and godly people should control the state. It is more like the perennial Catholic doctrine that the secular and religious realms exist in parallel, within the heart and mind of the believer and in public forms—church and state—each free from the supervisory management of the other. The feel and to some extent the content of the resolution differ from nation to nation depending on whether its people adhere very generally to one church (as in Ireland for the two generations after its constitution-making of 1937) or are as religiously divided as the United States, Australia, or India. But at bottom it is the same resolution, and it confronts two standing problems, one inbuilt, the other external.

The inbuilt problem is the one complained of by the monarch whom Bacon served in great offices of state. James I, addressing the first Parliament of his reign in 1604, acknowledged that his people belonged to three religions, as Protestants, Puritans, or Catholics, and denounced the political doctrine of the last-mentioned, a doctrine entailing that he and his law and government—any secular law and government—could have *only half* their loyalty:

As long as they are disconformable in Religion from us, they cannot be but half my subjects, be able to do but half service, and I to want the best half of them, which is their souls.[5]

The modern resolution, as I am calling it, rejects James's complaint, or at any rate his solution: state control of religious institutions and of private religious observance. But it is left with his problem. Religious loyalty is now not simply to the numinous immortal gods of our people, but to a message delivered with an authority believed divine, addressed to each

---

[5] James I, *Speech to the Parliament... 19 March 1603* [= 1604], C3. This followed his statement at York on Easter Day, 24 April 1603, on his way from Scotland to ascend the throne of England; Catholic courtiers having absented themselves from the service of the state church in York Minster, James declared: 'Who cannot pray with me cannot love me'. Shakespeare appears to comment ironically on both statements by telling the well-worn story of King Leir's [Lear's] love test for his three daughters in a new form, so that the (by play's end obviously Catholic) test-failing good daughter is for the first time furnished with an argument for refusing to match her sisters' maximal professions of love: 'Why have my sisters husbands, if they say / They love you all? Haply, when I shall wed, / That lord whose hand must take my plight shall carry / *Half* my love with him, *half* my care and duty': *King Lear* 1.1.98. The lord who does take Cordelia's plight in marriage has, like his rival (Burgundy), the name of a country and state (France).

person personally, and speaking of an eternal life begun and definitively affected, for better or worse, by one's choices and actions in this earthly, secular world. Whether or not the pastors dedicated to transmitting the message and administering the religious assemblies and cult make public declarations about the bearing of the revealed message on the state's affairs, government, and law, individual believers can and presumably should make such judgments for themselves. And such judgments may conflict with those of others, and with the judgments given authoritative secular form as laws and policies of state. That is the problem addressed, so clumsily, by Rawlsian 'political liberalism'.

The extrinsic problem is that the resolution itself may be attacked. For much of the twentieth century it was fiercely attacked by National Socialism and Bolshevism, whose fundamental thesis about all this is now taken up again by scientistic atheists. Religion is from top to bottom a falsehood, and a crippling distraction of the people (a term meant differently by Nazis and Communists) from its proper destiny, or of individuals from 'enjoying their life'.[6] So it is unjust for the state to allow children to be educated in a religious faith, or to permit the dissemination of religious claims or any but the most private religious ceremonies or manifestations. Alternatively, and of comparable contemporary relevance, there is religious rejection of the resolution, notably by those who put their faith in the message and vividly unambiguous example of a prophetic migration from which they date the era. For that migration resulted in conquest, near and far, and in installation of a unitary law, conceived as divine, regulating the whole of life, repudiating the resolution's fundamental division between secular and religious, and acknowledging no *de jure* boundaries short of the whole world. Rawlsian liberalism, being 'political not metaphysical', does not pretend to have anything to say to any of the secular or religious believers who reject the resolution.

The tensions intrinsic to the resolution are explored from different angles in a number of essays in this volume. Essay 4 ('Religion and State') considers the resolution directly, especially the form in which it is articulated and ratified by the central religion of our civilization. Essay 16 recalls and replays a historic moment—the Gladstone v. Newman debate—in the modern appropriation of the resolution; and points again, in its own way, to the ineluctability of tension at the resolution's complex core. If the fundamentally dualist structure of the resolution is kept in

---

[6] 'There's probably no god, so stop worrying and enjoy your life': the 'Atheist Bus Campaign' slogan launched by Richard Dawkins and the British Humanist Association on the Feast of the Epiphany 2009. (The 'probably' was demanded by the bus networks' marketing agency, on the plea that the state's 'advertising codes' required 'a grey area'.)

view—accepting the 'half–half' that James I repudiated—the tensions surfacing whenever a general and needed state law impinges on religious belief or organization, or a religiously motivated and reasonable individual or group decision is made to resist state law, are tensions that can be lived through without collapse, on either side, into the simplicity of secularist or theocratic monism. Essays 1, 2, 3, and 5 all explore the fragility and insufficiency of Rawlsian and other, more openly secularist conceptions of the resolution, conceptions that veer towards a dissolution of it by embracing the untruth of atheism or 'hard' agnosticism. And essay 1, like essay 4, considers in its final parts the extrinsic threat to the resolution.

Essay 6 is unlike these others, since it is addressed to a Catholic audience. In its last section it touches, like essay 21 ('The "Consistent Ethic of Life"'), on an under-discussed issue: the limits to the authority of bishops and other clerics to propose to the faithful in their care moral-political positions which rest on judgments on empirical or predictive issues about which clerics have no specific competence to judge. These essays conclude that such proposals should be framed carefully in conditional or hypothetical form, leaving to those addressed the formation of the factual judgments necessary—as with all practical syllogisms—to reach a conclusion. This is particularly the case with the application of affirmative moral norms (of which 'feed the poor' and 'befriend the alien' are only two among very many), an application which is always dependent on consideration of circumstances: causalities, commitments, conditions, consequences.... The history of Christendom is marked by very many examples of well-intentioned clerical presumption in secular affairs, to the prejudice both of the authentic clerical mission to bring their people to salvation, and of the political affairs of the state in which they exercise a jurisdiction which properly is ecclesiastical only. The attaining of the modern resolution has been, in some significant part, in response to clerical overreaching, to which James I's own overreaching was an oversimplified reaction. All this is not to deny that the Inquisitions which brought long-lasting and merited antipathy and suspicion upon Catholicism—and (under different names and forms) upon Anglicanism and Puritanism—were originally lay initiatives seeking clerical assistance and management.

The complexity at the resolution's core results not only from the dual loyalties and authorities it postulates within each citizen and each state, nor only from the additional complexity of multiple, competing religious voices within one political space, and multiple states to be addressed by a religion self-understood (and actually institutionalized) as universal. It also involves the complexity, widely ignored in contemporary secularist pronouncements, that there is at least one religion—indeed, the religion central, in its central form, to our history since not long after Cicero—which teaches, as part of its religious faith (creed), that its judgments of faith about morality are also the judgments to which *natural reason would properly come*, under favourable epistemic conditions, even without the benefit of any public revelation or resultant religious tradition.

More reasonable and politically sustainable than Rawls's exclusion from public deliberations (at least about constitutional fundamentals) of all 'comprehensive doctrines', that is, of all really justificatory philosophical arguments, is Aquinas's principle that one should be willing to argue out all questions of moral (and therefore political and legal) conduct and decision with all the intellectual resources one can get, addressing those who deny that religious authorities and testimonies are a resource with moral and political arguments that meet them on the plane of a reason that is 'natural' precisely as prescinding from (bracketing out) any such authorities or testimonies. But Aquinas's principle, like the whole modern resolution of which it is an intrinsic component, has to confront the challenge which I have called extrinsic: the presence and power of those who reject *debate*, that is, reject the openness of discourse in which no questions about justification are excluded. The problem whether to tolerate the waxing political power of those who are intolerant of the resolution, and of the constitutional order we summarily call democratic—the problem whose reigning European solution is therefore called 'militant democracy'—is opened up a little in the final section (VII) of essay I.

Our parents or grandparents wrestled with it in the form of the question whether to tolerate the organized activities of the Communist and/or National Socialist parties. They were clear, at least, that adherents of such intolerant political beliefs should be excluded from settling in our countries. With a negligence that before long will, I think, seem deeply surprising, that clarity was lost or repudiated. By a regrettable oversimplification, it was and still is generally assumed that because the nineteenth-century mass immigration of Catholics to the United States, at a time when their religion's doctrine was widely understood to be politically intolerant, turned out to be politically tolerable (and no real threat to toleration), it would have been wrong to exclude them then, and it now would similarly be wrong to keep members of another universalist monotheism from settling here. Both parts of this assumption seem mistaken, more plainly the second. The first can perhaps be given some sort of defence along the lines that Catholic political doctrine was always more complex and open to differentiation in itself and its application (as its subsequent history, like much in its earlier history, confirms). The peculiar error of the second is its assumption that the religious core of all religions has the same complexity, the same interest in debate, the same awareness of and respect for natural reason, and the same willingness to spread by using only such means as Christians for centuries used in spreading their message throughout the Roman Empire, by preaching (in public places when allowed), good example, and good works for believers and unbelievers alike. Catholic Christianity, in history's shifting complexities, moved away from that early freedom from entanglement with state power, and only after a long interlude affirmed with unmistakable clarity the properly developed implications of its original and lasting belief that faith must be free from coercion. That belief matches the life, words, and example of its founder. In judging the second part of the above-mentioned assumption or argument, everyone concerned should ask whether there could be any more reliable way to find, assess, and compare each religion's stable core than by comparing each one's (records of its) revered founder.

II. BASES FOR ACCEPTING REVELATION

In relation to the historical issues involved in claims about public revelation, the volume's most foundational essay is certainly essay 9, 'Historical Consciousness and Theological Foundations'. Like essays 10 and 11, it is in part concerned with controversies within Christian theology, but only in part; its main arguments go to the grounds for accepting that the Christian gospel is essentially true.

Truth is always a matter both of correspondence with data and reality and of coherence with other propositions reasonably judged true. So, among the grounds for accepting testimony, not least testimony about such a one-off event or series of events as a public divine revelation, are historical data, considered in the light of the philosophical grounds for judging that miracles are possible and, *pace* Hume, can in appropriate and feasible circumstances be entirely credible. But the grounds for accepting sifted testimony include also the criteria which natural practical reason supplies for assessing the moral character both of witnesses and of those about whose words and deeds those witnesses testify, and equally for assessing the significance for human life of the message revealed. For all these considerations bear on the *particular* 'antecedent probability', as Newman called it, that testimony to the extraordinary is, in the *particular* case, worthy of belief, indeed of faith (see essay 4 at pp. 82–4, and essay 9 at n. 53 and pp. 151–4). The sermons in this part, essays 12, 14, and 15, say something, albeit not very much, about this significance for human life.

III. CONSCIENCE AND FAITH

Essay 17 is another Oxford sermon, which I have coupled here with the
analytical essay on conscience in Newman because to speak of dispositions
such as humility and faith is to speak of elements of one's subjectivity,
one's personal experience and constitution. And to speak of conscience
is, likewise, to speak directly of a fact about one's personal condition,
namely, one's definite and carefully formed condition of believing/
judging something to be true/really the case. To say that doing X would
be against my conscience is to say that I judge my doing X would be
wrongful. The discussion could then properly focus on the non-subjective
question whether it is true that doing X would be wrong. But by talking of
conscience, one focuses attention, even if only momentarily, on the fact that
I have formed an opinion (on the [truth of the] wrongness of doing X). For
Aquinas, and I believe for More (see essay 10 at p. 169) and Newman, the
prestige and normativity of conscience is, first and last, the prestige and
normativity of truth. For much modern thought, conscience's claim is the
claim, rather, of personal authenticity. Aquinas, More, and Newman are
concerned enough about authenticity, but it is secondary to, and derivative
from, one's responsibility to pursue *truth* in one's judgments and opinions,
and to adhere to it when one (thinks one) has found it. Still, the personal,
'psychological' conditions under which that pursuit and adherence are
feasible are of interest, especially to Aquinas as master theologian of the
virtues and of the 'law' of grace,[7] the divine initiative of sharing which
(whatever our pride would like to have been the case) is a precondition for
virtue, even for real truth seeking.

IV. CONTROVERSIES

The flipside of Aquinas's position about natural reason—a position which
is little or no more than a rearticulation, for a university audience, of
St Paul's—is this. Church teaching about moral matters must pass the
test of inherent reasonableness. So Catholic theological reflection on moral
questions (and therefore on political and legal questions) is a search for a
reflective equilibrium between (i) the givens (*dogmata*) of revelation with
its extension in the authoritative teaching of the same church that judged
what is and what is not a 'source' of revelation, and (ii) what would be judged
morally reasonable even without revelation. Both limbs are such that first
(and second…) thoughts are liable to be corrected by the (provisional)

---

[7] Aquinas's main treatise on that gratuitously given capability of sharing in divine life which is
called grace follows immediately on his treatise on law, as qq.109 et seq. of *ST* I–II.

content of the other limb. This is not a Rawlsian or post-Rawlsian reflective equilibrium, as that is normally understood. For neither the dogmas nor the elementary prescriptions of morality are revisable. But the dogmas need interpretation, and the interpretative theological tradition likewise needs interpretation. And anyone's judgments about what is inherently reasonable should certainly be open to amendment in the light of experience, deeper and more critical understanding, new insights and information, and certainly not least, the teaching and example afforded by any true divine revelation. As the central community offering to transmit through human history the one-off events of public revelation, the Catholic Church has the resources—a teaching office and its cumulating and developing doctrinal judgments—to resolve disputed questions about the content (including moral) of the faith. These judgments, too, are put to the test of theological reflection which, if authentic, incorporates both natural reason and fidelity to definitive teachings of the faith.

The forty-five years since the closing of the Second Vatican Council of bishops in 1965 have seen extensive public controversies among Catholics. The essays in this volume's last part have these as their immediate occasion and context; the essays' context and immediate audience were inhouse. Because that community of believers is concerned in and with people's common good at large, as it works out in the secular world, even the most apparently intra-mural two or three of these controversies bear more or less plainly and directly on public matters of interest and concern to people quite outside the Church, and are argued out in terms meant to be accessible to those who deny that the Church or any other Christian body transmits any divine revelation. All the essays had as their main spurs (i) resistance to arguments that seemed to me bad or assumptions that seemed faulty, impacting on important moral and political questions, and (ii) a sense that not many others seemed interested in refuting these publicly.

Essay 18 should have conceded more about the extent to which the social teaching of the Popes and other ecclesiastical authorities follows or reflects, both in what it omits and what it says, the opinions of the secular milieus from which the clergy come. During the decades of these essays, the Church has fallen silent, or nearly so, about matters on which it laid much stress only a generation before: the centrality of the mother in a well-ordered home and the need for a family wage (which may involve state subsidies or credits) to make that practicable; the validity and importance of patriotism; the evil of pornography—for example. The Church has made no progress in resolving the moral question of deterrence by threat of massive retaliation against would-be enemies' 'highest-value asset' (their people, however described). It could make progress by teaching what is within the competence of pastors, namely as general and strictly conditional a proposition as: if a deterrent policy includes the intention, even conditionally, to destroy non-combatants it cannot be reconciled with morality, natural or revealed. The question whether a particular national policy does involve such an intention could and should be left to the informed judgment of the faithful and anyone else concerned to think rightly. But instead, the Church's teachers, apparently thinking that they need to make a non-hypothetical judgment, can bring themselves no further than the ambiguous statement, made to a political agency in 1982: 'In current conditions "deterrence" based on balance, certainly not as an end in itself but as a step on the way toward a progressive disarmament, may still be judged morally acceptable.'[8]

There is another matter, taken up in essay II.7's reflections on Rawls and John Paul II on 'cosmopolis' and nation-states, which directly affects the whole existence of political communities and peoples, but which meets, in contemporary Catholic social teaching, with silence on essentials. This silence is veiled, moreover, by a rhetorical drift towards equating the borderless, cosmopolitan Church—in which there is 'neither Jew nor Greek' but all are equally and everywhere at home—with political community envisaged as if it likewise ought to be substantially borderless even if that resulted (but such consequences are not articulated even for consideration) in the annulling of national cultures, constitutions, and peoples. This drift is perhaps an instance of clerical overreach, or simply of forgetting the resolution's dual pillars. But it seems, as much as anything, an instance of the phenomenon to which Edward Norman pointed in the lectures discussed in essay 18: pastors conforming to the prejudices of the secular groups from which clergy tend to come or from which they take their cultural bearings.

Essay 19 ('Morality and the Second Vatican Council'), written like essay 18 at the end of the 1970s, takes the fact of public revelation seriously, and therefore too the very considered teaching, on matters of faith and morals, of the community constituted to transmit that revelation through the whole course of history, from history's newly established centring point (at the change of the eras 2,000 years ago) to its quite hidden end. The essay investigates a thesis widely put about in the 1970s, that the worldwide council of bishops concluded in 1965 had made light of the classic doctrinal and philosophical-theological conception of natural law, in favour of a (supposedly) new primacy of

---

[8] Message to Special Session of the United Nations for Disarmament, para. 8 (11 June 1982), AAS 74: 879. Analysis and interpretation: *NDMR* 97–8, 103; also endnote to essay 20, at 290 below.

conscience. A conscience so conceived, it seemed to me, is only too likely to be a rationalization for personal convenience admixed with the prejudices and fashions of one's time and place. And the thesis proved to be quite mistaken as a matter of history—indeed, to be a mild version of other, more gravely manipulative progressivist fabrications of the historical record such as I allude to in essay 10 at n. 9 or document in 1994d (and summarily in 1994b).

Essay 24, on the reality or unreality of a permanently catastrophic personal end-state, takes its terms entirely from revelation and is a debate within theology. (I was a fellow member with Hans von Balthasar of the International Theological Commission in his last years.) Nonetheless, natural reason is not innocent of these questions, as Plato makes clear with his philosophical myths of retribution in a life beyond death. And as Shakespeare carefully explores in *Richard III* (published in the same year as Bacon's first essays), any divine *postmortem* will hardly be other than a ratification of one's own most truthful particular practical judgment—call it one's judgment of conscience—as it operates[9] in and after every moment of choice, moments which, in the very nature of the spiritual, last until if ever they are reversed by a contrary choice. That such choices to repent remain possible only during this life, before death, is—like other aspects of the intersection (so to call it) of time and eternity—mysterious, but is a clearly articulated and transmitted element in the founding words and actions that are public revelation's, indeed religion's, high point. The mystery is one aspect of the mystery of evil, which some readers of Bacon, particularly since Hume and popular Darwinism, may be surprised not to find mentioned by the Lord Chancellor among atheism's causes. Bacon's generation, even its atheists, it seems, were more mindful of the relevant issues of philosophical method and reach.[10] Philosophical questioning and reasoning (like common sense, too) requires us to affirm divine creative and sustaining causality. But this causality, though it cannot reasonably be envisaged as operating in a zone of power or arbitrary will beyond reason and wisdom, must nonetheless transcend the order of nature whose actuality it explains, and *so far* transcend it that we cannot discern any basis for applying to divine causality the standards by which, in any of the four

---

[9] We have the concept of conscience, it seems, because we need to be able to speak about such practical judgments not precisely as dateable acts nor precisely as the propositional content of such acts, but as the state of mind of one who has made such a judgment and holds it (without always 'having it before one's mind'). So 'conscience' will signify primarily the active *capacity* to do this.

[10] See *NLNR* at 391 and, for Aquinas's simpler, more graphic terms, see *Aquinas* at 304, quoted in essay 13 n. 8 below; both passages are quoted also on pp. 24–5 below.

basic kinds of order and human understanding, we reasonably judge something defective, wrong, evil, or failure.

*   *   *

The gaze of the intrepid Horrocks and Gill into an immensity of distance can be taken as one icon of the interest and attitude we call religion. Another, certainly, is the Baconian search for forms buried deeper by far in physical matter than had been suspected by the late Aristotelian tradition of transmitting science through teaching rather than investigation and replication. And another is the gaze of an Aquinas, awake in the priory chapel in the earliest morning hours to adore the eternal God hidden, as he believed, under the appearances of a wafer of wheat flour, and to make himself ready for the public work of collaborating in understanding everything that matters, and reasoning about truths and other goods.

Part One

Religion in Public Reason and Law

1

DARWIN, DEWEY, RELIGION, AND THE PUBLIC DOMAIN*

I

John Dewey was born in 1859, the year that saw the publication—celebrated worldwide this 150th anniversary—of Charles Darwin's *The Origin of Species*. It is Darwin, I shall argue, who is the better guide when we try to think about the place of religion in a society that aspires to be fair and sustainable. The question whether such a society would include the free exercise of religion among its constitutional guarantees has recently become a focus of debate amongst legal philosophers. The philosophy of law—frame for the series of endowed lectures in which this essay takes its place[1]—is in some ways the most humble, low-level of philosophy's branches. But that same lowliness entails that one cannot do legal philosophy well without investigating and taking positions in all the higher levels and domains of practical philosophy, not to mention the epistemology and metaphysics which practical philosophy partly presupposes and partly informs. So legal philosophy is like law and lawyering: a place where all the great questions come to a head and become truly practical—a place proximate to decisions and actions affecting real persons and their lives and fortunes, decisions and actions whose rational soundness will depend on access—through culture, insight, or philosophy—to the deepest principles of morality and most strategic truths about human beings and their environment. So: a privileged place to work in.

In the debate I mentioned, some contemporary American legal and constitutional theorists hold that there is nothing about religion or its free exercise that calls for particular respect, or any mention in constitutional bills of rights. That is the thesis which my essay concerns. Religion, these theorists hold, has no such dignity, though (they add) history's

* 2009c ('Does Free Exercise of Religion Deserve Constitutional Mention?').
[1] This essay was the annual John Dewey Lecture at the University of Minnesota Law School in March 2009.

testimony to the vulnerability of religions or their adherents, especially their vulnerability to oppression by other faiths, helps explain and in a weak sense justify the First Amendment's denial of Congressional power to make law either 'respecting an establishment of religion' or 'prohibiting the free exercise thereof'. Ronald Dworkin is a principal proponent of the thesis,[2] but its most energetic exponents over the past fifteen years have been Christopher Eisgruber and Lawrence Sager, whose joint work culminates in a book proposing a principle they call 'Equal Liberty', a principle which is demanded by fairness in religiously diverse societies and which 'denies that religion is a…category of human experience that demands special benefits and/or necessitates special restrictions',[3] or any 'special immunity for religiously motivated conduct'.[4]

In Eisgruber and Sager's theory or principle of 'Equal Liberty' there is much that may seem welcome. They argue strenuously against the metaphor of 'separation of Church and State', and their theory equally discredits not only that slogan but also the once prevailing Supreme Court interpretation of 'no establishment of religion' that forbad any state aid to religious or religiously affiliated enterprises. They offer to defend, not a secular*ism* that would reject, exclude, or disparage religion, but what they see as the healthy secular*arity* of non-religious institutions—say, secular public schools—which while declining to be (and prohibited from being) 'overtly or specifically religious',[5] 'aspire to constitute a practical realm in which various competing…philosophical *and religious* views may coexist and constructively interact'.[6] They have no time for Rawlsian proposals to expel from the public domain all religious arguments or grounds for decision-making;[7] they share, I think, Dworkin's (and Joseph Raz's) healthy scepticism about that ramshackle Rawlsian project—he calls it 'political liberalism'—which in all really important decisions about human rights and the common good would banish concern for truth and in its place put an imaginary overlapping consensus of the 'reasonable' views of all 'reasonable' people (views supposedly identifiable as reasonable without reflection on their truth). They hold—rightly, I think—that in these matters neutrality is not an option. As to free exercise of religion, Eisgruber and Sager support the approach in *Employment Division v Smith*,[8] the *Peyote* case, upholding 'neutral and generally applicable' laws even when they happen to restrict some religious practice and no 'compelling state interest'

---

[2] Dworkin, *Justice in Robes*, 134; Dworkin, *Is Democracy Possible Here?*, 60–2.
[3] *Religious Freedom and the Constitution*, 6.   [4] *Ibid.*, 13.   [5] *Ibid.*, 313.
[6] *Ibid.*, 216 (emphasis added).
[7] See *ibid.*, 48–50 (not explicitly mentioning Rawls's 'political liberalism').
[8] 494 US 872, 890 (1990), Scalia J for the Court.

required them to do so. That approach is much less welcome to many who recognize the particular good of religion and religious liberty, but when I revisit it later in this essay I will not be arguing against it. Yet for all this, the overarching theory of Equal Liberty proposed by Eisgruber and Sager is, I think, radically unsound, at the very least insofar as it denies to religion and religious liberty any moral or constitutional status distinct from other 'deep commitments'.

Their theory's first exposition was entitled 'The Vulnerability of Consciences: The Constitutional Basis for Protecting Religious Conduct'.[9] But the title can give a mistaken impression of their central thesis. For they *deny* that conscience as the rational faculty of practical judgment has any more claim than religion to constitutional privilege or even protection.[10] Rather, the proper object of constitutional protection is any 'deep concern', any and all 'deeply' motivated and self-shaping attitudes and behaviour. Whether or not these are religious *or even conscientious*, all alike are entitled to 'equal regard'. There is, they say, a 'grand diversity of relationships, affiliations, activities, and passions that share a constitutional presumption of legitimacy' because in them members of 'a modern, pluralistic society...find their identities, shape their values, and live the most valuable moments of their lives'.[11] Religious acts, they concede, have the same dignity and constitutional status as the 'relationships, affiliations, activities and passions' under discussion...Their essay did not say how far this wider category extends, and their book, too, is not much concerned to clarify the matter. But it does make clear that, in their view, the freedom of a religious association such as the Catholic Church to maintain a male priesthood is defensible only as an instance of the constitutional principle that

there are a variety of personal relationships in which members of our political community are free to choose their partners [as in *Lawrence v Texas*], associates or colleagues without interference from the state.[12]

And their 1994 essay had several times explicated the phrase 'deep concern(s)' (which in the book is usually rendered 'deep commitment(s)') as including 'passionate' acts and relationships.[13]

---

[9] 61 U Chicago L Rev 1245–315 (1994).   [10] *Ibid.*, 1263, 1268–70.

[11] *Ibid.*, 1266. In truth, identities are shaped, not merely found, and values are found (or imagined), not merely shaped.

[12] *Religious Freedom and the Constitution*, 65; *Lawrence v Texas* 539 US 558 (2003), involving partnership in casual homosexual sodomy, is cited on the preceding page.

[13] 'The Vulnerability of Consciences' at 1283. At the very outset (1245n), the authors say that 'an important theme of this essay is that religion does not exhaust the commitments and passions that move human beings in deep and valuable ways'.

Eisgruber and Sager are right to hold that religion, if it is (as they think) just one among the deep passions and commitments that move people, does not deserve constitutional mention on account of any special dignity or value. True, this hypothesis does not warrant their conclusion that mention of religion in constitutions is defensible—if at all—only because religious people (the authors always seem to assume religious *majorities*) have been so beastly to each other (they assume, to *minority* religions) so often that historical constitution-makers could reasonably treat the exercise of religion as needing protection just because it is specially vulnerable to religiously motivated discrimination. For the argument forgets the threat to religious practice that can come from atheist or other secularist hostility to religion. But much more important is the hypothesis itself: that religion is just one deep and passionate commitment amongst others. This is lethal to religion, and I want to try to show why.

Before setting out my positive argumentation, I think it is fair to remark that theirs is a thoroughly external view.[14] They treat religion in the way that Ronald Dworkin regularly treats views of legislators or 'majorities' with which he is unsympathetic, that is, not as propositions *about* rights or common good, or as any other proposition or premise arguably justifying a normative conclusion, but instead as mere expressions of distaste or disapproval, accompanied by an appeal to the power of those who hold these views—their power as a majority to give effect to their attitude, *their* passionate commitment.[15] Eisgruber and Sager fall into this Dworkinian sort of sophism in their book's last pages, where they reductively treat the concern of religiously minded people that America acknowledge its dependence on God as a mere concern for 'their [own] wellbeing', a mere complaint that '*they* [the religiously minded] are being deprived of an environment' that they value.[16] The externality of Eisgruber and Sager's view of religion—their treating religious propositions as propositions inherently incapable of conveying any understanding of, or rational response to, any feature of reality, and their failure even to contemplate a line of rational inquiry, reflection, and judgment such as might lead people to affirm the existence of a transcendent intelligent and provident creator—is an externality further manifested in their repeated remarks about 'intelligent design'. For in these remarks they go beyond the rational (albeit not wholly compelling) objection that gaps in experimental science

---

[14] In *Religious Freedom and the Constitution* at 103, they explicitly speak from, or on behalf of, 'an external, secular perspective'.

[15] I first pointed to this sophistic technique of Dworkin in essay III.1 at 24–6 (1985a at 309–11), and again, with reference to its pernicious echoes in recent Supreme Court doctrine, in essay II.6 at 107–10 (2008b).

[16] *Religious Freedom and the Constitution*, 284–5.

call for more experimental science to two additional claims: (1) that the 'suggestion' that there exists an intelligent designer is merely 'a vague kind of religious view', that is to say a mere 'hypothesis grounded in religion'; and (2) that any identification of the designer as *God* rather than gods, wizards, fairies, or 'transcendental pasta' (their scornful phrase), is a mere profession of religious faith.[17] Assessing these two claims will get us closer—indeed close—to the root of this essay's title question.

II

Is the 'suggestion' that there exists a transcendent intelligent designer a 'hypothesis grounded in religion'? At the age of 65, seventeen years after the publication of *The Origin of Species* and six years before his death, Darwin wrote an *Autobiography*, which he revisited occasionally to supplement. It was a little too candid, intellectually, for some in his family; so the posthumous first publication of it in 1882 was not quite complete; but the deletions were eventually restored. In a short paragraph, present in his first draft and never revised, he speaks of a 'source of conviction in the existence of God', a source which is 'connected with the reason and not with the feelings' and therefore 'impresses me [him] as having much more weight' than another source that he had mentioned, namely, 'the sense of sublimity', or more exactly the sort of 'higher feelings of wonder, admiration and devotion' that, as he had years before recorded in his journal, filled and elevated his mind whilst standing in the midst of the grandeur of a Brazilian forest. By now, in 1876, even 'the grandest scenes would not cause any such convictions and feelings to rise in my [his] mind'. But when he sets feelings and lack of feelings to one side, and attends instead to reason, that is to thinking about data and their explanation, then once again there arises a 'conviction in the existence of God' which

follows from the extreme difficulty or rather *impossibility* of conceiving this immense and wonderful universe, including man with his capacity of looking far backwards and far into futurity, as the result of blind chance or necessity. When thus *reflecting* I feel compelled to look to a First Cause having an intelligent mind in some degree analogous to that of man; and I deserve to be called a Theist.[18]

Now it is clear that Darwin, when he wrote this, had for some years had no religious faith, no religion, no desire to adjust his living and thinking, in

---

[17] *Ibid.*, 190, 281, 310 at n. 56.

[18] *Autobiography of Charles Darwin*, 92 (emphasis added). Some time after writing this, Darwin inserted, immediately after this passage: 'This conclusion was strong in my mind about the time, as far as I can remember, when I wrote the *Origin of Species*; and it is since that time that it has very gradually with many fluctuations become weaker.'

any way, to respond to the intelligent mind of any supposed First Cause. Doubts about whether the human mind can be trusted when 'it draws such grand conclusions', and about whether the felt, or rather adjudged, necessity of 'the connection between cause and effect' instead 'depends merely on inherited experience', had reinforced the source of doubt that earlier led him to abandon Christian faith, namely, the suffering and death of his own daughter and, beyond that, the spectacle of all the suffering and waste in the world of nature. So he concludes: 'The mystery of the beginning of all things is insoluble by us; and I for one must be content to remain an Agnostic.'

The structure and sequence of Darwin's inner debate—as traced in this autobiographical reflection on the cause of the world and of its evolution—are philosophically sounder than the debate's conclusion. His foundational judgment (when really *thinking*, not feeling) was: it is impossible rationally to ascribe the universe to chance or 'blind necessity', and necessary to ascribe it instead to an intelligence which is neither a part of nor the totality of the universe but nonetheless the universe's *cause*. That foundational judgment is reasonable, sound, and indeed inevitable, provided we correctly understand his phrase 'impossible to conceive', and that phrase's implicit counterpart or entailment 'necessary [compelled to conceive]' and, for that matter, my term 'inevitable'. Correctly understanding these key terms requires more precision than, I think, Darwin himself achieved. The impossibility in question is not the impossibility of the logically contradictory or incoherent, and the implicit necessity is not logical necessity or strict entailment. Nor is it a matter of 'psychological necessity', or again of that necessity-of-habit which Darwin, an avid *amateur* of David Hume, perhaps has in mind when he speaks of 'inherited experience'; and equally it would be gratuitous to appeal here, in a Kantian manner, to a 'structure' of the human mind. The necessity is, rather, the rational necessity of adhering to those norms of rational inquiry and judgment which articulate what experience of discovering reality shows is *needed* for overcoming ignorance, illusion, and error.[19]

Such norms guide all scientific inquiry, all scientific discovery, and all scientific achievements and applications—and are the source, equally, of all inquiry, discovery, and judgment in fields which lie wholly or partly beyond the methods of natural science, fields such as mathematics, logic, philosophy, history, and the interpretation of texts and conversations. In all these fields, truth is found and knowledge of reality is won by hypothesizing (and then, when evidence and argument fail to disconfirm it,

---

[19] See *NLNR* 68–9, 385[; and essay 9, sec. V].

appropriately *concluding* to) some explanation, some explanatory factor or state of affairs or reality—what Darwin reasonably calls some cause—in preference to mere chance or inexplicable ('blind') necessity. So, one of the many rationality norms is: an adequate explanatory reason why something is so rather than otherwise is to be expected, unless one has a reason not to expect such an explanatory reason. Chance, of course, there is aplenty in a world where events and processes, each of which has its own intelligible explanation(s), coincide. But science progresses constantly by treating chance as the residuum of coincidence in a domain dominated by what is explicable because it is not chance. (So Richard Dawkins' celebration, earlier this anniversary year, of Darwin and Darwinism ends by indignantly repudiating the thought that evolution works or has ever worked by chance!)[20] Absolutely no entity, process, or other state of affairs in the world we can in any way experience or know shows any sign of *necessarily*—or, for that matter, causelessly—being what it is; or any sign of either necessarily or causelessly being actual rather than non-existent, or necessarily or causelessly doing what it does or changing as it does. Postulating that the whole (the universe or cosmos or universe of universes) has existed for an infinite time—a postulate that philosophers like Moses Maimonides, and Thomas Aquinas are happy, indeed keen, to entertain[21]—does not make it reasonable to predicate of the whole either a necessity or a causelessness that is discoverable in none of its component entities or state of affairs. Far more reasonable is it to infer that the actuality and intelligibility of every entity, process, or state of affairs result from a *sui generis* reality which *has what it takes* both to exist—be actual—without being caused and to cause, intelligently, absolutely every such resultant ('created') entity, process, and state of affairs.[22] (Nor is it difficult to show that no *set* of gods, no wizard or fairy, and no transcendental pasta, could have what it takes to be sheer *actuality*, without trace of mere potentiality, the pure actuality needed to explain a universe in constant development from potentiality to actuality.)

If one does what Darwin it seems did not sufficiently do, and takes fully into account (i) the wholly *sui generis* character of this transcendent actuality and causality of everything else, and (ii) the accordingly quite *sui generis* character of what he like Aquinas called the *analogy* between

[20] Dawkins, 'Dawkins on Darwin'.
[21] See *Aquinas* 301, citing *ST* I q.46, a.2; *ScG* II c.38 n.8; and three other texts.
[22] Flew, *There is a God: How the World's Most Notorious Atheist Changed his Mind*, 74–158, surveys the state of the debate, with particular focus on argumentation (e.g. of scientists like Einstein, Heisenberg, Planck, and others) analogous to Darwin's, argumentation whose strictly philosophical respectability Flew briefly vindicates. For a more fundamental treatment of philosophical issues about the existence of God, see Grisez, *God? Philosophical Preface to Faith*, cited under the first edition's title in *NLNR*, ch. xiii.

the Creator's and our creaturely minds, then one will discern the proper response to the doubts which in Darwin's mind somehow seemed to make possible what he had rationally judged impossible, namely conceiving of this world as existing without an intelligent First—or better, transcendent, *sui generis*—Cause. For beyond (or behind) the doubt which arbitrarily reduced the rational demand for an explanation to mere habit, and the doubt which a priori declared untrustworthy the only available explanation, there lay the doubt—which is not arbitrary or a priori—that a transcendent intelligence would not have chosen to make *this* world with its apparent 'waste' and its all too real not apparent suffering. The proper response to *this* doubt looks to the very consideration which Darwin treated as ground for abdicating from the whole inquiry and for accepting, agnostically, the equal possibility of what he had already judged impossible—the non-existence of an intelligent and transcendent cause. What consideration was that? Darwin put it in various similes and metaphors, all acknowledging or asserting the *inadequacy* of our grasp of the relevant realities and possibilities involved in conceiving of a transcendent and ultimate explanation of everything (including, of course, of the domains of mathematics and logic, of knowledge of the past, of intending and understanding intentions, and of mind's effortless though not unconditioned mastery over matter, as in speaking, or pointing). As I summed up Aquinas's fundamental response to the 'problem of evil':

Straining to ascribe everything to chance rather than a creative intelligence, materialists object that in some respects the pattern and evolution of things is wasteful, pointless, badly ordered, *unintelligent.* They do not attend to the fact that much which seems to them pointless or wasteful is still somehow a describable and to that extent stable and intelligible pattern. And in judging it defective or unintelligent because they do not understand its point, they resemble a country bumpkin (*rusticus*; *idiota*; *ignorans*) who, from the true premise that he does not understand what is going on in a busy laboratory or hospital theatre, draws the conclusion that what is going on is random, unintelligible, pointless, or foolish, or perhaps just needlessly complex.[23] The intention of an intelligence capable of projecting and actualising the entire cosmos and all its interlocking orders vast and minuscule (including human minds with all their capacities to understand and reason logically, mathematically, and interpretatively) is not an intention we could ever reasonably hope to understand *fully* by reasoning from those truths

---

[23] See Aquinas, *Collationes Credo in Deum* 1; *ScG* I c.3 n.4; *Sent.* I d.39 q.2 a.2 ad 5; *De Veritate* q.5 a.5 ad 6; also *ST* I q.116 a.1c and *ScG* III c.92 n.12 [2678] (gravediggers who are not aware of their director's purpose of finding buried treasure in the graveyard). The flourishing of evildoers and the miseries of decent people in this world (see *Sent.* I d.39 q.2 a.2 obj. 5; *Expositio super Iob* prol.) are in accordance with the abyss of the incomprehensible judgments of God {secundum altitudinem incomprehensibilium iudiciorum Dei}: *Quaestiones de Quodlibet* III q.3 a.3c; also *Sent.* I d.39 q.2 a.2 ad 5.

about it which, in our fruitful but laborious inferences from experience, we do manage to understand.[24]

Or again, as I concluded a discussion of evil and creation in my *NLNR*:

The norms in terms of which we judge states of affairs to be evil, in any of the four orders [of human knowledge: nature, logic, morality, and technologies], are not applicable to D [the transcendent first cause] as creator. Thus we have no ground to judge that D's creative causality is defective.[25]

Let me pause to take stock. I asked: Is the 'suggestion' that there exists an intelligent designer a 'hypothesis grounded in religion'? The example of Darwin shows well enough why it is not. The lines of thought that converge on the conclusion that one should affirm a transcendent cause are lines of thought continuous with all our inquiries, reflections, and judgments in every field of science and rational discourse. They are philosophical, though in substance accessible to informal 'commonsense' reflection. They are the perennial root and cause, rather than a consequence, of religious belief. Indeed, in themselves they are not yet religious at all. Before we can speak of religion, we must add further affirmations, including at least one further philosophical affirmation, and also some affirmations within *practical* philosophy (ethics) and some response(s) of freely willing *relating* of oneself to the divine. These points merit some expansion.

III

The *philosophical* character of the arguments for and affirmation of God's existence is strongly suggested by the philosophical lengths to which thinkers tend to go who make it their business to reject that argumentation and affirmation. David Hume denies the reality of human *insight* and equally the reality of natural causation, trying in vain to replace the one with habitual conjunctions of images (misnamed by him 'ideas') and the other with mere correlation or repeated coincidence. Richard Dawkins's disproof of God, in his *The God Delusion*,[26] uncritically assumes, explicitly, that complex realities can only be caused by more complex realities— implicitly, that mind is no more than complexified matter—an assumption falsified by every move one makes, in thought, to clarify one's statements and avoid fallacious arguments, and indeed by every meaning-conveying word we utter, and every project one brings to fruition. John Dewey made even wider and higher the protective rampart against inquiries that reach out for ultimate explanations; he rejected as superseded the 'notion' that

---

[24] *Aquinas* 304.   [25] *NLNR* 391.   [26] Dawkins, *The God Delusion*, 136, 151.

'knowledge is a disclosure of reality, of reality prior to and independent of knowing' and the 'notion' that 'knowing is independent of a purpose to control the quality of experienced objects'.[27] The latter position was an instrumentalist pragmatism (significantly coarse compared with the philosophy articulated by pragmatism's founder Charles Peirce) that harmonized with Dewey's denial, in his legal philosophy, that there are any principles which are more than 'working hypotheses, needing to be constantly tested by the way in which they work out in application to concrete situations'—a position which rendered merely provisional, indeed unintelligible, various unalienable human rights which have had to be insisted upon in the aftermath of Nazism and the like.[28] And Darwin like any other serious scientist could scarcely have assented either to Dewey's denial that knowledge discloses reality or his assertion that knowledge is all for the sake of controlling experience—positions each of which cuts off both the sense of wonder that is the motor of science and blocks the search for a knowledge of the past (not least the past of evolution).

But now it is time to make the other point: the judgment that God exists as explanation or causal source of everything's actuality, existence, and intelligibility is no mere contemplation of the past. It includes or at least entails a judgment (indeed several judgments) about the relation between our own thought and action and the ongoing causal activity of the transcendent creator, the activity traditionally called divine providence. For first, since every entity, process, or state of affairs somehow caused by the transcendent source is contingent, not necessary, it is reasonable to think of divine causation as not only intelligent but also free—as if it were causing through free choice: to create something rather than nothing, and *this* totality rather than other possible universes. And secondly, it is clear to us that our own activity, including our own thinking things through, is dependent, for its happening and achieving anything at all, on the cooperation of providence. Both these inferences are still philosophical—thoughts we have no need or sufficient reason to call religious. We start to move into the zone of the religious only with a third line of thought about the relation between our activity and divine providence.

And that is this. The world we find and do not make includes not only the normativity or directiveness of logic, but also the normativity of basic practical principles such as those that pick out knowledge and truth as an

---

[27] Dewey, *The Quest for Certainty*, 43–4.

[28] The impact of Dewey's position can be measured by Posner's statement in *Law, Pragmatism, and Democracy* at 361–2: 'Not . . . that the judge has a duty to abide by constitutional or statutory text, or by precedent. That would be the idea rejected by John Dewey that law is entirely a matter of applying rules laid down by the past . . .'.

intelligible good to be preferred to ignorance and muddle, or again pick out harmony with other persons as another such good, to be preferred to hatred and war; and so forth. For both these reasons, it is reasonable to think of the creator—the transcendent, intelligent, and freely choosing source of reality and meaning, and of intelligible goods and our directedness towards them—as being somehow personal, and as personally, so to speak, anticipating human fulfilment and leading us, via our own understanding, deliberation, and free choices, towards such possible fulfilment.[29] To have thought so far, something which takes time to spell out as I have but which common sense grasps as quick as thought, is to have reached the very threshold of a new, equally effortless, but now fully practical insight: that it would be good to be responsive to and—in hope, because in awe of one's finiteness and dependence—cooperative with this transcendent personal source of whatever good any of us could achieve. That is the good whose pursuit *is* religion and its exercise.

To be more precise, it is, so far forth, the good of *natural* religion, of an understanding of providence, dependence, and cooperation which does not yet include (though it would reasonably be open to) the belief, the faith, that it has been informed by some interpersonal communication, private or public, from—some revelation of—the transcendent and divine. It is an understanding that understands itself still to be from end to end a series of rational inferences from experience, natural science, and philosophical reflection. This remains so, even when the interpretation of divine providence's governing of events is adventurously confident, as for instance in a passage near the beginning of the very first presidential inaugural address, exactly 220 years ago next month. (You should have in your mind's eye the President, not as the stiff, florid figure of later portraits, but as the intense, far-seeing man sculpted two years earlier, with admiration and genius, from a life-mask, by a fellow freemason, Jean-Antoine Houdon, who took the better version back with him to France.) Having begun by recounting the anxious process of deliberation and discernment by which he decided to accept his country's summons out of longed-for retirement, Washington observes that

it would be peculiarly improper to omit in this first official Act my fervent supplications to that Almighty Being who rules over the Universe, who presides in the Councils of Nations, and whose providential aids can supply every human defect, that his benediction may consecrate to the liberties and happiness of the People of the United States a Government instituted by themselves for these

---

[29] 1987f at 279–80. Nor is this line of thought foreign to pre-Christian philosophy, as is demonstrated by Plato's reflections on the moral and political importance of (acknowledging clearly) divine concern for human life and choices: see essay 3.

essential purposes: and may enable every instrument [official or other public servant] employed in its administration to execute with success the functions allotted to his charge. In tendering this homage to the Great Author of every public and private good I assure myself that it expresses your sentiments not less than my own; nor those of my fellow-citizens at large less than either. No People can be bound to acknowledge and adore the invisible hand which conducts the Affairs of men more than the People of the United States. Every step, by which they have advanced to the character of an independent nation seems to have been distinguished by some token of providential agency.

Those steps, you all recall, included for Major General Washington and his forces many defeats, retreats, disasters, along with many and eventually decisive victories, and then the peace settlements, confederation, and the making and adopting of the Constitution itself.

The natural, philosophical religion invoked by President Washington is articulated with maximum economy in the prayer (the Regents' prayer) that in 1962 was expelled from the public schools of New York by the Supreme Court in *Engel v Vitale*:[30] 'Almighty God we acknowledge our dependence upon Thee, and we beg Thy blessings upon us, our parents, our teachers and our Country.' Such is the core both of natural religion,[31] and of any paradigmatic form of religion that goes beyond philosophy and natural religion to elaborate a doctrine and worship informed or mandated by some kind of non-philosophical communication from or with the divine reality—a form of religion such as one finds richly elaborated in, say, Judaism or Orthodox or Catholic Christianity. (There are, of course, non-paradigmatic instances of religion, some of them historically highly significant such as Buddhism, in which the relation between the transcendent and the world is differently conceived.) The human good of religion is centrally the good of being aligned in one's intelligence, will, and freedom with the intelligence, will, and freedom of the Creator; notions such as fall, repentance, forgiveness, redemption all fall within the ambit of that generic *alignment*, that *assimilatio* and *adhaesio*, as Aquinas puts it, an alignment that even natural religion can at least envisage and esteem even when, like Aristotle, it responsibly judges that the divine is too transcendent for us to hope for a relationship such as friendship.[32] One does not get the measure of even merely *natural*

---

[30]   370 US 421.

[31]   On the importance of natural religion, and the idea of natural religion, in the thought of the founders of the American republic, see Bradley, *Religious Liberty in the American Republic*, 8–9, 29, 40–1, 46, and 1–46 passim. The report of the US Senate Committee on the Judiciary on petitions to abolish the office of chaplain, 21 January 1853, lucidly affirms that 'our fathers…did not intend to send our armies and navies forth to do battle for the country without any national recognition of that God on whom success or failure depends…'.

[32]   *NE* VIII.7: 1158b35, 1159a4; see *NLNR* 397.

religion's dignity and value if one remains with the conception of religion's value that Andrew Koppelman has proposed on the basis, not least, of the 'place-holder' sketch of a good of religion that I offered in chapter IV of *NLNR*.[33] Koppelman's intentions in this enterprise are good—he is a critic of Eisgruber and Sager's unadmitted secularism—but the content and dignity of the good of religion cannot be identified (as he attempts to identify them) with a mere human questing, considered without regard to the reasons that point both to the existence of God as proper and real object of such questing, and to something of the divine nature and activity.

Nor should we neglect the importance of natural religion's underpinning of the idea, the truth, of human equality, the equality of the one species of animal whose members, each and all unlike (as far as we can tell) all other animals, have the *radical* capacities of persons. Those capacities are to participate in the immaterial life of the spirit, the life of meanings, logic, errors, and truths (known by their consistency with evidence and principle, not by their correlation with any brain-state), about the past, the actual, and the possible. As one of the sub-clauses[34] in the Indian Constitution's clause on religious liberty reminds us, it is possible for a developed religion to distort natural religion's awareness of human equality under the supreme, creative spiritual reality. But a deeper threat to human equality is materialist, scientistic denials of spirit, denials which strip away the one aspect of human reality that makes us equals in dignity despite the manifold inequalities between us. It seems significant that those who expend the patrimony of a religious, anti-materialist civilization, the patrimony we call *rights*, by extending rights to subpersonal animals, are characteristically to be found denying the equal rights of young or disabled human persons. Prayer like the New York Regents' prayer, acknowledging to God our dependence and addressing to the unseen God, by thought, a petition, both presupposes and reinforces the anti-materialist truth so essential to the validation of human rights.

IV

Eisgruber and Sager admit that the rule in *Engel v Vitale*, expelling all such prayer from public schools even when opting-out is fully permitted and protected, cannot be adequately justified by simple appeal to the risk of coercion by social pressure. That sort of argument, they concede, certainly

---

[33] See Koppelman, 'Secular Purpose' at 130–1; 'Is it Fair to Give Religion Special Treatment?' at 593–4.

[34] Art. 25(2)(b): '[The state may make law] providing for social welfare and reform or the throwing open of Hindu religious institutions of a public character to all classes and sections of Hindus.'

could not justify such progeny of *Engel* as *Santa Fe Independent School District v Doe* (2000):[35] after all, anyone can stay away from a football game at which there will be school-sponsored prayer. They accept that these judicial prohibitions, picking out the exercise of religion for seemingly 'unique prohibitions that have no secular analogues',[36] seem on their face incompatible with Equal Liberty. But Eisgruber and Sager vigorously defend the absoluteness of the rule in these cases. They do so by appealing to a wide-ranging principle of *disparagement*:

> Government-sponsored prayer rituals involve a public embrace of the faithful... more precisely, of those whose faiths are consistent with mainstream public prayer. As a result, their social meaning includes this blunt message: *The real members of this community (the school community and by extension the larger community serviced by the school or school district) are practicing Christians of a certain sort; others dwell among us but lack the status of full membership.* The public rituals create a class of outsiders and thereby **disparage** those relegated to that status....Proponents...will no doubt object that neither they nor school authorities have any intention to disparage anybody; their goal is simply to make prayer rituals available to those who will appreciate them.... [But] the relevant question is not about the intentions of particular speakers, nor about the perceptions of particular audiences, but rather about the social meanings of rituals, practices, and religions.[37]

You are entitled to be puzzled by a 'meaning' which floats free both of the intentions of the speaker or acting person and of the perceptions of the audience. But this argument from unintended but supposedly real disparagement is now a mighty force in constitutional and political arguments against not only religion or religions but also against the institution of marriage, the primacy of our language within our own country, and every other aspect of our culture which is not universally shared and about which some people, whether or not part of our community by birth, are discontented. To require immigrants to speak our language, argues Joseph Raz, is to disrespect them, to express a judgment that their culture is inferior and to be eliminated.[38] Here Raz, for so many years a stern critic of Ronald Dworkin, implicitly throws in his lot with Dworkin's long-running sequence of arguments, each one springing up when its predecessor twin or cousin was refuted, all revolving around the claim that some state action manifests disrespect, or lack of equal respect, for those persons whose conduct it restricts or otherwise affects—restricts or

---

[35] 530 US 290.   [36] *Religious Freedom and the Constitution*, 161.
[37] *Ibid.*, 163–4 (emphasis added).
[38] Raz, 'Multiculturalism' at 200, referring also to Raz, *Ethics in the Public Domain* at 178. On all this see essay II.6 (2008b) at 110–15.

affects perhaps, in truth, out of lively concern to protect them from their own folly or weakness.

To all these attributions of disrespect, insult, or disparagement, unhinged from any intent, we should reply that they are gratuitous and groundless, essentially sophistic fictions. The meaning of the resolve to pray together is simply *not* that those who abstain or absent themselves are not full members of the community. They are full members of the community, with every single right that everyone else in it enjoys, and every single right enjoyed by those who engage in the corporate activity from which they are entitled to dissent, and with whom they have, *pace* Eisgruber and Sager, equal constitutional stature.[39] Similarly, those countries or legislatures or citizens who insist that immigrants learn the country's language, lest a Balkanized country be bad for all alike, need neither have nor convey any view that the immigrant culture is inferior, or any intent to eliminate or in any way disparage it. And in those cases where they do judge some cultural syndrome inferior, and hope or even plan for its elimination, their judgment need be no more unfairly disrespectful of persons than the judgment that sexual relations between grown men and 10-year-old girls are immoral, harmful, and, however revered the men who have indulged in them, are (like female genital mutilation) to be eliminated from our community.

V

Time to take stock again. I have assembled the main premises for a primary answer to my title question. Religion deserves constitutional mention, not because it is a passionate or deep commitment, but because it is the practical expression of, or response to, truths about human society, about the persons who are a political community's members, and about the world in which any such community must take its place and find its ways and means. Even the many seriously misguided religions tell in some respects more truth about the constitution's ultimate natural (transcendent, supra-natural) foundations than any atheism or robust agnosticism can.

This thesis is consistent with the kind of argument I develop in all chapters save the last in my *NLNR* and *FoE*—the argument that practical reason's first principles can be understood and acknowledged, and their normative implications extensively unfolded into rich, substantive moral, political, and legal theory, without relying upon, presupposing, or even adverting to, the existence of God or providential order. *But*: if it is true, as I argue in

---

[39] Cf. *Religious Freedom and the Constitution*, 130, where the authors gratuitously postulate that a (hypothetical?) 'mainstream Christian' majority consciously treat dissenters as 'less than full members of our community' who lack 'equal constitutional stature'.

the final chapter of each of those books, and of my *Aquinas* book, and have outlined again today, that the rationality norms which guide us in *all* our fruitful thinking also, and integrally, summon us to affirm the existence and providence of God, then we should expect that refusals to make such an affirmation will rest on arguments, or on other considerations, which do not leave reason, including practical reason, intact and undistorted. I have already alluded to this matter in my remarks about Hume, Dawkins, and Dewey. And those reflections can be taken a little further.

The first condition for the acceptability of a philosophical position is that it be coherent not only with itself but also with the worth of critically reflecting on it, proposing it, arguing for it, and communicating it discursively to others. So, for example, positions about legal obligation must not only satisfy the test which H.L.A. Hart showed[40] is failed by Holmesian Legal Realism, namely that it make real sense of the use of rules by judges, officials, and other rule-followers—a use in which rules function not as predictions but rather as guides, directives, and norms. Positions about legal obligation must also make sense of the willingness of such judges and others to treat positive legal rules in this way, in deliberations where at the time for decision the rules must either compete or cohere with the standing reasons for action that are supplied by moral requirements and other intelligible needs. Hart, as Nicola Lacey's biography shows, was tormented by what he knew to be the failure of his own legal philosophy to satisfy that condition.[41] Blocking his way to a satisfactory account was his deep uncertainty about the status, *as reasons*, of moral and other deep practical principles and reasons for action; he could not see how they could be true—really reasons—without being somehow 'part of the furniture of the universe', a metaphor he rightly regarded as discrediting what it purported to signify. And indeed the only ultimately satisfactory account of practical truth is one that first points to first practical principles such as I have exemplified by the principles directing us respectively to the good of truth and the good of friendship—and secondly understands these *as* principles that we do not select, fashion, or invent, and that have their truth by anticipating the human fulfilment whose realization is possible through actions in conformity with these (and other like) principles; and that thirdly observes that though this anticipatory correspondence to fulfilment is different from the correspondence of true propositions to reality in non-practical knowledge, the two kinds of truth are nonetheless analogous since in both cases there is a correspondence of the human mind,

---

[40] *CL* 1, 10–11.   [41] Lacey, *A Life of H.L.A. Hart*, 335–6.

and its objects, with the divine creative mind.[42] That account of practical truth, though it is not free from mystery or challenge to the imagination, is coherent and sufficiently intelligible, and with it in place, we can range up and down the whole reach of practical thought, making good sense of the authority and obligatoriness of positive law and its 'social fact sources'. We can escape the fate of all those narrow legal positivisms shipwrecked by their aspiration to explain the legal 'Ought' (which they rightly conceive as a kind of reason for action) by deriving it from some 'Is'—a form of explanation which Plato and Aristotle discerned was fallacious long before Hume did, and far more steadily than Hume ever did.

Similarly, legal philosophy's account of agency and responsibility in contract formation, tort, and criminal law must cohere with the facts of human freedom and responsibility to rational normativity which are instantiated, precisely as facts both experienced and at least partly understood, in one's critical questioning, reflecting, and reasonably judging in this or any other area of philosophy. For philosophizing is an activity, and carrying it forward is subject at every moment to our freedom to back off, opt out, cheat, or persevere in fidelity to norms of rationality (attention to evidence, relevant questions, and argument, and so forth). And the mystery of this freedom of choice, so scandalous to materialists, is alleviated by two reflections: (1) that divine causality must be such that it could explain not only the causality that natural science seeks out and recounts but also those orders of reality—evidenced, like the order or reality studied by natural sciences, in every deliberate human act—orders whose intelligibility is not the object of natural sciences at all, the orders of logic, of practical reasoning towards choice and self-shaping action, and of mind's mastery over matter in technologies from speaking and ballet-dancing to moon-shots; and (2) that the creator's choice to bring about this universe rather than none or some other had a freedom which is surely the archetype of any choice of ours that is truly free.

Nietzsche's famous account of guilt and punishment, and conscience, in his *On the Genealogy of Morals* (1887)—a prime inspiration of today's post-modernisms—is a paradigm of the havoc wrought in a train of thought, a course of thinking, which is in some sense philosophical but truncated and turned against itself by (as Nietzsche is well aware) that refusal of natural theology which he gives the absurd but sinister name 'the death of God'. Suffice it to recall the last part of the *Genealogy*, in which he declares that willingness to seek and hold on to truth is itself a product of that sickness we call conscience. The truths that conscience is a sickness and

---

[42] See 1987f at 115–20; *Aquinas* 99–100.

that God, the only ground of truth's value, is non-existent therefore put in question, render problematic, the will to truth, and the value of truth and being truthful: 'the value of truth must for once, by way of experiment, be *called into question...*' Nietzsche's phrase 'by way of experiment' reveals the ultimately frivolous character of his thought,[43] and the depth of the impasse to which his arbitrary assertions and denials have driven him. But he does not deny, indeed he here, at this juncture, admits that the 'core' of conscience is, in fact, the will to truth and truthfulness. As he says, again, the 'hard, severe, abstemious, heroic spirits...these pale atheists, anti-Christians, immoralists, nihilists...these men are far from *free* spirits: *for they still believe in the truth!*' And right here Nietzsche associates himself with the *secretum* of the highest grades of 'that invincible order of the Assassins, that order of free spirits *par excellence*', (a sect of Shi'ite Muslims in Syria, Lebanon, and northern Persia, whose operative killers called themselves *fedayeen*)—the *secretum* being, according to Nietzsche, that 'nothing is true, everything is permitted'. He calls this a 'proposition' (true? false?) with 'labyrinthine consequences' that will be worked out in 'the great drama in a hundred acts which is reserved for Europe over the next two thousand years...'.[44]

In all this we have, of course, left reason and responsibility far behind, and are witnessing the performance of a kind of atheistical magician, a performance rationally inferior, by far, to the paradigms of religious thought. One of the evidences of its real impact in legal theoretical writings of recent years was Judge Posner's 1998 lectures at Harvard on law and morality.[45] On the wider stage of the world, of course, such performances as Nietzsche's, such essays in decapitating reality by wilfully refusing to admit reasonable questions and to pursue the self-critical, collaborative, discursive search for real causes wherever it leads, have had drastically real consequences. Eric Voegelin traced in detail[46] the point at which the young Marx, some years before Nietzsche, issued to himself (as if to the world too) his decree against raising questions about ultimate origins, and gave himself over to the fantasy of self-creation which is at the root of his notion of revolutionary transformation of human nature and society, a notion for which so many paid so high a price with so little good fruit of any kind.

In short, decapitation of reality is dangerous to individuals and societies. Religion in principle repudiates what, as sound philosophy confirms, is

---

[43] We do not have to decide about Nietzsche's character, or about what truth may be found in his work. Voegelin, 'Nietzsche, the Crisis and the War' at 185–6 presents him as a teller of truth about Europe's cultural suicide; elsewhere Voegelin shows him as a paradigm of the destruction wrought by atheism and the nihilism that is its rationally consistent accompaniment.

[44] For citations and some further material, see essay III.12 at 169–71 (1999b at 92–4) esp. n. 17.

[45] 'The Problematics of Moral and Legal Theory' (see the opening quotation).

[46] 'Science, Politics, and Gnosticism' at 262–5, 268–71, 274, 279–80, 284–6.

indeed such a decapitation. Treating religion as a private concern with the same public status as casual private sex insinuates a serious public untruth about the reality in which political communities and their law have their place.[47] The political community's public duty to respect, that is, to leave uncoerced, the conscientious religious beliefs and acts of everyone, even beliefs that include much that is false and acts that are accordingly ill-justified, is a duty grounded in a serious *moral* (not legal) duty of each individual—one's duty: to seek the truth about reality's most fundamental shape and, having raised and pursued that question, to shape one's own life in line with what one judges one has discovered about such matters, a duty which is only fulfilled if it is pursued with an authenticity that would be prejudiced, corrupted, and even nullified by coercion and psychological pressure.[48]

VI

Before I conclude with a secondary reason or pair of reasons for giving free exercise of religion constitutional protection, I should say something on the appropriate form and measure of that protection. Forbidding or invalidating the prohibition of free exercise of religion is probably not as satisfactory as declaring a right such as that articulated in Article 25 of the Constitution of the Republic of India, brought into effect in January 1950 after more than two years of lucid and intelligent public debate in a constitutional convention:

Right to Freedom of Religion
25. (1) Subject to public order, morality and health and to the other provisions of
      this Part, all persons are equally entitled to freedom of conscience and the
      right freely to profess, practise and propagate religion.

---

[47] This damaging insinuation is analogous to (though significantly distinct from) the damaging insinuation (teaching) portrayed by Budziszewski, *What We Can't Not Know*, 162:

> A good many parents decline to give their children any religious instruction, saying that they think it is better to 'let them make up their own minds.' But declining to teach [religion] is itself a way of teaching…a very definite creed with eight articles: (1) It is not important for children to know anything about God. (2) The questions which children naturally ask about Him require no answers. (3) Parents know nothing about Him worth passing on. (4) To think about Him adequately, no preparation is needed. (5) What adults think about Him makes no difference. (6) By implication, He does not make any difference either; God is not to be treated as God. (7) If anything is to be treated as God, it will have to be something other than Him. (8) This is the true creed, and all other creeds are false.… [A person thus] raised to 'make up his own mind'…[will have] the habit of not taking important things seriously, and the habit of considering the way things really are as less important than what he thinks of them at the moment.

[48] That is the fundamental argument in Second Vatican Council, Declaration on Religious Liberty, 1965 (*Dignitatis Humanae*) (DH).

Later in the same year, the European Convention on Human Rights and Fundamental Freedoms (ECHR) articulated:

Article 9—Freedom of thought, conscience and religion
1. Everyone has the right to freedom of thought, conscience and religion; this right includes freedom to change his religion or belief and freedom, either alone or in community with others and in public or private, to manifest his religion or belief, in worship, teaching, practice and observance.

The European formulation has some advantages. It suggests one of the reasons why it is appropriate not to be content with declaring a right to freedom of thought and conscience. Much more clearly than 'thought' and 'conscience', the term 'religion' connotes activities which extend from the individual to the associative and social, and from the private to the public, even when the Indian Constitution's reference to propagation is omitted. The European formulation also makes explicit the freedom to change one's religion, something suddenly of importance again in the demographically altering west; and the Second Vatican Council's articulation of the freedom[49] makes helpfully explicit that, morally if not constitutionally, the right is to be 'immune from coercion whether by individuals or social groups and by every kind of human power'.[50]

---

[49] This is essentially a right to be *free from coercion* when one is exercising one's conscience in forming, holding, or giving effect in action to one's beliefs 'in matters religious' (*in re religiosa*). This freedom from coercion was often described by the drafting committee as an immunity. And though it is not an immunity in the sense stipulated by Hohfeld in his analysis of jural relations, there is no objection to using 'immunity' as a synonym for a claim-right not to be interfered with or coerced. The 'religious liberty' is nothing more, nor less, than a *claim-right not to be coerced in performing religious acts, individual or corporate within due limits.*

It follows that the fundamental topic of DH is in substance not a liberty-right (*stricto sensu*) but duty—the duty of state government and law, and of other groups and individuals in civil society, not to coerce anyone's religious acts unless they threaten the rights of others, public peace, or public morality. The right of religious liberty—freedom from coercion—that is the subject-matter of DH is nothing other than the correlative of that duty, i.e. it is *nothing other than that duty considered from the point of view of the beneficiary* of (the performance of) that duty. For analysis of the Declaration and its drafters' intentions on this issue, see essay 4 at 90–5.

[50] DH 2:

This Vatican Council declares that human persons have the right to religious freedom. This kind of freedom consists in this: that all human beings ought to be immune from coercion whether by individuals or social groups and by every kind of human power, so that in religious matters no-one is compelled to act against his or her conscience or impeded from acting according to his or her conscience, whether acting publicly or privately, alone or in association with others, within due limits.

The Latin is:

Haec Vaticana Synodus declarat personam humanam ius habere ad libertatem religiosam. Huiusmodi libertas in eo consistit, quod omnes homines debent immunes esse a coercitione ex parte sive singulorum sive coetuum socialium et cuiusvis potestatis humanae, et ita quidem ut in re religiosa neque aliquis cogatur ad agendum contra suam conscientiam neque impediatur, quominus iuxta suam conscientiam agat privatim et publice, vel solus vel aliis consociatus, intra debitos limites.

The modern constitutional and ecclesiastical documents all try to specify the boundaries of the right or freedom. The European Convention, for example, says (Article 9(2)):

Freedom to manifest one's religion or beliefs shall be subject only to such limitations as are prescribed by law and are necessary in a democratic society in the interests of public safety, for the protection of public order, health or morals, or for the protection of the rights and freedoms of others.[51]

In practice, despite the use here of the Convention's stock phrase 'necessary in a democratic society', this principle of limitation works much more like *Employment Division v Smith* than like the earlier US principle in *Sherbert v Verner* (1963),[52] which permitted limitations on free exercise of religion only when required by some *compelling* state interest. So we can ask about both *Smith* and Article 9(2): Do they give sufficient constitutional protection? Obviously, much could be said, and I will skip to the bottom line. There can be problems that are not really about boundaries but about abuses, moral errors by legislators or judges that can scarcely be protected against by sound constitutional provisions. The application of general and (in intent) religiously neutral laws against discrimination can be unjust and a grave imposition on religious or religiously organized and inspired enterprises. Such is the case with laws prohibiting discrimination against persons who make no secret of their engaging in same-sex sex acts but wish to be employed as teachers in Catholic or Evangelical schools or to make use of Catholic or Evangelical facilities such as adoption agencies, church halls, and so forth. The mentality which regards same-sex marriage as conceivable, let alone desirable or reasonable, involves a truly radical break with human experience and reason. The consequent unjust impositions on religious or religiously motivated activities and associations are probably

---

The scandalously inadequate translation currently on the Vatican website reads:

> This Vatican Council declares that the human person has a right to religious freedom. This freedom means that no one is to be forced to act in a manner contrary to his own beliefs, whether privately or publicly, whether alone or in association with others, within due limits.

[51] The Indian limiting provision is built into the text of Art. 25(1), and is amplified by Art. 25(2):

(2) Nothing in this article shall affect the operation of any existing law or prevent the State from making any law—

   (a) regulating or restricting any economic, financial, political or other secular activity which may be associated with religious practice;

   (b) providing for social welfare and reform or the throwing open of Hindu religious institutions of a public character to all classes and sections of Hindus.

DH 7 says the right can be made subject to legal limitations arising out of

> the need for an effective safeguard of the rights of all citizens and for the peaceful settlement of conflicts of rights, also out of the need for an adequate care of genuine public peace, which comes about when people live together in good order and in true justice, and finally out of the need for a proper guardianship of public morality.

[52] 374 US 398.

best resisted by pointing, not to religious liberty, but to the way these impositions infringe associational freedom and parental rights, while pointing in any case to their manifold wrong-headedness about sex and marriage, to their abuses of children's innocence, and to their recklessness about the common good and the nation's future. In short, I am rather disinclined to protest, as Congress has, against the principle in *Smith*; its requirement that any law limiting free exercise be neutral, given vivid effect in the Santeria animal sacrifice case,[53] should give religion the constitutional protection it deserves and in some eras may need.

VII

Two secondary, rather pragmatic reasons to judge religion deserving of constitutional protection come into view when we raise a final question. What if a religion rejects on principle the right to religious freedom as defined, for example, in the ECHR's reference to freedom to change one's religion, and rejects also other fundamental elements of our constitutional order? After all, it is only five or six years since the eighteen judges of the European Court of Human Rights (ECtHR) held unanimously, in *Refah Partisi (No. 2) v Turkey*, that:

...the Court considers that sharia, *which faithfully reflects the dogmas and divine rules laid down by religion, is stable and invariable.* Principles such as pluralism in the political sphere or the constant evolution of public freedoms have no place in it.... [A] regime based on sharia...clearly diverges from Convention values, particularly with regard to its criminal law and criminal procedure, its rules on the legal status of women and the way it intervenes in all spheres of private and public life in accordance with religious precepts.... [A] political party whose actions seem to be aimed at introducing sharia...can hardly be regarded as an association complying with the democratic ideal that underlies the whole of the Convention.[54]

On that basis the ECtHR upheld the Turkish Supreme Court's dissolution of Turkey's elected Government and of the country's main party, on the grounds that the Government in which that party was dominant was, or might well be, preparing to introduce sharia either as law applicable to all or as part of a scheme in which every citizen would be subjected to the law of his or her own religion respectively.

Contemporary American constitutionalists are deeply suspicious of this sort of 'militant democracy'—pre-emptive defence of democracy—even when practised, as here, by a court (initially the supreme court in

---

[53] *Church of the Lukumi Babalu Aye, Inc. v City of Hialeah* 508 US 520 (1993).
[54] *Refah Partisi (No. 2) v Turkey* (2003) 37 European Human Rights Reports 1 at para. 123 (emphasis added), Grand Chamber, upholding and adopting the language of the Third Section of the ECtHR in *Refah Partisi (No. 1) v Turkey* (2002) 35 European Human Rights Reports 3.

Turkey). They will tend to find it even more questionable when it asks you to focus steadily on the possibility that a particular religion—the private faith of fellow citizens or of hard-up immigrants—might be different from all other religions in its core beliefs about the Constitution, and about the legitimacy of long-term deception and intimidation in the cause of overthrowing it or, much more immediately, in the cause of rendering certain constitutional guarantees, and related moral rights, inapplicable within the religion's zone of dominance. For I should not conceal the fact that it was part of Turkey's case before the ECtHR that 'In order to attain its ultimate goal of replacing the existing legal order with sharia, political Islam use[s] the method known as "*takiyye*", which consist[s] in hiding its beliefs until it ha[s] attained that goal.' The Court did not make any explicit finding about Islamic *takiyye* (a practice which had not, it seems, been denied by the applicant members of the dissolved government and party), but it did observe more broadly that political parties and movements may conceal their aims and profess their adherence to democracy and the rule of law until it is too late to prevent them overthrowing both.[55] Still, for present purposes we do not really need to speculate about the possible secret intentions of particular members of the Islamic religion. We can study the open public documents and declarations of states publicly holding themselves out, and cooperating with each other, precisely as *Islamic* states, such as the Cairo Declaration on Human Rights in Islam, adopted by the governments of 45 states in August 1990[56] as superior to the Universal Declaration of Human Rights adopted by the General Assembly of the United Nations in 1948. This 1990 Islamic Declaration's article on religious freedom reads as follows:

(10) Islam is the religion of true unspoiled nature. It is prohibited to exercise any form of pressure on man or to exploit his poverty or ignorance in order to force him to change his religion to another religion or to atheism.

The barely equivocal 'to another religion' makes the second sentence a declaration of the unfreedom of all persons deemed by Islamic law to be Muslim. For good measure, Articles 24 and 25 add:

(24) All the rights and freedoms stipulated in this Declaration are subject to the Islamic Shari'ah.
(25) The Islamic Shari'ah is the only source of reference for the explanation or clarification of any of the articles of this Declaration.

---

[55] *Refah (No. 1)* at paras 48 and 80; *Refah (No. 2)* at para. 101. See 2009e and 2009f.
[56] UN GAOR, World Conf. on Hum. Rts, 4th Sess., Agenda Item 5, UN Doc. A/CONF.157/PC/62/Add.18 (1993). The declaration is by the Organization of the Islamic Conference, to which now (2009) belong 57 states (not all of them Muslim-majority or Islamic in constitutional form); approval of the document was by the organ of the Conference which meets annually, viz. the Islamic Conference of Foreign Ministers.

These realities put a question mark over more than one part of the orthodoxy of the American freedom to exercise doctrine. They raise a doubt about the part that says the law and the court must make no investigation of a religion's doctrines, and over the part, treated as axiomatic by justices of every shade of opinion, that forbids any discrimination between religions. What if the 'theological propositions of a religion' include *political* teachings 'wholly at odds with premises of our liberal democracy' or, to speak like the ECtHR, 'with the democratic ideal that underlies the whole of the [Constitution]' or, to speak I think more suitably, with the Constitution and other principles that we have taken as foundational for our law? Is it unconstitutional to discriminate between religions at the borders? Would doing so amount to a wrongful *disparagement* of adherents of the religion who are already citizens? Would it wrongfully impinge upon *their* free exercise of religion? Or violate the human right to religious liberty of those who would be kept out of the country in the interests of the nation's public order?

In thinking about the last question, we come across one of the secondary reasons for constitutionally acknowledging religious liberty: that that guarantee fittingly accompanies the appropriate principle of distinction between religion and state, the principle which the Constitution witnesses to, perhaps, by its exclusion of religious tests and prohibition of Congressional establishment of religion.[57] The distinction is, of course, of wide and fundamental importance. It is theme enough for another essay. The only implication of it that I wish to touch on is its relevance to thinking about control of immigration. In that precise connection we can see it at work in one of the present Pope's first statements:

[S]ingle believers are called to open their arms and their hearts to every person, from whatever nation they come, allowing the Authorities responsible for public life to enforce [*stabilire*] the relevant laws held to be appropriate for a healthy co-existence.[58]

Within a universal religious community such as the Pope's there is no distinction between citizen and foreigner. But, as his words make plain, it

---

[57] The principle appears in another way in the second reason given by DH for religious liberty:
The religious acts whereby men, in private and in public and out of a sense of personal conviction, direct their lives to God *transcend by their very nature the order of terrestrial and temporal affairs.* Government [*potestas civilis*] therefore ought indeed to take account of the religious life of the citizenry and show it favour, since the function of government is to make provision for the common welfare. However, it would transgress the limits of its power were it to presume to command or inhibit religious acts [*actus religiosos dirigere vel impedire*]. (DH 3, emphasis added.)

[58] Benedict XVI, Address to the Pontifical Council for Pastoral Care of Migrants and Itinerant People, 15 May 2006, AAS 98: 454. Nothing in the particularly vague paragraph on international migration in the encyclical *Caritas in Veritate* (29 June 2009), sec. 62, qualifies this.

does not follow that such a distinction may not have decisive relevance to the common good, and indeed the public order, of political communities.

So a nation-state—if not this one, any time soon, then one or more of the European states more immediately affected—might judge it reasonable to limit or forbid further immigration by persons unwilling to credibly renounce their religion's core theologico-political and numbers-dependent drive to impose political and legal domination.[59] But then—and here is the other secondary reason I want to mention for constitutionally guaranteeing free exercise—it would be all the more important, you may agree, firmly to protect the right—a qualified right, of course[60]—of *citizens* to practise that religion (as well as the right, not recognized by their religion's law or doctrine, to renounce it).

[59] Because numbers—critical masses—matter, times change. A legislature looking forward from now, or fairly soon, might responsibly decide that the only likely medium-term constructive *alternative* to forbidding immigration by persons unwilling to make that renunciation will foreseeably prove to be the *state-promoted* introduction—as is beginning to be ventured in France, Germany, and the UK—of a would-be emasculated version of that highly distinctive religion, a version supervised by state instrumentalities responsible for selecting its teachers and preachers in the hope of watering down its inbuilt focus on domination, violence, and submission, its division of the world into the world of submission and the world of war, its public and private subjection of women, and other features that (so the legislature might judge) make it at best inassimilable and at worst a clear and mounting danger to the public good. If the latter alternative (a state-sponsored form of that religion) is to be judged permanently unavailable here in the United States, because it would be a plain 'establishment of religion', still the resort to it by centrist European governments may go some way towards (a) showing a compelling state interest in not treating that religion and its followers in just the same way as others, and thus (b) surmounting the bar raised by the beguiling but curious doctrine of the Supreme Court that discrimination against one religion is not only unfair but also an establishment of all the others (and of irreligion?).

[60] See n. 51 above.

2

RELIGION AND PUBLIC LIFE IN
PLURALIST SOCIETY*

The identification of human flourishing's basic aspects can be made, and defended against objections and misunderstandings, without appealing to any idea of divine causality, still less to any idea of a divine will about what we should and should not choose. The inquiry into human flourishing can proceed without adverting to the question of divine existence; the good of relating appropriately to a transcendent and intelligent source of everything we know of can be postulated without being affirmed—can be left, that is, as a kind of space in the account of human flourishing, to be occupied by the good we call *religion* if, but only if, further inquiry shows that such a being must be judged to exist. Accordingly, when one pursues (a) the inquiry into the principles of practical understanding that direct us towards the basic aspects of human flourishing, and (b) the inquiry into the rational requirement that one remain open in all one's deliberation and choice to the directiveness of each of those first principles, and likewise (c) the inquiry into the implications of that requirement, implications we call morality, one can proceed, rather as one does in the natural sciences, without adverting to the *further question*: the question whether the fact that all these principles are true, and the fact that we have the capacity to recognize that and to shape ourselves and the world accordingly, aren't facts that can be explained only as effects of a causality that, by reason of *what* its causer is, needs no further explanation. That 'further question' could be postponed to the end, or at least to the end of my books *NLNR* and *FoE*; obviously, if its answer is positive, the implications need taking up and being given their due importance, in due course.

The decision to structure my books in that way was in some respects methodologically motivated: the study of metaphysics, of the

* 2009d (address to a conference on the place of religion in American public life, Princeton University, October 2004).

foundations of all knowing and being, properly comes last (as Aquinas and Aristotle say). But my procedure was also an exercise in what John Henry Newman, following the Alexandrian Church Fathers of the third century AD, called *economy*: the adapting of exposition to the receptiveness, the state of mind, of one's expected audience. The idea of economy, in this or related senses, has got a bad name: a recent head of an Oxford college, when he was in public life as Secretary of the Cabinet and Head of the UK Civil Service, was pilloried for testifying that he thought it proper in the interest of the state sometimes to be 'economical with the truth'.[1] Newman himself was given occasion to write his famous *Apologia pro Vita Sua* by widely applauded accusations of dishonesty made by Charles Kingsley and made precisely because that best-selling children's author and cleric equated economy with deviousness, evasion, deception. But from the outset of his teaching, Newman had insisted on the line separating those vices of dishonesty from a rightly discreet *stewardship of the truth* by presenting always what is true, withholding no more of the relevant truth than the ignorance or prejudices of one's hearers would prevent them from properly understanding and assessing.[2] My procedure was indeed less economical than the decision of my mentor and editor H.L.A. Hart to leave undisclosed in all his public work his own atheism and his vigorous doubt that there are any moral truths whatever. After all, chapter XIII of my *NLNR* is right there in the hands of every reader of the book, with its argument, pursued over some pages, that the 'further question' of the origin of everything we come to acknowledge can only be answered reasonably by judging that—to put the matter as shortly as it can be put—God's existence and intelligent and necessarily free choice to create is that needed explanation.

Practising a similar economy even more strenuously in my *Aquinas*, I abstracted from—passed over in silence—the great theologian's theological concerns and foundations until, again, the last chapter, where I set out a version of each of the five kinds of ways of posing and pressing the 'further question', ways which he rightly thinks show that it is unreasonable not to judge that the universe as a whole and in every aspect is the effect of the

---

[1] Sir Robert, later Lord, Armstrong, testifying on behalf of the British Government, in proceedings (to suppress publication of the book *Spycatcher*) in the Supreme Court of New South Wales, in November 1986.

[2] For Newman's thoughts on this economy, thoughts which like the tradition's draw upon several of the senses of the Greek term *oikonomia* and appeal to pertinent and telling Scriptural sayings (no pearls before swine, no crushing the bruised reed, the tares to be left among the wheat) and examples (Paul's address to the Areopagus in Athens: Acts 17: 22–31), see his *Fifteen Sermons Preached before the University of Oxford*, 341–50; *Apologia Pro Vita Sua*, 45–6, 270, 343–6; *The Arians of the Fourth Century*, 65–77.

creative action of a being that is pure actuality free from every shadow of mere potentiality, a reality whose *what* it is includes *that* it is, a being with all the uncaused and necessary existence that the entire universe would lack even if it happened to have existed from eternity, a being which has projected some of its own intelligent intelligibility into the universe that it has freely—from among all alternative possible universes—brought into being and actuality.

The causing, ordering, and sustaining of the universe must, therefore, be an intellectual act which in one and the same timeless act both projects (by practical understanding) and effects (by willing), in every detail, this world with all its causal/explanatory systems, its unimaginable galaxies, subatomic particles, and fundamental forces—a world, too, of genomes, cells, and brains; of mathematics and logic which (even without aspiring to) fit that world; of loyalty, justice, and remorse; of computers, symphonies, chess, and constitutions.[3]

In my book on Aquinas I turn from that point to try to explicate, in barest outline, how these conclusions affect the understanding of the ethical and political principles and virtues explored in the preceding eleven chapters. A part of this explication:

The principles of practical reasonableness are now understandable as having the force and depth of a kind of sharing in God's creative purpose and providence.[4] The good of practical reasonableness {bonum rationis} is now understandable as good not only intrinsically and for its own sake but also as a constituent in the good of *assimilatio* [making oneself like][5] and *adhaesio* [uniting oneself] to the omnipotent creator's practical wisdom and choice. The truth of the practical principles is now understandable not only as the anticipation of the human fulfilment to which they direct us,[6] but also as their conformity to the most real of all realities, the divine creative mind, the mind which is nothing other than the very reality of that pure and simple *act*, God.[7]

There is a lot more to be said along these lines, but there are two points to be made here, about what is going on in these and similar discussions. The first is that the whole course of reflection, heading towards the reasonable judgment that God exists and is relevant to understanding more adequately why our responsibilities matter, is an exercise in

---

[3] *Aquinas* 305.

[4] 'And so it is clear that the natural law is precisely the sharing out of the eternal law in the rational creature {participatio legis aeternae in rationali creatura}': *ST* I–II q.91 a.2c. It is *as* the natural law in this sense that the eternal law is the standard for human willing {regula voluntatis humanae}: I–II q.71 a.6c.

[5] Plato attributes much the same importance to achieving likeness with God: see *Laws* IV 716; *Republic* VI 501. The ideal is the more attractive when put in the frame of Christian revelation's disclosure of God as intelligent, free, self-possessed, and generous, as well as (to use the predicate that Plato regards as central) moderate. See *Aquinas* 314–15.

[6] See *Aquinas* 99–100.   [7] *Ibid.*, 308–9.

public reason. The second is that the argument's conclusion entails that neither atheism nor radical agnosticism is entitled to be treated as the 'default' position in public reason, deliberation, and decisions. Those who say or assume that there is a default position and that it is secular in *those* senses[8] (atheism or agnosticism about atheism) owe us an argument that engages with and defeats the best arguments for divine causality. Only if some counter-argument of this kind were successful would they be entitled to set aside the judgment of the countless many who, even when they could not articulate formal arguments for it, have been able to judge that the reality and intelligibility of this world has been brought (and is kept) from nothingness by something that utterly transcends it and whose 'glory', as the Psalmist says, 'is declared by the heavens'.[9] The heavens are the part of this world we most easily contemplate for what it *is*, without mixing in our own concerns with using or relating to it. They also arouse in us the thought that we are not in a world closed off in death and finitude, but in a reality that opens out—not spatially—into transcendence.

Still, public reason's deliberative, practical part does deal with matters that concern us because, unlike God, they can be brought into being, changed, or averted by our choice and action. These are the deliberations for which the principles understood in practical reason—of natural law, if you like—give their directions, their prescriptions. The purpose of all the earlier chapters in these books of mine was to show how moral rules and principles, not least those we use more or less uncontroversially throughout our law, are explicable by reference to the more general and first principles of intelligent thinking about what to do, taken with a sound and exact understanding of what—what kind of act—one elects to do when one has deliberatively shaped alternative proposals for action and made one's choice by adopting one of them. The common objection to this whole idea is that it fails because the principles it identifies command none of the consensus that, say, good science confidently expects and commonly gets. The objection uses the fact of pluralism as an argument for scepticism about natural law, but really (therefore) about all ethical propositions.

The objection is invalid. The truth of ethical claims is assessed, not by looking to facts such as people's agreement or disagreement with them, but by considering whether they correctly identify how the kind of action (or abstention) in issue relates to the well-being of human persons (human flourishing), and whether it rightly evaluates that relationship.

---

[8] On the legitimate secularism which is part of Christian doctrine, see e.g. *Aquinas* 322–5; essay 3, at 56.

[9] Psalms 19: 1; and see Romans 1: 19–20 et seq., which opens up into the Pauline account of natural law: 2: 14–16.

The standards of rightness and wrongness in such assessments are identified in the reflective, critically clarified practical understanding and reasoning we call ethics. Consensus around those standards is not what makes them true, and is not a necessary condition of that truth in any sense save this: that under *ideal* epistemic conditions, there would be consensus on them. For: that there would be consensus under ideal conditions on a proposition's truth is a 'mark'—not a criterion—of that proposition's truth.[10] But the conditions under which any and every moral proposition is in fact assessed are very far indeed from ideal. We have strong emotional interests in securing certain outcomes which would be blocked by any reasonable ethical standard. Our capacity to devise rationalizations for departing from reasonable ethical standards to secure those interests is very great. The tendency for language, institutions and culture to crystallize around such plausible (albeit unreasonable) rationalizations is very strong, resulting in local (but perhaps widespread and rather lasting) subscription to—and often enough more or less local consensus on—distorted standards and ethical falsehoods. The overall pluralism of ethical opinions about more or less specific kinds of action is precisely the kind of diversity one would expect, even though there is some impressively general consensus on some very general principles and standards.

The past forty years have provided illuminatingly clear examples of the way in which the descent from high-level general principles to specific moral rules and judgments is waylaid by emotions, mixed motives, and rationalization. Even in the mid-1960s, after eighty years of passionate feminist campaigning about birth control as a necessary alleviation of the difficulties and dangers faced by women in and after pregnancy, the idea that a mother has a right, moral or legal, to choose to seek the death of the child she has conceived was virtually unheard of, had no perceptible presence in the literature,[11] and had been implicitly repudiated as unethical and unacceptable by main leaders among the feminist advocates of birth control. But then, within ten years, that idea became, as it remains, a commonplace for many (albeit without consensus about its basis or limits). Yet it remained and remains in the view of many others a simply false claim of right. To me, its acceptance seems a paradigm instance of the process by which moral truth becomes obscured, and a vivid illustration of the way that non-ideal epistemic conditions block the attainment or retention of consensus on moral propositions. But there are plenty of other paradigmatic instances. In my book with Joseph Boyle and Germain Grisez

---

[10] For this use of 'mark' (a term much used by Newman), see the summary and discussion of David Wiggins's account of truth, in *FoE* 63–6.

[11] See my survey of the positions promoted in the medical literature in the 1960s: 1970c.

on nuclear deterrence, we trace the historical process on which a consensus that civilians should not be intentionally selected for destruction was lost, and the moral truth considerably though by no means wholly obscured, under the non-ideal epistemic conditions prevailing in Europe in 1941 and in the Pacific in 1945.[12]

But of course, epistemic conditions are never ideal, even in the natural sciences and mathematics, where ambitions, fears, uncriticized conventions and assumptions, and other such factors can and do distort rational inquiry and judgment. All the more so in moral reasoning. Moral reasoning always concerns premises and conclusions, principles and judgments that are liable to affect profoundly our *interests* and the passions, strong or calm, whose objects are wrapped up in those interests. And the impact of familial, local, and national conventions and prejudices is particularly formative of the elements with which we conduct our moral reasoning. (As Aristotle says,[13] you should pray that you happened to grow up in a morally more or less sound culture, since if you didn't your ability to do ethics soundly is all but irremediably weakened. He did not mean, of course, that culture or convention, even when morally sound, is the *criterion* of what is sound and unsound in ethics.)

Hence it is hard, though by no means impossible, to think soundly about moral matters, not least about the issues that do not concern the forms of human good realizable by our choice and action, but rather the given make-up and dignity of human persons, or the proper description of human acts—issues that, though not in themselves practical, normative, 'ought' questions, nonetheless directly enter into and affect moral judgments. Now if (1) consistently sound moral thought is difficult to achieve and maintain, and (2) at the same time it is the case that the moral principles which are the criteria of moral soundness and unsoundness are, like every other intelligibility that we find rather than make, to be attributed to the wisdom and will of a divine creator—as the arguments I sketched earlier indicate they should—then (3) it is reasonable to anticipate that this supremely intelligent creator of less adequate intelligences like ours might communicate those same moral principles in a way that renders them more clearly accessible and more palpably warranted. And that anticipation is satisfactorily met, fulfilled, as one aspect of the public revelation in Jesus the Christ.

So the issue at the heart of my reflections is the status of public revelation in public reason. Revelation of God's nature and intentions for us is 'public', in the focal sense, when it is offered in public preaching attested to by

---

[12] *NDMR* 38–44.   [13] *NE* I.4: 1095b4–8.

signs or miracles such as resurrection, otherwise inexplicable healing, fulfilment of prophecies, and so forth. But the evidentiary force of these is immeasurably enhanced by, perhaps even dependent upon, the further fact that the teaching to whose authenticity they are meant to attest, a teaching by word and deed, is itself *morally* attractive. As I once summarized Aquinas,

the revelatory power and credit-worthiness of Christ's teaching should be ascribed also to [besides miracles and other public signs] his persuasive authority and manifest personal virtue, and the inherent excellence of what he taught— something he deliberately left to be judged from the public preaching and writing of those who had witnessed his own public life and works.[14]

In other words, we bring to our hearing of the preaching and assessment of its teachers and witnesses our prior understanding of human good, an understanding that is, as I have argued, at root our natural reason. And we use that as a criterion in judging, for ourselves, the authenticity, the divine origin, of what is being proposed and displayed to us. Yet, in turn, the preaching, the witness, and the exemplary lives of the teachers can and do change our prior moral understanding, enhancing and correcting it. There is, to this extent, a reciprocity and a certain kind of epistemic interdependence of natural reason and divine public revelation, a reciprocity or interdependence which heads towards a kind of reflective equilibrium (as Rawls might say[15]).

That reflective equilibrium is not in all respects a once-for-all achievement, but rather is to some extent developmental, both in the life of the believer and in the teaching of the community established to bear the historical revelation through history. This does not exclude the making of definitive judgments by those with the authority to make them. But the implications of even such definitive judgments, and the meaning and implications of the rest of the revealed message, come to be understood more adequately. Experience provides the matter for more differentiated insights into the principles of practical reason, as well as into the data of revelation and the doctrine that rests upon and transmits revelation.[16]

---

[14] *Aquinas* 320–1, citing *ST* III q.40 a.1c and ad 4; q.42 a.1 ad 2 and a.4c.

[15] See Rawls, *Political Liberalism*, 45, where he expounds the idea without the phrase put into currency by his *A Theory of Justice*, 18, 40–5.

[16] See Vatican Council II, Dogmatic Constitution on Divine Revelation, *Dei Verbum*, 8.2:

...crescit enim tam rerum quam verborum traditorum perceptio, tum ex contemplatione et studio credentium, qui ea conferunt in corde suo... tum ex intima spiritualium rerum quam experiuntur intelligentia...Ecclesia scilicet, volventibus saeculis, ad plenitudinem divinae veritatis iugiter tendit...

For insight into the realities and words handed down grows, through the reflection and study of the faithful who ponder these things in their hearts, and through the penetrating understanding

A fine example of this process of developing reflective equilibrium is provided by the Second Vatican Council's Declaration on Religious Liberty (1965). This document, which repays study, identifies some of the soundest and steadiest foundations of the 'public square' (and much more). It often goes by the first two words of its Latin text, *Dignitatis Humanae*—of the dignity of the human person.[17] Its core teaching can be stated quite shortly. All persons have a right, as individuals and as groups, not to be coerced by government either to perform or not perform religious acts. This right is fully possessed even by people who hold false religious beliefs—indeed, even by individuals or groups who have formed their own religious beliefs without due care for truth. It is limited *only* by the needs of public order, that is, by the need to protect the rights of others, and uphold public peace and public morality. The document divides its consideration of the right into two parts. The first defines, explicates, and justifies the right by reference to natural reason (that is, natural law) alone. The second shows how it is rooted in Christian revelation and doctrine. The principal justifying argument from natural reason is this: *so important* is it for each human being to seek, find, and live according to *the truth* about God and man—religious truth—that coercion, since it prevents, distorts, or tends to render inauthentic that search for religious truth, is wrongful. The wrong done is a wronging of the person whose search for truth, had there been no coercive pressure to conform, might have been authentic and centred on truth (about the most important things) at least as an aspiration, ideal, or goal. So that person (and thus any person) has the *right* (claim-right) correlative to the government's *duty* not to commit that wrong. And all this reinforces the document's further justifying argument, which recalls the classic Christian distinction between the secular and the ecclesial, and the idea (already coming to flower in Aquinas)[18] of limited state government: religious matters as such transcend the sphere of state government [*potestas civilis*], which, though it should recognize and favour the religious life of its citizens, 'would have to be said to be exceeding its limits if were it to presume to control [*dirigere*] or inhibit religious acts'.[19]

The principal argument from revelation is this: God created human beings with the dignity, the elevated status, of rationality and freedom,

---

of the spiritual realities of which they have experience...Thus, over the centuries, the Church is constantly heading towards the fullness of divine truth...

[I have quoted economically.] On development of doctrine through differentiation, see e.g. *MA* 25–7.

[17] This should not be translated as 'of human dignity', since the document's first three words are 'Dignitatis humanae personae', and in the context of the whole sentence the adjective *humanae* qualifies *personae* not *dignitatis*.

[18] See *Aquinas* 222–8.   [19] DH 3.4.

and has added to that dignity by inviting all to share the divine life as his sons and daughters, an invitation which, for all who can choose, can only be fittingly accepted by a fully voluntary response:

Redeemed by Christ the Saviour and through Christ Jesus called to be God's adopted son or daughter, one cannot give one's adherence to God revealing Himself unless, under the drawing of the Father, one offers to God the reasonable and free submission of faith. It is therefore completely in accord with the nature of faith that in matters religious every kind of human coercion is to be excluded.[20]

The document treats as foundational for its newly accented teaching the historically continuous Catholic doctrine that no one can rightly be coerced into the faith:

It is one of the major tenets of Catholic doctrine that one's response to God in faith must be free: no one therefore is to be forced to embrace the Christian faith against his or her own will [citations omitted]. This doctrine is contained in the word of God and it was constantly proclaimed by the Fathers of the Church.... In the life of the People of God, as it has made its pilgrim way through the vicissitudes of human history, there has at times appeared a way of acting that was hardly in accord with the spirit of the Gospel or even opposed to it. Nevertheless, the doctrine of the Church that no one is to be coerced into faith has always stood firm.[21]

The underlying thought is this: reflection on historical experience leads the Church's teachers and members to the judgment that that doctrine (faith is not to be coerced), or certainly its rationale, has wider implications. The authenticity and reality of the search for religious truth—and of the act of faith in which that search under ideal epistemic and volitional conditions would end—are so prejudiced by threats of coercion that coercive measures for the sake of religious truth, whatever their apparent success, are self-stultifying and in opposition to the nature of human persons, because they are willy-nilly in opposition to the flourishing of human persons in one of its basic (and most overarchingly important) aspects, the willing and thus whole-person-shaping *adhaesio* to God.

The natural law version (and so one might say the economical version) of the Council's teaching is in the first part of the document, the fully

---

[20] *Ibid.*, 10.

[21] *Ibid.*, 10, 12.1. For critical observations on the coercion that from the 4th to the 18th century was often applied, with ecclesiastical and theological approval, against those who departed from the Catholic faith (as distinct from pagans, Jews, Mahometans, etc.), see *Aquinas* 292. The unbelief of pagans etc. was judged harmful to the common good (*ST* II–II q.10 aa.7c and 10c) but not culpable like heresy, which was (mis)conceived of as a breach of promise and met with punishment; the thesis that these positions and measures were distinguishable from compulsion of belief (a compulsion always rejected: see II–II q.12 a.2c and ad 2; Aquinas, *Sent.* IV d.13 q.2 a.3 ad 5) was inherently unsound.

explanatory version is in the second, or rather in the two parts taken together as an achieved equilibrium. Is the second part necessary? Cannot natural law and natural rights be affirmed confidently without the benefit of revelation? That is a question that I began to answer when I was pointing to the humanly necessary interdependence of natural reason and revelation. Consider, for example, equality.

That human beings are radically equal in dignity is entailed by the revelation that we are all made in God's image, and are called as sons and daughters into his household in the transcendent Kingdom.[22] Can we have much confidence that, without benefit of those revealed teachings, this radical equality would have been steadily understood and affirmed—practically, that is, precisely as ground for true entitlement of all to equality in basic rights—or much confidence that it will be long maintained if they are set aside?[23] I do not think so.[24] Without those revelatory insights, or confirmations of insight, into our nature and potential destiny, people—even people who understand human consciousness and character with the immense penetration of a Plato—gravitate towards some version of views that treat dignity as variable, waxing and waning, predicable of us at some time after the start of one's existence as a human being, perhaps at or perhaps quite some time after one's birth, and ceasing in 'terminal' debility or disability. Or towards some variant of the view that human dignity is merely *ascribed* or *attributed*, not without flattery and speciesist bias, to beings whose true condition is like that of the other animals and substances in an indifferent universe, and whose claims and acknowledgements of

---

[22] *Dignitatis Humanae* does not mention the concept of being 'made in God's image', but it was adopted and promulgated simultaneously with the much more expansive document *Gaudium et Spes*, the Pastoral Constitution on the Church in the Modern World, which devotes secs 12 to 22 to 'The Dignity of the Human Person', and begins sec. 12 with the heading *De homine in imaginem Dei*: on the human being as made in the image of God.

[23] Writing of Charles Larmore's (and, he might have added, Ronald Dworkin's) notion that equality of respect for persons requires state neutrality about the good life, Kent Greenawalt pertinently says:

> Although many defenses of equality rely on moral capacity, it remains unclear why people should be owed equal respect based on a capacity *if* the capacity itself is unequal among people and is exercised to unequal degrees. The problem is *resolved* by some comprehensive views, most notably by the religious idea that all human beings are equally loved by God and are equal in God's sight, but it seems doubtful if the basic principle of equal respect can be grounded without reference to some comprehensive view. (Greenawalt, *Private Consciences and Public Reasons*, 82.)

[24] In its discussion of atheism in *Gaudium et Spes*, 19–21 at 21, Vatican II states (rightly, I think) that acknowledging God in no way diminishes human dignity, a dignity grounded and brought to perfection in God, and that when people are deprived of [the] divine support [of hope in life to come, and knowledge that one has been placed in the world by God who created us as intelligent and free beings] 'their dignity is deeply impaired, as may so often be seen today'. The whole of this section repays study, not least its condemnation of discrimination by civil authorities between believers and unbelievers, and its invitation to unbelievers to weigh the merits of Christ's Gospel with an open mind.

rights are truly no more than conditions of peace affording a working basis for a life of comfort and satisfaction of desires while we may.[25]

Rawls's famous theory of political liberalism is that in one's decision-making as a citizen or public official, on matters of basic importance, one should never draw upon one's 'comprehensive worldview'—one's deeper reasons for assenting to the principles and propositions that inform and direct one's decision. Instead one should proceed only on the basis of those reasons that are part of an overlapping consensus, in the sense that all [reasonable] people could reasonably be expected to 'endorse' (that is 'affirm' or agree to)[26] them. The theory is crippled by its ambiguity and unprincipled exception-making, as I and many others[27] better have shown. Anyone who thinks a proposition true thinks, or should think, that under ideal epistemic conditions all reasonable people would assent to it. So if it refers to ideal epistemic conditions, Rawls's radically ambiguous criterion—'all [reasonable] people can reasonably be expected to agree'[28]—excludes precisely nothing (except perhaps the opinion of those who think that value judgments are all relative and have no truth to them). But if the criterion refers to the actual prevailing epistemic state of affairs, then it again excludes little or nothing, because Rawls accepts that reasonable people can and do hold some unreasonable views,[29] from which it follows that for all practical purposes there is no interestingly substantive view that *all* reasonable people agree to. So Rawlsian political liberalism's exclusionary principle rests on a mere *double entendre*, and once disambiguated proves quite empty. As for the arbitrary exception-making in his theory, one can see a good example when he envisages 'rationalist believers' confronting what would be a consensus, but for their beliefs. Helping himself to the assumption that 'we' are inside this would-be consensus and the believer outside, Rawls says that we should simply draw upon our comprehensive worldview to declare the rationalist believers' belief either false or so undemonstrated as to be, in either case, ineligible to affect the consensus (without our judging that the believers themselves are unreasonable).[30] Here Rawls achieves his 'consensus'-preserving exclusion by imposing on these rationalist believers a condition that he does not impose on 'us', who are

---

[25] See *Aquinas* 297.

[26] On the synonymity (in his articulation of the criterion for reasons being public) of 'endorse' and 'affirm' and 'agree', see Rawls, *Political Liberalism*, 39, 241.

[27] See e.g. Hampton, 'The Moral Commitments of Liberalism'; or essay I.16 (1998a).

[28] On the ambiguity of 'can *be expected* to' (or 'can reasonably *be expected* to'), see essay I.16 (1998a) at nn. 22–3.

[29] Rawls, *Political Liberalism*, lvi nn. 31, 32; 244 n. 32.   [30] *Ibid.*, 152–3.

never required by him to be able to 'demonstrate' any of our principles or positions to others.[31]

Rawls fails to take seriously the fact that 'political liberalism' of his or any other kind may need to demonstrate its positions in the face of an existing or emerging anti-liberal 'consensus' or would-be consensus, not to mention the curious and the uncommitted. We may not be able to ignore this indefinitely, if large Muslim minorities or even, a bit later, majorities emerge in, say, European countries, and if these adhere, for whatever reason, to that important variety of Islam—probably the religion's authentic central form—which teaches the legitimacy of compellingly induced conversion, expulsion of anti-Islamic views and practices from the public domain, and the capital guilt of apostasy from Islam.[32] Where is the defence of freedom of religious (including irreligious) expression and practice to come from? Even setting aside the unreasonable self-denying ordinances proposed in Rawls's theory of liberalism, where are we to find the bases for a defence of that freedom, or for a defence of the radical equality of men and women? Nowhere, I think, other—and certainly nowhere better—than from the developed Christian teaching. About that teaching, and the whole doctrine of revelation that underpins it, we have sufficient reason to be confident that its truth would be recognized under proper epistemic conditions of free and open-minded discourse—that is, of public reason, properly understood and participated in—conditions that have scarcely been allowed to obtain

---

[31] Cf. e.g. *ibid.*, lv: 'if when stand-offs occur, citizens invoke the grounding reasons of their comprehensive view' [as they do when they discount the rationalist believer's ideas] 'then the principle of reciprocity is violated'. In the same passage (in the Introduction to the Paperback Edition, lvi n. 31) Rawls says that, on questions like abortion, he doesn't know whether there are any 'most reasonable or decisive' arguments (within the domain of public reason). He continues to avoid confronting the question why it is outside public reason to argue from the premise that human rights belong equally to all human beings/persons, and the premise that unborn children are human beings/persons (as is obvious whenever the baby is wanted), to the conclusion that unborn babies have the equal right to life. In 1993 he seemed committed (*ibid.*, 243) to regarding such an argument as paradigmatically unreasonable; in 1996 he seems to regard it as perhaps reasonable or perhaps unreasonable but in any case capable of being either held or rejected by reasonable people, and to be decided in practice by voting. To me it seems reasonable, and his own position paradigmatically unreasonable. (NB: the issue as he sets it up concerns not obstetrical emergencies [on which see essay II.13, sec. III] but the unborn during early pregnancy and the overriding of their life by concerns such as 'equality of women' (with men) (243n).)

[32] Abdullah Saeed (Professor of Arab and Islamic Studies in the University of Melbourne) and Hassan Saeed (Attorney General of the Maldives), in *Freedom of Religion, Apostasy and Islam* argue, in relation to Malaysia (chosen because it is one of the most moderate Muslim-majority states) that *capital* punishment for apostasy is not warranted by the Koran. They note that 'there does appear to be general consensus within the Malaysian Muslim community that some form of action ought to be taken to check the growing influence of Christianity in the region' (164), and predict that legal penalties ('coated with euphemisms such as "rehabilitation" and "education"') for apostasy from Islam are likely to continue, despite their incompatibility with the Constitution adopted at the end of British rule. Their final word is that, throughout the Muslim world, 'only a few are arguing for doing away with apostasy laws that adversely affect the individual's basic rights as a person...').

in communities subject to Islamic rule.[33] If one should have that confidence in relation to a confrontation between Muslim and Christian claims to revelatory authenticity, one should, of course, also have it in relation to confrontation between the Catholic claims and atheistic or agnostic denials of them, denials which proceed from a position less reasonable than the Muslim (but also Christian) thesis that everything has its explanatory origin in the decision of the one eternal and all-powerful Creator.[34] In this discourse between atheistic secularism and Christian secularism with transcendent foundations, what generally makes the epistemic conditions non-ideal is not lack of political freedom from coercion but a complex of myths, images, and memories that block and distract from the Christian position and its evidences.

None of this is a prediction of what, in our world, will be the results of political freedoms of the kind that everyone has a right to participate in.[35] No one can foresee how the interaction between atheistic secularism, Islam, and Christian faith (with its affirmation of secularity alongside the sacred) will play out over this century[36]—or foretell the interaction between development of doctrine and fundamentalism or radical orthodoxy within the competing sects in Islam. Violations of rights[37] and of the other aspects of public order are indeed the responsibility of law and government to repress with judgment, equity, and an eye to consequences. But our

---

[33] In reflecting on the outcome of a free discourse about Islam and Catholic Christianity, recall that its core is necessarily a comparison between (the moral characters of) Mohammad and Jesus: see at n. 14; and *ScG* I, c.6 n.7.

[34] How that decision is to be understood is, of course, the subject of doctrinal and theological theses which differ radically as between Christianity and Islam respectively.

[35] The bible is the Catholic Church's book and confirms its teachings, but for many centuries the Church's leaders predicted that if it were generally available to everyone in their own languages, it would be extensively misunderstood and turned against the very doctrines that, understood as a whole, it fully supports. The prediction has been very amply fulfilled over the centuries since 1500. But it would be a mistake to infer that people do not have the right of access to all the materials of public revelation, and equally a mistake to predict that in the long run the result of giving effect to that right will be to defeat the Church's evangelical mission (a mission which includes providing, and encouraging educationally and in other ways, the truthful and adequate guides to proper understanding of those materials).

[36] Joseph Butler, who preceded Newman at Oriel College Oxford by about a century, and influenced his philosophical theology, prefaced his *Analogy of Religion, Natural and Revealed, to the Constitution and Course of Nature* (1735) with a page including this observation:

> It is come, I know not how, to be taken for granted, by many persons, that Christianity is not so much as a subject of inquiry; but that it is now, at length, discovered to be fictitious. And accordingly they treat it as if, in the present age, this were *an agreed point among all people of discernment*; and nothing remained, but to set it up as a principal subject of mirth and ridicule, as it were by way of reprisals, for its having so long interrupted the pleasures of the world. (Emphasis added.)

Predictions made by these social and intellectual elites of 1735 about the likely condition of Christianity two and a half centuries later would very probably have been wide of the mark.

[37] Note that 'any action which seems to suggest coercion or dishonest or unworthy persuasion, especially when one is dealing with the uneducated or poor ... must be considered ... an infringement of the rights of others': DH 4.4.

reflections and inquiries should be directed, not so much to speculations about the future, but to fulfilling the duty that is the foundation of religious liberty, of morality itself, and of all decent political existence and coexistence: to seek the truth about God, and to follow it when one has found it as best one can judge.

3

SECULARISM'S PRACTICAL MEANING[*]

I

'Secular' is a word minted by Latin Christians.[1] Translating the New Testament, Jerome used it for Greek words signifying the affairs of this world, sometimes neutrally the world of time rather than eternity,[2] and the daily life of any human society,[3] sometimes pejoratively as matters which distract us from realities and dispositions of lasting worth.[4] Aquinas uses it regularly, and often quite without negative connotations: he will say, for example, that in matters which concern the good of the political community (*bonum civile*), Christians should generally obey the directives of the secular rather than the ecclesiastical authorities.[5]

Aquinas is pointing out a distinction of competences which exemplifies a social process of differentiation that goes much wider. Modern historians and sociologists have often called this wider social process 'secularization'. Fields of life in which human enterprises and conditions were once scarcely within human control—bodily health, or the sowing of crops—become more or less subject to natural-scientific understanding and technological control, and attempts to manage them instead by prayer (as in Mary Baker Eddy's *Christian Science*) are laid aside as misdirected. This secularization commonly accompanies, therefore, the processes of urbanization and industrialization, which in turn promote the specialization of competence and the organizational autonomy that are required in directing complex communities and their politics. That theocracy is a recipe for mismanagement becomes clear even for people not governed by the firmly differentiating directive, 'Render to Caesar the things of Caesar...'

---

[*] 1998c, for a Notre Dame Law School conference on secularism and the common good, April 1997.
    ¹ In classical Latin the word *saecularis* never acquired the range of meanings of *saeculum*, which does extend to 'the world' in most of our senses of the word.
    ² 2 Timothy 1: 9; Titus 1: 2.   ³ 1 Corinthians 6: 34.   ⁴ 2 Timothy 2: 4; Titus 2: 12.
    ⁵ See *Sent.* II d.44 exp. textus ad 4: 'magis obediendum potestati saeculari quam spirituali'.

Neither the differentiating of the secular from the sacred, nor the social processes of secularization, entail the mind-set or cluster of ideologies we call 'secularism'. Like any significant reality, this mind-set is not tied to any one word or to the accidents of semantics. Without benefit of 'secular' or cognate terms, Plato has provided us with a profound analysis of secularism. In his great last work, *Laws*, he sketches a cluster of dispositions which shape up around one or another of three propositions: there is no God; no God has any concern with human affairs; or any such divine concern with the human is easily appeased by a superficial piety and requires no demanding reform of human vice.[6] The corresponding character types described by Plato are well recognizable in more recent times. And the three propositions—no God; God absent; and God soft-spirited[7]—match closely modern secularism's characteristic forms: atheism; a deistic assumption that human history knows no divine intervention,[8] no revelation of God's intentions for us; and a 'liberal' religiosity which presumes upon divine benevolence, and has no time for warnings of the alienation from God inherent in immorality and potentially final (as Plato too warns in his prophetic meditation on wrongdoing's retribution, the *Republic*'s myth of Er[9]).

Though Plato's strongest indignation is reserved for the position ascribing to God a soft-spirited fatuity contemptible in men and women, his most vigorous argumentation confronts the first and second positions, which deny mind's sway in the cosmos. Atheistic materialism's claim that all is ultimately sheer chance and brute inexplicable necessity truncates the investigative quest of science and philosophy for intelligibility and explanation wherever it can be found. And deistic denial of all-governing divine providence underestimates the all-creative, all-sustaining, and all-penetrating power of the maker's practical intellect.

But Plato judges that the practical significance of the three positions is in each case essentially the same: the withering away of reverence for God, of a steady, uncringing, inspiriting fear of the Lord.[10] We can readily see that secularism, in this practical inner manifestation or resultant, is part of the make-up even of a God-fearing believer, just insofar as one

---

[6]   See *Laws* X 885b, 888c, 901d, 902e–903a, 908b–d, 909a–b. Plato usually speaks of 'gods' or 'the gods', but when getting to the heart of the matter he switches to talk of God or 'the god'. *Ibid.* at 902e, 903d, 910b.

[7]   See *ibid.* at 901e, 903a; see also *Republic* 365d–e.

[8]   '[T]his very axiom, miracles do not happen, comes near the heart of that elusive shift in the European mind which we seek' in investigating the secularization of the European mind in the nineteenth century: Chadwick, *The Secularization of the European Mind in the Nineteenth Century*, 17.

[9]   See *Republic* X 614b–621d; see also *Laws* 903d; *Gorgias* 523a–527e.

[10]   See *Laws* XII 967d: '*bebaiōs theosebē*'. Plato does not speak of the Lord; but the divine 'mover of the pieces' (*petteutes*) has a similar dignity. *Ibid.* at 903d.

is sinning. In that sense, as Maritain could consider the Church a reality which occupies a part of the believer's spirit, so one can think of secularism as a kind of deficiency detectable to a greater or lesser degree in every human soul except the authentic saints'. All of us, with our friends and colleagues, seem to live in some sense as secularists; we have motives of sympathy and affection, as well as reasons of principle, to turn sharply aside from Plato when he plans fierce penal repression of secularists by the Guardians of the Laws.[11]

The secularism I consider in this essay is a public reality, the secularism which shapes public debate, deliberation, dispositions, and action, and dominates our education and culture. I shall be considering the ideas, not the people; and people are often less consistent, and better, than their theories. There is no profit in estimating whether secularism's dominance now is greater than in Plato's Athens or lesser than in Stalin's Leningrad. There is certainly a rich field for historical investigation of the particular and often peculiar forms taken by western secularism under the influence of the faith it supplants. But I shall not try to resume or repeat the illuminating investigations carried forward by De Lubac, Voegelin,[12] Fabro, MacIntyre, Chadwick, and many others. Still less do I join in the game of declaring this a postmodern, or post-baroque, or post-Christian, or historically minded and post-classicist[13] era, period, age, or epoch. Instead I want to explore secularism's practical significance, as it can be illuminated by understanding practical reason itself. We try to carry forward that understanding when we reflect on the basic reasons for action, the first principles (as Aquinas calls them) of natural law, on the choices, intentions, and commitments they guide and shape, and on the personal dignity of a being who can respond either integrally and reasonably or arbitrarily and deviantly to their intelligibility and directiveness.

II

What do I mean by 'directiveness'? Well, if one inquires into one's own and other people's achievements, and into the range of one's opportunities, the question 'Why? For what reason?' will, if resolutely pressed, disclose a set of primary reasons for action. Like other reasons, these have a propositional form. The propositions pick out, and direct one towards,

---

[11] See *ibid.* at X 907d–910d.

[12] See Voegelin, *From Enlightenment to Revolution.*

[13] On the ambiguities and misconceptions in the 'classicist v. historically minded' distinction adopted by Bernard Lonergan SJ (and thence many Catholic theologians) from the secularist historian Carl Becker's lectures at Yale Law School in 1931–32, see essay 9, secs I–V.

basic human goods, as opportunities-to-be-pursued, worthwhile to attain and maintain by one's acting, and giving point to everything one does. Thus, for example, the basic human good of knowledge is a reason for action and correspondingly the content or subject-matter of a primary principle whose directiveness can be articulated in the form, 'Knowledge of truth is a good to be pursued'. And similarly for the other basic human goods, such as life, marriage, friendship and peace with others, skill in work or play, and practical reasonableness. This directiveness of these first practical principles—the intelligibility of these primary goods precisely as *to-be-pursued*—is original; the goods are understood as good each for its own sake and in their own right, not as mere means to some further good.

Still, each of the basic goods is an aspect of human fulfilment or flourishing, and each is a good whoever the human persons in whom it is or can be instantiated. So reason further grasps the notion of an integral human fulfilment, that is, the fulfilment of every human person and community in all the basic goods. This notion does not signify a new basic good or reason for action, and does not point to a goal attainable by human planning and cooperation. But it does express the object (or subject-matter) of the combined directiveness of all the basic human goods taken together. The good of practical reasonableness, which Aristotle called *phronēsis* and Aquinas *prudentia* (with its object the 'good of practical reasonableness' [*bonum rationis*]), directs us to accept the integral directiveness of all the first practical principles, and not to allow emotions and sub-rational feelings to fetter or deflect it. And this integral directiveness of the first principles of practical reason can be articulated in a primary or master *moral* principle: all one's willing should be compatible with integral human fulfilment (the fulfilment of all human persons in all communities)—a highly abstract formulation of the more well-known statement that one should love and respect one's neighbour as oneself. High-level moral principles such as the Golden Rule or the principle forbidding intentional infliction of harms are, then, specifications (themselves in many cases further specifiable) of that primary or master moral principle; they identify forms of willing incompatible with a steady and undeflected will for integral human fulfilment. So the directiveness of the first principles is both rationally motivating (*contra* Hume and Kant), and morally restraining (as well as spurring on).

Thus one *finds oneself being* directed, as a matter of intelligence and reason. In this sense, the first practical principles, though not innate prior to all experience, have the status of *givens*—'given to' and grasped in our understanding. Both in their directiveness and their 'self-evidence' as knowable without deduction from higher premises, these principles have a kind of necessity. But as the propositional content of the acts of insight by which one comes to understand these opportunities and reasons for action (and of one's consequent habitual knowledge), the first practical principles—and likewise the master moral principle (with its specifications in less abstract moral principles)—are like all the other realities within our experience. For those acts of insight (understanding) are the actuation of a potentiality, and contingent on something which explains that change from potentiality to act(uality). So, like every reality which we can think of as *what* it is without knowing *that* it is, the practical principles have an actuality which calls for explanation, and that explanation can only be a reality whose *what-it-is* includes *that it is*, and so is without shadow of mere potentiality or of change from possibility to act(uality).[14]

And since the first practical principles not only *are* but are *directive*, and their directiveness cannot be explained by anything subhuman or by any human originating, it is also reasonable to conclude that the ultimate explanation or first cause which accounts for their being also accounts, of itself, for their directiveness. This inference is not to be confused with the contention of Kant's posthumous papers, or of John Henry Newman, that the commanding voice of, or in, one's conscience requires one to conclude to a transcendent commander. Kant and Newman were heirs to a long tradition of voluntarist misunderstanding of directiveness and 'ought' as ultimately a matter of commands or imperatives. In truth, first practical principles direct us to intelligent acts of will intending human flourishing. So we must take the first cause of their directiveness to be a non-human intelligence and will—we can only say, *person*—directing us thus towards our own goods, towards human fulfilment.

An argument to the existence of God from the data of practical reason converges, of course, with the more familiar arguments from other realities in which change and contingency are more evident. The conclusion on which all converge with a rational necessity[15] is that everything within our experience, including every form of intelligibility which (like the first practical principles) is prior to human willing, has as its ultimate explanation the still active action of divine creation. Here I should recall the warning of St Thomas, taken up with full seriousness in Germain Grisez's restatement of the philosophy of God. We can have no understanding of *what* a being is in which *what* it is includes *that* it is.

---

[14] See Grisez, *Beyond the New Theism*, 36–91; *NLNR* 378–88; *Aquinas* ch. X.
[15] This is a matter not of logical necessity, but of requirements of rationality in seeking explanatory knowledge ('rationality norms'). See Grisez, *Beyond the New Theism*, 132–6, 168–72; essay 9 at 150–4.

So 'we cannot know what God is, but only what God is not'[16] 'and how other things are related to God'.[17] Whatever we say about God must be taken with a drastic shift of meaning leaving nothing but what must be predicated of God to explain the very existence and character of the realities within our experience. But clearly we must predicate of God this act(ion) of Creation as the projection of immense structures and patterns of intelligibility, structures and patterns whose intelligibility still far outreaches natural and mathematical sciences dedicated to disclosing it. We must take divine creation to be somehow an act which carries out an intention. And it is an act which cannot have been necessitated. Being free from every trace of potentiality, lack, imperfection, or need, the Creator must be of a perfection that cannot conceivably be enhanced. So the creating of a universe—this or any other—could not be required, by any reason whatever. So the intention to create and sustain our universe must be somehow the adoption of a proposal by truly unnecessitated, free choice. Plato's *Laws* insists, and sketches a demonstration, that mind is the primary explanation of the cosmos. This argument is resumed in Aquinas's 'fifth way', and in the vindication of God's existence in John Haldane's recent dialectic with J.J.C. Smart[18]—a resumption deepened by Christian philosophy's clarity about Creation: the primary explanation of the cosmos involves both intellect and will, a reason not merely contemplative but fully practical.

In reflecting on divine creation we can go further in understanding the givenness of our practical reason's first principles. They outline for us the aspects of human flourishing, as object(ive)s of intelligent action. And, as Aquinas never tires of reminding us, it is by understanding objects of action that we understand action, and only by understanding a being's action can we understand its capacities, and only by understanding its capacities can we understand its nature. So our practical understanding of the basic goods, the primary objects of all intelligent action, is an indispensable source of our understanding of human nature. But in turn that nature—by which we have the *capacities* we have, and can *do* what we can do, for the *forms of flourishing* available by our activities—is obviously a sheer given. It is an outcome—via what processes of evolution matters not at all for a reflection on these fundamentals—the outcome of God's free choice to create. Integral human fulfilment, indeed any human fulfilment however fragmentary, will be the outcome of that same free choice, accompanying and sustaining our own unnecessitated free choices.

---

[16] *ST* I q.3 prol.; see also *ScG* I, c.14 nn. 2–3 [117–18].   [17] *ScG* I, c.30 n.4 [278].
[18] See Smart and Haldane, *Atheism & Theism*.

These valid inferences are available even to urbanized people in a fully differentiated, technologically organized way of life. Those who live closer to the givens of nature, say farming or fishing, can more immediately apprehend the conditions of and limits upon our capabilities, the radical and constant dependence of successful human work on the collaboration of nature, that is, of the divine providence which today, as completely as at the Big Bang, both originates and shapes our materials, our efforts, and their combined productiveness. A further basic human good is most readily within their understanding and interest, the good of harmony with the transcendent source of every other human good, and every form of fruitfulness. As harmony of minds and wills with the transcendent mind and will, this collaboration is nothing less than a community, not the less real for being between utterly unequal persons. This sense of community is the heart of what is often called 'natural religion'.

Human understanding of that natural community of divine and human beings was transformed by Jewish and Christian faith, which displays and denounces the illusoriness of the 'strange gods'—those products of an awareness of mind's omnipresence in nature, but an awareness dominated by imagination, and an imagination marked by the forms of habitual immorality mirrored in the sexual and other laxities of the gods and left unchallenged by idols capable neither of saving nor condemning. The created world, as grasped by human understanding, science, and technique, is now radically de-divinized, for God—the only divinity to be affirmed by a truth-seeking reason—is utterly transcendent, both to our understanding and to every reality within range of our experience, even though divine action must by its unnecessitated causality be somehow utterly intimate to every this-worldly structure and event. The *saeculum*, this contingent world and its time, is differentiated from its sole origin's eternal act of uncontingent being. We can no longer make room, as Plato still did in speech, for the pagan gods, and we cannot envisage a this-worldly community with ancestors or other spirits of material bodies; New Age outpourings cannot now be more than make-believe.

Moreover, the natural community of humankind with God, and the productive divine collaboration which natural religion prays for, are extended and deepened in the revelation completed in Christ. For this revelation is not merely a communication about the nature of things, but also and primarily the offering, and on our side the accepting, in faith, of a covenant. Perhaps the philosophy of law has something to contribute at this point. Of course, the covenant offered by the true God is radically different from a bargain, and transfigures our ideas and institutions of promise and contract. Still, the climate of secularist indifference to anything like a covenant between God and humankind has left us all struggling to explain and vindicate Contract as a valid category irreducible to Tort, Restitution, or Welfare Law. And we can, I think, make progress by revisiting Aquinas's insight that promising, like praying and legislating, is fundamentally an act of practical *reason*. Take legislating: this is essentially an act of reason, projecting an intelligible and reasonable order of future conduct and consequent benefits, yet also for the most part a sheer *determinatio* whereby one amongst two or more 'equally'[19] reasonable options (proposals) is adopted by creative choice (will) for the sake of common good (not least friendship and justice). So too the making of a promise by offer and acceptance is more fundamentally an act of reason than of will.[20] The offer on which valid contracts are characteristically founded projects an intelligible order of relationships between the parties in respect of some course of conduct by each of them for the sake of intelligible benefits for each; the corresponding acceptance by which such contracts are brought into being as sets of mutual obligations is, like the offer, an assent—a saying Yes—to that order of relationships and to the course of conduct which is the precise subject-matter of that order, and Yes to the proposal that as from this moment all the parties be able (entitled) to count the whole future relationship (and especially the future conduct, the obligations, of any other party) as part of their present stock of benefits, their 'own', their 'right(s)'.

That affirming Yes is not in vain, unless we are to say that persons simply lack the ability to confer on each other the present benefit of such rights to future beneficial conduct. The Yes indeed affirms *that* it is not in vain. So, if it is not to be mere impotent folly—or else a lie, sundering both the harmony of outer with inner self and the harmony, the trust, between speaker and hearer(s)—the assent of offer and acceptance must bring into being, create, the relationships, including the rights, the obligations of fidelity and commitment, which it projects and affirms. Still, the intention to undertake such obligations, and the communicated promise, presuppose the basic reasons for action, the basic human goods at stake (including friendship and/or justice) and the requirements of fairness (the Golden Rule). Whenever one knows that one's expression of intention will arouse another's hopes, one has some responsibility in fairness or friendship—quite independently of the practice of promising—not to disappoint those hopes. In making a promise one focuses attention on one's consciousness of responsibility not to disappoint the other, and one thereby greatly increases

---

[19] Properly speaking, 'incommensurably' rather than 'equally'. See Raz, *The Morality of Freedom*, ch. 13 esp. 325–6.

[20] *ST* II–II q.88 a.1c.

the extent to which friendship or justice is at stake, and so also intentionally increases one's responsibility (obligation) to the other person.[21]

God's promises, even more radically than ours, engage their maker's truthfulness, for the whole time of the promise's fulfilment lies open to God's view, so that his 'I will' excludes any change of mind in future circumstances. The duplicity in any affirming or asserting at odds with the virtue of *Veritas* is such an evil that the divine perfection must exclude it. Now in God's covenants, old and new, the benefits promised by God are identified as dependent upon our own adherence to the relationship and the conduct it demands of us—essentially, as the new covenant (perfecting the old) makes clear, the demands already inherent in the natural law, together with willingness to participate in the Lord's own saving acts as they extend through history in the life of his *ecclesia*.[22] Plato's special disgust at the third impious proposition, that God can be bought off, would surely extend to the assumption widespread among Christians today, that the Lord's warnings about final judgment are wholly or largely bluff.

Secularized Christian views about this seem, in fact, to oscillate between variants of Plato's second and third forms of impiety. Either the benefits God has promised and the loss he has warned against are undeliverable, are outside the reach of his power and providence, or God is supposed to be quite complaisant and unconcerned about moral integrity in communicating his covenant's conditions. Its promises will be delivered whether we keep our side or instead do exactly what we please. Thus the covenant relationship is treated as, on God's side, manipulation by empty warnings; von Balthasar, in his rough polemics about hell, misdescribes these as 'threats' and treats them as bluffs.[23] His thought remains trapped in the false alternatives presented by the pervasive voluntarist misunderstanding of law, promises, practical reason, and thus of the relation between Creator and created persons. Von Balthasar joins the secularist's understandable flight from the voluntarists' God, who chooses to inflict the pains of hell on those who disobey the divine commands; but, being still in the grip of that voluntarist legalism so widespread among Christians in recent centuries, he develops an argument which, like the assumptions of secularized Christians, fails to understand God as having real concern for what truly benefits us, and fails to understand the divine law's wisdom and goodness as directing us how to save ourselves from

---

[21] *LCL* at 412; see also *NLNR* at 298–308.
[22] On the old and new covenants, see Bouyer, *The Church of God*; *CMP* at 507–16.
[23] See Balthasar, *Dare We Hope 'That All Men Be Saved'? with a Short Treatise on Hell*; and essay 24 below.

injuring ourselves and one another by choices incompatible with openness to integral human fulfilment.[24]

On our side, the secularist emptying out of the covenant has more than one kind of practical implication. On the one hand, it can result in a generalizing of the manipulation found in every act of wrongdoing, even independently of revelation and covenant. For, as natural religion is more or less aware, in doing wrong one takes the goods provided by divine providence and exploits them without regard to the integral directiveness of the principles of practical reasonableness, principles which (as we have seen) point even natural religion towards an acknowledgement of that providence.[25] This exploitativeness can be generalized and radicalized in a kind of secularized Christian thought: 'Let's eat, drink, and be merry—do just what we feel like—for tomorrow we live forever!' But the emptying out of the covenant's conditions can have results less radical and consistent. Practical reasonableness, the natural law written on the heart, was brightly illuminated by the revelation that there is a Kingdom of God which transfigures the natural ideal of integral human fulfilment and has terms of citizenship extending and deepening natural love of neighbour as oneself. That illumination invites our will's response, and does not fade away, leaving the will relaxed and content, as soon as revelation is rejected or radically misapprehended in secularizing 'enlightenment'. So there emerges an earnestly secular Christianity which is not readily distinguishable from secular humanism; for in each the hope of heaven has disappeared *from practical life* as completely as fear of hell.

And this practical elimination of a transcendent hope should be no surprise. If X will happen, or not happen, regardless of anything one does, one cannot *intend* X. So, if one assumes that either everyone reaches heaven regardless, or heaven is mere myth, we know not which, then one cannot *intend* heaven. Hope, not as dream unconnected with practical deliberation and choice, but as standing intention of shaping one's choices and actions in the hope of being made fit for the integral human fulfilment—the life of heaven—on offer in the covenant, becomes *impossible*.[26] So it is practical reason's own logic that makes inevitable the shift from 'Christianity' without fear of hell (and so with certitude of heaven) to Christianity without hope of heaven (and so with some this-worldly hope)—the shift to secularism so widespread among so-called liberal Christians (and Jews),

---

[24] See the analysis and critique of Balthasar's position on hell in *DMQ* at 21–8.

[25] See 1987f at 141–7.

[26] See the very important analysis of the proper integration of hope and fear in Christian life in *LCL* at 91–4.

especially perhaps those who happen to be theologians or ecclesiastical bureaucrats.

Since public reason in the United States is shaped within a culture of subscription to the religions of the new or the old covenants, this religiose secularism has far-reaching practical consequences for your common good.

<h1 style="text-align:center">III</h1>

I have sketched some reasons (there are others) why the recognition that practical reason is grounded in God clarifies the goodness of the basic human goods, the freedom of free choice, and the reality of intention (irreducible to desire or foresight), and enhances, accordingly, the directiveness of the first practical principles, the coherence and inherent force of moral principles, and the perfecting of interpersonal collaboration in the making and fulfilment of promises.

Before turning to secularism's practical implications, I should indicate why that recognition also clarifies and enhances the equal dignity of all human persons.

To think of the freedom and practical intelligence involved in the creation and providential sustaining of everything out of nothing is to think of the reality of spirit—a reality to us most comprehensible and yet most incomprehensible. And, it is by thinking about one's own intelligent and free *acting* that one most directly and securely grasps[27] something which secularism has lost its grip upon. In its understanding of the human person, secularism (in the functionally atheistic form that was Plato's first target and today is dominant in university culture) oscillates between dualism and materialism. Dualism and materialism, each in its own way, deny the unity of the person (I, the bodily self) who lives, wants, chooses, tries, understands, senses, feels, moves, and is moved, as animated body, rational animal. They are each inconsistent with the data they seek to explain and with the thinker's own performance in choosing to seek and put forward explanations.[28] The only explanation consistent with our ability to choose, to seek, to find, and to communicate explanations is

---

[27] Prior to all accounts of it, this intelligible presence of my many-faceted acting self to myself is a datum of understanding; one and the same I—this human being—who am understanding and choosing and carrying out my choice and sensing, etc. is a reality I already truly understand, albeit not yet fully (explanatorily, with elaboration). See *ST* I q.76 a.1c; q.87 a.4c; q.86 a.1 ad 3; *Sent.* III d.23 q.1 a.2 ad 3; *Aquinas* 176–9.

[28] See Braine, *The Human Person*. For Aquinas's argument from the self-refutation of those who held that there is but one intellect, see *De Unitate Intellectus contra Averroistas* III 62, 79 (see McInerny, *Aquinas Against the Averroists* at 80–1, 94–5).

one which, like the accounts of human soul by Aristotle and Aquinas, identifies a *form* and lifelong *act(uality)* by which the matter of my bodily make-up is constituted the unified and active subject (me myself). As one experiences in making and carrying out a choice such as giving this lecture and so uttering this sentence audibly now, the *one* factor unifying and activating one's living individual reality is a factor at once animal (sentient and self-locomotive) and intellectual (understanding, self-understanding, and, even in the conduct of thinking, self-determining by judging and choosing).[29] Though the manifold activations of these bodily and rational powers depend upon one's physical maturity and health, the reality and powers of the soul are given to each of us complete (as wholly undeveloped, radical capacities) at the outset of his or her existence as such.[30] And here we have the root of our dignity as human beings, not as a 'status' to be conferred or withdrawn, but a reality to be acknowledged in every member of our species. This is indeed a truth already implicit in one's understanding of basic reasons for choice and action. For these reasons each direct us to goods good for me *and anyone like me*—anyone who shares my nature, any human being.

Dignity connotes both superiority (for example in power, excellence, status) and intrinsic, non-dependent worth.[31] The radical capacity and act(uality) which each human being has by virtue of his or her individual rational soul makes each of us superior in the straightforward sense that we thereby have and instantiate every level of being—physical solidity and dynamisms, chemical and biological complexity, and self-directedness, *and more*: the capacity to understand all these other realities, to reason about them and about reasoning itself, to replicate and transform other beings on all those levels of reality, and with self-mastery's freedom to choose these activities as part of choosing how to live. As for inherent worth, its paradigm is our living, knowing, playing, and loving, and the good we grasp in our friend's (and thus in every human person's) very being.

---

[29] Thus:

> the principle by which we understand is intellect...so this must be united to one's body as form, not indeed in such a way that the capacity of understanding is the act of some organ, but because it is a power of one's soul, which is the act of a physical and organic body. (*De Unitate* III c. 3 (McInerny, *Aquinas Against the Averroists* at 96–7).)

On soul as the primary 'act' of a living, physically organized body, see e.g. *ScG* II, c.61 n.2 [1397]; *ST* I q.76 a.4 ad 1; *In Anima* 1.1 n. 15 [227–9].

[30] The intellectual (and sensory and vegetative) soul by the creation of which I came into existence—existence as already a person—is not itself a person but only a 'part' (uniquely, the organizing part and indeed the very form and act) of me. *ST* I q.29 a.1 ad 5; q.75 a.4 ad 2.

[31] '"Dignity" signifies something's goodness for its own sake (*propter seipsum*)': *Sent* III d.35 q.1 a.4 sol. 1c.

In short: materialist secularism's denials or determined agnosticism about *soul* and *species* radically misrepresent our experience as choosers— an experience internal and private, but shared in kind, common to us all, and in that sense in the public domain of philosophical reflection and discussion. This materialism likewise renders unintelligible the public and private judgment that 'by nature all human beings are equal', and that there are *human* rights and requirements of justice which do not discriminate between male and female, intelligent and dull, race and race, young and old, healthy and infirm. All around us we find talk of human rights. But this can't hide the hollowness and fragility of rights to equal treatment, or opportunities, or concern and respect, on the assumptions of materialism, assumptions which are secularism's philosophically most popular basis—or is it consequence?

We see this loss of grip on human equality's basis in the will to treat the unborn—whose reality and nature is known to us better than ever before—as utterly without constitutional rights, and disposable at whim, simply because they are physically located within or even partially within their mother's womb. In the work of secularist philosophers like Peter Singer, what in the US Supreme Court's judgments about abortion is shameless evasion becomes instead a firmly asserted thesis: there are non-human animals who rank higher in status, dignity, and entitlement than newborn and other very young human children. And the widespread shift of thought and sentiment towards euthanasia proceeds in part on the assumption—characteristically secularist in its unstable amalgam of materialism and dualism—that with irretrievable loss of consciousness the life of the person is not only deprived of all worth but actually has come to an end.

IV

Philosophy's search for explanations yields the inference that our universe, including our practical understanding, its principles, and that inherent responsiveness to understood goods which we call will, all have as first cause a creative practical intellect and will. God's self-disclosure in the historical revelation completed in Christ teaches us to understand our practical reason and will—and indeed our whole life, by which rational soul as fundamental act(uality) of the body animates every aspect of our bodiliness—as an image of God's reason, will, and life (an existence unrefracted, however, by body's susceptibility to being acted upon and changed by division or augmentation). And our freedom includes, like God's, the capacity to envisage and bring into being a new order of interpersonal relationships, by covenants that bind. The world as understood in secularism is not open to these realities, or at least (in the case of secularized religiosity) takes them too lightly to matter.

John Haldane has raised what he rightly calls 'the interesting question to what extent those who deny the reality of causation are moved to do so by a concern to block' a certain type of proof of the existence of God.[32] Without pursuing that hypothesis about motivation ('concern') as a cause of theoretical positions, I want simply to take note of certain practical positions—including positions within the theory or philosophy or indeed the theology of morally significant action—positions which seem to be consequences, indeed natural consequences, of secularism's denials or oversights of God's existence, or providence, or holiness (purity, steadfastness, and seriousness).

As I have suggested, the first principles of practical understanding, picking out and directing us towards intelligible and intrinsic basic human goods, point towards their explanatory cause in a divine mind which envisages and makes possible integral human fulfilment, involving constitutively the cooperation of human free choices. Correspondingly, the denial of any divine mind, or at least of any efficacious divine concern with human fulfilment, is characteristically accompanied and supported, or at least protected, by a denial that basic human motivations are a matter of understanding, reason, and truth at all. At bottom are just the passions, of which practical reason is the busy and ingenious slave concerned with clever and effective means for attaining what we emotionally, sub-rationally want. In more recent philosophy, this Humean thesis, focused upon the account of motivation, is transposed into the emotivist account of moral discourse as, not judgment which can be right or mistaken, but simply an expression or projection of similarly sub-rational desires and aversions (including perhaps the desire to get other people to do what you want). These emotivist theses are scarcely plausible as accounts of psychology or of our discourse. But in their polite, schoolteachers' form, taken for granted by almost every freshman, they provide the more or less concealed foundations of the claim or assumption that practical reason is a matter of value judgments, and value judgments—at least, basic value judgments—are just 'a matter of opinion', subjective, not matters of truth on which one could, consequently, be in error. The professorial counterpart to this received wisdom of the schoolteachers is the self-refuting neo-Nietzschean patter that everything is interpretation and perspective or viewpoint.

---

[32] Haldane and Smart, *Atheism & Theism*, 136.

The thought that basic value judgments have no truth scarcely coheres with, say, the Constitution's proclamation and defence of fundamental human rights. So the polite form taken in this context by secularism's unreadiness to acknowledge basic human goods as *true* is the demand for a kind of constitutional neutrality about them. Counsel for the American Civil Liberties Union opened the oral argument in *Planned Parenthood v Casey*[33] by defining the issue as: 'Whether our Constitution endows Government with the power to force a woman to continue or to end a pregnancy against her will...'.[34] And the Court's judgment repeatedly appealed to the same implicit assumption of neutrality: *since* it is obvious that she has a right *not* to terminate the life within her and *not* to be forced to end a pregnancy against her will, she must equally have the right to terminate that life within, a right not to be prevented from aborting it. To support this value-neutral autonomy right, the Court points to a line of cases beginning in 1923 with *Meyer v Nebraska*[35] and running through *Pierce v Society of Sisters*[36] in 1925, *Skinner v Oklahoma*[37] in 1942, and the dissenting judgment of Justice Harlan in *Poe v Ullman*[38] in 1961, before reaching *Griswold v Connecticut*[39] in 1965 and *Eisenstadt v Baird*[40] in 1972. But if one reads these cases in sequence, it is instantly obvious that the decisions before 1972 utterly reject the conception that politics, government, and law must preserve neutrality about such basic human goods as education in good and useful knowledge (goods celebrated in the cases from the 1920s), or marriage (honoured in its procreativity in *Skinner* and in its domesticity and friendship in Harlan's dissent in *Poe* and even in *Griswold*). The break comes with the judgment of the radically secularized Justice Brennan in *Eisenstadt v Baird*, which assumes a double neutrality of values and corresponding symmetry of normative judgments: what is true of sexual relations that express, actualize, and support a mutual commitment making possible a good environment for children must equally, and obviously, be true of even the most casual act of lust; and what is true of the decision to try to beget and bear a child must be true of the decision to prevent the begetting of a child (or, as Brennan's clerks well understood he meant,[41] to abort the bearing of a child once begotten). There is just the single neutral category: 'the decision [of the individual, whether married or single,] ... whether to bear or beget a child'.[42] The key

---

[33]   505 US 833 (1992).

[34]   New York Times, 23 April 1992, at B10. For the origins of the argument, see *Griswold v Connecticut* 381 US 479, 486 (1965) (Goldberg J, concurring).

[35]   262 US 390 (1923).   [36]   268 US 510 (1925).   [37]   316 US 535 (1942).

[38]   367 US 497 (1961).   [39]   381 US 479 (1965).   [40]   405 US 438 (1972).

[41]   See Garrow, *Liberty and Sexuality* at 542.

[42]   *Eisenstadt* 405 US at 453 (Brennan J, for the Court).

word is 'whether'. What matters, according to this new, unprecedented, unargued doctrine of the Court is the ability to decide whether *or not* ... to do—or instead to destroy, damage, or impede—something the earlier, pre-secularist cases confidently identified as of basic human value.

The 'Philosophers' Brief' to the Supreme Court in the 'assisted suicide' cases (*Washington v Glucksberg*[43] and *Vacco v Quill*[44]) takes up the key sentence from *Eisenstadt* and deploys a similar argument from the symmetry and obligatory neutrality between good and evil: since patients and their doctors must be allowed to try to preserve life to the end, *so* they must be allowed to terminate life, at least degraded life, at their choosing.[45] *Since* you must be able to choose life, you must be permitted to choose death. It is as if the Supreme Court in *Meyer v Nebraska* or *Pierce v Society of Sisters* had said: since parents have the right to choose non-state education, they must have the right to choose for their children *no* education at all.

Of course, a group of philosophers such as these brief-writers, John Rawls, Ronald Dworkin, Thomas Nagel, and the others, will deny that they are advancing an emotivist, subjectivist, perspectivalist, or any other meta-ethical scepticism. They will say that their claim about neutrality is purely about political rights and the proper competence of the state's rulers, and the value or dignity of individual autonomy. And so, on its face, it is. But the weakness of all the arguments which these philosophers have put forward to justify their claim about individual rights and state competence is good reason to conclude that their position's real foundation is the concern to be 'let alone' to *do what one really feels like.*

Rawls, for instance, argued that people behind a Veil of Ignorance— ignorance as to (among other things) intrinsic, non-instrumental human goods—would choose the liberal state-neutralist principle. But, even on its own terms, the argument depended on assuming that people are far more risk averse than even self-interested 'prudence' requires. And no reason was given for the crucial Rawlsian assumption that principles which would not be chosen behind a Veil of Ignorance are unjust principles in the real world of intrinsic, 'thick' but intelligible human goods.[46] And it was on the same undefended assumption that the later Rawls proposed that we

---

[43]   521 US 702 (1997).   [44]   521 US 793 (1997).

[45]   Just as it would be intolerable for government to dictate that doctors never be permitted to try to keep someone alive as long as possible, when that is what the patient wishes, so it is intolerable for government to dictate that doctors may never, under any circumstance help someone to die who believes that future life means only degradation.

Dworkin et al., 'Assisted Suicide: The Philosophers' Brief' at 44 n. 1 [The Philosophers' Brief]. [The *amici curiae* were Ronald Dworkin, Thomas Nagel, Robert Nozick, John Rawls, Thomas Scanlon, and Judith Jarvis Thomson; the brief is signed by Dworkin and dated December 1996.]

[46]   See essay III.2 (1987c), sec. II esp. at n. 12; essay III.3 (1973a).

should 'endorse'—splendid equivocation between 'accept as true' and 'opt for'!—the 'principle' that no argument about either good and bad or right and wrong should be advanced in public discourse about basic matters if the argument's acceptability depends upon its being *true, all things considered* (say, philosophically considered).[47] Naturally, he could give no reason why those who think there are truths about human goods and rights should judge his 'principle of legitimacy' true. But he did offer an illustration of its reach: the 'principle' yields the conclusion, he said, that no one can have any acceptable reason to argue against the legal right of women to abort their unborn children during at least the first three months of life; better still, it enables us to reach this conclusion without even considering the arguments of those who contend that these unborn children instantiate the good of human life, that is, do really have human lives and human rights.[48]

The grounds which Ronald Dworkin has offered for state neutralism about basic values are equally weak. If the state were not neutral about the intrinsic goodness or badness of ways of life, it would deny *equality* (of respect). When this first argument was refuted by showing that equality of respect requires rather than forbids the state to promote good and discourage bad forms of life, Dworkin shifted to a new one. Such discrimination between good and bad ways of life requires people to accept a view they cannot accept without abandoning their self-respect. But this was just as unsound: for restrictions, prohibitions, or taxes on the basis of such a discrimination do not require those who disagree to accept a view about the good, and do allow them to keep their self-respect. As Bentham made his boast, one can combine obedience, even prompt obedience, with free censure (inner or outer) of laws one judges misguided and unjust.[49]

Then there was a series of arguments dependent on ignoring the law-makers' reasons for action and categorizing the law as a mere 'appeal to the majority's preferences'.[50] The game is to state those preferences from an external viewpoint, as if the individuals who happen to make up a majority were each concerned only with 'following or imposing majority opinion'

---

[47] See Rawls, *Political Liberalism*, 225 ('[T]he guidelines of inquiry of public reason, as well its principle of legitimacy, have the same basis as the substantive principles of justice'). For illuminating critiques of Rawls's 'principle', see e.g. Raz, *Ethics in the Public Domain* at 60–81.

[48] Rawls, *Political Liberalism*, 243 n. 32. For comment, see George, 'Public Reason and Political Conflict: Abortion and Homosexuality' at 2486–95, which also refutes a similar argumentation by Judith Jarvis Thomson. The similar principle of legitimacy advanced by Nagel, 'Moral Conflict and Political Legitimacy' at 221, is vulnerable to the same critique. [See also essay I.16.]

[49] On this series of Dworkinian arguments and their refutation, see essay III.2 at 51–3 (1987c at 437–8).

[50] See the analysis of Dworkin's equivocations on this theme in essay III.1 at 24–6 (1985a at 309–11).

rather than with the goods and evils, rights and wrongs which, according to such an individual's opinion, are at stake. And the neutralist liberal's game is won by proceeding asymmetrically, juxtaposing the 'majority opinion/will/preference' (content and rationale unstated) with the *content* of the threatened right or value. So, in the Philosophers' covertly euthanasiast Brief, the reasons or motives of the patient seeking assistance in suicide are stated from the internal viewpoint of one 'who believes that further life means only degradation', while the reasons for the law against assisting suicide (and mercy killing) are stated from an external viewpoint—'just because that is what some majority thinks proper'.[51] In *Romer v Evans*,[52] the Colorado Amendment 2 case, the presumption that the law-making 'majority' acts not on reasons but only on sub-rational preferences, emotions, prejudices, and a will to power was erected into the very 'principle' of decision. Systematically, the majority's judgments and decisions are denied the dignity which, by the accolade of 'autonomy', is accorded to the choices of individuals whose opportunity to do what they please would be hampered by the majority's law.

The Philosophers' Brief repeats like a mantra the 'mystery' passage(s) from *Casey*:

[M]atters, involving the most intimate and personal choices a person may make in a lifetime, choices central to personal dignity and autonomy, are central to the liberty protected by the Fourteenth Amendment. At the heart of liberty is the right to define one's own concept of existence, of meaning, of the universe, and of the mystery of human life ... [b]eliefs [which] define the attributes of personhood.[53]

Now one might wonder whether in that passage and the Philosophers' Brief, *autonomy* is accorded an objectivity which emotivist, Humean, or Nietzschean meta-ethics deny to all other values. And perhaps, in the thoughts of some who appeal to it, autonomy does have that status. After all, secularism as we know it inhabits the room not only 'swept' free but also 'furnished'[54] by Jewish and Christian faith—swept free of worldly divinities but furnished with a knowledge of good and evil, of freely adopted intentions, of the dignity of persons invited to be cooperators with the universe's very source of being, meaning, and value. In this room one finds not only the autonomy, the self-will of those whose desires are protected by *Eisenstadt* or *Casey* or *Evans*, and the Nietzschean will to power now recovering from the odium it attracted fifty-five to sixty years ago, but also the earnest, utterly dissimilar autonomy of a Kant, who understood that autonomy has

---

[51] Dworkin et al., 'Assisted Suicide: The Philosophers' Brief' at 44.
[52] 517 US 620 (1996).
[53] *Planned Parenthood v Casey* 505 US 833, 851 (1992).
[54] See Matthew 12: 44; Luke 11: 25.

no dignity unless it is freedom from the rule of the passions. But Kant also judged that the secularism he mistakenly associates with pure reason must give way to practical reason's 'inevitable postulate' of God as most holy, source of all moral directiveness, and omnipotent providential source of a final 'balance' between happiness and moral worth.[55] So Kant's conception of autonomy—especially when cleared of his own crude empiricist/ hedonist psychology, his expulsion of human free choice to the noumenal unknown, and his neglect of basic human goods and substantive practical principles—opens a road down which secularism declines to go. Rather than turn down that way to divine existence, providence, and intention for humankind—truths available to theoretical as well as practical reason— secularism will embrace the unprincipled freedom to do what you will which Kant rightly regarded as subhuman and irrational.

V

Just as secularism obscures the truth of the basic human goods, reasons for action, first practical principles, differentiated from sub-rational inclinations and passions, so also is it marked by a pervasive misunderstanding of *intention*. Creation, covenant, and the acts of salvation are supreme manifestations of intention, that is, of purpose. Reflection on the divine perfections makes it clear that the moral and non-moral evils in the created world, including human defections from the covenant, are not intended but rather foreseen and permitted since their prevention would entail the loss of great goods. Nor did Jesus intend or choose his death on the cross; it was not a suicide's terminating his life as a means to our salvation or anything else, but instead the free (and salvific) acceptance of that side effect of his fidelity to his mission of teaching and healing. Secularism characteristically collapses that distinction. In the heyday of the Victorian construction of a new radically secular ethics, the atheist utilitarian Henry Sidgwick said with characteristic directness: 'For purposes of exact moral or juristic discussion, it is best to include under the term "intention" all the consequences of an act that are foreseen as certain or probable.'[56]

Despite its very poor fit with reality, law, and professional ethics, this artefact—intention collapsed into foresight and causation—is powerfully attractive to the secularized. The Ninth Circuit's opinion in *Compassion in Dying*[57] was wholly reliant on it. The opinion derided the American

---

[55] Kant, *Religion Within the Limits of Reason Alone*, 4–7 (preface to first edn).
[56] Sidgwick, *The Methods of Ethics*, 202.
[57] *Compassion in Dying v Washington* 79 F3d 790 (9th Cir. 1996), rev'd sub. nom. *Washington v Glucksberg* 521 US 702 (1997).

Medical Association's distinction between giving analgesics with intent to suppress pain and giving them with intent to kill. It declared that doctors who respect a patient's decision to forgo life-sustaining treatment *intend* to hasten their patient's death, that the laws authorizing people to refuse treatment are simply laws for authorizing suicide, and even that laws for preventing suicide have 'an aim' of prolonging a dying person's suffering. The Second Circuit opinion in *Quill v Vacco*[58] followed the same route. In reality, of course, the New York legislature, in declaring the lawfulness of refusing medical treatment, did not intend to promote or protect any patient's intention to hasten or determine the time of death but intended rather to protect the intention to be free from unwanted burdens and interventions on the patient's body, even if the patient's death is a foreseeable consequence. True, the legislature foresaw that one consequence of its enactment would be that some people would use, that is, abuse, this right by exercising it *with intent to* hasten death. But as a legislative declaration made clear,[59] that was no part of the legislature's intent—no more than we intend the guilty to escape when we grant due process of law, or intend lawyers to conspire to lie when we grant an attorney-client privilege. When we grant or acknowledge a constitutionally protected *liberty to testify*, we foresee that some or even most defendants will exploit their right by lying for the purpose of deceiving the jury. Our foresight does not make that deception our aim or a part of the constitutionally protected liberty right—as if that great liberty could be accurately understood as '*the right to lie*', and as if counsel, after hearing a client's unambiguous confession of guilt, would nevertheless have the constitutional right to put that client on the stand precisely in order to lie.

This loss of grip on the reality of intention can be found in other contexts of great significance for our culture, for instance amongst Catholic theologians. The astonishingly rapid and far-reaching penetration of secularism amongst these moralists took the form, primarily, of adopting the quasi-utilitarian ethic of proportionalism: acts have their moral character from their end, that is, from a state of affairs which can be caused by human action, and which makes actions right when it is judged to promise the greater proportion of overall net pre-moral good or the lesser proportion of overall net pre-moral negative value. With equally astonishing completeness and casualness, leading theologians in this group—Schüller, Fuchs, Peschke, and others—began asserting both that the moral norms they were rejecting are about what is 'directly' rather

---

[58] 80 F3d 716 (2d Cir. 1996), rev'd sub. nom. *Vacco v Quill* 521 US 793 (1997).
[59] *Quill* 80 F3d at 734 n. 7.

than 'indirectly' *caused*, and that what one causes as a side effect is a *means* to the consequences one seeks to achieve by one's action. Intention virtually disappeared from their discourse. In the tradition they were seeking to overthrow, 'directly willed' means 'intended as an end or chosen or intended as a means', 'indirect' has a corresponding meaning by negation of such intention, and what is willed as a means is intended. But all this seems to have become simply unintelligible to these theologians.[60] They stand before it as uncomprehending (so it would appear) as Ronald Dworkin reading Justice Scalia's judgment in *Cruzan*,[61] noting Scalia's denial that the distinction between inaction and positive action is morally decisive, and concluding that Scalia thinks a patient who refuses life-saving amputation must be treated as a suicide.[62]

VI

Utilitarianism (consequentialism, proportionalism) is the peculiar symbol of secularism in reaction against but still illuminated (as I have already suggested) by the after-glow of Christian faith. It is an 'ism', an ideal, aspiring to much more than the 'eat, drink, and be merry', or the opportunistic *libido dominandi*, which are the untutored outcome of much unbelief. There is nothing new about Machiavellian politics or about the thought that it is better for one innocent to be killed 'lest the people perish'. But there is something new in ethics, these past 200 years, and it is utilitarianism or, more generally, consequentialism (or, more narrowly, religiose proportionalism).

Consequentialism is radically incompatible with belief in divine providence. For consequentialism's supreme or indeed single practical principle is to pursue states of affairs embodying greater overall net good. But the doctrine of divine providence is that God permits what is bad only to draw from it good and more good. So the principle taken *with* the doctrine yields the practical norm: Try anything! Do whatever you like! (For whether your project succeeds or fails, the result will providentially have promoted overall long-term net good.) But consequentialism is proposed as an ethics. So it does not tell us to do whatever we feel like. So, to avoid the *reductio ad absurdum*, it must suppress or ignore belief in divine providence.

Indeed, when one reflects on the phenomenon of consequentialism, one comes, I think, to see it as, wittingly or otherwise, an attempt to replace

---

[60] See 1991c at 74–7. For a recent example of such incomprehension, see Porter, '"Direct" and "Indirect" in Grisez's Moral Theory', esp. 621–7. [And see now essay II.13.]

[61] *Cruzan v Director, Missouri Dept. of Health* 497 US 261 (1990).   [62] See 1993e at 565.

divine with human providence, not in retail (as with the differentiation of secular from sacred that comes with all particular technical competences, as in agriculture, sewerage, or medicine) but wholesale, across the board. Though proposed as an ethics, its conception of deliberation does not belong to what Aristotle and Aquinas identified as ethical or moral practical reasoning, in which various irreducibly basic goods, each an aspect of the flourishing of human persons, are pursued in the unbounded horizon of 'human existence as a whole'. Instead, consequentialism adopts the form of technical reasoning, in which we seek the means which will effectively achieve an attainable goal, and can measure every action against alternatives for their respective cost-benefit efficiency.

Haunted by the inherent problems of incommensurability among the basic goods, by the future's unforeseeability, and by risk's incommensurability with value, consequentialism needs to make rational commensuration and aggregation seem possible in the real, open horizon of morally significant choice. First, then, it characteristically tries to eliminate the multiplicity of substantive basic human goods, and deal instead in a single maximand such as pleasure, or alternatively the absence of pain, or alternatively 'preferences' of any and every kind, or money value, or whatever. But this commensuration alone is not enough; the aggregation requires a bottom line, and so the real, unbounded horizon of human existence is characteristically blocked off, in consequentialist deliberation, by the adoption—necessarily arbitrary, on consequentialism's own assumptions—of some delimited horizon: my country's survival and prosperity during the lifetime of me and my children, or something of that sort.

Nor should we be surprised to find consequentialism also blocking off awareness of the reality of free choice—for two reasons. First, free choice is always between alternative, incompatible proposals each of which offers something attractive to practical reason. But if consequentialist aggregation could be done, it would identify one proposal as promising *all* the benefits of the others *plus* some more (including more certain) benefits; and then there would remain no possibility of rationally *choosing* any of the proposals that offer less (including less certain) benefits. One would simply assent to the proposal promising maximum net good, and spontaneously begin putting it into effect. So consequentialism is incoherent with its own undertaking to guide deliberation towards morally significant *choice*.

Secondly, if there is to be any computation of overall net good, and at least the appearance of aggregability, consequentialism will have to ignore the implications of free choice for moral character. For the shaping of character by free choices is an inherent, intransitive side effect, so to speak, of the spiritual aspect of the making of free choices. Such choices not only initiate their own transitive effects—their execution—but also *last*, endure, subsist, and persist in the soul, the character, of the chooser until such time, if ever, as they are reversed by a new and incompatible choice; for example, to repent of them and to resolve not to make them again. And this perduring of choices in character—perhaps the most valuable theme of Karol Wojtyla's own philosophical work—is a consequence of choices which is clearly incommensurable in significance, value, or disvalue with those choices' transitive consequences, that is their consequences outside the acting person's will and character. So it is no accident that the founders of utilitarianism were determinists.

And secularists. For secularism of one kind, the whole consequentialist method or cluster of ethical methods is attractive because it promises to dissolve all moral norms which exclude cheating and killing, and obstruct me in doing what I want. For secularism of another kind, consequentialism is attractive because it seems to be implied by concern for 'overall' human or sentient good. For secularized religious people, proportionalism offers both these attractions.

The attractiveness of consequentialism was of course immensely enhanced by its cultural context: it is in essence an extrapolation, certainly unwarranted and sometimes apparently hubristic, from the successes and the genuine utility of technologies. Quasi-technical economics, game theory, and the like, each suggest a reductive model for all practical thinking. So that extrapolated, reductivist model is found in many parts of our culture. We find, for example, that the *Model Penal Code* and some of the Restatements of the law were consciously modelled in some respects on utilitarian suppositions about action and value. And then, in quite another context, we find a scarcely secularist Christian philosopher like Maritain asserting that Christians have a 'temporal mission' quickened by a 'terrestrial hope' which must 'have as its comprehensive aim the ideal of building a better or a new Christian civilization'.[63]

Does anyone's temporal vocation require a 'comprehensive aim'? It seems to me a mistake to suppose that practical thought is impotent unless guided by such far-reaching envisagings of vast future states of affairs capable of being built up by efficient human effort. The envisaging or imagining of such states of affairs is not a prerequisite for our being oriented and motivated by concern for the common good of our communities (family, neighbourhood, cultural, political), a complex good involving respect for

---

[63] Maritain, *On the Philosophy of History*, 122. He goes on: 'At each new age in human history (as is, to my mind, our own age with respect to the Middle Ages and the Baroque Age), it is normal that Christians hope for a new Christendom, and depict for themselves, in order to guide their effort, a concrete historical idea appropriate to the particular climate of age in question.' *Ibid.* at 123.

rights and, as I have suggested against 'neutral liberalism', a substantive conception or range of conceptions of individual and communal flourishing. As it seeks to save itself from collapsing into nihilism, secularist thought—burdened as it is (as I have tried to show) with all its misunderstandings of human good and human action—will always be tempted (as this century has amply shown) by the envisaging of vast 'goals' or 'comprehensive aims', and by the passionate experience of technical efforts to achieve them: Ten-Year Plans, wars for carving out a Thousand-Year Empire's living space, and such like. These and all other such this-worldly hopes seem to correspond, obscurely and deviantly, to the hope for the only really possible and worthwhile 'comprehensive goal', the Kingdom which we are called upon to 'Seek first'.[64]

If we are right to accept it as true that providence includes divine revelation and God's extra-ordinary personal action in history, we are authorized to hope that that Kingdom will include—as Vatican II puts it in a fresh articulation of the givens of Scripture and Tradition—all the good fruits of human efforts made in obedience to the norms of truth and justice, love and peace,[65] even when such obedience had no comprehensive secular goal, and seemed to end in failure, perhaps even thorough-going failure, to achieve what one had hoped to do in this life.

---

[64] Matthew 6: 33.   [65] Vatican II, *Gaudium et Spes*, sec. 39.

4

RELIGION AND STATE*

I

These reflections will be philosophical and historical or factual, not theological. They will draw upon and propose considerations which are available in principle to everyone and do not rely on the content of any communication that may have been made to human persons from a transcendent source by means that depart, in some measure, from the patterns that are the subjects of empirical natural and/or social sciences.

This philosophical purpose and method does not, however, have the consequence that many would assume it has, or should have. Many people assume, and some hold with argument and tenacity, that in an inquiry pursued intelligently and without bias any such transcendent source of reality and value is no more than, at most, a bare possibility. They treat as ungrounded and altogether improbable any anticipation or judgment that there has been or may well be some such communication—revelation— from such a source. But the question whether the existence and character of our universe give cogent reason for affirming the existence of such a transcendent explanation is a philosophical question, and one which cannot reasonably and philosophically be given an answer without considering, carefully and with openness, the arguments supporting such an affirmation. They are philosophical arguments, and stronger than many an argument, in many a field of philosophy, that is widely thought philosophically acceptable and warranted. I have rehearsed a number of these arguments for the existence of God in my two main books on political philosophy.[1]

* 2006a, a Newman Lecture given in Washington, DC on 15 September 2006.
[1] *NLNR* 378–88; *Aquinas* 298–304. In each treatment, the rest of the chapter unfolds some relevant implications which tend to reinforce the bare initial arguments. The remarkable book by Germain Grisez which underpins especially the earlier of these two treatments has been republished with a new title and an introductory exposition of a further argument to God from practical reason's cogency: *God? Philosophical Preface to Faith.*

Two of them are taken up by practically every serious-minded person, with degrees of clarity and resolution that differ widely from person to person and culture to culture. The first of these arguments begins by noticing how the patterns of functioning that everyone observes or infers, and that modern natural sciences successfully describe and explain, always involve a shift, change, or movement from one state of affairs (call it P) to another (call it A), such that A is the *actual* functioning of the *potentiality* so to function constituted by or present in P—a change from potentiality to act which needs explanation and is explained by some further factor, X, acting upon P and thereby bringing about the change from P to A. This line of thought proceeds by noticing that (as natural sciences luxuriantly illustrate) any such X is itself an actuality (call it A_1) that was shifted from potentiality (call it P_1) by another X (call it X_1) and so on. Without presupposing any denial of the possibility that the universe has existed for an infinite length of time (a possibility vigorously and repeatedly defended by Aquinas), this line of thought moves to the conclusion that the universe would be radically under-explained, and indeed could not exist, unless there is some quite different sort of explanatory factor, some sort of reality which can contribute to the explanation of every X (and thus every A and the whole universe of As) but can do so without changing or ever needing to change from potentiality to act—a sheer act(uality), free from any mere potentiality, and capable of bringing into actuality and existence anything and everything which, but for that, would and could have had no actuality at all.

Such a creative bringing of states of affairs into being also makes it possible to point to the explanation sought in the second line of thought which is pursued by any serious-minded person. This line of thought seeks to explain the orderliness of things, the orderliness and directionality of states of affairs (events and things) which (not without fortuity and disorderliness) is so thoroughly characteristic of the world we know. And the explanation sought and proposed shows that such directionality is to be understood as a direct*ed*ness resultant from something not altogether unlike our intentionally putting into effect an intelligible plan of action. This second line of thought enhances the first by showing the need to think of the transcendent pure act(uality) as intelligent and free, albeit in a manner altogether surpassing our intelligence and freedom. Thus the two lines of thought converge in the judgment that there exists a reality such as is everywhere referred to by the name 'God'.

The second line of thought has a further consequence. Since we have intelligence, including the capacity both to project (express) meaning and to share it, and some freedom to choose between alternatives understood by us as more or less desirable, it is reasonable to hypothesize and anticipate that there might at some time be some projection, to us, of meaning and shareable purpose, from the infinitely greater intelligence and purposiveness needed to explain the existence of our universe including our own mysterious but commonplace sharing with each other of meaning and intentions. Philosophy here bids us cast about for historical evidence of such transcendent revelation, if any there be. In doing so, philosophy does not yet consign us to theology. The judgment that certain events are best understood as instances of a transcendently revelatory communication is one that builds on the philosophically (and commonsensically) grounded affirmation of the existence of a creator, and on historically warranted affirmations that certain words were spoken and deeds done with certain intentions. The judgment draws also on the complex range of presuppositions and insights that shape judgments about personal credibility. And it also draws (or needs to be in a position to draw) on an assessment of the array of theological arguments which show that the contents of the revelation or teachings of its messengers at no point contradict reason. But none of this amounts either to making an act of faith, that is of submitting one's mind and will to the revealing God,[2] or to doing or endorsing theology, the discipline that takes as axiomatic the propositional content of divine revelation.

The philosophical argument to God does, however, warrant and include judgments that are theological in a broader sense. What is traditionally called natural theology is that part of philosophy which, while remaining strictly and integrally philosophical, speaks of such things as God's existence and nature as intelligent, free, and so forth. Similarly, despite what many say, a historical judgment of the kind hypothesized above would not cease to be authentically historical merely because it affirmed that the most reasonable explanation of certain extraordinary events is their being acts of divine revelation.

Moreover, there can be (and is) a mutual support, and in that sense interdependence, between the philosophical and the historical, each capable

---

[2] On faith and its interrelationship with the rational judgment that God exists and that a specific set of events communicates the divine purpose of creating (and, as it may be, of restoring), see *LCL* ch. 1. I differ from this rich and penetrating treatment only insofar as sec. C.3 (pp. 13–14) says without qualification (such as Grisez might well wish to make) that Islam is one of the three 'biblical religions' which offer a sound account of God and human persons, an account which is true humanism, forestalls modern thought's problem with free choice and objectivity, and responds to human hopes and expectations. Islam appears to me to offer unsound accounts of God, and human destiny, and to be anti-humanist and unclear about free will. Above all, Islam's partial endorsement of the bible does not at all reinforce the grounds for accepting the bible, and where Mohammed departs from the biblical revelation and proposes an alternative account of God and salvation his teaching lacks philosophical, moral, or historical merit just insofar as it differs substantially from the bible read as it is read in the Church whose founding and teaching is witnessed to in the New Testament.

of giving the other a degree of clarity and certainty not available to it in isolation from the other. John Henry Newman's profound discussions of *antecedent probabilities*, from his twelfth Oxford University Sermon (1839), through his *An Essay on the Development of Christian Doctrine* (1845) to his *A Grammar of Assent* (1870), bear in good measure on this network, this virtuous upward spiral, of mutually supporting considerations, presumptions, and grounds for accepting hypotheses that go, in varying ways, beyond the warrant of the simply perceptible towards—go, indeed, all the way to—responsible, critical, and warranted affirmation or confirmation not only of the transcendent and divine (affirmations of which are *primarily* philosophical) but also of concrete revelatory divine intervention, more or less preternatural, in human affairs (affirmations of which are *primarily* historical). It is such a network of convergent considerations, starting with the antecedent reasonableness of anticipating some communication between the intelligent Creator and the other intelligences in the created universe—us—that (as Newman shows)[3] subverts David Hume's a priori argument that the probability that an apparent miracle is miraculous must always be lower than the probability that the laws of nature prevail without exception. Given the certain dependence of the laws of nature on the creative intelligence and will of an actuality not limited by any mere potentiality, it is neither contrary to nor beyond reason to expect that the course of human history might well include events, of communicative significance, going beyond or contrary to the laws that generally structure affairs. Nor need it be unreasonable to judge that such a communicative event did actually or very probably occur at such-and-such a time and place.

In making a responsible judgment of this kind, one will meet with another kind or instance of such rationally reinforcing interdependence: that between moral character (and the moral judgments which assess it) and the credibility of witnesses and prophets (and the factual/historical judgments which assess it). To the question whether a prophet asserting divine revelatory words or deeds is to be believed, one should indeed bring questions both about philosophical cogency and about historical evidence, but also questions about the moral creditworthiness both of the evidentiary witnesses and, perhaps even more importantly, of the supposed prophetic witness to divine communicative words or deeds of revelation. A self-styled prophet, however impressive are certain aspects of his theological teaching, undermines his credibility whenever he shows himself to be

---

[3] *An Essay in Aid of a Grammar of Assent*, 199. I have tried to put this in the wider frame of *rationality norms*: essay 9 at 152–3.

morally flawed, especially if his claim is to be the primary bearer of a new
revelation and founder of new institutions or arrangements for carrying
it forward in perpetuity, and especially if his moral flaws give reason to
judge his supposed messages self-serving—as, for example, when he says
that the God whose messenger he is has dispensed him from certain sexual
restrictions, or has authorized him and his followers to require of anyone
else adoption of their message on pain of death or servitude.[4] The same
goes for the character and methods, morally assessed, of those who hold
themselves out as witnesses to the principal prophet or founder. Apostles
who are willing to kill or otherwise coerce, or to offer carnally seductive
incentives ('the women that thy right hand possesses'), in support of their
testimony and of the Prophet's message, should be contrasted with apostles
who make no such threats but are willing to be killed rather than renounce
their testimony or message at the demand of ruthless persons. The contrast
gains in significance if it corresponds to differences in the contents of the
respective revelations which these differing sets of witnesses preach. Such
moral contrasts have great epistemic relevance. They bear directly on what
is the most reasonable answer to the questions both about evidence and
about substantive acceptability that are decisive for the primarily historical
judgment that such-and-such is or was, or is or was not, an instance of
divine revelation. And such moral contrasts also bear directly on any
consequent moral decision (choice) to take the revealed message as a guide
to one's actions.

II

So it was not merely a matter of taxonomy, or a mere academic concern
privileging method over substance, that led me to begin these reflections
on 'religion and state' by pointing out the overlap between philosophy and
theology, and between reason and faith. Any discussion of religion and state
derails from the outset if it presumes that, as Brian Leiter puts it, 'religion
is contrasted with reason'[5]—a theory for which Leiter, if he felt inclined,
might summon as a supporting witness the first definition of 'religion' in
Webster's New Universal Unabridged Dictionary (New York, 1992). And the
discussion equally derails if it presumes that no religion's claims about
God and man, world and society are reasonable, or that no religion's
claims are even discussable within the domain of public reason, that is, of

---

[4] See also Aquinas, *ScG* I, c.6 (on which, see Van Riet, 'La *Somme contre les Gentils* et la polémique
Islamo-Chrétienne').
[5] 'Religious Reasons and State Power', 26 July 2006, <http://leiterlawschool.typepad.com/
leiter/2006/week30/index.html>.

the discourse that one should find in universities, schools, and legislative
and other political assemblies, including discourse about what laws and
public policies to adopt. The discussion derails, again, if it presumes that
the philosophically neutral, default, baseline or otherwise presumptively
appropriate framework or basis for the discussion of religion and state
is that no religious claims add anything—whether content, certitude, or
probability—to what is established in moral or political philosophy, or in
natural or social science or social theory.

It derails, too, if it holds or presumes that religion's status is nothing
more than one way of exercising the 'right' proclaimed as fundamental and
'at the heart of liberty', in *Planned Parenthood v Casey* (1992): 'to define one's
own concept of existence, of meaning, of the universe, and of the mystery
of human life'.[6] Or again if, as Ronald Dworkin says, *the* basis of the First
Amendment's guarantee of religious freedom is simply that 'no one can
regard himself as a free and equal member of an organized venture that
claims authority to decide for him what he thinks self-respect requires him
to decide for himself'.[7] These celebrations of the right to 'decide for oneself'
and 'define one's own concept' trade, as we shall see, on an important truth.
But they abandon reason when they assert that the relevant intelligible and
basic good in issue is not the good of aligning oneself with a transcendent
intelligence and will whose activity makes possible one's own intellect and
will, nor even the good of discovering the truth about some meaningful
and weighty questions, but rather the good of self-determination or self-
respect. For these are no true goods unless the goods around which one
determines oneself deserve the respect due to what is true, rather than
self-interested make-believe.

In line with one reading of some remarks of mine in *NLNR*,[8] Joseph
Boyle's important paper on religion's place in practical reasoning argues
that even 'one who is not motivated by religious conviction[9] can be aware
of the reason to seek—can see the point of seeking—harmony with the
divine',[10] the harmony that is Boyle's working definition, rather like
Cicero's, of what *religion* is about. I agree with this insofar as it points
out that the line between ability and inability to recognize the good
of religion does not track the line between a sound theistic belief and

---

[6] 505 US 833 at 851. Celebrated in the *amicus curiae* brief of Ronald Dworkin, John Rawls, and
others submitted to the Court in *Washington v Glucksberg* 521 US 702 and *Vacco v Quill* 521 US 793
(1997): Dworkin et al., 'Assisted Suicide: The Philosophers' Brief'; see essay 3, sec. IV.
    [7] Dworkin, *Justice in Robes*, 134.   [8] See *NLNR* 90; cf. 410.
    [9] Boyle has in mind here, primarily, someone who *has* no religious conviction and perhaps
instead the conviction that all religious claims are false and there is no transcendent source of being
and meaning.
    [10] Boyle, 'The Place of Religion in the Practical Reasoning of Individuals and Groups' at 10.

confused alternatives. But there are non-believers and non-believers, and radically different senses of 'seeing the point' of some logically possible object of choice. One who thinks '*If* there were a divine source of reality and meaning, being in harmony with it would be a basic form of human good, but there is no *reason* to believe that there is any such source' may well, and reasonably, conclude that religion is not a basic good and indeed no good at all save as a kind—a rather imperfect, distorted, and distorting kind—of self-determination, of exercise of a *Casey*-style defining of *one's own* concepts, perhaps to fit some of one's raw desires and aversions. For all who hold this sort of view of what reason—if you like, philosophy— has to say about religious claims, the place of religion in schemes of constitutional or human rights is only historically grounded. They may have no intent to set the state or its government and law against religion, still less to scorn the instrumental personal and social benefits religious belief may sometimes (perhaps often) be instrumental in yielding; but, for them, religion's constitutional status and immunities are as instances (and scarcely exemplary) of the only really basic human good, the only intrinsically worthwhile *end*, at stake: settling for oneself one's stance in the world.[11] Like Boyle, I think it is important not to conduct one's reflections about religion and state on this false premise. The importance of not doing so is all the greater because self-determination itself is now widely regarded, not least among our constitutional lawyers, as a form, not so much of shaping up as best one can to what one judges in conscience to be reason's demands on one, but rather as the bundling of one's *strong desires*, one's 'deep concerns', most considerable when most *passionate*. In such a line of thought (formalized within a year or two of *Casey*),[12] religion is doubly discredited, first by the casual assumption that it is outside the domain of reason, and then by hostility to its unwelcome critiques

---

[11] Boyle's assumption, which his essay intends to test (and confirm), is 'that the good of religion has rational appeal prior to such articulate beliefs about God [as that God is a personal being with whom cooperation is possible]': *ibid.*, 15n. That assumption may in the abstract, and in certain contexts, be sound while being unsound in a context where an understanding of the personal God of Abraham and Isaac and Jesus has been made available (not altogether inadequately) to virtually everyone. One who rejects that understanding of God is poised to reject the thesis that it is good to consider oneself in harmony, through awe and worship, with a being one has imagined or postulated. And so a good many people object to, or are puzzled by, the inclusion of religion in the list of basic goods in *NLNR*. Just as 'religion presupposes some views about the divine and about the rest of reality' (p. 5), so too acceptance that religion has a distinct intelligible point presupposes the view that its views about the divine are not simply false (and demeaning).

[12] Eisgruber and Sager, 'The Vulnerability of Consciences: The Constitutional Basis for Protecting Religious Conduct' at 1266. (The title can give a mistaken impression of the authors' central thesis; they deny [at 1263, 1268–70] that conscience as the rational faculty of practical judgment has any more claim than religion to constitutional privilege or even protection; the proper object of constitutional protection is any 'deep concern', any and all 'deeply' motivated and self-shaping attitudes and behaviour, which whether or not religious *or even conscientious* are all alike entitled to 'equal regard'.)

of and constraints upon 'deep' desires. Its place in the constitution can be accepted only grudgingly as a historical relic and a monument to the threat that religions characteristically have posed to each other as well as to everyone's 'conscience' (reconceptualized as the articulation of their 'deep concerns').

Our reflections will go soundly if they treat affirming God as within the full reach of the critically disciplined reasoning we call philosophy, and treat affirming the political common good (including politically acknowledged human rights) as within the full reach of critically disciplined practical reason at its highest: political philosophy. *Each* of these affirmations—of God and of a true public interest or common good—confronts openly sceptical denials, and the fair-weather friendship of fideistic or merely conventional concurrence, and the masked scepticism communicated by concepts such as Rawls's 'burden of judgment' and 'fact of pluralism'. The 'inevitably' controverted character of each of the two affirmations or affirmation-clusters only challenges us to think more resolutely, and in no way robs them of their privileged status as, in each case, the truth of the matter (or a worthwhile part of it). It is a status that *each* is entitled to, by its rational soundness.

III

Before we turn to consider how all this bears on real-life political communities, we might reflect that claims about divine revelation do not rise to the level of the philosophically considerable unless the group which advances them is willing to defend the historical assertions which are the core (albeit not the whole) of its claims. Beginning about 120 years after John Henry Newman's conversion, the Church which he joined and adorned experienced a severe and still ongoing loss of faith among its members and of political and other influence in many parts of the world where it had been well established. Though the main causes of this are complex, and that Church's demanding moral teaching is prominent among them, they centre, in my estimation, on the loss of confidence in the truth of those Gospel teachings that warn insistently of the utterly grave and unending consequences of one's seriously wrongful and unrepented choices. And in turn this loss of confidence derives, in some large measure, I believe, from the weakening of belief that in the four Gospels and the Acts of the Apostles we have, albeit in theologically inflected form, a truthful and sober account of things actually said and done by a man whose divine authority and, indeed, nature was attested not only by his moral authenticity and virtue but also by his transcendence to the laws of time and nature. And this weakening of belief in the historicity of the testimony of the apostles and their confidantes has among its primary causes the adoption by many of that Church's scripture scholars, and accordingly by those whom they teach and advise, of a philosophically unsound presumption against that transcendence to laws of nature—against the miraculous.

The Gospels could be credible witnesses to everything they report even if they were written after AD 70. But scholars poison the root of the tree if a main reason for their concluding that a Gospel dates from after AD 70 is that otherwise its foretelling of the fall of Jerusalem[13] would outrun human knowledge and ignorance of the future.[14] For then the reports that Jesus foretold those events become historically discreditable, and efforts to save them from the status of falsehoods, by denying that they were intended to assert the happening or content of any actual event or statement, ripple out from these passages and change—infect—the reading of all other parts of the narrative in the Gospels (and Acts). All parts become not accounts or reports but 'stories', in the equivocal terminology of the modern preacher. Of course every historical inquiry should start with a definite presumption that the events under investigation transpired in accordance with the laws of nature. But that presumption can rationally, and should, be qualified (and in due measure, and with due caution) set aside, once a convergent set of considerations (bearing on *those* events' antecedents, concomitants, content, and sequels) make it probable that the events were part of a divine communicative intervention. For once that becomes probable, the philosophically warranted, indeed compelling, principles of methodological consistency demand that the investigation's initial presumptions, including the presumption against miracles, should be revised and indeed abandoned to the extent that the whole range of grounds for judgment makes appropriate. If Jesus of Nazareth was in any way divine, or even an authentic witness of the divine, he could speak with miraculous foreknowledge about the future of Jerusalem. So if he presumably didn't, he presumably couldn't, and so presumably wasn't divine. (The other category, 'merely human messenger of the divine', is inapplicable to this man, because, if we know anything significant about what he said and

---

[13]   Matthew 23: 37–9; 24: 1–2; Mark 13: 1–2; Luke 13: 34–5; 19: 41–4; 21: 5–6, 21–4.

[14]   Of course, just as scholars such as John A.T. Robinson, *Redating the New Testament* and John Wenham, *Redating Matthew, Mark & Luke* argue from the silence of the New Testament about the circumstances and sequelae of the fall of Jerusalem in AD 70 to the conclusion that the Gospels and Acts ante-date that event, so more conventional recent scholars may argue that features of and/or elements in the Gospels quite distinct from the *prophecies* of the fall of Jerusalem attributed to Jesus suggest a post-70 origin for Matthew and Luke if not also Mark. The point I am making does not touch the latter line of argument (though I do not find it persuasive), but concerns those who overtly or covertly assume that the prophecies are *ex eventu*—made up after the event—and employ that assumption in the approach to the dating and historicity of the Gospels.

did, we know that he claimed to *be* divine.) Of course, many scholars (and bishops who follow them) are inconsistent and inattentive to implications. They don't, I think, mean to run the theorem as I just did. But, like it or not, it does run that way, poison (to the proclamation of revelation) from root to leaf. A religion that remained at peace with such incoherence would drop below the horizon of philosophy, and could not claim the adherence of any earnestly inquiring mind. It would fail to live up to the demands of public reason.[15]

IV

What then does a sound philosophy of politics have to say about political communities in which there is no consensus about this world's dependence upon a divine creator, and still less consensus about whether and if so where and how there has been any communication to us from any such creator? Even assuming (as we should) that neither atheism nor agnosticism is the rational default position for political philosophy, what is to be said, within political philosophy, about the place of religion in political communities very many of whose members treat atheism or agnosticism as their default position in both their daily lives and in their political deliberations?

These questions can be answered well by considering first a society in which adherents of sound philosophy, both political/moral and religious, have procedurally fair and constitutional authority to settle the laws and their execution. How should the laws and public policies of such a state bear on religion? Answering that first form of the question will provide a sound basis for answering the question in its second form, today more engaging but inherently subordinate, about a society which is deeply pluralist in religious beliefs, if not also about political and individual morality. My discussion focuses on the first and basic form of the question, though some of the implications for more deeply divided societies should become apparent.

V

Political philosophy draws on experience, including experience which is only in a loose sense 'available to all' and is better called historical. And so it is not impossible, and indeed is positively fitting, to consider as essentially political-philosophical (and not merely positive law) that legal position on religion and state which is articulated in (1) the US Constitution

---

[15] On public reason, coherently and critically understood, see essay I.16 (1998a) or 2000c or 2005e; and essay I.2 (1999a).

First Amendment's protection of 'the free exercise of religion', in (2) the European Convention on Human Rights Article 9(1)'s guarantee that

Everyone has the right to freedom of thought, conscience and religion; this right includes freedom to change his religion or belief, and freedom, either alone or in community with others and in public or private, to manifest his religion or belief, in worship, teaching, practice and observance

(subject to the considerations of public order spelled out by Article 9(2)), and in (3) the Second Vatican Council's Declaration (*Dignitatis Humanae*) on Religious Liberty. The Council's identification of the right to religious liberty closely tracks the European Convention's. Much more clearly than the Convention, however, it identifies the right not as a Hohfeldian 'liberty-right' but as an *immunity*, of individuals and groups, from *coercion*—including coercion by private individuals or groups—in respect of religious belief, and all those expressions of religious belief, or other acts of putting one's religious belief into practice, that are compatible with laws motivated exclusively by concern to uphold just public order, that is (as sec. 7 of *Dignitatis Humanae* spells out) the rights of others, public peace, and public morality.

To show that this immunity from coercion is a natural law right, violation of which is '*intrinsically* unjust',[16] the Council puts forward two lines of argument. The first and much more extensively expounded has as its major premise: 'everyone has a moral obligation to seek the truth about religious matters, and adhere to whatever truth one finds'. Then its minor premise is: 'one cannot live up to that obligation in a manner appropriate to one's nature as a rational and responsible person unless one has immunity from external coercion as well as psychological freedom'. The minor premise, as is usual in practical syllogisms, is essentially one of fact (albeit not brute fact)—the fact referred to by the word 'cannot'—and this fact is what the Council is pointing to when in sec. 9 it says that 'the exigencies of the dignity of the human person have become more fully known to human reason through centuries of experience'. This is one of the kinds of historical experience that political philosophy needs to draw upon, and can draw upon without ceasing to be philosophical.

It might be objected that coercion in religious matters does work. True, in those immediately subjected to it it may induce little or nothing more

---

[16] *Acta Synodalia Sacrosancti Concilii Oecumenici Vaticani II*, vol. IV, pars VI (Vatican City, 1978), 761 (reply to modus 3 to sec. 10). But should it not be admitted that this is a weak form of *intrinsece malum* (intrinsic moral wrong), since the identification of the (morally excluded) object of choice involves a reference to (further) intentions and to circumstances—namely, that the proposed coercion is not intended (or needed) for the sake of preserving the rights of others, public peace, or public morality?

than a spiritually worthless conformity to the coercing authority's demands
for specified conduct or abstentions. But, so the objection goes, experience[17]
shows that the children and descendants of the coerced may well live an
authentic religious faith and practice in the form, or with the restrictions,
coercively imposed upon their parents or forebears. To which the principal
reply is that a good end, or end-state, cannot justify means which are
wrong intrinsically, that is by reason of their object, that is, their proximate
intention, not by reason of their further consequences. Insofar as coercion
applied to P_1 has as its object a change of mind by P_1 about religious matters,
it will be intrinsically wrong even if it has the consequence that P_2 and
P_3 later adopt true religious beliefs by an authentic process of inquiry and
reflection. That reply is not available where the object of the coercion is to
stop conduct which is a violation of the rights of others or of public peace
or public morality. Nor is it available where the intention in coercing P_1
is not to change P_1's religious beliefs but P_2's and P_3's. Here the reply will
have to observe that the final balance sheet of consequences of those uses of
coercion (just or unjust) has not yet been filled out, even from the viewpoint
of the persecutors. And it will give full scope to what experience has taught
about coercion's effects upon people's conceptions or misconceptions of the
transcendent creator, effects alluded to by Pope Benedict XVI in his lecture
on 12 September 2006 in the University of Regensburg:

The emperor [Manuel II Paleologus in his debate c. 1391 with a learned
Moslem], after having expressed himself so forcefully,[18] goes on to explain in
detail the reasons why spreading the faith through violence is something
unreasonable. Violence is incompatible with the nature of God and the nature of
the soul. '...[N]ot acting reasonably...is contrary to God's nature. Faith is born
of the soul, not the body. Whoever would lead someone to faith needs the ability
to speak well and to reason properly, without violence and threats...To convince
a reasonable soul, one does not need a strong arm, or weapons of any kind, or any
other means of threatening a person with death...'.

   The decisive statement in this argument against violent conversion is this: not
to act in accordance with reason is contrary to God's nature.

So, as the Regensburg lecture suggests, coercion for the sake of religion has
the very bad consequence of ruining people's understanding of that object

---

[17] Consider the realm of Islam, or the near extinction of England's once vibrant Catholicism
over the 250 years following Queen Elizabeth's accession to the throne in 1558, or the transformation of Mormon beliefs about polygamy by remorseless use of Federal coercive power between the
Morrill Act of 1862 and the Mormon Church's capitulation in September 1890. The issue here is
whether these repressions were effective, not whether they were justified.

[18] This alludes to a remark by the Emperor, just quoted by the Pope, which expresses 'forcefully'
an estimation of how Islam stands to biblical revelation and faith rather similar to that proposed in
n. 2 above and in the chapter of *ScG* cited in n. 4 above.

(subject) of inquiry that it is most important not to misunderstand. If it be objected that the violence and unreasonableness are contrary not to the nature of God but to the human good of religion, the proper reply is that they are contrary to both. Religion as a human good is the condition of being in harmony with the transcendent providential explanatory cause of the created world, and what it is to be in that harmony cannot be rightly understood or postulated without some conception of the nature (wise? whimsically violent?) of that transcendent and personal cause. So it was with good reason that the Council began its argument for religious liberty (as an entailment of the human good of religion) with some summary reminders of the divine wisdom and love (that is, will to favour true human good, precisely for its—human persons'—objective goodness and worth).[19]

To support its case that coercion of religious belief, expression, and religiously motivated conduct is 'intrinsically unjust', the Council adds a second, much less extensively articulated argument:

The religious acts whereby people, by their personal judgments, privately or publicly direct their lives to God transcend by their very nature the order of earthly and temporal affairs. The civil power therefore, whose proper responsibility is to attend to the *temporal* common good, ought indeed to recognize and favor the religious life of the citizenry, but must be said to exceed its limits if it presume to direct or inhibit religious acts.[20]

The repeated and key word here is 'temporal', which draws in the whole tradition of thought that I summed up in my book on Aquinas's political theory like this (I abbreviate):[21]

[Aquinas judged that] God's self-communication included propositions about complete human fulfilment in eternal life; and about the community which Jesus established both to transmit that divine promise of eternal life and to help people make themselves, by free choices, ready for that life (and indeed somehow already participants in it). . . .

So human associations are henceforth of two fundamentally distinct types. On the one side is the 'temporal' or 'secular': the names connote a time-bound association and role; Aquinas uses them, in relevant contexts, as synonymous with 'worldly' {mundanus} and 'civil' or 'political' {civilis}. The contrast is

---

[19] See DH 3.1, and note the parallel use of *suaviter* ('without force') in 1.3 and 3.1.

[20] Standard English translations such as that on the Vatican website are particularly poor. The text (which presents no genuine problems to translators):

Praeterea actus religiosi, quibus homines privatim et publice sese ad Deum ex animi sententia ordinant, natura sua terrestrem et temporalem rerum ordinem transcendunt. Potestas igitur civilis, cuius finis proprius est bonum commune temporale curare, religiosam quidem civium vitam agnoscere eique favere debet, sed limites suos excedere dicenda est, si actus religiosos dirigere vel impedire praesumat.

[21] *Aquinas* 321–2.

with a 'spiritual' association organised, by divine inspiration, towards eternal participation (albeit in a somehow bodily way) in the non-bodily (spiritual, mind-like) life of God.[22] The spiritual association par excellence is a church (in Latin *ecclesia*, transliterating the Greek synonym for Latin's *congregatio*); paradigmatically it is the society of 'the faithful' {congregatio fidelium} …

The sole organising purpose of the Catholic Church is that there be *beatitudo perfecta* in eternal life for, so far as possible, all human persons, of every family, association, state, and people. It has no 'secular' purposes. Responsibility for human affairs is thus divided between, on the one side, the Church and, on the other side, secular societies, most notably states and families.…

The rationale of secular authority is, for a parent, to manage a household in which the children are nurtured and protected, fairly dealt with, and educated by instruction and discipline, in the hope that they will gain eternal life; for the law-makers and other rulers of a state, the secular mission to secure peace and justice within its territory.[23]

Aquinas himself is very clear (at the level of principle) that the coercive jurisdiction of temporal political authority extends only to external and interpersonal acts—acts which implicate the community's peace and justice.[24] Though external acts are of course, as Aquinas explains better than anyone, behaviour shaped by and putting into action the internal acts which we call intending and choosing, Aquinas is firm in his assertion, if not altogether clear in his explanation, of several points. First: internal acts as such are inaccessible to human authorities;[25] main texts of his on this point were in the footnotes to *Dignitatis Humanae*'s first argument for the immunity of religious acts, in all drafts including the last.[26] Second: 'personal' acts of self-disposition such as whether and whom to marry, or whether to make a religious vow,[27] are quite beyond the jurisdiction of state government and law. Third, things like 'matters of faith and divine worship, and similar matters', even though everyone *ought* to do them in the same way and everyone benefits from their being done, nevertheless 'do not consist in community and pertain to each individual person in himself

---

[22] See e.g. *ST* II–II q.183 a.1c; a.2 ad 3.

[23] So the 'justice by which human society is governed in line with secular political good {ad bonum civile} can be sufficiently attained through the principles of natural right available to every-one {principia iuris naturalis homini indita}': Aquinas, *De Veritate* q.12 a.3 ad 11.

[24] *Aquinas* 222–45.   [25] *Aquinas* 241.

[26] Attached to the fourth sentence of sec. 3 of DH 3 ('For the exercise of religion, by its very essence, consists primarily in voluntary and free internal acts by which man directly orders himself to God: acts of this kind cannot be commanded or prohibited by merely human authority.') was the footnote:

Cf. S. Thomas, ST I–II q.91 a.4c: 'Man can make laws about those matters about which he can judge. But there can be no judgment of man about interior acts which are hidden, but only about exterior acts which are manifest'; cf. II–II q.104 a.5c: 'In matters which pertain to the interior movement of the will, man is not bound to obey man but only God.' …

[27] *Aquinas* 239–41.

[ad unum aliquem pertinet secundum seipsum]'.[28] Aquinas's philosophical arguments for these positions are the arguments deployed in *Dignitatis Humanae*—arguments from the essential interiority and inaccessibility of such acts, and from the limitation of the state's coercive jurisdiction to matters that are public, not purely private—though Aquinas supplements his arguments by appeal to the essential equality of persons, and *Dignitatis Humanae* raises the whole set of arguments to a new plane by making primary one's serious duty to pursue the truth about ultimates and to shape one's life in line with what one judges one has discovered about them, a duty which is only fulfilled if it is pursued with an authenticity which coercion and 'psychological pressure' prejudice, corrupt, and tend to nullify.

Adding clarity and certitude to the philosophical arguments both of Aquinas and the Council are the Declaration's theses of (as it asserts) divine revelation and divinely guided ecclesiastical tradition: the division of jurisdiction implicit in 'Render to Caesar the things that are Caesar's, and to God the things that are God's', and from the earliest apostolic times onward the unbroken refusal to countenance any attempt to coerce someone to embrace the Christian faith against his or her own will.[29] Indeed, all the elements of the Council's declaration of a natural, human right to religious liberty are taken from authorities as traditional as Aquinas, and none of the *principles* defended by Aquinas is contradicted. As the drafting committee advised the Council fathers orally and in writing in the two days before the final vote adopting *Dignitatis Humanae*, the old thought that error has no rights remains unchallenged. Understanding 'liberty' in its strict (Hohfeldian) sense—absence of duty—there is no moral liberty to proclaim a false religion.[30] But there is the human right (Hohfeldian claim-right) to be immune from coercion by individuals, groups, governments, or laws, in one's religious or religiously motivated acts, provided they are in line with public order; and the acts thus immune include adhering to and proclaiming a religion which one believes to be true but is in fact false. Taking common good in its widest extension, it is for the common good of the members of a political community that they find the truth about divine creation and redemption, live in accordance with that truth, and so enter and remain for ever in the altogether fulfilling fellowship of the divine family extending from this world into eternity. But the state is responsible only for temporal common good, and correspondingly the coercive jurisdiction of state government and law has as its defining objective not the widest common good which might include salvation itself, but what

---

[28] *ScG* III, c.80 nn. 14, 15; *Aquinas* 226, 253–4.   [29] DH 10.
[30] *Acta Synodalia Sacrosancti Concilii Oecumenici Vaticani II*, vol. IV pars VI (Vatican City, 1978), pp. 720–2, 725 (response to 'general *modus*' no. 2, repeated by cross-reference twenty times in subsequent responses to *modi*). [On the Hohfeldian analysis of rights, see *NLNR* 192–201.]

the Council calls a (or the) 'basic component of the common good', namely *public* order.[31] The entire shift away from mediaeval and early modern, ecclesiastically sponsored practices of state coercion of, or arising out of, religious beliefs and acts is carried out by a shifted emphasis among, a clarifying reordering of, a set of truly perennial principles.

<h1 style="text-align:center">VI</h1>

Philosophically assessed, without the philosophically unsound presupposition of atheism or agnosticism about creation and revelation, the natural law thesis articulated in *Dignitatis Humanae*, like its positive law antecedents in the US Constitution and the European Convention on Human Rights, constitutes a sound and true civilizational core. It is a centring pole between unsound secularist and theocratic alternatives.

Secularists, presuming or asserting that religion cannot be grounded in rational inquiry that issues in true judgments, may nonetheless remain within the tradition of their society and admit religious concerns and acts among the 'grand diversity of relationships, affiliations, activities, and passions that share a constitutional presumption of legitimacy' because in them (as Eisgruber and Sager put it) the members of 'a modern, pluralistic society...find their identities, shape their values, and live the most valuable moments of their lives'.[32] Religious acts, they concede, have the same dignity and constitutional status as the 'relationships, affiliations, activities and passions' under discussion...Eisgruber and Sager's essay does not say how far this wider category extends, but it seems they would include (and not merely marginally) the activities in issue in *Bowers v Hardwick*[33] and *Lawrence v Texas*,[34] and likewise those in *Roe v Wade*[35] and *Planned Parenthood v Casey*,[36] activities which often, it is not unreasonable to suppose, express not so much conscience or any other concern for truth as very strong (deep) emotional desires of the kind which are so often the subject of belated rational regret.[37] Secularists differently placed have often drawn conclusions less favourable to constitutional respect for or even tolerance of religion, as we have seen in many places over many decades of the twentieth century.

---

[31] DH 7.   [32] Eisgruber and Sager, 'The Vulnerability of Consciences' at 1266.

[33] 478 US 186 (1986) (casual homosexual sodomy).

[34] 539 US 558 (2003) (casual homosexual sodomy).

[35] 410 US 113 (1973) (elective abortion).

[36] 505 US 833 (1992) (elective and lifestyle abortions).

[37] True, sometimes acts of the kinds in question (acts of non-marital intimacy, elective abortions) are sought for conscience sake, and religious acts are sometimes or even rather often performed for reasons other than conscience. But Eisgruber and Sager's argument looks only to the 'deepness' (and in that equivocal sense authenticity) of the concern that underlies the protected class of activities, and sets aside any requirement (whether at the level of explanatory principle or of constitutional test) that the concern and self-determination have the *responsibility* (ultimately to truth and thereby also to other persons) and alertness to intrinsic *worth* implicit in conscience and religion.

And at the other end of the spectrum at whose centre stands *Dignitatis Humanae* are the theocracies. These are exemplified in the early modern world by Elizabethan and Jacobean England—in which citizens are directed to perform the religious acts of a worshipping community which is treated as coterminous with the state and whose leaders and ceremonies are specified directly by the state's government. Today they are exemplified by the two main Islamic forms, Sunni, in which like Anglican England the state appoints religious leaders, and Shi'ite, in which (like Puritan England and Calvinist Geneva) the political community and all its members are subject to the coercive control and jurisdiction of the religion's leaders. Radicalized, in ways which have not convincingly been shown to be unfaithful to the core texts or traditions of Islam's purported divine communication, these two forms can together be called Islamism, which in its outward-looking aspect often describes itself as Jihadism, and has a variety of forms which it is not necessary here to itemize.

It is worth adding one further factual observation about the present disposition or alignment of civilizational blocs, groupings, or 'forces'. Just as the Catholic Church's doctrine of religious liberty is pointedly aimed, in one direction against secularist (say American) devaluation of the earnest search for truth about religion and life and secularist (say Communist) repression of religion, and in the other direction against anti-philosophical and anti-Christian (not to mention anti-Semitic) theocratism, so too that Church's members, in their political and day-to-day involvement with issues very fundamental to the legal protection of life and freedom, find themselves allied, variously, with each of those ends of the spectrum against the other. That is part of what it is to be central to civilization.

VII

So state governments and legal systems have a negative duty: not to coerce religious acts unless these threaten the rights of others, public peace, or public morality. Have they other negative duties, perhaps the duty not to discriminate between adherents of one religion and adherents of another? And have they any positive duties, say (as we have seen *Dignitatis Humanae* saying) to encourage the religious activities of citizens, or again to perform what the Council calls[38] 'the moral duty of men and societies towards, the true religion and toward the one Church of Christ'?

Joseph Boyle gives the following positive formulation to the negative duty, and to the Council's arguments for it from authenticity and jurisdiction. His formulation is one that seems to enhance the duty's negative implications by

---

[38] DH 1.

cutting off any favour for a particular religion, any disfavour for a specific religion, and any favour for religion over irreligion or for irreligion over religion:

Political society is morally obliged to create the social space for people to fulfil their obligation to seek the truth in religious matters and live accordingly. *It cannot do this if political life is conducted as if a certain outcome of this inquiry—whether a particular kind of belief or nonbelief—were correct*; for such political action skews public life in ways that hinder rather than facilitate this inquiry, and inevitably and unfairly *coerces* some to support actions whose rationales are incompatible with deep elements of their worldviews. Rather, political society must recognize that its proper actions cannot be based on any particular outcome of this morally mandatory inquiry, since the correctness of any such outcome is for individuals, families, and voluntary associations, not political societies, to determine.[39]

Boyle here uses the notion of coercion a good deal more expansively than *Dignitatis Humanae*, since he includes governmental actions whose intentions are not to coerce anyone but to favour some, so that any coercive effect is a side effect. But, as a matter of political philosophy or natural law or human rights, may it not be true that (as Boyle seems to be saying) the immunity of religious acts from coercion extends to policies, especially governmental policies which, albeit as a side effect, have a coercive impact on those who do or might do religious acts? And may it not also be true that the state's favour for one religion over others, or over irreligion, might entail that the state was making religious judgments, something outside its proper sphere and responsibility? As the prospectus for the series in which this lecture is given puts it, seeming to take a view like Boyle's: 'the principled respect for the autonomy of the individual person expresses itself in the form of principled neutrality on the competing claims of diverse religious communities'.

A reflection in response to Boyle and to the prospectus might begin with the Equality Act 2006, s. 52(4)(g), which exempts from that UK statute's prohibition of discrimination on grounds of religious belief (or unbelief) the following class of decisions by public authorities:

(g)   a decision in connection with an application for entry clearance or for leave to enter or remain in the United Kingdom or anything done for the purposes of or in pursuance of a decision of that kind...if the decision is taken on the grounds—

   (i)   that a person holds an office or position in connection with a religion or belief or provides services in connection with a religion or belief, [or]

   (ii)   that *a religion or belief is not to be treated in the same way as certain other religions* or beliefs, *or*

   (iii) that the exclusion from the United Kingdom of a person to whom paragraph (i) applies is conducive to the public good...

[39] Boyle, 'The Place of Religion' at 22 (emphases added).

Though this authorization of discrimination between religions in immigration decisions is narrow, not to say timid, if it is to be understood as covering only a religion's functionaries, rather than any or all of its other non-national members, the provision nonetheless gives us one way of testing Boyle's thesis.

Suppose a general decision is taken by the British authorities that the functionaries of a certain religion are to be excluded on the ground that that religion 'is not to be treated'—regarded, assessed, and acted upon—in the same way as most or all other religions precisely *because* its functionaries teach, or incline its adherents to believe, say, (i) that any who speak adversely of its prophet or decline specific invitations to convert may appropriately be intimidated, assaulted, or killed, or (ii) that the British state and its institutions should be subordinated to this religion's laws authorizing coercion of religious acts, polygamy, and other violations of British constitutional law and what the British authorities regard as natural law and human rights. Such a general decision, even though restricted to the immigration or expulsion of such functionaries, would be a governmental decision precisely about the content of a religion (at least in the form in which it is ascertainably held by those functionaries and their followers). It would reasonably be taken by everyone to presuppose the judgment that the religion (as so held and professed) is false at least *pro tanto*. It would in both those ways skew public life against that religion, and would begin to put pressure on its adherents or potential adherents, pressure of a kind that Boyle's line of argument seems to treat as coercion by side effect if not by intent. Yet it might well, I suggest, be an entirely reasonable decision properly and perhaps urgently required by what the Act calls 'the public good' and what *Dignitatis Humanae* and the European Convention call public order, notably the rights of others and public peace.

For it is a very grave degradation of public order and the temporal common good that there has recently been imported into our polities religious intimidation, extending perceptibly into the operations of the media, the academy, the writing of essays such as this, and many other institutions of national life. The exclusion or expulsion of those non-nationals who give open or covert or tacit support to the religious doctrines and practices of intimidation is in principle compatible, I suggest, with the true right to religious liberty.

So I do not think that England's highest court must be said to have erred in *Shabina Begum's Case* in 2006 when, interpreting the European Convention on Human Rights, it dismissed the claim that a state school violated religious liberty when it banned its pupils from attending school clad not in any of the school's prescribed choice of western- or

Muslim-style alternative school uniforms but in a more austere garment of the kind demanded by more militant forms of Islam. The Law Lords used as the decisive premise in most of their judgments the factual and legal findings of the Constitutional Court of Turkey, adopted also by the European Court of Human Rights,[40] that (1) where Islam (as distinct from other religions) is socially influential, even the *option* of wearing to school or university a distinctively Muslim form of attire is regularly and predictably the occasion and opportunity for intimidatory pressures, and (2) state governments and laws and other public institutions are accordingly entitled to exclude and forbid that sartorial exercise of religious liberty, in order to preserve public order including the religious liberty of others (and even, sometimes—perhaps often—of the would-be wearer herself).[41] The Lords' decision implicitly accepts the premise that one religion may and should be treated—understood and dealt with—differently from others (just insofar as its beliefs and practices, perhaps even core beliefs and practices, adversely affect public order, public morality, or the rights of others).[42] And the Lords' decision should remind us that the right to be free from coercion in one's religious beliefs and acts is a right that is good not only against the state and its government and laws, but also against all other individuals and social groups. If a religion treats coercion of its own adherents, of potential adherents, or of anyone else as permissible, let alone mandatory, it is a standing incitement to violate the rights of others and public order, and those who adhere to it faithfully are rightly liable, in principle, to be kept, where morally possible, as far as is necessary from political communities that acknowledge the right to religious freedom.

VIII

Joseph Boyle might respond, however, that I have mistaken the focus and exaggerated the reach of his concern that unintended social pressure may impact as coercion impacts on the authenticity and worth of religious behaviour chosen under such pressure. His concern, he might respond, was not with governmental attempts to defend public order from real religious threats. Even though such legitimate defences of public order may

---

[40] Şahin v Turkey (2004) 41 EHRR 109; see R (Begum) v Headteacher & Governors of Denbigh High School [2006] UKHL 15 at paras 32 (Lord Bingham), 59–65 (Lord Hoffmann), 91 (Lord Scott), 98 (Baroness Hale). See 2009e and f.

[41] R (Begum) v Headteacher & Governors of Denbigh High School [2006] UKHL 15.

[42] Only if and to the extent that it is compatible with this rightful discrimination between religions should one accept the assertion of Habermas, Between Naturalism and Religion, ch. 6 text at n. 20, that: 'The principle of separation of church and state demands that the institutions of the state operate with strict impartiality vis-à-vis religious communities.'

presuppose the falsity of a part of the creed of a particular religion, they need not intend to teach or proclaim that falsity, or anything about the truth or otherwise of that religion or any other religion. Boyle's concern, he might say, was rather with constitutional or governmental declarations intended to identify the correct answer to the question whether there is a true religion. Such declarations cannot plausibly claim to be made for the sake of public order, and (Boyle might say) not only overreach the due limits of the jurisdiction of state government and law, but also create a social pressure prejudicial to the authenticity of religious inquiry and faith. So, he might conclude (and does already, I think, imply), there can be no positive duty of state government and law towards the true religion as true (but only the general negative duty owed to all religious communities respectful of the just limits of public order, the duty not to coerce their religious beliefs or practices[43]).

Inquiring whether a state's law and government can justly adopt a religion as true does not seem of urgent practical importance. But, urgency aside, it will clarify our political-theoretical reflections to keep that question before us, like a distant peak, and approach it via the foothills.

First, then, the main strands of my reflections entail that the state's government and law cannot justly teach that no religion is true. For such a teaching would be false, and false on a matter closely affecting a basic aspect of human well-being. And if a state does not teach that but its arrangements give rise, as a side effect, to widespread belief that the state's government has adopted them because it holds that no religion is true, the government has a significant duty to do what it reasonably can to rebut that inference. This it can do most readily by following, in ways that are for it to determine, the Council's injunction to 'recognize and favour religion'. It is hard to see how government might otherwise counteract the damaging side effect and false inference than by measures which carry a countervailing implicit message that some religion may well be essentially true and that if so the others, for all their errors, at least have the benefit of mediating the important truth that there is a transcendent source of being, intelligibility, and value.

The US Constitution's prohibition of 'establishment of religion', as that is interpreted, gives rise to problems hereabouts, which I need not dwell upon. British and other European constitutional arrangements which contain no such provision confront a different problem hereabouts. They can

---

[43] Here as earlier I leave aside the issue much debated in US constitutional doctrine whether religious acts are presumptively immune ('exempt') from the operation of legal commands or prohibitions of general applicability to religious and non-religious acts alike (i.e. 'neutral' as between religiously motivated acts and acts not so motivated).

favour religion to the extent needed in justice—namely, by implying if not asserting that some religion may well be true—and can do so by requiring or permitting the teaching and profession of religious faith in state-run or state-funded schools (with suitable opt-outs to preserve religious liberty). But the threat that some religious beliefs present to public order (essentially by authorizing or inciting intimidation), and present in the longer term to the constitutional order which enforces the right to religious liberty, may be such that it is necessary to explicitly withhold from those beliefs the advantages that parity with other religions, combined with weight of numbers, would otherwise require. Such discrimination, though justified, runs so strongly against widespread assumptions about 'equal protection of the laws' that governments will be sorely tempted to withdraw their favour from all religions, rather than make 'invidious comparisons and choices'. Yielding to the temptation would create, even if only as a side effect, the very bad consequence of seeming to express the belief that no religion is true. To incur that consequence deliberately is presumptively unjust. So the discrimination should presumptively be made, with all due care for accuracy and procedural fairness.

Secondly, however we should answer the peak question (about what if anything may be stipulated constitutionally and legally about the true religion), there is certainly an obligation not to hold out as true any religion that is not essentially the true one.

Thirdly, there is a duty not to make subscription to a particular religion, or to one of the many religions, a prerequisite for public offices or benefits. For, subject perhaps to some minor exceptions, such an affirmative 'religious test' does have coercive effects of the kind that Joseph Boyle points to as tending to negative authenticity, and does exceed the state's proper bounds. Only when the upholding of public order requires it can it be right to accept those bad side effects of imposing a negative test such that membership of a religious group threatening to public order becomes a *dis*qualification for public office.

Fourthly, there is a duty not to seek to *direct* the true religion by claiming a power to appoint its functionaries (say, bishops) or to give or withhold ratification of its doctrinal pronouncements or ecclesiastical arrangements.

Fifthly, however we should answer the peak question, it must be accepted that individual voters and legislators can rightly and should take into account the firm moral teachings of a religion if it is the true religion, so far as its teachings are relevant to issues of law and government. This duty extends only so far as the teachings do not depend upon premises which are essentially questions of present fact and prediction of consequences, for on such questions religious authorities cannot reasonably be supposed to have any special competence, or authority to teach with any decisive effect. In saying that voters and other bearers of public authority have this liberty and responsibility, I assume that the true religion itself holds out its moral teaching as a matter of public reason, that is, as accessible and acceptable by a purely philosophical inquiry and only *clarified* and/or made *more* certain by divine revelation or the theological-doctrinal appropriation of that revelation. And I assume that this holding out is no mere lip service or idle boast, but goes along with real willingness to shoulder the argumentative burden of making its moral and political teaching philosophically plausible, and maintaining the educational and scholarly resources for doing so.

Sixthly, then, I think we can give at least this response to the peak question: with the third duty firmly acknowledged as excluding *positive* religious tests for voting or other public office, and with the negative duties to abstain from coercion all firmly in place, it does not seem to be contrary either to what experience shows are the exigencies of authenticity in religious inquiry, or to what seem likely to be the conclusions of revelation as well as philosophy about limits to the state's coercive jurisdiction and temporal authority, to hold that in establishing their constitutional arrangements a people might without injustice or political impropriety record their solemn belief about the identity and name of the true religious faith and community.

Even when politically possible, making such a declaration might in many circumstances have such bad side effects that doing so would be unfair or otherwise unreasonable. And it would always be a quite unfitting declaration to make if the adherents of the religion so identified did not accept and act on the responsibility which I mentioned earlier, of showing how their faith embraces and is continuous with public philosophical, historical, and moral reason.

5

POLITICAL NEUTRALITY AND RELIGIOUS ARGUMENTS[*]

One of the many attractive aspects of this lucid and searching essay is the proposal that political theory—'answers to normative political questions'—must be consistent with the practical possibility of asking questions, pursuing inquiries, and reaching answers in a manner which complies with the 'logical and moral rules of [the] enterprise' of seeking reasoned agreement about political institutions. I have long thought that a most fundamental constraint on (i.e. rational requirement for) political theory (including the political-theoretical analogue of 'meta-ethics') is that its content must propose tenets, norms, and institutions consistent with the proposition that the raising of questions about any and all matters of serious concern, the orderly rational pursuit of critically satisfactory answers to them, and the adaptation of personal and social conduct so as to cohere with such answers, is a great and not merely instrumental human good which everyone who could engage in it should, so far as practicable, be entitled and materially, intellectually, morally, and culturally helped and encouraged to undertake. Both the proposition and the constraint it imposes on political theory are, I think, incompatible not only with radical scepticism about practical truth (i.e. about the objectivity or cognitive status of practical propositions) but also with voluntarist (e.g. imperativist or radically contractarian) theories of authority, political obligation, and law. But that of course is a long story, and not the one that Janos Kis is pursuing (at least, not in this essay).

In the essay, the primacy of the logic and morality of questioning is more closely allied to the essay's primary thesis: state policy and action must be based only on arguments and conceptions which are 'accessible to

[*] Unpublished comments on a then unpublished essay by Janos Kis, 'Political Neutrality: A Defence', for a conference in Oxford in July 1993. Quotations where not attributed are from the typescript of Kis's essay; the page references have been removed.

every normal person'—in respect of which 'everyone (in theory) has access to the relevant evidence'. This demand that laws and other deployments of coercive power be publicly justifiable seems to me thoroughly sound. The old-fashioned name for theories which sought self-consciously to live up to this demand is 'natural law theory'—the intended implication of the label being that the only constraints rationally acceptable to human persons are requirements intelligibly involved in, or identifiable by, the exercise of our native capacity to raise, consider, and respond intelligently to questions, that is, our reason.[1] I don't much recommend the label 'natural law', which is open to too many misunderstandings. Still less, however, would I recommend the comparable (and not incompatible) framework term regrettably adopted by Kis (and others), 'liberal'. Political theories should never, I suggest, be commended or opposed as being 'liberal', but only as reasonable, sound, true, appropriate, decent, just, and fair.[2]

The essay's primary thesis, about public justification or 'accessibility' is proposed by Kis as making possible his final (for this essay) resolution of the puzzle about how political institutions can be justified 'in a neutral way'. How can the demand that justification be neutral cohere with the fact that conceptions of the good, and thus of the right, and thus of the politically justifiable, vary greatly in a 'pluralistic society'? Must not the demand for neutrality fall into 'uncoherence', that is, be self-referentially inconsistent or self-destructing? Or, if we say that neutrality itself is demanded on the basis of the more fundamental demand of equality—that every person be treated with equal respect—how can government or the state be said to be respecting persons whose political views reject or ignore the demand for neutrality and for equality of respect? The answer: government respects such persons if (and only if) (i) it bases its adoption of neutralist policies and institutions on (ii) publicly accessible and only on publicly accessible arguments.

The thesis embodied in this answer obviously has two components of interest, which I have signalled as (i) and (ii). The first rests on the premise

---

[1] See *Republic* IV 444d; IX 585–6 on acting according to reason and *thus* according to nature. More explicitly, *ST* I–II q.71 a.2c:

> The good of the human being is being in accord with reason, and human evil is being outside the order of reasonableness.... So human virtue...is in accordance with human nature *just* in so far as it is in accordance with reason, and vice is contrary to human nature just in so far as it is contrary to the order of reasonableness.

[2] Little or nothing is to be gained from inquiring whether a theory is or is not 'genuinely' liberal (or socialist or conservative); such inquiries enmesh the would-be theorist in the shifting contingencies of political movements or programmes which, taken in their sequence since the term 'liberal' emerged in political use in the 1830s, have little or virtually nothing significant in common and, as movements, no principle for identifying a central case or focal sense. The only sensible way to deal with philosophical claims framed in terms of liberalism, liberal political institutions, etc. is to treat them as rhetorical code for 'sound', 'true', 'warranted', 'just', or the like; one translates accordingly and carries on with the consideration of the arguments on their merits.

that policies which are not neutral in this or some other plausible sense deny people equal respect. This premise has of course been argued for by Dworkin and modified if not abandoned by him under the pressure of counter-arguments.[3] Kis does not really seek here to defend it, or to attend to the counter-arguments. So I shall say only a little about it; without a theory, based on other premises, of the limits of the functions of the political community, it is quite implausible even in relation to straightforwardly paternalist, and even wrong-headedly paternalist, prohibitions. For one way in which people show their genuine respect for associates (even adult) who are damaging themselves by their foolish choices is by preventing them from executing those choices.[4] In any event, the thesis depends on its second component: institutions and policies based only on publicly accessible arguments can usefully be called 'neutral' and (more interestingly than that terminological point) will not include any ranking of different 'conceptions of the good life'.

Why should we accept that the arguments for ranking one conception of the good life over another are not publicly accessible? So far as I can see, Kis does not answer that vital question. Indeed, the relevance of the question seems to be what he has in mind in his last paragraph, when he faces the objection that perhaps the requirement of public accessibility will exclude 'nothing, short of religious revelation or mystic experience'. His reply refers us beyond the bounds of this essay; here he just suggests that this objection is not

compelling. I would argue, for example, that ultimate ethical values belong to the private domain while principles of politics [belong] to the public one.

Out of bounds or not, I want to dwell on this last suggestion, for which the whole essay has, in a sense, prepared us. The suggestion is remarkable, first, in assuming that 'politics' can reasonably be conceived of as a distinct 'domain'. This seems to me a manifestation of the 'statist' character of much 'liberal' thought. This statism we should have been prepared for, in particular, by the striking statement that 'the political community...encompasses the complete life of the individual' whereas, by apparent contrast, merely 'cultural communities normally do not claim authority over the entire life of their members'. This seems to me to get things seriously wrong. The political community is but one of several communities in which each individual will, in a decent life, participate: for example friendships, family, religious community, state, and mankind. Only an arbitrarily statist thought, unconsciously formed by the less

---

[3] See e.g. Raz, *The Morality of Freedom*, 151; *NLNR* 221–3; essay III.2 at 51–3 (1987c at 437–8).
[4] See *NLNR* 222; Hart, *Essays in Jurisprudence and Philosophy*, 214.

defensible parts of Platonic-Aristotelian political thought,[5] and by the spurious absolutisms of early-modern western state theory and subsequent practice, could peacefully accept that 'politics' (that is, the state/political community) is a 'domain' which can plausibly be supposed to have principles independent of, and with a radically different epistemological or rational status from, the principles regulating one's other communities (some of which, unlike the political, are directly and immediately instantiations of a basic human good and so, unlike the state, are not merely instrumental). Each of one's communities must have its proper standards for decent and fair relationships and dealings within it. In that sense, each must have its 'political' principles. But if these too, like the principles of state politics, can be in the domain of the publicly accessible, what are the principles left to the domain of the merely private and inaccessible?

This point can be made, perhaps more clearly, by noting a second remarkable feature of the notion that principles of politics might be public but 'ultimate ethical values' private. Every political actor/agent is a human person or at least, in the case of the social acts of groups (states, corporations, teams . . .), has no existence apart from the personal acts of the people who are the group's leaders and/or other members. Each person's reasons for choosing to perform some political act must either be reasons which for that person are ultimate/basic (in need of no further, rationally motivating and thus justifying reason) or must be based on some more ultimate/basic reasons; and all these reasons must be consistent with the acting person's other reasons or principles of action. One's public act is at the same time one's private act—it is part of one's one and only real life. That one is to undertake such-and-such a 'political' act must be not merely logically consistent with one's conception of 'the good life'; it must actually be rationally motivated by that conception (which after all can be nothing other than one's conception of what are good reasons for one's acting). One's 'public' reasons for acting must also be one's 'private' reasons (though it does not follow that all one's reasons for action need be 'made public', that is, published). Political actions often have the gravest consequences both for the actor and for others. So the public reasons are not good (adequate) reasons unless they justify the act, so to speak, all the way down—justify the actor in doing it. The picture summoned up in the essay's penultimate sentence, of political acts all being done for publicly inaccessible reasons, is a picture of a political order which refuses to offer its participants any good (adequate) reason for participating in it or for tolerating the burdens of citizenship. (So it must keep seducing their compliance with bread and

---

[5] See *NLNR* 148–50, 160.

circuses, or distracting them with chatter, until the barbarians break down the gates or radical reformers appear and restore the integrity of political life.)

(And here the spectre of self-referential inconsistency or 'uncoherence' reappears with a vengeance. For a state which aspires to the neutrality commended by Kis, and so acts in reliance upon his theory that ultimate reasons for action are non-public, precisely matches his definitive description of the non-neutral state as one which 'base[s] its claims on ... [say, Kis's] philosophical interpretations of reality which some of its citizens [e.g., the one writing this comment] cannot subscribe to without first abandoning their own world view as mistaken'.)

But of course, the whole essay has prepared us for this objection, which does no more than reprise some objections of Dworkin and Raz as reported by Kis. Indeed, the central theme of the whole essay is the neo-Rawlsian (weak-)independence thesis:

a political conception can be called weakly independent if there is a possibility to justify it without relying on principles and beliefs included in a wider moral, philosophical, or religious doctrine.... [P]olitical theory's being embedded in ... a comprehensive doctrine ... is not necessary for the defence of political theory.

My question, however, is: Does the essay offer us any reason to believe in this 'possibility'? So far as I can see, it does not. It gives us no reason to resist the conclusion that 'independent' political theories are theories which are without foundations, and whose proponents (if they behaved consistently with their own independence thesis) would simply be abdicating from their intellectual responsibilities as theorists and assuming the philosophically less demanding role formerly occupied by court theologians and the like.

Kis's first reason for accepting this independence or ungroundedness is: 'The idea of a public political culture implies the possibility of an independent justification of political theory.' But, given Kis's definition of weak independence, 'independent justification' is merely an oxymoron: independent 'justifications' of political action are claims that the action needs precisely no public justification which could be adequate to the demands of a critical conscience. I think Kis fails to notice this because he keeps moving back and forth between two different things:

(A) justifying a political 'conception', 'principle', 'statement', 'institution', or 'tenet';

(B) justifying a whole 'political theory'.

Now, to be sure, it is possible to offer some justification for particular political conceptions, principles, statements, institutions, or tenets, taken so to speak one by one, by merely displaying their logical consistency with other political conceptions, statements, etc. in the same 'public domain' of the commonly accepted. (Perhaps this is what Raz had in mind in talking of the 'shallow foundations' of political theory à la Rawls; otherwise Raz's phrase is too generous by half.) But none of this has much claim to amount to 'theory', or to a justification which could satisfy the critical conscience of serious acting persons.

Kis's second reason for accepting that political theory can claim 'independent justification' (or independence from intellectually serious justifying grounds) is set out in his reply to Raz and Dworkin:

> Weak independence is not incompatible with addressing each individual in both of two ways: first on the basis of the public political culture…, and also on the basis of his own wider convictions…, showing that the principles which he has a purely political reason to accept are entailed by or at least in harmony with his wider moral (and philosophical or religious) conception.… [I]f political theory can be given, at the same time, an independent justification, then it remains neutral between the competing moral conceptions…

If the last sentence is meant to add to the rest of the passage, then it seems to me simply to beg the question raised by Raz and Dworkin. As for the main part of the passage, one must ask: Who is supposed to do this 'addressing'? Who or what is meant to be 'showing' the relation of entailment or at least harmony between principles which are public and principles which by hypothesis are private? In the context, it seems to be 'political theory' that is supposed to be doing this. But since the 'public domain' is the domain of reasons (convictions, beliefs, statements) which are 'publicly accessible', I cannot see how 'political theory' can reach into a domain which by hypothesis is not publicly accessible. And what happens when (as Kis himself envisages) political theory discovers that something accepted in the public domain is incompatible with something supposed to be in the private domain? After all, 'political theory' has no life or activity of its own; it is just the thinking of inquiring people. So, when you or I, pursuing our questions, discover that some political tenet in the public domain is inconsistent with a principle which is not commonly shared but seems to us rationally grounded, warranted, sound, true, which should we take to prevail? The answer must be: reason should prevail. And notice: what we have discovered in such a case is precisely that something supposed to be in the private domain actually should be in the public domain (*qua* domain of commonly accepted opinions) and already is in the public domain (*qua* domain of principles accessible to people of normal intelligence—for who is so elitist as to maintain that people of normal intelligence cannot, even 'in theory', understand a moral or other practical principle which is sound, rationally grounded, true?).

Perhaps we should be more concrete, and at the same time take up again the issue with which we began. What is it for a statement or tenet to be publicly inaccessible (including under 'inaccessible' also instances of 'limited accessibility', that is, of accessibility too limited to be a proper basis for state action)? Kis gives only two examples.

The first is presented, not explicitly as a case of such inaccessibility, but as a 'tenet[] on which there is no social consensus'. I think this is not a mere slip; for the burden of the central sections of the essay can, I think, be reduced to this: where a political tenet is (to speak loosely) 'supported' by the sociological conditions of modernity, and so enjoys a wide public consensus, it does not need to be supported (in the sense of 'support' that is relevant to critical inquiry and judgment) by publicly accessible argument; the burden of providing publicly accessible arguments lies on those who challenge the tenets on which there is 'social consensus'—whatever that may be. This asymmetry of argumentative burdens ('reallocat[ion of] the burden of evidence') is expounded by Kis in relation particularly to the egalitarian presumption, and that, as we shall see, has its relevance to the first example of inaccessible arguments.

The first inaccessible argument, then, is this: '[i] The Catholic Church teaches that the moment of conception is also the moment of ensoulment; [ii] the embryo is, thus, a human being from the moment of conception, [iii] with the same right to life as any other human being...' (is, one might say, entitled to the benefit of the egalitarian presumption). Now I am disinclined to spend too much time examining whether proposition [i] and the associated implied proposition that what the Catholic Church teaches is worthy of belief is indeed inaccessible; for reasons suggested later, I don't think it is, but for the sake of discussion I grant that it is. I do so happily because in fact no one ever advances this proposition as a premise, for the good reason that it is well known to be false. The Catholic Church does not teach that the moment of conception is also the moment of ensoulment. The only teaching of the Church, clearly restated by its highest teachers in 1974 and 1987, is that the Church's teaching on abortion 'leaves aside the question of the moment of ensoulment'.[6] So if we want a realistic candidate for inaccessibility, we must omit the fictitious first part and consider the

---

[6] Declaration of the CDF, *Quaestio de Abortu* (1974), n. 19. The CDF Instruction on Respect for Human Life in Its Origins... *Donum Vitae* (1987) remarks that the Church 'has not expressly committed itself to an affirmation of a philosophical nature' (i.e. about ensoulment). It adds:

Certainly no experimental datum can be in itself sufficient to bring us the recognition of a spiritual soul; nevertheless, the conclusions of science regarding the human embryo provide a valuable indication for discerning *by the use of reason* a personal presence at the moment of this first appearance of a human life: *how could a human individual not be a human person?* (Part I sec. 1, emphasis added.)

actual argument used in political debate: '[ii] the embryo is a human being from the moment of conception, [iii] with the same right to life as any other human being…'. That pair of claims obviously needs defence, and there is a substantial body of public argumentation which offers to supply it.[7] Included in that body of argumentation are refutations of every argument advanced in the public domain by proponents of the ruling consensus that human beings who are or normally would be inside their mother's body are not entitled to the egalitarian presumption and can be attacked with the precise intention of destroying them if their mother regards that destruction as in her interests. I have no doubt, and am willing to argue in any temperate public domain, that the arguments in favour of giving the benefit of the egalitarian presumption to people still inside their mother's body not only are at least as publicly accessible as, but also are by all and only rational criteria clearly superior to, the arguments for the ruling anti-egalitarian (or limited egalitarian) tenet.

So the first example fails to illuminate the problem of accessibility. (And at the same time it happens to cast a rather eerie light over Kis's central assumption that the historical developments which have yielded the 'modernity' of his perhaps slightly deterministic and Euro-centric historical sociology have also landed us in a position where the supporters of the ruling consensus, who enjoy the new freedom made possible by wielding virtually unfettered power over a class of relatively vulnerable people, can safely and indeed reasonably, be excused from bearing the burden of evidence which they wish to impose on their critics.)

The second example of the inaccessible is a statement whose accessibility ('acceptability' for purposes of public and political argumentation and action) is defended by Joseph Raz,[8] and which I give in the following slightly adjusted form (more realistic than the one given by Raz and Kis): 'Jesus rose from the dead; the grounds for thinking so include a report that the guards[9] posted outside his tomb saw him come out of it.' Against the accessibility of this, Kis argues (in effect) that the guards' seeing Jesus come out of the tomb (if they did) does not answer the question whether there was a Resurrection in the theologically loaded sense proposed by the Gospels and the Catholic Church down to today. And that is quite correct. But the claim actually made by the Gospels (and so by the Church which

---

[7] See e.g. Grisez, 'When Do People Begin?'

[8] Raz, 'Facing Diversity' at 40 (now *Ethics in the Public Domain* at 90–1).

[9] Raz and Kis speak of a centurion, but seem to have transposed this character from the crucifixion on Friday to the garden on Sunday: cf. Matthew 27: 54, 66; 28: 11. Actually the Gospels do not clearly affirm that Jesus was seen coming out the tomb by the guards. They rely on other eyewitnesses.

proposes that the Gospels give a historically faithful account of what Jesus really did and said before, during, and after his resurrection[10]) is that when you take that evidence along with all the other publicly accessible evidence about what he said and did, and take that along with the publicly accessible evidence of revelation to the prophets of Israel, and take that along with the publicly accessible arguments for believing that there is a creator who might communicate with intelligent creatures, then (and only then) you have a publicly accessible reason for thinking that there was a resurrection in the sense that goes along with belief in life after death, immortality, divinity of Jesus, and so forth. Kis's position that only those who already believe in the Resurrection can rationally treat eyewitness accounts of the event as evidence for its occurrence seems to me simply confused; it is held today by many Protestant and some Catholic theologians, but not by the Church's authoritative teachers,[11] and overlooks the way in which an accumulation of various veridical grounds[12] can give rational grounds for accepting and interpreting an event. Even someone who in the end, or item by item, rejects the evidence in question should agree with Raz that many who judge the foundational Jewish or Christian beliefs rationally acceptable 'rely on nothing but acceptable reasons . . . and ordinary methods of reasoning . . .'.[13]

So it looks as if Kis's worst fears are going to be realized; 'nothing short of religious revelation or mystic experience will fall . . . in[to] the class of private beliefs'—but worse, the failure of Kis's argument about what Catholic theologians have long called 'public revelation' suggests that it is only what they call private revelation that, along with mystic experience in the narrower sense, is going to fall into that class.

To conclude. The perfectionists among us should unhesitatingly[14] endorse the requirement that political action be founded only on publicly

    [10]   Second Vatican Council, Constitution on Divine Revelation, *Dei Verbum* (1965), sec. 19.
    [11]   Nor will it be, for it would involve the Church in repudiating its own Gospels, which plainly convey that the witnesses to the Resurrection came to believe it *notwithstanding* their prior doubts about the credibility of predictions and reports of its occurrence. I became and remain a Christian in large measure because Catholic Christianity plausibly claims to be based *entirely* on publicly accessible reasons: everything foundational is open to view and nothing foundational depends on 'experiences' or 'conversion' or faith. Another factor making Christianity credible to me was and is that the Church's position on matters like abortion is supportable by arguments more genuinely accessible (simply, better) than the transparent rationalizations advanced by the 'liberal' position then emergent and now 'consensus'.
    [12]   [See now the Note to essay 12, with citations to works of N.T. Wright.]
    [13]   Raz, 'Facing Diversity' at 40 (now in his *Ethics in the Public Domain* at 91).
    [14]   Well, almost. But some 'liberals', e.g. Macedo, *Liberal Virtues*, 43, 46, 63, 212, maintain that justification must be accessible to 'people as we know them', must involve no difficult or complex argument, and must exclude any principle or tenet which would not be accepted by most people as they are [perhaps corrupt, biased, blinkered, ill-educated]. In other words he drops Kis's vital qualifying phrase 'in theory', and slides 'accessible' towards 'likely to be accepted here and now'. The

accessible arguments as Kis defines but not as he illustrates or exemplifies them. Equally we can endorse the proposition that 'government should not enforce mores against the ethical convictions of the individual', on the understanding that mores are a matter of moral beliefs held unquestioningly, uncritically, and without publicly accessible reasons. Mores, then, are one thing and ethical convictions are quite another. As I have suggested, there seem to be no grounds in the essay for denying that those whose decisions count as state action can proceed on the basis of ethical convictions held for publicly accessible reasons, enforcing those judgments against those who hold convictions which are different but (so far as the state can judge, using publicly accessible argumentation) rationally inferior or false. As Kis says, political theory need not 'seek a compromise with false claims', for example about the proper ambit of concern and respect.

But: the truth that the state, like every other human person and group, can rightly and should proceed on 'perfectionist' principles does not at all entail the over-simple claim of Plato, Aristotle, and Aquinas[15] that it is the state's proper function to lead people to virtue by coercively prohibiting indulgence, even adult indulgence, in vice. Still, this non-entailment can be shown only by an argument like the one which I sketched above: the state political community is in some important respects a less important and more merely instrumental and subsidiary community than friendships, families, or serious religious communities. And that, as I said before, is obviously another story, not at all Kis's. I add just this Parthian shot: if one can show, from premises such as those I hinted at, that the state goes outside its proper functions when it enacts paternalist prohibitions of adult private vice, then one has the beginnings of a case for saying that the adults in question are being treated without proper respect. What one can't reasonably do is find a premise for defining the state's proper function in the thought that prohibitions motivated by concern for adults' well-being ('perfection') are disrespectful, insulting, or inegalitarian.

justification he offers for this slide is that in political theory one must not be 'elitist'. But that is just an abdication of reason in favour of *mores* and prejudice.

[15] [Not Aquinas: see now *Aquinas* 222–54.]

6

CATHOLIC POSITIONS IN
LIBERAL DEBATES*

I

The term 'liberal' has no core of meaning sufficiently stable and clear for use in a general political philosophy or theory. We could accept that the first liberal ('the first Whig') was Thomas Aquinas, while also accepting the core of right judgment in Pius IX's Syllabus of Errors when it rejects the claim that the Church must simply 'reconcile itself to modern liberalism'. That claim was rightly rejected because modern liberalism, then (in 1864) as now, included opinions such as John Rawls defends— that no one should ever act in public life (for example as a voter) on the basis of the thought that such-and-such an opinion is *true*.[1] Aquinas was a liberal because, although he rightly defended institutions and practices important in public life on the basis that they are required or authorized by certain moral and metaphysical *truths*, he at the same time insisted that the proper functions of the state's laws and rulers do not include making people morally all-round good by compulsorily requiring them to abstain from immorality. The role of state government and law, according to Aquinas, is to uphold peace and justice; the requirements imposed, supervised, and enforced by state government and law concern only those sorts of choice and action which are external and affect other people.[2]

But though we can and should do our general critical political reflection without attempting to employ the term 'liberalism' as a framework category like 'just', we can accept the phrase 'western liberal societies', as used in my essay's title, and use it simply to pick out a set of states,

---

* 1999d ('The Catholic Church and Public Policy Debates in Western Liberal Societies: The Basis and Limits of Intellectual Engagement'), for a conference organized by the Linacre Centre for Healthcare Ethics on 'Issues for a Catholic Bio-ethic'.

[1] Rawls, *Political Liberalism*, 61, 127, etc. Truth, he argues, should be replaced, as the criterion of right political action, by an idea of the 'reasonable' which entails that many conceptions of public policy are 'reasonable' although quite untrue.

[2] See *Aquinas* 222–54.

political communities, politically organized nations, which inter alia allow the Catholic Church and its members the liberty of participating in public deliberation and choice, as one among many groups and individuals similarly participating in public decision-making. So my question, my title, comes to this: On what basis should we as Catholics participate in those public deliberations, and abide by or reject their outcomes (social choices such as legislation, adjudication, and administrative practice)?

My reflections in response to this question have three main parts. The first concerns the faith which, by God's grace and our decision, can shape and guide all our choices, including choices of the kind we are reflecting upon now (choices to participate in public debate, accept or reject its outcome, and so forth). The second concerns cooperation, and the question when it is wrong and when it can be right to choose to do what will assist others in their wrongdoing. The third concerns the role of the Church acting (for example speaking) precisely as Church, that is through its pastors.

II

A first condition for participation as a Catholic in public policy deliberations and debates is that one be quite clear about the relations between faith and reason. There are many propositions of our faith which are not accessible to natural reason, that is, to someone who is unaware of the particular set of historical realities which were the revelation culminating in the life and teaching of Christ. These propositions—e.g. that there are three persons in the one and only God—are proposed by the Church for our and everyone's acceptance on the basis of the Church's confidence that they are part of the revealed word of God; and that is the only basis on which we can accept them and propose them to others. But the Church also proposes for us to accept a good number of propositions—e.g. that God exists, that each human being is a body animated and unified by an intellectual soul, or that it is always wrong to choose to kill an innocent human being—which are indeed accessible to natural reason (reason unaided by revelation). Indeed, that there are such propositions (including those three) is itself a proposition of faith. And of natural reason.

If we are clear about these different types of relationship between the faith and natural reason, we can avoid mistakes common outside and inside the Church. Outside the Church, it is widely assumed and asserted that any proposition which the Catholic Church in fact proposes for acceptance is, by virtue of that fact, a 'religious' (not a philosophical, scientific, or rationally grounded and compelling proposition), and is a proposition which Catholics hold only as a matter of faith and therefore cannot be authentically willing to defend as a matter of natural reason. Inside the Church, there are a good many moral theologians who hold or presuppose the positions defended twenty years ago in Gerard Hughes SJ's little book *Authority in Morals: An Essay in Christian Ethics* (1978), in particular that revelation and its custodian the magisterium of the Catholic Church can never decisively settle an ethical question because to attribute to them that sort of authoritativeness would be to adopt an irrational fideism— irrational because one cannot reasonably decide to accept revelation in general, or reasonably interpret the sources of revelation in particular, without presupposing moral criteria which revelation and its sources, to be creditworthy and properly understood, must satisfy, criteria which must therefore be accessible to us independently of revelation.[3] (The independent criteria these theologians usually have in mind are the norms they rationalize by whichever version of consequentialism or proportionalism they take from the surrounding philosophical or popular culture.)

But the Catholic faith is coherent when it teaches both (i) that there are moral truths accessible prior to revelation, including truths which make it obligatory for us to search for the truth about God and to adhere to it when we judge that we have discovered it, and (ii) that these truths are clarified and decisively confirmed by the revelation which also makes accessible some moral truths that are not otherwise knowable with clarity and firm certitude (e.g. truths about mercy, or the impossibility of dissolving a valid and consummated marriage between Christians). It is quite fallacious to argue, like Frs Fuchs, Hughes, and Sullivan, that because revelation alone, without moral presuppositions, cannot settle all questions, therefore revelation, even when rationally accepted on morally compelling grounds, cannot settle any.[4]

Distinctions of this kind, clarified long ago by St Thomas but already proposed in the tradition by St Paul and by Irenaeus, and reposed by Vatican I and Vatican II, enable and entitle us as Catholics to participate in public policy deliberations on many matters without appealing to revelation or faith as the grounds for accepting and acting upon truths which are in fact part of revelation and the propositional content of the faith. These truths, for example about retributive justice, or killing, or enslavement, can be defended on the basis of arguments which are rationally accessible to people who, by ignorance or mistake, do not accept the revelation proposed by the Catholic Church. These arguments are rather confusingly called in the tradition principles of 'natural law' or 'natural reason', and

---

[3] See *MA* 92–3.
[4] See 1980b; essay 19, sec. II; and *MA* 92–3. [And on Hughes see now the endnotes to essay 16.]

could be called 'public reasons', in a sense of that term more reasonable and durable than John Rawls's use of the phrase 'public reason' to signify the propositions, true or false, in a truth-bracketing 'overlapping public consensus', or Stephen Macedo's related use to signify those truths which are accessible without any complex argument.

The fact that we could apply the new and fashionable phrase 'public reason' to the natural moral law and the natural or human rights defended by (amongst others) Catholics, taken with the fact that *those* public reasons are accessible to all independently of divine revelation, should not lead us to conclude that revelation itself is not a public reason. On the contrary, what in the Catholic tradition and the Second Vatican Council (LG 25) is called 'public revelation' is truly accessible to all, just as Peter proclaimed in the middle of Jerusalem on the day of Pentecost, reminding his listeners that 'Jesus of Nazareth was a man duly accredited [*apodedeigmenon*] to you from God; such were the miracles and wonders and signs which God did through him in your midst, as you yourselves know' (Acts 2: 22), and as Paul proclaimed 'in full view of the Areopagus' in Athens, informing his listeners that 'the man whom God has appointed [to pronounce just judgment on the whole world] he has accredited [*pistin paraschōn*] to all, by raising him up from the dead' (Acts 17: 31; cf. 2: 32). Thousands of Peter's hearers were persuaded, rather few if any of Paul's in Athens. What is accessible as creditworthy to all may in fact be accessed and accepted by most, many, some, or few; the de facto variation is explained in part by what Elizabeth Anscombe once called[5] the endless twistiness of the human mind. But the access*ibility* to reason, and the credit-*worth*iness, of evidence and argument and other premises for reasonable judgment are all independent of the facts about actual acceptance.

We ought to reject the reduction of Catholic faith to a private sentiment which happens to be shared with others. We ought to think of the truths of the faith as good and proper grounds for action, including one's activity as a voting citizen or a public official, even though they are grounds which many members of the political community do not accept and would denounce as improper. This does not amount to 'imposing Catholicism'; one of the truths of the faith is that everyone, even those who unreasonably reject Catholicism in favour of some false religion or some false denial of every truth about God, is entitled not to be coerced in relation to such beliefs so long as the actions which result from those beliefs respect (1) the rights of others (effectively safeguarded and peacefully harmonized),

---

[5] Anscombe, 'War and Murder' at 60.

(2) the decent public peace which is an ordered living together in true justice, and (3) public morality duly preserved.[6]

Here it is helpful also to recall (as I have already) St Thomas's rejection, in principle, of paternalistic laws restricting the truly private activities of adults.[7] He himself did not consistently adhere to this rejection, so far as it bore on the practice of employing state power to punish departure from the Catholic faith. For his defence of the practice relied on the premise that heresy is not merely infectious and corrosive of the true faith of naïve or wavering people,[8] and therefore contrary to the common good—as other unbelief (e.g. of pagans) can be—but is also, unlike those other forms of unbelief, a *culpable* infidelity consisting of, or closely analogous to, a breach of promise.[9] This analogy was always unsound: the faith was usually adopted by proxy in infant baptism, and even when this subscription was made by explicit act on conversion at or above the age of reason, it was not accurately regarded as having the character of a commitment made to other people. Rather, as Aquinas himself says elsewhere, the human good at stake in matters of faith, though it is a good which benefits not just one person but many, is not a good which consists in community but rather one which 'pertains to each person alone as an individual {ad unum aliquem pertinet secundum seipsum}' (*ScG* III, c.80 n.15 [2560]). And the 'medicinal' (that is, retributive, deterrent, and eliminative) punishment of heresy was too tenuously distinguishable from compulsion of belief, a compulsion which Aquinas (like the Church) always vigorously rejected. Aquinas tried to insist on the distinction (*Sent.* IV d.13 q.2 a.3 ad 5), but slipped into saying—inconsistently also with his own account of the nature of the assent of faith (e.g. *ST* II–II q.1 a.2c; q.10 a.8c)—that the punishment of heretics was justifiable as a matter of 'compelling them [back] to faith', 'physically compelling them to carry out what they promised and to hold fast to what they once accepted' (*ibid.*).

The requirement that faith be voluntary and free from coercive pressures is an implication of the basic good of religion as a personal search for, appropriation of, and adherence in practice to the truth about God as one can grasp it. Taken with the truth that faith as act and disposition of acceptance pertains as such to the individual person and does not as such affect civil justice and peace, the requirement that that act be free yields the conclusion which, as I have already mentioned, was stated by Vatican II: provided public peace, public morality, and the harmonised rights of others are respected, all persons have a right, as against political authorities, to

---

[6] DH secs 2 and 7.   [7] See *Aquinas* ch. VII; essay 9.   [8] *ST* II–II q.10 a.7c and a.10c.
[9] *Ibid.*, a.8c.

freedom from coercion in respect of all their expressions of religious belief. This right is not that mere tolerance of erroneous religious practices which Aquinas argued for (*ST* II–II q.10 a.11c).

We should not be nostalgic for, and do not need to defend, the paternalism defended by Plato and Aristotle, or the religious intolerance of the mediaeval and post-mediaeval Catholic (not to mention Protestant) states. Nor should we accept other package deals, in which Catholicism might be yoked to a restorationist politics of conservatism or a liberationist politics of socialism or state capitalism, or whatever. So far as anyone can see, the Catholic Church is still near the beginning of its long journey to the end of the ages; its Augustinian, mediaeval, and subsequent experiments with harnessing state power were no more than a passing phase in which faith and benevolence were harnessed together without sufficient attention to differentiations which the faith itself suggests and, when developed, ratifies. If we make and insist upon those differentiations, we can peacefully and without even implicit threat affirm, in our own reflections and when and as appropriate in public, that the centre of human history is the life and teachings of Jesus Christ, and that the truths which his Church conveys, even in periods when it is humanly speaking as decayed, confused, and weak as it at present is, are the true *centre* of the culture which can and should direct political deliberation in western liberal as much as any other kind of political society. The disarray within the Roman Catholic Church is surely a substantial cause (as well as a consequence) of the disarray within these societies, even those societies which for many centuries have had no reason to think (or have made it their business not to think) of Catholics as other than virtual strangers.

If we look for the roots of the present disarray and demoralization within the Church, we find I suggest two outstanding candidates: the muffling of the public, historical character of revelation by biblical scholars who have uncritically accepted some unsound tenets and presuppositions of Enlightenment philosophy; and the practical elimination of transcendent hope, the hope of heaven. I have said a little elsewhere about the first;[10] about the second, let me add a word to what Germain Grisez has just said to us.[11]

The doctrine of hell was as emotionally repugnant to, say, St Thomas More as it is to us.[12] But it is so clearly part of what has been revealed in the

---

[10] Essay 9.   [11] Grisez, 'Healthcare as Part of a Christian's Vocation'.

[12] See More, *Dialogue of Comfort against Tribulation*, 249. Cf. More's last written prayers: 'Give me thy grace, good Lord…/ To walk the narrow way that leadeth to life;/ To bear the cross with Christ;/ To have the last thing in remembrance;/ To have ever afore mine eye my death that is ever at hand;/ To make death no stranger to me;/ *To foresee and consider the everlasting fire of hell*;/ To pray for pardon before the judge come…': *Thomas More's Prayer Book*, xxxvii. [See also essay 10.]

life and teaching of Jesus that its undermining in Christian consciousness had to await radical confusion about, or denial of, the true relations between revelation and reason. I have mentioned already some instances of such confusion or denial. But many people have been quite needlessly surprised at the impact of the loss of hell on the hope of heaven. Their surprise is needless because if X will happen, or not happen, regardless of anything one does, one cannot *intend* X. So, if one assumes that either everyone reaches heaven regardless, or heaven is mere myth, we know not which, then one cannot *intend* heaven. Hope, not as dream unconnected with practical deliberation and choice, but as standing intention of shaping one's choices and actions in the hope of being made fit for the integral human fulfilment—the life of heaven—on offer in the covenant, becomes *impossible*.[13] So it is practical reason's own logic that makes inevitable the shift from 'Christianity' without fear of hell (and so with certitude of heaven) to Christianity without hope of heaven (and so with some this-worldly hope)—the shift to secularism so widespread among so-called liberal Jews and Christians.

It is obviously a precondition of sustainable engagement in public policy debates that one keep bright one's hope, and keep clear and firm the presuppositions of that hope. The Council, rearticulating the Church's perennial faith, stated the content of that hope in a way that makes full sense of participation in the affairs of this world, great or small, even when that participation seems doomed to failure. For it recalled and restated the promise of the covenant in terms recalled here by Cardinal Winning and again by Germain Grisez: that if we act on the Lord's command, we will somehow find again—but cleaned up and transformed—all the good fruits of our nature and our efforts, when Christ hands over to the Father the completed Kingdom of truth and life, holiness and grace, justice, love, and peace.[14]

III

Our engagement in public deliberation will be greatly facilitated if we are clear in our own minds, and can make it clear to other people, that the purpose of moral reflection is not to identify certain persons and their acts as *culpable*. Its purpose is rather to settle, for one's own conscience, the question: What should I do? What may I do? What options may I adopt, and what options must I not adopt however attractive they otherwise are?

---

[13] See the very important analysis of the proper integration of hope and fear in Christian life in *LCL* 91–4; also *DMQ* 21–8.

[14] Vatican II, Pastoral Constitution on the Church in the Modern World, *Gaudium et Spes*, sec. 39.

This clarification is important for many reasons. Public debate is frequently distracted and rendered fruitless by the question whether conduct of type X is *as bad as* conduct of type Y—e.g. whether intending the death of innocents as part of a strategy of nuclear deterrence which includes (as all militarily coherent policies of nuclear deterrence do) the options of city swapping and final retaliation is *as bad as* killing them in an act of city swapping or final retaliation on the night. In truth, the only fruitful and interesting question is whether it can be reasonable (morally acceptable) to form the intention. The question how much worse it would be to carry it out is a question we simply need not engage with.

Similarly, the important question for deliberation is never whether it is with feelings of repugnance or with thoughts of 'disapproval' that one is doing what one chooses to do. The question is always whether the option is choiceworthy, or is instead excluded from upright choice by its injustice, or by its opposition in some other way to the human goods (*bona humana*) which St Thomas describes as the content of the directiveness of the first principles of anyone's practical thinking, the basic reasons for action which the encyclical *Veritatis Splendor* (1993) refers to frequently and calls fundamental human goods.[15]

As that encyclical makes very clear, it is only in this perspective, the perspective of the person deliberating towards action, that one can understand what human action actually is, for the purposes of moral judgment:

The morality of the human act depends primarily and fundamentally on the 'object' rationally [whether reasonably or unreasonably] chosen by the deliberate will…In order to be able to grasp the object of an act which specifies that act morally, it is therefore necessary to place oneself in the perspective of the acting person. The object of the act of willing is in fact a freely chosen kind of behaviour…. By the object of a given moral act, then, one cannot mean a process or an event of the merely physical order, to be assessed on the basis of its ability to bring about a given state of affairs in the outside world. Rather, that object is the proximate end of a deliberate decision which determines the act of willing on the part of the acting person. (*Veritatis Splendor* sec. 78)

This is well understood in our society to the extent that most people still easily grasp the distinction between giving painkillers to kill the patient and giving the same dose to kill pain. It seems to be poorly understood to the extent that people assert that getting a patient dead by omitting nutrition and hydration cannot be murder;[16] or to the extent that people

---

[15] See e.g. *Veritatis Splendor* sec. 48.3; see also secs 13.3, 67.2, 78.2, 79.2.
[16] See essay II.19 (1993c).

think the fact that a bomb had a military target as its aim-point settles the question whether it was intended to kill non-combatants.

The question of cooperation in wrongdoing depends first on grasping firmly this understanding of the *object* of a human choice, and secondly on understanding that there are moral responsibilities which bear on what we foresee and cause even though those effects are not within the object or any other part of the intention with which one is choosing and acting. Formal cooperation is defined in terms of object and intention, that is, of the whole set of means and ends which one chooses and intends (including the ends which are means to yet further ends); material cooperation is defined in terms of foreseeable side effects, that is, effects not within one's intention (in that same sense of intention: the whole set of ends and means one chooses and intends). Joseph Boyle has taken us skilfully through all this.[17] Let me use an example closer to my theme of Catholic participation in the deliberations of partially corrupt societies.

In *Evangelium Vitae* (1995) sec. 73 you find two statements: (i) it is never licit to vote for a law permitting abortion; (ii) a Catholic elected legislator whose absolute personal opposition to procured abortion is well known can, in a legislative vote decisive for the passage of a bill, licitly give his or her support to a bill for a law which permits abortion but less permissively than the existing law or than a bill which will otherwise be passed and become law. Are these two statements consistent? Someone may say that they are not, because the vote which the second statement declares licit is for a law *permitting abortion* even though the permission is less extensive than the existing or a likely alternative law; but the first statement precisely judges illicit any and every vote for a law permitting abortion.

But the objection is, I think, mistaken, and the two statements are consistent. The kinds of acts which are always, exceptionlessly illicit are, as *Veritatis Splendor* sec. 78 made clear, acts defined by their object. The always illicit vote is for a law *as permitting*, precisely *to* permit, abortion. This is always illicit, even if one is personally opposed to abortion and is voting for it only to keep one's seat and prevent euthanasia or genocide laws, or only to equalize the position of the poor and the rich. The kind of vote which the second statement judges can be licit has as its object not: *to permit* abortions now illegal, but rather: *to prohibit* abortions now legal or imminently likely otherwise to become legal. Even though it is a vote for a law which does permit abortion, it is chosen by this legislator as a vote for a law which restricts abortion. That this restrictive law also permits abortion is only a side effect—when we consider the act of voting in the

---

[17] Boyle, 'Collaboration and Integrity: How to Think Clearly about Moral Problems of Co-operation'.

perspective of the acting person—even though the side effect of permission is as immediate as the object of restriction (the new law says abortion is lawful up to 16 weeks, the old law or the threatened alternative bill says abortion is lawful up to 24 weeks).

Sec. 73 of *Evangelium Vitae* concludes with the words: 'This [second sort of vote] does not in fact represent an illicit cooperation with an unjust law, but rather a legitimate and proper attempt to limit its evil aspects.' The wording is a little incautious, for the sentence is dealing with two things at once. It is implicitly saying *first* what I have been saying, that such a vote need not be *formal* cooperation in the wicked choice to permit abortion up to 16 weeks—sec. 74 will go on to say that formal cooperation in moral evil is never licit. But the sentence at the end of sec. 73 is also saying, secondly, that the legislator's non-formal but obviously real material cooperation in enacting the new law which does in fact permit[+] abortion up to 16 weeks can be justifiable. The incautiousness in the wording is twofold. On the one hand, the sentence says, not '*can be*' (as I did) but '*does in fact* represent a legitimate and proper attempt' etc. The legitimacy of material cooperation depends upon many factors, not all of which are considered by the paragraph. 'Does' should be read as meaning 'can in fact, provided all relevant conditions are fulfilled'. And on the other hand, the paragraph spoke of legislators who have made known their 'absolute personal opposition to procured abortion'. This phrase 'personally opposed' has the unfortunate side effect of seeming, in isolation, to give some blessing to a certain type of Catholic politician whose illicit formal cooperation in the enactment of permissive abortion laws and indeed of arrangements precisely to facilitate the procuring of abortion has been defended precisely by the slogan:

I am *personally opposed* (or absolutely opposed) to abortion but I vote to permit or facilitate or arrange for it because, in a pluralist society or a liberal democracy, no one is entitled to impose their religious beliefs or their private moral convictions on others in matters which go to the very heart of personal existence etc. etc.

Of course, taken as a whole sec. 73 of *Evangelium Vitae* gives no support and no room to such politicians, but it would have been better, I think, not to use their slogan 'personally opposed', in which the word 'personally' summons up a contrast foreign to the thought of *Evangelium Vitae* sec. 73—the thought that there can be true moral judgments about justice which are only private, not valid public reasons for action. The true question is not whether upright Catholic legislators are personally opposed to abortion but whether they are publicly opposed to it and will never vote *to* permit it, i.e. to make it more permissible, and will always take every reasonable opportunity to vote for its restriction, including if possible the absolute prohibition of all intentional killing by abortion.

Is this sort of object-centred analysis of acts perhaps too psychologistic and indeed dualistic or Cartesian and incompatible with healthy Aristotelianism or Thomism (which, as John Haldane argues, regards bodily behaviour as the best expression of the soul)? I think not. Neither *Veritatis Splendor* nor *Evangelium Vitae*, nor my own restatements of their position, are psychologistic in a dualistic or any other objectionable way. When Professor Haldane, in the course of his address, waved his hand and shifted his weight from one foot to the other to illustrate the bodily expression of the soul, we all understood the wave as precisely that: a manifestation of deliberate control of bodily functions at will, in this case to make a philosophical point. In the context his intentions were clear. Otherwise the shifting of weight might have been an animal reflex corresponding to nothing he wanted to show us about his soul, and his wave might have been a signal for a bomb to be thrown, or (in another forum) attracting the attention of the teller for the affirmative and thus the casting of a pro-abortion vote, or a cancellation of that vote and an expression of prompt repentance, or greeting a friend, or we know not what. As St Thomas so often says, one and the same type of behaviour (*actus in genere naturae*) can be one or more of many different types of morally significant human act (*actus in genere moris*),[18] and the moral judgment one should make about such acts, when deliberating about choosing them, will depend in the first instance on one's object in doing it (the act's object), and then on one's further intentions in doing it (the act's end or intention), and then on the circumstances including the side effects of doing it (the effects *praeter intentionem*). The envisaged outer act is assessed as the carrying out of one's inner act of intending and choosing and setting oneself to do what one chose, and as a manifestation (expression) of one's virtuous or negligent and vicious dispositions in relation to foreseeable side effects.

With a care and precision new in the tradition, Grisez's *Difficult Moral Questions*, volume 3 of his *The Way of the Lord Jesus*, traces out and articulates the various sorts of possible bad side effects of material cooperation[19] (they are also, as he points out, bad side effects of formal cooperation, but that is not the present issue). These bad side effects include the basic or primary bad effect of contributing to another's wrongdoing which necessarily has bad effects; and then a whole raft of secondary bad side effects of the cooperation. There are (1) the bad effects of one's very accepting of the primary or basic bad effects—the effects on one's feelings and dispositions of, say, voting for

---

[18] Essay II.9 (1991a).   [19] See *DMQ* 879–82.

a law which does in fact permit abortion up to 16 weeks in concert with people who think abortion should be freely available and are voting for 16 weeks only because they can't get something more permissive; (2) the occasion this cooperation offers for the grave sin of formally cooperating in some other immoral project of those whose collaboration one needed to enact the restriction to 16 weeks; (3) the comfort likely to be drawn by the principal wrongdoer from one's cooperation, understood by the wrongdoer as endorsement of the wrongdoing, and similarly the scandal to third parties who understand one's cooperation in the same way, the resentment of victims of the wrongdoing, and other forms of disharmony between the cooperator and them, and the impairing of one's witness to the moral truth, say about killing the innocent.

All the bad side effects which I just listed as that third set are of particular importance in reflecting on the engagement of the Church itself, through its leaders and representatives, notably the bishops. For the mission of the Church is precisely to bear witness to the truth, particularly the moral truths at stake in Jesus' summons to repent and live a life worthy of the Lord.

IV

So I reach my last theme, the role of the Church acting (e.g. speaking) precisely as Church, that is through its pastors, in a modern liberal society. My remarks about the meaning of 'liberal' left unstated one of the primary characteristics of these societies as we actually know them. I made some remarks about the loss of practical hope among Christians, and in doing so I was identifying, implicitly, the third of the three varieties of practical atheism which Plato long ago analysed in his last work, *Laws*.[20] That third sort of practical atheism or (as we now say) secularism Plato saw as the assumption that God is easily satisfied with human conduct or easily appeased and bought off. The other two sorts are at least as pervasive: that there is no God, or any god there may be is unconcerned with human affairs. The encyclical *Veritatis Splendor* takes up this theme in sec. 88:

The separation [between faith and morality] represents one of the most acute pastoral concerns of the Church amid today's growing secularism, wherein many, indeed too many, people think and live 'as if God did not exist'. We are speaking of a mentality which affects, often in a profound, extensive, and all embracing way, even the attitudes and behaviour of Christians, whose faith is weakened and loses

---

[20] See *Laws* X 885b, 888c, 901d, 902e–903a, 908b–d, 909a–b. Plato usually speaks of 'gods' or 'the gods', but when getting to the heart of the matter switches to talk of God or 'the god' (see 902e, 903d, 910b). [See also essay 3.]

its character as a new and original criterion for thinking and acting in personal, family and social life.... It is urgent, then, that Christians should rediscover the newness of the faith and its power to judge a prevalent and all-intrusive culture.

As the Council made clear, in line with the whole tradition, pre-eminent among all the principal responsibilities of the successors of Peter and Paul and the other apostles is to announce and confirm that faith.[21] If those who have that responsibility, and those whose duty it is to assist them, do not carefully assess and constantly reassess and vigorously respond to the 'profound, extensive, and all embracing' inroads of secularism in the Church's seminaries, teacher training colleges, and schools (and universities), and its bookshops, publishing houses, and newspapers—and if pastors fall silent about heaven and hell and therefore also about other unpopular teachings, and about the public good reasons for accepting the revelation in Jesus Christ—then no one should be surprised to find the Church ceasing to be even an interesting participant in the secular debate, and faltering in its own primary and irreplaceable purpose of leading people to salvation.

It is not, it seems to me, the responsibility of the Church itself, the bishop as such, to make the kind of assessment of complex contingent facts that is necessary to reach a deliberative judgment about, say, a social welfare policy or a strategy of nuclear deterrence. It is the Church's, a bishop's, role to teach in season and out all the moral principles and norms which any such policy must meet if it is to be morally acceptable to Catholics or anyone of good will. So ecclesiastical teaching on morals, and ecclesiastical participation in public deliberations, should in relation to many matters be framed strictly hypothetically. To give an example: *if* a policy of nuclear deterrence involves the intention to destroy non-combatants then it is immoral and may not in any circumstances be approved or formally cooperated in, whatever the consequences; and cannot be saved from that conclusory judgment by facts such as that the intention is conditional, or is formed with good motives, or has been and seems likely to be successful in facing down the enemy and avoiding war. Does the deterrence policy involve that intention? That question should, I believe, be left to the judgment of those whose responsibility it is to decide whether or not to participate in making and carrying out the strategy or policy, a responsibility about whose gravity and urgency the Church should not fall silent. The attempts of the US bishops, extended over years and conducted in the full blaze and buzz of secular publicity, to reach a non-hypothetical judgment about nuclear deterrence were skewed from the start by their committee's

---

[21] Vatican II, Decree on Bishops, *Christus Dominus* (1965), sec. 12.

own resolution, made privately in advance, that their contribution to the public debate would not condemn their country's deterrent, and were then waylaid by the willingness of public officials to contrive artful formulae to disguise the facts about national policy's intentions from the bishops' not too probing inquiries.[22]

Secular liberal societies and their public officials as such have a horizon of concern which (like the horizon of every secularism and every consequentialism)[23] is arbitrarily limited by emotional interests. In that horizon the Church and the collectivity of its members appear as walk-on bit players to be managed in the interests of whatever short-term goals are felt currently to be pressing. The horizon of the Church and of each of its faithful members is, as I have tried to suggest, far different. The transformation of this world into the new heavens and new earth will not be accomplished by the success of any human project or calculus, yet every reasonable human undertaking, every act of love of neighbour as oneself, will be taken up as material usable by God in the building up of that new world, discontinuous but in that mysterious way also continuous with this one. Philosophy even unaided by revelation can discern that kingdom of ends from far off, as an ideal, the only acceptable ideal of practical reason, the only principle capable of integrating the basic reasons for action. Reason's own trajectory, which every worthwhile public or private debate seeks to trace and track, is headed towards that same end. If we undertake the demanding disciplines of reasoning we should do so in that confidence.

NOTE

[†] *a law which does in fact permit abortion*...(p. 122). This phrase is seriously inexact, as I explain in essay IV.22, 459 (2004b) at n. 49, an essay which clarifies the whole treatment of legislating in sec. III of the present essay.

[22] See essay 21 at 326 n. 73; essay 20 at 277–8; *NDMR* 23–4, 36–7, 160–1.
[23] See e.g. *FoE* 126; *MA* 43–4.

Part Two

Bases for Accepting Revelation

7

THE SIGNIFICANCE OF
QUESTIONING*

I

Lawyers, as you know, have a notion of reasonable doubt. Correspondingly, they have a notion of unreasonable doubt. And since the pair of notions is a part of common sense, jurymen who are not lawyers can be asked to determine guilt 'beyond reasonable doubt'.

It would, of course, be most unwise to rely unquestioningly on common sense in dealing with all the problems that confront one. For one of the problems that confront us is, is it not, that common sense is not innocent either of unreasonable dogmatism or of unreasonable doubt, not to mention common-nonsense. And it would, I can tell you, be even more unwise to rely unquestioningly on the notions which lawyers offer you authoritatively.

Still, it seems that the notion of unreasonable doubt is going to play a part in the working of any critical intelligence. For if one has doubts about what in certain circumstances is alleged or supposed to be the case, still one can always add to those doubts one further doubt, namely, 'Is it sensible, is it warranted, to entertain these particular doubts of mine in these particular circumstances?' And often enough that question has a clearly appropriate answer: 'No; those doubts are not sensible, not warranted'—and thus, with that question answered, that doubt resolved, the other doubts are dissipated, and reasonably so.

Since the sixteenth century, when Sextus Empiricus's compendium of the sceptical arguments of classical antiquity was reintroduced into our culture, the term 'sceptic', like the term 'doubt', has carried the suggestion that faith, religious belief, and theology stand to reason, criticism, and science as complacency stands to intellectual concern, as naïve common sense stands to critical intelligence, as illusions and wishful projections

* Unpublished: the University Sermon, Church of St Mary the Virgin, Oxford, 28 October 1973.

stand to reality clearly seen and coolly accepted. Nevertheless, it was sensible then and it is possible now to raise some questions about these suggested equations, analogies, and contrasts. It is possible, for example, to inquire whether Hume's account of understanding and its objects takes any account of sheer intelligence, which goes beyond a comparison and association of impressions and images, and which by the act of understanding adds to the data of experience the intelligible content of those rational judgments through which we come to know what is the case. For such sheer intelligence Hume himself displayed in no small measure, notwithstanding his rather obvious oversight of that very fact itself. Or again, it is possible to inquire whether there is any reason to accept the explanation of explanation offered in the most recent Gifford Lecture, on 'The Claims of Theology': namely, that any explanation must yield a hypothesis 'which we can successfully project', a 'pattern in the course of events', 'one actual pattern in contrast to others which are logically possible'.[1] For indeed it is not in the least obvious that explanation by way of successful prediction is even a relevant form of explanation when the question is: What are the fundamental conditions on which we can affirm, rationally and critically, that there really is a course of events, any course of events, a pattern, any pattern, an actuality, any actuality, available to be contrasted either with mere logical possibility or with illusory appearances? When people begin to appreciate the need for an explanation of the very possibility of explanations, and will not be put off by a restrictive explanation that suits restricted ranges of questions, and demand an answer that fits their own actual and critical question, and when they insist on this question because without it one cannot give any account, that is both coherent and full, of what it is in any case to be factual, empirical, actual, or real—such people are not to be accused of complacency or uncritical common sense, or of legalistic kowtowing to the speech-habits of the tribe if at the end of the day they appropriate such terms as 'God' or 'creation' to signify that which they judge must be actual if anything at all is to be actual.

But how is our assent to these old terms to be made not merely a notional assent, but real-to-us? There is a dogmatism of the sceptic which parallels and responds to the dogmatism of believers who speak and even philosophize about God, creation, causality, and omnipotence before they have really opened their minds to the questionable character of what is taken complacently to be 'the world' and our 'knowledge' of it. As far as it goes, the response of scepticism to that dogmatic mode of unquestioning belief is quite fitting; the only fitting response to scepticism is to push

---

[1] Ayer, *The Central Questions of Philosophy*, 216–17, 222.

on with questions where the sceptic arbitrarily calls a halt. The reward for so pressing the question is the intelligible intimation of what St Paul, with full cognizance of the paradox, calls God's 'invisible nature clearly perceived in the things that have been made' (Romans 1: 20).

Very different from one another are the methods and very different the achievements of the many disciplines and sciences, ancient and modern. Still, you find in fact a language that is common to all of them. For you find that all of them express the judgments which they finally pass on hypotheses, in terms of what is plausible, what is elegant, what is fruitful, what is warranted, and so on. Someone who noticed this common language might suppose that, common to all the disciplines and sciences, there is some one test or criterion of sound or true judgment. But no. To know what is elegant or plausible within a discipline, so that one could use the terms 'elegant' and 'plausible' intelligently and critically within that discipline, there is absolutely no alternative but to submit oneself to the discipline of attending to the data of that discipline, of appreciating the questions raised with that discipline, of entertaining its hypotheses, of reflecting on its criteria. So, similarly, it is not possible to understand the terms in which theology and faith speak of God—or even the term 'God' itself—unless one first submits oneself to the *questions* which the assertions of theology and faith offer to answer. It is not enough that one understands how to use terms like 'cause', or 'power', or 'good', for other purposes, in response to other questions. For just as the meaning of 'plausible', 'elegant', 'fruitful', and 'warranted' shifts systematically from discipline to discipline, from set of questions to set of questions, so does the meaning of 'cause', 'power', and 'good'. We can know what is being said of God only to the extent that we understand what is being found to be questionable, insufficient, contingent, unexplained about the world as we know it in our experience and in all the other disciplines and sciences.

The reason why the shift of meaning of terms like 'plausible', 'elegant', and so on is a systematic shift of meaning and not a mere equivocation or accident of our language is this: that there is something, more than mere words, which is common to all disciplines and sciences—namely, the dynamic structure of the consciousness of scholars and scientists and indeed of all human beings 'in possession of their faculties' (as the saying goes). When St Paul spoke of 'clearly perceiving' the maker in the made, he was rather simplifying matters, in his strenuous way. Is truth indeed to be found by just opening one's eyes and looking? What one sees when one opens one's eyes and looks is not, of course, to be written off as mere appearance to be contrasted with reality. But is it not, for all that, a mere starting point for intelligence? If one is alert, questions arise. Why do things look like this? Suppositions and hypotheses are to be generated. Further questions compel revisions. And the judgment that such-and-such is indeed the case (the judgment which the original question was obscurely but recognizably heading for), the judgment in and through which one at last knows, is a judgment made, if made responsibly, only when one judges also that there are sufficient evidences or reasons to warrant that judgment and to render further doubt unreasonable.

II

Questions, then, introduce us to a labour, a work, a project to be carried on in time. As with our other works and projects, there is an end in sight (which we label truth or knowledge or whatever): and there is a choice between strategies and between means, between shortcuts and what my son calls longcuts, between the safe method and the untested hunch, and so on, and so on: you are very familiar with the problems. And they are the problems of a practice.

And so there comes into view an ethics of questioning and of scholarship and science—not for a moment as a deduction from or 'application of' some other, received or general ethics or morality (what could be more obscure in our age than the notion that there is a general ethics or morality?)—no! What I mean is: anyone who experiences, in himself or vicariously, the sheer thrust of curiosity, of questions, of the pure disinterested desire and intention to know, can grasp in that experience the good, the value, of truth and of knowing it, and of clearheadedness—as goods or values that are indeed universals, in the sense that they not only can be realized by getting a satisfactory answer to any particular question that happens to be engaging one, just now, but also can be realized in the attainment of answers, of knowledge of what is the case, by oneself or anyone and everyone *at any time or place*. Equally one can grasp the evil of wilful suppression of questions, of the temptation to obscurantism, of the temptation to affirm to oneself as well as to others the false, the half-true, what one would like to be the case rather than what critical questions and reflections would reveal is in truth the case. I could go on, but it is obvious how this complex of desire, grasp of universal forms of good, and temptation to (and aversion from) the wilful or careless falling away from those goods, all requires for its expression a use of the term 'ought' which goes beyond that merely instrumental use in which we say that 'if you want to be a good chemist you ought to learn some mathematics'. But how is our assent to these old terms 'ought', 'ethics', 'morality', to be made not merely a notional assent but real-to-us?

The tension and thrust of questioning breaks up our commonplace conceptions of ends and means, of wants and needs, of 'oughts' and 'cans'. The truth which we want may, as we well know in advance, turn out to be what we did not want to know. We cannot be satisfied with a judgment that is merely satisfying, for an unwelcome question insinuates itself and we want to know whether that judgment also is true. I said that in the practice of theory there is an end in sight. But that was the form of words in which we cover our predicament. The end is not in sight; it is luminously attractive; but it is unseen, unknown. So, in his old age, when he had graduated from politics to law, Plato amended his symbol of the life lived in pursuit of truth. No longer do we have the *Republic*'s symbol of the ascent from the darkness and shadows of the cave to the sunlit world above ground (though even here Plato takes care to offer no description of what is seen, no account of the form or idea of the Good); instead, we have in the *Laws* the symbol of the golden cord of understanding and judgment, which draws us gently and without force. That it is the golden cord, the lovely and worthwhile among the iron or leaden tugs of the passions below the passion of reason, that is clear. But where it is leading us is *not* known; it runs out, golden, into darkness. To follow it is the only serious goal we have, says Plato, but it is a goal we pursue as if in play; for, as in a game, we have nothing to say about what lies at its end and therefore we cannot say what point there is in following it.[2]

Precisely parallel are the paradoxes which the philosophers put their finger on, concerning self-love and friendship. If one loves oneself one wants good things for oneself, and a pre-eminent good for anyone is friendship; so friendship is indispensable for one's own flourishing; but friendship sought for one's own sake, rather than straightforwardly for the sake of one's friend, is not real worthwhile friendship at all. Start at the other end: if you love a friend, you want to secure what is good for him; but among the goods your friend treasures is you; so you must set about securing your own good. And, in either case, friendship can demand that one sacrifice all one's worldly goods for one's friend's sake. So where do one's reasonable interests lie? What is the point of friendship?

Together, then, the quest for truth and the claims of friendship introduce us to the sense of responsibility for our actions and inaction, that sense which we express in the language of duty, the so-called moral ought. Together the quest for truth and the claims of friendship stultify any suggestion that conscience cannot but be the product of parental suggestion, or of the after-image of the father, or of the mores of the tribe or class or cult.

---

[2] *Laws* 644, 803b–804c; [*NLNR* 407–9].

Both truth and friendship force us to revise the scheme of utility, of practical reasoning from wants to methods, ends to means. We find we have to introduce the category of the *worthwhile*, which is not a mere means, and yet is not an ordinary want since it is intelligently wanted above all intelligible calculi of interests and satisfactions. Finally, both the quest for truth and the claims of friendship require for their practical carrying-through the adoption of a peculiar third viewpoint. Thus, friendship demands that one adopt a viewpoint not precisely one's own nor precisely one's friend's, but a viewpoint from which to see and hold in tension the interests both of oneself and of one's friend, and from which can be plotted a strategy for realizing *both* interests in the measure suggested by *impartial* benevolence. From another direction, but with convergent implications, the pure disinterested thrust of questioning reveals as merely arbitrary (and thus demolishes, for reason) any and every form of self-preference which an impartially benevolent observer of the human scene, seeing all times and all places, all lives, deeds, and consequences, would consider unfair and unwarranted. And so the impartial benevolence of friendship takes its place within a wider perspective; for questions, demanding a *reason* for self-preference, can locate the circle of family and friends not at or as the horizon of one's practical interests but as one of many overlapping and concentric circles which, for each one of us, expand and recede to the horizon of the human race itself. And so we see why Plato, in his last days, grounded the very possibility of any ethics, politics, justice, or law on the possibility and attractiveness of participating in the divine viewpoint which is more than a mere observer's viewpoint, that divine dealing with human affairs *sub specie aeternitatis* which he expresses in the tersest formulation of his philosophy: 'God is the measure.'[3]

---

[3]   *Laws* 716. [And see essay III.3 (1973a) at 75.]

8

ETHICS AND REVELATION:
A FRAGMENT*

Plato's work, not least the part discussed in essay I.5, seemed to Christians in the first few centuries of our era to be highly convergent with what the revelation they believed to have been completed in Christ disclosed about God's existence, nature and will—so convergent that some hypothesized meetings or other communications between Plato and the prophet Jeremiah. St Augustine eventually concluded, in AD 416, that accurate computation of dates precludes that particular connection.[1] But he was deeply impressed by the way in which Plato and his successors (first among them Aristotle) went through and beyond natural science, epistemology, and ethics to a knowledge of God as cause of the organized universe, source of the light by which truth is perceived, and spring of human happiness and fulfilment.[2] Augustine wavers between thinking that Plato must have had some acquaintance with Israel's sacred books, and thinking that the sound parts of Plato's teachings about divine and human existence and goodness were made known to the philosopher by God by revelation, in that broad sense of 'revelation' which Paul puts near the beginning of his letter to Rome: 'what can be known about God has been *manifested* among them; in fact God has *manifested* it, for his invisible realities, indeed his power and divineness, have from the [time of] the world's creation'—that is, universally—'been made visible to [human] understanding through his created works'.[3] To which Paul adds, on the next page,

when nations that do not have the Law [revealed to Moses and the prophets of Israel] nevertheless do by nature what the Law [summed up in the Ten Commandments] requires, they ... show that what the Law requires is written on their hearts, to which their conscience testifies.[4]

* 2008a, sec. III; for secs I–II, see essay I.5 ('Bernard Williams on Truth's Values'); for secs IV–V, see essay II.7 ('Cosmopolis, Nation States, and Families').
[1] Augustine, *De Civitate Dei*, VIII, 11.   [2] *Ibid.*   [3] *Ibid.*, 12; Romans 1: 19–20.
[4] Romans 2: 14–15.

Here 'heart' and 'conscience' refer to the same reality—the activities of human reason—which the earlier passage called 'understanding'.

The 'Revelation' in this essay's title is that body of teachings which identifies itself as transmitted by God to a particular people by the series of intermediaries we call Moses and the prophets, and completed by all that Jesus of Nazareth said and did as witnessed and witnessed to by his apostolic disciples. It is a faith—a body of teachings and practices—which affirms that its foundations are established (*demonstr[ata]*) by reason,[5] that its accounts of the life and deeds of Jesus are true, sincere, *historical* in character even while keeping to the style of preaching,[6] and that the moral precepts it teaches are valid for all people everywhere and accessible to everyone's understanding and fully rational acceptance. In relation to those truths of faith (including moral truths) which are knowable by reason without revelation and faith, what divine revelation does is enable those matters to be known in a way which surpasses unaided reason in accessibility, certainty, and freedom from error.[7]

Morality (if you like, ethics and conscience) precedes faith in two important ways. It is by love of truth—by that responsiveness to the desirability of knowledge which I was recalling a little earlier[8]—that one (anyone) is moved to ask questions about the source of the world's existence, and of its astounding processes of orderly evolution and its stably and thus scientifically accessible orderliness, and to seek a really adequate explanation for these overarching realities of existence and orderliness as well as for the more specific realities studied by science and history. The moral obligation to seek such knowledge, or at least to be receptive to it when it comes one's way, and in either case to act upon what one has rationally judged to be true, turns out to be a compelling motivation to acceptance of a revelation whose content in part confirms reason's findings but in part far exceeds, without contradicting, what can be known by reason unaided by revelation. So this obligation is a part of *natural* morality, prior to religious faith.[9]

And ethics precedes faith in a second way. Revelation, in the sense I am concerned with, has been conveyed by particular human persons, most notably by this Jesus. The necessary judgment that he, his forerunners, and those who preached and wrote about him were persons of truth not imposture is a judgment with various foundational elements, not least—as

---

[5] Vatican I, *Dei Filius* (Dogmatic Constitution on the Catholic Faith) (1870), c. 4 (D-S 3019): foundations, but certainly not its whole content (D-S 3041).

[6] DV sec. 19.   [7] *Dei Filius*, c. 2 (D-S 3005).

[8] Essay I.5 at 98–101 (2008a at 30–3); see also essay 3 at 59, above.

[9] As is stated in DH sec. 2.3.

Aquinas's review of these elements makes clear—his and (in more mixed ways) their manifest personal virtue and the inherent excellence of the way of life he proposes to us.[10] A prophet whose message is mixed with self-serving permissions for acts of lust, hatred, and vengeance thereby not only rivets immorality, injustice, and intimidatory menace into the permanent content of any faith he (or she) founds, but also shows his (or her) message to be unworthy of belief.[11] (And here it is worth recalling that in the teaching of the community of faith founded by Christ, public revelation is closed with the age of the apostles, so that 'no new public revelation is to be expected' thereafter,[12] a teaching of faith which entails that any later proclamation of a subsequent revelation proposed to all must be taken to be a delusion or an imposture.)

Revelation, then, is a remarkable evidencing of truths universal in their significance and application to all human persons, by really particular, unrepeatable historical events and choices. To the reasonable assessment and appropriation of these evidences, philosophy however soundly done can be no more than a preparation and then an ancillary means, among others, of clarification, and of some conceptual contributions to 'the growth in understanding of the words and realities handed on [by *traditio*] from the apostles'.[13] This process of handing on involves the adoption of the revealed truths into particular human cultures which it more or less reforms but does not obliterate. Some elements of the reform are in themselves cultural, for some elements of revelation are themselves cultural, that is, the product of human choices that could morally have been rightfully different. The paradigm of an element which is in this way both cultural and universal is the Lord's Prayer (*Pater Noster*...), established by the choice of a particular human individual and referring, as it does, to a cultural artefact (bread) that is not inherent in the natural world, not required by reason, and not universal.

The two-way inter-dependence between revelation and reason includes this: that the moral precepts of the Catholic faith are understood by the Church as—and indeed are—*also*, at the same time, truths of public reason, accessible to any reasonable person even if and when de facto widely rejected. Like the rational preambles to faith, such as Plato's, Aristotle's, or Aquinas's proofs of the existence of God,[14] or the refutation of Hume's sophistries about the possibility and knowability of miracles,[15] these

---

[10] See *Aquinas* 320–1. Other leading elements in Aquinas's list are the miracles worked by Christ, and the self-sacrificial heroism of his apostles and other witnesses.

[11] See Aquinas, *ScG* I, c.6.   [12] DV sec. 4.   [13] DV sec. 8.

[14] On the main lines of some of the many proposed by Aquinas, see *Aquinas* 298–304.

[15] See e.g. 'Hume on Miracles' in *FHG* 40–8; and essay 9 below.

ethical positions and their political applications are matter for open public debate, to be proposed and defended as defensible and acceptable without appeal to the authority of revelation or its author. Those believers who accept them simply on faith, lacking the ability, education, or leisure to appropriate them by unaided reason, can reasonably rely on them in making political decisions, without needing to appeal to the 'Proviso' that John Rawls belatedly introduced into his 'liberal' but highly restrictive theory of public reason when he said we can appeal to religious considerations 'provided that, *in due course*, we give [what he calls] properly public reasons to support the principles and policies our [religious] doctrine is said to support'.[16] Christians of the central tradition do not have to hope that 'in due course' such public reasons will become available; if a moral teaching is proposed as a matter of doctrine in their tradition, public reasons both including and supportive of that very position are already available.

The position I have just stated is part of the general position about revelation that it clarifies and confirms God-related propositions and judgments of reason, including moral/ethical judgments about the good for human persons. And this, at least in anticipatory outline, is what is suggested by Plato's philosophical thesis[17] that perception of the divine archetype and cause of all human good enables those who have that perception—that glimpse of understanding—to judge better about the issues of individual, social, and political life.

---

[16] Rawls, *The Law of Peoples*, 144.
[17] See essay I.5 at 94–7 (2008a at 26–9).

9

HISTORICAL CONSCIOUSNESS AND
THEOLOGICAL FOUNDATIONS*

I

A number of theologians have adopted Bernard Lonergan's distinction between historical consciousness (or historical-mindedness) and the classicist worldview. Richard P. McBrien and Richard M. Gula, for example, appeal to Lonergan's authority for this synopsis: the classicist worldview sees the world as complete, fixed for all eternity, marked by the harmony of an objective order to be spoken of in terms of well-defined essences using abstract universal concepts; historical consciousness sees the world as dynamic, evolving through historical development, marked by progressive growth and change, and to be spoken of in terms of individual traits using concrete, historical concepts. Classicist method begins with the abstract and derives principles from universal essences, is primarily deductive, and opines that its conclusions are always the same and secure provided the deductive logic is correct; the historically conscious view begins with experience and derives principles from accumulated experience, is primarily inductive, leaves room for incompleteness and possible error, and is aware that its conclusions will be revised as the empirical evidence changes. And so forth.[1]

---

* 1992d, Etienne Gilson Lecture No. 15, in the Pontifical Institute of Mediaeval Studies, University of Toronto.

[1] Gula, *Reason Informed by Faith*, 32–3, codifying McBrien, *Catholicism*, 941–3 ('Catholic Moral Theology: From Classicism to Historical Consciousness'). Might one perhaps apply, *mutatis mutandis*, to such passages what Lonergan says in one of those places where he accepts that the great leaders of the tradition are in good measure exempt from the charge of classicism?

> While…the Greek philosophers did not know about the techniques developed by more recent exegetes and historians, it remains that a more exact understanding of the normative [i.e. classicist] approach is to be had by turning from the Greek philosophers to the humanists, the orators, the schoolteachers, to the men who simplified and watered down philosophic thought and then peddled it to give the slow-witted an exaggerated opinion of their wisdom and knowledge. (Lonergan, *A Second Collection*, 234.)

Some questions arise. First, is it significant that this rather far-reaching distinction is announced, by Lonergan as by the others, in essays, chapters, and books on moral matters?[2]

Secondly, when did the reported shift from one worldview to the other actually occur? In McBrien and Gula, the answer is fairly clear: it began with 'the Age of Enlightenment'; within Catholic theology it happened rather close to the Second Vatican Council.[3] In Lonergan, things are not so simple. Sometimes he presents classicist theology as a late seventeenth-century product, and seems to exculpate Aristotle and St Thomas from its inadequacies.[4] At other times, and more prominently, he suggests the McBrien/Gula interpretation, by stating, for example, that the distinction involves 'enormous' differences between positions, viewpoints, worldviews which 'differ in their apprehension of man, in their account of the good, and in the role they ascribe to the Church in the world.... [D]ifferences in horizon, in total mentality.'[5]

Thirdly, what is being asserted about the truth of the positions maintained within the respective worldviews? Proponents of historical consciousness do not explicitly raise this question, and they answer it only by insinuation. Obviously, they are telling us to see the world with historical consciousness. But they leave unanswered several questions which come to mind when one considers whether to take their advice. Are there really no universal principles, in any field of inquiry or knowledge? Is it really so clear that, from the data of sense, imagination, and emotional inclination, there can be no induction warranting assent to such principles?

---

[2] Notably, Lonergan, 'The Transition from a Classicist World-View to Historical-Mindedness', *A Second Collection*, 1–9; 'Natural Right and Historical-Mindedness', in Crowe, *A Third Collection: Papers by Bernard J.F. Lonergan, S.J.*, 169–83; Gula, *Reason Informed by Faith*; McBrien, *Catholicism*; Himes, 'The Human Person in Contemporary Theology: From Human Nature to Authentic Subjectivity', excerpted in Hamel and Himes (eds), *Introduction to Christian Ethics*; at p. 7, the editors say,

> Perhaps no single factor is more important for understanding moral theology today than an appreciation of how history shapes our self-understanding. This is precisely the subject of Michael Himes' essay. In it he describes how historical consciousness, an awareness of the time-conditioned nature of human existence, has influenced contemporary theology through a revision of what it means to be human.

[3] Gula, *Reason Informed by Faith*, 30–1.

[4] Lonergan, *A Second Collection*, 57, 67, 234. Sometimes the distinction seems to be little more than: between having an education focused on the Greek and Latin classics and then expanding one's horizons by reading early Christopher Dawson on comparative religion (*ibid.*, 264).

[5] *Ibid.*, 2 (address given in 1966). Though the neo-scholasticism affected by rationalism is to be distinguished from the philosophy and theology of St Thomas and the Fathers, and is open to important criticisms which are inapplicable to Thomas, there would be no plausibility in a claim that these differences have the character asserted in this passage. Hence, if there are such differences in total mentality, the classicist mentality, if it includes the neo-scholastics, must include Aristotle and Thomas (as McBrien and Gula suggest).

Fourthly, don't the terms of the proposed distinction—'worldview,' 'viewpoint', 'consciousness', 'mentality'—perhaps share in the almost pre-Socratic confusion of sense (or imagination) and understanding that we find again in, say, the Lockean or Humean equivocation on 'idea'? Has this something to do with the bracketing of the question of truth?

Fifthly, is the distinction self-referentially consistent? After all, a proposition is not made 'concrete' by its abstract reference to the abstraction 'concreteness' as something preferable to 'abstractness'.

In sum, is the distinction perhaps philosophically confused and historically inaccurate? But then, even if it is, must there not be some relevant truths which give it the measure of plausibility it has? I think so. They have something to do with the massive growth of historical information and with the bearing of that information on theology's sources, as well as with the pre-Vatican II treatises in Catholic moral theology and philosophy, and with the method and content and presentation of the philosophical work on which such treatises drew.

II

In reflecting on the relation between historical concern and theology, one might initially react with some scepticism to talk of a shift from ahistorical to historical-mindedness. One might, like Gilson, doubt the historical unconsciousness of, for example, the Middle Ages—

when all minds lived on the memory of an historical fact, of an event to which all previous history led up, from which was dated the beginning of a new era; a unique event...the Incarnation of the Word and the birth of Jesus Christ. The men of the Middle Ages were possibly unaware that the Greeks dressed otherwise than they did themselves; more probably they knew it well enough and cared very little; what they did care about was what the Greeks knew and what the Greeks believed, and still more what they were able neither to know nor to believe.[6]

Fifty years after Gilson's Gifford Lectures, one might doubt the historical-mindedness of mid- and late-twentieth-century theology and the catechesis it inspires. At the end of the 1970s, Martin Hengel prefaced his book on early Christian historiography with a warning about today's unhappy convergence of fundamentalist ostracism of historical and critical methods with a widespread *critical* 'retreat from any historical research worth taking seriously': 'theologians today increasingly lack historical knowledge and an interest in history'.[7] In the same year Ben Meyer noted how very

---

[6] Gilson, *The Spirit of Mediaeval Philosophy* at 384.
[7] Hengel, *Acts and the History of Earliest Christianity* at vii, viii; quoted with approval in Hemer, *The Book of Acts in the Setting of Hellenistic History* at 13.

few key exegetes in the liberal mainstream have been deeply interested in understanding the Jesus of ancient Palestine or had any delight in history as such;[8] more recently he has observed how fashions in literary criticism have diverged even further from the historical. René Latourelle lately remarked wistfully how few exegetes attempt a serious *historical* criticism of the Gospel miracles.[9] To a very wide field of recent biblical studies one might reasonably extend Lagrange's ironical remark to Batiffol in 1904: 'into documents [M. Loisy] digs deep down to extract the idea [!] they contain', but 'when the discussion turns on an historical or topographical fact, [he] passes on quickly'.[10]

True enough. But these initial reactions should also take into account that only sixty years ago a standard Catholic catechism for American schoolchildren could still present the creation of the universe and the human species as events to be dated much as they were dated by the seventeenth century's most erudite scholars, at around 4,000 BC. Today it is fundamental to our understanding of things—as of course it was for a Lagrange before the twentieth century began[11]—that human history spans scores or hundreds of thousands of years, and the universe millions. Pius XII's *Divino Afflante Spiritu* did not exaggerate in saying that many things, 'especially in matters pertaining to history, were *scarcely at all…* explained by the commentators [on Sacred Scripture] of past ages', since they lacked

---

[8] Meyer, *The Aims of Jesus*, 19.

[9] Latourelle, *The Miracles of Jesus and the Theology of Miracles* at 40.

[10] Lagrange, *Historical Criticism and the Old Testament* at 226. Compare successive recent editions of works which mediate scriptural scholarship to the wider theological community, such as the *Jerome Biblical Commentary* and *New Jerome Biblical Commentary*; consult, e.g. the treatment in such works of the question whether the synoptic prophecies of the fall of Jerusalem, and in particular the more detailed and striking form of the Lucan prophecies, require or even suggest that *Luke*, at least, be dated after AD 70. Do the more recent treatments show any signs of considering the historical and archaeological records of the actual siege and destruction? There is no sign of attention to the historiographical question: Can anyone as interested in Jerusalem and the Temple as the author or redactor of *Luke* be plausibly imagined constructing *ex eventu* [retrospectively] a detailed 'prophecy' which not only seems to foretell aspects of Jerusalem's fall that have left no trace in Josephus's history of the siege, and seems to counsel flight from the encircling armies when in the event most of the thousands who tried to flee were crucified or equally horribly killed just outside the walls, but also, and above all, completely omits the single most striking and central fact about Jerusalem's fate, a fact stressed by Josephus on the first page of his *History*, recorded by him in its proper place in all its awesomeness, theatrically portrayed to the citizens of Rome and the Empire in enormous mobile street displays in the imperial triumphs of AD 71, and recalled with horrified fascination in the rabbinic sources: the fact that the Temple, along with a crowd of thousands who had sought refuge in its porticos, and indeed with most of Jerusalem, went up in flames—was not simply destroyed but destroyed *by fire*? See Staudinger, 'Die Zerstörung Jerusalems bei Flavius Josephus und im Evangelium des Lukas' at 179–80. Attention to such matters is required if even the literary character of the texts is to be understood with historical mindedness, and if a theologically precise explication is to be given of the Church's teaching concerning the Gospels' historicity and reliability and their authors' intention to communicate, through the various forms of kerygma, a true and sincere account (*vera et sincera*) of Jesus (*Dei Verbum*, 19; Instruction *Sancta Mater Ecclesia* AAS 56 [1964] 713–16).

[11] See e.g. Lagrange, *Historical Criticism and the Old Testament* at 190, 203, 206–9.

almost all the information which was needed 'for an accurate exposition of such matters'.[12] The reliable information now available about chronology, sequence, and antecedents disqualifies many otherwise reasonable hypotheses about events and interpretations of texts, including many hypotheses once universally accepted as givens. The enhancement of information and means of information about human history has for several centuries, particularly the last two, become almost exponentially vast.

So vast, that we may be tempted to an untenable extrapolation about the necessity and effects of historical knowledge. An example lies close to hand. Lonergan attributed the origin of the name 'historical-mindedness' to the Anglican theologian Alan Richardson. But Richardson in fact adopted it from a passage in which the unbelieving American historian of Enlightenment, Carl Becker, is explaining to the Yale Law School—in the same year as Gilson's Gifford Lectures—why neither he nor any modern man can understand St Thomas's definition of natural law.[13] That fact about the history of the phrase in no way weakens the historical or philosophical validity of Lonergan's thesis. But Richardson's explanation of historical-mindedness, inspired by Becker's, is this:

Because we are nowadays historically minded, we can understand an idea or a doctrine only when we relate its history; we can identify a concept only by regarding it, not as something static...but as a living, developing entity.[14]

Richardson's extrapolation there leads him to assert two self-refuting doctrines: that we can understand a doctrine *only when* we relate its history, and can identify a concept *only by* regarding it as developing. If these doctrines could only be understood by relating their history (something attempted neither by Richardson nor Becker), that historical relation would only lead us back to other doctrines, and indeed could only be understood if we could get back to other doctrines which could only be understood if...and so on: a doubly vicious regress. And if a concept could be identified only by regarding it as developing, we could not now identify what Richardson meant when he uttered this statement twenty-five years ago or

---

[12]   Encyclical, *Divino Afflante Spiritu* AAS, 35 (1943) 309 at 313 (emphases added).

[13]   Richardson, *History, Sacred and Profane*, 253; Becker, *The Heavenly City of the Eighteenth-Century Philosophers*, 19.

[14]   Richardson, *ibid.* at 256. The passage continues, 'Becker is right when he thus describes what is involved in the fact of historical-mindedness' (Richardson's book is better than this on the history of historiography). Cf. Becker, *ibid.*:

Historical-mindedness is so much a preconception of modern thought that we can identify a particular thing only by pointing to the various things it successively was before it became that particular thing which it will presently cease to be.

Whether Richardson and the exponents of historical consciousness mean to assert the almost Heraclitean universal-evolutionism implicit in Becker's statement is unclear.

Becker his similar statement thirty-five years earlier still. And of course, the statement is inconsistent not only with its own claim to intelligibility but also to much else in the practice of science and philosophy, not to mention the preaching by which revelation was passed on and theology initiated.

What I have said about the self-referential inconsistency of these assertions of the early promoters of the term 'historical-mindedness' must be said, too, of the assertion (at least on one reasonable reading of it) by Wilhelm Dilthey, from whom I suppose[15] Lonergan took the term 'historical consciousness': '...the development of historical consciousness destroys faith in the universal validity of *any* philosophy which attempts to express world order cogently through a system of concepts'.[16]

III

Most prominent in Lonergan's own description of the classicist worldview are the terms 'necessary', 'unchanging', 'abstract', and 'normative', contrasted with the 'probable', 'changeable', 'concrete', and 'empirical'.[17]

Here in this Institute I need not expand on the historical facts about the tradition which are overlooked in such a description. For Aristotle and Aquinas, 'necessity' and 'science' are analogical terms. For them, science extends, in principle, beyond the necessary to the *ut in pluribus* and beyond that to the *per se* which embraces the intention in even one-off intentional actions.[18] It could thus extend to basing a whole *scientia*,

---

[15] Lonergan of course cites Dilthey directly on various matters, but prefers to expound his views as described or mediated by Gadamer: see e.g. Lonergan, *Method in Theology*, 212. Gadamer, *Wahrheit und Methode*, makes extensive use of the category 'historical consciousness' and some use, analogous to Lonergan's but more occasional and unthematic, of 'classicism' (see e.g. II.I.l(b)(i)).

[16] Rickman (ed.), *Wilhelm Dilthey: Selected Writings*, 135 (emphasis added). The statement is elusive and vague through want of quantification: Does 'express world order...' refer to the making of any and every claim about the world? Or only to a Hegelian or other rationalist complete 'system'? If the former, it is self-referentially inconsistent.

[17] One compressed formulation among many:

For, in the first place, the classicist believed that he could escape history, that he could encapsulate culture in the universal, the normative, the ideal, the immutable, that, while times would change, still the changes would be minor, accidental, of no serious significance. In the second place, the classicist judged modern science in the light of the Aristotelian notion of science and by that standard found it wanting, for modern science does not proceed from self-evident, necessary principles. (Lonergan, *A Second Collection*, 112.)

[18] Central to Lonergan's set-piece account of classicism is the remark, 'every good Aristotelian knows that there is no science of the accidental (Aristotle, *Metaphysics*, VI.2, 1027a19f.)': *Second Collection*, 3. But from the same page of the *Metaphysics* one can learn that science extends to what happens for the most part (*ut in pluribus*), and from the next page that the accidental of which there is no science is nothing other than that which has no cause, no explanation at all. And even for one-off ('concrete,' 'historical') events there are, in Aristotle's view, accounts which, though they do not show that the event itself happened by necessity, do give a genuine knowledge-by-causes of why it happened (or, if it be still in the future, the grounds for a well-founded prediction): *Metaphysics* VI.3: 1027a29–b16; Aquinas, ad loc.; Aquinas, *Commentarium in Libros Perihermeneias* I lect. 14, nn. 187, 194: if someone got thirsty because he ate spicy food, and so went outside to get a drink, and there

theology, primarily on an identification of the *sensus litteralis seu historicus*, the set of propositions which the witnesses to the revelation and its transmission through history actually intended to assert as true.[19] For Aquinas, though that science has an unchanging, ahistorical subject, God, it relates everything back to God, and so deals with salvation history: fall, *praeparatio evangelica*, incarnation, and life of Jesus, the instituting of the sacraments and founding of the Church...many things that involved change, radical concreteness, one-off events, the necessity only of freely adopted intentions....

As for the claim that classicists work 'from the abstract and universal towards the more concrete and particular',[20] and assume that any adequate knowledge proceeds *from* self-evident, necessary principles,[21] you will wonder why there is here no mention that the first principles of an Aristotelian science come to be known, by the *sapientes*,[22] by induction from experience of particular cases; and that, in outlining the Aristotelian organon, St Thomas points to a *dialectica*, or *logica inventiva*, which directs the rational processes whereby we reach truth *ut in pluribus*, even though not with necessity, by rational judgments which full-bloodedly (*totaliter*) adopt positions while yet not excluding all possibility of revision or even reversal.[23]

Then there is classicism's 'normativity'. The contrast asserted is with the 'empiricism' of historical consciousness, which is above all (in Lonergan's account) the consciousness that our world is made by man by intentional acts informed by meanings, including common meanings. Historical consciousness is consciousness of the diversity, development, and decay of *cultures*;[24] classicism's idea of culture is not empirical but normative.[25] Again you will need no elaboration of the facts this overlooks. In the preface

met a violent death because robbers were lying in wait for him, we have not only the kind of necessity which everything past has, just because it now *cannot* be the case that it did not happen, but also the per se, non-accidental causing of thirst by spicy food, and the per se, non-accidental character of whatever is intended.

[19] *ST* I q.1 a.10c; *In epistolam ad Galatas*, c.4 lect. 7; cf. Vatican II, *Dei Verbum*, 12: '...interpres Sacrae Scripturae...attente investigare debet, quid hagiographi reapse significare intenderint...'.

[20] *A Second Collection*, 3.   [21] *Ibid.*, 112.

[22] *ST* I–II q.66 a.5 ad 4 ('...sapientia non solum utitur principiis indemonstrabilibus, quorum est intellectus, concludendo ex eis, sicut aliae scientiae; sed etiam iudicando de eis, et disputando contra negantes.' One needs wisdom to judge which terms are admissible in such principles, the wisdom which consists in 'an accumulation of insights that stands to the universe as common sense stands to the domain of the particular, incidental, relative, and imaginable': Lonergan, *Insight*, 306; see also Lonergan, *Verbum*, 66–94).

[23] *In libros Posteriorum Analyticorum*, proem., 5–6. Within this field of dialectics seem to lie, inter alia, those judgments of *certitudo probabilis* which according to Aquinas are available to courts and other judges of fact, *circa contingentia et variabilia*—as we might say, historians: *ST* II–II q.70 a.2. See Gardeil, 'De la "certitude probable"' at 236–66, 441–85.

[24] *A Second Collection*, 4, 51, 61 141; *A Third Collection*, 170–71, 177.

[25] *A Second Collection*, 92, 141, 160, 181.

to his *Commentary on the Ethics* St Thomas identified four great fields of human *scientia* or *philosophia*, among them two fields entirely constituted by intentional acts of meaning, the fields of morally significant action and of the manifold of forms of culture.[26] The great twentieth-century debate about the possibility of a purely 'empirical', 'value-free' account of cultures has vindicated an epistemological position scarcely distinguishable from Aristotle's, as I have explained elsewhere in reference to the last 150 years of legal theory.[27] And there remains the issue which is suppressed by programmatic distinctions between the classical or historically-minded, the issue of truth. Is there indeed no ranking of cultures, of chosen forms of social life, of political or legal orders? Is there indeed no *catholic* church, and has it indeed no universal culture created, at once 'empirically' and 'normatively', by its founder's choices (as in the Lord's Prayer, or in the Mass in which is offered the same true and proper sacrifice once offered on Calvary)?

IV

In distinguishing classicism from historical consciousness, Lonergan and the others are attempting to describe a change, but also are urging us to join them in shifting to the latter, better view (and higher viewpoint). Their distinction is at once empirical and normative. It needed some argument, and the argumentation offered repays attention.

In his last major exposition of the distinction, Lonergan traced what he called the dialectic and experiment of history. (Observe the non-historical metaphors, 'dialectic' and 'experiment', to which the understanding of history's course is thus subjected.) This proceeds in terms of a succession of plateaus of developing human meaning, the first plateau having to do

---

[26] *In Eth.* I lect. 1 (nn. 1–2); lect. 2 (n. 31).

[27] *NLNR* ch. 1. If there is to be a general sociology, or theory of any human culture or cultural artefact (say, legal systems), there must be a formation of interpretative and explanatory concepts by the theorist, and this formation and selection must be guided by notions of what is important and what unimportant in human existence—notions which are by logical necessity normative. Nor need this involve theorists in blindly imposing on the data their personal or 'Platonic "ideals"' (*pace* Lonergan, *A Second Collection*, 4); for sensitive interpreters find in the data a source of information or reminders of human opportunities, which assists them in converting their prejudices about the right and the good into truly reasonable judgments. There is thus an indispensable movement to and fro between the normative and the empirical; without this there can be neither a sound ethics nor a sound description of human affairs: *NLNR* 16–19. The reflective equilibrium may be articulated separately in an ethics and descriptive human sciences respectively, or it may be articulated in more or less unified form, as in Aristotle's *Politics*, where great masses of empirical historical information gathered by Aristotle are presented in generalizations, in some respects shown by subsequent historical experience to have been premature but in other respects of lasting application and still unsurpassed penetration of the perennial problems of human social existence. See Voegelin, *Plato and Aristotle*, ch. 9.

with doing, the second (on which is to be found classical consciousness)[28] mainly with speaking, and the third with 'the human understanding where developments originate';[29] this supreme level (which is also historical consciousness in its fullness) seems to be reached precisely with the author's own unfolding of the 'generalized empirical method'.[30] The whole process is one which 'has its origin in the tensions of adult human consciousness'.[31]

Now 'adult human consciousness' is as 'classicist' a category as one could wish for, and has been rather carefully explored by the tradition. Central to individual and social development, default, and decline, according to the tradition, is the tension between reason and feeling, between intelligence and emotion or affectivity. Virtue, in the tradition, is no suppression or despotic mastery of one's affectivity. Every intelligent and good action will be supported by some emotion, and in a well-ordered person even conflicting and dissonant emotions would take their place in an inner harmony or resolution. But intelligence grasps goods, values, benefits which one's affectivity, as such, cannot apprehend, and these are the principles of all reasonable deliberation. Lonergan made very little of this central theme of the tradition, for he came to the view that the apprehension of values *rests on* affectivity,[32] that 'apprehension of values and disvalues is the task *not of* understanding but of intentional response', that is of 'sensibility' and 'feelings'.[33] Sin's root, then, is stupidity: inattention, oversights, irrationality, irresponsibility[34]—the account is vague, but its drift is clear; sin is rooted in intelligence's failure to do its job of integrating and serving the feelings which, in this account, are the *ultimate* principles of right action. Now Chapters 6 and 7 of *Insight* are subtle and helpful in tracing the origins of such failings of practical intelligence. Whether they capture the intelligible root of sin and decline is doubtful. My point here is simply that the pertinent issues lie well within the boundaries of 'classicist' philosophical method, and are treated by Lonergan in a thoroughly classicist style, with just the sort of philosophical tools which he assigned to the second plateau of history's dialectic. The *methods*

---

[28] *A Third Collection*, 181. [29] *Ibid.*, 177.
[30] See *A Third Collection*, 176–8, especially the last paragraph of 177. [31] *Ibid.*, 178.
[32] *Ibid.*, 181. See the analysis of texts in *FoE* 42–4, 49, 54. Even in his earlier, more intellectualist period, the intelligible 'good of order' was for Lonergan no more than the 'thin', empiricist conception of good as *whatever* ensures the recurrence of all effectively desired instances of particular objects or actions which meet anyone's wants of *every* kind. In *A Third Collection*, 179 there is a single mention of a distinction between 'satisfactions' and 'values'; in *Insight*, 630, 631 there is unelaborated mention of one's intelligence, reasonableness, and willingness standing 'in opposition with sensitive and intersubjective attachment, interest, and exclusiveness', 'attached, interested, and narrow sensitivity and intersubjectivity'. But the issue goes unexplored.
[33] *Method in Theology*, 67, 115, 247. See also *A Third Collection* at 173 ('Feelings reveal values to us') and 141 ('On affectivity rests the apprehension of values').
[34] Lonergan, *Method in Theology*, 117.

employed in generating Lonergan's account of the dialectic seem to me no more historically conscious or historically critical than those employed by Aristotle in tracing various patterns of social, political, and philosophical development in the *Politics* and the *Metaphysics*.

Indeed, in significant respects they are less so. The study of intellectual development and method is assigned to a third plateau, not by virtue of any historical knowledge or reasoning, but by extrapolating from a form of argument which, like the extrapolation, is (whether right or wrong) straightforwardly (classically) philosophical. Now the form of argument extrapolated from is the one which Karl Rahner recalls when he talks of certain 'objective structures of human nature' being 'implicitly affirmed by a transcendental necessity even in the act of their denial'.[35] It is the one which Lonergan gestures towards when he claims, in Chapter XI of *Insight*, that any attempted revision of his explanatory account of knowledge would be 'necessarily fallacious'.[36] And the extrapolation from this form of argument has much the same significance in Rahner as in Lonergan, for Rahner assimilates historicity (in the sense of historical-mindedness) to 'anthropocentricity (i.e. the explicitly transcendental perspective of modern times)'.[37] But, setting aside the extrapolation, the form of argument itself is employed by Plato, Aristotle, the Stoics, quite extensively by Augustine, much less extensively by Thomas[38]—in each case, to refute some sceptical or reductivist assertion by showing its self-referential inconsistency, that is the inconsistency of the proposition asserted either with itself or its own entailments, or with what is involved in the sceptic's own performance in making the assertion (or both with itself and with its assertion). Examples of self-referentially inconsistent assertions of the first sort are: 'It can be proved that nothing can be proved', 'All propositions are false', 'All propositions are true'; examples of the second sort are 'No one can communicate by language', 'I do not exist', 'No concept can be understood without tracing its history', 'Knowledge is not worthwhile', 'No one can make a free choice', and so on.

Now the logic of arguments from self-referential inconsistency has been soberly and well explored in recent years, not least by Joseph Boyle,

---

[35] Rahner, 'Natural Moral Law', 305. Lonergan speaks approvingly of this essay in 'The Transition from a Classicist World-View to Historical-Mindedness', *A Second Collection*, 6.

[36] *Insight*, 336. But Lonergan makes no attempt to expound the argument from self-referential inconsistency with the necessary rigour, and in fact fails to show that such a revision would be self-refuting—in particular he fails to show that his account of knowledge is not seriously deficient through, e.g., its failure to attend to *reasoning*, which cannot be reduced to insights and judgments, and without which there can be no *causal*, explanatory account of anything. (See Grisez, *Beyond the New Theism*, 121–9, 230–1.)

[37] Rahner, 'The Historicity of Theology', IX at 73.

[38] See the citations in essay I.3 at 70–2 (1977a at 257–8).

Germain Grisez, and Olaf Tollefsen (who have shown in detail how to *use* this form of argument in defending a variety of metaphysical positions such as the reality of free choice).[39] And this exploration makes it clear that, for all their potency (signalled in the old title *consequentia mirabilis*) in refuting metaphysical positions mistakenly denying some major portion of reality,[40] such arguments both presuppose unrevisable propositions about some features of the portion of reality they defend, and require supplementation by additional propositions of the same sort to build up an adequate metaphysics, epistemology, or ethics. Philosophical explanation of what is involved in the making of assertions has no special method; the truths it may attain have no special metaphysical necessity, no 'transcendental' necessity, even though their defence is peculiarly facilitated by the special *proximity* (so to speak) of the facts which are given in the performance of denying them.[41] Thus there disappears the most plausible reason for claiming that studies of human understanding or 'method' have a peculiarly 'transcendental' character and a unique 'concreteness'.[42] So too there disappears the apparent ground for claiming to identify a third 'plateau' in a 'dialectic of history'. Philosophical reflection on human understanding and method is valuable, but must be content to employ the same sorts of method as the philosophical reflections to be found on the supposedly transcended 'second plateau'.[43]

V

For all that, there are some important truths which lend plausibility to the flawed historicist critique of the tradition.

[39] See Boyle, 'Self-referential Inconsistency, Inevitable Falsity and Metaphysical Argumentation'; Boyle, Grisez, and Tollefsen, *Free Choice: A Self-Referential Argument*, 122–38; Grisez, *Beyond the New Theism*, 111–13, 133–4, 172–80.

[40] i.e. one or more of the four orders discussed in sec. V below.

[41] Cf. Lonergan, *Insight*, 342:

Finally, cognitional theory differs from other theory; for *other theory reaches explanation only by venturing into the merely supposed*; but cognitional theory reaches explanation without any such venture; and since it contains no merely hypothetical element, it is not subject to radical revision. (Emphasis added.)

This claim involves an arbitrary and indefensible use of the term 'mere supposition', and devaluation of knowledge of matters other than the subject-matter of cognitional theory, a knowledge without which cognitional theory itself can make no justified assertions or is reduced to solipsism.

[42] Cf. *A Second Collection*, 6, where Lonergan claims, e.g., to have articulated a 'concrete and historical apprehension of man ... with its appropriately concrete foundations in structural features of the conscious operating subject, by a method that has come to be named transcendental'. For the reasons suggested in the text, one should avoid dramatizing the overcoming of empiricist error as 'intellectual conversion'.

[43] Cf. Rahner, *Theological Investigations*, IX, 46: 'modern philosophy (seen as man's transcendental and existential-ontological interpretation of himself)'.

St Thomas speaks of the *via inventiva* or *dialectica*, but undertook no commentary on the *Topics*. True, St Albert did; but what was really needed was to get decisively beyond Aristotle's confusion of dialectics as 'a process wherein lies the path to the principles of all inquiries'[44] with dialectics as a non-philosophical process of debate between one person and another.[45] The rational processes by which one comes to assent to those foundational principles whose assertibility is known only to the wise remain unthematized. Inductive logic and method is neglected. Historical knowledge is assumed to rest wholly on the testimony of credible witnesses,[46] and no thematic attention is given to the various types of indirect evidence by which the credibility of witnesses should be tested and by which we can warrantably infer past intentions and other facts without perhaps any testimony; nor to the range of presuppositions involved in any inference from any evidence. Above all, the tradition failed to investigate the norms of sound historical thinking: for example that one can reason from signs or effects to actions, and from actions to intentions; but that in doing so, one may not draw conclusions at odds with antecedent probabilities unless there are strong grounds for doing so.

The norms I have just mentioned have some interesting features in common with the many other norms of sound thinking, norms such as Ockham's razor, or that logical principles are to be adhered to in all one's thinking even when doing so requires one to give up some belief based on experience, or that nothing inexplicable is to be accepted as possible.[47] Norms such as these must, I think, be involved in the wisdom by which one recognizes the assertibility and warrantedness of the foundational principles of a body of knowledge; an account of that wisdom must involve more than Aristotle succeeds in articulating at the end of the *Posterior Analytics* (experience plus unspecified *nous*), and more than the willingness to pursue questions for understanding and judgment, of which Lonergan speaks in *Insight*.[48] Wisdom will involve also adherence to norms each of which bears directly not on propositions (as do the principles of formal or deductive logic) but on affirming and confirming them, and guides the making of affirmations not by describing facts which would confirm them but by identifying legitimate and illegitimate moves from reasons or evidence to conclusions. Such norms are not physical 'laws of the human psyche', nor logically necessary truths, nor mere technical means to any

---

[44] Aristotle, *Topics*, I.7: 101b3.   [45] e.g. *Topics*, VIII.1: 155b5–15.

[46] See e.g. Gardeil, 'De la "certitude probable"' at 462.

[47] For lists, see Boyle, Grisez, and Tollefsen, *Free Choice*, 144–5; *NLNR* 68–9.

[48] Rationality norms are related to, but go beyond, whatever is sound in Lonergan's 'canons of empirical method' (see *Insight*, ch. III; cf. 586–8 on 'canons of methodical hermeneutics').

goal shaped by adoption of some purpose. They are not norms, therefore, of the first, second, or fourth of the four orders which St Thomas identifies in his neglected analysis of reason's fields of operation, in the preface to his *Commentary on the Ethics*. They seem to be norms, rather, included within the third order, the order which reason brings into deliberation and choice by identifying fundamental goods—in this case, the good of truth and knowledge—and ways of instantiating, damaging, or failing to instantiate them. They regulate choices in the work of inquiry and judgment, for example the work of historians, philosophers, and theologians; they are *internal* to all sound historical, philosophical, and theological work.[49] So understood, they can be called 'rationality norms'.

An important and very strong rationality norm is the one which bears on the form of argument I have already discussed: the norm that self-referentially inconsistent theses are to be abandoned, and not merely rescued from formal logical contradiction by gimmicky escape clauses, ad hoc postulations of meta-levels of discourse, and the like. Failure to reflect on the role this rationality norm plays in his refutation of empiricism, and in other instances of argument from self-referential inconsistency, and failure to reflect on other rationality norms as *such*, allowed Lonergan not only to exaggerate vastly (as I have already suggested) the philosophical peculiarity or transcendental character of philosophical work on human understanding and method, but also to give an account of method which in the end is curiously *external*.

What I have in mind by 'external' could be illustrated by many parts of his *Method in Theology*. I take an example from a paper of 1975, 'Christology Today': 'Where earlier history was a matter of believing testimony, contemporary history is a matter of understanding evidence.' So far, so good, provided one retains the testimony as part of the evidence.[50] But Lonergan goes on:

Any relic or trace of the past may be evidence, but what it might be evidence for emerges only from the accumulated expertise of the history-writing community, and what it actually does establish results only from a consensus based on investigations that have been carried out by competent researchers and submitted to the scrutiny of competent reviewers. This contrast between precritical belief in testimony and critical understanding of evidence is of the greatest theological significance.[51]

---

[49] See Grisez, *Beyond the New Theism*, 168–72, 392; Boyle, Grisez, and Tollefsen, *Free Choice*, loc. cit.

[50] A good deal in Lonergan's subsequent discussion treats testimony as if it were no evidence at all.

[51] *A Third Collection*, 80.

But the contrast remains broken-backed because the norms of critical judgment which are internal to, that is, directive of, any rational consensus on anything remain outside the field of Lonergan's attention. The history of historical research into the New Testament during the past 125 years is one of rather frequent reversals of 'assured results of criticism', that is, of 'a consensus' of 'competent researchers and reviewers'; some of the most competent researchers in that field have remarked on the grave damage done to research and understanding by the pressure of consensus.[52] Certainly there must be a norm or set of rationality norms enjoining anyone interested in the truth to *have regard to* the consensus of the competent, and not to depart from it without reason. But that norm is restricted by the indispensable qualifying clause, 'without reason', and is only one norm among others applicable to the field in question; it is by reference to the whole set of applicable norms that one judges critically what reason(s) would warrant departing from the consensus.

In the historical field to which New Testament exegesis is relevant, any consensus must have taken a view on the rationality norms formally and informally proposed by the historiography of the Enlightenment. A very important norm is the one most conscientiously elaborated and defended by Hume but central to the mainstream of historical-critical exegesis since Strauss; the 'maxim' (Hume's word for rationality norm) that 'no human testimony can have such force as to prove a miracle' or even such force as to render the testimony credible unless its falsity would be an even greater miracle than its truth. Newman's reply (though not expressed with all the precision an exegete could reasonably desire) gets near the heart of the matter. Hume's rationality norm is stated too absolutely, too unrestrictedly:

> the question is not about miracles in general, or men in general, but definitely, whether these particular miracles...are more likely to have been or not, whether they are unlikely, supposing that there is a Power, external to the world, who can bring them about; supposing they are the only means by which He can reveal Himself to those who need a revelation; supposing He is likely to reveal Himself; that He has a great end in doing so; that the professed miracles in question are like His natural works, and such as He is likely to work, in case He wrought miracles...[53]

And so on. But this appeal to presuppositions—like the comparable appeal, couched in Lonergan's mode of discourse, by Meyer in the methodological part of his *The Aims of Jesus*[54]—could have gained significantly in

[52] See e.g. C.H. Dodd, letter of 19 June 1972, in Robinson, *Redating the New Testament*, 360; Hemer, *The Book of Acts in the Setting of Hellenistic History*, 352.
[53] *An Essay in Aid of a Grammar of Assent*, 306–7.   [54] Meyer, *The Aims of Jesus*, 101.

philosophic cogency had Newman—and Meyer—been in a position
to draw on a reflective account of rationality norms in general, and on
other examples of rationality norms rendered false by the omission of
qualifications or exceptions. (What examples? Well, take an example
from the rationalist rather than the empiricist camp, yet quite relevant
to a genuinely critical historical consciousness: the principle of sufficient
reason, in the unqualified form stated and employed by Leibniz and the
whole rationalist tradition ending in Hegel. Properly understood, the
rationality norm of sufficient reason directs us to expect and look for causal,
explanatory accounts. And it is always reasonable to do so. Everything but
God can be accounted for in most respects, and there is a sense in which
what God is accounts for him. But there are certain realities that simply
cannot be accounted for: for example in the case of free choices, whether
God's or ours, why just this choice *and not some other* was made. If that
could be accounted for, there would be no free choices. So the erection
of the rationality norm of sufficient reason into a principle by Leibniz and
the rationalists was an epochal blunder.) But my point here is only that
the norms of rational dialectics or inductive logic or informal inference
were insufficiently explored in the tradition, and the neglect, which is not
yet adequately repaired, left it inadequately prepared to give guidance
in the truly critical assimilation of that vast mass of relevant historical
information which became available when technological and other cultural
conditions reached a take-off point.

As I said before, the significance of rationality norms goes well beyond
historical research and judgment. It is the normativity of a strong
rationality norm that constitutes the non-logical but cogent necessity
of the argument for an uncaused cause. Different rationality norms
direct us to the judgment that the uncaused cause is personal and may
intend establishing a personal communication with human persons. The
comprehensive failure of Enlightenment philosophers to adhere to these
principles of truth-seeking inquiry had many results. Among those results
are the self-referential inconsistencies which make Kant's philosophy
worthless as a general guide to reflection. Another is the denial that there
are events (words and deeds) which cannot be reasonably explained or
interpreted as anything other than divine communication (that is, miracles,
signs, revelation properly so called).[55] Another is the denial of any source
of meaning and value save the human psyche. There resulted, in short,
the manifold of post-Hegelian relativisms (all with their own disabling

---

[55] See *CMP* 479–80. For a thorough critique of the denial of the possibility of miracles, see
Grisez, *Beyond the New Theism*, 326–42; Nicolau and Salaverri, *Sacrae Theologiae Summa*, 156–71;
see also Charlton, *Philosophy and Christian Belief*, 46–54, 95–9.

but insouciantly tolerated self-referential inconsistencies) among which we live. (One seemingly paradoxical but actually intelligible result of assuming that meaning and value have only human sources is the absolutizing of the importance of *current consensus*...a phenomenon characteristic of today's academe.)

Rationality norms are of different sorts. The weaker ones will lead, via evidence which seems certain, to conclusions which are reasonable, yet in this or that case mistaken. Rationality norms are understood and accepted in a context of experience and cumulated knowledge; experience of mistakes in historical and natural-scientific judgment, and in philosophical speculations which relied on those mistaken judgments, gives reason for an enhanced caution about the sources employed in inferences, a caution greater than St Thomas showed in working with the various sources of theological speculation and judgment. He tended to read the sources available to him as if the main problem with them was their as yet imperfect unity, as if they were pieces in a jigsaw puzzle which could fit together as a whole without drastic reworking. But in fact his sources contained not only the mistakes induced by reasonable following of weak rationality norms in a context of very deficient historical information, but also mistakes due to the ubiquitous human desire to systematize by extrapolation—extrapolations which readily outrun the evidence actually available to the systematizing thinker and any genuine or applicable rationality norm for handling it. Human knowledge, in short, needed and doubtless needs much more development than St Thomas envisaged. So, while his way of doing theology was reasonable in his time, the proponents of historical consciousness are correct, in my judgment, in thinking that sound theology today not only must use a more complex method but needs to identify and correct important deficiencies in even the greatest work in the Catholic theological tradition.

VI

As I said near the beginning, those who programmatically announce historical-mindedness and denounce classicism have done so most prominently and extensively in relation to matters moral. So, to illustrate both what needs to be done in correcting and developing Catholic theology, and the way in which the 'historically minded' have obstructed rather than promoted the necessary work, I shall outline some types of mutability or relativity, neglected both in pre-Vatican II *moral* treatises and in the work of the 'historically conscious'.

I start with the latter. Their distinction between classicism and historical consciousness was and is promoted as context for two claims, most prominently articulated by Rahner, that concrete human nature is changing and that these changes deprive certain moral judgments and teachings of the premises which (it is granted, if not conceded) were once true.

The claims are confused. For, first, the principal exponent of classical moral theology was clear (though many neo-scholastics were not) that moral judgments have as their premises, not propositions about human nature or Being (transcendental, concrete or otherwise), but principles of practical reason which outline all the basic aspects of human fulfilment (and thus, incidentally, make possible an adequate conception of human nature in both its determinacy and its openness).[56] And, secondly, Rahner's conception of human nature (one which Lonergan explicitly promoted) makes the fallacious division which I foreshadowed in my discussion of the extrapolation underpinning claims about 'transcendentality'. On one level is placed an unchangeable transcendental nature comprising only those features necessitated by the very concept of thought and action (that is, by the very act of expressing scepticism); on a second level is placed the merely 'categorical' and 'concrete' nature which is postulated to be (in some unexplained way) the source of most moral norms but which, not being transcendental, *must* be subject to change.[57]

To this Rahner adds an assertion that sounds empirical; 'nowadays', he says, 'man himself in his concrete nature' is subject to 'swift changes', indeed 'to a most far-reaching process of change'. But to those who would like evidence, he replies only that 'up to the present we have not been able to experience much change in this concrete nature "in our own person" in so brief a space as is constituted by an individual life-span'.[58] Not even one concrete example emerges from his historical consciousness.

Any illustration he might have offered would need careful philosophical interpretation. In its historical actualizations human nature of course changes, for the worse by way of sin and corrupt cultures, for the better by putting on the new man in grace. But the relevant question, never confronted even historically, let alone philosophically, by Rahner and Lonergan and the exponents of historical consciousness in moral theology, concerns not human nature in its de facto actualizations, but human nature

---

[56] See e.g. 1987f, 99–151 [also 1991d, vol. 1: 236–89]; essay I.9 (1987a).

[57] Obviously, this distinction and opposition between transcendental and categorial nature has self-referential inconsistency problems (as does its Kantian antecedent, the distinction between the transcendental or noumenal self and the phenomenal self): Rahner claims to tell us how human nature really, unchangeably is, also in its empirical aspect: subject to change, at the mercy of the natural and socio-cultural environments, etc.

[58] Rahner, 'Basic Observations on the Subject of Changeable and Unchangeable Factors in the Church', 15.

in its basic possibilities of fulfilment, possibilities which are adequately known only by adverting to the basic forms of human flourishing which are understood in our grasp of fundamental reasons for action. Is there, then, anyone for whom it was not or is not or will not be the case that life and health, knowledge of truth and beauty, excellence in work and play, the harmony in friendship with others, the procreative friendship of marriage with another, personal harmony in interior integrity and peace and outer authenticity, and harmony with the source of all meaning and value, are the basic reasons for action, the basic forms of the human fulfilment in which he or she would wish to share and outside which no benefit or goal could seem really worthwhile? No. No such human person can be identified, and the talk of human nature's changeability—equivocating between nature as actualized and nature as basic possibilities of fulfilment—fails to impinge on the foundations of morality.[59]

But many forms of change need to be understood by the moral philosopher or theologian. Let it be supposed, for example, that among the basic goods, intrinsic to human persons and their communion, is the good of marriage. Marriage so understood does not change; it remains such an intrinsic human good for every era which we know of or can anticipate. But understood as an object of socially sponsored and ratified agreement between two parties, and consequently as a lived reality, marriage is culturally shaped. Marriage's reality is not only in the first order (of nature itself, independent of all deliberation and choice) but is also—like the reality of other legal or conventional institutions—in both the third order (of deliberation and doing) and the fourth (of making and technique), and thus varies with time and place (though by no means as widely and radically as, say, languages). As a culturally determined form, the institution of marriage available to the members of a community will embody both the insights and the relevant mistakes and oversights of that community. Many societies, while understanding the intrinsic good of marital communion, fail to understand that exclusivity is an indispensable requirement for realizing that intrinsic good, and almost all societies fail to understand that indissolubility is another such requirement. In such societies, the full reality of marriage which is available within the Catholic Church (even leaving aside marriage's sacramentality) is simply not held out for adoption by choice. The members of such communities (unless endowed with eccentric individual creativity) can consent only to imperfect marriages, which both are and are not marriage (properly understood); as marriages though imperfect, such relationships are not simply invalid, illicit

[59] See *CMP* 182–3.

concubinage; as imperfect and so far forth *not* marriage, such unions—though in good faith intended as marriage (imperfectly understood)—are dissoluble. When one understands the historicity of every legal and conventional institution, even institutions directly instantiating a basic good natural to humankind, one can envisage a theological account, better than those hitherto standard, of Old Testament marriage and divorce *ad duritiam cordis* (Matthew 19: 8) and of marriage's other historical vicissitudes among non-believers, Protestants, and others.[60]

More well known, perhaps, is the historicity of those legal and conventional institutions which directly instantiate not basic goods but merely instrumental goods, for example such forms of property and property relationships as money, leases, credits, options in futures, the markets associated with such forms of wealth, the realities defined by such markets, such as prices, and so forth. It is right to speak of true marriage, perfectly or imperfectly understood and instantiated in various historically given forms, but talk of the true nature of a loan is appropriate only as saying something about certain legal or other conventional institutions current in certain societies and similarly organized societies in certain other times and places. Of course, institutions which thus have *only* a 'historically relative' nature remain subject to assessment by unchanging moral principles of fairness, respect for basic goods, and so forth. The principle that it is wrong—unfair—for one who does not need property to take advantage of another's need by charging him for it is unchanging, and in all historical circumstances makes it wrong to charge interest on a loan in virtue of the very making of the loan (rather than in virtue of some factor related to the loan which provides a basis for fair compensation, for example transaction costs, premiums for insurance (or an equivalent allowance as self-insurance) against non-payment, taxes, inflation, and the forgoing of other good uses to which the property might otherwise have been put). When a capital market develops, so that funds can readily be put out for shares in productive enterprises or for bonds whose return is linked with the return on productive enterprises, the nature of money changes. From being a material object whose bearer uses it up in exchange, typically for consumables,[61] it becomes at least equally capital, a means of sharing in the risks and rewards of productive enterprise in a non-stationary (non-equilibrium) economy. Thus, while the moral norm specifying what is always unfair in charging for a loan remains unchanged, lending money at 12 per cent per annum interest within one socially given form will be

---

[60] Such an account is offered in *LCL* ch. 9, questions A and B.

[61] But not always, and this common feature of usurious lending is not of the essence of usury: see Langholm, *The Aristotelian Analysis of Usury*, 134–48. [On usury, see now *Aquinas*, 200–10.]

immorally usurious while lending at 12 per cent within another socially given institution (form of lending) will not. Outwardly similar or identical *behaviour* in 1292 and 1992 can involve essentially different objects (both in the third order and the fourth) and different relationships between the wills of those engaging in it and the relevant human goods and principles of reasonableness: same behaviour, perhaps even the same cultural vocabulary ('interest on a loan'), but different intentions and choices and thus different *actions* (acts *in specie moris*); and hence the possibility of different moral judgments accurately applying the very same moral norms.

Again, conceptual clarification not infrequently transforms moral judgments and the options with which they are concerned, particularly when the options are participation in complex forms of social life. So a correct but undifferentiated moral judgment on the position which mingled religious freedom with indifferentism[62] can be transformed into two correct moral judgments on alternatives now adequately differentiated.[63] Again, emotional biases and established social structures which blocked differentiation, for example between penal servitude and chattel *servitudo*, can be removed by changed social conditions, allowing the latent moral insight to be clearly articulated, as in the specific moral absolute which excludes slavery. Or new or apparently new forms of behaviour, such as taking the pill, can raise the question whether they are instances of a familiar and more or less well-understood form of action, such as contraception, a question which can clarify and deepen understanding of that action and of precisely why one does wrong in willing it. Finally, other new behaviour may prove, on analysis, to be indeed a new form of action, such as ('in vitro') baby-production—a new form of action, but one which turns out to possess a morally decisive feature in common with the (fairly recently clarified) moral evil of slavery.[64]

Underlying many of these particular conceptual developments is the distinction between intending and permitting. The history of that

[62] Or with the opinion that religious liberty entails that religious vows are neither morally binding nor even morally proper (e.g. the decision of the French revolutionary Constituent Assembly of 12/13 February 1790); or with the opinion that liberty of forming and publicly expressing opinion must be absolutely untrammelled (e.g. the teachings of Lamennais's liberal Catholic newspaper *L'Avenir* beginning in 1830 and condemned by Pope Gregory xvi's *Mirari Vos* in 1832: see Harrison, *Religious Liberty and Contraception*, 34–42).

[63] In short, religious practices which though based on false belief are compatible with the rights of others, with the public peace and orderly coexistence in true justice, and with public morality, must be permitted by the state; religious practices which do not meet those preconditions should not be permitted: Vatican II, *Dignitatis Humanae*, paras 2 and 7.

[64] See *Donum Vitae* (Congregation for the Doctrine of the Faith, Instruction on Respect for Human Life in its Origin and on the Dignity of Procreation, 22 February 1987), II.B.4–5 (AAS 80 [1988] 70–102 at 90–4); see also 1988e(ii) at 95–7; [and essays II.16 (1993a) and II.17 (2000b)].

distinction is significant for any reflection on the relation between theology and theology's sources. The distinction between intending and permitting is appreciated but scarcely articulated by Hippolytus of Rome and Origen, emergent in Augustine and Fulgentius, insisted upon in John Damascene, clear but not thematized and generalized in St Thomas, taught by Trent, and thematized but with inadequate attention to the distinction between behaviour (*in genere naturae*) and action (*in specie moris*) by the late- and neo-scholastics.[65] To the Old Testament, as to Philo Judaeus, it is all but unknown. So, since God creates everything, the Old Testament seems to assert that he causes evil. But authors should not be read as asserting what they had no clear concept to assert. The statements in question mean something that is both right and wrong— undifferentiated (in a neutral historical description), confused (in a philosophical account). An exegesis and hermeneutics taking seriously both the unity of the inspired scriptures and the still wider *analogia fidei* will not suppress the historical fact of the confusion in the sources, but will allow their mediation of the right proposition to emerge as an implication of the revelation taken as a whole and understood with that 'growth in understanding' (*perceptio cresc[ens]*) of which Vatican II speaks in *Dei Verbum* 8.

VII

The historical developments in moral matters which I have just mentioned and briefly illustrated require for their clarification a set of distinctions fundamental to a sound moral philosophy and theology. I have mentioned most of them: (1) between reason and feeling, and in particular between intelligible goods which are reasons for action and the merely emotionally motivating goals of feelings; (2) between intelligible goods intrinsic to human persons and their communion, and intelligible goods which have their intelligible attractiveness mediately, as means to the instantiation of basic goods; (3) between each distinct basic reason for action, each basic human good, and the at least heuristic ideal of the unity of those reasons in the overall reason for choosing which can be called 'integral human fulfilment'—the good of the whole human person and of all human persons and communities; (4) between the first principles of practical reasoning and the further 'intermediate' principles (such as the Golden Rule, or the Pauline principle that evil may not be done for the sake of good) in accordance with which the pursuit of basic human goods through

[65] See 1991c, 74–7.

chosen acts has the thoroughly reasonable character of full compatibility with integral human fulfilment—moral rightness;[66] (5) between types of act specified by physical characteristics (*in specie naturae*) or by merely conventional descriptions, criteria, or classifications, and types of act specified precisely by the description which they have (*in specie moris*) in the practical deliberations of the agent, that is, by what he intends as end and chooses as means in the proposal which he adopts by choice;[67] and (6) the closely related distinction between what is intended and chosen (whether as end or as means) and what is knowingly caused, permitted, accepted, but not intended—sometimes expressed (though at the risk of seeming to refer to physical characteristics as such) as the distinction between what is 'directly' and 'indirectly' willed.[68]

Reflection on these structuring ethical concepts enables us to understand not only the continuity of moral doctrine, but also that diversity of moral cultures which even today provides moral relativists or sceptics with their principal argument. For since the intelligence which should make these distinctions must do so in a context confused by images, feelings, culturally formed concepts, and vested interests (starting with one's own), it is easy prey to confusion and mistake. But if even slightly confused or deflected in fundamentals, practical reason will reach deformed conclusions in the many particular situations of individual and social choice, and these deformations will in turn obscure the fundamentals for whole eras and cultures.

---

[66] On the various formulations of the Pauline principle, see *FoE* 109–27; for a further defence of the attribution of this principle to (inter alios) St Paul (in Romans 3: 8) see 1991c 59–63.

[67] The importance of this distinction for a proper understanding of the ethics of St Thomas, and of Christianity, has been rightly insisted upon by, e.g., Rhonheimer, *Natur als Grundlage der Moral*, 61–2, 81, 91–7, 327–45, 352–3, 367–74, 375–7, 398–400. To illustrate it (by reference to the Golden Rule), consider a sharp blow to one's back by a colleague—struck jocularly and condescendingly to 'congratulate' one on a *faux pas*; or struck, perhaps over-anxiously, but with friendly intent to get one's attention and save one from compounding the *faux pas*. The Golden Rule of fairness cannot be applied to the behaviour *in genere naturae*: a sharp blow struck to a man's back by a colleague. But it can and must be applied to the two different acts which I described by describing the choices they respectively carry out.

[68] For the equivalence, in this context, of 'direct' and 'as an end or as a means', see Pius XII, Discourse to the St Luke Medical-Biological Union, 12 November 1944, *Discorsi e Radiomessagi*, VI (1944–5) 191–2, cited in Paul VI, *Humanae Vitae*, n. 14, and in the Congregation for the Doctrine of the Faith, *Declaration on Procured Abortion* (1974), para. 7 at n. 15 ('Pius XII clearly excluded all direct abortion, that is, abortion which is either an end or a means'); also Congregation for the Doctrine of the Faith, *Donum Vitae*, 22 February 1987, at n. 20. To illustrate this distinction (by reference to the Pauline principle), consider the administration of a certain quantity of analgesic drugs—this may be done for the sole purpose of relieving pain, though in the knowledge that life will be shortened; or it may be done for the purpose of shortening life so that death will bring relief from pain. Here there is not one human act, but two different acts according as the identical behaviour carries out two differ-ent choices, the latter (but not the former) a choice to do evil—to destroy or damage, or to impede the continuance of, human life—for the sake of good. [And see essay II.13 (2001a).]

But a characteristic pre-Vatican II moral theological treatise such as Josef Fuchs, *Theologia Moralis Generalis, pars prima* (1960)[69] deployed not one of the six distinctions, and examined not one of the developments and changes in moral understanding and moral matter which I have mentioned. Treatises such as this were very deficient in theoretical underpinning. Their conception of the first principles of practical reason was confused, obscure, question-begging; their exposition of reason's advance from first principles to further principles, norms, and judgments was almost non-existent, and where attempted was both incoherent and inconsequent (a series of *non sequiturs*). The work of inducing true foundational practical principles, of dialectically defending them against objection, of identifying the true premises of moral judgment in practical principles and analysis of morally significant acts, and of carrying forward valid inferences from these premises, all had to be done again. This work (in progress) illuminates the good sense of the moral-doctrinal tradition and the points at which it invites development.

For productive work in moral theology, a properly understood historical consciousness remains of the first importance in many ways. Some I have tried to suggest. But there is one which I have left almost unspoken. A fruitful Catholic moral theology takes seriously the figure who has virtually disappeared from the 'moral theology' books of those who styled themselves historically conscious.[70] I mean Jesus of Nazareth, whose historical choices of fidelity to his vocation last through history as redemption and sacraments, whose moral perfection reveals the possibilities of human fulfilment otherwise known only uncertainly and with admixture of error, whose promises and resurrection are our warrant for believing that integral human fulfilment is no merely heuristic ideal but a kingdom which our own choices are even now building up (or bearing us away from), and who in all these ways not only ratifies the natural moral law but makes intelligible certain options and norms otherwise senseless such as mercy and love of enemies. He, having assumed human nature, is thus in a certain

[69] To call it characteristic is not to deny that Fuchs's treatise has some rather personal, indeed more or less problematic, features: e.g. the emphasis on the 'call of God in the situation' (*Deus vocans in situatione concreta*, 40); the claim that, quite ordinarily, a man's situation itself has a '*sensus et intentio*' which come from God and are to be 'realized' by that man here and now (40–1); the claim that in *synderesis* 'the whole man is present to himself, in the depth ("*scintilla*") of his soul' (154); and the claim that there is a real and important distinction between my judgments of antecedent conscience about the-act-to-be-done-by-me (which he thinks somehow 'theoretical' judgments) and my judgments of antecedent conscience about my-doing-the-act (which he thinks truly 'practical' judgments) (164, 152).

[70] An extreme case is O'Connell, *Principles for a Catholic Morality*. Gula, *Reason Informed by Faith*, 172–97 offers some discussion of the significance of Jesus for moral theology; the poverty of this treatment may be fairly appreciated by comparing it with that in a work of comparable length, Grisez and Shaw, *Fulfilment in Christ*, 222–90. Far richer still, of course, is *CMP* 459–626.

basic way united with every human being; by being perfect in fulfilment of that nature he is the key and focus and *telos* of human history, and discloses man to man himself.[71] This disclosure is not of the thin, formal, and partial nature which some hope to find by 'transcendental deduction'. It is a disclosure whose content and implications cannot be theologically known without drawing upon all the resources of our knowledge, natural and revealed, of human fulfilment in moral goodness. And it is a disclosure from which we would be cut off unless the Gospels, having the historicity the Church unfailingly affirms, communicated to us a sincere and true account of the human life, death, and resurrection of the Word, the Jesus Christ of faith and history.[72]

NOTE

In 2009a sec. V, after reporting Anscombe's view (see now essay II.3 at 72 n. 17), I said:

> Was she right to say that that sort of removal of obstacles is 'the only possible use of a learned clever man' (such as her), and to leave everything else to revelation and faith as such? She asked 'Could a learned clever man inform me, on the authority of his learning, that the evidence is that God has spoken? No.' (*FHG* 18). Her scepticism about the *probative* force of the traditional evidences of and preambles to faith has a good deal in common with Newman's in the last chapter of his *A Grammar of Assent*, and her 'royal road to the Catholic faith,' through the Old Testament (*FHG* xxv; *FHG* 34–39), has much in common with Newman's in that chapter. But even if the learned are not in a position truthfully to say 'the evidence is…' (= all the evidence points to this, or at least the weight of the evidence excludes any reasonable doubt), must it not still be the case that they, or the relevant specialists among them, should be (and are) in a position truthfully to say 'there is good evidence that God has spoken, and these are the elements of this evidence'?

---

[71] Vatican II, *Gaudium et Spes*, 10, 22, 45.

[72] *Dei Verbum*, 19 (for a translation, see p. 260 n. 26 below):

…Ecclesia firmiter et constantissime tenuit ac tenet quattuor recensita Evangelia, quorum historicitatem incunctanter affirmat, fideliter tradere quae Iesus Dei Filius, vitam inter homines degens, ad aeternum eorum salutem reapse fecit et docuit, usque in diem qua assumptus est.…Auctores…quattuor evangelia conscripserunt…formam denique praeconii retinentes, ita semper ut vera et sincera de Iesu nobiscum communicarent.

Cf. Instruction *Sancta Mater Ecclesia*, AAS 56 (1964) at 713–16.

10

FAITH, MORALS, AND THOMAS MORE[*]

In the afternoon of Low Sunday 12th April, a week after Easter 1534, Thomas More was summoned to appear next morning, at Lambeth Palace, to take the public oath required of all adult subjects by the new Act of Succession—an oath to observe and maintain 'the whole effect and contents' of the Act of Succession, which declared that the marriage of Henry VIII and Catherine of Aragon was against God's law and utterly void notwithstanding the Papal dispensation in reliance on which it had been entered upon twenty-five years before. That Sunday evening, and again in the morning, More went to confession. After morning Mass he said goodbye to his family and went to Lambeth Palace, then as now the Archbishop of Canterbury's residence. The Commissioners for the administration of the Oath had summoned, that Monday morning, a large number of London clergy and one layman, More. And it was More who was called in first. He silently read through the Act of Succession, and the Oath drawn up under the Great Seal, and refused to swear that oath. After failing to get him to state his reasons, the Commissioners sent him from the room to reflect.

Out of the windows of another room in the Palace, looking into the garden below, he could see—as 'doubtless he was meant to—the clergy of London passing through the garden; most were cheerful enough, slapping each other on the back and calling for beer at the Archbishop's buttery'.[1] All took the oath, save one who was hurried through the garden on his way to the Tower, where he would languish for three years until he accepted the Reformed and Protestant order.

Why did More refuse to take the oath, incurring the automatic penalty of life imprisonment (which began, in effect, that morning), and

---

[*] 2003c, an address in August 1989 to the Thomas More Society, Melbourne.
[1] Kenny, *Thomas More*, 72. Kenny's summary closely follows the account given by More in a letter written by him in the Tower to his daughter Margaret Roper on 17 April 1534: see Wegemer and Smith, *A Thomas More Source Book*, 311–15.

confiscation of all his goods? His reason, I believe, was one which neither then nor later could More explain without incurring the immediate penalty of death for treason. And when, more than a year later, he was found guilty of treason and was thus in a position to speak freely, the focal issue had shifted by virtue of the later statute under which he was condemned to death, the Act of Supremacy. So More never did directly explain his original and really decisive decision, the decision to refuse the Oath. And historians and biographers have often been obscure about it. But the reason, I think, is clear and not in doubt. More believed, in 1534 as in 1529 when he became Lord Chancellor, that Henry's marriage to Catherine was consistent with divine law and perfectly valid, whether because of the Papal dispensation or because Catherine's marriage to Henry's brother Arthur had in fact never been consummated. More did not think that the validity of Henry's marriage to Catherine was an issue about which all honest and competent persons must agree; but he had made his own study of the theological issues and had himself reached the conclusion that the marriage was valid. (If he needed confirmation, he may have found it in the judgment of the Pope, delivered only a few weeks before Easter, after years of delay: the marriage was indeed valid.) To take the Oath would be to swear that he, More, maintained the marriage to be invalid, when in his own mind he maintained it to be valid. Thus, taking the Oath would be, for him, asserting publicly, and with God as his witness before men, a deliberate falsehood, intended to deceive others about the state of his own belief—in short, it would be to lie.

So: More went to the Tower on a point of morality, the absoluteness, the unconditional truth and force, of the quite ordinary and universal (though specific) moral norm which excludes lying, most clearly lying on oath.

The Reformation, whose incoming tide we see if we stand with More looking down into the garden, or if we go back with him to face the Commissioners again, was among other things a crisis of morality—symbolized in a mild but real enough and representative form by the Chief Commissioner, Thomas Cranmer, the 500th anniversary of whose birth was celebrated (rather quietly) in 1989 in England. There he sits (as More chooses to stand), the Archbishop of Canterbury who less than a year ago swore publicly an oath of obedience to the Pope, having just previously sworn secretly not to mean or intend that great public oath—in other words, who lied, publicly and on oath, in order to secure the opportunity to advance decisively the Protestant cause in England.

More's own catalogue of what he calls 'Luther's conclusions and most shameful opinions', a catalogue he drew up in his *Dialogue concerning*

Heresies in 1529, gives pride of place to the crisis of morals inaugurated by Luther's teachings:

Item, he teacheth that only faith sufficeth to our salvation with our baptism, *without good works.* He saith also that it is sacrilege to go about to please God with any works and not with faith only.

Item, that no man can do any good work.

Item, that the good and righteous man alway sinneth in doing well.

Item, that no sin can damn any Christian man, but only lack of belief. For he saith that our faith suppeth up [consumes] all our sins how great soever they be.

Item, he teacheth that no man hath no [any] free will, nor can anything do therewith, not though the help of grace be joined thereunto; but that everything that we do, good and bad, we do nothing at all there in ourself, but only suffer God to do all things in us, good and bad, as wax is wrought into an image or a candle by a man's hand, without anything doing thereto itself.

Item, he saith that God is as verily the author and cause of the evil will of Judas in betraying Christ, as of the good will of Christ in suffering of His passion.[2]

The Council of Trent, twenty years later, was to pick out that last statement of Luther's for explicit condemnation, along of course with many others. Today, the ecumenical movement may encourage us to suppose that a list such as More's or Trent's of Luther's errors is a list of regrettable misunderstandings. But such a supposition would be rash. The possibility that a laudable desire for reconciliation between Christians today leads those who review the Reformation controversies to misunderstand the historical data is at least as likely a possibility as that the rage and shock of dissent and controversy led participants in those controversies to misunderstand the fundamentals of their opponents' positions. The possibility that someone of the intelligence, learning, self-discipline, and balance of Thomas More understood Luther better, and represented his views more accurately, than do most late-twentieth-century theologians is greatly enhanced by this undeniable fact: that the principal positions of the early Reformers, such as Luther, Zwingli, Tyndale, and Oecolampadius, are positions which during the succeeding centuries, and in some cases during the succeeding *decades*, were more or less thoroughly abandoned by the mainstream Protestant churches. Who today holds anything really like Luther's position on predestination; on the utter absence of free will; on total depravity; on salvation by faith alone; or even on the independent entire sufficiency of Scripture?

The Protestant Reformation was above all a movement for sincerity and simplicity in Christian faith and life. Why did it attract the opposition,

---

[2] Campbell, *Erasmus, Tyndale, and More*, 150–1, quoting More, *Dialogue concerning Heresies [Tyndale]* [1529], bk IV, ch. 2, where the list of items continues.

pre-eminently, of a man whose Christian faith and life were of truly outstanding sincerity, inwardness, uncluttered simplicity, and freedom from empty forms? Let me hold that question in play while raising the question suggested by a repeated, almost mocking comment of More's latest biographer, Richard Marius, in his very interesting, in some respects perceptive and considerable, biography—the comment that More's thousands of pages of controversial writing against the Protestants (many hundreds of those pages written even while he was a Lord Chancellor who cleared up and kept cleared the great backlog of cases in Chancery) were a labour futile and pointless. Why did More write so? Why did he regard the Reformers and their cause with the horror that kept him moving through his vast project of refuting each and every one of their teachings?

It wasn't a conservative's love of or respect for what he had been taught like his parents before him, or for the social forms in which he had grown up, a love and respect which shies away from questioning their foundations and from seeking an exact understanding of what is essential in them and what contingent, of their vulnerability to critique and reform. For example: the same English Catholic hierarchy who in the mid-1530s would abjectly defect, with most of their clerisy, had in the previous decade (as before) rejected the project of translating the Bible into the vernacular; but that was a project warmly favoured by More (and accomplished by the Catholics in France, Germany, and Venice many years before the Reformation). Or again: More's reflective testing of the moral, political, and economic foundations of social organization in his *Utopia* needs no retelling here.

So More's response to the Reformers is not conservative. It is the response of someone who, unlike the English bishops (less learned than him) and unlike Erasmus (more learned than him), understood that the Protestant demands for Reformation in faith and morals put in question, more or less unwittingly, the very foundations of Christianity, of belief in a God who both creates out of nothing and discloses himself in human history by the definitive public revelation constituted by the incarnation, life, and deeds of Jesus of Nazareth, God made man. More's protest is against a subjectivizing of faith, against finding the criterion of belief in one's own inward experience, rather than in the reception of God's revelation by the apostles and its transmission through history by the common corps (body) of Christendom, the Church gathered about and led by the successors of the apostles as provided for by Jesus Christ.

The Reformation succeeded in overthrowing Catholic faith, sacraments, and worship just to the extent that it persuaded Christians to put that faith and sacramental order to the test of experience, of feeling what it does or does not *do for you*. As Tyndale put it in his *Answer to Sir Thomas More*

(1531), the question whether the Pope and the bishops in communion with him are the Church, with authority to teach definitively, is to be put to the test of one's own experience:

Judge whether it is possible that any good should come out of their dumb ceremonies and sacraments unto thy soul. Judge their penances, pilgrimages, pardons, purgatory, praying to posts, dumb blessings, dumb absolutions, their dumb patterings and howling, their dumb strange holy gestures, with all their dumb disguising [vestments], their satisfactions and justifyings. And because thou findest them false in so many things, trust them in nothing.[3]

The Catholic sacraments are dumb (Tyndale expects his readers to agree) because, in the precise sense of today's idiom, they don't *speak to me*, they *do nothing for me*. Catholicism offers me, says Tyndale, only an '*historical faith*', a faith which he defines as hanging on 'the truth and honesty of the teller, or [on] the common fame [opinion] and consent of many'. What I want and can have (he says) is a 'feeling faith'—'a sure feeling, and therefore ever fruitful'.[4]

More accepts that Catholic faith is indeed an historical faith, a faith which trusts those who witnessed Christ's words and deeds, his miracles, his prayer, his suffering, his resurrection, and witnessed to their reality by preaching them even to martyrdom, handing on their own supremely historical faith to us, through the transmission of the whole deposit of faith in the unwritten traditions and written Scriptures of the Church. The Reformers may believe that their feeling of faith is true, objective, common, and communicable, because it is communicated by the Holy Spirit. But they can't know about the Holy Spirit, save from the teachings of Jesus; and these they admit they can't know, save from the Scriptures; and the Scriptures they can't rationally judge to be reliable and true, save by relying on the judgment made, many centuries ago, by the Church, whose books they were and are, the judgment that *these* books, in all their assertions, are reliable and true while countless other purported testimonies to Jesus were misleading and false. And the same Church which made that definitive judgment on the canon of Scripture offers equally its definitive judgments on the meaning of those Scriptures, and on matters (such as abortion) on which the Scriptures say nothing explicit but about which the Church's tradition has spoken from times even before the New Testament writings were half completed.

---

[3] Campbell, 203 quoting Tyndale, *Works*, III 8–9; for More's response, see his *Confutation of Tyndale's Answer*, bk VI, 631–4.
[4] Campbell, 204 quoting Tyndale, *Works*, III 50; for More's response, see More, *Confutation*, bk VII, 741–63, 780–3.

Spurring More on, then, is a sense of the sheer folly, the muddle, the intellectual confusion, of a movement which will not recognize its own incoherence in relying on the Church's definitive judgment about what is and what is not Scripture while denying that the Church can ever judge the truth of anything definitively. Similarly stark muddles were manifest to More in the rejection of free will and in other principal positions of Luther and his followers.

It was also clear to More that such muddles could be attractive and effective only because each intellectual component, each proposition, in the overall incoherent teaching was necessary in order to *rationalize* a position reached and held *not for reasons* but to answer to, to satisfy, to express *feelings.*

More wrote and wrote. He did so because to write for publication is to act in the public realm, to participate in the realm of common, ideally of *universal* discourse, about things which are in that realm as the faith of the Gospel supremely is. What is reasonable can integrate feelings if it is not dominated by feelings, by private experience, but expresses the insights and judgments which any reasonable being would make on the available evidence, including the evidence of witnesses. What the Catholic Church hands on in her faith and worship expresses the insights and judgments of a vast succession of reasonable human persons who received, tested, and handed on the whole tradition (*including* the Scriptures) in which the divine act of publicly accessible revelation is to be made effective until the end of human history. For that act was ineffective unless what was taught by Jesus was heard and appropriated, and what was done by him was noticed and appropriated. The apostles' appropriation of what they had heard and seen took them time. But the act of divine revelation was itself completed when its appropriation by them was complete, in other words by the time of the death of the last apostle. From that time on, our access to the divine revelation is by appropriating what the apostles had appropriated, no more and no less; and an interpretation of it is acceptable only if consistent with the whole of it, and with the fact that it is borne through history by the community whose inauguration is one of the principal subjects of Jesus's discourse and action.

The deposit of faith is available to every individual member of that community, and indeed to everyone who could become a member by his or her own free choice; but each individual's private understanding of it will be irrational if it is not coherent with the understanding of it which has been accepted and proposed definitively by those who have been charged with transmitting it in its entirety, and those saints, fathers, and doctors of the Church who have appropriated it integrally. The whole Gospel speaks to the individual heart—by the power of the Spirit, More insists, and not 'fruitlessly'—but it belongs essentially to the vast public realm inhabited by the faithful of *every* era. The faithful of every era, then, participate in a vast common and public discourse with each other, and with the more or less unbelieving world to whom the Gospel must be proposed (as by St Paul to the Athenian intelligentsia), and with 'the new men' (*novi homines*, 'new people', as More calls them), Christians who have fallen away into what we call dissent and More called heresy.

I go back to More, in Lambeth Palace that hot April Monday morning. What had he said to the Commissioners when asked to swear the Oath? As he wrote to his daughter a few days later:

I showed unto them that my purpose was not to put any fault either in the Act or any man that made it, or in the oath or any man that swore it, nor to condemn the conscience of any other man. But as for myself in good faith my conscience so moved me in the matter…that I could not swear without the jeoparding of my soul to perpetual damnation.[5]

In the late twentieth century, the term 'conscience' is likely to be heard, as it is used by many, in a way profoundly affected not only by the Protestant appeal to inner experience, but also by the post-Enlightenment conception of a world in which the only source of meaning and value is the human mind, which settles meaning and value by its own, autonomous, self-constituting and self-constituted act, an act expressive of its own inner experience, its sense of individuality and selfhood. That conception of conscience is attributed to More by Robert Bolt in the play and film *A Man for All Seasons*. But, as Anthony Kenny argues in the last chapter of his little book, *Thomas More*, this conception of conscience is utterly opposed to More's. For More, as for St Paul and St Thomas Aquinas and John Henry Newman and the Second Vatican Council, conscience is nothing other than (i) one's intelligent grasp, one's understanding of the fundamental forms of intrinsic good and evil and fundamental principles of practical reasonableness, of right and wrong, and then (ii) one's judgment, in particular situations, about how those principles truly *apply* to the situation. When one's understanding of good and evil, right or wrong, has been stabilized and clarified and supplemented by the divine revelation which the Church preaches, one will understand those principles as precepts or norms of *divine law*. As Aquinas says, and Thomas More certainly agrees:

The binding force of conscience, even mistaken conscience, is the same thing as the binding force of the law of God. For one's conscience does not say that X is to

---

[5] Wegemer and Smith, *Sourcebook*, 311–12.

be done or Y avoided unless one believes that Y is contrary to, or X in accordance with, the law of God.[6]

In refusing the Oath, More was (I believe) relying on two conscientious judgments: (a) that the marriage to Catherine was valid and in conformity with divine law, and (b) that to declare on oath that something is *not* the case when one actually judges that it *is* the case is to lie, which is always against divine law. In saying that he did not denounce the conscience of others, he was saying no more than that he considered it possible for someone to come to a mistaken conclusion about Catherine's marriage (namely the conclusion that Catherine's marriage was invalid) without dishonesty, bad faith, corruption of conscience. Such a person, in taking the Oath, would neither be lying (as More would be if *he* took the Oath) nor manifesting wilfully corrupt conscience—though such a person would, in More's judgment, be mistaken. And, of course, More is not for a moment denying that many of those who took the Oath were, no doubt, lying, and many others, who were not lying, were in sinful bad faith, having preferred political convenience, or the like, to a careful and impartial inquiry into the truth about Catherine's marriage in particular, or about the Church's theology and discipline of marriage in general.

One of the most brilliant tales in More's wonderful *Dialogue of Comfort against Tribulation*, written in his final year of imprisonment in the Tower, recalls in homely terms how susceptible one's conscience is to being corrupted, whether by the cynicism and self-love of Father Renard (Father Fox) and Master Wolf or by the blinding stupidity of poor scrupulous Master Ass.[7] More's actual opinion about the leading Reformers of his day was that many of them, though he wished it were not so, were in bad faith, had sinfully 'framed themselves a conscience' (cf. *Dialogue*, 187) to suit the dictates of pride, resentment, or lust. But remember that that opinion of More's concerned not those who judged a disputable matter such as the validity of Henry's marriage differently from himself, but those who set aside the whole common consensus of historic Christian faith save where it coincided with their feelings and their too easily supposed direct private inspirations by the Holy Spirit.

The crisis of faith and morals in our day is in some respects more profound and far-reaching than the crisis in which More lived and died. One of its manifestations is the misunderstanding and abuse of the idea of conscience in relation to Christian moral teachings—particularly those

---

[6] *In epistolam ad Romanos,* c. 14 lectio 2 (ad v.5).
[7] *Dialogue of Comfort Against Tribulation,* 93–8 (in the very readable, modernized but not 'edited' edition by Monica Stevens).

teachings, about sex and about respect for innocent human life, which contradict the morals of the surrounding non-Christian and half-Christian culture. Of course it is true, as Aquinas says in the most explicit terms, that if someone after serious reflection judges that he *should* contracept or she should abort her baby (Aquinas's examples are: fornicate and deny Christ's divinity), then he or she sins gravely in not acting accordingly. But if one is going to recall that truth, one had better recall its companion: if one reaches such a judgment one has made a grievous moral error, is entangled in ethical incoherence and corruption, has wandered away from God's law and therefore from God's wisdom and from the terms of the divine offer of friendship and adoptive sonship; and, if one has heard the Gospel, preached in its integrity, such an error is scarcely possible without a sinful failure of faith, hope, and love, threatening salvation at its root. For, to repeat, in forming one's conscience one is not so much seeking to form oneself, or to secure one's personal integrity and authenticity, as to discern the truth about the meaning and worth which human existence is meant by its divine author to have, and does in each human life have, for good or ill, for heaven-haven or shipwreck.

But the follies of a legalistic moral and pastoral theology, which swings between presenting morality as if it were ecclesiastical law and proposing conscience as a licence to ferret out loopholes, are follies quite superficial, compared with other expressions and sources of today's crisis in moral theology and pastoral practice.

Some of those expressions and sources are interestingly close, even in content, to the moral teachings which More and soon the Council of Trent had to confront and reject. Thirsting for the feeling of certitude of salvation, Luther glorified and made central to Christian life a certain experiential surrender to Christ in faith, a feeling faith which was not itself chosen and which rendered particular free choices of moral good and ill, right and wrong, at best irrelevant. Quite reminiscent of that is the teaching of those who today profess as Catholic a theology in which no sin can be mortal, can exclude one from the grace of God's friendship, however freely and knowingly it is committed, unless it amounts to a reversal of one's so-called 'fundamental option', an orientation of one's whole self towards or, as the case may be, away from God, an orientation which (on one theologically widespread version of the theory) occurs, mysteriously, below the level of consciousness and reflective self-consciousness and is indeed not itself a free choice between alternatives. A Catholic theology of course knows of a fundamental option, and identifies it plainly enough: it is the option of faith, and it is a free choice to accept, consciously, the proposal to believe in God and to accept his offer of adoption into his family, here on earth his Church.

This faith is not itself abandoned when one freely and consciously makes a seriously immoral choice, such as adultery or abortion or contraception: but it is rendered ineffectual—'dead' is Trent's term (after James 2: 20)—because by an immoral choice of that sort one turns one's back on the divine friendship whose existence and availability one's faith acknowledges. Only the choice, by God's grace, to repent—again an unmysterious particular free choice—enables that friendship to be resumed. Thus Trent, John Paul II, the Church's millennial sacramental practice, the New Testament, the tradition of the Two Ways—of Life and of Death—which we find even earlier than most of the New Testament...

But in the teaching of the new men, which you will find amply represented, and virtually unopposed, in the theology and catechetical shelves of (I dare say) your local Catholic booksellers, the neo-Lutherite conception of fundamental option is only one thread in a web of positions that offer to replace the Catholic conception of morals, which More would have acknowledged as his own, whether in writings of the second-century fathers or documents of the Second Vatican Council and John Paul II. All the threads in this replacement web radiate out from, and circle about, a certain state of experience and a certain conception of the foundational role of experience in the reality of faith.

The widespread but unjustifiable theory of fundamental option as the only instantiation of mortal sin articulates a recoil from, a passionate unwillingness to accept, the tension of living in a relationship (with God) which can be broken off by a single, simple choice to do what one's friends are doing, and restored by a single choice to repent, to be reconciled, for example in a standard, mundane sacramental act. And what shall we say of the widespread theory that there are no specific moral absolutes, no exceptionless negative norms or precepts, but that all the precepts which every previous generation of Jews and Christians took to be (when exactly stated) unconditional, exceptionless, are really no more than generalizations of the way in which, subject to exceptions to be identified by individual conscience, the one true moral principle applies—the principle that one should bring about the states of affairs which involve greater good, or less evil in the world? This theory, which has no support in the Church's tradition or Scripture, and which is exposed to devastating philosophical objections well developed by secular as well as Christian philosophers, is supported really by an appeal to the 'experience of the faithful today', of those contemporary Christians who feel that there are situations in which they can do more good, or avoid greater harm, by aborting babies, trying out sexual compatibility before marriage, winning wars or securing peace by carrying out or planning massacres of civilians, finding a new sexual partner after a failed marriage, contracepting to prevent the bad effects of having another baby now—and so forth.

These opinions of contemporary Christians are ascribed by the theological 'new men' to a movement of the Spirit, who is guiding the faithful to mirror faithfully these moral opinions of the surrounding pagan culture of the wealthy West and the Marxist East, and who is not guiding the Pope or the bishops faithful to his teaching on these matters. Divine revelation they locate really in religious experience and conscientious judgments, witnessed by a supposed contemporary 'consensus' or *'sensus fidelium'*, and is only *imperfectly symbolized* in scripture and traditional dogmas and doctrines on matters of faith and morals. To the extent that the Church's magisterium clings (as they put it) to a different conception of revelation and therefore reasserts the old doctrine, including moral doctrines, in the very sense and with the same content [judgment] that they had in the tradition—*eodem sensu, eadem sententia*[8]—to that extent the magisterium (they say) is a less truthful witness to revelation than is the *'consensus theologorum'*, the consensus of those theologians who reflect 'contemporary Christian experience' and articulate it directly to and for 'contemporary Catholics', thereby correcting the magisterium (partly expressly and mainly by extensive omissions and tacit negations).

If this view of revelation and faith finds no support in Vatican II or the tradition, no matter—it can be given the support of a version of John XXIII's opening address to that Council, in which (they say) the Pope declared that what matters is (only) the *substance* of the tradition. The Pope (they say) never said to the Council what he is recorded in the *Acta Apostolicae Sedis* and in *Gaudium et Spes* 62 (the Council's final document) as saying to the Council—that the Church and Council and faithful must hold— *eodem sensu, eadem sententia*—to the *very meaning* of, and *position affirmed* in, traditional doctrines. The new men's favoured version of Pope John's address you will find in the Abbott and Gallagher *Documents of Vatican II*, p. 715 (fourth paragraph; but cf. the first paragraph on p. 715).[9] It is argued to be authentic in Peter Hebblethwaite's widely marketed biography (published 1984) of John XXIII, which claims that the Vatican bureaucracy subsequently falsified the Pope's opening address by inserting into the

---

[8]   1 Corinthians 1: 10 (Vulgate); More, *Dialogue concerning Heresies*, II, 9; GS 62.

[9]   The origins of this version are an unofficial Italian translation [of an early draft of the address] published by *L'Osservatore Romano* alongside the Pope's own Latin words on the day after the address. [On Hebblethwaite's wholesale fabrication and falsification of history, see now my letters to *The Tablet* (London), 14 December 1991, 4 and 18 January, and 1 and 8 February 1992, and Hebblethwaite's letters of 11 and 25 January 1992; the true content of the tape recording (to which Hebblethwaite's book had appealed) emerged, along with much else to the same effect, in the course of this correspondence.]

Acta, the Vatican's official Gazette, the words which you find attributed to
Pope John there and in *Gaudium et Spes* and in the Council's own official
record of the Pope's address. When one discovers that no changes were
made in the version in the *Acta*; that *L'Osservatore Romano*'s report of John
XXIII's address the day after it was given (*Oss. Rom.*, 12 October 1962,
p. 2 col. 3) says exactly what the *Acta* weeks later said [and exactly what
the Vatican Radio's tape recording of the Pope's address records]; that
Hebblethwaite's tale of subsequent curial falsification is itself, therefore, a
reckless falsehood; and that the mythical version of John XXIII's address is
far more widely quoted and known than the one which he actually delivered
(reaffirming, at this precise point, the First Vatican Council's teaching on
revelation and the immutability of the affirmed content of doctrine); one
then experiences something of More's *exasperation* at the sheer scale of
falsification of Catholic teaching to be found in the Reformers' writings,
and at the success of bad money in driving out good in the small change of
theological currency which finds its way into everyone's pocket or purse.

Against the conception of revelation, faith, and doctrine proposed or,
more often, presupposed by the new men much may be said. But in meeting
it at the level to which and at which it appeals, Thomas More's constantly
reiterated appeal is most helpful—his appeal to the true *sensus* and *consensus
fidelium*. This is not the judgment of our generation of Christians more
or less comfortable in a secular culture. It is the judgment of the many
generations of Christians before us, very many of whom like More knew
vast tracts of the Scriptures by heart, prayed not for minutes but for hours
daily, and yet who lived in cultures which posed moral questions no less
complex than today's.

This appeal neither denies nor ignores the development of Christian
doctrine. Development of moral teaching can involve the identification of
new options for morally upright choice, as when there emerges, alongside
the old, immoral option of usury the new or newly clarified option
of charging interest on loans at a rate, established by a capital market,
which fairly reflects the lender's entitlement to compensation for his risk
and for forgoing participation in the equity, the profit, of other economic
enterprises. Or such development can occur whereby one undifferentiated
and erroneous position or conception is replaced by two—as the one
conception of 'religious liberty' which the French revolutionaries said
was incompatible with religious vows and indeed with any unconditional
religious profession, and with any moral restrictions on religious speech
or conduct, and which was therefore condemned by the Popes, comes to be
replaced by two, differentiated positions, one position the still erroneous
and still condemned 'religious liberty' of indifferentism, or of rationalist

rejection of religious commitment or vows, or of freedom from every moral restraint, but the other clearly distinguished from the first, and affirmed, as the religious liberty proclaimed by Vatican II. But such developments, though they may involve some amendment and even reversal of some verbal formulations, involve no contradiction or reversal of any *proposition*, any position (*sententia*, judgment) which was accepted in the tradition as a position which Christians must definitively hold to—positions such as exclude the intentional killing of any innocent person, whether as an end or as a means, or adultery or any other way of securing sexual satisfaction outside marriage, or preventing one's act of sexual intercourse from having the procreative consequence which *it* might otherwise have had. On matters of the last-mentioned sorts, our situation is in all essentials humanly the same as our Christian forebears; our options, however elaborated at the level of technique, are in terms of intentionality (and therefore of moral assessment) the same options; and the moral judgment to be made on them is in all essentials to be found in the public revelation completed in Christ and the reception of his words and deeds by his Apostles and thence by the apostolic community established by Christ to transmit those words and deeds through the remainder of human history.

In the Catholic conception of faith for which More died, one's personal faith, which one has by the grace of the Holy Spirit, is only a fully adequate and appropriate response to that grace when it is a sharing in the faith of the Church. And that faith is (a) a reception of a divine revelation completed by the historical words and deeds of Jesus, and (b) a transmission of what God thus entrusted to the community of those, the Apostles, who had thus received him in faith. So More, in his very last work, *De Tristitia Christi* (On Christ's Sorrow), in the very midst of what is a devotional meditation on the Passion, and very much as part of the devotional purpose, goes about and about to establish (a) the factual truthfulness of the Gospel accounts, and to vindicate their historical credibility against sceptical doubts. And in all his defences of the faith, he strives (b) to put us in the presence of the great company of our fellow Christians of every earlier age: as we make our way through life, as 'through the broad High Street of a great long city',[10] we are accompanied on the one side by the voices and gestures of our dissenting contemporaries but on the other side by a much more numerous and honourable company, the communion of those who have gone before us to heaven, along that way, and whose voice we can hear in the writings of the saints and doctors of the Church, and in the acts of its Councils, Councils which in turn direct us to the successors of Peter.

---

[10] *Dialogue of Comfort against Tribulation*, 237.

The present crisis of faith and morals, like the crisis in More's time, centres on the clergy, their formation, their *esprit de corps*, their preaching. When did I last hear a sermon which tried to explicate, vindicate, or make real the factual truthfulness of what they commonly and misleading call the 'stories' of the Gospel? Or which explicated the appointed scriptural readings by putting us in the presence of the meditations and explanations of one or more of the Fathers, or by showing us the interpretation of that text in the Councils? Or indeed which expounded for us a sentence, let alone a paragraph or a page or a chapter, of any of the constitutions of Vatican II, a Council which simply has never been preached and which remains substantially unread even by many quite learned clerics? Anyone who today would like to learn from Thomas More could do no better than to read and re-read (ideally with the texts cited in its precise footnotes) the twenty pages of Vatican II's Dogmatic Constitution *Dei Verbum* on Divine Revelation, unprejudiced by the misleading claims of those, far or near, who invite you to be less impressed by the text than by its differences (which they hugely exaggerate) from earlier drafts.

If More strives to put us in the presence of Jesus of Nazareth and into the presence of the saints and doctors who have gone before us, he strives also to show us the true horizons of our earthly existence, the true range and depth of our morally significant choices. He wants to put us always in mind of heaven and hell, which have disappeared from the moral/theological treatises of the new men and which in most contemporary preaching appear only in the form of a fatuous, unexamined presumption that God, before whom no one need stand in holy fear, will with the entirely limitless indulgence of an irresponsible late-twentieth-century father somehow extend the comforts of our prosperity forever.

Few things are more foolish than the claim of the new men that the Bible has been newly opened to our generation of Catholics, when in fact it has never been so heavily censored as it is by a theology and catechesis which covers with silence the Bible's supreme themes of Genesis and Apocalypse, of creation which initiates time, and redemption which is completed only in eternity at the close of historical time. The faith and vision of Thomas More is closed to us if we do not live within the horizons thus pointed out to us.

We now cross the river from Lambeth Palace to Westminster where More, on Thursday 1 July 1535, after nearly sixty weeks' imprisonment, stands before his eighteen judges (including the new Queen's father and brother). They have just condemned him for the capital treason of attempting (allegedly in a casual conversation with the Solicitor General in the Tower while the Privy Council's servants were taking away all More's books) 'wholly to deprive our sovereign Lord the King of his dignity, title and name of Supreme Head in earth of the Church of England' (the title statutorily conferred by the Act of Supremacy 1534 along with the royal power to judge errors and heresies with finality). More has just been condemned—at that point, to be hanged, disembowelled alive, and quartered. He is allowed a final speech:

More have I not to say, my Lords, but that as the blessed Apostle St. *Paul*, as we read in the *Acts* of the Apostles, was present, and consenting to the Protomartyr *Stephen*, keeping their Clothes that stoned him to death, and yet they are both now holy Saints in heaven, and there shall continue Friends to Eternity; so I verily trust, and shall therefore heartily pray, that albeit your Lordships have been on Earth my Judges to Condemnation, yet that we, may hereafter meet joyfully together in Heaven to our everlasting Salvation…[11]

Left unspoken, but hanging in the air between More and his judges, in the Christian consciousness they shared, is the precondition of Paul's salvation: his conversion and repentance. In his *De Tristitia Christi* More had prayed that the new men would repent and come home to God, as Judas could have repented even after his betrayal of Jesus. In the top and bottom margins of his own Latin prayer book in the Tower, More penned a prayer: 'Give me thy grace, good Lord', it begins, and after various other petitions: 'Give me thy grace, good Lord…

    To walk the narrow way that leadeth to life;
    To bear the cross with Christ;
    To have the last thing in remembrance;
    To have ever afore mine eye my death that is ever at hand;
    To make death no stranger to me;
    To foresee and consider the everlasting fire of hell;
    To pray for pardon before the judge come…'[12]

The prayer's final reflection is that the thoughts expressed in the prayer's petition are 'more to be desired of every man than all the treasures' of this world's rulers all gathered together in one heap.

    The most urgent task for a truly Christian theology and catechesis of faith *and* morals is to recover, for us all, the treasure of the truth conveyed in so many words of Jesus, and presupposed in his willingness to remain faithful to his vocation at the cost of gruesome execution: the truth that this life is lived towards a destiny that, body and soul together, far outruns the existence of all other bodies known to us, the whole matter of our apparently expanding universe; and that this destiny of adoption into the

---

[11]   *A Complete Collection of State Trials* (3rd edn, 1742), I, 62.
[12]   *Thomas More's Prayer Book*, xxxvii.

family of the Creator is, for one who can freely choose, conditional on one's choices. And it is conditional, not according to a will and judicial judgment and order along the lines of the resolutions, judgments, and orders or commands (however just) of human legislators and judges, but by an appropriateness, a fittingness, an inevitability (given, on the one side, God's promises of salvation and, on the other side, the inherent power of free choice to terminate an interpersonal relationship) in the structure of personal relationships between Creator and created persons. That structure is a vast set of relationships to live within which completely and everlastingly is heaven, and to break off which will prove to have been the beginnings of a loss that, when things are seen and felt without distraction, is all that Jesus holds before us as the fire of hell. (The Lord's discourse here is not, as some theologians like, dismissively, to say, 'threat-discourse'; it is warning-discourse, utterly serious but devoid of threat. God makes promises, but no threats.)[13]

More's *Dialogue of Comfort against Tribulation* shows that he knows that atheists are not rare,[14] and that he knows how even the faithful recoil with revulsion from reflecting on the prospect of hell.[15] The four-and-a-half centuries since More's death have not only brought atheism even closer in to the Christian consciousness, but have also greatly deepened that revulsion, have made more intolerable anything savouring of arbitrariness, of a divine voluntarism, in the structure of human destiny, and have therefore made more urgent and necessary the responsibility of taking this part of the Gospel seriously. The failure to take this responsibility seriously, a failure which has many more aspects and origins than I have been able even to touch upon, is the heart of the crisis of faith and morals. Only if we do understand and take heed of that responsibility can we have a hope, going beyond mere words, such as of meeting St Thomas More, joyfully, in heaven.

---

[13] See now essay 24 at 373, below.   [14] *Dialogue of Comfort*, 194.   [15] *Ibid.*, 249.

11

ON CREATION AND ETHICS*

I

The reflective theoretical work of ethics begins from practical reason's understanding—the 'habitual' conscience, *synderesis*—of the primary principles in which we know and are directed towards the basic human goods. These goods are known in practical reason as truths about possible human fulfilment. As *per se nota*, these principles, their truth and their directiveness, have a kind of necessity. But as known in the human mode of knowing, that is, in the form of propositions, these truths and their directiveness have also a kind of contingency: they exist as the propositional object of acts of understanding and knowing. In this latter aspect, they are like all those other realities of which we have experience: contingent, in the precise sense that one can know *what* they are without knowing *that* they are. Like every contingent reality, their existence therefore needs a transcendent explanation: the existence of the contingent is ultimately explicable only by reference to a state of affairs—let us call it the act of Creation—which includes within it a reality—God the Creator—which needs no explanation because what this reality is is all that it requires to exist (so that to know *what* it is would be to know *that* it is).[1]

Thus, like every reflective discipline of the understanding, ethics finds in its own first principles a subject-matter for those further questions which head towards the rational affirmation of the divine creative reality. And the pressing of these further questions in ethics has a special significance.

* 1989c.

[1] For this argument to the existence of God—an argument adumbrated by Aquinas, *De Ente et Essentia*, c. 4, and as far as possible from any kind of Anselmian 'ontological' argument—see Grisez, *Beyond the New Theism*; shorter versions: *NLNR* 382–7; *FoE* 145–6; Grisez, *CMP* 65–6. The application of the argument to the contingent reality of first practical principles is first indicated in 1987f at 141–2; 143–7 explore other themes touched on in secs I to III of the present essay. A profound theological treatment of most of the matters touched upon in this essay: *CMP* 42–5, 50–2, 151–5, 460–1, 586–7.

For: philosophical reflection on the creative causing of contingent realities of every kind can hardly fail to envisage the Creator as intelligent and free. The act of Creation cannot be necessitated by any factor within the totally uncontingent reality of the Creator, still less by anything in the nature of the created realities themselves. Philosophical reflection therefore envisages the Creator in the mode of: intelligent, free, and active, that is, *personal*. But this conclusion has particular force in the light of the foregoing argument from the contingent and therefore dependent reality of practical reason's first principles. For those principles have their inherent directiveness precisely by being intelligible pointers towards human fulfilment. So we cannot but think of *their* transcendent source as being one who anticipates human fulfilment as an intelligible good, and who wills that it be (more or less) realized precisely by guiding human action intelligently towards it.

In short, the first principles of ethics have a particular significance among the *res creatae* by which the Creator provides us with evidence of himself (DV 3; Romans 1: 19–20) and from which natural human reason can securely know God as *rerum omnium principium* [origin/source of everything] (DV 6; Vatican I, *Dei Filius* cap. 2 (D-S 3004)).

II

Ethics not only has *praxis* as its subject-matter, but is also practical in its very origin and purpose.[2] Not only is the basic good of knowing truth one of the primordial elements in the content of ethical knowledge. It is also a good whose intelligible attractiveness as an aspect of human fulfilment directs us to inquiry and reflection, including (indeed, architectonically) ethical inquiry and reflection itself.

But more. So evident are the contingency and derivativeness of the being of experienced realities, and their need for a transcendent explanatory source, and the presumably *personal* character of that transcendent uncaused cause, that practical reason grasps, among its primary principles, the following distinct basic good: harmony with that personal source of all meaning and value. That basic good, *religio*, takes its place alongside other basic goods of harmony: the good of harmony between one's emotional and rational capacities (practical reasonableness as order in the soul), the good of harmony between one's judgments, one's choices, and one's behaviour (practical reasonableness as order in *praxis*), and the good of harmony between human persons (*pax* and *amicitia*).

---

[2] See *FoE* ch. 1.

But what this good of harmony with the transcendent source of meaning and value involves and requires of us is not evident. Within all the intelligible orders of reality within which human life is lived, lack of evident harmony is readily apparent: technical blunders, immoral choices, muddled reasonings, crop failures, sickness, hurt, death. Harmony with the creative source of order and reality is not simply found, but is to be pursued. Thus there emerges a basic human *responsibility*: to seek the truth about this transcendent source (i.e. religious truth), to embrace what to one's best judgment seems to be that truth, and to live in accordance with it.

This responsibility is one of the primary truths of the natural moral law, and just as such grounds also that right to religious liberty which the Second Vatican Council with good reason traced to the impossibility of adequately fulfilling that responsibility otherwise than in the conditions of psychological freedom which presuppose an immunity from external coercion: DH 2 and 3.[3]

III

Just as evident as the human need for harmony with the Creator is a fact which, however, is less obscured in 'primitive' than in technologically sophisticated societies: that whatever fulfilment one hopes for is not in one's own power to secure. Human fulfilment depends on human choices and action, but these cannot accomplish it without the concurrence of other factors which remain more or less outside one's own or anyone else's power. In acting, one hopes for the best.

This hope, if fully understood and lucid, is a hope for yet another gift. Already one recognizes that one's given reality is created—a gift—and that the principles by which one is intelligently directed towards the basic aspects of integral human fulfilment are themselves another gift. And now one acknowledges that whatever fulfilment is attained will be the gift of the one whose directing towards fulfilment—through the created directiveness of those principles—is the very source of the intelligibility of the good(s) for which one is acting. So, in intending an anticipated and hoped-for benefit, one in every action wills that the benefit come about both through that action and through whatever other causal factor is required insofar as that fulfilment is beyond one's own knowledge and power.

---

[3] [H]omines cuncti…personali responsabilitate aucti, sua ipsorum natura impelluntur nec-non morali tenentur obligatione ad veritatem quaerendam, illam imprimis quae religionem spec-tat. Tenentur quoque veritati cognitae adhaerere atque totam vitam suam iuxta exigentias veritatis ordinare. Huic autem obligationi satisfacere homines, modo suae propriae naturae consentaneo, non possunt nisi libertate psychologica simul atque immunitate a coercitione externa fruantur (DH 2).

See also GS 22.

But one also realizes that the being and concurrence of all those other necessary factors also is contingent, and will be actualized only if that same ultimate source wills that they be. Thus, in short, one envisages one's action as *cooperating* with that source which both directs us towards our fulfilment and helps us to bring it about.

This fundamental natural willingness to cooperate with the Creator is the fundamental natural love of God. For, properly understood, this cooperation is envisaged as mutual. As God's creative causality cooperates with human choices and actions to attain human fulfilment, so those human actions work towards God's 'fulfilment'. But since natural reason's argument to God identifies him precisely as the reality which needs and lacks nothing whatever, one must understand God's 'fulfilment' in a way which excludes all such lack. In other words, one must understand it as God's glory, the *expressing* of his goodness (his utter lack of imperfection).[4] So understood, one's cooperation with God is not to be understood as a means used by God to some ulterior purpose. Rather, our fulfilment is a part, an important part, of the self-expression God intends in creating.[5]

At the same time, there is to be excluded any sense that God is a means to one's own or any other human fulfilment. For: a *means* is something within one's power. But God is not in one's power, for everything is contingent on him but he cannot be contingent on anything. Moreover, God is related to human agency, as we have said, precisely as the one who directs human persons prior to any exercise of their own agency, and who brings about what is *not* within their power (which is not to say that their power is itself not altogether dependent on God's creative efficacy).

Thus there emerges this fundamental natural *amor Dei*, in which God's fulfilment (glory) is willed not only as an accepted and welcome side effect of one's own fulfilment through cooperation with God, but also precisely as it does fulfil God, that is, in the manner that one who loves a friend wills the good of the friend. And like every friendship, this love entails that the fulfilment of each party to it calls for fulfilment of the other, in communion each with the other.[6]

---

[4] What reason itself requires, revelation confirms:

> ...Deus bonitate sua...non ad augendam suam beatitudinem nec ad acquirendam, sed ad manifestandam perfectionem suam per bona, quae creaturis impertitur, liberrimo consilio...condidit creaturam...(Vatican I, *Dei Filius*, cap. 1 (D-S 3002); and see can. 1 (D-S 3025).)

See also AG 2:

> ...Principium sine Principio..., ex nimia...benignitate sua libere creans..., bonitatem divinam liberaliter diffudit ac diffundere non desinit, ita ut qui conditor est omnium, tandem fiat omnia in omnibus, gloriam suam simul et beatitudinem nostram procurando.

[5] For the texts of St Thomas, and discussion, *CMP* 460.

[6] Without revelation to give it an assured clarity, reason hesitates to envisage the proper relationship with God as a friendship: cf. *NE* VIII.7: 1158b35, 1159a4; *NLNR* 395–8. But unaided reason

Thus, taken together with the natural love of truth which aspires to understand all created things as they are understood by the Creator, this natural love of God as the creative and cooperative source of all human intelligent directedness and practical efficacy both envisages and evidences that a certain communion with God in his wisdom and for his glory is somehow an inseparable component of human fulfilment. In this sense, at least, and still *naturali rationis lumine e rebus creatis* [by the natural light of reason and from created things], God comes to be known as *rerum omnium finis* [the last end/point of all things] (DV 6; Vatican I, *Dei Filius* cap. 2 (D-S 3005)).

IV

Once ratified, extended, and deepened by divine revelation, the truth of divine creation (in the beginning, and ongoing) illuminates the status of the human person, the very subject of ethics. And a peculiarly significant sign of the human person's status as an *imago Dei* is our freedom of choice (GS 17). Free choice is a reality almost universally misunderstood and denied outside the peoples formed by the Old and the New Covenants. The Enlightenment, of course, sponsors much and diverse talk about freedom. Hume, Kant, Hegel, Nietzsche, Dewey, Heidegger, Sartre all affirm one or more kinds of freedom, even a kind of self-creative freedom (Nietzsche, Sartre...). But all these, along with nearly all today's psychologists and sociologists, deny the reality of the free choice affirmed by the people of the Book. The reality in question is this: choosing between intelligibly attractive open but incompatible alternatives, such that *nothing* settles which is chosen other than the choosing itself—so that in the strongest sense I am responsible for my choice because I really *could have chosen otherwise*, and there is thus in my choosing a kind of image of the sovereign freedom of creation *ex nihilo*.

One rather common source of misunderstanding and denial of free choice is the belief that nothing can come about without *sufficient reason*, i.e. without a reason which excludes any competing reason and explains why *this* (such-and-such) and only this came about. Those who accept the

---

can certainly apprehend that the morally bad will *exploits* God's creative causality. For the morally bad will is, by definition (i.e. in its essence), a will which rejects part of the intelligible direction it receives, in favour of a cut-down fulfilment that appeals to a reason *fettered* by feelings. Cutting-down on integral human fulfilment, it rejects some of the benefit (the glory) which would accrue to God through morally good actions. Yet still the morally bad person needs the benefit of the help of others including God. So the bad will is marked by want of mutuality; it subordinates the fulfilment of others to the benefit it seeks for itself. Thus man seeks to *use* God, to coerce, trick, manipulate, bargain with God, to evade his claims, and ultimately to try to get along without him.

supposed 'principle of sufficient reason' will conclude that this must be the best of all possible worlds, since otherwise God would not have chosen to create it. And they will propose that free will consists in no more than this: that the principle of our choices is not external but lies within us.

But those who understand divine creation (and, indeed, redemptive re-creation too) as it is understood in Scripture and the Fathers deny that God's creative and providential choice could be necessitated by anything. With St Thomas, they deny that the freedom of free choice consists merely in the absence of an external constraint or in the dominance of some principle of actions which is internal to the agent.[7] In one's free choices, one's exercise of will is neither constrained, nor even moved, by any other power, not even by the intellect which makes the will's act possible by presenting intelligible goods and intelligent proposals for realizing them.[8] The freedom we exercise in our free choices is the self-determining freedom of one who stands before two or more incompatible options (proposals for action), each option promising intelligible benefits and no option promising all-the-good-that-the-other-offers-and-some-more. And the diversity of the goods God richly creates for his glory—including the many-sided good of persons whose fulfilment depends in part upon their free and self-shaping choices—renders incoherent the notion of a 'best' of all possible worlds, yet leaves intact the biblical and philosophically appropriate judgment that the created outcome of a wisdom which guides without determining the divine generosity is an outcome *valde bon[um]*: 'God saw that it was *very good*' (Genesis 1: 31).

If one asks why, until the 1960s, no Catholic theologian entertained a proportionalist ethic, commending pursuit of the overall net greatest good (assessed prior to moral judgment), the answer will, I think, include the following: Catholic moral teaching is profoundly shaped by reflection on the doctrine of creation (understood always as including that creative *conservatio in esse a Deo* which is an essential aspect of the divine *gubernatio*

---

[7] [Q]uidam posuerunt quod voluntas hominis ex necessitate movetur ad aliquid eligendum. Nec tamen ponebant quod voluntas cogeretur: non enim omne necessarium est violentum, sed solum illud cuius principium est extra.... [V]iolentum enim repugnat naturali sicut et voluntario, quia utriusque principium est intra, violenti autem principium est extra.... Haec autem opinio est haeretica' (*De Malo*, q.6c (*de libera electio*)).

Cf. also D–S 1939. [On free choice and 'the principle of sufficient reason', see now also Introduction to vol. II, at p. 7 n. 13.]

[8] [D]e intellectu et voluntate quodammodo est...dissimile...quantum ad exercitium actus, nam intellectus movetur a voluntate ad agendum, voluntas [autem] non ab alia potentia sed a se ipsa (*De Malo*, q.6 ad 10m).

See also q.6c: 'Cum...voluntas se consilio moveat, consilium autem est inquisitio quaedam non demonstrativa sed ad opposita viam habens, non ex necessitate voluntas se ipsam movet.'

and *providentia*⁹); but such reflection is conspicuously absent from proportionalist theologizing.

This is not to say that, as many proportionalists claim, the classic Catholic moral theology (say, St Thomas's) confuses God's 'creative will' with his 'moral will'. The supposed distinction between 'creative' and 'moral' will in God seems groundless. But as Aquinas makes clear, a proper philosophy and theology of the natural moral law does not claim to draw practical conclusions from premises purporting to identify God's will, at all.¹⁰ Rather, to say that Catholic moral teaching, in rejecting proportionalism, is drawing on the doctrine of creation is to make the following two points.

(1) Proportionalism offers to guide moral judgment by a criterion which at best confuses human with divine providence. This criterion seems inappropriate, indeed unavailable, even as an aspect of the wisdom guiding divine creation and providence. What is certain is that it is inappropriate as a criterion of human moral judgment. It is philosophically inappropriate because incoherent with the very essence of moral judgment, which is to guide free and rational choice. For if one could identify one option as promising overall net greater good (or lesser harm), all other options would fall away, and there would be no need for free and rationally motivated *choice*. The incommensurability of the goods involved in morally significant choices makes impossible the proportionalist's calculations, while making possible the very choices which proportionalism offers to guide.

And the proportionalist criterion and moral method is theologically inappropriate, too. For if rationally combined with the doctrine of divine providence, it would have an absurd consequence: those in doubt could rightly choose *anything* to which they felt inclined—for even at the stage of deliberation one could see that, if one were to accomplish what one attempted, one could be certain that what one did had satisfied the proportionalist criterion by tending toward net good in the long run (since God's providence permitted it), while if one were to fail to accomplish what one attempted, one could be certain that one's failure had satisfied the proportionalist criterion by tending toward net good in the long run (since God's providence excluded the success of one's effort, yet answered to one's overall intention of enhancing overall net good). Proportionalists, of course, have no desire to propose the morally absurd injunction to 'Try

---

⁹ See e.g. *ST* I q.104 a.1.

¹⁰ 'Voluntas enim Dei ratione investigari non potest, nisi circa ea quae absolute necesse est Deum velle: talia autem non sunt quae circa creaturas vult, ut dictum est [q.19 a.3]': *ST* I q.46 a.2c. It is for these proportionalist critics to make sense, if they can, of their distinction between divine 'creative' and 'moral' wills.

anything' or 'Do what you feel like'. But within the context of Christian faith their method strictly entails that unwelcome implication.

(2) The second way in which many proportionalist moral theologians overlook the Christian doctrine of creation and providence is this: they assert that, for the sake of good, man can fittingly and uprightly *intend* evil, that is, *choose to do harm*, for example to persons in some basic aspect of their being and fulfilment, and that the distinction between intending to harm as a means and permitting/accepting harm as a side effect is of no moral significance. But Christian thought has insisted that man, made in the divine image and called to be holy as God is holy, must imitate the God who hates nothing that he has made and does not intend evils, not even as means, but only permits them, as a side effect of what he does intend.[11]

The distinction between *intention* (including intention of means) and *permission* (that is, accepting the foreseen side effects of one's own choices) is central to one of Trent's canons on justification, defending the reality of free choice:

If anyone says that it is not in man's power to make his ways evil, but that God performs the evil works just as he performs the good, not only permissively but also properly and per se...: *anathema sit.*[12]

What does 'per se' mean here? Aquinas explains the relevant usage thus: 'In those things which are on account of an end (*propter finem*), something is spoken of as *per se* when it is intended (*intentum*), and is said to be *per accidens* when it is outside the intention (*praeter intentionem*)' (*ST* II–II q.59 a.2c). Or again: 'In moral matters..., what is intended is *per se*, whereas what follows *praeter intentionem* may be regarded as *per accidens*' (II–II q.39 a.1c).[13] Trent's terminology is to like effect: neither as end nor as means does God in any way intend human evil (the canon gives an instance: Judas's treachery); God merely permits it. True, the defined dogma of faith

---

[11]   In Christian faith the 'Be holy as I am holy' (Leviticus 19: 2) becomes the moral principle of affiliation as children (1 Peter 1: 14–16; Ephesians 5: 1) in the divine family, 'Be perfect, as your Father' (Matthew 5: 48), which, in the context established by Matthew 5: 43–7, can be understood as teaching: Be perfect—always will good to all—as God does. See Spicq, *Dieu et l'Homme selon le Nouveau Testament*, 53; *Théologie du Nouveau Testament*, 96–9, 694–706.

[12]   Sess. 6 (1547), can. 6; D-S 1556.

[13]   Among the numerous passages in which Aquinas distinguishes thus between the *per se* and the *per accidens*, and in which the linking idea is the distinction between what is intended and what lies outside the agent's intention, there are many making it clear that, in these contexts, 'intention' extends not only to ultimate ends but also to proximate means (see e.g. *ST* I–II q.76 a.4c; II–II, q.37 a.1c; q.39 a.1c.; q.43 a.3c; q.64 a.7c; see also I–II q.12 aa.2c and 4c: 'intending' an end and willing the means are a single act of will, and moral analysis considers that whole act of will); the fundamental reason for this inclusion of means within intention is that every chosen means is also an end (i.e. an end of one's exertion): see *In II Phys.* no. 181 (ad 194b35); *In V Meta.* no. 771 (ad 1013a35–b3); *De Veritate* q.5 a.4c. See also Boyle, '*Praeter Intentionem* in Aquinas' at 649–50. [See essay II. 9 (1991a), sec. II.]

pertains to God's permission of human sin—a foreseen and permitted side effect of his creation of human free choice.[14] But the whole classic tradition of theological reflection on divine will and providence, most clearly expressed in John Damascene and Aquinas, insists that for God to will (intend) *anything* which intelligence would call an evil is inconsistent with his holiness.[15]

Christian reflection on the Creator's holy will, and Christian reflection on the morality of human choosing and doing, develop together in mutual support. Together they mark a large advance in differentiated understanding over pre-Christian philosophy and philosophical theology. Philo Judaeus, like Plato, will insist that God is neither the cause of evils nor responsible for them; but his explanations derail into a strange theory of agency in which the principal is not answerable for the acts of his agents; corruption and destruction are brought about not by God but 'by certain others as ministers [of the sovereign King]'.[16] Christian thought, in its dual reflection, replaces the undifferentiated concept of 'cause' with the act-analytical distinctions between willing (choosing or intending) and permitting (accepting). Today, many proportionalist moralists,[17] giving little sign of having reflected on the doctrine of creation, have fallen back into the undifferentiated problematic of 'causing' evils, at the same time accepting the Enlightenment extension of 'cause' to include whatever one could have prevented but did not—a concept incompatible with Christian understanding of divine holiness.

[14] Some proportionalists, following B. Schüller, wish to draw a sharp distinction: God's holiness is incompatible with his in any way intending human sin; but God, and therefore also human persons, can rightly intend pre-moral evils. They have difficulty explaining (i) why—on proportionalist principles—one may not rightly intend the sin of another as a means to reducing the overall number or gravity of sins, and (ii) why the difference between intending and permitting should be relevant in relation to one's involvement in the wrong-doing of others, but irrelevant in relation to one's involvement in any and every other kind of evil.

[15] See John of Damascus, *De Fide Orthodoxa* II, 29; *ST* I q.19 a.9; Lee, 'Permanence of the Ten Commandments' at 435–6. Especially illuminating is *De Veritate* q.5 a.4, stressing that natural defects are 'means' only in the sense that God turns them to good effect; they are not 'means' in the sense that every chosen means is, for every chosen means, however proximate, is not only a means but also an (intermediate) end (and thus is intended). One may add: To say that God intends any evil whatsoever would be either to hold that evil is a positive reality or to deny that God's will is creative.

[16] Philo, *Questions and Answers on Genesis*, I q.23; see also qq. 68, 78, 89, 100; II q.13; *De Confusione Linguarum*, c. 36 para. 180. Cf. Plato, *Rep.* II 379b–c; X 617e.

[17] e.g. Schüller, 'La Moralité de moyens' at 222:

Quoique l'on choisisse, qu'on néglige d'aider l'un pour ne pas avoir à nuire à un autre, ou qu'on nuise à l'un pour pouvoir aider les autres, les conséquences négatives qui resultent du choix sont un pur moyen en vue des conséquences positives qui en résultent. Cela découle du concept de vouloir et de choix préférentiel.

For a thoroughgoing confusion of 'willing' with 'causing', in the interests of proportionalism, see e.g. Peschke SVD, 'Tragfähigkeit und Grenzen des Prinzips der Doppelwirkung' at 110–12.

V

The foregoing observations in no way exhaust the significance of Creation for ethics, philosophical, or theological. I have not touched upon what God's continuing fecundity in creation signifies for the human *ordo amoris* in which provision for new lives has a certain priority.[18] I have said nothing about how an understanding of each human person's existence as a divine gift, indeed an altogether special gift,[19] can illuminate the moral understanding of questions touching the killing and the 'producing' of human persons. Above all, I have said too little of what could be said about how moral categories, even of natural reason—categories such as *obligation* and *right*—silently draw upon the disposition to *gratitude*, the appropriate consequence of acknowledging the creative and utterly mysterious generosity which grounds all that we are and have and do and can become.

---

[18] See *ST* II–II q.26 a.9 ad 1 and ad 3.
[19] See D-S 3896; Paul VI, *Professio Fidei* in AAS 60 (1968), 436; CDF, *Donum Vitae* (Instruction on Respect for Human Life in its Origin and on the Dignity of Procreation, 22 February 1987) at fn. 17.

12

ST CUTHBERT'S FAITH AND THE BISHOP OF DURHAM'S UNBELIEF[*]

Dominus illuminatio mea… The Lord is my light, and my salvation: whom then shall I fear? The Lord is the strength of my life: of whom then shall I be afraid?

(Psalm 27: 1)

In sixty-one days, 1,300 years will have been measured since the saint whom University College accounts its patron, and has always portrayed upon its seal, died on rocky Farne and was buried in St Peter's church on Lindisfarne: Wednesday 20 March 687. And the *Lives* of St Cuthbert show us a man who could indeed apply to himself the words of the same psalm:

On a rock fastness he lifts me high…
I will sing, and speak praises [*psalmum*] to the Lord

(Psalm 27: 5, 7)

Those who, across these 1,300 years, try to envisage Cuthbert (or any of the remarkable company of Celtic and Saxon saints) can feel themselves, perhaps, like the monk who secretly followed Cuthbert one night as he stole again out of the sleeping monastery. Watching from the cliffs, the monk could see and hear Cuthbert as he stood, chest-deep in the northern sea, from midnight until dawn, chanting the psalms and other prayers of the divine office.

In Cuthbert we don't have a scholar like his biographer Bede, or our founder William of Durham. Rather we see a life of extraordinary contrasts: years of priestly visitations in places too remote and villages

---

[*] Unpublished: the University Latin Sermon, the University Church (of St Mary the Virgin), Oxford, Sunday 18 January 1987. The Latin as delivered was published in the *University College Record 1987*; both texts were available to those present. The nomination of the preacher for this annual sermon rotates among the colleges, in a cycle of about once a generation. My college was founded by a benefaction of William, Dean of Durham, in 1249.

too rough for other priests, and years of a hermit's solitude; the press of episcopal responsibilities among a people ravaged by plague (and by the accompanying fears and superstitions), and what Bede calls 'repose of divine contemplation' on remotest Farne; departure from the well-found monastery of Ripon sooner than accept the Romanism[1] imposed by its royal sponsor, and later the arduous diplomacy of persuading his island monks, after the Synod of Whitby, to accept 'the decrees of the apostolic see or indeed of the universal Church'.

As we peer down through the darkness of centuries at Cuthbert shouting out his psalms across the waves, we can infer that his largeness of spirit included, richly though in a manner not the scholar's, the very same acknowledgement as we take for the motto of this University's studies. *Dominus illuminatio mea*: our everyday but truly astonishing understanding is a God-given light—the capacity of relating intelligently to reality precisely because created reality is really intelligible to human intelligence. The objective pole and the source of this created relationship are identified in Bede's scientific work *de Natura Rerum*:

From the seeds and primordial causes of this…creation, the whole world's movement is evolved by a natural law wherein even up till now the Father works, and the Son, and wherein, too, the ravens are fed and the lilies clothed by God.

The gospel most loved by the Celtic church and, it seems, by Cuthbert himself—*John*—is anticipated in its prologue by a psalm in whose meaning the saint, all his senses absorbed by the sea's sway and the night sky's lights, will surely have been immersed:

> By the word of the Lord were the heavens made,
> by the breath of his mouth all the stars.
> He gathers up the waves of the ocean,
> He stores up the deep as in a treasure house…

(Psalm 32: 6–7)

This world, in its course, its seasons, and all its unimaginable variety, is *enarratio Dei*, a telling-forth of God: here is a truth as accessible to us as it was to Bede and Cuthbert, if like them we question, look, and listen.

But what is best understood in silence and solitude still is to be passed on by words and action. Cuthbert's preaching and its effect are summarized by Bede:

…no one left his presence without consolation's joy…He knew how to refresh the soul by his exhortation; he could summon to the memory of the afflicted the joys

---

[1] i.e. the Latin-rite formalities.

of the heavenly life, and show them how fleeting were both the pleasures and the sorrows of this world...

'summon up the joys of heavenly life'; or as Psalm 27: 13 puts it: 'I believe I shall see the Lord's good things in the land of the living'. What the Psalmist could not know is the full richness of the hope rather thinly expressed by Cuthbert's, or Bede's, words but a little more amply put by the apostolic see's latest universal council (1,301 years after the Synod of Whitby):

> When, in the Spirit of the Lord and in conformity with his commandment, we have cultivated in the world the goods of human dignity, brotherly community, and liberty—i.e., all the good fruits of our nature and our activity—we will find all those goods again, cleansed from stain, illuminated and transfigured, when Christ returns to the Father the eternal and universal kingdom...a kingdom which is already present in this world, in mystery.
>
> (*Gaudium et Spes*, 39 (1965))

Cuthbert's goal, missionary and contemplative alike, was to make that 'mystery' transparent for its consummation in what he envisioned as a young man, before entering the monastery: the 'glory of the heavenly mission' and 'its king, who is Christ'.

Durham's cathedral was built for the body of Cuthbert. Bede reports that the body was found incorrupt, eleven years after death. It was found still incorrupt, by crowds of witnesses, some initially very sceptical, at the cathedral's inauguration in 1104. It seems to have been in that state—save the missing tip of its nose—when Henry's commissioners came to uproot the cult in 1537. All this is matter for historical investigation, and for reflection, not of Christian faith.

But the *cathedra* of Durham is occupied now by one who publicly doubts that 'that which was sown in weakness and corruption' (the body of Jesus of Nazareth, or of anyone who might be raised from death to share his Kingdom) could in bodily fashion 'put on incorruption' (the true incorruption which is not the preservation of a corpse but the transformed restoration of bodily life). For (it is said) if God could, or would, perform such a miracle in Jesus, how could he fail to snatch the doomed from Auschwitz or Hiroshima?

Some reverse the argument. Since Jesus taught and did works of mercy and was raised from the dead, we can be sure (they say) that God will not permit the destruction of this human world by nuclear fire and poison.

St Cuthbert's faith and hope is different. His island community, and even the whole world to his horizon, was all but exterminated by plague, and lay under the shadow of invaders who might stop at nothing. But he preached and lived a gospel which, like every bishop until the Lord's return, he was charged with handing on as both historically true and a matter of faith. That gospel's assurance is summed up in God's resurrection of Jesus. The assurance is of no more (and no less) than this. Free choices (say, to accept or reject faith, or do or omit the works it requires) can last into eternity, and those who have chosen (or who have been included in the choices, the prayers, and the merits of another) will, in a world physical but divinely transformed, duly meet with whatever a redemptive justice secures or permits for one who chooses *thus.*

Just in that sense, we, like Cuthbert (and with the benefit, one can hope, of his merits and prayers), may pray and believe

The Lord is ... my salvation: whom then shall I fear?
The Lord is the strength of my life: of whom then shall I be afraid?

NOTE

David Jenkins, for many years Tutor in Theology at Queen's College, across the High Street from University College, became bishop of the Anglican see of Durham in mid-1984, despite his disavowal of belief in the bodily resurrection of Jesus of Nazareth, a disavowal which he maintained, not least in the Synod of the Church of England in 1986, where many seemed swayed by argumentation of the kind summarized in one sentence above. His successor in the see from 2003 to 2010, N.T. Wright, another Oxford teacher of theology, has given excellent accounts of historical grounds for believing the Gospel accounts of the emptying of Jesus' tomb by his bodily resurrection: see, listed in 'Other Works Cited', below: most pithily, 'What Happened at the Resurrection?'; of intermediate length, the other articles listed from 1998 and 2002; the long book, *The Resurrection of the Son of God*; and the 2005 discussion of four scholarly responses to that book.

13

PHILOSOPHY AND GOD'S NATURE:
SECOND THOUGHTS*

Mark Murphy[1] thoughtfully debates the question how the basic human goods and the requirements of practical reasonableness are related, in my thought, to a transcendent, divine cause, the question how far the affirmability of the goods and moral requirements is 'detachable' from the affirmability, if such it is, of God's existence and nature. The question, so far as it relates to my thought, is complicated by the fact that *NLNR* takes a very austere, minimalist view of what can be affirmed on the basis of reason alone about the nature of God. The argument that we are, not logically, but rationally required to affirm the existence of a transcendent explanation/cause 'which exists simply by being what it is, and which is required for the existing of any other state of affairs' is said on p. 389 to be unable, 'I think', to take us further. That God's nature is personal, that 'the uncaused cause of all the good things of this world (including our ability to understand them) is itself a good that one could love, personal in a way that one might imitate, a guide that one might follow, or a guarantor of anyone's practical reasonableness' is said on p. 398 to be a set of propositions of which 'it is impossible to have sufficient assurance... without some revelation more revealing than any that Plato or Aristotle may have experienced'. Hence the negative conclusion stated bluntly on p. 405: '... what can be established, by argumentation from the existence and general features of the world, concerning the uncaused cause of the world, does not directly assist us in answering' the practical questions set up in the chapter's first pages—about the possibility of a deeper explanation of obligation, the reasonableness of self-sacrifice in human friendship, 'the point of living according to the requirements of practical reasonableness',[2] that is, 'whether any *further* sense can be made

---

* 2008d, Part V of a five-part comment on discussions of my work at a conference in Atlanta on my work on the grounds of law and legal theory.
[1] Murphy, 'Finnis on Nature, Reason, God'. [2] *NLNR* 405.

of the whole situation ...'.[3] This limitation of 'natural reasoning', I added, though it

leaves somehow 'subjective' and 'questionable' the whole structure of basic principles and requirements of practical reasonableness and human flourishing...does not unravel that structure or affect its internal order or weaken its claim to be more reasonable than any logically possible alternative structures.

Before saying how I think the just-mentioned negative conclusions ought to be revised, let me review the *NLNR* position. (1) The first thing to observe is that it is not at all the 'secular' position attributed to me by Perry when he says:

It is a presupposition of the secular position—Finnis's position—that *it* [the natural law] *holds even if* the *universe is just what Clarence Darrow and Steven Weinberg...have proclaimed it to be: a cosmic process bereft of ultimate meaning.*[4]

For it is one thing to say, as I do at *NLNR* 49, that the theory of natural law can be set out '*without needing to advert to the question* of God's existence or nature or will' and something quite different to say that the theory of natural law would be unaffected if reason established that there is no divine existence, nature, or will and that the universe *is* bereft of ultimate meaning. To hold, as I did and do, that norms, not precisely of logic, but certainly of rationality demand that natural science's myriad affirmations of causal explanation be under-girded by an explanation of the availability both of those explanations and of the realities they explain is to hold, by an entailment whose necessity again is that of rationality norms, that denial of that meta- or transcendent explanation unravels the rationality norms on which natural science itself depends. A good explanation of molecular motion, as I say on p. 49, can be provided 'without adverting to the existence of an uncreated creator of the whole state of affairs in which molecules and their laws of motion obtain'. But non-advertence is very different from denial. Nietzsche's progression from denial of God's existence (jokily or confusedly framed as 'God is dead') to denial of all metaphysical order is not unreasonable. Of course there are countless natural scientists and others who are confident in affirming the laws of their science while confidently denying that they have any divine source or at least that the affirmation of such a source is rationally required. But that does not show that Nietzsche's inference was mistaken, any more than the existence of dissent shows that the majority are wrong, or the outnumbering of the dissenters shows that they are wrong.

---

[3] *Ibid.*, 372.   [4] Perry, 45 (his emphases).

So too, (2) the *NLNR* position is not, as Murphy (p. 197) takes Leiter to be asserting, that 'natural law theory [is] safe for nontheists'. No aspect of the world's existence and multiple orders is safe for non-theists, for the affirmation of those intelligible orders, including the (third-order) order of moral principles,[5] invites the further questions pursued in Chapter XIII through to the thesis that rationality norms require the abandonment of non-theism. I think Murphy's conclusion about Leiter's position is stated near the end of his essay, and is right:

> ... once he [perhaps Finnis, perhaps anyone who affirms the natural law] has raised this set of issues [about ultimate intelligibility] and decided [I would say judged] that only a theistic solution will do, he has committed himself to the position that adherence to the natural law is rationally unstable in the absence of a certain sort of theistic stance. (208)

I agree, and would add that an analogous rational instability must, in the absence of a 'theistic solution', be attributed to the rest of human knowledge, too, by anyone who judges that the rationality norms which guide us in the acquisition of such knowledge require us also to affirm the 'theistic solution' (divine causality).

Though it is not clear to me that *NLNR* ch. XIII set out to 'explain the natural law',[6] it is equally not clear that it fails (a) to 'explain the necessary relations between universals that constitute the natural law' and (b) to show that 'there is some further point beyond' the basic goods, some point to 'acting on [the natural law's] categorical norms given that their status is indexed to mere human needs and interests'. For, as to (a) the necessity of the connections between the relevant universals, the principles of natural law, is the necessity of our given nature (and therefore our opportunities of flourishing) having many aspects and being instantiated in many persons, which is a necessity only because the divine creative (and unnecessitated) choice opted for this world rather than none and rather than a world containing beings of radically other nature. And as to (b), I think it is logically unsound to say that the participation of our pursuit of basic goods in the divine play gives that pursuit no added intelligibility because 'if there is any trouble about ... basic goods being relative to us in some sense, the trouble should reappear here in the explanation' (Murphy at 202). For if the trouble about the basic goods is not about their content but about (briefly) the perishability of their instantiations in fleeting lives, why should not the

---

[5] See the whole passage at *NLNR* 404 from which Murphy, 192 at n. 17 quotes a main part. [In *NLNR* the moral order is called 'fourth order', and the technical is called third; but in all subsequent work I retain Aquinas's original enumeration, in which the moral is the third and the technical the fourth.]

[6] Murphy, 200, first sentence of sec. III, and 197, 201.

recontextualization of those instantiations in the eternal play add to the intelligibility of our willingness to make choices in line with them?[7]

Murphy is right that, in the end, *NLNR* does not say that the goodness of the basic goods is explained by the *goodness* of the transcendent cause. The book attributes to that cause 'the perfection of being all that is required to make all states of affairs exist' (406), but declines to explore that perfection. In the book *Aquinas*, by contrast, the divine causing, shaping, and sustaining of the universe is treated as explaining 'the actuality, existence, specific reality, goodness and orderliness of every being without exception' (305), and the divine nature, as 'pure act…free from every trace of potentiality, lack, imperfection, or need' (309), 'includes…every kind of benefit of being, every kind of power (in act, not potentiality), and every kind of perfection' (312).

On the one hand, then, God cannot have chosen to create the universe to meet any need; lacking nothing, reality as a whole could not be improved by God's choice to create. On the other hand, creating, directing, and sustaining the universe need not, and could not, have been pointless, lacking in intelligibility; like every other aspect, so to speak of the single divine act of being, the idea and act of bringing into being this universe cannot be deficient in intelligibility. [So] the point, the common good, of the universe must be the expressing, representing, and communicating (somehow sharing) of the divine perfection of actuality by bringing into being a universe of creatures which are each *like*…God in having actuality, perfections, intelligibility, and so forth.…By [their] flourishing, creatures and systems of creatures become more similar to…and more apt to represent…God, each in its own way; and all together they can express the inexhaustible divine perfection by their plurality and diversity,…and their intelligibility each in itself and all as parts of the whole order (312–13).

To these thoughts of his, with which I fully concur in judgment, *Aquinas* adds that (again in my close paraphrase):

This flourishing of human beings is not as *mere* parts of a system. For we are persons, and when we are functioning well we act not simply by following the dynamisms of some system whose pattern is built into us, but rather by our mastery over our own acts. By thus having an authorship of one's own life through acts of free choosing, one acts on one's own account and, in a sense, for one's own sake, and in the plan of divine creation each of us is a *per se* end; the plan is directed towards one's personal flourishing, for one's own sake…[8] [H]uman existence,

---

[7] Of course, much more intelligibility still would be added if that recontextualization placed our instantiations of basic goods in the framework of personal immortality or resurrection, and of an eternal community in which the good deeds of this life will be 'found again' (as Vatican II puts it); and about immortality and resurrection *NLNR* is silent even when it outlines 'speculations and hopes' (406) well beyond natural reason.

[8] In the face of the often crushing calamities to which human beings are prey, one must regard the disorder as somehow within the stable and intelligible order, and abstain from judging it defective

understanding, willing, and acting thus re-present and image God's actuality in a way that sub-personal creation cannot. They do so in a specially close and vivid way when they have all the practical reasonableness, all the unfettered openness to human goods, that we have traced in outline in earlier chapters. (313–14)

So I agree with what I take to be the fruit of Murphy's investigation, though I would not myself say that this explanation through participation and likeness is 'through unification' or that the human goods are or are identical with 'theistic facts', or that these explain human goods or 'normative facts' by 'the immediacy of identity' (Murphy, Part V). My interest in any of the kinds of 'detachability' that Murphy's exploration summoned up never went much beyond the simple thought that, as it is possible to do physics without raising or pressing further questions, so to some extent it is possible to have a practical and theoretical understanding of practical reason's principles and their implications for reasonable choice and individual and communal self-constitution without raising further or pressing questions. When setting out the short ways through *NLNR*, on the first page of its preface, I said that someone interested only in legal theory could omit Chapter XIII, but not someone 'interested in natural law simply as an ethics'.

But I think it is important not to follow the example of Perry's 'Sarah'. She confronts Nietzsche without benefit of philosophy, without grappling in dialectics with his dialectic. Quoting and it seems relying on the seer who wrote the *First Epistle of John*, she affirms simply that God is love.[9] She does not notice that in that letter, the assertion about divine love is preceded by the affirmation that God is light—both intelligibility and the blaze of glory—and that the letter presents itself as an extension of the Gospel which begins by affirming God as source of all that is, as *logos* (intelligibility and practical intellect), and, again, as glory.[10] The affirmation that God is love has to be earned. It might be earned by the stupendous judgments made by John and the other disciples about the divine nature

---

or unintelligent because one does not understand its point, lest one

> resemble a country bumpkin {rusticus, idiota, ignorans} who, from the true premise that he does not understand what is going on in a busy laboratory or hospital theatre, draws the conclusion that what is going on is random, unintelligible, pointless or foolish... The intention of an intelligence capable of projecting and actualizing the entire cosmos and all its interlocking orders vast and minuscule (including human minds with all their capacities to understand and reason logically, mathematically, and interpretatively) is not an intention we could ever reasonably hope to understand *fully* by reasoning from those truths about it which... we do manage to understand. (*Aquinas* 304.)

[9] Perry, 'Morality and Normativity' at 220 ('Sarah' is evidently an alter ego of that essay's author).

[10] It is not the case that (as *ibid.*, n. 29 approvingly quotes John Caputo as saying) 'God is love' is 'as close as the New Testament [gets] to a "definition" of God'.

of the suffering servant. Or it might be earned by metaphysical reflections on an implication of divine actuality and perfection: that 'since God, being pure actuality, can have no lack or need of any kind whatsoever, all the good in the created universe—creatures and everything from which any creature ever benefits—must be given out of God's sheer generosity',[11] which is to say: out of 'the liberality—that is to say, the love—by which God enables us (and not out of any need of his but rather for our sake) to somehow share in the goodness of his actuality'.[12]

And those metaphysical reflections and inferences need, I think, to begin with the reflective vindication of metaphysical order against all Nietzschean, Calliclean, and other sceptical doubts. Such order, along with order in all the other three kinds of order, can be found, for instance in the undeniable reality that I can put questions to myself, think them through, and answer them or hold them in suspense; and can put to myself the very same question as Nietzsche or the other sceptics put to themselves, in another language and another era, in the same though altered Europe. My picking up the book (to see what Nietzsche thought) is an event, an element, an episode, intelligibly linked to countless others, in an indubitably metaphysical and indubitably orderly order, as well as in the orders of logic, rational choice, and technical art, the four kinds of order in which every human person's life is lived.

---

[11] *Aquinas* 310.
[12] *Ibid.*, 311. See nn. 76–78 which include a discussion of the reason for using the masculine pronoun (and implicitly for eschewing modelling creation and providence on the womb—cf. Perry, 18).

14

THIS WORLD AND THE NEXT*

When it became clear, a few months ago, that Robert Mugabe, not the Bishop,[1] was going to inherit the white dominion of Rhodesia, the newspapers went to ask him about himself. Everyone knew that he had been a Christian, indeed a practising Roman Catholic. But not now. Now, he said, 'I don't agree with the practice of Christianity. The notion that material things don't matter, that this world is only a stage to another world about which we know nothing, I don't accept.'

Some people reject Christianity because they don't accept its claims about what *has* happened in this world—the stark claim that the creator and sustainer of the entire universe has revealed himself with utter particularity in words spoken and deeds done, in the flesh, at a few moments of time in one patch of this little Earth; that the immortal put on mortality and committed his fate to the hands of a few ordinary men and women, those who killed him and those who testified to his risen bodily life after that death. These claims are what seem to many people to matter most; and many of those who reject Christianity do so because they don't believe that all this *happened*. They won't believe the witnesses and don't want to be led by wishful thinking. Other people *accept* Christianity when they judge that all this *did* happen; they don't perhaps see the significance of it all, or *want* to believe it, or want to see the world and its future as Jesus portrayed it; but they judge that they ought to because, Yes, the witnesses were truthful and so those *were* the words and signs of the Creator.

Those were the judgments that seemed to me to matter, and that I made—first of unbelief, then in due course of belief. But there are others who reject or accept Christianity because of the meaning or significance it gives or attributes to human existence, the world, and the future. If he spoke truly

* Unpublished sermon, Evensong, University College Oxford, 11 May 1980.
[1] That is, Abel Muzorewa, Bishop of Rhodesia in the United Methodist Church; Prime Minister of Zimbabwe Rhodesia from early 1979 until the elections won by Mugabe's party in March 1980.

and was reported rightly, Robert Mugabe is one of those; 'I don't agree with the practice of Christianity. The notion that material things don't matter, that this world is only a stage to another world…I don't accept.' When he speaks of a 'stage', he may possibly be using the metaphor of rocketry; certainly it's vivid and relevant: the first-stage rocket is burned up and jettisoned; leaving it (and any other stage) altogether behind, the nodule floats freely under its own momentum in the emptiness of space. A great deal of preaching of Christianity can be summed up in that sort of picture; the reward of heavenly existence lies wholly in the future and has no more intrinsic connection with this life than a gold medal has with running 100 metres; the connection is made simply by the will of the prize giver and the ambition of the runner—an ambition which, if extended to the whole of life, would seem an ignoble because self-centred one. Indeed, if that is what it's all meant to be about, no wonder there's so often a discreet silence about heaven.

So we ought to attend to the full meaning and significance of the Resurrection of Jesus—not merely to the sheer fact of it, which has always seemed to me the main thing, *the* great evidence of God's revealing of himself in history; but rather to what it tells us about the meaning of history and of the end of history.

One could start in lots of places. Because of the second reading appointed for Evensong today, let me begin with the last words of that: 'in the Lord, your labour'—your 'work'—'is not in vain'.[2] This looks back to chapter 3, where Paul says that on the Day of Judgment

each man's work will become manifest, because it will be revealed with fire, and the fire will test what sort of work each one has done; if the work which anyone has built…survives, he will receive a reward. If anyone's work is burnt up, he will suffer loss, though he himself will be saved, but only as through fire.[3]

Christian meditation on this should not stop, and has not stopped, at the imperfect analogies of fire and reward. You might like to hear what the Bishops of Robert Mugabe's ecclesial community and mine make of it, in the teaching of the Second Vatican Council about the meaning and fulfilment of human activity:

Some people are called to testify openly to the yearning for a heavenly home and keep the human family's awareness of it vivid; others are called to dedicate themselves to the earthly service of man and in this way to prepare the material [the matter, the stuff, *materia*] of the kingdom of heaven…We do not know the way the universe will be transformed…[but] we are taught that God is preparing

---

[2] 1 Corinthians 15: 58. The labour that is not in vain is the 'work [*ergon*; *opus*] of the Lord'.
[3] 1 Corinthians 3: 13–15. Throughout these verses, 'work' is *ergon* (Latin, *opus*).

a new heaven and a new earth…Then with death overcome, the children of God will be raised in Christ and what was sown in weakness and corruption will put on the imperishable: charity *and its works*[4] will remain and all of creation which God made for mankind will be set free from its bondage to futility.…Far from diminishing our concern to develop this earth, the expectation of a new earth must spur us on to cultivate this earth, for it is *here* that the Body of a new human family is growing, which even now foreshadows in some way the age that is to come. That is why, although we must be careful to distinguish earthly progress clearly from the increase of Christ's Kingdom, such progress is of great moment to the Kingdom of God, insofar as that progress can make for the better ordering of human society. *For* when we have spread on earth the goods of human dignity, brotherhood and freedom—that is to say, *all the good fruits of our nature and of our enterprise* [*industria*]—according to the command of the Lord and in His Spirit, then we will *find those goods and good fruits again,* cleansed this time from the stain of sin, illuminated and transfigured, when Christ presents to the Father an eternal and universal kingdom…the realm which is mysteriously *present on this earth* and which will when the Lord comes be *perfected.*[5]

That is the teaching which, it seems, didn't get through to Robert Mugabe, just as it certainly hasn't got through to countless other Christians, former Christians, and non-Christians. Eternal life somehow begins here. Good works—in every sense, including study and contemplation and acts of friendship and sportsmanship and endurance and statesmanship, and so on—good works themselves operate not only to build up this world in the ways we can understand and work for, but also, in ways now mysterious to us, to build up, now, the new order of things and the renewed human family that are to be fully constituted and apparent on the other side of death. The image of the individual soul launched out of this world by a rocket that is then ditched and left behind is quite misleading; even Paul's analogy of the seed[6] is incomplete. The good works of men and women and children now, the good lives lived, are somehow the *material* of the City of God, even when they by chance or adversity fail, end in disaster, go unnoticed, and disappear from 'history'. Still, Paul's image of the seed has its point as one powerful representation of the coexistence of the already and the not yet, an image of the tension between the continuity and discontinuity between this world, this order-of-things that we understand, and the next world (beyond death), the heavenly order-of-things that is really present but quite hidden to us now. Paul himself shifts his metaphor; the perishable *puts on* the imperishable—as the Book of Revelation says, the guests at the Lord's wedding feast wear 'the fine linen which is their good works'

[4] '…*caritate et eius* opere *manente* (1 Cor.…3: 14)'.
[5] Vatican II, *Gaudium et Spes*, sec. 39 (emphases added).
[6] In the Evensong reading from 1 Corinthians 15: 37–8, 42–4.

(Revelation 19: 8). But this too is only an image, only partially adequate: the important thing is, as the same writer says, that 'the works of those who die in the Lord accompany them' (Revelation 14: 13), are not left behind—indeed, we may say that those works go to make up, constitute, the realm which is now developing (really but in mystery) in the material acts and facts of this life and which will then—on the other side of suffering, death, dissolution—become apparent.

A full reflection on these truths of the Christian faith would take us far afield. It would not dissolve their mysteriousness, though it would add to the density of meaning that they give to, or rather disclose in, our world and our lives. Let me just say this: their mysteriousness should make it easy to remind ourselves that though it is *our* bodies and *our* minds and *our* efforts that have this everlasting significance, that this is so is *entirely* the work of the merciful generosity of God.

15

THREE AND ONE[*]

Trinity Sunday 1988, sixth week of Trinity Term, a late spring holy day for what is most central to the Christian faith. The cycle of readings for Evensong makes us listen to Peter, near the beginning, it seems, of a baptismal sermon he preached in the early spring of AD 65, in Nero's Rome which he calls Babylon. And Peter like us is looking back, as well as forward, in the effort to understand what he repeatedly calls 'the revelation of Jesus Christ'.

He is looking back to 'the prophets who prophesied of the grace that was to be yours', and who, centuries before, had 'searched and inquired about this salvation' which he himself was now preaching. From the prophets, he will quote, mostly, Isaiah and the anonymous successor whom we call Deutero-Isaiah and heard in the first reading and whose work, with its four evocations of a Suffering Servant, is in mind when Peter speaks of the prophets 'predicting the sufferings of Christ and the subsequent glory'.

Looking back, Peter can say of the prophetic undertaking: they 'searched and inquired', and 'inquired what person or time was indicated by the Spirit of Christ'. And we, looking back, can observe how Peter attributes the prophetic predictings not to the human imaginings of the prophets but to 'the Spirit of Christ within them'—whereas the good news which has been preached to you—to those in Rome and Asia Minor and now in Oxford, who all must believe in Jesus Christ 'without having seen him'—this good news is preached, he says, 'through the Holy Spirit sent from heaven'. And this good news, as he said at the outset, is precisely the revelation of the great mercy of 'the God and Father of our Lord Jesus Christ'.

[*] Unpublished sermon, University College chapel, 29 May 1988. The readings for Evensong were Isaiah 40: 12–31 and 1 Peter 1: 3–12. [See Robinson, *Redating the New Testament* 150–69.]

Thus we can observe that these compact sentences from and to the first generation of Christians confidently, though implicitly and doubtless unconsciously, use the principle which, 250 years later, the Christian community—which must hand on the revelation until the end of human time—would use to settle the controversies about God's nature as three persons of one being: the reflective principle that whatever is truly said of God the Father is to be said of God the Son, except that the Son is Son and not Father; and likewise in respect of the Holy Spirit. So, if it is true that the Holy Spirit conveys the good news to Christian believers, it is equally true—as Peter sees and says—that it was Christ, the Son of the Father, who revealed to the prophets (centuries before his own incarnation as Jesus of Nazareth) some foreshadowing of his own human coming, suffering, and glorious resurrection from the dead.

So the hymn to God's greatness which we heard from Deutero-Isaiah—to God the everlasting Creator, the Judge who blows away earthly rulers like stubble, the Governor whose providence holds in being every one of the unnumbered stars and can see the way and protect the right of even the weakest among us—this hymn will be understood by Christians just as they have always understood the opening words of John's Gospel: the Word who became flesh and dwelt among us was with God, and was God; everything that has had a beginning was made through him, and nothing that has been created has been created without him.

If the man Jesus Christ is God, and if there is but one God, then Athanasius' principle holds good: whatever is truly said of God the Father is to be said of God the Son, except that the Son is Son and not Father. And if God's nature is supremely personal—a supremely active, self-directing centre of understanding, love, and will, as our Isaian passage like the rest of Scripture attests—then there follows the whole Trinitarian doctrine which you may find expressed in the *Quicunque Vult*, after the order of Evensong in the Book of Common Prayer. This so-called Athanasian Creed, probably emanating from fifth-century France, is, as John Henry Newman said,

not a mere collection of notions, however momentous. It is a psalm or hymn of praise, of confession,...with which we warn first ourselves, then each other, and then all who are within its hearing...who our God is, and how we must worship Him, and how vast our responsibility will be, if we know what to believe, and yet believe not...For myself I have ever felt it as the most simple and sublime, the most devotional formulary to which Christianity has given birth...Even the antithetical form of its sentences, which is a stumbling block to so many, as seeming to force, and to exult in forcing a mystery upon recalcitrating minds, has to my apprehension...a very different drift. It is intended as a check upon our reasonings, lest they rush in one direction beyond the limits of the truth, and it turns them back into the opposite direction.[1]

And Newman summed up the doctrine of the Trinity in nine propositions, each accessible to our mind and in a certain sense to our imagination, and mysterious and utterly beyond our imagination only in their combination: there are three who give testimony in heaven, the Father, the Word or Son, and the Holy Spirit; from the Father is, and ever has been, the Son; from the Father and the Son is, and ever has been, the Spirit; the Father is the one eternal personal God; the Son is the one eternal personal God; the Spirit is the one eternal personal God; the Father is not the Son; the Son is not the Holy Spirit; the Holy Spirit is not the Father—nine propositions.[2]

Such a series of propositions, like its expansion in the *Quicunque Vult*, or its contraction into Augustine's supremely terse 'tres et unus', is rather different from the method and culture of the Bible; but none of the propositions asserts anything not equivalently asserted and evoked in countless scriptural images and statements such as the fragments we heard this evening. Still further from the method of biblical discourse, yet equally appropriate to appropriating its full sense and significance, is the vast, centuries-long theological enterprise of rationally exploring the credal propositions. This enterprise has profoundly enhanced our understanding of what it is to understand and what it is to love—for the relation between one's coming to understand something and the concept(s) which such an act of understanding generates and makes intelligible is one of the closest analogies by which we can conceive some part of the relationship between the Father and the only-begotten Son; and the relation between one's understanding of something or somebody as truly desirable or lovable and one's intelligent desire for and love of that something or somebody is perhaps the closest analogy we can conceive to the proceeding of the Holy Spirit from the Father and the Son.

And like every other doctrine of the Christian faith, this has a practical significance all the greater because it is not a doctrine *about* human *praxis*—dispositions, choices, and actions—at all. In particular, this doctrine illuminates what we heard Peter calling 'the salvation of your souls'—something which has become opaque and unsettling, but which we can begin to appreciate from the great Trinitarian fact: that God is a unity of distinct persons, perfectly united and perfectly distinct. For if in God there is already a communication of divine life without any dissolution of selfhood—a communication between persons without absorption or annihilation—then 'the salvation ready to be revealed at the last time'

---

[1] Newman, *An Essay in Aid of a Grammar of Assent*, 133.   [2] *Ibid.*, 135.

cannot be supposed to be either self-centred or self-extinguishing. Rather, what Peter calls our living hope is for a freely chosen participation in the community which God is establishing by his own freely chosen initiative of extending, by creation and redemption, the familial unity which already is exemplified by the exemplary community of his own Trinitarian life.

The conditions of cooperation with this divine initiative are stated by Peter a few verses later: 'if you invoke as Father him who judges each one impartially according to his deeds, conduct yourselves with fear'...not fear of violating some arbitrarily imposed divine norms, but fear of choosing to turn away from God's initiative and life to follow passions and futilities attractive, as Peter says, when one ignores that 'living hope'—that is, when one ignores or loses faith in those possibilities which we have reason to believe realizable just because, thanks to the testimony of Peter and his fellows and successors, we have reason to have faith in Christ and in what his words and life disclose about the life and personalities of God.

Part Three

Conscience and Faith

16

CONSCIENCE IN THE *LETTER TO THE DUKE OF NORFOLK**

Gladstone's *Expostulation* made little use of the word 'conscience'. But others besides Newman saw that conscience was the pamphlet's theme. Bismarck wrote personally to Gladstone to express his

> deep and hopeful gratification to see the two nations, which in Europe are the champions of the liberty of conscience encountering the same foe, stand henceforth shoulder to shoulder in defending the highest interests of the human race.[1]

The Reich Chancellor's expression of favour for 'liberty of conscience' recalls for us the ambiguity of that phrase, and the experiences which now stand between us and the Gladstone–Newman debate.

Newman's *Letter*[2] does not concern the freedom of religious conscience from state coercion,[3] the freedom which, within due limits of public order, respect for others' rights, and public morality, is defended by the Second Vatican Council.[4] Nor does the *Letter* restate Newman's argument that

---

* 1990e.

[1] Letter dated 1 March 1875: see Conzemius, 'Acton, Döllinger and Gladstone: A Strange Variety of Anti-Infallibilists' at 51. Bismarck's own circular-despatch of 18 May 1872, claiming that Vatican I established a papal totalitarianism, had been first made public on 29 December 1874. The response of the German bishops, written in January 1875, had been signed by them all by February, and includes the sentence 'es ist wahrlich nicht die katholische Kirche, in welcher der unsittliche und despotische Grundsatz, der Befehl des Obern entbinde unbedingte von der eigenen Verantwortlichkeit, Aufnahme gefunden hat' ('it is not the Catholic Church that has accepted the immoral and despotic principle that superior orders release one unconditionally from personal responsibility'): D-S 3115; *Irenikon*, 29 (1956), 143–8, quotation from p. 146. Some chronology: Gladstone's *The Vatican Decrees in their Bearing on Civil Allegiance: A Political Expostulation* was published on 5 November 1874; Newman's reply was signed by him on 27 December 1874, finally corrected on 8 January and published on 14 January 1875. Gladstone's response, *Vaticanism: An Answer to Replies and Reproofs*, appeared on 24 Febuary 1875, and Newman's rejoinder appeared, by way of postscript to the fourth edition of the *Letter*, on 5 April 1875. The written exchanges between Bismarck and the German bishops and between Gladstone and Newman thus will have proceeded entirely independently.

[2] Cited from Newman, *Certain Difficulties Felt by Anglicans*, ii [hereafter *Letter*], 175–378; page numbers are given in parenthesis in the text.

[3] *Pace* D'Arcy (in an otherwise valuable essay), 'Conscience and Meta-Ethics: Newman vis-à-vis Anglo-American Philosophy Today' at 181.

[4] *Dignitatis Humanae*, Declaration on Religious Freedom, 7 December 1965, esp. paras 1–8. For Newman's apparent indifference to this political freedom, see *Letter* 204, 267, 271, 274; these pages

the experience of conscience justifies belief in God's existence, power, and providence.[5] Another lifelong theme of Newman's which is likewise helpfully absent from the *Letter* is the contrast he often drew between conscience and reason.[6] Indeed, the *Letter* has its peculiar power from its celebration of conscience precisely as an 'intellectual endowment' (248) enabling the 'rational creature' (246) to share in 'the Divine Light' (247), the Divine Law, 'Divine Reason or Will of God' (246)—as against the theories of 'the great world of philosophy now', which dethrone conscience as 'but a twist in primitive and untutored man', a 'simply irrational' product or manifestation of 'imagination' (249).

I

How does this high philosophical theme emerge?

Newman saw two charges to be met: (1) Catholics cannot now be trustworthy subjects, since the council has given the pope a hold over their consciences such that he can interfere with their civil duties and allegiance (179, 180, 181, 195, 349); (2) the same dogma of papal infallibility equally requires Catholics to renounce their mental and moral freedom and uprightness (179, 180, 350). Already, in the ground-clearing polemics about the Irish bishops' opposition to the Irish University Bill of 1873, and about the eighteenth- and early nineteenth-century assurances of Irish and English bishops that papal infallibility was no dogma, Newman reminds his readers, with lightest touch, that popes and bishops, too, have claims of conscience, duty, principle (183, 185). And he artfully recalls, in passing, a case where every reader would reject the claims of civil

---

also express his antipathy to the modern liberal ideal of a morally 'neutral' state which will allow 'free love' and even 'infanticide', which for Newman are 'atrocities' which 'the good sense of the nation would stifle and extinguish' even when they are practised in the name of conscience (274).

    [5] *Letter* 248 states in passing that non-Catholic Christians, like Catholics, consider conscience 'to be the internal witness of both the existence and the law of God'. The argument to God from conscience had been most recently stated by Newman in his *Grammar of Assent*, 47, 72–7, 251–2.

    [6] In the word 'felt' there is just a hint (*Letter* 349) of that distinction between reason and conscience which, in relation to the same decision (to join 'that Catholic Church, which in my own conscience I felt to be divine'), is drawn in Newman's letter of 30 March 1845 to Maria Giberne:

> My own convictions are as strong as I suppose they can become: only it is so difficult to know whether it is the call of *reason* or of conscience. I cannot make out, if I am impelled by what seems *clear*, or by a sense of *duty*…Then I am waiting, because friends are most considerately…asking guidance for me: and, I trust, I should attend to any new feelings which came upon me, should that be the effect of their kindness. (*Apologia pro Vita Sua*, ed. Svaglic, 208.)

For Newman's contrast between reason (i.e. reasoning) and everything concerned with the 'antecedents of an act of reason(ing)' (moral sense, intuitions, *nous*, the dictates of conscience, the inspired Word, the decisions of the Church, etc.), see e.g. 'Revelation in its Relation to Faith' (1885–6) in *Theological Papers on Faith and Certainty*, 141–2, 152–5.

allegiance: 'a heathen State might bid me throw incense upon the altar of Jupiter, and the Pope would bid me not to do so' (187).

Similarly, the chapter on the 'Ancient Church' presents the whole history of the Church as 'the very embodiment of that tradition of Apostolical independence and freedom of speech which in the eyes of man is her great offence now' (197). While Anglican and Oriental Churches are ashamed before kings, or lie under their bondage, 'Rome is now the one faithful representative, and is thereby heir and successor, of that free-spoken dauntless Church of old' (198), fulfilling 'the very mission of Christianity to bear witness to the Creed and Ten Commandments' (197). The chapter on 'The Papal Church' reinforces the point: Gladstone's objection cannot be merely to 'the Pope's special power' (209).

It is not the existence of a Pope, but of a Church, which is his aversion. It is the powers themselves, and not their distribution and allocation in the ecclesiastical body which he writes against (209–10).

Whenever Christians act in the political realm, they are responsible to God and conscience (211); when the pope acts as supreme judge of Christendom, the 'basis and rule' of his sentence must 'appeal to the supreme standard of right and wrong, the moral law' (221).

The chapter on 'Divided Allegiance', which immediately precedes the central chapter on 'Conscience', is announced as the beginning of 'a long explanation, and, in a certain sense, limitation' (223) of what Newman has been saying about the sovereignty of the Church and of the pope as its head. The explanation will extend to the end of the *Letter* (224). It will show why Newman can reject Gladstone's conclusions (the charges of allegiance to a foreign power, and moral slavery) while accepting his premises: that the pope claims infallibility in morals, and that there are no departments of human life which fall outside the domain of morals (224).

Newman says he will 'put aside for the present and at first the Pope's prerogative of infallibility in general enunciations, whether of faith or morals', and confine himself to considering the pope's 'authority (in respect to which he is not infallible) in matters of conduct' (224). The implications of the pope's prerogative of infallibility are not formally taken up, I believe, until the last substantive chapter, Chapter 9, 'The Vatican Definition'. But, as we shall see, the questionable thesis there developed is aired in the fifth chapter, on conscience.

Meanwhile, the long fourth chapter on 'Divided Allegiance' proceeds to make two broad points: that the pope's interpositions into 'our private affairs, . . . our routine of personal duties' (228) are so rare as to be 'absolutely unappreciable' (229); and that, while there are cases (particularly involving the performance of religious duties) in which 'we should obey the Pope and disobey the State' (240), there are cases, hypothetical, in a sense 'impossible' (241, 244), but imaginable, in which 'I should side, not with the Pope, but with the Civil Power' (241). In relation to each point, Newman's argument is clouded by unclarities about the logic of the Church's *moral* teachings, unclarities which will later cloud his discussions of conscience's relation to the Church's infallibility *de moribus*.

For, in his treatment of the first point we find Newman bundling together papal directives on 'matters sacramental, ritual, ecclesiastical, monastic, and disciplinarian' (230) with papal teachings on matters moral. The whole discussion sets morality firmly within a framework in which moral truth and positive law, though distinguished in principle, are commingled in the practice of moral formation.[7] In our 'ordinary duties', Newman says, we are guided by books of moral theology and casuistry,

based on the three foundations of Faith, Hope, and Charity, on the Ten Commandments, and on the six Precepts of the Church, which relate to the observance of Sunday, of fast days, of confession and communion, and... to paying tithes (229).

The books give 'directions' which are 'little more than reflexions and memoranda of our moral sense', though sometimes their answers, like those of 'private conscience itself', may be 'difficult to us or painful to accept'. Our 'private judgment' need not in every case give way to the books, which after all 'are no utterance of Papal authority' (229). And when that authority has intervened in moral matters it has been by condemnations which

relate for the most part to mere occasional details of duty, and are in reprobation of the lax or wild notions of speculative casuists, so that they are rather restraints upon theologians than upon laymen (230).

Newman here instances 'at random' two of the sixty-five laxist propositions condemned by the Holy Office in 1679 under Innocent XI: that domestics who think themselves underpaid may compensate themselves by stealing from their employers,[8] and that public persons may head off otherwise unavoidable calumny by killing the intending calumniator (230).[9] Are even these so wild, so speculative, so removed from the passions of lay people? In any event, today's reader will think instead of the moral

---

[7] On legalism in the moral theology and casuistry to which Newman is referring, see *CMP* 13, 15, 292–5, 304–6.

[8] Proposition 37: see D-S 2137, which editorially identifies Leonard Lessius SJ, Antoninus Diana, and Matthaeus de Moya SJ as proponents of the condemned proposition.

[9] Proposition 30: see *ibid.*, 2130 which editorially identifies Martinus Becanus SJ as affirming the proposition, and implicates also the Jesuits Vasquez, Filliucci, and Escobar, 'and many others' including Jesuits and non-Jesuits of high theological standing.

teachings on which twentieth-century popes and council have had to insist, not against a few 'speculative casuists' but against many priests, some bishops, very many influential clerical moralists, and numerous 'private Catholics' (cf. 231) who wish to feel justified in accepting what is accepted in their affluent cultures: intentional abortion, contraception, euthanasia, baby-making, adultery, remarriage after divorce, and the area-bombing of enemy cities.[†]

Newman does not deny or overlook, of course, the authority of the pope 'to speak definitively on ethical subjects', and he affirms that what the pope thus propounds 'must relate to things good and bad in themselves, not to things accidental, changeable, and of mere expedience' (231; similarly 331). But by casting his discussion in the terms (common to virtually all the moral theology of his age) of law and obedience, and by granting (if not conceding) that moral teachings are a weight on conscience, Newman here encourages rather than dissipates the confusion of teaching with *law-making*, a confusion he would have deplored had he confronted its modern manifestations. This is a passage where we feel, again, our distance from his age.[10]

What of Newman's other broad point in this chapter, that one can imagine cases where Catholics should 'act with the Civil Power, and not with the Pope' (241)? The theological authorities he cites (pre-Reformation, Counter-Reformation, and nineteenth-century) establish convincingly that papal orders *ought* to be disregarded and disobeyed when they contradict 'Holy Scripture, or the articles of faith, or the truth of the Sacraments, or the commands of the natural or divine law' (242).[11] But Newman's two examples scarcely instantiate a clear-cut contradiction between papal orders and faith or morals, and today seem problematical.

The first example supposes that a member of Parliament or privy councillor has sworn not to acknowledge the right of a Catholic to succeed to the throne, and that a pope has purported to release him from that oath and commanded him to acknowledge a Catholic succession. As Newman

---

[10] Only twenty years before, Newman had written, 'never was the Church less troubled with false teachers, never more united'. He had treated as distant (though not necessarily merely in the past) the miserable times 'when a man's Catholic profession is no voucher for his orthodoxy, and when a teacher of religion may be within the Church's pale, yet external to her faith': 'A Form of Infidelity of the Day' (1854) in *The Idea of a University*, 318. In 1874 there possibly are slight, but certainly only the slightest, intimations of a return of those times: see *Letter* 208–9.

[11] Newman here cites Cardinal Turrecremata, '*Summ. de Eccl.*, pp. 47, 48'; see Ioannis de Turrecremata (Juan de Torquemada, OP (1388–1468), named *Defensor fidei* by Eugenius IV in 1436 for his theological defence of papal authority), *Summa de Ecclesia* (1448–9; Venice, 1561), lib. II, cap. 49, p. 163'. (In this edition, at least, the phrase translated or emended by Newman 'truth of the Sacraments' is 'veritati sanctorum'; cf. e.g. Gregory IX's letter of 7 July 1228; theologians ought to expound theology 'secundum approbatas traditiones Sanctorum', i.e. of the Fathers ('sanctorum Patrum'): D-S 824.)

himself observes, the Catholic councillor can avoid the clash between Church and state by resigning his office, thereby ridding himself of the binding force of his oath.

The other example is more interesting. A member of the armed forces, serving in a war which he cannot in conscience see to be unjust, is with all his fellow Catholic servicemen 'suddenly' ordered by the pope 'to retire from the service' (242). Here all turns on Newman's word 'suddenly'; we must read it as excluding the case which is rather easier to imagine: the pope judges that the war, though just in its cause and objectives, is being prosecuted by an immoral strategy of taking and killing non-combatant hostages and destroying and threatening to destroy whole cities and their inhabitants in the manner denounced by Vatican II as a crime against God and man; and the pope, having stated his judgment, and his further judgment that combatant service in a state campaigning under the protection of a counter-civilian terror strategy amounts to participation in the immoral acts of terrorism, 'bids' (242) all Catholic servicemen to retire from the service unless their government immediately renounces the immoral strategy. The question is not whether this is a likely contingency, but whether, confronted by the pope's (or a council's) moral judgment about the immorality of any combatant service under the umbrella of a terrorist strategy, one should follow that judgment even if one's own moral assessment were that only those who personally authorize or execute the terrorist acts are participants in terrorism.

You will say: that is not the sort of case Newman was considering, and his 'suddenly' shows that he had another case in mind. All he needed was *some* case in which a Catholic might rightly disobey a papal injunction. I agree, and wish only to note that Newman's example raises for us certain questions which he and his readers felt unreal, but which later events and our own predicament make real.

The chapter on divided allegiance thus concludes with a proposition which Newman, in effect, formulates in two different ways: (1) one should disobey papal orders *which are contrary to morality*; (2) one should disobey papal orders *which are contrary to one's conscience*. The first is the more fundamental formulation, the second derivative. Their propositional equivalence consists in this: when judgments differ on the question whether a papal order is contrary to morality, the judgment one must follow (after testing it as best one can against the arguments and opinions of others) is one's own; so (1) and (2) are each equivalent to: (3) one should disobey papal orders *which one judges to be contrary to morality*.

In short: talk of following one's own conscience has a distinct point only when there is *disagreement* about whether the moral norm to which one is appealing has indeed the truth or the application which one judges it to have:

I should look to see what theologians could do for me, what the Bishops and clergy around me, what my confessor; what friends whom I have revered: and if, after all, I could not take their view of the matter, then I must rule myself by my own judgment and my own conscience (243–4).

But throughout, the object of one's inquiry is not to discover one's own conscience, but to discover what (as best one can see) is the *truth* of the matter. That my judgment is *mine* adds not a jot to my grounds for thinking that it is true. Hence the priority of formulation (1). Newman would be the first to agree that his preference for formulation (2), in ending the chapter on divided allegiance and in opening that on conscience (246), arises not from any doubt about the priority of (1), but from concern to show that Catholics are not mental and moral slaves, since they make their own judgments.

II

In the depths of conscience, man discerns a law which he does not dictate to himself but which he ought to obey. Always summoning him to love and do the good and to avoid evil, the voice of this law[12] sounds when necessary in the ears of his heart as 'Do this, shun that'. For man has in his heart a law written by God; to obey that law is his very dignity, and according to it he will be judged [Romans 2: 15–16]. Conscience is the most secret core and sanctuary of man, in which he is alone with God, whose voice resounds in his inwardness [citation to Pius XII, 23 March 1952]. Conscience, in a wonderful manner, makes known that law which is fulfilled by love of God and neighbour.... [T]o the extent that a correct conscience holds sway, persons and groups turn away from blind choice and seek to conform to the objective norms of morality.[13]

This teaching of Vatican II 'on the dignity of the moral conscience' is, of course, the teaching proposed by Newman in the powerful opening pages of his chapter on conscience. Not that the council takes the teaching from Newman; Mgr Delhaye's book on conscience in Christian thought, published shortly before he became involved in the drafting of this part of the council's work, refers to well over a hundred classic Christian sources, in which virtually every element and phrase of this passage can be found.[14]

---

[12] Not 'the voice of conscience', as mistranslated in Abbott, *The Documents of Vatican II*, 213.
[13] GS 16.
[14] Delhaye, *La Conscience Morale du Chrétien:* see esp. ch. 3, 'Patristic Signposts'.

Newman is not among them. This is no surprise; these pages of the *Letter* are what they profess to be: a statement of what is 'acknowledged by all Catholics' (246).

With rhetorical economy and power, Newman begins by showing that Catholics acknowledge 'the prerogatives and the supreme authority of conscience' (246) precisely because they acknowledge the 'sovereign, irreversible, absolute authority' of 'the Divine Law [which] is the rule of ethical truth, the standard of right and wrong' (246), the eternal law of which Augustine wrote, the natural law which Thomas Aquinas called 'an impression of the Divine Light in us, a participation of the eternal law in the rational creature' (247).[15] For:

> This law, as apprehended in the minds of individual men, is called 'conscience;' and though it may suffer refraction in passing into the intellectual medium of each, it is not therefore so affected as to lose its character of being the Divine Law, but still has, as such, the prerogative of commanding obedience (247).

At this stage of his exposition, Newman is discussing what many theologians since Aquinas have called the 'habitual conscience'. One's understanding of the fundamental principles of practical reasonableness, like one's understanding of fundamental non-practical principles (e.g. of logic), is not so much a special power (as Newman sometimes seems to suggest (e.g. at 248)) as, rather, a state of mind, a disposition or *habitus*, whereby one is in a position to proceed to other, derivative, and more particular acts of understanding and of reasoning to particular conclusions. The theological tradition has been inclined to reserve the term 'conscience' for one's last, best judgment, whereby the principles which one 'habitually' knows are brought to bear in a fully specified act of judgment that a particular practical proposal is good or bad, right or wrong. But Christian tradition has from the outset used the term 'conscience' (*syneidēsis, conscientia*) to refer to our grasp of natural and divine law in all its universality and immutability *as well as* to our grasp of a particular option's rightness or wrongness or eligibility here and now. So theologians came to call the former the 'habitual conscience', while the latter they called the 'actual conscience', that is, conscience *qua* one's last best act of practical judgment. (The scholastic jargon does not matter, but the distinction it signifies is real and important in any explanation of how conscience can both illumine and deceive.)

---

[15] Here Newman vaguely cites 'Gousset, *Theol. Moral.*, t. i. pp. 24, &c.', namely T.M.J. Gousset (Archbishop of Reims), *Théologie morale à l'usage des curés et des confesseurs* (Paris, 1845), where the passages from Augustine and Aquinas which Newman quotes both appear on p. 48, in the chapter on 'Divine Laws' (which, as in the treatise of Gousset's master St Alphonsus Liguori, follows rather than precedes the chapter on 'Conscience' from which (24) the other passages quoted by Newman are taken). (Cardinal Gousset, 1792–1866, was a notable defender of papal infallibility, and opponent of Gallicanism and Jansenism.)

Later in the chapter, as we shall see, Newman will abruptly switch to speaking of the actual conscience. At the outset, however, his magnificent portrayal of the conscience which philosophers condemn and 'the popular mind' (249) counterfeits is a portrayal of the habitual conscience.

To speak of conscience, in this sense, is to speak of *principles*, the principles one's understanding of which simply *is* one's having a (habitual) conscience. Hence Newman's defence of conscience against Enlightenment reductions is centred on his rejection of the moral principles proposed by the Renaissance and the Enlightenment:

The rule and measure of duty is not utility, nor expedience, nor the happiness of the greatest number, nor State convenience, nor fitness, order, and the *pulchrum*. Conscience is not a long-sighted selfishness, nor a desire to be consistent with oneself; but it is a messenger from Him, who, both in nature and in grace, speaks to us behind a veil, and teaches and rules us by His representatives (248).

And these representatives are two: nature and grace, conscience and revelation. For by 'conscience...we mean, the voice of God in the nature and heart of man, as distinct from the voice of Revelation' (247). So:

Conscience is the aboriginal Vicar of Christ, a prophet in its informations, a monarch in its peremptoriness, a priest in its blessings and anathemas, and, even though the eternal priesthood throughout the Church could cease to be, in it the sacerdotal principle would remain and would have a sway (248–9).

That is, if the voice and vehicle of revelation were stilled *(per impossibile:* Matthew 28: 20), the Word would still be heard, in as much as habitual conscience could still grasp what the Creator intended as the rule and measure of the rational creature's choices and actions—could still be aware of the 'truths which the Lawgiver has sown in our very nature' (253), the 'Natural Law' (254), and 'the rights of the Creator,...the duty to Him, in thought and deed, of the creature' (250).

Still,

Natural Religion, certain as are its grounds and its doctrines as addressed to thoughtful, serious minds, needs, in order that it may speak to mankind with effect and subdue the world, to be sustained and completed by Revelation (254).[16]

In the 'insufficiency of the natural light' (253) is the justification of the pope's 'very mission...to proclaim the moral law, and to protect and

---

[16] Cf. Vatican I, *Dei Filius*, Dogmatic Constitution on the Catholic Faith, 24 April 1870, ch. 2:
It is by virtue of this divine revelation that those things which *in rebus divinis* are in themselves not inaccessible to human reason can, even in the present condition of the human race, be known by all with ease, with firm certainty, and without contamination of error. (D–S 3005; Vatican II, DV 6.)

strengthen that "Light which enlighteneth every man that cometh into the world"' (252). For conscience is weak:

the sense of right and wrong...is so delicate, so fitful, so easily puzzled, obscured, perverted, so subtle in its argumentative methods, so impressible by education, so biassed by pride and passion, so unsteady in its course, that, in the struggle for existence amid the various exercises and triumphs of the human intellect, this sense is at once the highest of all teachers, yet the least luminous; and the Church, the Pope, the Hierarchy are, in the Divine purpose, the supply of an urgent demand (253–4).

But revelation, though going beyond 'a mere republication of the Natural Law' (254), has its point not by being independent of, or without relation to, the natural law known to the (habitual) conscience, but rather by being the 'complement, reassertion, issue, embodiment, and interpretation' of that natural law (254). Thus, if the pope were to speak against conscience in the true, 'high sense' (255) of the word, 'he would commit a suicidal act...cutting the ground from under his feet', denying his mission and undercutting 'both his authority in theory and his power in fact' (252). When popes such as Gregory XVI and Pius IX have scoffed at 'liberty of conscience', enclosing the phrase in their own quotation marks, they have been speaking against conscience only 'in the various false senses, philosophical or popular, which in this day are put upon the word' (251) and which Newman has just sketched with memorable animus and force:

Conscience has rights because it has duties; but in this age, with a large portion of the public, it is the very right and freedom of conscience to dispense with conscience.... Conscience is a stern monitor, but in this century it has been superseded by a counterfeit, which the eighteen centuries prior to it never heard of, and could not have mistaken for it, if they had. It is the right of self-will (250).

III

Newman's direct and 'distinct' (255) answer to the charge of mental and moral slavery employs two arguments for its correct conclusion. Of these, the first and most prominent has premises which, I shall argue, are mistaken:

conscience is not a judgment upon any speculative truth, any abstract doctrine, but bears immediately on conduct, on something to be done or not done. 'Conscience,' says St. Thomas, 'is the practical judgment or dictate of reason, by which we judge what *hic et nunc* is to be done as being good, or to be avoided as evil.' Hence conscience cannot come into direct collision with the Church's or the Pope's infallibility; which is engaged on general propositions and in the condemnation of particular and given errors (256).[17]

Both the premises of this argument are mistaken. For: (1) Conscience is 'engaged on' and makes 'judgment upon' propositions more general than that *this* particular option is not to be made *now* by *me*. (2) And the general propositions which are the proper object of the Church's infallibility include negative universals which, by absolutely excluding all actions of a specified type, exclude *this* particular option which could be made by *me now*.

As to (1): Newman's discourse has here shifted, without warning, from the 'habitual' to the 'actual' conscience. There can be no objection to that; both are legitimate senses of 'conscience' and there is no incompatibility between them. But his argument here forgets that the actual conscience, being a rational (even if mistaken) judgment about a particular option, is an *application* of rational (even if mistaken) norms and principles of judgment—at the highest level, the principles understood and affirmed in the habitual conscience.

The quotation which Newman ascribes (256) to St Thomas does indeed represent Aquinas's opinion. But the words are those not of Aquinas but of St Alphonsus Liguori;[18] reading p. 24 of Gousset's *Théologie morale*, Newman's eye has slipped from footnote 2 to footnote 3.[19] The passage to which the latter footnote is attached gives the relevant teaching of St Thomas: 'Conscience is simply the *application* of knowledge to a particular act'.[20]‡ The whole point of the Church's teaching about conscience, as

---

[17] This or a very similar argument seems to be recalled prominently in the concluding chapter: since the

prerogative of infallibility lies in matters speculative...infallibility bears upon the domain of thought, not directly of action, and while it may fairly exercise the theologian, philosopher, or man of science, it scarcely concerns the politician (342–3).

[18] Gousset's citation is 'S. Alphonse de Liguori, Theol. Moral., *de Conscientia*, n. 2'; see Alphonsi de Ligorio, *Theologia Moralis*, lib. I, cap. 1, para. 2 (ed. L. Gaudé) ([9th edn, 1985] Rome, 1905), 3; it is Alphonsus's primary definition of (actual) conscience.

[19] See Gousset, *Théologie morale*, 24. It is amusing to see the US bishops, in the section on conscience in their joint pastoral letter *Human Life in Our Day* dated 15 November 1968, saying (just before quoting from Newman's *Letter*) that 'Thomas Aquinas describes conscience as the practical judgment or dictate of reason, by which we judge what here and now is to be done as being good, or to be avoided as evil'; they give no citation to Aquinas; they are unwittingly quoting Alphonsus via Newman. More serious is the inappropriateness of the US bishops' extended quotation from the *Letter*; the passage (257–8) concerns the pre-conditions for conscience 'to prevail against the voice of the Pope' (257) in his 'laws', 'commands', 'acts of state', 'administration', and 'public policy' (256, 258), not in his enunciation of 'general propositions' or his 'condemnation of particular and given errors' (256), still less in his restatement of truths which, like the central propositions in Paul VI's encyclical *Humanae Vitae*, 25 July 1968 (on which the US bishops were then commenting), had already been infallibly taught by the Church's ordinary magisterium even though they were not formally defined *ex cathedra* by the encyclical itself.

[20] Gousset correctly cites *De Veritate* q.17 a.3. Aquinas first states this clearly in the preceding article, where he adds that, when we say that conscience is the application of *knowledge*, we do not

recalled by Newman in the early pages of the chapter, is that in obeying one's conscience one is unconscious of any mistake one may in fact be making[21] and so considers oneself to be obeying the divine *law*, that is, the natural and/or revealed *general* and *universal* rule and measure of human acts.[22] One's reasons (right or wrong) for judgment are necessarily general propositions, and are present to one's conscience in one's conscientious final judgment, which therefore can 'come into direct collision' with a general proposition which in fact has been infallibly proposed.

As to (2): This is especially evident when the general proposition infallibly proposed by the Church is a negative universal of the form 'Acts of type X [for example directly killing an innocent human being] are always wrong, whatever the circumstances'. As Karl Rahner rightly put the point:

it goes without saying that a man must obey his conscience....It is right that the Christian conscience should be mature. But this maturity of the Christian conscience is not an emancipation from and casting off of the universal norms preached by the Gospel and the Church...it is the ability to apply these norms oneself to a concrete situation without needing help in every case....When the whole Church in her everyday teaching does in fact teach a moral rule everywhere in the world *as* a commandment of God, she is preserved from error by the assistance of the Holy Ghost, and this rule is therefore the will of God and is binding on the faithful in conscience, even before it is expressly confirmed by a solemn definition. A moral norm is by nature universal but, precisely as a universal law, is intended to be the rule for the individual case. And so when it is fully grasped and rightly understood and interpreted (that is, understood as the magisterium means it, not just as an individual thinks fit to interpret it), and bears on an individual case, then this unique individual concrete case is bound by the norm and obliged to abide by it. When, for example, the Church teaches

---

imply that the 'knowledge' is always really knowledge, i.e. *true* belief; in mistaken conscience it is only *seeming* knowledge: *De Veritate* q.17 a.2c and ad 2.

[21] As Aquinas says, *De Veritate* q.17 a.4c:

one who has a mistaken conscience, and believes that it is correct (*otherwise he would not be mistaken*), clings to his mistaken conscience because of the correctness he believes is there; indeed, speaking *per se*, he is clinging to a correct conscience, but one which is as it were mistaken *per accidens*, insofar as this conscience which he believes to be correct happens to be mistaken. (Emphasis added.)

[22] A precept does not bind save by force of [one's] knowledge [of it], nor does [that] knowledge bind save [by mediating] the force of the precept. So, since conscience is simply the application of knowledge to an action, it is obvious that conscience is said to bind by the force of divine law. (*De Veritate* q.17 a.2c.)

Or again:

The binding force of conscience, even mistaken conscience, is the same thing as the binding force of the law of God ('idem est ligamen conscientiae etiam erroneae et legis Dei'). For conscience does not say that X is to be done or Y avoided unless it believes that Y is contrary to, or X in accordance with, the law of God. (Aquinas, *In ad Romanos*, cap. 14 lect. 2 ad v. 15.)

that *every* directly induced abortion is morally wrong...then this applies to every individual case quite regardless of the circumstances.[23]

The only clarification that need be added to Rahner's lucid statement is that there are many universal norms and principles which cannot by themselves supply sufficient premises for a secure application to the particular case, but must be supplemented by additional premises which one's conscience will find in one's own prior commitments, in the responsibilities of one's special roles (such as parenthood), in the applicable civil or ecclesiastical laws and directives, and, quite generally, in one's own chosen vocation. This is true of all the norms and principles which specify *affirmative* responsibilities—to do such and such (honour parents, educate children, serve the community, etc.).

Still, the same cannot be said of the few but vital norms which specify the *negative* responsibilities common to all human beings. To these negative moral norms there are no true exceptions. In their application, they are the exception to the 'rule' (generalization), reiterated throughout the *Letter*,[24] that to every rule (generalization) there are exceptions. An example? In Vatican II's words: '*Every* warlike act aimed indiscriminately at whole cities...is a crime against God and man.'[25]

From (1) and (2) together it follows that Newman's conclusion that 'conscience cannot come into direct collision with the Church's or the Pope's infallibility' (256) is mistaken. His statement can be made true only by taking 'conscience' here to mean exclusively a conscience which correctly acknowledges all the infallible moral teachings of the Church. (There are hints on pp. 255 and 257 that this is what Newman may here have had in mind;[26] and Newman will later say that the Church's infallible moral teachings are 'such as in fact will be found to command the assent of most men, as soon as heard' (332)—another sign of his distance from our age.) But, if 'conscience' be taken thus, his argument distinguishing general from particular becomes redundant, irrelevant. And his denial of

---

[23]   Rahner, 'Dangers in Catholicism Today: The Appeal to Conscience', 96–100. Later writings of Karl Rahner SJ seem to overlook this position, but offer no reasons for departing from it.

[24]   See *Letter* 243, 261, 338, 342, 359. There can be no doubt that Newman, in reiterating this generalization and in other aspects of his argument in the *Letter*, had no thought of questioning the Church's teaching of negative moral absolutes, or of proposing that they are subject to the exceptions alleged by modern theologians who do not share Newman's conviction that the pope is 'appointed by his Divine Master to determine in the detail of faith and morals what is true and what is false', with 'dogmatic authority' (278).

[25]   GS 80: 'Omnis actio bellica...'. For the distinction between affirmative moral norms, which bind 'semper sed non ad semper' [always but not for every occasion], and negative moral norms which bind 'semper et ad semper' [always and on every occasion], see e.g. Aquinas, *In ad Romanos*, cap. 13 lect. 2 ad v. 9; *De Malo*, q.7 a.l ad 8; *ST* II–II q.33 a.2c, etc.; Alphonsus Liguori, *Theologia Moralis*, II–II I, tract. 2, cap. 1, dub. 1, para. 101 (ed. Gaudé, 82); [*Aquinas* 164].

[26]   See below, n. 28.

the possibility of collision between (such a) conscience and the Church's *de fide* teaching *de moribus* becomes tautologous, scarcely an answer to those who regard acceptance of the Church's infallible teaching authority as slavery.

The primary true reply to that accusation is that the Church's irreformable teachings are not a burden but an enlightenment.

A secondary reply is the one developed by Newman in parallel with his mistaken argument about general and particular:

a Pope is not infallible in his laws, nor in his commands, nor in his acts of state, nor in his administration, nor in his public policy (256).

In relation to these, one's conscience has (that is, one has) the responsibility of identifying the bearing of one's affirmative responsibilities (vocation) in the circumstances—something which no moral teaching, infallible or otherwise, could fully settle. Moreover, in these matters one is not merely *bound* to follow one's conscience; one's conscience can even be said to have, on certain conditions, 'the *right* of opposing the supreme, though not infallible Authority of the Pope' (257, emphasis added). In the practical matters which are the primary subject-matter of the Church's infallible teachings *de moribus*, that is, as to 'things in themselves good or evil' and 'necessary for salvation' (331), the whole theological school from Aquinas and before (259) to Newman and after will willingly say that one has a *duty* to follow one's conscience[27]—for though one may indeed be culpable for erroneously rejecting what the Church has taught (259), and though one has a duty to correct one's conscience by conforming to that teaching, still one is certainly culpable if one fails to do what one's *conscience* (not mere self-will) bids one do. But this *duty* is not a *right* of opposing papal authority, such as Newman speaks of in relation to the many matters in which the pope does not act infallibly.[28] That 'right', manifesting an aspect

---

[27] The solidity of this theological teaching is not affected by the fact that the striking dictum 'Quidquid fit contra conscientiam, aedificat ad gehennam' which Gousset (*Théologie morale*, 24; the sentences quoted from him in *Letter* 247 are an amalgamation of passages from paras 55 and 57) and Newman (259: 'He who acts against his conscience loses his soul') ascribe to the Fourth Lateran Council is taken not from that council but from a letter of 1201 by Innocent III touching the 'difficultas quasi perplexa' of a wife who is ordered by an ecclesiastical court to return to a marriage bed which she believes ('habet notitiam') incestuous: 'propter sententiam oporteret eam reddere debitum, et propter conscientiam debitum reddere non deberet'. The pope's canonical solution is prefaced by the reflection that she ought not to disobey God by obeying the judgment, but ought humbly to accept the excommunication which will follow disobedience to the court: 'quoniam omne, quod non est ex fide, peccatum est, et quicquid fit contra conscientiam aedificat ad gehennam'. See *Corpus Iuris Canonici*, ed. Richter (1881), ii. 287 (Decretales Gregorii IX, lib. II, tit. xiii de restitutione spoliatorum, cap. 13). Theologians of the thirteenth century treated Innocent III's dictum [from Gratian's *Decretum* II, Causa 28 q.1 c.14 (Friedberg I 1088)] as of quite general significance, 'generaliter verum', as Bonaventure says in his *Commentary on the Sentences* (c. 1250) II d.39 a.1 q.3 ad 4.

[28] The distinction I am drawing seems to be implied in what Newman says on p. 257: 'infallibility alone could block the exercise of conscience, and the Pope is not infallible in that subject-matter in which conscience is of supreme authority'. This passage makes best sense if 'conscience' is taken

of conscience's autonomy overlooked in the allegation of mental and moral slavery, is simply an entailment of the fact the magisterium's divine mission is to hand on the deposit of revelation and faith, not to coordinate the political communities and other lesser groups to which each of us belongs, nor to supersede personal discernment (and choice) of vocation.

IV

I add one remark. Certainly, if I am obliged to bring religion into after-dinner toasts, (which indeed does not seem quite the thing) I shall drink—to the Pope, if you please,—still, to Conscience first, and to the Pope afterwards (261).

These closing words of the chapter on conscience seem to have been intended to anticipate the remark, three pages later, about 'what Bentham calls Church-of-Englandism, its cry being the dinner toast, "Church and king"' (264). But Newman's toast has made its way in the world quite divorced from its context—not merely the now unimportant context just mentioned, but the essential context established by the whole *Letter*: reverence for the truth of divine law disclosed by conscience; 'generous loyalty towards ecclesiastical authority' which 'a true Catholic…must have', 'accept[ing] what is taught him with what is called the *pietas fidei*' (339; similarly 258); the horror of false consciousness, that 'miserable counterfeit' (257) masking self-will.

At the end of a penetrating exposition of the Christian philosophy of conscience, and of this century's philosophical explorations of the corrupt consciousness engendered by corrupt societies, the Episcopalian philosopher Alan Donagan recalls Newman's toast, and drily adds:

Were we obliged to bring morality into toasts, we should not refuse to drink to conscience; but we should beg to drink to a truthful consciousness first.[29]

For our generation, Donagan's toast expresses better than Newman's the essential premise, and something of the spirit, of the *Letter*.

---

here to mean 'well-instructed Catholic conscience'. Otherwise, the statement is another version, even more questionable, of the failed argument that general cannot collide with particular. See also p. 345, where Newman reaffirms that, for the Catholic, 'private judgment' is liked, possessed, and maintained 'just so far as the Church does not, by the authority of Revelation, *supersede* it' (emphasis added). See, likewise, Newman, *Development of Christian Doctrine*, 86:

Revelation consists in…the substitution of the voice of a Lawgiver for the voice of conscience. The supremacy of conscience is the essence of natural religion; the supremacy of Apostle, or Pope, or Church, or Bishop, is the essence of revealed…Thus, what conscience is in the system of nature, such is the voice of Scripture, or of the Church, or of the Holy See, as we may determine it, in the system of Revelation.

[29] Donagan, *The Theory of Morality*, 142.

NOTES

† *Moral teachings on which twentieth-century popes and council have had to insist*...(212–13). For an instance of the problem confronted by the papacy—an instance trivial in itself but symbolic of much—take the polemic against the present essay in Gerard J. Hughes SJ, 'Newman and the Particularity of Conscience'. As part of his effort to avoid acknowledging that there are 'moral teachings on which twentieth-century popes and council have had to insist...', for example, on the kinds of act listed (in descriptive, not morally loaded terms) from intentional abortion to area-bombing of enemy cities, the Jesuit moralist informs his readers (69) that I give a list (the one at 213 to which this endnote is cued) of 'exceptionless moral principles which Finnis claims we infallibly grasp' (a claim I have never made), as examples of 'the doctrine that we have an immediate and infallible grasp of some moral truths' (a philosophical 'doctrine' I have never affirmed and often rejected). He goes on (70n.) to wonder at the 'very various' character of 'Finnis's examples', and to contend that the list is an instance of 'manipulative terminology or persuasive re-definition instead of reasoned argument'. Adultery, for example: 'if Finnis means some action which *he would consider* to be adultery, then, of course he simply begs the question by using a morally loaded term'. 'And surely nobody can be against baby-making quite generally? Or does Finnis have in mind some particular *method* of making babies; and if so, on what grounds?' By such means, Hughes is able to go the entire length of his essay without having to ask how Newman would have regarded—and how Newman's argument as it stands applies to—the specific moral teachings of the twentieth-century Catholic magisterium against the kinds of action recalled in my list of those 'various' teachings—teachings in which my summary term 'baby-*making*', for example, stands for all the methods of *producing* human beings by methods separate from intercourse (methods describable fully in morally neutral terms), and in which the adverse moral judgment has the reasons (particularly producer-product inequality) articulated in, for example, the Instruction *Donum Vitae* (22 February 1986) (see also 1984c and essay III.17 at 278–9). Nor is it the case that, in the moral teachings recalled in my list, 'adultery' is a 'morally loaded' term used so that 'adultery is always wrong' becomes true merely 'by definition', as Hughes here implies and plainly affirms (67) in relation to Aristotle's remarks about adultery—very questionably in relation to Aristotle, as I show in *MA* 31–3 (briefly in essay I.12 (1990a) at nn. 15–19), and certainly falsely in relation to Aquinas and the twentieth-century popes and the intervening doctrinal and theological consensus as well as its New Testament foundations: *MA* 7–8, 31–8. Equally, these misrepresentations enable Hughes to avoid mentioning that between my essay and his, each of which concerns Newman's thoughts on papal moral teaching, there lie such notable papal affirmations, general and particular, of exceptionless negative moral truths as the encyclicals *Veritatis Splendor* (1993) and *Evangelium Vitae* (1995). In 1980b (and more briefly and incompletely in essay 19 at 258–9, 261–4) I show in some detail how far Hughes misunderstands and rejects both the authority of Christian teachings and the foundations of moral thought—misunderstandings and denials still on display in his 2004 essay on Newman and conscience.

‡ *Conscience as the application of knowledge*...(219 at n. 20). Hughes (62–3) says that my criticism of Newman 'wholly misunderstands Newman's theory of moral judgment. It interprets Newman against a scholastic background, and indeed against the version of that background which Finnis himself accepts...' But as the citations hereabouts in my essay make plain, Newman himself proposed his teachings about conscience against the scholastic background that I here cite, and Hughes adduces no evidence at all that he rejected it, even when his arguments slid away from it (just as they slid away from his own teaching about the Church's 'mission...to proclaim the moral law' in moral doctrine which, with the aid of revelation, is the natural law's 'complement, reassertion, *issue*, embodiment, *and interpretation*'). What Aquinas says about conscience as 'application' must be taken with his distinction between affirmative and negative norms or principles; it is in the application of the former, without which one cannot decide *what to do*, that one finds the 'particularity' on which Hughes insists (which, however, is not to be understood in the intuitionistic way he proposes, but rather as the rational though rationally under-determined process of specification that the essay briefly recalls—as a process involving many 'additional premises'—in the paragraph after the quotation of Rahner (221 after cue 23)). On the general ethical issues of principle and method ventilated by Hughes, see e.g. *Aquinas* 163–70.

17

GRACE AND HUMILITY[*]

Among the dozen texts specified for this sermon by William Master, its benefactor, is one from the first of Paul's letters to the Greek Christians at Corinth. It is verse 7 of chapter 4, and comprises three questions. How to understand the first is as disputed amongst modern translators as it was amongst the Fathers: *Tis gar se diakrinei?* Jerome: *Quis enim te discernit?* King James: 'For who maketh thee to differ [from another]?' Ronald Knox, similarly: 'After all, friend, who is it that gives thee this pre-eminence?' The Revised Standard Version, rather differently and, I think, opaquely: 'For who sees anything different in you?'

The second and third questions, at any rate, are clear:

What have you that you did not receive? If then you received it, why do you boast as if it were not a gift?

This verse, like others in these pages of the letter, attracted much reflection in the Christian community. Its questions, particularly the central question, not only promote humility by indicating the deepest *reason for* humility (reason to be humble, in the precisely relevant sense of that word). They also indicate the deepest *cause of* the virtue (the right disposition) of humility, namely divine grace, and do so in a way which helps us understand what sort of relationship is established between God and us in *any* gift of grace, and in *any* such virtue. And identifying this quite general cause promotes (I do not at all say guarantees), again, that specific effect, that very specific mode of personal response, which we call humility.

We can begin to get the measure of all this by hearing one of the canons of the Second Council of Orange, held in AD 529, in that great decade or so in which Europe, our Europe, finds two of its most formative influences: the drawing up of Justinian's *Corpus Iuris Civilis*, the European law library, inaugurated with the publication of the First or Old Codex a few months

[*] 1992e: the annual University Sermon on the Grace of Humility, February 1992.

earlier; and the settling of St Benedict's Rule, a charter for monastic life which unfolds under the direction of its author's twelve 'strata [or steps] in humility [*gradus humilitatis*]', by which one may ascend to the perfect love of God which casts out fear, by a progress grounded upon fear of the Lord.[1] Here, then, is the Second Council of Orange's sixth canon on grace:

If you say that mercy is divinely extended to us when, without God's grace, we believe, will, desire, strive, work, pray, keep watch, make busy, inquire, investigate, or knock, and that it is not by the outpouring and inspiration of the Holy Spirit that we believe or will, or are empowered to do each of these things when appropriate;[2] or if you treat the help of grace as subordinate to humility or human obedience and fail to accept that our being obedient and humble is a gift of grace itself; then you are contradicting the Apostle when he says, 'What have you got that you did not receive?'...

Humility, then, is the *particular* gift which enables one to orientate oneself, choose, and act in harmony with one's awareness that *every* good thing one has and does and achieves is a sheer gift.

But is humility not a virtue intelligible to those who do not see their life as gift, who do not know or have no use for Creation and Redemption? Plato, for example. He speaks of humility (using the same terminology as the Bible's) at the very heart of his teaching about justice and right, in Book IV of *The Laws*:

God...holds in his hand the beginning, end and middle of all that is, and straight he travels to the accomplishment of his purpose, as is [his] nature; and always by his side is Right [*dikē*: justice] ready to punish those who disobey the divine law. Anyone who wants to be fulfilled [*eudaimonēsein*: happy] follows closely in the train of Right, with humility...What line of conduct, then, is dear to God and a following of him?...Well, it is God who is for us the measure of all things...So, to be loved by such a being, one must strive as far as one can to become like that being; and following out this principle, the person who is temperate and ordered is dear to God, being like him.[3]

This Platonic conception of a humble imitation of God's ordered moderation is set in the context of a portrayal of human existence as the existence of playthings of God, as puppets whose strings, worked by the divine puppetmaster, are the passions of audacity and aversion and the golden cord of law and reason, with whose soft and gentle pull we are to cooperate, lest the pulls of pain, pleasure, and passion prevail over us.[4] In this imposing

---

[1] As St Thomas says in his commentary on the twelve *gradus* of Benedict, the *gradus* which goes to the root is the one put first by Benedict (last in Aquinas's enumeration), that one fear God and be mindful of all his directives: *ST* II–II q.161 a.6c.

[2] Cf. Augustine, *De Dono Perseverantiae*, 64.   [3] *Laws* IV 715e–716d.

[4] *Laws* I 644d–645b; VII 803c.

vision of the relations between God and humankind, our existence is not understood as gift, though certainly as somehow analogous to a gift in its radical dependence.

Plato's understanding and misunderstanding of divine causality and human action I shall return to. His highly deliberate association of humility with temperance, moderatedness, and self-mastery we find again in the Thomistic synthesis of Greek, Roman, and Christian reflection. In this synthesis, humility is closely allied to temperance in preserving equilibrium amid feelings.[5] It is a species of Cicero's *modestia*, modesty.[6] Its specific role is to temper and restrain the mind lest one press forward immoderately towards high things, great matters, things above one's abilities.[7] In contrast to courage and magnanimity (Aristotle's greatness of soul), the role of humility in the moral life is not to spur one on, or stiffen one against hopelessness and disheartenment, but to brake and bridle pushiness and self-confidence.[8] Its root is in reverence for God, which prevents you from thinking yourself more than you actually are, and from claiming more than is due to you according to your God-given lot.[9] It not only establishes a whole style in one's thinking about and relating to other people—for one can, without sham, acknowledge that one's own secret faults are worse, and that others have from God gifts which one cannot see.[10] It also has a highly strategic role, for it gives one's reason sway over one's passions not merely in some particular field (as with other moral virtues), but in every field.[11]

That then, in summary, is Aquinas's resumé of the philosophical and theological tradition, and it has the integrating power and truth we should expect. But we may wonder whether it says all that should be said, or even identifies humility's most fundamental intelligibility. In what seems to me the most helpful work of moral theology since Aquinas's own, Germain Grisez shows how the data of the tradition allow us to understand humility not as a virtue of restraint but as a gift whereby, if one is receptive to it, one overcomes discouragement and is encouraged in activities of the most worthwhile kind (not excluding contemplative activities).[12]

How can this be? Well, we can go back to St Paul: 'What have you that you did not receive?' In the following verse Paul turns on the Corinthian Christians with irony: 'Already you are filled! Already you have become rich!' Riches induce complacency, a sense of power, control, self-sufficiency, the antitheses of humility. With good reason, then, the Fathers most often

---

[5] It is a *pars potentialis* of temperance: *ST* II–II q.155 proem; q.161 a.4c.
[6] II–II q.160 a.2c.   [7] *Ibid.*, q.161 aa.1–2.   [8] *Ibid.*, a.1c; a.2 ad 3.
[9] *Ibid.*, a.6c; a.2 ad 2.   [10] *Ibid.*, aa.3 and 6, esp. a.6 ad 1.   [11] *Ibid.*, a.5c.
[12] *CMP* esp. ch. 26.

understood the blessing spoken of in the first of the Beatitudes of the Sermon on the Mount as the gift of humility: 'Blessed are the poor in spirit, for theirs is the Kingdom of Heaven' (Matthew 5: 3).

'...for theirs is the Kingdom of Heaven'. That Kingdom is being built up already in this world by good human choices and actions made and done within the acting person's response of faith to God's supreme and all-embracing gift of the Spirit: charity. (We should understand this as the Church understands it: the response of faith which I just mentioned can be quite real and effective even when it is the response of 'those who, though ignorant of the Gospel of Christ and of his Church through no fault of their own, still seek God with a sincere heart and who, responding to grace, struggle by their works to fulfil his will, known through the dictate of conscience'.[13]) Now in the same page and passage as our text, Paul indicates how our choices and actions can build up the Kingdom: good works, done or built on the foundation which is Jesus Christ, will be disclosed on the last Day as having survived.[14] The Church takes up this teaching: human activity which, in an upright way, promotes and respects human goods thereby 'prepares the material of the heavenly kingdom', for if we obey the Lord and in his Spirit nurture on earth the goods of our nature *and our work*, we will *find these goods* and their good fruits *again*, but freed of stain, and burnished and transfigured, in the completed kingdom of truth and life, holiness and grace, justice, love, and peace.[15]

So: 'Blessed are those who...for theirs...'—the Beatitudes each speak of the same final reality (whether as the Kingdom or as adoption as God's children or as obtaining mercy or comfort or satisfaction in goodness), and of a blessing not merely appended by some extrinsic decree to certain choices and actions (as human rewards and punishments are appended extrinsically to actions). No, the blessings referred to in the Beatitudes are blessings in which choices and actions which express the attitudes to which the Beatitudes refer already themselves participate. For, to repeat, such choices and actions can last forever and are themselves, by divine grace, already somehow part of the Kingdom which when completed will be the embodiment of human fulfilment, *beatitudo*. (So Paul, in unfolding to the Greek Christians of Ephesus the prospect of sitting with Christ Jesus in the heavenly places, and reminding them that this place in God's household is won by a faith which is God's gift and not by works in which one might boast, adds immediately that choices and actions done in response to this gift are themselves no less a gift: 'For we are...created in Jesus Christ for

---

[13] Vatican II, *Lumen Gentium* (1965), 16; 'for they also, in a number known only to God, are able to achieve salvation': Paul VI, *Profession of Faith*, 30 June 1968.
[14] 1 Corinthians 3: 10–14.   [15] GS 39, citing 1 Corinthians 3: 14 and 13: 8.

good works, which God prepared beforehand that we might walk in them'
(Ephesians 2: 10).)

Blessed, then, are 'the poor in spirit', for theirs is the Kingdom of
God. The poor in spirit, whose choices and actions already build up and
participate in the Kingdom and its as yet unconsummated blessings,
are those who have humility—anyone, if, when and *as* humble. They
understand that their own undertakings and achievements (including this
understanding itself) are only some share, given freely and generously by
God, in the prodigious fullness of his creative and redemptive activity.
They see that, as Paul puts it at the beginning of our passage (1 Corinthians
3: 6; cf. 4: 6), one plants, another waters, but God gives the growth—that
all the good fruits of one's work (like one's very doing of good work itself)[16]
will be God's gift.

The poor: those who are aware of their need—anyone, when and *as*
aware of that dependence. (The rich: those, anyone, who—as the book
of Revelation starkly puts it—not knowing that they are poor, blind, and
naked, think they need nothing.)[17] So humility, poverty in spirit, is rooted
in awareness of one's need for God's gifts, for the charity which he can
pour into human hearts (Romans 5: 5), for the faith which can be one's
fundamental option in response to and in that divine love, for the vocation
within which one can commit oneself to implementing that option through
cooperating in one's own way with the Lord, for the good choices and
actions by which one can carry out that vocation, and for the good fruits
which one hopes one's activities will yield in all one's communities in
this world and the next. In this awareness, this understanding which is
fundamental to (not alone sufficient for!) humility, one finds the *reason* for
setting aside the debilitating assumption that one's choices and actions,
however well intentioned, well prepared, and vigorously carried out, can
yield no good fruit that really matter and really last.

That enervating presupposition is, of course, well grounded in our
experience, which is the experience of a fallen human condition manifestly
subject to sin and death. Most good works depend for their intended effect
on the cooperation of others, and this fails no less often than we fail to
bestir ourselves to really helpful cooperation with others, not to mention
the times we carelessly or meanly disrupt such cooperation as there is or
might otherwise be. The presumption that human efforts consistent with
fairness and human decency will all sooner or later end in dust, in manifest
futility, is the well-grounded wisdom of the world of which Paul speaks
in the alternative passage from 1 Corinthians which William Master

---

[16] See 1 Corinthians 15: 10.   [17] Revelation 3: 17.

appointed for this occasion—the wisdom by whose measure what Paul preaches is folly:

For Jews demand signs and Greeks seek wisdom, but we preach Christ crucified, a stumbling block to Jews and folly to Gentiles, but to those who are called, Christ the power of God and the wisdom of God. (1 Corinthians 1: 22–4.)

The folly is precisely this: of believing that fidelity to one's vocation can, by divine action, yield a harvest, indeed an unimaginably rich harvest, even though—and in a sense because—its way lies through humiliation and suffering. As Paul will say to the Greeks of Philippi:

Christ Jesus, though he was in the form of God, did not count equality with God a thing to be grasped...And being found in human form he humbled himself and became obedient unto death, even death on a cross. Therefore God has highly exalted him...(Philippians 2: 5–6, 8.)

Now, the Lord's humble acceptance of death was no pointless deprecation or abnegation of self, but an implication of his willingness to remain faithful to his chosen purpose of teaching and healing, to the commitment made in that first Lent. And in his second letter to Corinth, Paul, in explaining what he *is* willing to boast of, restates the folly of Christian faith in words he had from the Lord: 'my power is made perfect in weakness' (2 Corinthians 12: 9).

We judge this folly to be wisdom, realism not vanity, for the reason Paul states in the first letter to Corinth: because Christ was raised from the dead. What is sown in dishonour is raised in glory; what is sown in weakness is raised in power (1 Corinthians 15: 43). And the conclusion must be the one drawn by Paul himself, ending his discourse on the resurrection (and the substance of his letter) in words intended for all:

Be steadfast, immovable, always doing your full share in the task the Lord has given you, knowing that your labour in the Lord's service is not in vain. (1 Corinthians 15: 58.)

The action (including the dedicated contemplation) of the saints, that great-souled labour, is rooted in humility, in an integration of feeling and disposition with their understanding that by God's gift they *can* build up one tiny corner of God's vast project, and with practical reason's norm: do not let felt inertia deter you from acting for those human goods which revelation has made intelligible and grace makes available.

And if we thus should perhaps revise the Thomistic synthesis, we should certainly correct Plato's image of the relation between divine initiative and human action. Grace—whether it be the all-embracing grace of charity (the love of God poured into human hearts) or the more specific gifts (such as the grace of humility) by which charity bears on specific aspects of our existence—grace is not a set of spiritual pulls on or via the cords of the passions or of reason. It is not some set of unconscious influences on us, such that the more grace we were given the less would be our real freedom of choice. The image of the divine puppetmaster attributes both too little and too much to human freedom. Too little, because free choices—one's seeing reason to act and freely choosing to follow that reason in preference to other competing reasons—cannot be understood on the model of being pulled or tugged, howsoever 'spiritually' and 'gently' or imperceptibly. Too much, because to think of responding to grace as cooperating with a divine pull is still to think of our human choices and acts as somehow independent of God's giving, and tacitly to claim for ourselves a certain *independent* credit for good choices when we make them. And wrongly so. Of course, the causality of God's redemptive giving (his grace), like the natural causality (knowable even to reason) of God's creative giving (his causing my voice to carry to your ear, and my words to your understanding), is quite mysterious to us. But since we do not know *how* divine causality works, there is no obstacle in reason to affirming what the whole revelation completed in Christ proposes: that we can and do make choices in which nothing but our own choosing settles what we choose; that those choices, however marginal to the events which seem to us world-historical, greatly matter not only for us but for others and for the world's real history, the building of the Kingdom; *and* that the entire reality of any good choices we may make, of any good works, and of all their good fruits known and unknown, is bestowed upon us by God the Father, Son, and Holy Spirit.

Part Four

Controversies

18

CHRISTIANITY AND WORLD ORDER[*]

I

The themes, and the strengths and weaknesses, of E.R. Norman's Reith Lectures are all to be found in his final paragraph, which offers any Christian much for reflection:

What Christians most need in our day, therefore, is to see that *the complicated mixture of the Infinite in the structures of time* is explicable according to the spiritual interpretations of religious tradition—and does not require them to turn, instead, to the inappropriate explanations of secular culture. Both in daily life and in the worship of the Church, the prevailing emphasis upon the transformation of the material world has robbed men of their *bridge to eternity*. Around them, as in every age, they hear the clatter of disintegrating structures and the shouts of outraged humanity. But the priest in the sanctuary no longer speaks to them of *the evidence of the unseen world*, *discovered amidst the rubble* of this present one. He refers them, instead, to intellectualized interpretations of the wrong social practices and political principles which have, in the view of conventional wisdom, brought suffering to the society of men. Around us, however, the *materials of eternity lie thick upon the ground*, ambiguous in relation to time, *lucid as pointers to celestial realities*. For *the mysteries of the Kingdom* are not the commonplaces of the mere inquirer, but the *pearl of great price*, which only they possess who *dispose of all their other goods*.[1]

I have emphasized the metaphors and images which Norman uses to convey his understanding of that 'complicated mixture' (itself a weak and secular metaphor) of eternity and time. The limitations of those metaphors and images as bearers of Christian faith can be appreciated if we compare them

---

[*] 1979 ('Catholic Faith and World Order: Reflections on E.R. Norman, *Christianity and the World Order*'). The essay was read at the 1979 annual meeting of the Commission for International Justice and Peace of the Episcopal Conference of England and Wales.
[1] *Christianity and the World Order* [CWO], 84–5 (emphasis added here and throughout the essay).

with a passage from Vatican II about the 'mysteries of the Kingdom' and the ultimate disposition of 'all our other goods':

After we have spread on earth (in accordance with the Lord's command and in His Spirit) the goods of human dignity, brotherhood and freedom—that is, all the good fruits of our nature and our enterprise—we will find those goods again (but washed of all stain, brightened and transfigured) when Christ hands over to the Father the eternal and universal kingdom: 'a kingdom of truth and life, a kingdom of holiness and grace, a kingdom of justice, love and peace'. On this earth the Kingdom is already present in mystery; when the Lord comes it will be perfected.[2]

That passage is Vatican II's explanation (it begins 'Bona *enim...*' [*For,* the goods...]) of the balanced truth that

although earthly progress is to be carefully distinguished from the building up of Christ's Kingdom, still, inasmuch as it can contribute to the better ordering of human society, it is of great concern for the Kingdom of God.

Norman's image of the Kingdom was of the pearl, waiting to be discovered in the rubble of human calamity. In the Lord's saying (Matthew 13: 45–6) that is a valid image of the supreme significance of the Kingdom, *apart from which* all human goods are of no ultimate value, and for the sake of which one should be prepared to give up all that one has. But for an understanding of the presence of the Kingdom now, in this world, in mystery, and of the ways in which the Kingdom grows and is built up by the goods that are not 'apart from' it, one needs a richer vocabulary. And that vocabulary is going to come, as Dr Norman rightly says, 'from the inherited and learned traditional knowledge about [God's, Christ's] presence among men'[3] (we could say, from Scripture and Tradition), not from the conventional wisdom of secularized intellectuals.

II. SOME HOME TRUTHS FROM DR NORMAN ...

Although he devotes lectures to Christianity in Russia, Latin America, and South Africa, Norman's real interest throughout, I think, is in 'the politicized Churches of the old world, where Christianity is in radical decay',[4] the 'western Churches' which, 'in their death agonies' are 'distributing the causes of their own sickness—the politicization of religion—to their healthy offspring in the developing world'.[5] So I will concentrate on his home truths, not on his excursions into foreign parts.

'In the world, the Christian seeks to apply the great love of God as well as he can in contemporary terms. And that will actually involve corporate social and political action'.[6] Norman is an historian, and so a primary focus

---

[2] GS 39.   [3] CWO 83.   [4] *Ibid.,* 5.   [5] *Ibid.,* 6.   [6] *Ibid.,* 79.

of his interest is on 'the immediate motivations of Christian involvement with political issues',[7] and with the 'social mechanics' of 'the relationship between social fact and the adoption of ideology',[8] for example the adoption by Christians of political and social ideologies. He is looking for 'realism about the conditioning of knowledge'.[9]

Here he hints that Marxism gives a 'realistic appraisal' of those social mechanics (though not of 'the nature of the purposes they convey').[10] And earlier he had remarked that 'aspects of Marxist social analysis are extremely valuable'.[11] I wondered what he had in mind; for the more I become acquainted with Marx's writings, the lower I rank their value. So I found it helpful to see what Norman had written in the introductory chapter of his big book *Church and Society in England 1770–1970*, published in 1976. The question of Marxism is in fact peripheral to Norman's purposes in the Reith Lectures, and to my own discussion; but a passage from that earlier book will help to clarify his concept of *politicization*, which dominates the Lectures:

Only the 'vulgar' Marxists have supposed that the Church [in, say, the nineteenth century] ignored social evils and the sufferings of the working classes. Philosophical Marxists know better. They see that churchmen were full of concern for the poor; but they also see that they were victims of their own class moralism, presenting solutions which comprehended neither the subtleties of working class social custom nor the possibility of social reconstruction.[12]

And again:

Several general conclusions emerge from this survey. The most obvious is the class basis of the social ethics the Church has adopted. It has, of course, long been assumed in the 'vulgar' Marxist attitude to social history, that the clergy propagated the morality and politics of the ruling class...In such a version of things a few men of conscience and 'prophetic' discernment were believed to have emancipated themselves sufficiently to promote social radicalism... [and thus] to have transcended the ordinary assumptions of their class. It is the contention of the present study that most of the social attitudes and ideas adopted by churchmen were a reflection of class-consciousness—*including the radical and critical ideas. Receptivity to new influences was strictly limited to ideals promoted by sections within the intelligentsia*, of which the clergy were themselves a part. *Social radicalism was as much the result of class moralism as was the more prevalent conservatism.*[13]

Remember, in those passages Norman was speaking of English churchmen (mainly but not exclusively Anglican) of the nineteenth and early twentieth centuries. He was willing, however, to cast his net wider:

...another general conclusion of the present study [is] that the social attitudes of the Church have derived from the surrounding intellectual and political culture

---

[7] *Ibid.*, 13.   [8] *Ibid.*, 84.   [9] *Ibid.*, 82.   [10] *Ibid.*, 84.   [11] *Ibid.*, 19.
[12] *Church and Society in England 1770–1970* (CSE), 3.   [13] *Ibid.*, 8.

and not, as churchmen themselves always seem to assume, from theological learning... This is, no doubt, the way of *all truth; it takes on the form and the idealism of the intellectual preoccupations of each generation.*[14]

And this fact did not, of itself, arouse Norman to denunciation. Rather, he adopted the irenic remark of Bishop Hensley Henson: 'Christian theology, Christian ethics, Christian institutions, have all been demonstrably shaped by contemporary non-Christian influences; it is a condition of the Church's terrestrial mission from which there is no escape'.[15]

The easiest way to misunderstand the Reith Lectures is to read them as a denunciation of the *borrowing*, by contemporary Christians, of secular political ideas. There are many passages that can be read that way.[16] But it is *contemporary* Christians that he is denouncing, and as he says at the beginning of his last lecture, it has *always* been the case that the political and social ideas used by Christians are 'derived from the secular values of the time'.[17] What, then, is different about contemporary Christians? Norman's answer, in the next sentence, fails to say what he really means:

The main difference between the present experience of Christian adaptation, and past ones, is that the culture of the modern world is becoming frankly secular.[18]

As it stands, this will not do as an answer. For one thing, the preceding sentence had said that Christians of all epochs borrow from the *secular* values of their time. And for another thing, Norman himself had pointed out, in an essay on 'Christianity and Politics', published shortly before he delivered the Reith Lectures, that

Today, *as in the first centres of Christian experience*, the surrounding culture is frankly antipathetic to the unique spiritual outlook of revealed Christianity... [19]

Now Norman has no complaint about the first Christian centuries (the Apostles and Fathers who transmitted the revelation to us) for *their* borrowings from the secular and antipathetic culture that surrounded them. So what, again, is his complaint about the Christians of today?

You will have guessed by now. His complaint is that modern Christians, in borrowing from the secular culture of this age, are failing to *preserve* 'the unique spiritual outlook of revealed Christianity'.

Christians are losing their faith

This, then, is the key to Dr Norman's notion of 'politicization'—*not* that Christians are borrowing secular political and social ideas and ideals and treating them as theologically warranted or even as part of the Gospel;

---

[14] *Ibid.*, 10–11.   [15] *Ibid.*, 11.   [16] CWO 11, 15, 18, 31, 44, 56, 74.
[17] *Ibid.*, 72; also 32.   [18] *Ibid.*, 72.   [19] 'Christianity and Politics' (CAP) at 72.

but that the Christians who are doing this are 'little concerned to preserve the Christian heritage'[20] and are losing, forgetting, repudiating 'any distinct sense of the historical claims of Christianity'.[21] 'The evaporation of any sense that religious tradition conveys a unique understanding of human life has been one of the most decisive changes in modern Christian experience'.[22]

'Lacking a distinct sense of the uniqueness of the Christian revelation',[23] these Christians not merely incorporate the teachings of Liberalism, or Marxism or Humanism into their Christianity; they see these teaching as *the essence* of the Christian message'.[24] 'Contemporary Christians are *re-defining the very essence* of their religion' around human rights, or majority rule, or the extinction of racism or economic exploitation.[25] They 'identify' Christianity (in the strong sense of that ambiguous word, 'identify') with one or another of those ideologies,[26] or, more generally they make an '*identification* of the content of the faith with human attempts at social improvement'.[27]

That is why Norman does not attack the political opinions of the politicized Christians. Again and again he states that Liberalism (which in western churches today is, he says, the characteristic message of politicized Christianity[28]) 'may well be…perfectly acceptable for all kinds of political and moral reasons'.[29] His concern is 'not to say that the actual social and political ideas adopted by Christians are in themselves untrue'. His concern is not, he says, to argue that such ideas are 'not in correspondence with a legitimate understanding of the faith'. 'It is, however, to suggest that they are far too relative to be regarded as *central* in the *definition of Christianity itself*'.[30] Norman's point is that the politicized Christians are *losing* Christ:

> At the centre of the Christian religion, Christ remains unchanging in a world of perpetual social change and mutating values. To identify him with the passing enthusiasms of men…is to lose him amidst the shifting superstructure of human idealism.[31]

The Christians of earlier times, for example the subjects of Norman's many studies of church and society in seventeenth- to twentieth-century North America[32]—all *these* Christians derived 'their moral seriousness and their political ideals from the surrounding culture'.[33] But they, unlike so many

---

[20] CWO 17.   [21] *Ibid.*, 44.   [22] *Ibid.*, 11.   [23] *Ibid.*, 75.   [24] CWO 31–2.
[25] *Ibid.*, 73.   [26] *Ibid.*, 44.   [27] *Ibid.*, 3; see also 32, 44.   [28] *Ibid.*, 6–7.
[29] *Ibid.*, 7; also 17, 73.   [30] *Ibid.*, 12.   [31] *Ibid.*, 77.
[32] *The Conscience of the State in North America* (1968); Ireland: *The Catholic Church and Ireland in the Age of Rebellion 1859–1973* (1965); *The Catholic Church and Irish Politics in the Eighteen-sixties* (1965); *A History of Modern Ireland* (1971); and England: *Church and Society in England 1770–1970* (1976).
[33] CAP 75.

contemporary Christians, remembered 'the true Christ of history',[34] 'the
Christ who said he was before Abraham, and who is for ever reminding
men that heaven and earth shall pass away'.[35] The churchmen of earlier
times knew that 'Christians *are* directed by the Gospel to be concerned
with their neighbours and that [this] does imply political activity'.[36]

But *for most of the period* covered by [Norman's study of English Christian social
thought], churchmen had another priority. They regarded the alleviation of
social ills, and care for the temporal welfare of mankind, as important aspects
of the Divine Will for ordered and just life, but not as the essential purpose of
the Church's mission. The pursuit of eternity remained the first and absorbing
preoccupation of organized religion.[37]

But with so many leaders of Christian thought and action today, it is not
so. That is the home truth that Norman wished to proclaim. And he is
right. As Michael Dummett says in his critique of the Reith Lectures,
there is a 'kind of here-and-now theology that enjoys a certain vogue
at the moment'; it is 'an example of the so-called demythologization of
Christianity' and is governed by the same ('most irrational') principle as
governs 'much modern exegesis of Scripture':

You know the sort of thing: the future tense, in Scripture and the creeds, is
interpreted, not as referring to what is yet to come, but to the present, only in a
deep, rather than a surface, sense; conventional apocalyptic imagery is being used
to convey a spiritual truth about the present. There is to be no Second Coming
as a future historical event: rather, Christ has already come again and is present
with us, who make up his body. We are not to be raised again *after* our deaths;
rather, we have already died and been raised with Christ. We should not look to
be delivered from death by its *subsequent* annulment; rather, we already possess
eternal life and are liberated from death by the equanimity with which we are able
to regard it.[38]

On this point, at least, Dummett and Norman are at one—that about the
vocation of man to eternal life, any ambiguity or silence is intolerable. And
so, too, John Paul II puts at the forefront of his first encyclical, *Redemptor
Hominis*, the passage from St John: 'God so loved the world that he gave his
only Son, that whoever believes in him should not perish but have eternal
life'.[39] What is the truth by which the Church lives?

…she lives by the truth about man, which enables him to go beyond the bounds
of temporariness [*brevis huius temporis spatium*, the space of this short time—our
short span] and at the same time to think with particular love and solicitude of

---

[34] CWO 78.   [35] *Ibid.*, 83.   [36] CAP 79.   [37] CSE 4.
[38] Dummett, 'Catholicism and World Order', 14–15.
[39] John 3: 16; John Paul II, Encyclical, *Redemptor Hominis*, 4 March 1979 (RH), 1 and 10.

everything within the dimensions of this temporariness [*huius finiti temporis*, this limited time] that affect[s] man's life and the life of the human spirit (RH 18).

And what precisely is this truth? It is that Christ

'(the Word) gave power to become children of God' [John 1: 12]. Man is transformed inwardly by this power as the source of a new life that does not disappear and pass away but lasts to eternal life [cf. John 4: 14]. This life, which the Father has promised and offered to each man in Jesus Christ, his eternal and only Son, who, 'when the time had fully come' [Galatians 4: 4], became incarnate and was born of the Virgin Mary, is the final fulfilment of man's vocation. It is in a way the fulfilment of the 'destiny' that God has prepared for him from eternity. This 'divine destiny' is advancing, in spite of all the enigmas, the unsolved riddles, the twists and turns of 'human destiny' in this world of time. Indeed, while all this, in spite of all the riches of life in time, necessarily and inevitably leads to the *frontier of death* and the goal [*metam*: limit or turning-point] of the destruction of the human body, *beyond that goal* we see Christ... In Jesus Christ, who was crucified and laid in the tomb and then [*inde*: thence] rose again [*resuscitato*: was restored to life], 'our hope of resurrection dawned... the bright promise of immortality' [*futurae immortalitatis*: of *future* immortality], *on the way to which man*, through the death of the body, shares with the whole of visible creation the necessity to which matter is subject. [Literally: the future immortality which man attains through (*ex*) the death of the body, thus participating, with the whole world, in that necessity to which matter is subject.] We intend and are trying to fathom more deeply the language of the truth that man's Redeemer enshrined in the phrase 'It is the spirit that gives life, the flesh is of no avail' [John 6: 63]. In spite of appearances, these words express the highest affirmation of man—the affirmation of the body given life by the Spirit.[40]

This is the great truth that Norman, quite correctly, sees obscured or even rejected in the thought and preaching of so many contemporary Christians who are 'redefining their own moral identity and their own claim to significance in society... in terms of an external context dominated by ideologies *which have no other end for man in prospect except as part of the material process*'.[41] Hence his very first definition of the politicization that Christianity has undergone 'during the last twenty years':

By the politicization of religion is meant the internal transformation of the faith itself, so that it comes to be *defined* in terms of political values—it becomes *essentially concerned* with social morality rather than *with the ethereal qualities of immortality*.[42]

The home truth that Norman wishes above all to convey is expressed thus by Paul VI in his Apostolic Exhortation, *Evangelii Nuntiandi* (8 December

---

[40] RH 18.   [41] CWO 58.   [42] *Ibid.*, 2.

1975), to which John Paul II so often referred in his visit to Latin America. It is the truth,

... the fact that many, even generous Christians who are sensitive to the dramatic questions involved in the question of liberation, in their wish to commit the Church to the liberation effort are frequently tempted to reduce her mission to the dimensions of a simply temporal project. They would reduce her aims to a man-centred goal; the salvation of which she is the messenger would be reduced to material well-being. Her activity, forgetful of all spiritual and religious preoccupation, would become initiatives of the political or social order.[43]

'Reduction' and 'ambiguity' (EN 32, section title)—those are the dangers that Norman, Dummett, Paul VI, and John Paul II are all in their various ways calling to our attention—the absence of a

prophetic proclamation of a hereafter, man's profound and definitive calling, in both continuity and discontinuity with the present situation: beyond time and history, beyond the transient reality of this world, of which a hidden dimension will one day be revealed—beyond man himself, whose true destiny is not restricted to his temporal aspect but will be revealed in the future life (EN 28).

The Reith Lectures are, first and foremost, a cry of alarm that this proclamation of the true salvation offered to all men in Jesus Christ (EN 27) is being stifled, muffled, drowned out by a well-intentioned but fundamentally secular moralism.

We ought not to heed any criticism of Dr Norman's Reith Lectures that does not echo his concern about the fate of a Christianity which allows its content to be 'drained away into the great pool of secular idealism'.[44]

III. AND SOME HALF-TRUTHS: NORMAN'S DEFICIENT THEOLOGY

I have taken many pages to identify and set out what I believe to be Norman's main thesis, since that thesis does not emerge from the Reith Lectures as clearly as one could wish. It must be said that the Lectures give an impression of hasty composition. Dummett is right to say that it is difficult to arrive at any exact formulation of Norman's central thesis, and that different passages (taken in isolation) suggest different standpoints. But it should by now be clear that, in my view, Dummett is mistaken in thinking that Norman's main concern was to argue that 'Christian leaders

---

[43] Paul VI, Apostolic Exhortation, *Evangelii Nuntiandi*, on Evangelization in the Modern World, 8 December 1975 (EN), 32.

[44] *Ibid.*, 13.

have no business to be advocating' the particular political and social views they do (even if those views are true).

A striking example of looseness in the composition of the Lectures is the following:

...the Churches now see Human Rights as *the essence* of the Christian message. 'The Church', according to one of the documents uttered by the Second Vatican Council, 'by virtue of the Gospel entrusted to her proclaims man's rights and acknowledges and esteems the modern movement to promote these rights everywhere'.[45]

It is plain at a glance that the passage here quoted from *Gaudium et Spes*, sec. 41, in no way treats human rights as 'the essence of the Christian message'. So there is no need, really, to mention such additional facts as that four sentences after the sentence quoted by Norman, we find the Council declaring that 'the proper mission which Christ entrusted to his Church, does not belong to the political, economic or social order: for the end which he set before her is religious';[46] or that the sentence following the one quoted by Dr Norman is: 'This movement [to promote human rights] must, however, be imbued with the spirit of the Gospel and guarded against every kind of false autonomy';[47] and so on.

More embarrassing still is the fact that Norman really does know about Vatican II's nuanced teaching on the relation between Christianity and politics. In his last lecture he adopts the Council's own formulation at a crucial point in his argument:

'By virtue of her function and field of action', as the Second Vatican Council rightly declared, in contrast [to the contemporary understanding of Christianity], 'the Church is quite distinct from the political community and uncommitted to any political system; she is at once the sign and the guarantee that human personality transcends the field of politics'.[48]

And there is more; in his essay 'Christianity and Politics' (1978) Norman, having said that 'Christians *are* directed by the Gospel to be concerned with their neighbours and this does imply political activity',[49] goes on to ask: 'How then, are Christians to know what to do?'

Surely the answer, which has had, in this century, the weighty support of Maritain and William Temple and was spelled out by the Second Vatican Council in the document *Gaudium et Spes*, is that the Church, as a corporate entity, should restrict itself to the identification and endorsement of general principles for the ordering of human society (which it believes to be in accordance with God's will for men)...[50]

---

[45] *Ibid.*, 31–2.
[46] Vatican II, Pastoral Constitution on the Church in the Modern World, GS 42.
[47] GS 41.   [48] CWO 78, citing GS 76.   [49] CAP 79.   [50] *Ibid.*, 80.

And he adds, realistically, that 'there is no agreed device by which to distinguish between general principles and particular applications'.[51]

Since Norman thinks that, in the matter of political pronouncements by Christian leaders, Vatican II got it right, you might wonder what more needs to be said by me. But again I must stress that Norman is not fundamentally interested in determining what sort of political pronouncements—general? applied? particular?—can properly be made by Christian leaders. He is interested in ensuring that, when Christian leaders make political pronouncements, they remember the essence of the faith, by which, 'as it was delivered by the saints and scholars of the centuries, men are first directed to the imperfections of their own natures, and not to the rationalized imperfections of human society'.[52] And here, where he gets down to describing the essence of Christianity, there *is* room for dissent from much that Norman has to say—that is, for dissent from what he says fairly clearly and often and in various of his works (and not merely from exaggerated remarks which he does not really mean, such as 'An awareness of social values is actually involved in [Christianity,... but] this should not lead, as, alas, it now often does, to the Christian espousal of social *principles*...').[53] My criticism, then, will focus on: (i) his version of Christian anthropology and his consequent denial of natural law; (ii) his lack of acknowledgement of divine law and of development of doctrine; and (iii) his doctrine on faith and works. (Anyone who thinks that the issues raised by the Reformation have somehow disappeared from Christian life is sadly mistaken; Norman's theological deficiencies are the ones that worried Trent, though I have to admit that I didn't really notice this fact until I sat down to write out this critique—my concern is not to disturb the ecumenical peace but to explore some fundamentals of the Catholic social teaching on true justice and authentic peace.)

(i)   Of human nature, human goods, and natural law

Dr Norman says that

Religion is centred...on the facts of human nature, and a human nature properly understood—from a Christian point of view—as corrupted and partial, so that even in our most noble attempts at altruism we find ourselves constantly involved in moral ambiguity and flawed intention.[54]

---

[51] *Ibid.*, 81. Paul VI thought that distinction simplistic and inadequate: Apostolic Letter, *Octogesima Adveniens*, on the occasion of the Eightieth Anniversary of *Rerum Novarum*, 15 May 1971, 42.

[52] CWO 76–7.   [53] *Ibid.*, 77, original emphasis.   [54] *Ibid.*, 76.

The last part of that remark recalls some fine pages in his 1978 essay 'Christianity and Politics', in which he develops some themes scarcely stated in the Reith Lectures: the fact that human frailty and wrongdoing find a niche in idealism as well as in *recognizably* evil deeds; the fact that good reasons, even intensely believed, can cloak bad or flawed motives; that moral campaigns tend to depend for their success on self-dramatization and on the arousal of morally dubious *punitive* feelings; and that the sin embodied in bad social arrangements will not be overcome by sweeping away those arrangements but will reassert itself in some new or other forms.[55]

But does Christianity teach nothing about human nature save that it is corrupted and partial? To read Norman, one would think so. Christianity, he says, 'ought...to be dogmatic in its insistence that what is permanent in human nature is revealed in moral frailty and in the universal incidence of sin...'.[56] 'Christianity...is an account of basic human nature, of man's fallibility; of sin and the need for redemption'.[57]

Now human nature is, in fact, understood in some degree by all of us through our fundamental *practical* understanding of the basic forms of human good, i.e. the basic human values, the basic aspects of human well-being or flourishing: life, including health, the transmission of life, knowledge, play, aesthetic experience, friendship, self-direction, practical reasonableness, and relationship to the divine. So if one thinks of basic human nature in terms of failings, corruption, and partiality, one will no doubt also be thinking of the human goods as somehow not really goods (though one will still be left with the problem of explaining what corruption is corruption *of*). And sure enough, Norman speaks, without discomfort, of 'the relativity of all human values',[58] and seems to use this phrase interchangeably with 'the worthlessness of human values'.[59]

Now, as Thomas Aquinas puts it, the practical propositions in which we express our grasp of the basic and self-evident human goods are 'the first principles of the natural law'.[60] So we are not surprised to find Norman affirming that 'the content of natural law is quite arbitrary'.[61] He says 'It is a matter of record that seemingly *any* claim to personal choice is capable of being represented as a natural law right',[62] and he is quite content to rest with this 'matter of record', and not to ask whether *some* such claims are not simply wrong, unreasonable, for example because they defy that requirement of practical reasonableness which Christ expressed in the

---

[55] CAP 77–9.   [56] *Ibid.*, 72.   [57] *Ibid.*, 77; notice the punctuation of that sentence.
[58] *Ibid.*   [59] *Ibid.*, 82; cf. 'the relativity of men's values', in the same paragraph, 83.
[60] ST I–II q. 94 a.2.   [61] CWO 30–1.   [62] *Ibid.*, 30, emphasis added.

Golden Rule (known to all traditions of moral thought), or that other requirement of practical reasonableness that forbids us to choose directly against any basic value in any act (the requirement that Kant formulated as the 'categorical imperative': 'Act so that you treat humanity, whether in your own person or in another's, always as an end and never as a means only').

Vatican II, following in the whole tradition of 'saints and scholars', teaches that there is a 'universal natural law' whose principles have 'permanent binding force'—a natural law that includes such principles (at once 'general' and 'particular', i.e. immediately applicable in a concrete case) as—'*Every* warlike act which tends indiscriminately to the destruction of entire cities or of extensive areas along with their population is a crime against God and men'.[63]

Behind such teaching lies the high Christian doctrine that the natural goodness of things comes from God who as Creator has established them according to his plan;[64] that the 'goods of our nature' which 'we will find again…transfigured' in the complete Kingdom of God include the goods of 'truth and life…, justice, love and peace';[65] and that we somehow 'participate in the light of the divine mind',[66] through our conscience, which (when we really care for truth and goodness) discloses to us a law which we do not dictate to ourselves but which we ought to obey, the law expressed in the 'objective norms of morality',[67] norms derived from the nature of the human person and of his acts.[68]

Behind the Christian teaching on natural law lies also the high Christian doctrine (restated by Vatican II in *Gaudium et Spes* to show how Christ 'fully reveals man to man himself') that Christ is the 'perfect man', who 'assumed and did not annul human nature' itself.[69]

That is why Norman's dictum that 'the wise aspirant to eternity will recognize *no* hope of a better social order in his endeavours…'[70] seems both unreasonable and offensive to pious ears. The natural law is, as Paul VI put it in *Humanae Vitae*, 19, 'the law which is truly proper to human life restored [by Christ] to its own authentic truth'; to say that there is no hope of a better social order is to say that grace is not restorative, or that it is offered in vain. Dr Norman is right to point to Original Sin, to be pessimistic about human nature left to its own devices, to question the constantly rising expectations of what can be achieved by social change

---

[63] GS 80.
[64] Vatican II, Decree on the Apostolate of the Laity, *Apostolicam Actuositatem*, 7; Decree on Bishops, *Christus Dominus*, 12.
[65] GS 39.   [66] GS 15.   [67] GS 16.   [68] GS 51.   [69] GS 22.
[70] CWO 79.

and political action,[71] and to deny that the Christian virtue of hope has for its object the social progress that can or could be achieved by human effort in this world. He is right to warn against the facile optimism of many theologians; we should recall that even 'progressive' bishops from 'the Rhine' had to warn the Council, publicly, that the drafts of *Gaudium et Spes*, right up to the last, were marred by this optimism (which last-minute amendments only reduced, not eliminated). But none of this suffices to justify a denial of the real possibility that human effort can create social arrangements *more* in conformity with the natural law. It is permissible to predict, as an historian, that 'our foolishness here will make a desert of the world'[72] but it is not permissible to make that prediction a matter of Christian faith, as if it were something that 'Christianity sees'.[73]

(ii) Of the commandments of God

I have just been, in effect, reasserting the teaching of Trent that 'no one should use that rash statement, once forbidden by the Fathers under anathema, that the observance of the commandments of God is impossible for one that is justified' (D-S 1536). For everywhere the Church's teaching about natural law takes for granted the teaching of St Paul (Romans 2: 14–15) and Irenaeus (*Adv. Haereses*, IV, 13, 1 and 4) that the moral precepts of the Decalogue are precepts of natural law. The Church does not sponsor any philosophical doctrine about the connexion between the most basic principles of natural law (which do not of themselves give *moral* direction) and such stringent *moral* conclusions as that the innocent are never to be directly killed; indeed, theologians until quite recently have not seriously explored that connexion. For its certainty about such conclusions, the Church relies on the revealed commandments of God, repromulgated by Christ, for example to the rich young man who came asking him what one must do to inherit eternal life.[74] Even the teaching of *Gaudium et Spes* (as developed in *Humanae Vitae*) that sexual intercourse must in every act retain the full sense of mutual self-giving and of human procreation[75] is as much an inference from the revealed teaching on sex as it is an application of the principle, available to unaided 'natural reason', that the basic human goods must be respected in every act.

In short, as Vatican II teaches, 'the outstanding cause of human dignity lies in man's call to...colloquy with God',[76] and that colloquy, in this life,

---

[71] *Ibid.*, 5.   [72] CAP 81.   [73] *Ibid.*
[74] Matthew 19: 16–20; Mark 10: 17–19; Luke 18: 18–21.
[75] GS 51; Paul VI, Encyclical, *Humanae Vitae*, On the Right Ordering of Procreation, 25 July 1968 (HV), 12–14.
[76] GS 19.

takes the form, *first* of God's 'speaking', in the depths of man's conscience, through the voice of that law which God has written in man's heart [we call it the natural law]; 'to obey that law is the very dignity of man',[77] and *secondly* the form of God's public self-revelation, known to us now by hearing 'the word', 'the human expression of Christ',[78] the gospel which is 'the source of all saving truth and all moral teaching'.[79]

So it is not satisfactory to speak of the human rights movement elevating western liberalism 'to the apparent authority of eternal truth'[80] or 'of the laws of God';[81] for *some*, at least, of the human rights being proclaimed today *are* a matter of 'eternal truth'—for example, those rights guaranteed by the divine command not to murder.

Nor can we leave it at that. The moral teaching of Scripture, like the rest of the revealed teaching, awaits interpretation and development by the tradition and theology[82] of the Church. As Vatican II puts it:

> …what was handed on by the apostles includes everything which contributes to the holiness of life…[and] develops in the Church with the help of the Holy Spirit. For there is a growth in the understanding of the realities and the words which have been handed down. This growth in understanding arises from the contemplation and study of believers who treasure those things in their heart…, from the intimate understanding of the spiritual things they experience, and from the preaching of those who with the episcopal succession have received the sure charism of truth.[83]

The field of Catholic social teaching offers many examples of doctrines which are 'not expressly affirmed in revelation' but which 'have their roots' in a revelation understood more profoundly through centuries of such personal experience and ecclesial life: the teaching on the human right to immunity from coercion in religious matters (within the limits only of public *order*) is a good example of this—indeed it is also a good example of the interrelation, or interpenetration, between 'faith' (revelation) and 'reason' (natural right): see the two parts of *Dignitatis Humanae*.[84] Other good examples are the teachings on (i) *private* ownership as a legitimate and desirable form of stewardship of the resources created by God for *common* benefit, and (ii) the *subsidiary* function of social organizations.

Development is not invention. We cannot say, with Norman, that Christians 'recognize that their language of principles, and the cultural materials in which they are expressed, are wholly unstable'.[85] For our moral language and 'cultural materials' are permanently related to the

---

[77] GS 16.   [78] RH 19.
[79] Vatican II, Dogmatic Constitution on Divine Revelation (*Dei Verbum*) [DV] 7.
[80] CWO 30.   [81] *Ibid.*, 33.   [82] See RH 19.   [83] DV 8.
[84] [See essay 5, sec. V.]   [85] CWO 79.

language and cultural materials of Christ, the stable 'centre of human history' (GS 10; RH 1). The parable of Dives and Lazarus will retain its meaning for the rest of history, as will

the scene of the last judgment according to the words of Christ related in St Matthew's Gospel, [a scenario which] must always be 'applied' to man's history [and] made the 'measure' for human acts as an essential outline for an examination of conscience by each and every one.[86]

And, to revert to those strict negative commands of the Decalogue which are the first charter of human rights, the meaning and implications of 'killing', 'adultery', 'stealing', and 'false witness' may not fittingly be described as 'wholly unstable' or even as 'relative'.

(iii) Of faith and works

In the introductory paragraph of this essay I quoted Vatican II's notable statement of the eternal significance, for the Kingdom, of the good works done in obedience to the Lord and in his Spirit. So I need not here dwell too long on Norman's view that morality—'works'—is no more (apparently) than (i) 'the discipline which best enables men to order their lives that they might discern the shadow of eternity cast over time... an education of the soul' and (ii) 'an essential sign of the operation of faith'.[87] No; in the Catholic faith eternity is not merely something whose 'shadow' can be discerned here; it is not simply 'unearthly',[88] still less 'ethereal'.[89] Rather, eternal life somehow begins here. And good works do not merely manifest the operation of faith; they themselves operate, not only to build up this world (in the ways we understand and work for) but also (in ways now mysterious to us) to build the new heaven and new earth and new human family that are to come. The discontinuity is as important as the continuity; neither is to be suppressed. 'Charity *and its fruits* endure' (GS 39); they are not overwhelmed in the clatter and rubble of this world's disintegrations, but accumulate as a kind of hidden treasure, in a 'hidden dimension that will one day be revealed'.[90] This Christian doctrine about the real but hidden world order is not a commonplace optimism; for its teaching, the Council refers us back to St Paul:

the Day [of Judgment] will disclose each man's work, because it will be revealed with fire, and the fire will test what sort of work each one has done. If the work which any man has built on the foundation [of Jesus Christ] survives, he will receive a reward. If any man's work is burned up, he will suffer loss, though he himself will be saved, but only as through fire.[91]

---

[86]   RH 16.   [87]   CWO 80.   [88]   *Ibid.*, 79.   [89]   *Ibid.*, 2.   [90]   EN 28.
[91]   1 Corinthians 3: 14; adding vv. 13 and 15 to give the sense.

The Christian doctrine of eternal life is amazing. As John Paul II put it in *Redemptor Hominis*, sec. 10 (all of which should be read):

...the name for that deep [*maxima*: utter] amazement at man's worth and dignity is the Gospel, that is to say: the Good News. It is also called Christianity. This amazement determines the Church's mission in the world...

19

MORALITY AND THE SECOND VATICAN COUNCIL[*]

In 1965, the Second Vatican Council declared in *Gaudium et Spes* (The Pastoral Constitution on the Church in the Modern World):

Today the human race is entered upon a new era of its history.... Profound and rapid changes, triggered by the intelligence and creative energy of man, recoil on man himself, on his judgments, his individual and collective desires, and his manner of thinking and acting both about things and about people. So we can now speak of a true social and cultural transformation....[1]

History itself is speeding up on so rapid a course that individuals can scarcely keep pace with it.... And so the human race is passing from a relatively static conception of the scheme of things to a more dynamic and evolutionary conception—whence there arises a new set of problems, calling for new analyses and new syntheses.[2]

The remainder of *Gaudium et Spes* is devoted to just such new analyses and new syntheses. And in the last words of the Introduction, the Council offers a methodological reflection on all that is to follow:

The Church believes that Christ, through his Spirit, provides man with light and strength so that man can respond to his high calling.... Likewise she believes that in her Lord and Master are to be found the key, the centre and the goal of the whole history of mankind. And the Church affirms, too, that underlying all changes there are many things that do not change, and which have their ultimate foundation in Christ who is the same yesterday, today, and forever. So it is in the light of Christ, the image of the unseen God, and the firstborn of every creature, that the Council is setting out to speak to everyone, to clarify the mystery of man and to cooperate in finding a solution to the principal problems of our time.[3]

---

[*] 1980c.
[1] GS 4. Translations of Vatican II documents are my own, and are intended to be as close as possible to the literal structure of the Latin texts. All emphases throughout the essay are mine, unless the contrary is indicated.
[2] GS 5.   [3] GS 10.

Gaudium et Spes and *Dignitatis Humanae* were promulgated on the same day, and we may usefully weave the great themes of those documents together to find the pattern of those underlying realities which, in the teaching of the Council, do not change, being founded on Christ, the Word of God and, as crucified and risen, the centre of human history.

I. THE OBJECTIVITY OF THE NATURAL LAW

In the final paragraph of *Gaudium et Spes*, the Council recalled that most awesome saying of Christ: 'Not everyone who says "Lord, Lord" will enter into the kingdom of heaven, but those who *do the will of the Father*...'.[4] As *Dignitatis Humanae* puts it:

The highest norm of human life is the divine law[5]—eternal, objective and universal—whereby God orders, directs and governs the whole world and the ways of the human community according to the plan of his wisdom and love. God makes man a sharer (*particeps*) in this his law so that, by divine providence's sweet[6] disposing, man can recognize more and more the unchanging truth.[7]

At this point, in a footnote missing in the English and some but not all other modern language translations, the Council referred us to three texts of Aquinas, including one obviously uppermost in the mind of those who drafted the document:

The eternal law is unchanging truth, and everyone somehow knows the truth, at least the general principles of the natural law (even though in other matters some people share more and some less in the knowledge of truth).[8]

So it was no accident that the Council said that the human person is a sharer (*particeps*) in the eternal law. Aquinas's 'definition' of the natural law is: 'the participation of the eternal law in the rational creature';[9] for, as Aquinas says in the same place, the rational creature is subject to divine providence in a more excellent way than other creatures, in as much as the rational creature *provides* for himself and others and thus is a sharer (*particeps*) in divine providence.[10]

---

[4] GS 93 quoting Mathew 7: 21; for the full sense, see vv. 22–3 also; cf. *Lumen Gentium*, 14, n. 13.

[5] Cf. the passage from St Thomas quoted in *Pacem in Terris* (1963) (D-S 3573): *ST* I–II q.19 a.4.

[6] *Suaviter disponente*: a covert reference to Wisdom 8.1: 'Adtingit enim a fine usque ad finem fortiter et disponit omnia *suaviter*'—'Wisdom deploys her strength from world's end to world's end, and orders all things sweetly'. There is thus a further covert reference, viz. to Vatican I's dogmatic Constitution *Dei Filius*, c. I (D-S 3003): 'God protects and governs by His providence all things which He has made, "reaching from end to end mightily, and ordering all things sweetly" (cf. Wisdom 8. 1)'.

[7] DH 3.

[8] *ST* I–II q.93 a.2; the other texts are q.91 a.1 and q.93 a.1 (both concerning the eternal law).

[9] I–II q.91 a.2.   [10] *Ibid.*

The Council's text, where we left it, was speaking of the unchanging truth that human beings can increasingly recognize. This looks back to the previous paragraph of *Dignitatis Humanae*: '...all men...are by their own nature impelled, and are morally bound, to seek the truth' (DH 2). And the truth that they are to seek is no merely abstract or speculative truth. For 'they are bound, too, to adhere to the truth they know and to order their whole life according to the requirements of the truth' (DH 2); their duty is 'prudently [that is, reasonably, by practical wisdom] to form right and true judgments of conscience' (DH 3). For the human being 'perceives and recognises the dictates of the divine law by means of his conscience' (DH 3).

More about conscience in due course. For the moment I want to reinforce the clear implication of *Dignitatis Humanae* that these 'dictates of the divine law', which are the 'supreme norm of human life', include the requirements of the natural law.[11] This emerges sufficiently from a later paragraph of the Declaration:

...by the will of Christ the Catholic Church is the teacher of truth and it is her responsibility to proclaim and authentically [or authoritatively: *authentice*] to teach the truth that is Christ himself and, at the same time, by her authority to declare and confirm the principles of the moral order *that flow from human nature itself* (DH 14).

As *Gaudium et Spes* put it: 'The Church, in preaching the Gospel on the basis of her divine mission, contributes to placing the brotherly common life [*consortionis*] of individuals and peoples on a solid basis: namely, a knowledge of the *divine and natural law*' (GS 89), that is, of a law that, as natural, is also divine. This is made very clear in the famous paragraph about birth control: the divine law which, in the light of the gospel, is unfolded (GS 51) and authentically interpreted by the Church's magisterium (GS 50) provides, or consists of, objective standards based on the nature of [human] persons and of their acts [*objectivis criteriis, ex personae eiusdemque actuum natura desumptis*] (GS 51).

The Council's teaching that the natural law is an aspect of the divine law is not an idle, arbitrary, or formal assertion. For the 'natural goodness' of things (including human life), their 'value', comes from God,[12] who as Creator has established them according to his plan.[13] And in the finest

---

[11] Fuchs, *Natural Law: A Theological Investigation*, 10: '...the natural law itself is divine. This is made plain in Canon 27 of the Code of Canon Law'; 9: 'The Code of Canon Law understands the revealed positive law, with the natural law, as being divine law (CIC, can. 6, 6° and can. 27; cf. can. 1038 §1; can. 1529; can 1926)'. See also D-S 3272 (Leo XIII [letter] against duelling, 12 September 1891), and generally Aubert, *Loi de Dieu: Lois Des Hommes*.

[12] *Apostolicam Actuositatem*, 7.   [13] *Christus Dominus*, 12; cf. also *Lumen Gentium*, 36.

paragraph of *Gaudium et Spes* we find that the Lord's command [*mandatum*] is to 'spread on earth the goods of human dignity, brotherly unity, and liberty, *that is to say* all the *good fruits of our nature* and of our effort'—the goods which 'we will find again . . ., transfigured' in the 'completed kingdom of truth and life, holiness and grace, justice, love and peace'.[14] A group of six Council fathers suggested that this reference to the goods, or good fruits, *of our nature*, be deleted, on the ground that in the context of human culture today it is not too felicitous to speak of 'our nature'; these things are the fruits not of our nature but of free human work.[15] Their objection was rightly rejected, though the reference to 'our effort [*industria*]' was added to make the point (as traditional as it is modern) that human nature is fulfilled (bears its good fruits) only in action (including, of course, such action as contemplation).[16]

All in all, it is easy to see that, in the teaching of the Council, the objectivity that a judgment has by being in accordance with the divine creative understanding (that is, in accordance with the divine law) and the objectivity that a judgment has by discerning and/or choosing what is really good for a being constituted as we are (that is, a being with our nature) are two aspects, only notionally distinguishable, of (a) the objectivity of the 'objective moral order' (DH 7 and *Inter Mirifica*, 6; cf. also GS 16: 'objective norms of morality'), and (b) the rightness and truth of a 'right and true conscience' (DH 3).

Against this background we can get a clearly focused understanding of the Council's teaching on conscience, the dignity of the conscience, and indeed on human dignity in general. The Council spoke of human dignity more than sixty times, and always as a kind of shorthand for the complex of reason/freedom/responsibility we find referred to in that sentence I quoted partially above:

In accordance with their dignity, all men—since they are persons, i.e., endowed with reason and free will and thus raised to personal responsibility[17]—are by their own nature impelled, and are morally bound, to seek the truth (DH 2).

---

[14] GS 39.   [15] *Acta Concilii Vaticani II*, Vol. IV, pars VII, p. 443.
[16] See the *relatio ad* n. 38 (G) in *ibid.*, p. 463 ('aspectus contemplativus et renunciationis huic mundo'); and GS 38.
[17] Clearly an echo of John XXIII, *Pacem in Terris* (1963) (D-S 3957):

. . . every human being has the character of a person i.e. is a nature endowed with intelligence and free will; and so, as such, each has rights and duties which flow, directly and together, from his nature: rights and duties which, moreover, are general and inviolable and therefore cannot be alienated in any way. Now when we consider the dignity of the human person as conveyed in the truths of divine revelation. . . .

John XXIII and Vatican II both refer explicitly at this point to Pius XII's Christmas Broadcast of 24 December 1942 for this careful interrelating of dignity with responsibility and fundamental rights.

Reason, freedom, responsibility, obligation: perhaps the nearest the Council gets to a formal account of human dignity is in *Gaudium et Spes*, in the central paragraph of the chapter on the dignity of the human person,

Man attains [his] dignity when, liberating himself from all captivity to the passions, he pursues his end, in the free choice of good and procures for himself, effectively and by skillful effort [*industria*], appropriate aids to that end (GS 17).

And what is that end? It is, as the Council says in the next sentence, an 'ordination toward God'. So the Council can venture an even shorter 'definition' of what it means by dignity: the dignity of man *is*, consists in, obeying the law written in his heart by God (GS 16). And here, of course, the Council cited the foundation text for Catholic reflection on natural law, Romans 2: 15–16:

[When the Gentiles who do not have the Law do by nature [*naturaliter*] what the Law requires] they show that what the Law requires is written on their hearts, while their conscience also bears witness. . . .

For conscience, too, is another in the cluster of concepts that we use in understanding this subtle intersection ('participation') of the human with the divine. As the Council said in the first sentence of its treatment of 'the dignity of moral conscience':

In the depths of conscience man discerns a law which he does not dictate to himself but which he ought to obey; always summoning him to love and do the good and to avoid evil, the voice of this law [*not*, as the standard English translation has it, the voice of conscience!][18] sounds when necessary in the ears of his heart as 'Do this, shun that. . . .'

'Conscience', continues the Council, quoting Pius XII, 'is the most secret core and sanctuary of man, in which he is alone with God, whose voice resounds in his inwardness' (GS 16). Fidelity to conscience means a 'search for *truth*' and for *true* solutions to moral problems; conscience can indeed err 'through invincible ignorance without losing its dignity' (provided there is sufficient 'care for the search for the true and the good'); but 'to the extent that a correct conscience holds sway, persons and groups are turning away from blind choice and seeking to conform to the objective norms of morality' (GS 16).

---

[18] The Latin is quite unambiguous:

In imo conscientiae *legem* homo detegit, *quam* ipse sibi non dat, sed *cui* obedire debet, et *cuius* vox, semper ad bonum amandum et faciendum ac malum vitandum eum advocans, ubi oportet auribus cordis sonat: fac hoc, illud devita. Nam homo legem in corde suo a Deo inscriptam habet, cui parere ipsa dignitas eius est et secundum quam ipse iudicabitur.

The French and Italian translations are accurate enough on the point. [But the error was not confined to English speakers. Fr (now Cardinal) Georges Cottier OP, shortly before being appointed theologian to the papal household by John Paul II in 1990, expressed to me his amazement that anyone could think it was not 'the voice of conscience'.]

In short, it was the Council's unwavering teaching that the dignity of conscience consists in its *capacity* to disclose the objective truth about what is to be done, both in particular assessments and in general norms,[19] and that that truth has its truth as an intention of God whose voice is our law. This law is knowable by us because we 'participate in the light of the divine mind' (GS 15). The teaching corresponds to this, indeed, it is an explicitation of it, the even more frequently repeated teaching of the Council that human dignity consists of the capacity to *understand*, to some extent, what God expects of us, and to choose *freely* to relate ourselves to God in faith, hope, and love by acting and living in accordance with that understanding. Let us now add a last statement:

The outstanding rationale [*ratio*] of human dignity consists in the vocation of the human being to communion with God. To converse [*colloquium*] with God, the human being is invited right from his very origin; for he would not exist were he not constantly preserved (as he was created) by God's love, and he cannot live fully according to truth unless he freely acknowledges that love and commits himself to his Creator (GS 19).

In all the Council's many references to human dignity, there is no trace of that arbitrary, 'picture-thinking' conception of dignity that we find, for example, in the working paper (dated 27 May 1966) of the 'majority theologians' of the Pontifical Commission on Population, Family, and Birth, in which they sought to *explain* why, if contraceptive intercourse is morally good, nevertheless various other masturbatory acts between spouses are not. In relation to the latter acts, they said:

The new theory is extremely strict…since it does not permit them. For in these acts there is preserved neither the dignity of love nor the dignity of the spouses as human persons created according to the image of God.

---

[19] Karl Rahner expresses the common teaching of theologians at the time of Vatican II:

It is right that there should be a 'conscience' which tells the individual man what he must do *as* an individual. That is to say: that the individual is not just one member of the human race with a common human nature (he is this too), but also unique and irreplaceable, he has a sphere of moral choices which cannot be clearly decided by universal norms and laws alone, but needs a special individual function of his conscience…. But because the individual does not take away the universal, but by God's will lies within what is universally human in him [not a happy way of putting it] there is an individual morality only within a universal normative morality… [M]aturity of the Christian conscience is not an emancipation from and casting off of the universal norms preached by the Gospel and the Church… [I]t is the ability to apply these norms oneself to a concrete situation without needing help in every case…A moral norm is by nature universal but, precisely as a universal law, is intended to be the rule for the individual case. And so when it is fully grasped and rightly understood and interpreted (that is, understood as the magisterium means it, not just as an individual thinks fit to interpret it), and bears on an individual case, then this unique individual concrete case is bound by the norm and obliged to abide by it. When, for example, the Church teaches that *every* directly induced abortion is morally wrong…then this applies to every individual case quite regardless of the circumstances. (Rahner, *Nature and Grace*, 96–100.)

This is no explanation at all, since an act accords with human dignity in the morally relevant sense by being reasonable and right in accordance with God's call to us. As *Gaudium et Spes* said (citing Corinthians 6: 13–20 on the indignity of fornication): '...human dignity itself involves that one glorify God in one's body' by 'not allowing it to serve the depraved inclinations of one's heart' (GS 14); that is, once again, by turning aside from blind choice toward the objective norms of morality, toward God's law, which is discerned in the conscience (GS 16) *somehow* by all who have intelligence at all and *fully* by one who has that wisdom which 'perfects the intelligent nature of the human person' (GS 15).

And so, when the Council comes to speak in *Gaudium et Spes* 51 of the need to reverence the conjugal sexual act as 'directed according to genuine human dignity', it explains this norm (so to speak) of dignity by exactly the same line of thought as we have just observed in GS 14–16; indeed it makes its explanation even clearer by beginning the next sentence with a 'therefore' [*igitur*]:

Therefore, the moral character of [this] action, when the harmonizing of conjugal love with the responsible transmission of life is in question, does not depend only on a sincere intention and a consideration of motives, but ought to be determined by objective criteria, derived from the nature of the human person and of the human person's acts....

That is what human dignity demands: an objective (that is, real) relationship to basic human goods, basic aspects of human personality as they are inevitably involved in certain sorts of human acts: these 'objective criteria', therefore, 'in an ambience of true love, *respect the whole sense of mutual* [*self-*] *giving and of human procreation*', and this objectively adequate respect for those basic human goods (and thus for authentic human dignity) 'cannot be had unless the virtue of conjugal chastity is cultivated serious-mindedly [*sincero animo*]' (GS 51).

II. NATURAL LAW: ULTIMATE AUTHORITY FOR CHRISTIAN LIFE?

It is said by various contemporary theologians that the objective or 'natural law' ethics with which moral theology must work is an 'experiential' ethics, that is, an ethics based on ordinary knowledge of the facts.[20] These theologians differ among themselves about what sorts of 'facts' really

---

[20] See e.g. O'Connell, *Principles for a Catholic Morality*, 145–6; Hughes, *Authority in Morals: An Essay in Christian Ethics*, vii, 63.

count for these purposes.[21] But their appeals to experience and/or ordinary facts have a common purpose, which is twofold. The *first* purpose is to suggest that it is the relevant sort of experiential or factual knowledge, and not revelation, that provides the 'ultimate' foundation of ethical knowledge so that the 'ultimate' authority in any inquiry into natural law (and thus in human, including Christian, life) is *not* revelation but these experienced facts. And the *second* purpose of these theologians is to argue that the alternative to 'experiential' moral knowledge is a legalism which, whether it be based on 'natural law, understood in some juridical sense' or on 'commandments of some kind', is 'an injustice to both the Creator and his creation'.[22] Let me take up these two arguments.

First, the argument that, if we believe in natural law, we cannot believe that revelation has 'ultimate authority' in morals. The argument and its implications are spelled out most clearly by Fr Gerard Hughes: 'Belief in revelation is irrational unless that revelation somehow fits our antecedent convictions, and, in particular, with our antecedent moral convictions'; our response to revelation 'must inevitably include moral reflection which is not in turn dependent on the revelation it is trying to interpret'; such moral reflection is 'epistemologically prior to our appeal to revelation, which cannot therefore be ultimately authoritative'; *therefore*, according to Hughes, appeal to revelation *cannot* 'enable us to solve moral dilemmas to which there is no other adequate solution'; there *could not* be 'a specifically Christian ethic, the conclusions of which cannot be firmly established without appeal to revelation'; and if one can find no *conclusive* arguments, say, against the legitimacy of divorce and remarriage *before* one appeals to revelation, it necessarily follows that there *could not* be any basis in revelation for concluding that divorce and remarriage are illegitimate.[23]

You will have noticed the *non sequitur*; it is, I'm afraid, extremely glaring. Revelation (since it cannot settle the question whether I ought to believe it and adhere to it—I must have some prior grasp of the moral importance of truth) cannot settle *all* questions; 'therefore' revelation cannot settle *any* questions. Revelation is not the 'ultimate' source of Christian life, which must 'ultimately' begin with a free response to what is divinely proposed for belief and acceptance; the 'ultimate authority' is the truth, respect for which motivates and justifies that response; 'therefore' revelation is not an 'ultimate' authority in any aspect of Christian life. Either *all* moral truths

---

[21] Thus for O'Connell, the experienced facts include 'values' ('independent of our wishes and our needs') such as beauty, honesty, compassion, etc.: O'Connell, *Principles*, 118, 221. For Hughes, however, the relevant facts are the 'wants' of particular persons and the ordinary non-moral knowledge of human nature and the world in which we live: Hughes, *Authority*, 60–3.

[22] O'Connell, 168; see also 169, 146.   [23] Hughes, *Authority*, 10, 24.

receive their ultimate justification or verification from revelation, or *none* do. (Three ways of expressing one and the same invalid reasoning to a false conclusion.)

The middle position—the Catholic position clearly expounded by Vatican I and frequently implied by Vatican II—was simply overlooked or brushed aside by these writers, viz., the position that moral truth about *some* matters *can* be securely known without (supernatural) revelation but the moral truth about *other* matters can be *securely* known only because God has revealed what objectively ought to be done.[24] Both parts of the position were developed in *Dignitatis Humanae*. Prior to their acceptance or even awareness of divine revelation, 'all men…are by their own nature impelled, *and morally bound*, to seek the truth, especially religious truth' (DH 2). That this is an objective moral demand can be securely known in advance of hearing the Word. So can the further objective moral demand that all 'adhere to the truth, once it is known, and order their whole lives in accord with its demands' (*ibid.*). And then, when the Word has been heard, there arises 'the duty of believing the word of God' (DH 9, 11), that is, the 'gospel,…source of all saving truth and all moral teaching [*morum disciplina*]' (DV 7), including that 'sacred and certain doctrine' by which the Church 'declares and confirms by her authority those principles of the moral order which have their origin in human nature itself' (DH 14).

Thus, Vatican II supplied the materials for a more profound exposition of the relations between natural law, gospel, and conscience than the Council itself formally expressed. Classic expositions of natural law as the participation of God's eternal intention in the human understanding have used, and rightly used, the metaphor of light, 'irradiating' our minds, enabling us to 'see', for example, moral truth. Without questioning that metaphor, indeed making use of it, the Council in effect invited us to consider another. It is not precisely or merely the metaphor of hearing; rather it is the richer metaphor (drawn not from the order of bare 'nature' but from the order of social interaction) of coming to understand (and love) a person better through conversation or colloquy. For our dignity, to be found in our obedience to God's law (the voice of which sounds in the depths of our conscience) (GS 16), is rooted in our vocation, our calling, '*ad colloquium cum Deo*' (GS 19).[25] That *colloquium* begins in this life with our questions, 'our' suppositions and 'our' judgments (ours, because we are responsible for them; 'ours', because we do not simply 'make them up'), for example about what really is good, and about what response the really good requires of

---

[24] Vatican I, *Dei Filius*, c. 2 (D-S 3003, 3004, 3005).
[25] See Hamel, 'La Théologie morale entre l'Écriture et la raison' at 282.

us: about the natural law. But that is a conversation in a space crowded with our relatives and acquaintances and communities and enemies, and noisy not only with their voices but also with the voice of our own self-interest. Into that Babel the Word of God has been spoken publicly, so that it may be heard and taken to heart by each of us. That voice can be recognized for what it is, since its tones and its message are not foreign to our anticipations; but it can reply to questions whose answers otherwise seemed muffled and indistinct to us; and it summons us to closer converse—*colloquium, participatio*—with the loving and therefore demanding and judging One whose voice, whether recognized or unrecognized, it always has been, in truth, whenever we judge rightly.

One could pursue and amplify this analogy extensively. But I want to sharpen the point by turning to the *second* argument of those who oppose 'experience' to 'revelation'—the argument that the alternative to experiential moral knowledge is *legalism*. Now I have just finished a long book defending the classic theses *not only* that one can understand, without revelation, the basic forms of human good and the basic requirements of practical reasonableness and thus a number of quite precise moral obligations, *but also* that one can understand, without referring to the will or commandments of God, the idea of real moral obligation. So I should like now to show how those classic theses do not imply that a respect for the commandments of God must be inappropriate, childish 'legalism'. These reflections of mine on legalism will continue through most of the rest of this essay, even when I am discussing other themes.

Why speak about the commandments at all? Well, as you know,[26] a rich young man came up to Jesus one day, and asked him, 'Teacher, what must I do to have eternal life?' And (as all the Synoptics report, with interesting but immaterial variations) Jesus began his answer by saying to him, 'If you would enter into life, keep the commandments'. 'Which?' '*You must not kill. You must not commit adultery. You must not bring false witness. Honour your father and mother,* and: *you must love your neighbour as yourself*' (Matthew 19: 16–20; Mark 10: 17–19; Luke 18: 18–21).[27]

---

[26] How? It is easy to forget, when one is discussing the consequentialist theologians, that one is doing theology, not apologetics. But since we *are* doing theology, suffice it to recall Vatican II's *Dei Verbum*, 19:

> Holy mother Church firmly and most constantly has held and holds that *the four Gospels* just mentioned, whose historical character she unhesitatingly affirms, *faithfully convey what Jesus* the Son of God, while living among men, really did and *taught for their eternal salvation*...(Emphasis added.)

This does not, of course, foreclose exegetical and hermeneutical questions.

[27] These verses are amazingly neglected: Spicq, *Théologie morale du Nouveau Testament* does not even mention them; Schnackenburg, *The Moral Teaching of the New Testament* gives them no discussion. The treatment in Irenaeus, *Adversus Haereses* IV, 12, 5, is as fresh and helpful as it was

Now if the rich young man had recently been reading *Principles for a Catholic Morality*, these words of the Lord would have come as quite a surprise. For in that book there is no suggestion that Jesus made the specific moral commandments in the Decalogue his own; the most Fr Timothy O'Connell will allow is that it is a 'great exaggeration' to contrast 'Jesus' teaching of the two New Commandments' with 'the Ten Commandments of the Old Law' which, however, were 'not particularly concerned about *individual* morality in any form' and did not have a 'precisely ethical' importance.[28] Well, the rich young man might reflect that, whatever may have been the case when the Decalogue was originally revealed or incorporated in the inspired Scriptures, and whatever may have been its original relationship with similar moral conceptions in Egypt and Babylon, these commands, *repromulgated to him* by the good teacher who spoke with the authority of the Creator who offers eternal life, are the very paradigm of what in late western society would come to be called 'precisely ethical' and 'individual morality'.

If the rich young man might well have lost confidence in the adequacy of Fr O'Connell's discussion of the Decalogue, so he would be unlikely to listen any longer (if ever he had) to Fr Hughes's suggestion that Christ's Revelation is not concerned with 'the details of morality' but only with 'the general importance of being morally good'—the suggestion that, in direct contradiction to the words that the rich young man had just heard, 'particular teachings on particular moral issues' are not 'taught as salvation-truths' but are 'offered simply because it is in general a salvation-truth that to take such issues seriously is required of us....'[29]

But he might have been reading Frs Schüller, McCormick, and O'Connell on parenetic discourse, inviting him to conclude that Christ's commands here do 'not convey information about the specific content of...moral demands' but are merely 'hortatory to what is presumed to be known and agreed on',[30] so that they were 'not meant to be taken literally and not intended to be really exceptionless'.[31] Rather every command, such as 'Do not kill', 'Do not commit adultery', can be read subject to a tacit

---

1,800 years ago. See also Kittel's *Theological Dictionary of the New Testament*, vol. 2, 548–9 (s.v. *entolē*). For Christ's attitude to the Decalogue, see also Matthew 5: 17, 19; Fuchs, *Natural Law*, 33–7.

[28]   O'Connell, 129–30.

[29]   Hughes, 18. The suggestion is advanced tentatively, but recurs in later argument: see e.g. 95.

[30]   McCormick, 'Notes on Moral Theology' (1975) at 84–5. It must be said that McCormick et al. use a rather simplified notion of parenesis; Hamel, 'La théologie morale entre l'Ecriture et la raison' at 317 distinguishes between *paraclesis* (an urgent reminder or restatement of fundamental duties, made with considerable authority) and *parenesis* (more gentle and orientative, appealing more to generosity).

[31]   O'Connell, 220.

rider of the form: 'except when there is a proportionate reason',[32] i.e. except when killing or committing adultery would 'maximize good and minimize evil'.[33] An 'absolute' or 'exceptionless' command would be sheer legalism, i.e. would be a betrayal of the natural law itself.

Can we help the rich young man sort out these claims of the new 'moral theology'? The claims are of two sorts. One is about the need to interpret the promulgated commands (and implicitly, to interpret them in the light of our *prior* grasp of natural law). The other claim is specific: what the natural law requires, or makes appropriate, is a consequentialist interpretation of those 'commands'. Let us take these two sorts of claims separately.

III. NATURAL LAW, REVELATION, AND INTERPRETATION

No one doubts, or has doubted, that the commands of God that Christ entrusted to his apostles to be taught to the ends of the earth and the end of the world (Matthew 28: 20; cf. 1 Corinthians 7: 10, 25) are in need of interpretation. As *Dei Verbum* put it:

…through contemplation and study by believers who treasure those [words] in their hearts…, through the intimate understanding of the spiritual things they experience, and through the proclamation of those who with the episcopal succession receive the sure charism of truth, the understanding of the words handed down grows (*Dei Verbum*, 7).

Moreover, this interpretative understanding will be achieved by Christians, that is, by persons who bring to their contemplation and study of the divine words that (at least) elementary grasp of basic values and fundamental requirements of practical reasonableness which enabled them, under God's grace, to recognize the moral obligation to accept the revelation of Christ by reason of its truth. And if we, prior to that acceptance, can understand that truth is an objective good which, as objective, makes authoritative claims on us, equally we can grasp other basic aspects of human good such as life, and friendship, and practical reasonableness, and such basic requirements of practical reasonableness as impartiality. Indeed, it is the

---

[32] McCormick, 98.

[33] O'Connell, 147, 152–4. See also Hughes, 75:

Bert killed Bill…Perhaps…he thereby *obtained a great deal of money* on which he lived happily ever after. Perhaps the doctor who performed an abortion thereby *saved a marriage*? Clearly enough, the additional information about the relationship between the behaviour and human needs will not in every case lead us to change our moral judgment about whether the behaviour was right or wrong. *What cannot be said in advance*, however, *is that these features need not even be considered* before we make a moral judgment on what was done. (Emphasis added.)

What Hughes says 'cannot be said' is, of course, said (and 'in advance'!) by Scripture and the whole tradition.

grasp of these goods and requirements that enables us to perceive the publicly offered word as divinely uttered. As Fr Hughes says, 'Revelation commends itself to us in part because it does harmonize with our moral aspirations', which must therefore have been 'present antecedently (at least in a logical sense)'.[34] So far so good; but then Fr Hughes (openly, and many another theologian tacitly) falls for the hermeneutical circle:

The attempt to use the biblical tradition as ultimately authoritative [i.e., as providing final and certain solutions applicable to *us*] is viciously circular, since it must invoke precisely those processes of independent moral reason which it is the purpose of the attempt to circumvent.[35]

Alas, Fr Hughes's argument would prove that learning, in any field, is logically impossible! For learning, in any field, very commonly involves a *self-correcting* process, whereby the understanding with which one began a particular inquiry (and which enabled one to undertake the inquiry) is not only amplified but also partially qualified and partially corrected by the new understanding yielded by the inquiry.[36]

So, if we accept the Pauline thesis that 'Gentiles who do not have the Law do by nature what the Law requires... [and] show that what the Law requires is written on their hearts' (Romans 2: 14, 15), or the equivalent thesis of Irenaeus and the whole Catholic tradition that the moral precepts of the Decalogue are matters of natural law,[37] we are not thereby challenging the 'ultimate authority' of God's publicly revealed word, that is, (in *this* use of 'ultimate'), the capacity of that divine word to reform and correct as well as supplement and make precise our prior (and continuing!) understanding (whether articulated or not) of natural law, that is, of the *same* 'eternal, objective, and universal' plan of God's wisdom and love as is disclosed to us through our natural capacity to understand the goods to which we created beings find ourselves inclined.

A command such as 'Do not kill' has this capacity and 'ultimate' authority to correct and refine (notwithstanding its own need for interpretation) precisely because it is not a single set of words on a page but one part of a larger revelation made by word and deed. It is not my intention to make a foray into either biblical exegesis or biblical hermeneutics. But recent appeals to the notion of parenesis are calculated to suggest that the moral teachings of revelation are all in need of an interpretation which, in respect of all specific and material norms of conduct, must be effectively

---

[34] Hughes, 8; also 5.

[35] Hughes, 19. Hughes adds: 'This hermeneutical problem is quite a general one, and does not apply only to ethics, but to the interpretation and translation of any text from a different language or culture.'

[36] See Lonergan, *Method in Theology*, 159, 208–9.

[37] Irenaeus, *Adversus Haereses* IV, 13, 1 and 4; Aquinas, *ST* I–II q.100 aa. 1, 3.

controlled by some 'natural law' (or autonomous, philosophical reasonings; or by 'experience' yielding, I suppose, some sort of intuitions). (This argument from the parenetic character of scriptural moral teaching is thus an alternative argument toward the thesis about the 'ultimacy' of natural law, which we saw fallaciously defended by Fr Hughes.) So I wish to give an indication of the *sorts* of reasons there are for supposing that revelation contains within its own resources *sufficient material to control its own interpretation* and thereby sufficient to correct the philosophical or 'natural law' reasonings that might have seemed persuasive without it. To say that revelation has these resources and thus this corrective capacity is not to say that the resources of revelation could override a strict demonstration that an alleged moral norm cannot be morally acceptable. Nor is it to say that, where revelation does not confirm what would otherwise have seemed to be required or permitted by natural reasonableness, revelation must be *adding* something over and above the natural law. Rather it is to warn against the all too common slide *from* 'the law of God/Christ is fundamentally natural law', or 'nothing in revelation can in principle be contrary to reason', *to* 'whatever I find morally opaque (or: whatever I cannot demonstrate to be part of natural law) cannot be part of the gospel's saving *disciplina morum*'.

So, to go back to particular but not fully specific commandments: each of them is one of a number of commandments, one or more of which are *explained* by Christ and his apostles in terms that make clear the proper *strategy* for interpreting the parenetic (non-explanatory) 'Do not kill'. For example, as against the Jewish interpretation, Christ by explanatory discourse makes plain certain aspects of the stringency and 'material' content of the command 'Do not commit adultery' (Matthew 5: 27–8, 31–2; and par.), and this strategy, identified as Christ's, is applied (as against Gentile incomprehension of the moral significance of sex) by St Paul to the whole range of non-marital sexual activity.[38] So too, the context of revelation supplies the materials for an explanatory specification of what counts as the 'killing' forbidden in the commandment which, when thus made fully specific, applies as an exceptionless rule of life; the process of specification begins in Exodus itself (the 'Do not kill' of Exodus 20: 13 becomes the 'Do not kill the innocent and righteous' of Exodus 23: 7); the distinction between direct and indirect killing can be approached by asking whether Jesus committed suicide; and so on. The interpretative process always envisions distinctions in terms of real human goods and real modes of involvement with those goods, but never proposes a calculus of consequences, and never degenerates into the merely formal 'Do not kill unjustly'.

---

[38] See Jensen, 'Does *porneia* mean Fornication?', esp. 179–84.

And do not forget that, just as the call of Christ to the rich young man extended beyond the Decalogue itself and indeed beyond the other commandments that I quoted (see Matthew 19: 21), so the resources of revelation that control its own interpretation extend far beyond the expressed commands, the vice lists, the house tables, and other overtly moral argumentation. These resources include such fundamental perspectives as Vatican II recalls for us in the passage I have already partly quoted:

> We do not know the time of the consummation of the earth and of humanity, nor do we know how the universe will be transformed. The figure of this world deformed by sin is passing away.... [But] all the good fruits of our nature and our effort (after we have spread them on earth in the Spirit of the Lord and according to his command) we will find again ... transfigured, when Christ hands over to the Father the kingdom ... of truth and life ... now on this earth present in mystery, and to be consummated when the Lord comes (GS 39).

Christians, then, are not to count only the good consequences that can be humanly seen and foreseen in a world that is passing away; the morality of Christ counts the good that cannot be seen, that hidden treasure of good works, which is hidden to us in the calamities of ruin and oppression but known by faith to be real and really constitutive of the kingdom of God that is now, in mystery, being built up by obedience to the Lord (GS 39, 93).

IV. REVELATION, NATURAL LAW, AND CONSEQUENTIALISM

The consequentialist theologians argue that Christ's commands are all subject to riders such as 'unless there is proportionate reason for doing (the otherwise forbidden act)', or, less obscurely though in fact absurdly,[39] 'unless doing (the otherwise forbidden act) would maximize good and minimize evil'. They argue that the parenetic form of the commands leaves them open to such 'explanatory' qualifications. But the writings of these

---

[39] 'Proportionate reason', when used 'at large', is a highly obscure phrase: see e.g. McCormick, 'Notes on Moral Theology' (1978) at 110–15 (where 'inherent' or 'essential' links are contrasted with empirical probabilities ranging up to practical certainties, and *this* contrast is then said to be 'in other words' a matter of 'proportionality', i.e. of finding the 'lesser evil'). 'Maximizing good and minimizing evil' *seems* relatively clear, until one asks (a) how one is supposed to measure incommensurable goods, and (b) whether one is to prefer a large surplus of 'good' (at the cost of much evil) to a very small amount of 'evil' (at the cost of forgoing much good), or vice versa. Question (b) shows that T.E. O'Connell has not begun to think through the logic of utilitarianism; the aphorism 'Maximize the good and minimize the evil', which (O'Connell, 223) he says 'has come to be known as "Schüller's Preference Principle"', is *flagrantly* absurd; competent philosophical utilitarians have been formulating their principle in terms of the 'greatest possible *surplus*' of good over evil since, at the latest, Sidgwick, *The Methods of Ethics*, 413; and the problem of whether to prefer 'much good' or 'little evil' was vigorously explored by Cicero, *De finibus* II, 6–25, esp. 17.

moral theologians themselves provide a refutation of this thesis. For do they really have any use for the commands as formulated in revelation? An audience or congregation that has learned that the commands of the Decalogue 'do not give us any information', are 'not oriented toward the material of a particular situation', 'are really tautologies', and 'somehow involve circular logic', are 'contentless'[40] and just amount to saying that wrong actions are wrong, is not going to be impressed or 'challenged' or 'motivated' by a homiletics that appeals to such 'commands'.

By contrast, the architecture of Catholic moral teaching is, I venture to say, profoundly biblical in its methodology; even when presented as if simply an unfolding of the natural law, it has in reality been also an intelligible exposition and development of the words and deeds of revelation. Much of this architecture is visible in the moral teachings of Vatican II. The Council taught that there is a 'natural and Gospel law' (*lex naturalis et evangelica*, not well translated in the Abbott edition as 'natural law and the Gospel') which establishes 'limits' that must be observed even by one who is defending his rights against unjust oppression (GS 74). It proclaims, not that there is only one universal principle of the natural law with unchanging binding force (as the consistent consequentialist argues) but that there are many (GS 79). It offers several examples of types of action that 'are deliberately opposed' to those universal and unchanging principles: 'above all, those actions which by intention and design exterminate a whole people, nation or ethnic minority' (GS 79); and again, '*every* warlike act which tends indiscriminately to the destruction of entire cities or of extensive areas along with their populations is a crime against God and man...' (GS 80). It proclaims that the magisterial unfolding of the divine law can involve the condemnation of particular 'ways of regulating births', not surely because the magisterium is in a position to assess '*authoritatively*' the 'facts' about good and bad consequences of, say, contraception, but because some 'ways of regulating births' fail to preserve the 'integral meaning of mutual self-giving and of human procreation...' (GS 51). The Council itself condemned abortion and infanticide as dreadful crimes (*ibid.*). Then, in a context dealing not with revealed divine law but with 'the high dignity of the human person...and his universal and inviolable rights and duties' (GS 26), the Council spoke in terms that cannot be reconciled with consistent consequentialism:

Whatever is opposed to life itself, such as any sort of homicide, genocide, abortion, euthanasia and willful suicide itself...; all these and others of their like [some of which the Council identifies in the same passage, e.g., slavery, prostitution, and

---

[40] O'Connell, 161; see also 162.

torture] are indeed shameful; while they poison human civilization, *they degrade [or harm] those who so act more than those who suffer the injury...*(GS 27).

This last observation by the Council is, of course, as well known in the tradition of natural law philosophizing (see Plato, *Gorgias*, 469B, 508B) as in the biblical revelation, which would clearly be understood as teaching that 'evil may not be done for the sake of good' even if Paul had not expressly said so (Romans 3: 8; cf. 6: 1).[41] So too the biblical and conciliar proclamation of prohibitions of types of act meshes in with the tradition of purely human ('natural') reason and custom that Aristotle summed up in the remark that there are actions about which we should never be asking ourselves 'When? How? With whom? etc.'; the mere commission of such acts (e.g. adultery) is wrong, and circumstances do not affect the matter (*NE* II, 6: 1107a9–18; similarly, *Eudemian Ethics*, II, 3: 1221b18–26). Again, the scholastic maxim 'Affirmative precepts are always valid but do not have to be carried out on every occasion; negative precepts have to be respected on every occasion'[42] is an induction from the scriptural data faithfully interpreted—indeed, the distinction between affirmative and negative precepts can be discerned even in the reordering of the commandments by Christ, addressing the rich young man—but it is also a principle of reasonableness, which insists that, though an omission to act can be as murderous, say, as a positive act, the distinction between act and omission is frequently of decisive relevance in assessing one's responsibilities (or guilt).

Thus, between the scripturally controlled theological tradition and the products of philosophical reflections intended to be 'without revelation', there is an interpenetration so profound that when we are confronted by, say, Kant's 'categorical imperative'—'Act so that you treat humanity, whether in your own person or in another's, always as an end and never as a means only'[43]—we cannot say (even as historians of philosophy) how much this owes to 'natural reason' and how much to the revealed commands treasured in the hearts if not the deeds of Europeans for 1,750 years. So too it is virtually impossible to determine (and unprofitable to try) whether the consequentialist theologians have been led astray *primarily* by bad philosophy (for consequentialism, which rejects all the principles, maxims, and distinctions I've just mentioned, *is* incoherent and philosophically

---

[41] Consequentialists sometimes think that they can give some sense to the Pauline dictum: e.g. '*moral* evil is not to be done for the sake of *premoral* good'. But since, on their view, moral evil consists in not doing what is required to maximize net pre-moral good, they have to attribute to St Paul the absurdly empty dictum 'Do not fail to maximize premoral good for the sake of premoral good'.

[42] *ST* I–II q.71 a.5 ad 3; II–II q.33 a.2c; q.3 a.2c; Supp. q.6 a.5 ad 3; etc.

[43] Kant, *Foundations of the Metaphysics of Morals*, 47.

indefensible)[44] or primarily by a loss of faith in the scriptural/traditional *disciplina morum*.

But there is another side to all this. The controlling clarity of the main lines of revealed moral teaching has encouraged a certain philosophical slackness amongst moral theologians; we are now seeing the bad consequences of that neglect. And we will be unable, I think, to respond adequately to the philosophical/theological crisis unless we identify and correct certain defects in, for example, Aquinas's treatise on natural law, defects left uncorrected, indeed exacerbated, in the neo-scholastic revival of moral theology.

For instance, Aquinas distinguished three levels of principles or precepts of natural law: (i) most general principles, 'not so much precepts as, so to speak, the ends or point of precepts', recognized by anyone who reaches the age of reason and has enough experience to know what they refer to; (ii) precepts that state the most elementary and easily recognizable moral implications of those first principles; precepts that can nevertheless be obscured or distorted for particular people and indeed for whole cultures; and (iii) precepts that state solutions to moral questions which can be answered rightly only by someone who is *wise* and who considers the question searchingly. Now this set of distinctions, though vague, is quite reasonable.[45] But, secure in his faithful grasp of revelation, Aquinas was casual in giving examples of the first-level principles, and some of the examples he gave encouraged the neo-scholastic thesis that certain precise, negative moral precepts (corresponding to items expressed or implied in the second table of the Decalogue) are intuitively known by an act of intuition which is truly self-validating (that is, which is not really a conclusion from suppressed premises that could be brought to light by analysis). That neo-scholastic thesis is not true; theologians who have recently discovered that it is not true tend to become (more or less consistent!) consequentialist theologians of the sort I have already mentioned. That is to say, they leap to the conclusion that therefore the strict negative precepts of the Decalogue cannot be precepts of natural law; they fail to make the patient survey of the various truly self-authenticating requirements of practical reasonableness (or modes of responsibility) which, when brought to bear on particular basic values (i.e. on the pre-moral first principles of practical reason which Aquinas spoke of), do yield fully 'material' moral precepts such as those of the Decalogue as interpreted in the Catholic tradition. For Aquinas, too, failed to identify these (so to speak) methodological

---

[44] See Grisez, 'Against Consequentialism' at 21–41, 48–9.

[45] (i) *ST* I–II q.94 a.6c; also a.2c; q.99 a.2 ad 2; q.100 a.5 ad 1, a.11c; q.58 a.5c; q.77 a.2c; (ii) *ST* I–II q.100 a,1c; q.94 a.4c, 6c; (iii) *ST* I–II q.100 a.3c, a.11c. [*NLNR* 30.]

requirements of practical reasonableness (or modes of responsibility). He was aware that his first-level practical 'first principles of natural law' are not moral principles, and he had enough philosophical acumen, and enough faith in the revealed word, not to fall for a consequentialist methodological norm (such as 'maximize net pre-moral goods'); but he did not identify the intelligible links between the basic goods and the moral precepts that give definite guidance in particular cases.

Secondly, Aquinas (when he was doing meta-ethics, not when he was doing ethics) tried to force his account of natural law into a distinction (unhappily transposed from the distinction in Aristotelian physics between necessity and chance) between universals (*communia*) and particulars (*propria*). This led him to make those remarks of his (quoted everywhere today, as authoritative, by people who, however, disbelieve the greater part of Aquinas's philosophy and theology) to the effect that the precepts of natural law apply to particular cases not universally but only 'in most cases' (*ut in pluribus*) (*ST* I–II q.94 a.4). This is false to his own ethical reasonings, which everywhere (and rightly) presuppose (i) that the morality of particular acts is not affected by the 'accidental' features of the case (such as that it is *Bert* who is killing and *Bill* who is being killed), and, correspondingly, (ii) that there are valid moral precepts that apply determinatively to *all* particular intentional performances that are instances of the class of acts to which the relevant precept relates, for example, 'Innocent people are not to be intentionally and directly killed', or 'Sexual intercourse outside marriage is always wrong'.

Some neo-scholastics, of course, were more or less aware that precepts of such specificity are not primary and self-authenticating, and so were unwilling to account for them by appeal to intuition (or to such equivalents of intuition as moral consensus, or the '[consensus of] Christian conscience'). Building on some rather unclear argumentation of Aquinas about sexual vice and about lying (*ST* II–II q.153 a.2; q.110 a.3), they developed the thesis that it is a primary principle of natural law that natural human functions be respected and, more particularly, be not deflected from their 'natural ends'. This supposed principle was then employed to explicate the rational (i.e. natural law) character of the Church's constant proclamation of that divine command, which is fairly obviously implicit in the scripturally expressed divine commands about the use and abuse of sex: I mean the implicit command not to engage in sexual acts in themselves inapt for procreation, acts that do not 'preserve the full sense of … human procreation …' (GS 51). When that command came under hedonist and consequentialist pressure, first in relation to contraception and then, logically enough, in relation to other forms of heterosexual, homosexual, or solitary masturbation, the supposed higher principle of natural law proved to be far from self-authenticating.

That is not to say that the principle about respect for natural functions is simply false. At least in relation to some human capacities, the principle amounts to something true, namely, that the exercise of those capacities is so structured that it will involve one willy-nilly in either respecting or choosing against a basic form of human good (such as the good of human-life-in-its-transmission, i.e. the good of procreation). And this fact is relevant morally, since there is a truly primary and self-authenticating requirement of practical reasonableness (i.e. of natural law) viz. the requirement that every basic human good be respected in every act. This requirement is the intelligible core (perhaps only dimly perceived by its author) in the version of Kant's categorical imperative that I recited before ('...treat humanity in oneself and others as an end not a means'); for every basic human good (such as life, knowledge, play, aesthetic experience, friendship, practical reasonableness, and religion) is an aspect of human personhood or, in Kant's word, of the *humanity* of a human individual.

The basic requirement of practical reasonableness that I have mentioned affords an 'explanation' of many of the strict negative commands known to us in faith through Christ's revelation of himself and of the will of the Father. With this explanation we have a more than sufficient rebuttal of the charge that the authentically and infallibly[46] proclaimed Catholic moral teaching is legalistic. That is to say, we have a demonstration that our observance of those commandments of God is a reasonable service, a *rationabile obsequium*,[47] objectively and really adequately related to the goods-of-persons that God loves. And I say that this rebuts the charge

---

[46] O'Connell, 95, 202, takes it for granted that there are no infallible moral teachings; he simply overlooks the infallibility of the ordinary magisterium, clearly taught by LG 25. See Rahner, *Nature and Grace*, 98–9:

> The fulfillment of the Commandments is an essential part of Christianity as such.... Furthermore, the Church teaches these commandments with divine authority exactly as she teaches the other 'truths of the Faith'... [A]lso through her *ordinary* magisterium, there is in the normal teaching of the Faith to the faithful in schools, sermons and all the other kinds of instruction... binding on the faithful in conscience just as the teaching through the extraordinary magisterium is.... When the whole Church in her everyday teaching does in fact teach a moral rule everywhere in the world *as* a commandment of God, she is preserved from error by the assistance of the Holy Ghost, and this rule is therefore really the will of God and is binding on the faithful in conscience, even before it has been expressly confirmed by a *solemn definition*. (Original emphasis.)

Note that because of his dubious distinction between transcendental and concrete human nature, Rahner now thinks that 'hardly any particular or individual norms' could be infallibly proclaimed; but he still affirms that such a proclamation can be by the ordinary magisterium: see his 'Basic Observations' at 14. On the infallibility of the ordinary magisterium, see Grisez and Ford, 'Contraception and the Infallibility of the Ordinary Magisterium'; and 1978b (where the remarks at 415 are mistaken: see my letter in *The Month* 240 (1979) 216).

[47] See Romans 12: 1; Vatican I, *Dei Filius*, c. 3 (D-S 3009); Wojtyla, *The Acting Person*, 166; *Redemptor Hominis*, 19 at n. 144.

of legalism 'more than sufficiently' because that charge is, in my view, quite sufficiently rebutted by establishing the *possibility* that there is some explanatory principle that supplies the desired link between material moral norms and real human good. In other words, the charge of legalism could only be made out, in the face of God's word, by a demonstration that no such explanatory principle is possible, for example because consequentialism is true. But, of course, no such demonstration is forthcoming. And as for consequentialism, it is not merely undemonstrated; it is demonstrably untrue.

Well, the requirement that basic goods be not turned against in any act is not at all the only fundamental requirement of practical reasonableness; seven or eight others can be identified, including the requirement of impartiality, and the requirement of efficiency, that is, of concern to secure maximum net good consequences within those limited contexts (defined by one's non-consequentialist commitments) in which such a computation is in principle feasible. Together these eight or nine requirements supply the missing link in Aquinas's theory of natural law, the link between the first, pre-moral practical principles (in which we grasp the basic forms of human good as 'to-be-pursued-and-realized') and the specific moral precepts that structure the virtues of justice, chastity, religion, and so on—the moral precepts (or *objectiva criteria ex personae eiusdemque actuum natura desumpta*) that express the discerning demands of the love of the Christian. For love of God and neighbour, which fulfils (Romans 13: 8, 10) and keeps (James 2: 8–12) all the commandments of God, makes Christians unwilling to usurp the role of God's providential concern for the ultimate consequences of actions (cf. Genesis 50: 20; Romans 8: 28; Matthew 6: 25–34), or to treat their fellows as building blocks in the construction of some imagined 'optimal' future, or to regard themselves as consistent consequentialists must regard themselves, as tools in that construction holding themselves ready to do *anything* to themselves or their hostages to avert the bad consequences threatened by nature, chance, or the opportunism of the wicked.[48]

---

[48] Thus O'Connell, 162, prepares us to 'drop a bomb that will kill a million people'. He 'prays' that the need to do this will not arise, neglecting the fact that preparations for doing so are well advanced, and that this *sort* of action regularly took place in the Second World War and that (*qua* indiscriminate) it is solemnly condemned by GS 80 as a crime against God. McCormick is aware that, in the consequentialists' numbers game, willingness to kill one million to save two million is no different from willingness to kill one million to save one million and ten (i.e. to 'save ten'): cf. his 'Notes on Moral Theology' (1978) at 109. He seeks to reconcile Christian teaching about indiscriminate bombing with his 'mixed teleological' method by arguing that by such actions 'one equivalently denies the freedom' of those whom one wishes to deter or dissuade from their hostile actions since 'one supposes by his action that the cessation of others from wrongdoing is necessarily dependent on my doing harm' (113). This argument fails; one's supposition is not about '*necessary* dependence' but about extremely *probable* correlation; nor is the supposition of continuance (otherwise) in

V. NATURAL LAW AND 'HISTORICITY'

I began this essay by quoting Vatican II's affirmation of profound and rapid changes amounting to a true social and cultural transformation, of a shift from static to dynamic and evolutionary conceptions of things, and the need for new analyses and syntheses. What, then, should we be saying about the 'historicity' of human nature and the possibility of 'changes in the natural law'?

The first thing to say is that the philosophico-theological literature on this matter is of little value. Even very substantial writers fall into a cloudy rhetoric about the significance of cultural change,[49] or become entangled in an inadequately thought-out metaphysics in which 'nature' is sometimes interchangeable, but at other times contrasted, with 'essence', sometimes by definition unchangeable while at other times capable of change, and sometimes equated with the 'transcendental' (epistemologically conceived, so that it includes only those human elements that are inevitably 'affirmed' in any affirmation whatsoever).[50]

The second thing to say is that, so far as it is directed toward ethics and the natural law, the existing theological literature that proclaims the significance of historicity and changeable nature seems to *presuppose* an indefensible conception of practical reasoning, that is, an indefensible conception of method in ethics. In the case of English-speaking theologians such as Fr Timothy O'Connell or Fr Gerard Hughes, the presupposition is typically of consequentialist ethical method—about which I will say no more here. In the case of continental theologians, the presupposition seems often enough to be neo-Suarezian: that one by speculative (metaphysical/descriptive) reasoning establishes first what is human nature, and then what is 'in accordance with' (*conveniens*) that nature and thus a matter of

---

wrongdoing a denial of freedom (sin is free). (Moreover—*ad hominem*—at 112–13 McCormick treats contraception as justified where lack of intercourse 'can easily harm the communicative good and *thereby* the procreative good itself'—as if acting on the basis of this fear were not a radical denial of the freedom of spouses.) The failure of the theological consequentialists (after sustained attempts) to integrate into their ethics even the most elementary Christian norms about direct killing of the innocent should be borne in mind when one is evaluating their incessant references to the marginal *quaestiones disputatae* of traditional Catholic ethics (e.g. Abraham and Isaac; 'masturbation' to obtain semen; evacuation of the uterus to enable life-saving surgery).

[49] e.g. Lonergan, 'The Transition from a Classicist World-View to Historical-Mindedness' in his *Second Collection*, 1–9. [See now essay 9.]

[50] See e.g. Rahner, 'Basic Observations' at 15–16 (contrast between 'transcendental necessity of human nature' and 'concrete human nature'); Rahner and Vorgrimler, *Concise Theological Dictionary*, 305, s.v. 'Natural Moral Law' (natural law flows from 'the objective structures of human nature which...are implicitly affirmed by a transcendental necessity even in the act of their denial...[and which] objectify the will of God, their Creator...'); *Lexicon für Theologie und Kirche*, Bd. 7 (1962), col. 827 (distinction between essence and nature); cf. *Theological Investigations*, vol. 9, 214–17, 230–4. The criticisms in Dorr, 'Karl Rahner's "Formal Existential Ethics"', are not superseded by Rahner's later work.

'natural law'. But this is a misconception of practical (including ethical) reason, which (as is emphasized both in Aquinas and in the recent developments I have spoken of) begins with a practical grasp of basic forms of human (personal) good as 'goods to-be-pursued and realized and done', and continues through the discernment of the requirements of one of those basic goods (the good of practical reasonableness)—requirements that structure the pursuit of the other aspects of human well-being.

In short, general discourses about the changeability of human nature need not be taken seriously unless and until they get down to the serious business of considering someone for whom life (bodily life, including bodily health), or the transmission of life, or play, or aesthetic enjoyment, or speculative knowledge, or friendship, or religion, or authenticity, or self-integration, or practical reasonableness are not really good. Not surprisingly, such considerations are not to be found in the literature.

Beyond this, there is the more practicable task of evaluating the real changes in human culture, including not only such relatively superficial changes as have affected, say, human economics and thus the rights and wrongs of interest-bearing loans but also such relatively profound cultural changes as are effected by humans as makers of their own symbols, including the symbols (e.g. the Platonic dialogues, or the prophetic proclamation of personal responsibility) which bear and transmit changes in self-consciousness and which thus could (I suppose) affect, say, the rights and wrongs of penal servitude in its extension to dependants and descendants. All this is a necessary but immensely delicate task, threatened always by the too easy assumption that our forebears (Plato! Aristotle! St John! St Paul!...) lived in some *infancy* of human personality.

Against such easy assumptions, and indeed against much loose talk about changing human nature, we should set the Christology affirmed by Vatican II: 'Christ fully manifests man to man' (GS 22, the last paragraph in the chapter on human dignity). He is the 'perfect man' (GS 22, 38, 41, 45; and this perfection of his human nature is not affirmed merely in the eschatological sense). 'In him, human nature is assumed, not annulled' (GS 22). 'By his incarnation he has somehow united himself with every human being' (GS 22; *Redemptor Hominis*, 13, 18). For '*all* human beings...have the same nature and the same origin' (GS 29; *Lumen Gentium*, 19), a single nature (*Lumen Gentium*, 13) which is 'more fully manifested by the experience of past ages, the advance of the sciences and the treasures hidden in the various forms of human culture' (GS 44); and all have the 'same calling and divine destiny' and so, fundamentally equal both in nature and in supernatural calling (GS 29), can be citizens of the one People of God regardless of race or place or time (*Lumen Gentium*, 13).

So the Council did not forbid us to accept, if we choose, such apparently ad hoc and certainly simplifying categorizations as that which contrasts 'the classicist' with 'the historical-minded worldview'. But it did remind us that, if we want to be 'historical-minded', we had better recognize that human history has a structure that is not straightforwardly 'linear': Jesus Christ is the *centre* of history (as well as its key and goal) (see GS 10 and 45, the end of Part I; and also *Redemptor Hominis*, 1). And no one has given us intelligible reason to doubt those further affirmations of the Council, each given a certain solemnity and formality of wording:

The Church affirms that underlying all changes there are many things that do not change, and which have their ultimate foundation in Christ who is the same yesterday, today, and forever (GS 10).

The Council seeks to recall before all else the unchanging [*permanens*] force of the natural law of peoples and of its universal principles (GS 79)

—the law that the Council had not hesitated to call 'natural and gospel' [*lex naturalis et evangelica*]: (GS 74).

So 'the Church proclaims the rights of man, *by virtue of the gospel committed to her*' (GS 49) those rights which are a principal component (DH 6) of the common good of the human race as directed by the eternal law (GS 79). For 'the fundamental law of the Christian dispensation' is this: '...who is Saviour is the same God who is also Creator, the same too who is Lord both of human history and of the history of salvation' (GS 41). Christ restored our dignity (GS 41, 22) by taking our nature (GS 22), and so, reflecting surely on these teachings, Paul VI could say that the divine and natural law of right reason (HV 27, 22), one fragment of which he had to proclaim again in *Humanae Vitae*, is 'the law which is truly proper to human life restored [by Christ] to its own authentic truth' (HV 19; cf. also 7).

20

NUCLEAR DETERRENCE AND
THE END OF CHRISTENDOM*

If there is, as I believe, a temporal mission for the Christian, how would it be possible for the terrestrial hope by which such a mission is quickened not to have as its most comprehensive aim the ideal of building either a better or a new Christian civilization?…At each new age in human history (as is, to my mind, our own age with respect to the Middle Ages and the Baroque Age), it is normal that Christians hope for a new Christendom, and depict for themselves, in order to guide their effort, a concrete historical ideal appropriate to the particular climate of the age in question.

Lecturing *On the Philosophy of History* in the United States in 1955, Jacques Maritain thus restated a theme he had elaborated in Spain in the high summer of 1934, 23 months before Franco's uprising. And he added a concrete assessment:

as a matter of fact, America is today the area in the world in which, despite powerful opposite forces and currents, the notion of a Christian-inspired civilization is more part of the national heritage than in any other spot on earth. If there is any hope for the sprouting of a new Christendom in the modern world, it is in America….

I shall argue that we should answer Maritain's rhetorical question, No: it is a philosophical and theological mistake to suppose, as he did, that the temporal vocation of the Christian—or the Christian's conscience in political matters—*requires* a 'comprehensive aim' such as the 'concrete historical ideal' of building a new or a better Christendom. And the facts, properly assessed, suggest that, even if it did, the hope of locating such a 'really and vitally Christian-inspired civilization' in the US is firmly blocked.

In March 1955 Prime Minister Churchill, speaking in the House of Commons, used words which have survived as expressing the reality

* 1988b.

of the nuclear age, and the hope which has guided the masters of the age: 'safety will be the sturdy child of terror, and survival the twin brother of annihilation'. The threat of annihilation would, he was warning, become mutual, reciprocal, when the Soviet Union acquired the thermo-nuclear weapons then recently unveiled by the US. Still, the west's new armaments would increase 'the deterrent upon the Soviet Union by putting her...scattered population on an equality or near-equality of vulnerability with our small densely-populated island'—a vulnerability matched by the equal, mutual vulnerability of the west's populations.

The threat expressed by Churchill, to destroy Soviet populations by 'a crushing weight of nuclear retaliation', has remained the indispensable element in the deterrent threats and accompanying operational plans of the US, Britain, and France ever since.

To understand why Christian consciences responded as they did, or reposed as they did, recall that the threat to destroy Soviet people became fundamental to western strategy, and to the preservation of western freedom, only in the mid- to late 1950s, when the Soviets became capable of devastating the population of the US. Well before then, to be sure, everyone understood that western contingency plans for war included an atomic bombing campaign against the Soviet Union. But citizens, even philosophers, who gave the matter an ordinary degree of attention, might have assumed that those plans were essentially a continuation of the bombing strategies of the Second World War.

The position in the late 1950s, however, was clear enough. John Courtney Murray, SJ, put it thus in 1959:

the two controlling American policies [are]: We shall never shoot first, but if anyone shoots at us the answer will be 'massive retaliation' by weapons of indiscriminate mass slaughter. These are, I take it, the two correlative policies, of the highest order, that embody the most profound thought about war that our government has been able to elaborate.

Against this shallowness, Murray proposed a return to 'the traditional doctrine', which, in the light of the present facts,

asserts that the use of nuclear force must be limited, the principle of limitation being the exigencies of legitimate defense against injustice.... Since limited nuclear war may be a necessity, it must be made a possibility. Its possibility must be created.

Murray's hope that limited nuclear war could be made possible is, I suppose, the hope which guided many of the US and some allied bishops at the Second Vatican Council in their successful resistance to a condemnation of nuclear deterrence.

In the real world, however, it remains as impossible as it was in Murray's time to plan to fight a limited nuclear war *without threatening one's adversaries with indiscriminate mass slaughter should they overstep the limits.*

The proposals which citizens of the US and their elected representatives are invited to approve in relation to possible nuclear war have been stated, in detail, every January, February, or March for twenty-five years, by each Secretary of Defense in his annual report and funding request to Congress. These remarkable source records of strategic doctrine's evolution in details and constancy in essentials are supplemented by the ample records of the annual cross-examination of the Defense Secretary and his officials. All seem to have been overlooked by the US bishops in the preparation of their 1983 Pastoral Letter on War and Peace, *The Challenge of Peace.*

While it is possible that the terror of imminent annihilation might keep a limited nuclear war limited, it is certain, and stressed by every Secretary of Defense and every competent strategist without exception, that no one can fight, or even threaten to fight, a limited nuclear war without credibly threatening to resort to annihilation of cities in the event of the adversary making nuclear attacks on targets in cities of our own.

So the US—in documents which, as I said, also make proposals for adoption and approval by the US public—includes in its strategic policy two threats: the threat to *city swap* (that is, to retaliate against a Soviet city or cities in the event of Soviet attack on a US city or cities), and the threat of *final retaliation.* Both threats appear—to take one example from scores—in Defense Secretary Harold Brown's 1979 report to Congress:

> To have a true countervailing strategy, our forces must be capable of covering, and being withheld from, a substantial list of targets. Cities cannot be excluded from such a list, not only because cities, population, and industry are closely linked, but because it is essential at all times to retain the option to attack urban-industrial targets—both as a deterrent to attacks on our own cities and as the final retaliation if that particular deterrent should fail.

In drafting *The Challenge of Peace,* the US bishops found 'particularly helpful', they said, a letter from the President's National Security Adviser, William Clark, and a sentence in Secretary Weinberger's report of January 1983. Clark wrote to the bishops: 'for moral, political, and military reasons, the United States does not target the Soviet civilian population as such'. Weinberger wrote: 'The Reagan Administration's policy is that under no circumstances may such weapons be used deliberately for the purpose of destroying populations'. But only four pages earlier Weinberger had stated what the essence of US deterrence policy is: the maintenance of the assured capability of destroying 'those political, military and economic assets that they [the Soviets] value most highly'. A few days before the bishops adopted *The Challenge of Peace*, Weinberger wrote to the Senate Armed Services Committee: US forces, he said must 'be able to retaliate effectively against the full range of Soviet high value assets; regardless of the scope, duration, or intensity of the conflict'. And the first of these assets he listed was: 'their urban-industrial society'.

I dwell on these matters because they illustrate some of the realities of the present relationship between Church and state. The Church's teaching against the counter-city use of nuclear weapons is not accepted as a norm of national policy, but it affects the language in which that policy is, on appropriate occasions, presented. So, when addressing specifically Catholic audiences, in the months running up to the adoption of *The Challenge of Peace*, officials like Clark and Weinberger produced, respectively, such really duplicitous statements as: 'We do not threaten the existence of Soviet civilization by threatening Soviet cities', and: 'The United States rejects a strategy which targets nuclear weapons against population centers'.

Other audiences, and other occasions, resulted in very different formulations. Speaking in Oxford in 1984, Weinberger deployed the official justification for the Strategic Defense Initiative: its purpose *will be* to 'defend people instead of avenging them' as *present* policies propose; its weapons *will* 'go after weapons rather than people' as *present* weapons do. In his post-summit broadcast to the nation from the White House on 13 October 1986, President Reagan said that 'our only real defense' is still 'a policy of mutual destruction and slaughter of civilians'.

The Christian citizen must learn how to read official statements. In our book *Nuclear Deterrence, Morality and Realism*, Germain Grisez, Joseph M. Boyle Jr, and I include a detailed study of the British Government's duplicity about its war-time bombing, a duplicity consciously aimed at satisfying leaders of religious and humanitarian opinion while leaving operational policy just as it was.

The real meaning of the policy of not targeting civilians 'as such' or per se becomes clear when one takes into account a few dates, for the policy was not introduced by the Reagan Administration; it was announced by Defense Secretary Elliot Richardson in 1973 and formulated in secret nuclear planning and targeting directives signed by Secretary James Schlesinger in April 1974. *At the very same time*, Schlesinger stated to Congress:

an attack on our cities…would inevitably result in the destruction of their cities…. It is this assured capability to retaliate decisively against Soviet cities even after absorbing the full weight of a Soviet nuclear attack that offers the best hope of deterring attack and thus protecting our cities.

His successor Harold Brown, a Defense Department professional, told the House Armed Services Committee that: 'We have never targeted populations, as such.' *In the same breath* he added that it had been the Department's objective to destroy 30 per cent of the Soviet population and that, though that figure had been revised downward as American second-strike capability diminished, it still in 1979 remained 'a very large number, 200 or 400 Soviet cities . . . a lot of people'.

Great masters of state policy like Schlesinger and Brown have well understood that, to attain the desired deterrent effect of the threat of final retaliation, it is quite unnecessary to target population 'as such'. In an attack targeted on 'political and economic assets' (to use Weinberger's 1983 phraseology) or 'vital interests' (to use his 1986 phrase), the civilian casualties will be so horrendous that the question whether they could have been made higher by deliberate anti-population targeting can be of little or no interest to rational Soviet leaders. In a 'no population per se' Major Attack Option in the US Single Integrated Operational Plan (SIOP), each of the 200 largest Soviet cities would be struck by, on average, nineteen nuclear warheads amounting to 6.33 equivalent megatons, or about 500 Hiroshima's-worth for each of the 200 cities. We would kill so many Soviet people anyway that we do not need to target them.

But there is a deeper sense in which targeting is not the issue in a moral assessment of deterrence. Only in the last few years has the moral analysis been pressed with sufficient vigour and precision to disclose this feature of deterrent intentions, a feature I believe decisive for a moral judgment on the deterrent in its present and any foreseeable form. The understanding of *intention* which this analysis employs will reappear in my later remarks about the responsibilities of citizens in a nation publicly committed to grievous wrongdoing.

The intention of a military attack is not *defined* by the targeting of the attack. One's intent is defined by what one chooses to do, or seeks to achieve through what one chooses to do. Consider, for example, the intent in a city swap.

Even in a limited nuclear war, the destruction of a single city or a few cities might be needed to dissuade the Soviets from repeating an attack they had made against a western city or cities The Soviet city selected for destruction might well contain military personnel and installations; the targeters might well select some such installation for the aim-point or desired ground zero—just as the targeters of Hiroshima selected a point alongside the army encampment there. But *all* those killed in the attack would be killed for a reason having nothing to do with their status as combatants or non-combatants. All would be killed simply as people present in a city to be destroyed for the purpose of showing western resolve and deterring further Soviet attack.

No one killed in Hiroshima was killed as a combatant; no Japanese civilian in Hiroshima was killed as a mere 'side effect' or by merely 'collateral damage'; *all* were killed as inhabitants whose mass destruction would shock Japan out of the war. No one killed in a city-swapping duel would be killed *as* a combatant; all would thus be killed *as* non-combatants—that is, *as* innocents. Everyone threatened in the threat to carry out such 'limited nuclear options' as city swaps is threatened as an innocent. The term 'as' which I have been stressing is the word which introduces the description which identifies the morally significant intent of the threatened attack.

Similarly, *all* those killed in the execution of the threat of final retaliation, even members of the Soviet leadership and armed forces, would be killed simply *as* surviving members of Soviet society upon which the west, having then *nothing left to lose* (that is, nothing capable of being defended), would be imposing the now threatened 'unacceptable losses'. Some of those killed would no doubt be war criminals who might have been tried and executed for horrific war crimes against the west. But the west's threatened final retaliation does not propose to destroy such persons *as* war criminals, or as military personnel still engaged in unjust military operations against the west. For the threat of final retaliation is to be carried out only after the west has lost what it went to war to defend. When a war has been lost, it is over. And when it is over, there are neither combatants nor non-combatants. There remain only criminals, who cannot be justly killed without a trial, and the innocent. The threat of final retaliation is a threat to kill them simply as Soviet people. In Weinberger's and Reagan's homely language, final retaliation would avenge people rather than defend them; it will go after people rather than weapons; it is the enduring underpinning, now as in the mid-1950s, of a policy 'based on the threat that if they kill our people, we'll kill theirs', as Reagan put it in 1985.

I have used the term 'innocents' exactly in the sense of Christian teaching, as summed up in the *New Catholic Encyclopedia*:

It is a fundamental moral principle unanimously accepted by Catholic moralists that it is immoral directly to take innocent human life except with divine authorisation. 'Direct' taking of human life implies that one performs a lethal action with the intention that death should result.... Non-combatants are in this sense innocents and enjoy the immunity of the innocent from direct attack.

Let us take stock. US and NATO deterrent strategy includes many options. Some of these are probably so limited and precise that they could, considered in isolation, be judged discriminate and, in intention, respectful of innocent human life even though causing many deaths of innocents as a foreseen and certain side effect. But none can be considered in isolation. For none could sanely be undertaken or even threatened unless embedded in a strategy which seeks to deter the adversary by threatening counter-retaliation in the form of selective attacks on cities, in retaliation for limited attacks on our cities, or a devastating attack on 'the full range of Soviet high value assets', in final retaliation for an attack which had devastated our society and left us with nothing more to lose. The US and NATO distinctly threaten, and adequately prepare, both such forms of retaliation. In so doing, our nations threaten to kill Soviet citizens simply as such. The proposal adopted by our nations is this: in those circumstances to kill people under a description *other than* 'combatants to be stopped' or 'war criminals to be punished' (namely a description such as 'high value assets'). They thus propose to kill people *as* innocents.

But, as Pope John Paul has said, 'the whole tradition of the Church has lived and lives on the conviction' that 'there exist acts which are always and everywhere in themselves and of themselves illicit', and that among those acts is 'the direct killing of an innocent person' ('Address to Moral Theologians', 11 April 1986). 'Direct', in this tradition, means no more and no less than: intended, as an end or as a means. The deaths threatened and proposed to be imposed in city swaps or final retaliation would be fully intended as part of the plan to impose on the Soviets limited or unlimited losses of things they value most highly, including the lives of their population. City swapping and final retaliation are therefore acts which, whatever the circumstances, are utterly excluded from Christian life.

The choice to do such acts—the intention, the willingness to do them—this too is excluded from Christian moral life. For in the Ten Commandments and in the words of Jesus, the Church has always found confirmation of the rational principle that *what it is wrong to do it is wrong to intend*: what makes one worthy or unworthy is what proceeds from one's heart; voluntary anger and lust, even without issuing in deeds, are morally evil (see e.g. Exodus 20: 17; Deuteronomy 5: 21; Matthew 5: 22, 15: 17; Mark 7: 18–23; Aquinas, *ST* I–II q. 74 a.1). The willingness, now, to do a great wrong if certain conditions are fulfilled, is a seriously wrongful choice, even if one might, when the conditions are fulfilled, repent of one's choice and choose not to carry it out.

A careful analysis of conditional intentions would extend over many pages, as in our book [or essay II.12 (1994a)]; it will only confirm that conclusion. We devote many more pages to analysing attempts to evade the necessity, in any deterrence between superpowers, of maintaining credible threats of counter-city retaliation. These attempts include the Strategic

Defense Initiative (SDI), which would indeed make those threats redundant if it could be put in place, and itself defended, in the way some now dream of. But it is one thing to imagine perfect defences, and another thing to acquire them. No official now claims that SDI could replace deterrence within several decades. A moral judgment on your or my involvement in the deterrent cannot wait so long, or at all.

I have said enough to indicate, in barest outline, why we conclude that suggestions, such as John Courtney Murray's, for solving the moral problem of the deterrent by transforming it into a limited threat, to destroy not cities but enemy forces, are suggestions as remote from realization as they were thirty years ago.

There remains a different suggestion for resolving the moral issue in favour of the deterrent: that we should regard the deterrent as a bluff, or convert it into a bluff. Few, save Christians, ever seriously advance this notion. Suggestions which sound rather different, such as that the whole system is 'mere possession' without any determinate intention, or is no more than 'keeping open our options', turn out on analysis to include the notion that it is or could be a bluff, a threat which is not backed up by any corresponding intention, choice, or willingness.

What all such suggestions overlook is that the deterrent is not some weapon or device wielded by the President or a tiny inner circle. It is a vastly ramified public act, defined by a public policy—the policy stated year after year by Secretaries of Defense in their requests to Congress for funding. That public policy is not a policy of bluffing the Soviets; it is a policy which states, inter alia, that we can *and will* destroy them, impose on them disproportionate and unbearable (the official word is 'unacceptable') damage, if they destroy us. That proposal is integral to the deterrent, in which one participates by one's own individual free choice by voting for the proposal and policy—for example in Congress—or by taking any part in a team of tens of thousands who define their military or supporting civilian role in terms of making the system (which the policy publicly explains) *ready to go* (as indeed it is).

The President could personally be bluffing. A few others could be. Most who participate in the system *cannot*—that is, logically cannot—be bluffing; for they have done their part, now, in making the execution of the threat possible, but have no part in any eventual execution itself: Congressmen; those who build and arm silos and submarines and missiles and bombers, or who transmit the never ceasing flow of information to the underground or airborne command posts; none of these can be bluffing.

They may hope the President is. They may hope that those who would execute the deterrent on the day will turn out to have been secret bluffers, or dissidents who will disobey orders. They have no ground whatever to judge that this President or any President has been bluffing. And they have solid ground to anticipate that the military hardware in the silos and submarines will prove reliable on the day. But the crucial point is: *they* themselves cannot be bluffing, but can choose only to do, now, or not to do, now, their bit for the effecting of the proposal, the maintenance of the system, the performance of the vast and ongoing public act.

The act goes under the name 'deterrence', and has deterrence as its motive, but is defined, publicly and unambiguously, by its visible capacity to carry out the official *proposal*, the officially stated intention or willingness, to impose unacceptable losses in city swaps and/or final retaliation. That is the proposal and intention in which one participates, whatever one's reluctance and whatever one's hopes or even expectations, when one voluntarily does one's bit for the deterrent.

The conclusion seems inescapable: the nuclear deterrent is not acceptable to Christian consciences and cannot in the foreseeable future be transformed into an acceptable form of deterrence.

The deterrent is a public act, which comes to be in and through many individual choices which propose that act, accept proposals to adopt it, participate in it, or in some other way support it. Everyone's fundamental responsibility is: not to choose or do anything which itself adopts, participates in, or supports that public act or any of the subordinate acts by which it is sustained. Because the public act includes, essentially, a proposal no one should ever adopt, one must never accept any invitation to support the deterrent or to help, however reluctantly, to bring about its continuance.

This basic negative responsibility has far wider implications than one might at first think. For western deterrents underpin all the many policies and acts (military, political, economic, etc.) which western nations would not choose maintain or perform in the face of the Soviet challenge, if they could not adequately deter Soviet power. Thus, the western nations' deterrents are necessary means for their pursuit of the ends of all those other policies and acts. But persons who rationally choose one means to an end also intend all the other means they know they must use to enable their chosen means to attain that end effectively. So: well informed and rational citizens of the US, Britain, and France who judge nuclear deterrence wrong will see that they cannot adopt, participate in, or support *any* national policy or act which presupposes that balance of power with the USSR which their nations need and use the deterrent to maintain, even policies and acts morally good in themselves and perhaps urgently needed.

For example: one must be prepared to decline tempting invitations to support a national policy of standing up to the Soviets in the Middle East. Such invitations are indeed tempting, because the Soviets deserve to fail in the Middle East, and their hegemony there would entail very far-reaching evils, including grave political and economic injustices for many parts of the world, including our own societies. But the invitations must regretfully be declined, because standing up to the Soviets means intending the deterrent; the proposal to resist them cannot succeed unless one's nation maintains or participates in a nuclear deterrent in order to underpin all its other power to resist the Soviets.

Or again: one must decline and refuse to take part not only in the strategic forces which would execute the deterrent but in all those military forces which, if engaged in a zone of Soviet interest, would depend for the security of their military operations on ultimate underpinning by the threats to city swap and execute a final retaliation.

May one pay all one's taxes, or should one withhold the part one calculates corresponds to the proportion of total government expenditure which goes toward readiness to execute those wicked proposals? The answer, I think, is that taxes must not be withheld unless such withholding meets all the criteria for legitimate civil disobedience—criteria which I shall here state without discussion in only twelve words: openness in one's violation of law, non-violence, ready submission to legal penalties. Our taxes are paid into a consolidated fund; payments are not earmarked for a particular governmental project. So one can *intend* that one's tax payments be spent on worthy projects which one is morally bound, as a citizen, to support, and merely *accept*, as an unwanted side effect, that some portion of these payments will be diverted to immoral purposes. Moreover, no one can reasonably judge that the withholding of tax payments will in any way affect the amount spent on the nuclear strategic system; the authorities give every sign of regarding the maintenance of that system as a high priority. So it is morally certain that the only effect of withholding one's taxes will be that other citizens will have to pay more, and/or that worthy projects which one has a duty to support will suffer.

What about voting? If one sees the immorality of the deterrent, may one vote for any congressional candidate other than a unilateralist? If not, one will have virtually no one for whom one can vote in such elections. But it seems to me that one certainly *may* vote for candidates who support the deterrent. One does not share in the guilt of the deterrent merely by voting for a candidate who supports its immoralities, provided one is doing so in order to prevent the election of candidates who support morally similar policies and who are less suitable in other respects, or who support other immoral public policies, such as the funding of abortion. Votes for candidate A do not morally associate these voters with all the policies of candidate A, if the voters' intention is no more than to do what they can to prevent the election of candidate B. The subsequent use which candidate A makes of his powers as a member of the national legislature can be (even though fully foreseeable) a true side effect, which such voters can legitimately accept and for which they need not be morally responsible.

I have touched on a few actual or possible *negative* responsibilities of citizens. *Positive* or affirmative responsibilities are, as always, harder to specify in general terms, and will vary from country to country and from citizen to citizen. But the general positive responsibility of all citizens, anywhere, who recognize the deterrent's immorality, is to take such opportunities as their prior responsibilities permit to bear witness to their alienation from their nation's deterrent policy.

In many cases one's opportunities will be very limited indeed. And in any event, one's expression of alienation should be responsible. For example, one should be alert to the grave risks created by 'peace' movements which advocate unilateral nuclear disarmament but fail to acknowledge, steadily and clearly, that a side effect of doing what they advocate would very probably be Soviet domination. Electorates that adopted a unilateralist policy without clearly recognizing Soviet domination as a likely outcome would probably backslide when that outcome became manifestly imminent. And then their clamour for nuclear rearmament might well precipitate war and holocaust. And if unilateral disarmament became a politically serious movement in the US, those considering active support for it would have a duty to measure their *positive* responsibilities in view of a possible immediate consequence: backlashes might well deliver US forces into the hands of persons more likely than others to make direct and extensive uses of nuclear weapons.

So Christians, whether (as I am) reaching their own verdict now, before any eventual verdict of the Church against the nuclear deterrent, or following that verdict if and when it comes (I know not when), are still to consider how their choices bear on their nation's common good. But they will do so knowing that they can make no choice which participates in or itself supports a policy which, though indispensable for securing that common good against terrible disruption and damage by foreign, unjust, and anti-Christian forces, is simply excluded from Christian life because murderous.

And they will do so without holding before their minds' eye any 'comprehensive aim' such as Maritain's building of 'a new Christendom'. As an *ideal*, such a civilization is an appropriate object of contemplation.

But utopias are not appropriate objects of striving. And as a *goal* of practical reasoning, deliberation, and hope, I cannot see how it could ever be other than utopian. And if it could, its attainment in our era is blocked by such massively present obstacles that it has now no proper role to play in the practical reasoning of any of us about his vocation. Of those obstacles, the most massive is the brutal fact I have been dwelling upon: the vicious threats to city swap and inflict a crushing final retaliation truly are indispensable to resisting subjugation by the superpower which we confront and cannot overcome.

If one dismisses from one's practical reasoning all 'comprehensive aims' defined in terms of future states of affairs as broad as 'a new Christendom', one in no way stultifies that reasoning or frustrates the responsibilities which such reasoning seeks to identify and fulfil. It is a philosophical error to suppose (as Maritain did) that practical reasoning is impotent unless guided by such envisagings of far-reaching future states of affairs.

It is a more serious error to suppose (as Maritain did not, but many contemporary theologians do) that one's fundamental responsibility and vocation is to do what one can to secure overall net good states of affairs in the world—and a new Christendom as Maritain envisaged it would indeed, were it attainable, be a good state of affairs. But the goodness of the choices by which one seeks to attain it is not determined simply by their motive. There are other goods at stake, for instance: the other good states of affairs which one might have brought about by alternative choices (for no one can do everything worthwhile); the commitments one is fulfilling or breaking by making one's choice; the fairness or unfairness with which one is dealing with those whose interests one affects by one's choice; the personal dignity of those whom one chooses to destroy or harm in carrying out one's choice. And none of these goods can be commensurated with the good of the state of affairs one hopes to achieve; neither singly nor together can they be identified as objectively *lesser* goods.

Suppose, for example, that one's choice involves intending to destroy or harm some basic human good, not merely to accept such destruction or damage as a foreseen side effect but to include the causing of it as part of the proposal one adopts by one's choice. Suppose, in other words, that one's choice is in that respect like the choice to maintain a nuclear deterrent. Then we must say: the doing of such harm cannot be objectively weighed and found to be outweighed by the overall future good of that hoped-for state of affairs. And this is why the moral absolutes of the commandments repromulgated by Jesus, and transmitted by the Church, as a precondition of eternal life, are no affront to reason.

The attempts of philosophers to assess objectively the goods and bads involved in the alternative options—maintaining the deterrent at the risk of nuclear holocaust, or renouncing it with the probability of unjust subjugation—have made it plain that there is no balance, no metric, to give rational form to the hazy metaphor of balancing human goods and harms of such radically disparate kinds.

It is impossible not to laugh with dismay at the recent adoption—by theologians such as Richard McCormick, Garth Hallett, Bruno Schüller, Gerard Hughes, Jack Mahoney, and Josef Fuchs—of an ethics of consequentialism, utilitarianism, proportionalism, call it what you will. The insuperable problems of any such ethics, problems ignored by most of these theologians and solved by none of them, were mostly identified long ago. Indeed, they were identified by the secular successors to the philosophers who proposed such an ethics.

And here we may recall that consequentialist ethics were first proposed 200 years ago when for the first time, in the hubris of the Enlightenment, men began to forget that providence is God's. It is no accident that theologians and philosophers have been pointing out to the consequentialist theologians for years, without response, that their new ethic entails a theological *reductio ad absurdum*. For intrinsic to Christian, as to Jewish, faith is the doctrine that God permits what is bad only to draw good from it. Those who accept both the new ethic and the doctrine of providence are rationally committed willy-nilly to the following moral principle: if in doubt about what is right, one should choose whatever one is inclined to! For if one accomplishes what one chooses, one can be certain that on the whole it was for the best, since that choice must have fitted into the plan of providence.

Now, a moral principle of the form *Do what you feel like* is absurdly at odds with Christian faith. Consequentialist methods of Christian moral judgment confuse human responsibility with God's. Related to this confusion is their oversight of the fact that our choices do not merely shape states of affairs in the world (the 'consequences'), but also shape and constitute our *character*. The worth of Socrates' refusal of the Thirty Tyrants' invitation to join in political murder, like the human significance of Christ's overcoming of the temptations, of Caiaphas's *raison d'état* and Judas's and Peter's succumbing to the world's blandishments, was utterly profound but utterly immeasurable even in the earthly lifetime of these choosers. The further consequences of each of these choices are still, millennia later, immense and not even beginning to be exhausted. The consequentialist proposal to sum up consequences and identify the greater overall net good or lesser net evil cannot even begin to be carried out in any of these cases. It cannot be carried out in any situation of morally significant choice.

Perhaps I have said enough to indicate the conception of vocation which I believe the faith proposes to us. In this conception, the Christian is called to cooperate in the Father's work of creation, the Son's of redemption, and the Spirit's of sanctification. The public life of one's own political community is certainly one field of such cooperation. But our life, for each one of us, must be spent on a small detail of the great edifice the divine persons are building. That edifice is not a new Christendom. Society and polity are never identical with the Church. Only the Church has a comprehensive goal—the Kingdom of God, which is not of this world, though it is in this world such that here its materials are assembled and the divine construction of it mysteriously begins.

As the Second Vatican Council teaches, the good fruits of our nature, and of any chosen efforts we do in obedience to the Lord's command, will be found again in the Kingdom of truth and life, holiness and grace, justice, love, and peace. Any choice that authentically honours those goods thus goes to build up that Kingdom, even if the choice results in, or accepts, some loss of those goods as states of affairs (see *Gaudium et Spes*, 39). The choice to reverence human life, for example, by refusing to participate in public or private choices to destroy it, is thus a choice which is material of the Kingdom and has real and truly lasting effects even when worldly wisdom understands it only as a choice of 'greater evil'.

The horizon of worldly wisdom is limited to the future of whichever worldly society or state one happens to be concerned for; such 'wisdom' is guided to its commitments by a principle of *bias*, generating mere rationalizations which pose as calculations of greater good and lesser evil. But there is a specifically Christian ethics because there is a specifically Christian horizon—the Kingdom and its building up by choices to follow in the way of the Lord Jesus—a horizon which relativizes every ethic that measures choices by their aptness to preserve or secure any temporal state of affairs.

The vocation to heal the world's weaknesses, wounds, and sickness certainly encompasses active participation and, for some, leadership in the public affairs of one's particular polity. But it is of the essence of the nuclear age, for as far ahead as any can see, that mastery in polities such as the US, the UK, and France will go to those who are willing to devastate the innocent in adversary nations. So, in all such polities, a Christian's vocation can now no longer include what once it could, a share in executing the supreme policies of national leadership; nor can it any longer include the vocation, honourable in itself, of forcibly resisting the nation's adversaries, if those credibly threaten the cities of one's own nation or its allies.

A mere accident of technology has indeed radically changed the relationship between Church and state in the forum where that relationship has its central reality and role: the conscience of the individual Christian.

In the nineteenth and twentieth centuries, Catholics came to see themselves, by and large, as the best of good citizens. Giving up on that will be hard, indeed.

Any theologian who today thinks the Spirit is guiding and strengthening Christian consciences to experience no guilt when they work out the most satisfying sexual arrangements they can, or choose to kill when that seems for the best, is doubtless going to judge that the Spirit guides Christians to conform to the world's judgment that surrender is intolerable and therefore deterrence is the right option, on a 'balance of values'. The Christian who holds that Revelation was consummated in Christ and is transmitted by his Church will leave such theologians to their new religion.

Very many Christians will be extremely reluctant to accept that our ancient faith could suggest, at this juncture in history, leaving our nations militarily defenceless against a cruel and deceiving ideology. They can perhaps be helped a little toward a sound resolution of their crisis of conscience by an orientation often proposed by Cardinal Ratzinger:

it is time that the Christian reacquire the consciousness of belonging to a minority and of often being in opposition to what is obvious, plausible and natural for that mentality which the New Testament calls—certainly not in the positive sense— the 'spirit of the world.' It is time to find again the courage of nonconformism, the capacity to oppose many of the trends of the surrounding culture...[1]

NOTE

For some years around the time of this essay and *NDMR*, Cardinal Hume, Archbishop of Westminster, convened and presided over a Nuclear Issues Committee of about a dozen members more or less equally divided between supporters and opponents of nuclear deterrence; the principal supporter, by any criterion, was Sir Michael Quinlan, a principal architect and exponent of the then and still current British nuclear deterrent. With his and the Committee's encouragement and critical input I prepared for publication a debate-dialogue on the ethics of nuclear deterrence; but at its completion the chairman forbad its publication and dissolved the Committee. The positions elaborated and argued for by the actors in the dialogue can be found, in substance, in Quinlan's final book, *Thinking about Nuclear Weapons* at 49; at 50–5 he gives his judgment, which is correct in concluding that there are only two coherent positions, not three; and mistaken, I believe, in concluding that 'position III' is morally acceptable in holding that 'some use of nuclear weapons, in ways and on a scale the prospect of which could provide effective deterrence, might in extreme circumstances be morally tolerable; and that their possession for war-prevention can therefore be legitimate' [even in a situation where each side is capable of destroying the other's cities]. The mistake in Quinlan's careful and sensitive discussion is most clearly evident in the paragraph where he (rightly) dismisses the relevance of possible uses of nuclear weapons (depth charges, or exo-atmospheric interceptors, etc.) which would 'not cause huge loss of life to non-combatants'. His grounds for dismissing the relevance of such uses appear in the appendix to which he refers readers at 52; the pivotal proposition in that appendix,

[1] Ratzinger, *The Ratzinger Report*, 36–7.

at 186, is para. 9 (which makes explicit what is muffled in para. 6's response to the question identified in para. 5 as key):

> 9. To be both effective in deterrent prospect and justifiable in execution, the level of nuclear strike would need to be such that the expected damage to the aggressor should suffice to rob him of will or capability to go on, while at the same time the unpurposed harm expected to non-combatants was less than the evil expected if the aggressor prevailed. It is not obvious that there could never be a level of strike satisfying these two conditions together.

It is clear that the harm to non-combatants 'need[ed]' to achieve the strategic purpose of deterring or ending enemy attack would—precisely because needed—be 'unpurposed' only in the sense that it could be *achieved* without targeting cities or non-combatants 'as such' (the phrase used in para. 6's vaguer statement of the point). For the reasons set out at 278–81 above, this truth about targeting does not negate or render less certain the conclusion that the intent of such a nuclear strike would be to impose 'huge loss of life on non-combatants' as the only available means of deterring or ending attack. Quinlan's rejection (51) of 'Position II' (possession of nuclear weapons while renouncing their use) amounts—though he does not put the point quite clearly—to conceding, indeed insisting, that deterrence is not possible without willingness to form such an *intent* (not merely pretend such willingness).

Quinlan's argument for rejecting Position I (defended in *NDMR* and this essay) is that the consequence of abandoning deterrence is an intolerable subjection to evil regimes. The argument has all the power that we allow, and expound, in *NDMR*. In mentioning some hypothetical instances of the intolerable, he recalls the situation of Israel in face of Iran; it is indeed an agonizingly powerful appeal to consequences. Though it does not meet his point in the event that Iran acquires the capability to overwhelm Israel unless deterred, it is worth noticing that nuclear deterrence in the form practised by Israel hitherto is arguably morally acceptable; no threat is articulated, since no admission is made that nuclear weapons are possessed; and the deterrence is substantially unilateral, at least if no relevant adversary has comparable counter-value capabilities and all likely adversaries could be deterred by the prospect of nuclear destruction of their military capabilities.

In the month that this essay was published (July 1988), the US Catholic Bishops issued two documents supplementary to their 1983 Pastoral Letter. Quinlan (51–2) takes these [he names the first but the page reference is pertinent and is to the second, the detailed committee report] as clarifying the bishops' 1983 position by rejecting 'Position II' (possession, renouncing use) in favour of Position III (Quinlan's and the US/UK/French position). All that is clear, in my view, is that the bishops did not accept Position I; that, as already noted, is the position articulated in *NDMR*, which the bishops refer to at n. 42 of 'Report [by Ad Hoc Committee on the Moral Evaluation of Deterrence] on "The Challenge of Peace" and Policy Developments 1983–1988' (approved in 'A Pastoral Reflection on the Response to "The Challenge of Peace"'). But it is true that their non-condemnation of Position III, and non-articulation of Position II, amount to a de facto acceptance of Position III (notwithstanding all manner of hand-wringing caveats which leave its substance and actual reality untouched). Quinlan at 51 quotes John Paul's Message to the UN Second Special Session on Disarmament, 11 June 1982: 'In current conditions "deterrence" based on balance, not as an end in itself but as a stage on the way toward a progressive disarmament, may still be judged morally acceptable', and remarks that the Pope, in 'ruling out Position I', 'did not either then or later indicate whether his view rested on…Position II or Position III'. It was suggested in *NDMR* 97–8 (see also 103) that the papal statement '*affirms* no more than that the Catholic Church has not yet clarified and reached firm conclusions on the relevant issues'. The US bishops chose to take it as affirming the moral legitimacy, now, of policies substantially like those of the US (and the UK and France); in so taking it they made no progress at all towards clarifying the issues, or in suggesting any reasons at all for not adopting the clarification proposed in *NDMR* (and this essay), a clarification which would entail, given the moral principles which they declared, that the deterrent policies in issue are immoral. Over twenty years later, the unsatisfactory state of Catholic teaching on the matter remains just as it was in 1988.

21

THE 'CONSISTENT ETHIC OF LIFE'*

PRELIMINARY CLARIFICATIONS

The phrase 'the consistent ethic of life' is a name, not a thesis. Philosophical reflections seek first the propositions which the phrase's author[1] intends, and which must be borne in mind when studying the discourses in which he uses or recalls it.

In speaking of 'a consistent ethic of life', Cardinal Bernardin calls for such an ethic to be *developed* or *constructed*.[2] But he speaks as a bishop. Thus he presupposes, with his hearers, that Catholic moral teaching is, already, *consistent*—contains no contradictions or arbitrary truncations. And he

---

* 1988a ('The Consistent Ethic: a Philosophical Critique', written for a conference hosted and attended by Cardinal Bernardin and dedicated to discussing the theses he had been publicly proposing as 'a consistent ethic of life'; the footnotes in square brackets were in the version of the essay published in the resulting book, as responses to the reply to the essay by James Walter in that book).

[1] Cardinal Joseph Bernardin, in the discourses listed below. The phrase has, however, an episcopal pre-history in e.g. Archbishop Medeiros's 1971 address, 'A Call to a Consistent Ethic of Life and the Law', noted in McCormick SJ, *Notes on Moral Theology 1965 through 1980*, 399. Cardinal Bernardin's discourses are cited herein by number, as follows; page numbers in parentheses refer to the above-mentioned book in which this essay appeared.

1: Fordham University (Gannon Lecture), 6 December 1983, *Origins* 13 (1983) 491–4; (1–11).
2: University of Chicago, 16 January 1984, *Origins* 13 (1984) 566–9.
3: St Louis University (Wade Lecture), 11 March 1984, *Origins* 13 (1984) 705–9; (12–19).
4: Kansas City (National Right to Life Convention), 7 June 1984, *Origins* 14 (1984) 120–2; (20–6).
5: Cincinnati (National Consultation on Obscenity, Pornography and Indecency), 6 September 1984; (27–35).
6: Georgetown University, 25 October 1984, *Origins* 14 (1984) 321–8.
7: Report to US bishops on Committee for Pro-Life Activities, 14 November 1984, *Origins* 14 (1984) 397–8.
8: Catholic University of America, 17 January 1985; (36–48).
9: University of Missouri, 7 March 1985, *Origins* 14 (1985) 759–61.
10: Loyola University, Chicago, 8 May 1985, *Origins* 15 (1985) 36–40; (49–58).
11: Criminal Court of Cook County (Criminal Law Committee), 14 May 1985; (59–65).
12: University of Notre Dame, 1 October 1985, *Origins* 14 (1985) 306–8.
13: Seattle University, 2 March 1985, *Origins* 15 (1986) 655–8; (77–85).
14: Catholic Medical Center, Jamaica, New York, 18 May 1986; (66–76).
15: University of Portland, Oregon, 4 October 1986, *Origins* 16 (1986) 345–50; (86–94).

[2] See e.g. 9: 759. Such an ethic is 'needed': 1:493(7); 3:707(14).

presupposes, too, that Catholic teaching includes, already, at least the essential moral principles and norms applicable to, and linking the elements of, the whole spectrum of issues he has mentioned: genetics, abortion, war, capital punishment, euthanasia, pornography, hunger, homelessness, unemployment, education...[3] Indeed, none of his discourses suggests a need for any new moral norm, and all assume and imply the following proposition—the first of three which I shall formulate as articulating the essence of Cardinal Bernardin's call:

> CEP1: Individual Catholics must seek a self-consistent and positive acceptance of the whole framework of linked values, principles, rules, and applications in Catholic teaching over the whole spectrum of linked human life issues, old and new.

Thus: 'The consequence of a consistent ethic is to bring under review the position of every group in the church which sees the moral meaning in one place but not the other. The ethic cuts two ways, not one: It challenges pro-life groups and it challenges justice and peace groups'[4]—and, of course, each of their individual members.

But if there is already, in essentials, a Catholic ethic to be found and lived consistently by every Catholic, what is still 'needed'? What is still to be 'developed' or 'constructed'?

Cardinal Bernardin's answer is clear: what must be developed are 'our ways of thinking, our attitudes, our pastoral response'.[5] These must be *made* consistent, not with the facile 'consistency' of those who commit themselves to nothing, but with the active concern of all those committed to the well-being, life, and dignity of others. If *our* ways of thinking, attitudes, and activities are thus made consistently responsive to those goods, then we (believers) may hope for the development of 'an attitude or atmosphere in society' at large, a social ethos which is the precondition for any successful, nationwide defence and promotion of those goods.[6]

---

[3] Sometimes this pre-supposition surfaces, more or less clearly: e.g. 10:40(58) on the framework for moral analysis provided by the consistent ethic of life which is 'primarily a theological concept, derived from biblical and ecclesial tradition'.

[4] 13:657(83).   [5] 15:347(88).

[6] 1:493(9), see also 2:568–9 on 'setting an atmosphere' in society; 3:708(17) on a 'systemic vision of life' which 'seeks to expand the moral imagination of a society'; 4:122(25) on 'the need to cultivate within society an attitude of respect for life' and to 'build a network of mutual concern for defense of life'; 5:11(34) on the 'comprehensive moral vision which the consistent ethic of life promotes'; 6:325 on the 'posture' to be developed in the 'analytical setting' of the seamless garment; and 6:326 on the effort 'to 'see the helpless among us'; 8:4(39) on the need to 'make space for the faces of the poor...in the public agenda'; 9:761 on creating 'space in the public debate'; 10:38(52) on 'quality-of-life pos-ture'; 11:3(61) on the need to respond to 'all the moments, places or conditions which either threaten the sanctity of life or cultivate an attitude of disrespect for it'; 13:656(77 et seq.) and 658(77 et seq.) on developing a 'moral vision', and 657(77 et seq.) on the consistent ethic's 'function...to gather a constituency' against certain social forces; 15:348(86) on the desperate need for a 'societal attitude

So, Cardinal Bernardin says:

The purpose of proposing a consistent ethic of life is to argue that success on any one of the issues threatening life requires a concern for the broader attitude in society about respect for life. Attitude is the place to root an ethic of life, because, ultimately, it is society's attitude—whether of respect or non-respect—that determines its policies and practices.[7]

Hence, a second proposition named by 'the consistent ethic of life':

> CEP2: Catholics have a responsibility to foster in themselves, and thereby in their fellow citizens, an ethos of respect for human life in all its forms and stages, and a readiness to promote the dignity and quality of life of every person across the whole spectrum of threats to life, dignity, and quality of life.

The link between CEP1 and CEP2 is made clear by Cardinal Bernardin: Catholics cannot adequately fulfil the responsibility identified in CEP2 unless they share a common judgment about what the ethical requirement that human lives be respected implies for such great issues of national policy as abortion, capital punishment, and nuclear deterrence and war.[8] But this Catholic consensus can scarcely arise unless Catholics individually each seek what CEP1 calls for: consistency in their individual thinking and attitudes concerning human life.

A third proposition conveyed by Cardinal Bernardin's discourses about the consistent ethic is related to the very fact of his making those discourses as a bishop and indeed as the chairman of the US Bishops' Committee for Pro-Life Activities. But he does not leave it merely to inference. Instead, it is a theme of the discourses that a Catholic bishop has, as such, *responsibilities* in relation to the fulfilment by society and individuals of their affirmative responsibilities identified in CEP1 and CEP2. Indeed, 'the consistent ethic challenges bishops to shape a comprehensive social agenda'.[9] So we can articulate

> CEP3: To foster the desired consensus amongst Catholics and thus the desired ethos in society at large, Catholic bishops should publicly commend not only the principles of Catholic teaching on the whole spectrum of 'life' and 'quality of life' issues, but also policies which appropriately apply those principles right across that spectrum.

---

or climate that will sustain a consistent defense and promotion of life', given that it is attitude that determines social policies and practices.

[7] See 11:10(65); 14:5(69).

[8] On the urgent desirability of Catholic consensus on these issues, see 1:493–4(10); 13:656–8(77 et seq.).

[9] 13:658(77 et seq.). See also e.g. 6:327; 8:12(47).

Later I shall disengage and discuss other positions mentioned or implied in Cardinal Bernardin's discourses on these themes. But these three primary formulations will provide the structure of my essay: CEP1 is the theme of sec. I, CEP2 of sec. II, and CEP3 of sec. III.

Three further preliminary observations.

First: it would be rash for a foreigner to try to assess the impact of Cardinal Bernardin's discourses on the public ethos in the United States or the thought and morale of America's Catholics. Nothing I shall say will imply any such assessment.

Secondly: however, I do not doubt the prediction that the non-Catholic public will, in some measure, be favourably impressed by seeing that the concern of Catholics is limited *neither* to one or two issues given an emphasis so exclusive as to appear eccentric and sectarian, *nor* to issues which, according to the believers' varying predilections, seem selected to fit all too smoothly into the platforms of one or another political party.

Thirdly: CEP1 and CEP2 can be understood as stating propositions which should, I believe, be accepted, and accepted as important. Thus far, at least, an episcopal call for a consistent ethic of life is surely fitting. But, CEP3 seems to me open to doubt, so far as it states and argues for an episcopal *obligation* to promote 'prudential' judgments in national politics, a course with side effects quite adverse to the fulfilment of a bishop's undoubted responsibilities.

More generally, the discourses in which the consistent ethic has been promoted seem open to helpful clarification. Even in relation to CEP1 and CEP2, the discourses *can* be understood or misunderstood as conveying questionable or mistaken propositions. So, too, can those two formulations: CEP1 can be misunderstood as suggesting that the relevant moral norms are constructed by a Church which shapes rules it judges will best promote human life or well-being over the long run; CEP2 can be read as proposing an impossibly wide range of affirmative individual or group responsibilities, and an impossible search for the 'best policy' to fulfil them.

The following reflections, then, are offered in the hope that they may serve not only the good ends which Cardinal Bernardin's discourses so clearly identify and so vigorously pursue, but also the philosophical precision which Christian teaching, like Christian theology, has always sought.

I. WHICH CONSISTENT ETHIC?

The consistent ethic is presented by Cardinal Bernardin as 'primarily a theological concept, derived from biblical and ecclesial tradition about the sacredness of human life, about our responsibilities to protect, defend, nurture and enhance this gift of God'.[10] '[B]ehind the consistent ethic' stand certain themes:

the theological assertion that the human person is made in the image and likeness of God, the philosophical affirmation of the dignity of the person and the political principle that society and state exist to serve the person.[11]

My philosophical reflections will range over all these sources and themes, using the freedom of the philosopher to seek the concepts and premises required to give sense and justification to the relevant biblical, ecclesial, theological, and political affirmations.

My first reflection, then, is that some of the conceptual resources required for a consistent ethic acceptable to Catholics are omitted from the foregoing list of 'themes', and are generally overlooked in the fifteen discourses I have seen. The seamless garment explicitly tailored in the discourses is not big enough to clothe the Christian. Moreover, if seamless, it has gaps and loose ends which, left unstitched, could expose the Body of Christ to 'every wind of doctrine…'.

The duty which CEP1 urges, to find and hold a consistent ethic of life, and of life's protection and promotion (including its promotion by provision of life's basic necessities), has a basis which everyone will agree to: love of neighbour. Christian morality's primary principle is 'Love your neighbour as yourself' (understood within the frame of 'Love God above all things' and 'Seek first the Kingdom').[12] And that principle is, I suggest, the true seamless garment not to be divided by impious, uncomprehending, or self-interested hands.

Philosophically, that first principle of morality can be formulated more abstrusely: one ought to choose and otherwise will those and only those possibilities whose willing is *compatible with integral human fulfilment*, that is, with the good of all persons and communities, conceived not as a goal attainable by some worldwide billion-year plan but as a guiding ideal which inspires and rectifies practical thinking by the general principles and more specific norms it implies.[13]

For, of course, this first moral principle in both its biblical and its more philosophical articulations needs specification. The principle's implications for human choice among the various basic human goods—life, knowledge, friendship, etc.—need to be identified. Love of neighbour needs to get down to cases.

---

[10] 14:16(76); see also 10:40(58).   [11] 15:348(91).   [12] e.g. Matthew 19: 19; 22: 39; 6: 33.
[13] For a much fuller discussion of the ground, sense, and force of the first moral principle, see *NDMR* 282–4; 1987f, secs VII–VIII.

Some of the necessary specifications no one wants to argue against. The Golden Rule as Jesus stated or restated it[14] is one such specification—highly general, no doubt, but still an implication of the first principle and potent in its own implications for moral reasoning; a will marked by egoism or partiality does not love or respect neighbour as such and cannot be open to integral human fulfilment.[15] Derived, in turn, from the Golden Rule of fairness are such more specific but still general norms of common morality and common law as 'equality before the law' or 'equal protection of the law', and such fully specific moral judgments as: Jill who wants her husband Jack to be faithful acts unfairly in sleeping with Sam.

But Jesus and St Paul stressed the *breadth* of morality's seamlessness: love fulfils *all* the commandments[16]—all the key moral norms. And in the constant traditional understanding, some of the commandments go beyond the demands of fairness. 'Thou shalt not commit adultery', for instance, is read as absolutely exceptionless, even though adultery committed by a couple who find it mutually agreeable to have an 'open marriage' is not unfair. Now, right here, we find a serious problem for Catholics who want to identify (as CEP1 bids) a consistent ethic of life. Does 'Thou shalt not kill' state (or imply) a moral absolute, or not?[17]

Published theological statements on this have been guarded; prudent contemporary theologians avoid listing kinds of cases in which they might or might not approve killing the innocent. Even so, a significant number of significant theologians publicly suggest that killing (in a full sense, direct, intentional, of innocents...) is sometimes justified.[18] Popular opinions

---

[14] 'Treat others the way you would have them treat you': Matthew 7: 12; Luke 6: 31.

[15] For a clarification of this intuitively obvious relationship between the first moral principle and the Golden Rule, see *NDMR* 285. On other intermediate principles such as this, *ibid.*, 285–7; *CMP* chs 8, 10; *FoE* 68–76.

[16] Cf. Galatians 5:14; Romans 13: 9; Matthew 22: 39–40.

[17] Throughout, I mean by '(moral) absolutes' specific, exceptionless moral norms which exclude types of act described or describable without evaluative terms and without reference to further circumstances and motives falling outside the description: e.g. 'adultery (sexual intercourse with one not one's spouse) is always wrong'. This is the sense in which the term 'absolute' is used in Cardinal Bernardin's discourses, too: e.g. 13:656(77 et seq.). Like the rest of Catholic moral doctrine, the teaching that some specific but universal norms are absolute is proposed and transmitted on the basis not of some natural law philosophy but of the sources mentioned in the teaching's recent magisterial reaffirmation (in the post-Synodal Apostolic Exhortation *Reconciliatio et Paenitentia* (1984) sec. 17):

> there exist acts which, *per se* and in themselves, independently of circumstances, are always seriously wrong by reason of their object... This doctrine, based on the Decalogue and on the preaching of the Old Testament, and assimilated into the *kerygma* of the Apostles and belonging to the earliest teaching of the Church, and constantly reaffirmed by her to this day...

[18] See e.g. McCormick in McCormick and Ramsey, *Doing Evil to Achieve Good*, 261–3; McCormick, *Health and Medicine in the Catholic Tradition*, 131–2; Fuchs, *Christian Faith in a Secular Arena*, 82–4; Fuchs, 'Christian Faith and the Disposing of Human Life' at 678–9, 681–2. I believe that Charles E. Curran was correct in stating, already in 1973, that 'there is a sizable and growing number of Catholic theologians who do disagree with some aspects of the officially proposed Catholic teaching that direct abortion from the time of conception is always wrong': Curran, *New*

among Catholics today (clergy, catechists, and others) are not so guarded; the principle that killing is justified when it is the 'lesser evil' finds wide acceptance and is resorted to across a spectrum of cases—for example abortion when the mother's life or health is seriously jeopardized, or in cases of rape or incest, or of a probably defective child, or multiple pregnancy (quintuplets etc.), and perhaps in other cases such as pregnancies amongst young girls and middle-aged women, or generally in cases where it seems to them that contraception was justified or required for 'responsibility' but a contraceptive failed or, alas, wasn't used.

Two 'consistent ethics' of killing are held before every individual Catholic who tries to follow CEP1's injunction to identify and live a consistent ethic of life. There is the seamless garment one finds in the *New York Times* or the *Washington Post* (or, in London, in *The Guardian* or *The Sunday Times*); wide sectors of Catholic opinion are picking it up, trying it for fit, and finding it rather comfortable, at least when worn conservatively. And there is the seamless garment one finds in the teaching proposed or approved by John Paul II, in continuity with the Catholic tradition.[19]

Cardinal Bernardin's discourses leave careful readers in no doubt which of these two contradictory 'consistent ethics' of killing he proposes. The discourses insist upon the absolute character of the 'basic moral principle that the direct killing of the innocent is always wrong'.[20] As the Pastoral Letter on War and Peace over whose preparation he presided states: 'the lives of innocent persons may never be taken directly, regardless of the purpose alleged for doing so', and '*no* end can justify means evil in themselves, such as the executing of hostages or the targeting of non-combatants'.[21]

Perspectives in Moral Theology, 193; for Curran's own view, then, that abortion is justifiable in certain cases of grave harm (including psychological harm) to the mother, and of rape, see *ibid.*, 191–2. I believe that the ninety-seven clerical, religious, and other signatories of the 'Catholic Statement on Pluralism and Abortion' in the *New York Times*, 7 October 1984 (reprinted in the *New York Times*, 2 March 1986, E-24) were correct in stating that: 'A large number of Catholic theologians hold that even direct abortion, though tragic, can sometimes be a moral choice.'

[19] No more than Vatican II or Trent or the Popes does Cardinal Bernardin propose a teaching such as 'Directly killing the innocent is always wrong' for acceptance as being the 'conclusion' of the 'deductive systematic method' of some natural law theory or social ethics. *No* part of the Catholic ethic has been authoritatively proposed in such a fashion. An old-fashioned consensus of theologians like Francis Hürth SJ or Gerald Kelly SJ explained Catholic moral teachings with bad philosophical arguments; the philosophical arguments deployed against those teachings by new-style moral theologians like Scholz, Schüller, Fuchs, Knauer, Janssens, et al. are at least as bad as their predecessors. Yet the teachings remain matter for a non-fallacious philosophical reflection, which not only defends them against ungrounded criticisms but also could make them more accessible and fruitful.

[20] 4:121(23); also 1:493(8) ('the principle which prohibits the directly intended taking of innocent human life' as 'always wrong'); 3:708(16) ('the prohibition against direct attacks on innocent life'; 'this principle is . . . central to the Catholic moral vision'); 13:657(77 et seq.) (the 'absolute prohibition' 'against the intentional killing of the innocent').

[21] United States Catholic Bishops, *The Challenge of Peace* (1983), paras 104, 105 (emphasis added); see also paras 148, 332.

Still, I have already suggested that Cardinal Bernardin's discourses do not deploy all the resources available to him as a Catholic bishop for illuminating the sense and the strength of the tradition which he wishes to uphold. Now I should add that some features of his exposition of the moral norm on killing are likely to confuse Catholics who look for guidance in clarifying the issues in dispute between the two competing 'consistent ethics'. My purpose in commenting on these features will not be to lay out any full-dress argument on any of them, as I and others have laid out the relevant arguments elsewhere. I shall attempt no more than a *clarification* of the issues. Success in this attempt might be of some help to Cardinal Bernardin in his own project: upholding and passing on the constant and very firm moral teaching which should guide the faithful in their response to CEP1, and thus shaping the Catholic consensus needed to promote the social ethos called for by CEP2.

Let me take a representative passage in which the issues seem to me misstated:

Precisely because life is sacred, the taking of even one life is a momentous event. Traditional Catholic teaching has allowed the taking of human life in particular situations by way of exception—for example, in self-defense and capital punishment. In recent decades, however, the presumptions against taking human life have been strengthened and the exceptions made ever more restrictive.[22]

The traditional teaching, however, has a form and logic different from that suggested by this passage. It is not that killing is a bad thing, to cause which is *generally* wrong but in exceptional cases right; nor that there is a desirable presumption that the exceptions be limited, and tightened whenever possible—a presumption which is, however, 'overridden'[23] in at least two types of case. Rather, the traditional interpretation of 'Thou shalt not kill' is: The direct killing of the innocent is always wrong, except when divinely authorized in particular cases (e.g. Abraham and Isaac).

The traditionally stated exception just mentioned is, of course, a theological issue not relevant to the issues raised by Cardinal Bernardin; so I shall here set it to one side.[24]

---

[22] 15:347(89); see also 10:37(51); 14:3(68).   [23] See 13:656(81).

[24] [Note that I say the 'traditionally stated exception'. On a more adequate account of moral absolutes, which Aquinas *sometimes uses*, cases such as Abraham and Isaac, even using the mediaeval exegesis, are *not* to be considered as 'exceptions' to or 'dispensations' from the moral absolutes of the Decalogue, but are rather cases in which God so changed the usual conditions in which the relevant act was chosen that the choice fell outside the moral absolute against killing, which is thus truly *exceptionless*. See the comprehensive explanation in Lee, 'Permanence of the Ten Commandments'. There is here no question, as Walter gratuitously asserts, of 'requir[ing] the divine to intervene and direct personal conscience' in order to remedy some unspecified essential lack in creation.]

Nor will I dwell here on the concept of *innocent*. As used in this context, it refers to persons *not* within one of the two classes whose killing is justifiable according to the traditional common morality: those guilty of capital crimes and those engaged in forcible violation of society's just social order. The sources of this concept of innocence have been analysed in our recent book on nuclear deterrence.[25] But the clarification needed in the context of the 'consistent ethic of life' can better begin with the traditional teaching's concept of *direct* or *intentional* killing.

Why 'directness' in killing matters

The idea of direct killing is that one intends the death. In indirect killing, though one's behaviour brings about the death, and one foresees that, and accepts it, one does not intend it. And one intends the death when it is either the end *or a means* which one adopts (whether gladly, indifferently, or reluctantly) by one's *choice*. Popes who use the term 'direct' to enunciate the moral norm about killing, for example Pius XII, Paul VI, and John Paul II, have many times explained the term thus: 'either as an end in itself, or as a means of attaining another end'.[26]

But some say that this distinction—between direct and indirect, that is, between the intended and the merely accepted, that is, between end or means and side effect—is a scholastic artefact, not essential to Christian teaching. Others add that the artefact was crafted as a device for lightening the otherwise intolerable burden of moral absolutes, and for achieving objectives more frankly acknowledged by a moral theory which looks always to the 'lesser evil' and the 'proportionate good'.[27]

---

[25] *NDMR* 87–8.

[26] Thus Pius XII, Address to the Italian Catholic Union of Midwives, 29 October 1951, 43 AAS 83: 8–9:

> …no man,…no…'indication'…can show or give a valid juridical title for *direct* deliberate disposition concerning an innocent human life—which is to say, a disposition that aims at its destruction either as an end in itself, or as a means of attaining another end that is perhaps in no way illicit in itself…for example, to save the life of the mother…a most noble end…

The equivalence, in this context, of 'direct' and 'as an end or as a means' is clearly stated in Pius XII, Discourse to the St Luke Medical-Biological Union, 12 November 1944 (*Discorsi e Radiomessagi* VI (1944–45) 191–2, cited in Paul VI, *Humanae Vitae*, n. 14), and in the Congregation for the Doctrine of the Faith, *Declaration on Procured Abortion*, 18 November 1974, AAS 66: 735, para. 7 at n. 15 ('Pius XII clearly excluded all direct abortion, that is, abortion which is either an end or a means'); also in CDF, *Donum Vitae*, 22 February 1987, at n. 20. The phrase 'directly intended', sometimes used by Cardinal Bernardin [e.g. 1:493(8)], is an uneasy combination of two traditional ways of speaking.

[27] e.g. McCormick in McCormick and Ramsey, *Doing Evil to Achieve Good*, 255; McCormick, *Notes on Moral Theology 1965 through 1980*, 506; Fuchs, *Christian Ethics in a Secular Arena*, 79. [McCormick's paper says that any rule or principle using the term 'direct' is 'not clear in one of its most relevant and urgent terms; for Germain Grisez's understanding is certainly not that of popes and theologians who appealed to the rule'. But if one referred to Grisez's writings since 1966, one would see that he understands 'directly willed' in just the terms I mentioned: intended as an end or chosen as a means. There are cases where it's not easy to say whether some occurrence or state

Both these claims seriously mistake the sense, force, and justification of the norm in its traditional understanding, and of the distinction which the norm embodies.[28]

The use of the distinction begins in Scripture: wilful murder, punishable by death, is distinguished in the Pentateuch from unpremeditated manslaughter and accidental killing, whose perpetrators find asylum in a city of refuge (Exodus 21: 12–14; Numbers 35: 16–23; Deuteronomy 19: 4–6 and 11).

But much more important, I believe, for the clarification of the morality of killing have been Christian reflections on God's will, reflections made directly relevant to ethics by the fundamental principle of Christian anthropology: that human beings are created in the image of God. The relevant Christian understanding is expressed in a canon of the Council of Trent:

If anyone says that it is not in man's power to make his ways evil, but that God performs the evil works just as he performs the good, not only permissively but also properly and per se...: *anathema sit.*[29]

Trent here speaks of God's relation to the sinful human will. But no adequate Christian understanding of creation, of providence, or of predestination, can do without the distinction, in God's willing, between direct and permissive willing.[30] The same understanding is decisive for Christian anthropology and ethics because human beings face the same problem (and not merely because of sin): in making choices, one brings about bad side effects, including side effects which one can confidently predict.

of affairs is included within the means, and where Grisez has suggested (for the reflection, not the practical guidance, of Christians) one or two applications of the term 'means' marginally different from those proposed by the Holy Office and the pre-Vatican II *consensus theologorum.* But in most of its applications, the term 'means', and thus the term 'direct', remain all too clear for the comfort of those who dislike their implications. As with the letter 'a', or the colour orange, or the term *human,* there are marginal cases where we're not sure whether to apply the term or not, but the concept of the letter 'a', or of the colour orange, or of humanity, remains in each case clear and in many central cases indisputable in its application; such terms are fit for use in definitive teaching, as when the Church teaches that Christ died for all humankind although one might legitimately wonder whether monsters or day-old embryos fall within the reference of the term 'humankind'.]

[28] For a much fuller philosophical exposition, see *NDMR* 288–91; essay II.8 (1987b), secs IV and V (the latter section includes a detailed critique of the positions of Bruno Schüller and Richard McCormick which deny the per se moral significance of this distinction).

[29] Decree on Justification, can. 6, DS 1556. [Walter thinks it curious that I omitted the last words of the canon; but they add nothing relevant here, and their omission conceals nothing—it is obvious that Trent is here concerned with God's responsibility for sin ('man's power to make his ways evil'). See further nn. 31 and 38.]

[30] [This is one of the passages which Walter cites to illustrate his astonishing thesis that I presuppose a priority of will over intellect. Such a priority is inconceivable, in my view, since the *will* manifested in upright intentions is nothing other than a pursuit of what *intellect* identifies as reasonable. In none of the passages mentioned by Walter is there any question of the relationship between intellect and will. See further n. 39.]

And from the outset, Christians have understood that Jesus did not choose to kill himself, did not choose to be killed, but did (as the Second Eucharistic Prayer puts it) 'freely accept' his death as a foreseen effect of his own choice to remain faithful to his mission. In the Christian understanding, God cannot directly will what is bad; to do so would be inconsistent with his holiness.[31] Jesus as man, then, cannot either. Nor may those who follow him.

Why choices to kill innocents are always wrong

We are now nearing the foundations of the traditional doctrine on killing. The wrongness of killing the innocent is not just that they get dead—a 'bad thing to happen', a 'sad state of affairs', or even (in Cardinal Bernardin's above-quoted words) 'a momentous event'. Nor is it even that their being dead at our hands is unfair to them (as it very often is). Christian morality is more in the heart than in the results; one's intention is morally more basic and important than any performance or behaviour by which that intention is carried out.[32] Any performance—that is, any outward action, considered as the execution of a choice—has its primary moral significance from the act of the will (the choice or intention of means or end) which it embodies and carries out, or on which it depends in some other way. Directly killing the innocent—that is, carrying out a choice (intention), to kill the innocent—is excluded from Christian life precisely because it is straightforwardly a choice against human life.

---

[31] On God's foresight and permission of evils he does not per se intend or will, see Aquinas, *De Veritate* q.5 a.4 ad 11; *ST* I q.19 a.9 and 3; q.49 a.2c; I–II q.39 a.2 ad 3; q.79 aa. 1–4. (The 'direct'-'indirect' *terminology*, in the sense used by the modern magisterium, emerges long after Aquinas, who conveys it with terms such as *per se* as opposed to *per accidens, praeter intentionem,* etc.) Behind Aquinas lie Augustine and John Damascene. [Walter thinks that *ST* I q.19 a.9c establishes that Aquinas thought 'God wills (*vult*) the evil of natural defect...'. My reason for citing here the ad 3 to that article was precisely to indicate to careful readers that a reading such as Walter's of the body of the article utterly falsifies Aquinas's thought; for in the ad 3 Aquinas adds two essential precisions, (i) that the *only* sense in which God wills natural defect is that he *wills to permit them,* and (ii) that God does *not* choose even non-moral evils whether as ends *or as means* (not even 'for the sake of the preservation of the natural order'), but only *permits* them by a *providentia concessionis.* See generally Lee, 'Permanence of the Ten Commandments' at 435–6. Walter also here claims that 'throughout the *Summa*' the meaning of *per se* is 'for the sake of itself' as opposed to 'for the sake of something else'. This too is a very serious mistake: start the very long list of counterexamples with II–II q.64 a.8c where what is willed or intended *per se* (i.e. either as end or as means) is contrasted with what is willed or intended *per accidens* or *casualiter.*]

[32] If one says: 'When human life is considered "cheap" or easily expendable in one area, eventually nothing is held as sacred and all lives are in jeopardy' (15:348(89)) one will—*unless one differentiates between event/happening and human choice/doing*—be met with the thought that since we tolerate many deaths for the sake of rapid to-ing and fro-ing on our roads (and do little to eliminate infant mortality in Africa), we cannot consistently regard human life as sacred and therefore can, in consistency, choose to kill for the sake of alleviating misery or poverty or discrimination between rich and poor or whatever other value is felt to be at least as weighty as rapid transit.

Given the Christian understanding of the significance of choice and action, the traditional norm thus follows from the first principle of Christian ethics: love of neighbour. For human life is intrinsic, not extrinsic, to the human person. A choice against human life is thus a choice against the person: anti-life, therefore anti-person. It is thus incompatible with love of the person, i.e. with that first principle of Christian and rational ethics.

The link I am tracing between the first principle and the specific norm against killing is—like the Golden Rule—an intermediate principle of wider application: one may never choose to destroy any *basic* human good—any intrinsic aspect of *personal* well-being—for the sake of any ulterior good, however important. 'Evil' (e.g. destruction or damaging of a basic human good) 'may not be done' (willed, intended, chosen as means) 'for the sake of good'.[33]

Reflection on the foregoing clarification of the traditional norm should not omit its tight relationship to the Christian understanding of *free choice* (a reality which philosophy vindicates against denials, but which pre- and post-Christian philosophies more or less fail to grasp). In Christian understanding, human choices are not merely events or states of affairs like the events and states of affairs which they initiate and bring about. They have a twofold further significance.

First, they *last*, beyond the behaviour which executes them, until, if ever, one changes one's mind. Choices thus can last into eternity, and they can be understood as Vatican II (building on St Paul) does in *Gaudium et Spes* 38–9, as contributing here on earth the material of the heavenly Kingdom. The 'material' of the Kingdom includes persons, with the moral selves they have shaped by their choices.[34]

---

[33] [In the most comprehensive misunderstanding of my ethical theory which I have ever encountered, Walter attributes to me a thesis which I have regularly denied and which has no even remote counterpart in my writings. According to this thesis, I assume (without proof or argument) that the basic human goods are moral goods; or alternatively, I attribute a moral significance to them because I 'identify the creative and moral aspects of God's will vis-à-vis the basic human goods' and so assume that 'the mere fact of [the basic goods'] existence as such must also constitute the moral will of God for humanity'. Walter repeats this claim again and again, but it is sheer invention; in my fundamental ethical work, *NLNR*, I regularly repeat and adopt Aquinas's position that the will of God for creatures (including humankind) cannot be discovered by reasoning and so (I say) cannot be appealed to in any philosophical argument about basic goods, or about the moral significance of those goods (which in themselves are not 'moral goods': *NLNR* 59, 101) as that significance is rationally expressed in the requirements of practical reasonableness, and the specific moral norms (*ibid.*, 49, 130, 403–4). So too, here, the clarification of the norm against choosing to kill the innocent makes no appeal, however covert, to the will of God, creative or moral.]

[34] [Note the word 'includes'. Contrary to Walter's assertion, I never 'define' the material of the Kingdom and never claim that it is moral selves that 'make up' that material. As the texts cited in the next note make clear, the point *for which* one acts uprightly is *not* the shaping of one's moral self which might endure into the Kingdom, but the this-worldly realization or protection of human goods in persons (e.g. 'what actions do to and for people in conflict situations'). What the proportionalists overlook, however, is that the *effect* of such choices includes the reflexive effects on the character of the chooser, effects which are real (even when the hoped-for this-worldly effects of the choice

For, secondly, choices *reflexively* shape the character, the personality, the soul of the one who chooses.[35] The reality of these reflexive consequences is easily illustrated. Over the past decades, we have so often seen how someone who decides to resolve *one particular* moral issue in a certain way becomes a 'different person'—one who resolves whole ranges of moral issues differently, and who adopts new attitudes to the human body, the course of history, the nature of salvation and human destiny, the proper conduct of scholarly controversy...

Here, then, is a dimension of consistency in ethics which should not be overlooked. And reflexive consequences like these are similarly strikingly manifest in the life of whole societies such as yours or mine. Societies, like individuals, can of course live with a large measure of inconsistency and intellectually incoherent compromise. Still, the adoption of an approach—constitutional, statutory, administrative, judicial, or in custom—to one social problem suggests, provokes, or even demands, and certainly often meets with, the adoption of similar approaches to other problems, if only for the sake of consistency. (My colleague Ronald Dworkin has illuminatingly studied some of the dimensions of this rational pressure for consistency, under the name 'integrity'.)[36] Thus, the social consequences of the social adoption of a solution—any solution—in a 'conflict situation' include indefinitely ramifying reflexive changes in the character of the people, their stance in the international arena, the content of their laws and institutions, their education of their young...

A special and contemporary challenge has made more evident than ever before, perhaps, the significance of these reflexive dimensions of individual and social choice for an understanding of the bases of the traditional distinction between direct and indirect. That distinction, we can now see, is integral to the Christian understanding of divine and human nature: what is directly willed (intended) is *adopted*—however reluctantly or disapprovingly—and embraced by and *integrated into* the will. What is not chosen as end or means, but merely permitted (accepted) as a foreseen result of one's behaviour, is not.[37] The challenge I refer to can be labelled 'proportionalism'. I shall explain what I understand by that term. Here it is enough to note that theologians who embrace a proportionalist ethical

---

fail to be realized), and potentially everlasting, and incapable of being commensurated in the way that any non-irrationalist proportionalism requires. As Vatican II states (GS 39), the material and growth of the Kingdom, 'must be carefully distinguished from earthly progress', notwithstanding the Christian ethic's vital concern for such progress.]

[35] See *CMP* 50–9; Wojtyla, *The Acting Person*, 149–52; *FoE* 136–42.

[36] *LE* chs 6–7.

[37] See also the excellent account by Boyle, 'The Principle of Double Effect', 250–1. The interpretation of this passage offered by McCormick is simply confused, and impossible.

methodology suggest that we could, in an authentically Christian way, reread and re-think the tradition so as to dispense with the direct-indirect distinction (at least in relation to all the norms relevant to the consistent ethic of life).[38]

The proportionalist challenge

The 'proportionalist' or (the names matter little) 'consequentialist' proposal is this. In situations of morally significant choice, the overall net pre-moral human value or disvalue involved in and resulting from the various alternatives available for choice can be rationally assessed, prior to moral judgment. Choice intended to, say, destroy human life can sometimes be thus identified as the choice of the greater net value or lesser net disvalue.

Discussing that claim, Chapter IX of *NDMR* shows with some fresh arguments and illustrations (which I shall here not even summarize) that the commensuration of goods and bads which would be needed so to guide morally significant choice is not merely impracticable but logically impossible.[39] Where commensuration is possible, morally significant choice is out of the question.

As common speech suggests, of course, *many sorts of commensuration of goods and bads are possible.* That chapter lists many senses in which one thing or state of affairs can be said to be 'better' or 'worse' than another— many intelligible and coherent senses of 'greater good' and 'lesser evil', and of 'proportionate good' (e.g. as used in traditional formulations of

---

[38] For e.g. McCormick's rejection of the moral relevance of the traditional distinction in all cases of causing 'non-moral evil', see McCormick and Ramsey, *Doing Evil to Achieve Good,* 254–65. As McCormick admits and explains (258–9), this makes it difficult to understand why the same direct-indirect distinction is vital in the case—where both he and Bruno Schüller wished to retain it—of inducing another to act wrongfully. [Walter, in speaking of 'Finnis' allegations', overlooked this note, and further seems to have overlooked the pages I here cite, in which McCormick with commendable frankness lays bare the fragility of Schüller's position which he had summarized on the page cited by Walter; what McCormick is rightly observing is that proportionalists lack any *reason* to preserve the direct-indirect distinction in relation to moral evil. The point has been noticed by many secular philosophers, e.g. Scheffler, *The Rejection of Consequentialism,* ch. 4 and works there cited. Consider the case where one can confidently judge that, by inducing someone to commit adultery (or a murder) with full freedom and deliberation, one will prevent a number of murders.]

[39] See also *FoE* 80–120. [The arguments of those pages, and of the chapter from *NDMR* cited in the text, establish the irrationalism implicit in Walter's assertion that moral good can be 'discerned' 'after all the various goods (non-moral values) and evils (non-moral disvalues) are assessed'. No rational justification for, or even explanation of, such 'discernment' can be offered; and what is freely asserted is freely denied, as we illustrate at great length in relation to the rival 'discernments' of the risks and benefits of nuclear deterrence. There is no question of my 'distrusting' human reason or intellect or believing that 'reason cannot...make reasonable distinctions where they exist' (I simply deny, with reasons, the possibility of making rationally the distinctions which the proportionalists claim to 'discern' without reasons); nor am I interested in 'erecting moral absolutes in reason's place to guard against the uncertainties and potential abuses of human moral discernment and judgment'—which is essentially the task explicitly undertaken by McCormick and other proportionalists: see n. 51 below.]

the 'principle of double effect', rightly understood).[40] *None* of them, we there show, is what proportionalists need; none is rationally based on the sort of overall, *pre-moral* commensuration, *capable of rationally guiding morally significant choices*, which is required by the proportionalist or consequentialist proposal. As meant by proportionalists, the proposal to guide morally significant choice by identifying the 'lesser evil' or the 'greater good' is like other plausible-sounding but incoherent proposals, for example to identify the largest natural number, or to prove any point provided it is the most obvious one.[41]

The *reflexivity of choice* which I discussed above is worth recalling in this context. It creates one of the many dimensions of incommensurability which render incoherent the proposal to guide choice by identifying greater and lesser proportions of pre-moral human goods and bads.[42] How could one conceivably assess the overall net pre-moral value and disvalue of the more or less comprehensive changes of attitude—or, similarly but even more extensively, of social ethos and practice—which so often result from a single choice? Some secular consequentialist philosophers have felt obliged to admit that, by seeking to settle a specific problem of choice by attending to anticipated proportions of pre-moral goods and bads, one becomes a different sort of person—one who stands ready to sacrifice personal commitments and stable identity, for the sake of achieving 'greater good' or preventing 'lesser evil'. Indeed, such philosophers[43] sometimes feel obliged to concede that this reflexive consequence of adopting proportionalism might make that adoption the greater evil! But we should not seek this concession; we should be content, instead, with the more accurate reflection: this sort of consequence simply cannot be commensurated with

---

[40] The Pastoral Letter, *The Challenge of Peace*, explains the proper sense of 'proportionate' and 'disproportionate', with helpful philosophical precision (after affirming a principle—'no end can justify means evil in themselves; such as the executing of hostages'—which in proportionalist thought is false or devoid of relevant meaning):

> even if the means adopted is not evil in itself, it is necessary to take into account the probable harms that will result from using it *and the justice of accepting those harms.* (Para. 105, emphasis added.)

The paragraph continues, very pertinently:

> It is of the utmost importance, in assessing harms *and the justice of accepting them,* to think about the poor and the helpless, for they are usually the ones who have the least to gain and the most to lose when war's violence touches their lives. (Para. 105, emphasis added.)

[41] [I of course do not assert, as Walter claims, that the latter two proposals are part of the proportionalist project; they are merely analogous instances of plausible-sounding incoherence, *like* proposals to identify the overall greater pre-moral good in situations of morally significant choice.]

[42] Kiely, 'The Impracticality of Proportionalism', rightly emphasizes proportionalism's failure to take coherently into account the reflexive or immanent consequences of human acts.

[43] See e.g. Scheffler, *The Rejection of Consequentialism*, 7–10, 41–70, attempting to accommodate the arguments of Bernard Williams in Williams and Smart, *Utilitarianism: For and Against*, 116–17; Williams, *Moral Luck*, 40–53; cf. also Parfit, *Reasons and Persons*, 24–8, 42–3.

the other consequences of one's particular choices. Instead of re-arguing these points, elaborately argued elsewhere, I simply suggest that one consider an example of a type of morally significant choice: abortion. Even in the rather narrow range of cases in which some Catholic theologians will allow direct abortion as 'the lesser evil', the commensurations they suggest or assume are grossly impressionistic and manifestly deniable. Partly, because one cannot foresee the future. But above all, because one cannot know, compare, and commensurate the everlasting realities with which one is dealing when one decides to blot out that individual human being. The goods at stake, in that individual—not to mention in his or her mother (as mother, and as the chooser) and in all who must choose to adopt or reject this choice to kill—are goods not adequately distinct from persons. And so the shortest reply to the proportionalist challenge is: *persons* cannot be weighed and balanced.[44]

Persons include embryonic human individuals

Some, of course, object that the unborn are not persons, at least not at the early stages. But these 'early stages' are stages in the life of biologically living, human individuals. Nobody can demonstrate, and the Catholic Church has never asserted, that these youngest of human individuals are always certainly persons. But the Church does teach that they should be presumed to be. And rightly. For what can we point to as common to all whom we consider persons, other than that they are living human individuals? Thus it is manifestly arbitrary to deny that some or (as in US law's contemporary denial) all of the unborn living human individuals are

---

[44] [To understand *choice* is also to understand the acting persons who constitute themselves most fundamentally through their free choice in serious issues. Underlying the difference between the consistent Catholic ethic and the consequentialist or proportionalist transformations of it are differences in conceptions of the person—just as the difference between the Catholic ethics of sex life and proposed transformations of that ethic is traceable not to any contrast between 'nature' and 'person' but to contrasting conceptions of the person. Thus, the foundational consideration in the CDF's March 1987 Instruction on AIH and husband-wife IVF (*Donum Vitae*) is not at all what McCormick's essay asserts. For that foundational consideration concerns not biological facticity, nor an 'intention of nature' forbidding the separation of unitive and procreative, but a conception of the dignity of the person, that is of the child as 'equal in personal dignity to those who give him life' and therefore as 'not to be desired or conceived as a product', not to be *made* as *object*, in that relationship of domination which necessarily exists between *maker* and *made* and which is 'per se contrary to the dignity and equality that must be common to parents and children': *Donum Vitae* (1987) II.B.4–5. The human and personal good being defended by the Catholic teaching against manufacturing babies is that basic good of inter*personal* harmony which is the ground and substance of justice, friendship, and charity, and the root of the consistent ethic. This is one of the respects in which Catholic teaching on sex/life ethics has appropriated more and more deeply its understanding of the absolutes entrusted to it by the New Testament and the tradition, by a fifty-year development involving collaborative discussion going far beyond past statements and earlier *consensus theologorum*—a course of development which is, *pace* McCormick, even more 'biblical, communal, dynamic, personal' than the development of Catholic *social doctrine* (as, *pace* McCormick, it is called in all the relevant Vatican II documents and very many magisterial statements, not to mention Puebla itself, down to today).]

persons, or to be treated as persons. The denial is plainly motivated by the desire to allow them to be disposed of or used as material for destructive experiments or other useful exploitation.

But are there not bona fide objections based on twinning and on the non-immediate development of neural organs and capacities? These objections seem to appeal to elements of the tradition—notably to St Thomas's doctrine of matter and form, and his conception of the successively vegetative, animal, and intelligent stages in human generation. (They pass over in silence the Church's unfailing teaching, unchallenged by St Thomas, that killing at any stage of human generation is gravely wrongful.)

Such an appeal to Aquinas's opinions about human generation is misconceived. It overlooks their strict dependence on empirically false biology. What Aquinas thought he knew about human generation was this. The formative principle is male semen, *neither organic nor living*, and generation proceeds by sudden (*subito*) generations *and corruptions*: semen corrupts into bloody matter with a plant's life and soul, which perishes and is replaced by animal life and soul, which perishes and is replaced by human life informed by the sensitive and intellectual human soul.[45]

Had Aquinas known about the *organic life* which organizes the one billion items of molecular information in the one-cell conceptus with a *self-directing* dynamic integration which will remain continuously and identifiably identical until death perhaps ninety years later, he would I believe have concurred with most of his followers (and almost everyone else) since the eighteenth century: the fertilized human ovum is specifically human; indeed, the youngest human embryo has already a body which in its already specified (but quite undeveloped) capacities is apt for understanding, knowing, and choosing; he or she already has the biological capacity appropriate to supporting (given only metabolic transformations of air, water, and other sustenance) specifically human operations such as self-consciousness, rationality, and choice.

Similarly, objections about twinning (and about the assumed possibility of human mosaics) misconceive the biological facts. Biologically, one always finds just individuals. If these split, or combine to form a mosaic, one then simply finds one or more different individuals.

Such replies to the objections do not demonstrate that the fertilized human ovum is a person. They show that there is no factual ground whatever for denying that it is a person. Thus, since one picks out human persons in other cases by picking out living human individuals, one must

---

[45]   *ScG* II, c. 89; *ST* I q.118 a.2; *de Potentia* 3, 9, and 12.

presume that the youngest of living human individuals are persons, too; to presume otherwise is just arbitrary discrimination.

Capital punishment and just war

An issue which I set aside in beginning these clarifications now returns in the shape of an obvious objection to their strategy. How can the traditional allowance for killing the innocent—by capital punishment, and in just war—be other than a proportionalist 'exception', a permission to adopt an anti-life will when that is the 'lesser evil', that is, is necessary to preserve a greater good, the common good?

Scripture and Church teaching give no support to that reading, though it may perhaps find some support in some pre-conciliar theologians (who did not contemplate the proportionalist challenge). Rather, capital punishment and war are envisaged in the sources as *authorized* by God because doing *justice* to one who has violated or is violating, the community's order of reciprocal rights and duties, the just order willed by God; in the Old Testament there seems also to be the further dimension of purifying God's holy community from the corruption of evil.

Reflecting on the proportionalist challenge, and on the fundamental structure of a rational (and of a Christian) ethics, I and others have offered (in Chapter XI of *NDMR*) a philosophical account which excludes *all* choices to kill—but which shows the justifiability of all, or nearly all, the types of death-dealing action which the tradition clearly allowed in order to protect the rights of the innocent.

We begin from the simplest case, self-defence. Even in the tradition, that is not an accepted 'exception' to the norm excluding choices to kill. (Here, then, is another amendment I propose to the text from Cardinal Bernardin quoted above at n. 21.) Following Aquinas's classic account of lethal self-defence—an account which entirely excludes any intent to kill one's assailant—we show that self-defensive behaviour, known to be likely to bring about the assailant's death, need involve no choice to kill but only accepting that death as a side effect.[46] Provided that that acceptance of the side effect is consistent with *other* moral principles (such as fairness)—if you like, is morally 'proportionate'—the choice to use these lethal means of self-defence is fully justifiable.[47]

---

[46] *ST* II–II, 64, 7c: 'it is wrongful for one human being to intend to kill another, for the sake of defending himself'. Cf. n. 49 below. See also Grisez, 'Toward a Consistent Natural-Law Ethics of Killing' at 73–9; *FoE* 131.

[47] Thus, Scholz and McCormick are simply mistaken to treat the fleeing horseman's trampling of the blind and crippled as a *means* to his escape. That trampling in no way assists his purpose, is no part of his proposal—it succeeds totally even if the hooves miss every one of these potential victims. What he cannot do—and this is the source of Scholz's confusion—is *ignore* the effects he's accepting

The analysis of individual self-defence is then expanded to the context of social defence, as in war against internal or external assailants. Here, too, our account is anticipated by certain theologians in the tradition; their accounts of just killing in war require, like ours, that military action be always directed toward stopping the enemy's unjust use of force, not toward killing even those who are bringing that force to bear—and whose deaths must never be more than a side effect.[48]

Arguably, even capital punishment could be included within this form of justification for death-dealing behaviour. Aquinas, for one, did not think so: 'It is not right to intend harm to anyone except in the manner of punishment, for the sake of justice.'[49] My two co-authors of *NDMR* judge that capital punishment involves choosing to destroy or damage a basic human good, bodily life, and thus cannot be justified; it is a choice of a bad means to a good end (retributive justice). I am inclined to think that the intentions of a public official seeking to restore the violated order of justice have a unique structure; the death of someone capitally punished is not an end in itself, but neither need it be regarded as a means to an ulterior end, since it can be intended precisely as *itself* a good, namely the good of restoring the order

by choosing to flee down this occupied road. The distinction between object and side effects, between choice and acceptance, is not a carte blanche; there remains the question posed in the manualists' ambiguous word 'proportionality', as in the fourth of their fourfold set of conditions of legitimate 'double effect'. The question they were posing amounts to this. *Granted* that what is not chosen, but merely accepted, falls outside the principle that evil may not be done for the sake of good—more broadly, the principle that one must never *choose* to destroy, damage, or impede any instantiation of any basic good of any human person—still there remain all the other relevant moral principles derivable from the first principle of love: e.g. the principle of fairness, or the principle that one should carry out one's commitments, and so forth. So, *if* we revolt at the horseman's act, it is because we regard it as deeply unfair to those whom he allows to be subordinated to a self-interested purpose of escape. (Here Fr van Beeck's proposed norm, 'No self-serving killing', has its place, *alongside* the norm against direct killing.) The scenario is not, however, described with enough precision to know whether or not the horseman's purpose is self-interested, his action with its side effects unfair, or our appropriate reaction one of revulsion. One thing is clear: the question is not decided by showing that what was done and accepted was done and accepted with reluctance. All manner of wickedness is done with reluctance, in that emotional sense 'unwillingly' and even 'disapprovingly'—but yet with full reflection and freedom, by the free choices which constitute the human *heart* with which Christian morality is through and through concerned. (One chooses to perform abortions, reluctantly and disapprovingly, because that is the only way to become a successful obstetrician and gynaecologist these days...)

[48] Regan, 'The Worth of Human Life' at 241–2; *ibid.*, *Thou Shall Not Kill*, 77–9, argues that this restriction is implicit in the main Christian just-war tradition as it emerged once an essentially punitive conception of the justice of war began to break down with the rise of nation-states in the sixteenth century.

[49] *ST* II–II, q. 65 a.2c; see also I–II, q. 95a.2c. In II–II, q. 64 a.7c; he allows rightness of a public official intending harm (to kill) by way of suppressing activity which, if completed, would be worthy of punishment; cf. q. 64 a.2 ad 3 (note the objection to which this is a reply); q. 65 a.2c; *Sent.* II dist. 42, q.1 a.2c. He does not adequately show that it is acceptable for such an official, for justice's sake, to have an intention different from private citizens' intention in legitimately defending themselves, viz. to repel the unjust attack by all necessary means, even means foreseeably certain to cause death (in which case the killing is a side effect of the morally significant choice).

of justice.[50] Clearly, the act of capital punishment calls for further analysis in the light of a fully adequate theory of human action.

In sum, Chapter XI of our book shows that the lines drawn by the norm identified in our philosophical account—forbidding every choice to kill (every direct killing)—are very close to those drawn by the traditional norm against killing the innocent. Someone who agreed that human life is a basic good of the person, and that evil (e.g. destruction of a basic good of a person) may not be done for the sake of good, but who lacked an analytic apparatus explicitly distinguishing what is chosen as means from what is accepted as side effect, could hardly express the implication of those agreed principles more accurately than by saying: 'Killing the innocent, except by accident, is always wrong.'

Developing the tradition consistently

True, our philosophical account differs somewhat from traditional morality at its present stage of development. But the difference runs with the grain of the tradition's development. I would not say what Cardinal Bernardin says in the quoted text, that presumptions against taking human life have been 'strengthened' and the restrictions 'made' more restrictive. These formulations can suggest the position that moral teaching is a matter of prudent law-*making*, establishing moral norms fashioned or 'honed' for proportionately best consequences.[51] (Cardinal Bernardin's discourse at Seattle University identifies this position about the *source* of specific moral norms, apparently in order to reject it, but fails to disentangle it from the position which he does clearly argue against and reject, viz. that the *content* of the moral norm about killing includes proportionalist exceptions.)[52]

---

[50] McCormick, 'Notes on Moral Theology: 1984' at 52 n.4, says of this retributive notion of pun-ishment, as advanced in my *FoE* 128–35: 'One must ask whether such a notion makes any Christian sense.' He omits to mention that the notion is not peculiar to me but (as I showed, *ibid.*, 135) is the notion advanced by St Thomas (*ST* I–II, q. 87a. 6c; *ScG* III, c.140, para. 5; c.146, para. 1), a moralist whom McCormick frequently invokes as a sound embodiment of Christian sense. Pius XII judged this retributive conception to be, indeed, *the* Christian conception of just punishment: Discourse to the Sixth Congress of Penal Law, AAS 45 (1953) 739 et seq. [Against capital punishment: *Aquinas*, 280–3.]

[51] See e.g. J. Bryan Hehir in Gessert and Hehir, *The New Nuclear Debate*, 48–9, 92. More elabo-rately, McCormick has argued that the norm prohibiting direct killing of non-combatants in warfare is 'a law established on the presumption of common and universal danger', viz. the danger arising from 'human failure, inconstancy, and frailty, and our uncertainty with regard to long-term effects'. See McCormick and Ramsey, *Doing Evil to Achieve Good*, 44–5; see also 227, 232, 251–3, 261 on our, or the Church's, 'adoption' of a hierarchy of values, as the basis for 'exception-making'. On this 'tele-ological character of exception-making', see also McCormick, 'Notes on Moral Theology: 1984' at 51, 54.

[52] See 13:656–7(80). Certain of the Cardinal's formulations of the issue can, moreover, arouse rather than allay misunderstanding: e.g. 'Nor can we allow the moral principle protecting innocent life to be subordinated to other claims *because the consequences of such a process would not be confined to abortion*': 6:325, emphasis added.

The moral teaching which shapes the traditional ethic of life is not a law-making but an identification, ever more adequate, of *truths* about human good and human action—about the *intrinsic* demands of love or respect for persons. So I would say that the tradition is developing by penetrating ever more deeply to the full implications of its underlying principles and presuppositions—those I have here been seeking to indicate.

Perhaps the pace of the tradition's development has been quickening, or will quicken, in response to the challenge of proportionalism. It is easy to underestimate how radical that challenge is. If one adopts proportionalism only as a limiting strategy to deal with 'conflict situations' within a substantially traditional ethic, one will not notice how drastically it departs from the Christian conception of divine providence and human responsibility: God knows what is for the best but we do not. But if one adopts proportionalism at all, by what principle does one limit it? After two decades of theological debate, no coherent limiting principle has emerged; nor will one ever be found, for none is consistent with proportionalism's master principle.[53]

If on the other hand, with some theologians, one abandons the attempt to limit that master principle, one falls into a *reductio ad absurdum*. For, given the Christian doctrine of providence, one should then accept the following as a moral principle:

If in doubt about what is right, *choose whatever you are inclined towards*! (For if you accomplish what you attempt, you can be certain that on the whole it was for the best, since it must fit into the plan of providence.)

Moral absolutes, of the specific kind unfailingly taught in the tradition and rejected by proportionalism, fit the Christian conception of our subordinate human role as workers in the divine plan, who share in the eternal law without having it all laid out before us. In that conception (elaborated in the final chapter of *NDMR*), such dependence on a providence truly shared but only partially understood is accepted as the real matrix in which one's choosing and action have their most important significance: not as bringing about the this-worldly results one hopes for, truly important though that may be (if they occur at all), but as preparing material for the Kingdom, especially people and their own moral selves as shaped by their moral choices.

The difference between traditional and proportionalist ethics goes, however, much wider. On the traditional approach, Christians identified their affirmative responsibilities—what works of mercy to do—by

---

[53] For a critical examination of one influential theologian's attempt to find a limiting principle, see *FoE* 99–104; *CMP* 161–4.

considering their vocational commitments, their opportunities to bear witness, and so forth. A Carmelite in her cloister did not need to feel guilt about not being an activist for poor women in the ghetto, but prayed for them, lived simply, perhaps shared with them excess donations she received.

But once one adopts proportionalism, it seems that one should consider everything one could do, what results one could hope for, and what will be the results of not doing all that one *could* do—and then seek to achieve the results embodying greatest overall good. Of course, no one really takes this seriously and consistently: who tells an American couple to forget *whose* children are the ones going to college and whose are the ones starving in Africa (though the cost of a year in college might keep a multitude of starving children alive that year)?

Here, as in attempts to identify or establish a stable limiting norm about killing, acceptance of the proportionalist method destroys but cannot build; the method yields nothing but mere rationalizations for doing what is chosen on some other ground—feelings, social conventions, etc., or a residual, inconsistent acknowledgement of the principles, norms, and counsels taught in the tradition.[54]

In short: one's whole ethic of life will be different if one approaches it consistently in a traditional way with moral absolutes and affirmative responsibilities specified by diverse vocations, or if one approaches it consistently in a proportionalistic way, trying to weigh and measure. The latter approach yields no substantive, consistent ethic, but generates an unbounded number of ethics each shaped according to the varying feelings, the degrees of respect for traditional or cultural norms, and the hunches of their authors and adherents. No compromise which admits a proportionalistic component into the traditional ethic can be anything other than internally inconsistent; elaborated consistently, it must tend to dissolve (in the minds of its exponents) whatever moral norms conflict with the surrounding culture. It, too, yields a consistent ethic only in that negative sense.

So one might rephrase the heading of this section. The contest is not, strictly speaking, between two 'consistent ethics', but between two consistent ethical approaches only one of which could yield (as it does) a consistent ethic. Yet contest there is, and any attempt to promote or fulfil CEP1 must face and resolve it.

---

[54] On the inevitable reduction of proportionalism to rationalization, see *FoE* 94–105.

II. IMPLICATIONS FOR SOCIAL ACTION

I now turn to a question raised by CEP2: Should a Catholic be concerned to promote particular social/political policies across the whole range of issues mentioned in Cardinal Bernardin's discourses?

The text on which I shall focus in this section is particularly well known; the Cardinal has re-affirmed it in the face of criticism. I shall argue that, read in its more obvious sense, it is open to justified criticism. It is this:

> Those who defend the right to life of the weakest among us must be *equally visible* in support of the quality of life of the powerless among us…(e.g.) the hungry and the homeless…Such *a quality of life posture translates into specific political and economic positions* on tax policy, employment generation, welfare policy, nutrition and feeding programs, and health care. Consistency means we cannot have it both ways: We cannot urge a compassionate society and vigorous public policy to protect the rights of the unborn and then argue that compassion and significant public programs on behalf of the needy undermine the moral fiber of the society or are beyond the proper scope of governmental responsibility.[55]

To simplify my discussion, I shall focus on just two of the many issues there mentioned by Cardinal Bernardin: (i) *infanticide*, and (ii) *feeding the hungry*. And I shall focus on those questions of social policy or action which involve *the law* (whether as prohibiting or exempting conduct or as authorizing expenditures and administrative procedures). These simplifications are to be kept in mind throughout.

In their fundamental logical structure, infanticide and feeding the hungry are representative, both of the Cardinal's spectrum of life and dignity issues, and of the further dimensions of that truly seamless garment, love of neighbour as oneself, for the sake of God and his Kingdom (philosophically speaking: of a will for integral human fulfilment). Infanticide is the subject of a moral absolute, applicable always and everywhere to everyone. Feeding the hungry is the subject of a grave affirmative responsibility, whose implications for particular individuals depend upon their other responsibilities.

Even before we explore the difference between moral absolutes and conditioned affirmative responsibilities—a difference which the discourses advert to[56] but do not explore—it is evident, I suggest, that the text I

---

[55] 1:493(8–9) (emphasis added); re-affirmed in 13:657(77 et seq.); see also 10:38(52); 14:6(69–70).

[56] Cardinal Bernardin has alluded to this distinction, but only in rather generic terms. He has repeated that 'a consistent ethic of life does not equate the problem of taking life (e.g. through abortion and war) with the problem of promoting human dignity (through humane programs of nutrition, health care and housing)' (3:707(15); also 13:657(77 et seq.)). And he has stressed the 'analogical' character of the consistent ethic, and its irreducibility to a single type of problem (2:568; 5:707(17–18); 10:37(51); 15:348(81)).

have quoted needs a clarification or amendment. No individual (or group) need, or even could reasonably, be 'equally visible' in support of the consistent ethic's requirements in each and every one of the relevant issues. People do *and should* have different commitments and responsibilities. A conscientious Congressman should not be expected to be a right-to-life activist; he should vote consistently with the norm excluding any intent to kill the innocent, and he should work for less unjust laws and policies; he might focus his high-visibility activities on welfare reform or some other just policy. A person deep into the picketing of abortion clinics and baby-starving maternity wards (and perhaps in and out of jail) should not be expected to be knowledgeable about and working at welfare reform.

Cardinal Bernardin has in fact made this point: the consistent ethic does not mean that everyone must do everything.

There are limits of time, energy and competency. There is a shape to every individual vocation. People must specialize; groups must focus their energies. The consistent ethic does not deny this.[57]

So the phrase 'those who...', in the earlier-quoted text, must have been used in a sense which many hearers and readers will, I think, have misunderstood: *that community* (e.g. the Church) *which* opposes infanticide must also, as a community, be equally visible in support of the hungry and homeless... Even with this clarification, the statement seems rather imprecise: even in a community rich in diverse talents and charisms, *equality of visibility* seems scarcely the relevant measure of fulfilment of very diverse responsibilities—some absolute, some affirmative, and all arising in ever-shifting contexts of urgency.

But perhaps I have been pressing this fragment of the text too hard. So I turn to the main questions of this section.

Infanticide

My first question is: What social policy should Catholics support in relation to the *law of infanticide*? Should the intentional killing of a child, by 'act' or 'omission', whatever the circumstances, be prohibited and punishable as a crime?

Throughout the civilized world, now as in Aquinas's day,[58] the criminal law of homicide closely follows, 'translates', indeed transcribes the community's common morality. Each community tries to identify what forms of killing and of death-dealing behaviour or omission are *morally* wrongful, and then declares those forms of conduct unlawful

---

[57] 13:657(83).   [58] See *ST* I–II, 95, 2c.

and criminal.[59] Despite the severe strains introduced into the common moral-legal tradition by social acceptance of Dresden, Hiroshima, and Nagasaki, and of abortion, the Anglo-American law of homicide remains essentially consistent with the common law's and Christian morality's absolute exclusion of killing the innocent.[60]

This virtual coincidence of moral law and state/national law in relation to the definition and prohibition of homicides (including infanticide) is to be expected and supported. The fundamental moral principle of love of neighbour has its most immediate political application through the mediation of the Golden Rule, the rule of fairness which yields the fundamental political and constitutional principles: equal dignity of persons, equality before the law, equal entitlement to the law's protection. The first condition of fair human interrelationships is that one's own life and death be not at the disposal of another's choice. Hence the law of homicide should conform to morality's exclusion of all choices to kill any human being. The legal rule's most immediate source is the principle of equal dignity; the moral norm's most immediate source is the sanctity of life as a basic human good never in any instance to be destroyed as an end or as a means. But the two sources coincide in their implications.

How different from the ancient world! How different, too, from the new world which consistent utilitarians, and other consistent consequentialists and proportionalists, envisage and promote! Those are ethico-legal universes in which there is no (or no consistent) acknowledgement of human bodily life's sanctity—the more than instrumental significance of that life

---

[59] An exception now relates to the act of suicide (as distinct from assisting another to commit suicide), which can be regarded as having no *necessary* direct implications for justice (fairness). In other respects, the dominant trend of modern American and English legal thought and policy is tightening the coextensiveness of the legal and moral judgment on homicide. Where nineteenth- and early-twentieth-century law defined as murderous *any* death-causing act done in the course of committing felony, and in other circumstances a jury finds intention on the basis that a *reasonable* man would have *foreseen* death as a consequence of his actions, the modern law tends more and more to reject these divergences from the moral conception of murder, i.e. of intentionally causing death. The process of assimilating the law of murder to the ethics of murder is not quite complete, insofar as, e.g., *foresight* of the likelihood of causing grievous bodily harm (short of death), is treated as an 'intent' sufficient to sustain a charge of murder.

[60] Thus our law continues to accept not only that consequentialist rationalizations of choices to kill give no moral ground for admitting such choices, but also that human acts must be analysed in much the same way as I sketched in sec. I. Indeed, such an act analysis—identifying ends and means in proposals adopted for choice, and distinguishing both ends and means from side effects foreseen and caused but not part of the proposal adopted by choice—gives an unsurpassedly adequate theoretical account and explanation of almost all the actual decisions of Anglo-American courts concerning intention and *mens rea* in homicide, though not yet of all decisions nor of the terminology used and accounts offered by many judges and legislators. Similarly, the law accepts what a sound analysis of intention proposes, in relation to omissions, namely that one who has an affirmative responsibility such as feeding the hungry *can* choose to make non-fulfilment of that responsibility a *means* of killing by omission, in which case there is a violation of the moral and legal absolute forbidding intentional killing of innocents.

as an intrinsic and basic human good,[61] and its immunity in every instance from any choice to destroy it as end or as means. Nor do they acknowledge the equal dignity of every human person: those who lack 'quality of life' to some level selected by others, and some of those whose existence is thought likely to lower the quality of life of another, are removed from the protection of the law's prohibition.[62] They are deemed 'better off', or even just 'better', *dead*; the deliberate bringing about of their death is declared to be a 'necessity' or at least 'the lesser of evils'. Those in power are thus permitted—sometimes at their own free initiative, sometimes only after legal formalities—to kill those who are thus under their dominion.

(In periods when a culture, or an individual, is in transition from the ethic and law consistently founded on love of neighbour and equal dignity to the ethic and law founded on 'balancing of values' by those in power, the fact of transition may be veiled—diaphanously—by a requirement that the choice to kill be carried out only by 'omissions', 'letting die', withholding of sustenance...[63] Consistent value-balancers regard such veils with understandable contempt.)[64]

In short: those who wish to make exceptions to the law of infanticide accept that they must argue, or assume, that deliberately killing some human beings is *morally* justified. They rightly acknowledge that this is no place for a gap between law and morality. The implications of love of neighbour, as understood in Catholic morality, make clear (I have suggested) why such a gap, here, would be deeply unjust, and why both morality and the law must absolutely exclude the killing of babies as of other human persons.

Thus my question about the social policy that Catholics should support in relation to infanticide has a single, straightforward answer.

More generally, the moral absolutes of the tradition have a number of direct 'translations' into social policies which in the strictest sense

---

[61] See e.g. Fletcher, *Morals and Medicine*, 211: '...the body and its members, our organs and their functions—all of these *things* are a part of what is over against us...'. For reflections on the influence of such dualism amongst certain influential Catholics, see *CMP* 198 with n. 42 thereto. For philosophical critique, see *ibid.*, 137–8; Grisez and Boyle, *Life and Death with Liberty and Justice*, 372–8; *NDMR* 304–9.

[62] See the citations to, and quotations from Glanville Williams, Joseph Fletcher, Michael Tooley, and H. Tristram Engelhardt Jr, in Grisez and Boyle, *Life and Death with Liberty and Justice*, 218–20, 488–9. See further, e.g., Glover, *Causing Deaths and Saving Lives*, 154–69; Singer, *Practical Ethics*; Tooley, *Abortion and Infanticide*; Harris, *The Value of Life*, chs 1, 2, 4, 5.

[63] See e.g. the testimony of eminent and influential English and Scottish physicians at the trial of *Regina v Arthur* (November 1981), quoted in Linacre Centre Report, *Euthanasia and Clinical Practice*, 86–7. Cf. also McCormick, 'To Save or Let Die' at 175; Jonsen et al., 'Critical Issues in Newborn Intensive Care' at 760–2; McCormick, 'A Proposal of "Quality of Life" Criteria for Sustaining Life'.

[64] e.g. Harris, *The Value of Life*, 29–47.

apply—are *deducible* from—the absolute moral norm. So, for example, the Pastoral Letter on War and Peace rightly judged that the absolute norm, 'the lives of innocent persons may never be taken directly' (para. 104), *does* translate directly into such applications, or norms of 'policy', as: 'It is not morally acceptable to intend to kill the innocent as part of a strategy of deterring nuclear war' (para. 178).

But how far, if at all, are such translations, or applications *stricto sensu*, available in relation to the affirmative moral norm, 'Feed the hungry'?

'Feed the hungry'

This norm, like the norm against infanticide, is an implication of love of neighbour via the Golden Rule: since one wants the means of sustenance for oneself, one must feed the hungry when and in the way that one's other responsibilities fairly allow. Since people's other responsibilities vary widely with their commitments and opportunities, the responsibility articulated by the norm 'Feed the hungry…' will be fulfilled by a vast variety of individual and social acts at various levels. It will be violated by various forms of unfairness.

Some of these violations are quite straightforwardly identifiable, and straightforwardly translatable into law. Failures to feed the hungry can be omissions chosen in order to hasten death, and thus violations of the ethico-legal absolute excluding killings—itself, as we have seen, a norm articulating the requirements not only of the sanctity of life but also of fairness. Or such failures to feed can be negligence which unfairly flouts all accepted standards of responsibility of parents or guardians (including the standards of care which those parents or guardians expect from their own medical and other attendants).

Another of the many forms of unfairness emerges from Cardinal Bernardin's reference (at the end of the quoted text) to those who resist state-funded welfare on the score that it undermines society's moral fibre. What undercuts their argument is not some proportionalist computation that the undermining of moral fibre is disproportionate to, outweighed by, the survival or health of the needy; it is that those who make the argument make it with a biased selectivity. They support constitutional, economic, educational, and other social policies which also result in, or risk, undermining the moral fibre of some or many of those affected by them—undermining it by materialism, consumerism, indulgence in frivolity and baseness, indifference to the responsibilities which go with rights and advantages, and other immoralities commonly accompanying prosperity.

The demands of fairness, then, are one main respect in which the consistent ethic's consistency indeed 'means we cannot have it both ways'.

But how far does this mean that a fair 'quality of life posture *translates* into specific political and economic positions...'?

From consistent ethic to specific policies

The suggestion is ambiguous. In many issues and contexts, a fair respect for the basic needs of one's fellow citizens, one's fellow human beings, entails that there be *some* specific measures to meet those needs, yet fails to identify (leaves under-determined) *which* specific measures. In these many instances, the moral norm does not 'translate' into 'specific political and economic positions'. Instead it requires that individuals, groups, and political communities *choose* from among various possible appropriate measures (and nothing can be chosen without being fully specific).[65]

There are many morally significant criteria for detecting *inappropriateness* in proposals for such choice. But these criteria cannot be expected to identify as inappropriate all proposals save one policy, uniquely appropriate to the issue in question. There can be few if any issues or contexts in relation to which there is only one right answer to the questions how 'best', that is, how *rightly*, to fulfil such affirmative responsibilities as 'Feed the hungry'.

The Pastoral Letter of 18 November 1986, *Economic Justice for All*, puts a similar point thus—

the movement from principle to policy is complex and difficult and...although moral values are essential in determining public policies, they do not determine specific solutions (para. 134).[66]

That statement needs a little clarification. Its context concerns affirmative social and individual responsibilities, not moral absolutes. The denial, 'Moral values do not determine specific solutions', should be read as

---

[65] The classic exposition of this matter remains Aquinas, *ST* I–II q.95 a.2 on *determinationes* (as contrasted with quasi-deductive applications) of natural law; see also q.99 a.3 ad 2; q.100 a.3 ad 2; *NLNR* 281–90, 294–5; essays IV.2 (1984b) and IV.13 (1985c).

[66] The passage continues:

They [moral values] must interact with empirical data, with historical, social, and political realities, and with competing demands on limited resources. The soundness of our prudential judgments depends not only on the moral force of our principles, but also on the accuracy of our information and the validity of our assumptions.

One must add that prudential judgments can be sound without being correct (or incorrect): for many of the necessary assumptions relate to future consequences which are simply indeterminate and unknowable, not least because they involve the future free choices of many people. Thus there can be, and often are, alternative and *competing* sound prudential judgments on one and the same issue.

meaning: moral norms articulating affirmative responsibilities such as 'Feed the hungry' do not entail uniquely correct specific 'solutions', though they enable many possible public policies to be identified as incorrect, that is, unjust or in some other way immoral. Read in this sense, the Pastoral Letter seems to be correct in denying that the quality of life posture 'translates' into *specific* political and economic positions.

Now this has some implications often overlooked. I shall identify two.

Rightful opposition between adherents to the consistent ethic

Even with (an impossible) unanimity on the facts and likely consequences, it is possible for some members of our society to oppose, *rightly*, social programmes which other members *rightly* propose and support in fulfilment of an affirmative norm such as 'Feed the hungry'.

I take as my first premise a judgment of the US Bishops' Pastoral Letter *Economic Justice for All*, para. 185: the disparities of wealth and income in the United States are such as to be 'unacceptable…inequities', offensive to justice. I take (not from the Pastoral Letter) one further premise: it is now politically impossible, and no substantial US political party now proposes, to reduce those disparities to the extent required by justice.

Consider now a welfare programme to feed the hungry, to be funded (a) by taxation on income, sales/purchases, etc., and (b) by reducing the funds which might otherwise have gone to housing, education, health care, and pensions for all the relatively poor (above as well as below the 'hungry-poverty' line).

The burden of such a programme upon those who are just above the hungry-poverty line is inequitable, relative to the burden on the very rich who after paying their taxes retain an inequitably high level of income of wealth. And the burden on those just above the hungry-poverty line makes it more difficult, if not impossible, for them to fulfil their serious affirmative responsibilities for the education and health of their children.

In such a situation, those hungry poor who live responsibly, and who need the welfare programme, can rightly support it. Yet those only a little better off (who may be very numerous) may rightly *oppose* the programme. In doing so, they need not be manifesting a wrongful indifference to the needs of the worst off. They need only be manifesting a rightful concern to fulfil their own responsibilities to their children, and expressing a rightful judgment that a prior responsibility for funding the relief of the worst off falls, in justice, on those who are, inequitably, very rich.

For the programme is both really just and really unjust; its justice is only relative.

(As for the very rich, they are in a moral perplexity by reason of the prior injustice of their position. They cannot oppose the programme without compounding their injustice to the worst off, nor support it without compounding their injustice to the not quite so badly off. *This* programme, with its attendant injustice, would not have been needed if they had not been hanging on to their inequitable advantages.)

Legislators as such, finally, whether personally poor or rich, can rightly either support or oppose the just/unjust programme, for the competing good reasons I have mentioned. But all legislators have a serious responsibility not so to act as to leave the worst off starving. For, since everyone would rather accept many unfair deprivations than starve, it is grossly unfair for anyone specifically responsible for the public good to accord to per se reasonable protest against the starvation-preventing programme's unfair features an ultimate practical priority over preventing starvation.

This analysis could of course be refined. But it may already suggest one of the serious problems inherent in asserting, without some clarifying distinctions, that:

CEP3:... Catholic bishops should publicly commend not only the principles of Catholic teaching on the whole spectrum of 'life' and 'quality of life' issues, but *also policies* which appropriately apply those principles right across that spectrum.

All who express or insinuate support for a specific welfare programme— except perhaps legislators at the decisive moment of voting—not only express *acceptance* (I do not say 'approval') of the serious injustices involved in carrying out that programme, in our inequitable societies. They also become open to the charge of preferring the imposition of those particular injustices to lending active support for alternative specific welfare programmes which would involve neither those nor, perhaps, any other injustices.

Such a charge might be resisted by arguing that support for those alternatives is futile—the rich are not going to allow their privileges to be taken from them. This sort of defence may suffice for the politician. But if tried by the preacher it is considerably less convincing, insofar as it depends on contestable assessments of probability, and an overtly pessimistic attitude to the leaven of the gospel. Those among the preacher's flock who suffer the injustices involved in the programme he supports may well hear the defence with scepticism, in more sense than one. (More about the preacher's predicament in sec. III.)

Now to a second implication of the difference in 'applicability' between moral absolutes and affirmative responsibilities.

A litmus test available to voters

Single-issue voting is absurd, but in considering how to choose among candidates for high political office it is reasonable to give their views on infanticide a very different weight from their views on various public programmes for feeding the hungry.

Single-issue voting for candidates makes no sense, strictly speaking. For our constitutional systems require us to vote, not for programmes (responses to 'issues'), but for people to hold office. Candidates who profess to hold the view one favours on one's preferred 'single issue' may in fact not hold it, or may be unable ever to act on it, and/or may hold views one reasonably deplores on other issues, including important issues one has not even envisaged.

What one reasonably desires, then, are candidates who have ability and good character—who will try to act on what they publicly profess, and who will respond with justice to the whole range of issues (including unforeseen issues) which will fall within their authority during their tenure of office. *Character*, after all, is the foundation and substance of that attitude or ethos which Cardinal Bernardin's discourses invoke as a primary concern (see CEP2).

So it is reasonable for a voter to use candidates' discoverable convictions about (or 'positions on') infanticide as *a litmus test of bad character*, to give little or no weight to their preferences among possible policies regarding feeding the hungry, and (subject to exceptions) to vote accordingly.

For since the social and legal application of the moral truth about infanticide is quite straightforward, those who are willing to relax the legal prohibition of infanticide show themselves to have very bad character, at least so far as justice is concerned.[67] Those who oppose particular policy approaches toward feeding the hungry may be unjust. But usually that is not so clear. (An exception would be any who admit indifference to the hungry, let alone any who propose their elimination by starvation.) For the opposition to particular programmes may be motivated by preference for alternative programmes, or different methods of funding, or for policies which would more or less rapidly and more or less completely shift the undoubted responsibility for feeding the hungry back to the neighbourhood and family communities (where, in many societies, it rests to this day), leaving the organs of the national community with, in this field, only the most strictly subsidiary function.

---

[67] Their ultimate personal culpability is another matter, which their fellow citizens cannot reasonably be concerned to assess.

I do not insinuate any preference for the last-mentioned view. But I do say that a candidate who preferred it might well be of good character, in relation to all the norms of, say, Catholic social teaching. Such a candidate might well hold a truly consistent ethic of life—an ethic which not only applies absolute moral and legal norms protecting innocent life from assault and intentional neglect, but also extends to all the many 'quality of life' issues Cardinal Bernardin has mentioned (and to all the other aspects of justice), and requires a sincere recognition of the relevant affirmative norms and responsibilities.

Two footnotes

What I say about infanticide as a litmus test of politically relevant bad character applies also, it seems to me, to abortion. To an educated person, the sort who seeks high office in our societies, abortion is no more obscure an issue of justice than infanticide. (The countless protestations to the contrary, the endlessly shifty rationalizations for killing children while unborn, the market for 'probable opinions' of theologians and philosophers, are signs of pervasive bad conscience, of that *mauvaise foi* for which Christian doctrine has another name.)

The same is true of abortion funding, though here there may be more room for a kind of self-deception whose implications for character are more difficult to assess.[68] A politician who supports the provision of public funds for abortion, as means of alleviating poverty or disparity of 'opportunity' between rich and poor, violates the absolute norm which excludes intending to kill the innocent.[69] Those who thus choose to fund abortions, whether or not with feelings of disapproval and repugnance—'We're personally opposed but...'—*personally will*, that is, choose as a means, *that abortions be done*, with public funds. They act as prime contractors, procurers, in arranging for the disposal of unborn children presented (for destruction) to the healthcare providers whose destruction services are secured by the government's prior undertaking that *these* services will be paid for when performed. In a consistent ethic of life, as in common and Christian morality, the moral absolute excluding killing obviously excludes the procuring of killings, and—being itself an implication of 'love of neighbour'—conditions the fulfilment of one's serious responsibilities to diminish poverty and the unfair balance of opportunities between rich and poor.

---

[68] For a discussion showing the complexity of an accurate analysis of ends, means, and side effects in some voting situations, see *NDMR* 344–7, 357–62.

[69] Cf. McCormick, 'Medicaid and Abortion' at 716–17. Grisez, 'Public Funding of Abortion', 45–51, carefully demonstrates the point made above.

In short, though single-issue voting, strictly speaking, makes no sense, one may reasonably vote according to this rule of thumb: willingness, however reluctant, to relax the legal prohibition on infanticide, or to support the judicial permission of abortion as a means of securing 'privacy' or maternal health or 'fairness to the poor', or to promote the public funding of abortions for any such end, or as a means of securing or retaining public office lest worse people be elected, is sufficient manifestation of unsuitability for high office; few of the politically relevant positions on poverty and welfare are such a manifestation.

Of course, sometimes one may vote for a candidate who manifests this sort of bad character. But only as a way of doing what one can to prevent the election of a candidate who also manifests relevantly bad character and who has some other or wider unsuitability for public office. And sometimes one may find the test unusable because one has insufficient evidence to discover the truth about what the candidates are willing to do if elected.

III. AN OBLIGATION OF BISHOPS?

The discourses distinguish between 'moral principles' and 'the application of these principles to particular policies'—more briefly, between 'principles' and 'specific solutions', 'specific political and economic polices', 'particular strategies', 'policy proposals', 'policy conclusions', or 'policy judgments'.[70] They state that Catholic bishops, though speaking with 'a different authority' when they do so, offer 'policy conclusions' in order to foster public debate, to 'give a sense of how the moral principles take shape in the concrete situations our society faces', and 'to stimulate the public argument'.[71] The discourses recall with approval a distinction drawn in the Pastoral Letter on War and Peace (paras 9–10), between 'universally binding moral principles' and 'applications of these principles', applications which involve 'prudential judgments...based on specific circumstances which can change or which can be interpreted differently by people of good will'. The Letter adds that 'the moral judgments that we [the US Catholic bishops] make in specific cases' are 'not binding in conscience'.

All this calls for clarification. Being universals, the absolute moral norms can be called principles. Their direct application does call for judgment (sometimes so straightforward that errors in application are almost inconceivable), but not for any additional *moral* deliberation or judgment. No further moral norms or responsibilities can require or authorize any

---

[70] See e.g. 1:493(8); 6:327; 8:12(43); 14:6(70).
[71] See 8:12. Cf., similarly, *Economic Justice for All*, para. 20: 'we feel obliged to teach by example how Christians can undertake concrete analysis and make specific judgments on economic issues'.

choice other than: not to do what the moral absolute identifies as morally unacceptable.

It seems incautious, therefore, to speak as if a teacher whose mandate is authoritatively to identify and propose universal (general) moral principles cannot authoritatively apply the moral absolutes to particular policies. If the particular policy is overtly or obviously inconsistent with a moral absolute, it can and should be condemned by those who have authority to propose that principle.[72] When, however, a public policy is open to interpretation, to differing characterizations, then a judgment on it will carry the full authority of a teacher of moral truth only if expressed hypothetically:

If this policy requires or authorizes any person to attack non-combatants either as an end or as a means, then it must not be proposed, supported, or implemented, even if the consequences of not supporting or implementing it seem likely or humanly-speaking certain to be very bad...

So it is not universally true that the immediate applications of moral principles call for 'prudential judgment', unless 'prudential judgment' includes the simple and straightforward application of moral absolutes to instances falling under them. But the virtue of prudence is indeed fully engaged when the 'application' is of affirmative norms, and the fulfilment is of affirmative responsibilities.

For no affirmative norm can be applied without considering and assessing other *moral* norms, including the very specific norms which apply to some individuals, groups, or political communities but not to others, because of differences in their respective commitments, formal and informal. (I have already said something about such commitments in the constitutional, legal, or political sphere, when discussing the dimension of consistency called by some communal 'integrity'.) Every choice has bad side effects, and the range and content of one's moral responsibility to avoid, prevent, or minimize those side effects depend upon one's situation, one's opportunities and alternative options, and one's vocation with its responsibilities. Assessing all this well is the role of prudence, the intellectual disposition to make uprightly reasonable choices.

Now CEP3, as implicitly deployed in Cardinal Bernardin's discourses, seems to propose that Catholic bishops have an obligation to be ready to make, regularly and frequently, prudential judgments of the following form: it is appropriate for me as a Catholic bishop to fulfil my affirmative responsibilities as teacher and pastor by making a particular public

---

[72] This seems at least implicitly suggested by Cardinal Bernardin, when he says that the Pastoral Letter's 'most stringent [and] binding' conclusion is that 'directly intended attack [] on civilian centers is always wrong', and that this 'conclusion' or 'principle' has two 'implications' or 'extensions': 'such attacks would be wrong even if our cities had been hit first', and 'anyone asked to execute such attacks should refuse the orders' [1:493(8)].

statement intended to affect the national political debate on a specific 'policy issue' (say, a welfare programme to feed the hungry, or house the homeless).

Now, both episcopal affirmative responsibilities and civic affirmative responsibilities are undoubtedly serious. But the decision to be an actor in national political life, and to urge fellow believers to be actors, promoting or lending direct support to specific proposals for national policy, is a decision likely to have some notable bad side effects which I shall shortly sketch. If, however, the making of such decisions is an episcopal *obligation*, then accepting those side effects will in many cases be obligatory, since not to make the decision will also have bad side effects. If, on the other hand, the making of such decisions is not within the obligations of a bishop as bishop, then acceptance of the side effects of making them should be assessed rather differently by episcopal prudence.

What, then, are the bad side effects I have in mind?

The episcopal office carries the responsibility of catechizing believers about their duties as Christians, and primary among those duties is the affirmative responsibility to find and accept a personal vocation which, in all its richness and complexity, will shape a life by faith, hope, and love. Now the vocation of most Christians, while not negating their responsibilities as citizens, will be far removed from involvement in national or state political life. Yet contemporary secular humanism insistently teaches that the most truly significant arena, 'where the action is', is the arena of 'world history' or 'national life', where great worldly power is exercised. Christianity seems to teach otherwise—that the kingdom it hopes for is built up, through faith and good works in this life, in *mystery*, and as really by the faith and good choices of those who are utterly marginal to the transactions of 'world history'. Can one confidently affirm that in contemporary western societies Christian believers are receiving from their bishops a catechesis which challenges the secular humanist assumption, and effectively communicates that faith should shape every believer's vocation however far most elements of that vocation may be removed from publicity and 'public life'?

Again, episcopal office includes the responsibility of calling non-believers to conversion. Among those needing conversion are the non-believers who hold or seek political office. If bishops, in the interests of political relevance and of 'being taken seriously by important people', were to base their public pronouncements on some kind of ground rule excluding from serious attention any 'impracticable' or 'other-worldly' option—such as unilaterally ending nuclear deterrence, or taking from the wealthy *all* the property they do not administer in accord with the Christian conception of property as social responsibility—they would be passing over an opportunity to preach the Gospel, in its prophetic integrity and its unembarrassed denunciation of clear and sure evils, to many who might otherwise have heard its radical challenge.[73]

Again, episcopal office now disqualifies its holders from actually exercising any high political responsibility and participating directly in the actual choice of national or state policies. And their own responsibilities prevent bishops acquiring the detailed knowledge of options, opportunities, costs, and other realities which is needed and often possessed by those who do make and execute high political decisions. In both these ways, bishops are prevented from making *truly prudential* judgments about the political community's fulfilment of its affirmative responsibilities. For prudence, strictly speaking, is wisdom in *choosing*, and only those whose position requires them to choose are well placed to have the appropriate knowledge of the options. Insofar as actual decision-makers are wicked people and/ or unbelievers, they are unlikely to be impressed either by the authority or by the wisdom of episcopal pronouncements on matters of state. Where, however, they are believers, they are likely to be distressed by the authority just insofar as their own prudent judgment, made in accordance with Christian teaching, differs from that of their bishops.[74]

Finally as I argued in sec. II, support for specific polices for fulfilling affirmative social responsibilities in an unjust society involves material cooperation in moral evil. What sort of material cooperation in evil is appropriate is properly judged by those who, each in their own specific situation and vocation, must choose. What is appropriate for one believer

---

[73] It is alleged that the Ad Hoc Committee which drafted the Pastoral Letter on War and Peace adopted as a 'firm groundrule' that 'it would not, under any circumstances, support unilateral nuclear disarmament': Castelli, *The Bishops and the Bomb*, 79. The book making this allegation is not fully reliable. I do not suggest that the motives of such a decision, if it were made or proposed, were anything other than a sincere belief that unilateral renunciation of nuclear deterrence is not morally justifiable. The eventual Pastoral Letter asserts (para. 333) that 'surrender' is an 'indefensible choice'; I do not deny that unilateral renunciation of nuclear deterrence would be tantamount to surrender, but I can discover no argument in the Letter which even attempts to justify the claim that unilateral renunciation is an indefensible choice. I am also among the many readers of the Letter who find it lacking any coherent argument for its apparent conclusion that the retention of a nuclear deterrent which includes (like all existing and foreseeable western deterrents) proposals for counter-value retaliation can be a morally defensible choice.

[74] The difficulties confronting a bishop in assessing specific policies for discharging complex sets of affirmative responsibilities are illustrated by the multiple mistakes made by the US bishops in assessing US nuclear deterrent policies in relation to the straightforward moral absolute which they called 'discrimination' (and which they stated with precision and force). They failed to describe actual US nuclear policy; they failed to attend to official and unofficial strategic writings which stress the need for a deterrent to include threats and plans to destroy cities as such for intra-war deterrence and for final retaliation; through inattention to the historical use and thus the meaning of the relevant formulae, they misinterpreted certain ambiguous formulae put before them by government officials intent on influencing their Letter; they confused targeting policy with strategic intent. (See *NDMR* 18–28, 36–8, 160–1, 172–4.) These are all the mistakes of *outsiders*. Truly prudential judgments are the judgments of insiders.

may be inappropriate for another, given differences of role and responsibility. Most believers are likely to be confused, and find the truth of their faith somehow obscured, when a bishop takes stands which involve him in approving material cooperation in evil, and in taking sides with some believers against others on matters which the faith itself leaves open.

My purpose in sketching these bad side effects is not to argue that American bishops have erred in prudential judgment, or that their choices have been more liable to create these effects than the comparable choices of popes or of bishops in other places. The prudential judgment in question can be made only by Catholic bishops. And many popes and bishops, for many years, have judged it good to accept these side effects (assuming they were aware of them), in the interests of good causes, which have varied, in detail, from time to time and place to place.

Several good causes are proposed in Cardinal Bernardin's discourses: the stimulation of public debate, for the sake, in turn, of developing consensus among Catholics and thus promoting a life-respecting and life-enhancing ethos in society at large (CEP1 and CEP2).

But are these truly good causes sufficient to justify the position that Catholic bishops have an obligation to promote, in the public forum, specific policies for fulfilling non-absolute, affirmative social responsibilities? Or is the promoting of such policies rather something which a bishop *may* do, if and when in his prudent judgment doing so will achieve some good for the sake of which he is prepared to accept bad side effects such as I have indicated?

Philosophical reflections can do no more than pose the question. But they can extend to one final observation.

Suppose that bishops made the prudential judgment and decision *not* to 'shape a comprehensive social agenda'[75]—that is, *not* to accept, save in exceptional cases, the bad side effects of participation in political debates, or the contest of candidates, about specific policies on the national issues listed in Cardinal Bernardin's discourses: such a decision would not imply that the many Catholic lay people have erred, who have regarded such participation as squarely within their own personal competence and vocation in faith—and thus as among *their* affirmative obligations—and who in many cases have sought to work together, giving joint and public witness to that faith in doing so.

---

[75] 13:658(83). See text at n. 9 above.

22

SECULARISM AND 'THE CULTURE OF DEATH'*

I

Culture is what we add, by our choices, to nature, that is, to all that we find given in our minds, bodies, and environment, prior to human decisions to believe, plan, make, and do. So culture comprises ways of thinking, communicating, and behaving that have been shaped by decisions between alternative possibilities, and that last because they are carried on by more or less deliberate adoption.

When we hear of *a* culture, we need not think of some worldwide or nationwide reality, as wide as 'civilization'. The Queens' College Cambridge doubtless has a culture subtly different from University College Oxford's. There is a recognizably English culture of football hooliganism. Can it be said to be part of 'English culture'? In a sense. But most or perhaps all of us, even those of us who are immersed in English culture, can truthfully say that we are in no way involved in English football hooliganism. So it would be misleading to say that 'English culture *is* a culture of football hooliganism', or that English culture as such is hooligan.

Similarly, the phrase adopted by the Church in recent years, 'the culture of death', need not and, I think, should not be taken to say that modern culture as such, or western culture as such, or the secular world as a whole, *is* a culture of death. Rather, it says that there is very powerfully present in our contemporary world a distinguishable set of interrelated practices, conventions, laws, institutions, ways of responding, thinking, and communicating, and learned and learnable patterns of ambition and desire, which as a set can well be called 'a culture of death'. As *Evangelium Vitae* puts it, 'our societies and cultures, strongly marked though they are by the culture of death',[1] also contain within them forms of familial and

---

* 2002b (address to an international conference held at The Queens' College Cambridge in the summer of 2000).

[1] Encyclical, 25 March 1995, *Evangelium Vitae* (*EV*), sec. 26.1.

other associative culture radically opposed to that culture-within-our-culture.

As an ongoing reality, any culture centres on *intentio* in both main senses of that Latin word: meanings and purposes. It centres on what people *mean*, in both main applications of that English word: what they mean by their words and other signs and communications, and what they mean to be doing, bringing about, achieving. It is meaning in this latter sense, essentially intention or intendings as purposes and choices, that is referred to by the word 'culture' in the phrase 'culture of death'. These kinds of intention and choice are the decisive moment in a structure or pattern which extends from dispositions and willingness to act, through conditional choices, to unconditional choices to act here and now, carried out by actual conduct (acts and deliberate omissions or forbearances). The word 'culture' always picks out some more or less *lasting* reality, so 'culture of death' is a phrase picking out a more or less settled and shared *willingness* or disposition to make and carry out choices of a certain kind, a more or less stable and overt, publicly unashamed, pattern of *intention*.

'Of death'. What is distinctive of this set of attitudes and practices is that those who share in them are willing to *intend* death. Properly speaking, one intends what, and only what one chooses to try to bring about either as an end wholly or partly for its own sake, or as a means to some such end. So a culture in which the death of human persons is *not* chosen, but also is not shuffled out of sight or veiled in euphemism or other tricks of evasion and denial, but is a subject of open discussion, artistic representation, contemplation, and personal preparation, is not what 'culture of death' refers to. No, the phrase refers to a more or less systematized willingness to intend death, as an end or as a means.

'Intending death': more precisely, choosing to bring about or hasten the death of a person. For when we speak of *life* in contexts such as 'the right to life', or 'the basic and inviolable good of life',[2] we properly mean the life of a person. And since the persons whose life we can preserve or terminate are human animals, we properly mean the life of a human being, a person from the time of his or her conception because from then until death a single organism at all times radically capable of participating, under the right conditions of health and maturity, in acts of meaning, choosing, and carrying out choices. A human being's life, like the life of any organism, is a coordinated system of physico-chemical processes maintained in dynamic equilibrium by homeostatic controls,

---

[2] Note that the Latin title of *EV* is *De vitae humanae inviolabili bono*—On the inviolable good of human life.

and one's death is correspondingly the collapse of that integrated organic functioning and its irreversible decomposition. So one's life, the life of any human being, is one's very reality as that being, that person, who came into being at conception, unless anomalously at the time of an event such as twinning by extrinsically initiated embryo-splitting. Death, and only bodily death, ends that personal reality (leaving a spiritual remnant of so reduced a kind that St Thomas could say, and repeat, *anima mea non est ego*: my soul is not me, and if only my soul is saved, I am not saved). The death we are considering, then, is the termination, the destruction of the very reality of a human person. There is a culture *of death* when and where there is a more or less systematized willingness to *choose to* hasten or otherwise bring about the death of human beings, that is, a readiness, however reluctantly, to act or forbear from acting with a purpose of killing someone.

Since one's reality as a person can be promoted, protected, respected, neglected, damaged, or destroyed by human choice, life, human life, figures most commonly in one's thinking as a *good*, a value, a *reason* for acting. But talk, accurate though it is, of the good or value of human *life* should not be allowed to obscure the fact that what we are talking of is in every case the very existence and reality of an individual *person*. A society in which people are treated as having the right to suppress life, whether of themselves or of others, is a society whose culture approves of acts *against the person* (*EV* 4.2), and thus is willing that some people (characteristically the strong) exercise a kind of power over others that is unbounded or absolute in as much as it is power over their very existence (cf. *EV* 12.1, 20.3, 23.4).

Experience shows that in our culture, neither of the facts to which I have been drawing attention is welcome to those whose attitudes and practices I am considering. There is much reluctance to admit that those whose lives they are willing to terminate are human persons. And there is much reluctance to admit that these deaths are *intended*, or that it matters that they are intended rather than simply accepted as a side effect of something else. There is something healthy about this reluctance, though nothing healthy about what it generates by way of spurious argumentation or mere rhetoric and evasion. Conversely, there is something intellectually satisfactory but humanly deplorable about the clear-cut willingness of those who, like the American liberal philosopher Jeffrey Reiman, plainly articulate and defend the thesis that the constitutional and moral right to abortion is precisely the right to *kill* the unborn child, and to make sure that it dies, and that this great right would be unjustly denied if it were interpreted as merely the right to remove the fetus, or have it removed, from one's body[3] (the right famously defended in the early days of 'pro-choice' abortive feminism by Judith Jarvis Thomson). There is the same combination of the clear and the callousing in Reiman's associated thesis that—contrary to our law and tradition—even after birth one has no rights until one has a self-reflective consciousness, some years on in childhood. Positions like Reiman's remain uncomfortably advanced for the main body of those who treat abortion as a right and, in its way, a good—but 'advanced' is the right word: his position is at the point of their culture's, that is, their sub-culture's, trajectory or dynamic.

II

In seeking the deepest roots of the struggle between the 'culture of life' and 'the culture of death'...we have to go to the heart of the tragedy being experienced by modern man: *the eclipse of the sense of God and of man*, typical of a social and cultural climate dominated by secularism...(*EV* 21.1).

...[T]he loss of contact with God's wise design is the deepest root of modern man's confusion...By living 'as if God did not exist', man loses sight not only of the mystery of God, but also of...the mystery of his own being (*EV* 22, 3–4).

That is how the encyclical of 25 March 1995 makes the causal link suggested in the title of my reflections. The encyclical's proposal of this causal link is a theological reflection rather than a teaching of faith; it has some grounding in theology's sources, as the encyclical itself reminds us by quoting Romans 1: 28: 'since they did not see fit to acknowledge God, God gave them up to a debased mind and to improper conduct'. But that is only a phase in a more extended and complex causal analysis by St Paul, running from verses 21 to 32 of Romans 1, and this larger analysis the encyclical does not take up. All in all we have good reason to undertake our own reflections about secularism's bearing on the two issues I have pointed to: the worth and significance of human existence and personal reality, and the significance of intention and of misconceptions or misrepresentations of intention, in shaping a culture and shaping it as 'a veritable *structure of sin*' (*EV* 12.1).

What is the secularism that the encyclical says is a fundamental root of a more or less systematized contemporary willingness to kill some sorts of weak and dependent people? It is not respect for the secular, that which is not divine, sacred, or ecclesiastical. After all, 'secular' is a word minted by Latin Christians. Jerome's Latin New Testament uses it for Greek words signifying the affairs of this world, sometimes neutrally the world of time

---

[3] Reiman, *Critical Moral Liberalism*, 190. See further my debate with him in 2000c, and essay I.16.

rather than eternity,[4] and the daily life of any human society,[5] sometimes pejoratively as matters which distract us from realities and dispositions of lasting worth.[6] Aquinas uses it regularly, and often quite without negative connotations: he will say, for example, that in matters which concern the good of the political community (*bonum civile*), Christians should generally obey the directives of the *secular* authorities rather than the ecclesiastical.[7] Nothing startling about that: the Lord's 'Render to Caesar the things that are Caesar's, and to God the things that are God's' (Matthew 22: 21 and par.) points us away from theocracy or any other general supremacy of states over the Church or of the Church over states or their governments, laws, and citizens.

No doubt this Christian differentiating of the secular from the sacred is only one instance or aspect of wider processes called by social historians 'secularisation', processes which involve the extension of human understanding and control over fields of life formerly so little accessible to human science and technology that it seemed reasonable to attempt to manage them instead by prayer. Christianity encourages secularization of this kind, by insisting on the transcendence of God and the intelligibility of creation, with its consequent accessibility to the *natural* sciences and, accordingly, to technological exploitation. Secularism is another matter.

Like all significant realities, this mindset or family of mindsets is not tied to any word such as 'secular', 'secularization', or 'secularism'. What we call secularism, Elizabethan philosophers and academics called atheism. The philosophical works of John Case, Oxford's and England's leading academic philosopher of the last quarter of the sixteenth century,[8] are the first 3,000 pages of academic work published by the Oxford University Press, of which he was in many respects the real founder. In their introductions and dedicatory letters to the great politicians of the age, they express a strong sense that atheism has made vast inroads into English culture. To some extent what John Case was pointing to was literally the belief that there is no God; to a greater extent it was what Vatican II was to call forgetting God[9] and *Evangelium Vitae* was to call losing the sense of God and 'living "as if God did not exist"' (*EV* 22, 4). But here it will be useful to make some distinctions offered to us by Plato, who reflected deeply on secularism and atheism, without using those words.

---

    [4] II Timothy 1: 9; Titus 1: 2.   [5] I Corinthians 6: 3–4.
    [6] See II Timothy 2: 4; Titus 2: 12.
    [7] *Sent.* II d. 44 exp. textus ad 4: ... magis obediendum potestati saeculari quam spirituali.
    [8] For an introduction to Case, see Schmitt, *John Case and Aristotelianism in Renaissance England.*
    [9] GS 36.

In his great last work, *Laws*, Plato sketches a cluster of dispositions—if you like, cultures—which shape up around one or other of three propositions: there is no God; or, no God has any concern with human affairs; or, any such divine concern with the human is easily appeased by a superficial piety and requires no demanding reform of human vice.[10] The corresponding character types described by Plato are well recognizable in more recent times. And the three propositions—no God; God absent; God soft-spirited[11]—match closely modern secularism's characteristic forms: atheism; or a deistic assumption that human history knows no divine intervention, no revelation of God's intentions for us; or a 'liberal' religiosity which presumes upon divine benevolence, and has no time for warnings of the alienation from God inherent in immorality and potentially final (as Plato too warns in his prophetic meditation on wrongdoing's retribution, the *Republic*'s myth of Er).[12]

Though Plato's strongest indignation is reserved for the position ascribing to God a soft-spirited fatuity contemptible in men and women, his most vigorous argumentation (foreshadowing Aristotle in *Metaphysics* book I.4) confronts the first and second positions, which deny mind's sway in the cosmos. Atheistic materialism's claim that all is ultimately sheer chance and brute inexplicable necessity truncates the investigative quest of science and philosophy for intelligibility and explanation wherever it can be found. And deistic denial of all-governing divine providence underestimates the all-creative, all-sustaining, and all-penetrating power of the maker's practical intellect.

But Plato judges that the practical significance of the three positions is in each case essentially the same: the withering away of reverence for God, of a steady, uncringing, inspiriting fear of the Lord.[13] We can readily see that secularism, in this practical inner manifestation or resultant, is part of the make-up even of a God-fearing believer, just insofar as one is sinning. In that sense, as Maritain could consider the Church a reality which occupies a part of the believer's spirit, so one can think of secularism as a kind of deficiency detectable to a greater or lesser degree in every human soul except the authentic saints'. Many if not all of us, with our friends and colleagues, seem to live in some sense as secularists; we have motives of sympathy and affection, as well as reasons of principle, to turn sharply aside from Plato

---

[10] See *Laws* X 885b, 888c, 901d, 902e–903a, 908b–d, 909a–b. Plato usually speaks of 'gods' or 'the gods', but when getting to the heart of the matter switches to talk of God or 'the god' (see 902e, 903d, 910b).

[11] See *Laws* X 901e, 903a. Also *Republic* 365d–e.

[12] *Republic* X 614b–621d; see also *Laws* X 903d; *Gorgias* 523a–527e.

[13] See *Laws* XII 967d: *bebaiōs theosebē*. Plato does not speak of the Lord; but the divine 'mover of the pieces' (*petteutes*: 903d) has a similar dignity.

when he plans fierce penal repression of secularists by the Guardians of the Laws.[14] In reflecting on secularism, one is considering a public reality, the secularism which shapes public debate, deliberation, dispositions, and action, and is strong in our education and culture. One is considering the ideas, not the people as such. People are often less consistent, and better, than their theories and dispositions. There is little profit in trying to estimate whether and in what ways secularism's dominance now is greater than in Plato's Athens, or John Case's Oxford and London, or is lesser than in Andropov's Leningrad. Western secularism takes many different forms, often under the influence of the faith it supplants. What concerns us now is the inherent link between 'the loss of contact with God's wise design' (*EV* 22, 3) and the willingness to use the killing of human beings as a culturally approved, indeed publicly cultivated means if not also have it as an end (as it is in the nuclear final retaliation which remains a part of US and, in another way, UK public policy).

I think I see in one of Shakespeare's plays an extended and elaborate comic and bitter-sweet reminiscence of John Case, presented on stage for good reasons, a few months after his death. Be that as it may, one of the questions which the playwright, like Case, took up again and again, in work after work, is whether God intervenes in history by acts outside the order of nature. As the wise 'old lord' Lafeu says in *All's Well that Ends Well* (2.3.1ff.): 'They say miracles are past; and we have our philosophical persons to make modern [usual] and familiar things supernatural and causeless.' 'Thing causeless' means perhaps something without natural, this-worldly causes, perhaps the uncaused cause itself, doubtless (in Shakespeare's way) both. Lafeu is commenting on the healing of the king by the heroine Helena, and in a moment will say that it was by 'the very hand of heaven', showing 'In a most weak and debile minister great power, great transcendence'. In this he echoes what Helena had said when offering the king this healing:

> He that of greatest works is finisher
> Oft does them by the weakest minister:
> So holy writ in babes hath judgment shown,
> When judges have been babes; great floods have flown
> From simple sources; and great seas have dried,
> When miracles have by the greatest been denied.

'I must not hear thee...', the King breaks in to say. Helena responds: 'Inspired merit...'—resonant words indeed in late Elizabethan Protestant England—

---

[14] See *Laws* X 907d–910d.

Inspirèd merit so by breath is barr'd:
It is not so with Him that all things knows
As 'tis with us that square our guess by shows;
But most it is presumption in us when
The help of heaven we count the act of men.

The proposition that 'miracles are ceased' was a Protestant teaching—
one favoured by the Bishop of London of the day—which Shakespeare
with knowing anachronism had earlier put on the lips of the Archbishop
of Canterbury at the outset of *Henry V* (1.1.68). In that earlier play, as in
All's Well, the drama sets itself against the proposition, and suggests the
opposite thought, which the king himself articulates after Agincourt:

> O God, thy arm was here,
> And not to us, but to thy arm alone
> Ascribe we all. When, without stratagem,
> But in plain shock and even play of battle,
> Was ever known so great and little loss
> On one part and on th'other? Take it God,
> For it is none but thine.
> EXETER   'Tis wonderful.

And so on for several more exchanges, concluding with Henry's 'Do we
all holy rites: Let there be sung *Non nobis* and *Te Deum*…'—*Non nobis*: Not
to us, O Lord, but to your name give glory…Our God is in the heavens;
whatever pleases him he does.[15] As the editor of the play's current Oxford
edition remarks, commenting on the night scene where Henry goes about
his camp before the battle: 'Out of that night's anguished recognition of
his utter dependence on God comes the wonder of "O God, thy arm *was*
here" (4.8.104)—a line which demonstrates how easily, in performance,
"The platitudes of piety can become ultimate statements of overwhelming
power".'[16]

When Owen Chadwick in Cambridge investigated what his book title
calls *The Secularization of the European Mind in the Nineteenth Century*, he
concluded that 'near the heart of that elusive shift in the European mind' is
'the axiom, miracles do not happen'. My point is not that we should locate
the line between what is immediately from nature and what is immediately
from beyond nature just where John Case or Shakespeare's heroes and
heroines locate it, but that in 1600 thoughtful and penetrating minds like
Case and his philosophical junior William Shakespeare could see a main
hub of cultural change—or epicentre of cultural disintegration—just

---

[15] Psalm 115: 1, 3.   [16] *Henry V* (ed. Gary Taylor, *The Oxford Shakespeare* [1982], 1998), 48.

where the cultural historian of the period running up to 1900 can locate it. The 'axiom' that Protestants levelled against transubstantiation and the interventions of the saints had, perhaps unrecognized by those who wielded it, hidden premises, and these would before long be turned against all sacred history and revelation itself—against the Resurrection of Jesus and the resurrection of anyone at the last day, against all sacraments and all petitionary prayer, and so, in the end, against the twin truths of Creation and Providence, in their clear Christian articulation (for what could be more miraculous than creation of the universe out of nothing?) and in their less clear but very firm prototypes in the philosophy, the searching judgments, of Plato and Aristotle.

It is a truth of the faith that the spiritual soul, 'that by which [the human person] is most especially in God's image',[17] is in each and every case 'created immediately by God'.[18]

The human *body* shares in the dignity of 'the image of God': it is a human body precisely because it is animated by a spiritual soul...[and] the unity of soul and body is so profound that one has to consider the soul to be the 'form' of the body.[19]

St Thomas puts this even more vigorously when he insists, again and again, that in animals (including us) soul is the body's very *act*, so that in human beings the immortal spiritual soul, whose most distinctive acts are of insight and free choice, is, in each of us, what makes one a *live* body and makes all one's bodily functions, even the least 'mental', *human* bodily functions. God's creative causality *initiates* and is *in* one's life—one's very reality—in a way more direct and immediate than his causality of everything else in the order of nature, which is a causality that works not 'immediately' but through the natural causes which with their effects are the subject-matter of the natural sciences.

So for each of us the gift of life, of our very self as given prior to our free choices, is more radically because more directly the *gift of the Creator* than is any other kind of reality in the universe known or knowable by the empirical natural sciences. This gift is in the first instance a set of radical capacities, capacities which are actual and present in one as a zygote even though as yet in their initial and least developed way of being. There is no evidence of any substantial change—from something else into me—after the time of conception, save perhaps in the case of monozygotic twinning. So: then and there, each of us was actually capable, albeit as yet only radically, of understanding, reflecting, judging, laughing, choosing, promising, and praying. So even then and there, as zygotes, each of us was

[17] *CCC* 363.   [18] *CCC* 366; also *EV* 43 n. 32.   [19] *CCC* 365.

by God's gift *superior* to the most sensitive, alertly conscious, responsive, and lovable mature dog or great ape, because even then we had capacities which included all the kinds of capacity that dogs or apes have *and some more.*

And the *some more* that we had and have, and that sub-rational animals cannot have, are those that are not only God-given but god-like, God-imaging, far more directly and essentially than any other kind of thing whose activities, capabilities, and nature we can study.

Our reason for judging that human capacities image God's actuality in a specifically close way is this. Our natural, that is common sense and philosophical knowledge that God created and sustains in act the universe—knowledge attainable independently of any divine acts of self-revealing communication—is reached by a process of inquiry, understanding, reflecting, and judging, a process in which one is conscious, to be sure, but with a consciousness not so much of undergoing experiences or having responses as of *acting*—in this case, of carrying forward the action of responsibly raising questions, pursuing reflections, wrestling with objections or counter-hypotheses, and following one's inner argument to its conclusion in the act of judgment. All this is an exercise of freedom, for the opportunity of turning aside from the process is always available, and can have many attractions. And all this is a paradigm, a salient instance, of that 'interiority' (*interioritas*) in virtue of which, as Vatican II's *Gaudium et Spes* says, each of us outstrips / excels (*excedit*) the entire universe of things (*universitatem rerum*) (GS 14.2), an interiority described a little earlier as one's having been, or being, created 'capable [*capax*] of knowing and loving one's Creator' (GS 12.3; *EV* 34.5). But this inquiring reflection is, moreover, an imaging of *God.* For, in freely and responsibly following these ways of seeking the ultimate explanation of each and every thing, the explanation of each and every system and process in this universe, what we conclude is that there is a reality that needs no explanation, and needs no explanation because always and inherently and essentially *actual*, in need of nothing because never needing to be moved or changed from potentiality to act, never needing to be brought into existence or developed or sustained. And this reality (God)—unlike all other realities because its *what it is* includes *that it is*—has all that it takes to explain not only the reality of everything, of every system and process with which we are or can become acquainted, but equally the intelligibility, the orderliness which, though not unmixed with fortuity and disorderliness, is so characteristic of our world. The explanation of this orderliness is as, ultimately, a directedness: God has projected and is projecting the whole order of things and each of its sub-systems in something like the way one projects an intelligible proposal into reality by adopting it—choosing it—and putting it into effect—carrying out one's intention(s).[20]

The empirical scientific and philosophical understanding of the material world is a great work of spirit, that is, of human intelligence, purposeful mental effort, and intellectual and moral responsibility. The creation of the material world, even if it had not included intelligent bodily realities such as human beings, would have been an inconceivably greater work of spirit, of divine intelligence, and freedom in envisaging the infinite range of possible universes, and choosing the one which would come into actuality by being intended and chosen for existence. Plato and Aristotle stand, as it were on Mount Nebo across the Jordan from Jericho, on the very edge of and as if seeing by anticipation the promised land, the philosophical understanding reached and articulated by their Christian successors that human willing includes free choices in which *nothing* either external or internal determines which of the options one will adopt, and that the universe is not only ordered by and to the supremely actual being but actually created *ex nihilo* by an utterly transcendent free choice, a choice among infinitely many incompatibly alternative and incommensurably very good universes, a choice determined by nothing save the act of choosing, the divine will(ing) itself. Contemplation of the truth of God's transcendent freedom and power, in creating and sustaining and ordering the entire universe of everything there will ever be beyond Himself, has vastly deepened philosophical and commonsense understanding and appreciation of human dignity, and of the significance of intention in human life and action. When the truth of creation and providential sustaining and ordering is misunderstood, rejected, or forgotten, there emerge as if inherently caused and reinforced by, and reinforcing, the misunderstanding, rejection, and forgetfulness of intention in human moral life, and the explicit or implicit denial of the equality of all human beings in personal dignity.

To speak of dignity is to speak both of superiority (e.g. in power, excellence, status) and of what has intrinsic worth for its own sake. Our capacity for acts of free choice is a capacity both bodily and intellectual, material and spiritual, for in human beings all that is material and bodily is informed and actualized by a soul that is not only living and animal but also intellectual-spiritual. So each of us has every level of being—the physical solidity and dynamisms of a star or a galaxy, the chemical and biological complexity and self-directedness of a genome, a tree, or a lion, *and* then some. The *more* we have is the capacity to understand all these other kinds of reality, to reason about them and about reasoning itself,

---

[20] See *Aquinas* 298–312.

to replicate and transform other beings on all those levels of reality, and with self-mastery's freedom to *choose* whether or not to do so and in these and other ways *how to live*. These spiritual capacities subsist even when our bodily make-up is too immature, injured, or decayed to allow them to be actualized fully, or perhaps perceptibly at all. It is possession of these capacities that makes us each human and the equal of each other of us in basic dignity, worth, value, and so in human rights.

Nietzsche denied the existence of God because (in the last analysis) he could not bear that there be any being so transcendently his superior.[21] So he surrendered the truth to his own feelings, to a kind of spiritual passion, to pride itself. With the truth about God there disappeared the truth about human equality, dignity, and worth as such, and there opened up the way to Nietzsche's expression of active contempt for the weak and impatience with anyone willing to prefer care for them in their weakness to terminating their impaired existence. It is not so easy, usually, to trace the motivations of standard contemporary academic materialism. John Searle testifies against some forms of that materialism, while also exemplifying another form of it himself, and his testimony is that there are unstated assumptions behind the drive to adopt positions which are as absurd, but as commonplace among contemporary philosophers, as the denial of the existence of the mental—the denial even that anyone is conscious. And the most significant of these unstated assumptions, in his view, is what he calls a 'terror' of what seem to be the alternatives, among which he gives prominence (right alongside 'spiritualism') to 'belief in the immortality of the soul'.[22] One can only speculate whether some such terror lies behind Searle's own stated belief that one of 'the obvious facts of physics' is 'that the world consists entirely of physical particles in fields of force'[23]—as if physics were qualified to establish the non-existence of facts or realities of a kind other than those it studies, facts such as that I *mean* this, or that so-and-so was being economical with the truth when he said he was going to the Law Library to put 'the finishing touches' to his conference paper. But in general it would be rash to assume that fear of one or another element in Christian moral teaching plays no great part in the genesis, defence, and successful diffusion of materialistic 'scientific worldviews'.

What the Holy See calls the culture of death is, as I said earlier, a culture or sub-culture constituted by two main dispositions: willingness publicly to regard and treat some human beings as not persons, inherently entitled to basic rights and justice; and publicly unashamed willingness to

---

[21] This is demonstrated from Nietzsche's writings by Voegelin, *Science, Politics, and Gnosticism*, 53–73.

[22] Searle, *The Rediscovery of the Mind*, 13.   [23] *Ibid.*, xii.

choose and intend to kill such human beings, and to carry out, promote, and legally protect such choices and intentions. The opposing 'culture of life', then, is the culture or sub-culture—aspiring and entitled in reason to be a universal culture—which rejects those dispositions. Accordingly, the culture of life defends not only the reality of soul which is the root of human dignity, equality, and rights, but also the significance of *intention* in one's conscientious deliberations and accordingly also in moral teaching.

Thus the whole teaching of the *Catechism of the Catholic Church* about the kinds of act which are excluded by the fifth commandment, that is, the *Catechism's* entire treatment of legitimate defence as distinct from the intrinsic homicidal wrongs of murder, abortion, euthanasia, and suicide, is all placed under the distinction between carrying out an intention to kill and doing what causes death only as a side effect. Of course causing death as an unintended side effect is often an injustice,[24] but that wrong is relative to the circumstances whereas the commandment protecting at least innocent human beings is not; in line with natural reason, it excludes all intentional killing, exceptionlessly, whatever the circumstances—as *Evangelium Vitae* 75.1 puts it, 'always and everywhere, without exception'. Intentional killing, sometimes called 'direct' killing in one of the senses of that ambiguous word, is killing done in carrying out a choice to deprive someone of his life either as an end in itself or as a means to some other end, good or bad: see *Evangelium Vitae* 57.5, 62.1; *Catechism* 2271.

The teaching of the Church in defence of life, marking out the minimum elements and backbone of the culture of life, is thus a teaching founded precisely on intention understood in terms of what is chosen, willed, as an end or as a means, as distinct from what is *caused* perhaps with full *foresight* of lethal consequences but is for the chooser and causer neither an end nor a means (i.e. is a side effect, or, as is sometimes less clearly said, an indirect killing).

So one of the important results of secularism in our culture is loss of grip on the reality of intention, and its distinction from bringing about as a side effect. One finds this result of secularism in many contexts besides the pronouncements and decisions of certain British ministers of health and American courts. Germain Grisez, Joseph Boyle, and I recently wrote a long essay exploring the significance of intention in common sense, Roman Law and common law, and in Catholic moral teaching, and developing a philosophical analysis of the concept, on the basis of which we responded to criticisms which the Notre Dame theologian Jean Porter had levelled against our earlier discussions of it, and made our own criticisms

---

[24] *CCC* 2290.

of some of the discussion of intention in the works of some of our friends and collaborators such as William E. May and Fr Kevin Flannery SJ.[25] Since our work on intention had been the entire subject-matter of Jean Porter's essay in *Theological Studies* in 1996, we submitted our essay to the same journal, the leading Jesuit theological periodical at least in America. The editor, Fr Michael Fahey SJ, after six months' consultation, wrote praising the essay for its quality, but rejecting it for its subject-matter. The distinction between intention and side effect, or 'direct' and 'indirect', is, he said (summarizing the advice of the moral theologians he had consulted), a distinction which

admittedly has relevance for some and indeed might have importance in interpreting parts of the encyclical *Veritatis splendor*. But in the long run, it was seen, the logic is not judged as generally helpful for most moral theologians, let alone other theologians whose ministry lies elsewhere.[26]

I think this is probably all true. The distinction has indeed relevance for 'some', such as John Paul II and other bishops responsible for the *Catechism*, and *Evangelium Vitae*, and for the entire tradition running from Aquinas to Pius XII and Paul VI, and behind Aquinas back to Augustine and implicitly the author of the Bible's book of Wisdom. But these 'some' seem to count for little with 'most moral theologians'. Secularism has made an astonishingly rapid and far-reaching penetration among them. With striking completeness and casualness the leading theologians responsible for disseminating proportionalism began to make two particular errors. One error was and is about the tradition, the doctrine, that they were rejecting: it was their claim that the moral precepts they were rejecting, mostly in the field(s) of killing and sex, are precepts about what is 'directly' or 'indirectly' *caused*,[27] when in truth those precepts concerned kinds of intending, choosing, and carrying out one's intentions and choices. The other error was not historical but analytical or philosophical: it was and is their claim that what one causes as a side effect is a *means* to the consequences one seeks to achieve by one's action. In the tradition, properly understood and clarified, and in a sound analysis, whatever is willed as a means is intended, and chosen, and is part of what *Veritatis Splendor* 78.1 calls the object of one's act. That object, as this encyclical makes clear, must be understood from 'the perspective of the acting person', and is *not* 'a process or an event of the merely physical order, to be assessed on the basis of its ability to bring about a given state of affairs in the outside world',

---

[25] Essay II.13 (2001a).
[26] Letter of Michael A. Fahey SJ to John Finnis, 13 January 2000.
[27] See the quotations from Peschke and Fuchs in *MA* 77 n. 38.

but is rather 'the proximate end of a deliberate decision which determines the act of willing on the part of the acting person'. Understanding action from the perspective of the deliberating and acting person is the key to understanding the backbone of morality in the life and death issues that are our concern here. Adopting this perspective, I should add, makes demands on the thinking of those who uphold the 'culture of life', and upon 'traditional' theologians as well as on those who would sideline them as 'some'.

I have discussed elsewhere the collapsing of intention into foresight and causation in such witnesses of much contemporary culture as the judgments of the federal Courts of Appeals in the assisting suicide cases *Compassion in Dying v Washington* (9th Circuit, 1996) and *Quill v Vacco* (2nd Circuit, 1997).[28] These misunderstandings of intention or purpose were prominent in official and semi-official reactions to recent attempts in England to declare illegal the withholding of treatment, care, and sustenance 'with a purpose of hastening or otherwise causing death'. They reappear in many places, notably among those who write and speak explicitly or implicitly as 'secular humanists'.

I have already said here a good deal about why secularism can never be a genuine humanism. The loss of an understanding of intention and its significance among the many teachers of Catholic morals who are in revolt against Catholic faith and life should be of concern also to those theologians whose ministry, in Fr Fahey's engaging words, 'lies elsewhere'. For as James J. Walter remarked not so long ago, neither he himself 'nor any other proportionalist can see here how God's moral will is only disposed indirectly or permissively vis-à-vis non-moral evil (natural defect)'.[29] But the great tradition of theological reflection on the divine will and providence, expounded by St John Damascene, the last of the Fathers, and by Aquinas, insists that God indeed does not will even *natural* defects to *be*, but only wills to permit them, because for God to intend *anything* which intelligence would call an evil is inconsistent with his holiness.

God's holiness seems faint indeed in the works of proportionalist theologians—read them and see—and is denied, one way or another, in each of the forms of secularism differentiated and discussed by Plato. But we too can forget it, in one or other of the ways which the Lord speaks of in the parable of the Sower: lack of understanding of the Word (stony ground), lack of endurance in the face of trial (shallow roots), and lastly

---

[28] 79 F 3d 790, reversed sub nom. *Washington v Glucksberg* 521 US 702 (1997); 80 F 3d 716, reversed sub nom. *Vacco v Quill* 521 US 793 (1997).
[29] Walter, 'Response to John Finnis' at 74–7.

what Shakespeare's Bastard Falconbridge transposes to 'los[ing] my way among the thorns and dangers of this world'[30]:

Other seeds fell among thorns, and the thorns grew up and choked them.... [T]his is the one who hears the word, but the cares of the world and the lure of riches choke the word, and it yields nothing.[31]

The cares of this world: *he merimna tou aiōnos—sollicitudo saeculi istius—* our Lord's warning against a kind of secularism by default.

---

[30] *King John* 4.3.140.   [31] Matthew 13: 7, 22.

23

ON RETRANSLATING *HUMANAE VITAE*[*]

I

In May 2008, to mark the encyclical's fortieth anniversary in July, I did a retranslation of *Humanae Vitae* for the Catholic Truth Society (CTS), who are the Holy See's publishers in England and whose pamphlets on Catholic doctrine and culture are a principal resource for the faithful and for inquiring people throughout Britain. The CTS have always had an English translation of *Humanae Vitae*; as I recount in the notes at the end of my translation, they published one in September 1968, a revision of the one published in Rome at or about the time of the encyclical's publication at the end of July 1968, and they issued in 1970 a revised version of this revision, a version that remained in print down to 2008. The most well-known American translation, which appears on the Vatican website, dates from 1969 and is itself another revision of the CTS's September 1968 version. All these English translations are essentially translations of the Italian version published by the Holy See itself in July 1968; the English versions' revisions are intended to line up better with the Latin.

My belief is that, even if it was first drafted in French, the preparation of the encyclical would largely have been done in Italian, but that toward the end of the process the Pope would have worked with, and signed off, the Latin version, which is the only fully authentic text. So when I was asked by the CTS to advise on and perhaps tweak the best English translation, and then found myself dissatisfied with almost everything in detail, I decided to translate strictly from the Latin, and to point out in endnotes where and how this diverges from the Italian and the contemporaneous French, English, Spanish, and so forth. My translation is, I hope, very close to the style, feel, and meaning of the Latin.

Anyway, what I have to offer here is simply some reflections on an encyclical on which I commented in the leading English law journal

[*] Unpublished: the Josef Pieper Lecture for 2008, Notre Dame Center for Ethics and Culture.

in August 1968 (because its editor and I were at lunch together in our college on the day the encyclical came out),[1] and then again in an English theological journal in 1970,[2] and now, forty years on, have retranslated.

II

The former CTS translation had a regrettable blurb or covernote, prudish, evasive, and legalistic. So I wrote a new one:

In its profound teachings on marriage, the Second Vatican Council in 1965 stated precisely what difficulties husband and wife can face in relating their mutual love and the parenthood which naturally arises from expressions of that love. The Council reiterated the ancient and once universal Christian teaching that the morality of married intimacy depends on 'preserving the full meaning of mutual giving and human procreation in a context of true love'. It said that some questions about ways of regulating procreation were being studied by a commission (set up when the 'pill' became available), so that the Pope could give his judgment on how God's law applies to those ways.

Humanae Vitae is Pope Paul VI's judgment, issued in 1968, applying the Council's teaching to those new questions, and later solemnly reaffirmed by Pope John Paul II and the Synod of Bishops. It is a momentous restatement of how love must, and must not, be expressed if it is to be *marital* love, true to the nature of human persons and of real marriage as a high and most significant calling.

I said it was momentous because I think any papal document that failed to reaffirm the teaching that had been universal in Christendom until the early twentieth century would have been even more momentous for the fate of Christianity; and continued failure to issue any document after the expectation had become widespread in 1967 that change in the teaching was imminent would have been equally momentous for the future of the Catholic Church. That the document was issued, and both reaffirmed and clarified the teaching, was therefore momentous.

But the first paragraph of my blurb is more to the point. The very close relationship between the 1968 encyclical and the 1965 Council document *Gaudium et Spes* is left understated in the encyclical and is largely overlooked and forgotten. From its first sentence,[3] and through the doctrinal exposition that runs from sec. 7 to the decisive judgment in sec. 14, *Humanae Vitae* very closely echoes the five core sections of the part of *Gaudium et Spes* that deals with marriage. These teachings of the Council in its ambitious

---

[1] 1968e.   [2] 1970b.

[3] The transmitting of human life, a most serious role in which spouses share freely and responsibly in the activity of God the Creator, has always brought them great joys, and sometimes no few difficulties and deprivations.

Pastoral Constitution on the Church in the Modern World head toward its teaching about birth control in sec. 51. This teaching, like *Humanae Vitae* after it, begins with a brief statement of the real difficulties that lead married couples to consider contraception and/or abortion. Having condemned abortion and infanticide as unspeakably wrongful, sec. 51 finally comes to the marital intercourse (the acts proper to marriage) whose human and moral character is what is at stake in deciding whether or not to contracept. Without ever articulating the concept of contraception, the Council concludes:

So, where it is a matter of harmonizing conjugal love with responsible transmission of life, the moral character of a way of acting does not depend solely on a sincere intention or a weighing of motives, but must be determined by objective criteria drawn from the nature of persons and of their acts, criteria that, in a context of true love, *preserve the full sense of mutual self-giving and of human procreation*—which cannot be done without whole-heartedly cultivating the virtue of married chastity. In regulating procreation, sons and daughters of the Church faithful to these principles cannot rightly follow ways judged wrongful by the Magisterium [the teaching authority of the Church] in its interpreting of divine law.[4]

In the footnote to this, it adds references to the condemnations of contraception by Pius XI in 1930 and Pius XII in 1951, and finishes:

Certain questions which need further and closer investigation have been referred by order of the Pope to a Commission for the Study of Population, Family and Birth, so that when it has completed its task, the Pope may give judgment.[5]

What did Paul VI, in approving this footnote, think he would have to give judgment about when the Commission had finished its studies? All the evidence is in line with what is recounted by Germain Grisez, who was closer to these matters, from June 1965 through early July 1966 (the Commission's report having been delivered to the Pope in the last

---

[4] Moralis igitur indoles rationis agendi, ubi de componendo amore coniugali cum responsabili vitae transmissione agitur, non a sola sincera intentione et aestimatione motivorum pendet, sed obiectivis criteriis, ex personae eiusdemque actuum natura desumptis, determinari debet, quae integrum sensum mutuae donationis ac humanae procreationis in contextu veri amoris observant; quod fieri nequit nisi virtus castitatis coniugalis sincero animo colatur. Filiis Ecclesiae, his principiis innixis, in procreatione regulanda, vias inire non licet, quae a Magisterio, in lege divina explicanda, improbantur.

[5] Cf. Pius XI, Litt. Encycl. *Casti Connubii*: AAS 22 (1930), pp. 559–61; D-S 3716–18; Pius XII, *Allocutio Conventui Unionis Italicae inter Obstetrices*, 29 October 1951: AAS 43 (1951), pp. 835–54; Paulus VI, *Allocutio ad Em.mos Patres Purpuratos*, 23 iunii 1964: AAS 56 (1964), pp. 581–9. Quaedam quaestiones quae aliis ac diligentioribus investigationibus indigent, iussu Summi Pontificis, Commissioni pro studio populationis, familiae et natalitatis traditae sunt, ut postquam illa munus suum expleverit, Summus Pontifex iudicium ferat. Sic stante doctrina Magisterii, S. Synodus solutiones concretas immediate proponere non intendit. (Fn. 14 to GS 51.)

week of June), than perhaps anyone still living today: Paul VI, recounts Grisez, wanted *Gaudium et Spes* to say that what Pius XI and Pius XII (like the tradition before them) had judged wrongful (contraception as then understood) is indeed always wrong; but he was not certain, in 1965, whether using the pill *is* a kind of contracepting in that sense, or not.[6] So that was what he expected to have to judge, and what the Council expected him to judge when it said in its footnote that it was not intending to articulate 'concrete solutions' itself—*immediate* (Latin), that is directly, without an intermediary—but only mediately, through the eventual papal judgment.

As we know, the Commission's work,[7] and his own reflection, led Paul VI to see with complete clarity what is nowadays also clear to everyone, that there is no moral difference between using the pill and any other way of contracepting (except insofar as the pill, or some kinds of pill, can also induce abortion by preventing or even disturbing implantation). His decisive judgment is given in *HV* 14 without using the word contraception and without mentioning any particular method. It identifies the relevant *kind of act* which *of its nature*, its identity, the kind of act it is, is always, intrinsically, wrong. And this identification is entirely by reference to one's *intention* as a choosing person or couple: 'any act which—when marital intercourse is anticipated, being engaged in, or leading to its natural consequences—is *intended* (either as an end or as a means) to impede procreation'. This defining intention is not any *further-out* intention such as is referred to when GS 51 says that the morality of means of birth regulation does not depend on sincere intention or motive—the intention, for example, to avoid over-burdening the mother, or the family. Rather, the intention specified in *HV* 14's moral judgment on contraception is one's *close-in*, proximate, intention to do something *so that* a past, present, or future act of intercourse (including any in a series of future acts of intercourse) shall not result, or shall be made less likely to result, in the procreation that *it*—that act of intercourse—might otherwise have

---

[6] See Grisez and Boyle, 'Response to Our Critics and Our Collaborators' at 257.

[7] 'Germain Grisez on "Humanae Vitae", Then and Now' (2003) <http://www.zenit.org/article-7791?l=english>:

> The final report of the commission was not one of the documents that were leaked to the press, and, so far as I [Grisez] know, it has never been published. The leaked documents, which were misleadingly labeled, were among the appendices to the final report, and none of them was agreed upon by the majority of the 16 cardinals and bishops who made up the commission after it was restructured in February 1966, although they did approve sending those documents along to Paul VI. True, the majority of the theologians, who were then among the periti [experts] advising the cardinals and bishops, had argued that contraception was morally acceptable, and nine of the 16 cardinals and bishops agreed with their position. But *virtually all the theologians and all but one of the cardinals and bishops also agreed that the pill was not morally different from other contraceptives, which had long been condemned.* (Emphasis added.)

resulted in—that is, might have resulted in if one had not done what one in fact did choose (or is about to choose) to do, namely to contracept (use contraception). Since we are talking intention here, all these references to what might result or might have resulted from an act of intercourse are references to what the contracepting person or couple *think* might result—it's that thought which close-in, proximately, motivates them to take the steps we call contracepting. The fundamental idea is of course utterly simple: to have sexual intercourse and prevent *that* act resulting in procreation.

III

As is well known (because one or more people wanting change violated their promise of secrecy by publishing selected Commission papers in the American press in mid-April 1967), Paul VI's Commission reported in late June 1966 that a majority of its members thought the Church's teaching could change so as to acknowledge that contraception, at least when non-abortifacient, can be rightly used by married couples in some, indeed many circumstances. But Paul VI was more interested in reasons than in voting numbers. In giving *his* reasons, he alludes first to the majority's reasons in secs 3 and 6 of *Humanae Vitae*. In sec. 3 the proponents of change speak, in the Pope's paraphrase, putting questions that arise against the background of rising populations, growing hardship, a revaluation of the personhood of women, and the new opportunities for rational control of nature, and concluding:

Given present conditions of life, and the significance that acts of marital intercourse have for spouses' harmony and mutual fidelity, wouldn't it be appropriate to rethink the present moral norms, especially if it is felt that they cannot be adhered to without sacrifices, sometimes requiring heroic effort? Again, applying the so-called principle of totality, couldn't it rightly be accepted that the purpose of making fecundity less prolific but more rational might transform a physically sterilizing act into a morally acceptable and provident birth control? In other words, wouldn't it be right to accept that procreation as a goal applies to the totality of married life rather than to each and every marital act? And given that people today are more aware of their responsibilities, hasn't the time come when the role of transmitting life should be entrusted to their intelligence and will rather than to their bodily rhythms?

The key argument here is that respecting marriage's orientation to procreation need not be a matter of preserving that orientation in each and every marital sexual act; preserving it over 'the totality of married life' can be morally sufficient. The argument is a response, the only response available short of mere rejection, to the Council's teaching that

> where it is a matter of harmonizing conjugal love with responsible transmission of life, the moral character of a way of acting... must be determined by objective criteria drawn from the nature of persons and of their acts, criteria that, in a context of true love, *preserve the full sense* [*sensus*, Italian *il significato*, the meaning] *of mutual self-giving and of human procreation.*

The Commission majority thought the full 'sense' [meaning] of procreation need not be preserved in every act, but need only be preserved in the couple's marriage taken somehow as an enduring whole. Paul VI's judgment about the soundness of that suggestion is given first in sec. 6:

> certain ways of resolving the question... emerged [within the Commission] which were at variance with the moral doctrine on marriage which the Church's magisterium has taught with firmness and constancy.

IV

That reference to the moral doctrine on marriage anticipates the last words of sec. 10 and the first words of sec. 14. Section 10, on 'responsible parenthood', ends by speaking of a morally decisive 'design [*consilium*] manifested in the very nature of marriage and of married acts, and set forth in the Church's constant teaching'.[8] From there sec. 11 moves to its conclusion about what 'the precepts of natural law... interpreted by the Church's constant teaching' require of 'each and every marital act': that each such act 'remain oriented in itself to the procreation of human life'. And sec. 14, which as we've seen defines and condemns contraception, begins: 'On the basis, therefore, of these primary principles of the human and *Christian doctrine of marriage*, I must again declare...'

The full force and meaning of these references to the Christian doctrine of marriage never get articulated in the encyclical. *Humanae Vitae* seems to take for granted what everyone knows: that Christian doctrine on marriage is Christian doctrine about sex and Christian doctrine about natural law. It is Christian doctrine about sex because its central proposition is that sex acts—by 'sex act' I simply mean a sequence of behaviour intended, rightly or wrongly, to lead to someone's sexual satisfaction—are rightful only within marriage. And it is Christian doctrine about natural law because its central proposition is not addressed only to the acts of Christians and

---

[8] '...consilium Dei Creatoris accommodare teneantur, quod hinc ipsa matrimonii eiusque actuum natura exprimit, hinc constans Ecclesiae doctrina declarat.'

doesn't mean rightful or wrongful only for Christians, but is that nobody's sex acts are reasonable and morally acceptable unless they are marital; and this is proposed as part of the content of practical reasonableness, of human moral reasoning accessible even without the aid of any divine revelation. Both the teaching about all non-marital sex acts and the teaching about this being a matter of natural law have been the Christian teaching from the very beginning, as you can see by reading the first two chapters of St Paul's letter to the Romans, not to mention other epistles of his or Jesus's teaching about what marriage *truly and rightly* has been 'from the beginning [*ap archēs*]' (Matthew 19: 4–6). That the claim about reasonableness is not arbitrary is made clear enough by close attention to what Plato and Aristotle and the pagan Roman philosopher Musonius Rufus say, in the midst of a culture for the most part hugely indifferent to male chastity. You can get the gist of Plato's teaching from the conclusion reached, disapprovingly, in the careful study of 'Plato's Sexual Morality' by Anthony Price in his 1989 study of love and friendship in Plato and Aristotle:

Plato's position is like that to which [Pope] Paul [VI] adhered [against the majority recommendation of his Commission that particular acts of contraception should be permitted within a marriage so long as its overall purpose remains non-contraceptive].[9]

(And Price is saying that this line of thought is controlling for Plato's judgment about all sex acts, homo- or heterosexual.)

   You could say, a bit crudely but as a first approximation, that Christian doctrine about sex outside marriage is for the sake of sex inside marriage— more precisely, it is for the sake of marriage and thus of all those persons, in the first instance the children, who are benefited by marriage. And I will now suggest some reasons why and how this is so. I'm not saying that the line of thought I sketch in the next two paragraphs corresponds to anything that Paul VI or his advisers or the Council fathers would have mentioned if asked about the reasons for the classic Christian teaching that sex outside marriage is wrong. It is a line of thought suggested to me by some of Aquinas's teachings about marital intercourse, but extends those teachings in a way that I have not come across elsewhere. I have elaborated it in several writings in and since 1998,[10] and will here only sketch it in

---

   [9] *Love and Friendship in Plato and Aristotle*, 223–35 at 233. We don't have to agree that Paul VI's position is altogether like Plato's; where Plato sees procreation as what makes good moral sense of sex, Paul VI (and the Christian tradition) sees marriage as what makes good moral sense of sex (and sees procreation as what shapes and, along with friendship, makes sense of the institution of marriage).
   [10] Essay III.22 (1997d), secs IV–V. At nn. 120–8 of that essay I respond (in effect) to Price's challenge (*Love and Friendship in Plato and Aristotle*, 232 n. 17) to say why it is morally relevant that

barest outline. The Christian teachings about sex and marriage certainly do not stand or fall with it.

The marital act enables the married couple, husband and wife, to actualize, experience, and express their marriage. But their physical intimacy cannot be really marital, cannot enable them to actualize, experience, and express their marital commitment, unless they are resolved that such intimacy will be, and should have been, exceptionlessly reserved to marital acts before and during marriage. Moreover, their intercourse will be non-marital if, while they're engaging in it with each other, (i) one or both of the spouses *would be willing* (is conditionally willing) to have sex with some other attractive person then and there, or (ii) one spouse (or both), though resolved to have sex only 'within marriage', is so indifferent to the identity or personality of the other that the spirit of his or her engagement in their sexual activities is just as if he were doing it with a call girl or she with a toyboy. (Those are the cases often discussed by Aquinas in his exploration of marital *fides*—about which more in a moment.) Such forms of conditional willingness to engage in non-marital sex acts, indeed any and all forms of conditional willingness to do so, make the intercourse of spouses not truly marital, and are thus against marriage—their marriage and the institution of marriage. But approval of anyone's non-marital sex acts is itself a subtle form of conditional willingness. So married people, and anyone who sees the point of marriage, its indispensable goodness as a form of life needed for children and the survival and well-being of society, must not approve anyone's non-marital sex acts. Doing so implicitly denies that choosing to engage in such behaviour *has the meaning* (or, as we shall see, the conjoined *meanings*) that marriage needs the marital act to have, for it to enable the spouses without illusion to actualize, experience, and express their marriage and its commitment.

Thus the judgment about the need to reserve sex acts to the marital implies also the wrongness of the many more or less manifestly non-marital kinds of sex acts—between persons who are not married to each other, or who could not be married to each other because they are of the same sex, or between a person and a subpersonal animal, or solitary sex, and so forth. Hence the Christian norm, or rather the norm declared in

no homosexual couple can reproduce but not that *this* heterosexual couple cannot. The case of the permanently sterile married couple is a secondary instance of a clear central case (fertile marriage), and the parties to it can do together all the acts of mating that the fertile can do together, and in the same way; any homosexual couple, including one whose partners have made promises to each other of commitment, is part of a spectrum of relationships that have no central case; none of them is an act of mating, any more than oral sex between heterosexuals is, and in the absence of joint biological parenthood any commitment to exclusiveness or permanence as a couple has no intelligibly sufficient point.

Christian teaching to be 'natural', that is universally reasonable—true and right for all—as Jesus and St Paul and the whole tradition certainly declare it to be.

Of course, this teaching against fornication and much else, this teaching of the chastity required in relation to any and every actual or possible human sex act, has always been regarded as severe and difficult, something that separates Christians or Jews and Christians from almost all others, certainly from the pagan world (despite the flickering insights of its very best philosophers). It marked out a dramatic equalizing of the status of men and women. As Elizabeth Anscombe, the leading English Catholic philosopher of the twentieth century, puts it in her booklet *Contraception and Chastity* published by the CTS in 1975 and maintained in print to accompany *Humanae Vitae* ever since: 'Christianity taught that men ought to be as chaste as pagans thought honest women ought to be'.[11] And it went along with the other teaching that dramatically separated Christians and Jews from pagans: rejection of infanticide and abortion. The link, of course, is that chastity is needed for sound marriage and sound marriage is needed for the well-being of children, the fruit of sexual and properly the fruit of marital intercourse. Every pagan knew why a wife's adultery wronged her husband; Christians pointed out, as that rare pagan Musonius Rufus did too, that the *husband's* adultery wrongs the *wife*; their sexual rights in marriage are—naturally, that is to say, in right reason—equal. But this teaching of equality in sexual rights only makes sense if the reserving of sexual acts to marriage and, within marriage, to truly marital acts, is essential to marriage's point and well-being just as the wife's not introducing into the marriage the fruits of her adultery obviously is. And that *reserving* only makes sense if, in Anscombe's words, 'the good and the point of a sexual act is marriage'.[12]

V

What then is marriage's point? Paul VI states it in the first section of his exposition of doctrinal principles, sec. 8, the first of two sections about marital love. This statement successfully sums up the complex teaching about marriage in *Gaudium et Spes* 48–50, and is stated as an explanation of the phrase we have already heard from sec. 10, a phrase introduced in sec. 8: God's design, *consilium*. Marriage, says sec. 8, is no mere product of blind evolution, but rather is a matter of a wise and provident design of love.

---

[11] Geach and Gormally, *Faith in a Hard Ground*, 170–91 at 171.   [12] *Ibid.*, 185.

So husband and wife, through a mutual self-giving which is properly theirs and exclusive to them, develop a communion of persons by which to perfect one another *so as* to cooperate with God in procreating and educating new living beings.

Here beautifully captured is the irreducibly *dual* point and good of marriage: loving union (communion) and responsible procreation, the latter making sense of the exclusiveness and permanence of the former. The *commitment* to this 'mutual self-giving which is properly theirs and exclusive to them [this husband and wife]', is what the tradition called *fides* and Aquinas showed is the proper object of conjugal love and of every marital act (marital intercourse). This *fides* is not merely fidelity in the modern sense of shunning infidelity; it is also, as Aquinas shows,[13] a completely proper, indeed the most fitting, *motive* for choosing to engage in marital intercourse, and if thoroughly shaping that sex act, makes it a marital act. One of the important reasons why Paul VI's Commission became confused was that John T. Noonan's huge and pioneering 1965 book on contraception in Catholic teaching[14] completely misunderstood Aquinas's statements about why marital intercourse for the sake of and shaped by *fides* is morally right even when there is no possibility or intent to procreate. And what Aquinas calls *fides* is the core of what Vatican II and Paul VI call marital or conjugal love.

And now, with that sentence of sec. 8—'... through a mutual self-giving which is properly theirs and exclusive to them, [husband and wife] develop a communion of persons by which to perfect one another *so as* to cooperate with God in procreating and educating new living beings'—the argument of the encyclical is provided with its key premise for the conclusion stated fully in sec. 14 and summarily in sec. 11. Section 11 concluded, as we have seen, that it is morally 'necessary that *each* marital act remain oriented in itself to the procreation of human life'. And then sec. 12 states the encyclical's argument with maximum brevity:

This doctrine [that every marital act must remain oriented in itself to procreation], often expounded by the Church's magisterium, is based on the indissoluble connection—established by God and not rightly severable by human volition—between the two inherent meanings of marital intercourse: unitive and procreative.

A key to understanding this is the phrase 'not *rightly* severable'. Many translations say 'cannot be severed', or 'cannot be broken', and then people start thinking that there is something about sexual intercourse itself that,

---

[13] *Aquinas* 144–54; essay III.22, sec. II.
[14] Noonan, *Contraception: A History of its Treatment by the Catholic Theologians and Canonists*: see essay III.22, secs II and III.

in any context, makes it 'inherently' and inescapably both unitive (body- or mind-and-body joining) and procreative (genital)—which is to miss the point entirely. But the Latin is unambiguous: *non licet* can only mean that it is not morally permissible or right...in this case to choose to sever unitive meaning from procreative. And while we're about it, we should notice that this states the same thesis as GS 51, replacing the word *sensus* with the better Latin word of the same meaning, *significatio*: 'meaning'.[15] GS 51 said that morality requires the spouses to preserve the full meaning of mutual giving and procreation; Paul VI just adds the precision or clarification necessary to show that the Council's teaching is in line with the whole Christian teaching about reasonable sex acts: that they must each and every one of them be marital, and therefore—since marriage has the dual point and meaning of union/communion/mutual self-giving and procreation— they are rightful only if in each case the sequence of behaviour intending sexual satisfaction retains both these two meanings, neither meaning being severed or repudiated. To make a choice against the procreativeness of any sex act is one way to guarantee that it is not a marital act and therefore, in the Christian understanding of human reasonableness, is not a morally suitable act for anyone. That is what *Humanae Vitae* is about.

Of course, any act of intercourse by husband and wife can accurately be called a marital act. Any set of premises that could persuade someone of a conclusion can accurately be called an argument. Anyone with whom one has a friendly relationship can be called a friend. But if the argument, though persuasive, is logically invalid it is more accurately described as no argument—that's how a logician would tell the truth about it. And if one's friend, though friendly, betrays you for money, he's more accurately described as no friend—that's the human truth about him. So too, the intercourse of spouses, though between spouses and perhaps experientially 'great sex', is more accurately—morally truthfully—described as non- marital if one or both are fantasizing or conditionally willing sex with someone else or (in a different way) if—and this is *Humanae Vitae*'s point in sec. 12—the procreativeness that the spouses foresee their act might have is eliminated from it by something they choose to do with intent precisely to prevent or impede that procreativeness.

I should add this. There are two related, mutually supportive ways in which the 'cannot be severed' or 'cannot be broken' translation, inspired by 'indissoluble' a few words earlier, was not completely wrong. First, the act (intercourse) *cannot* be *marital* if either the unitive or the procreative

---

[15] Later in sec. 12, the word used for the same purpose is *ratio* which I there translate by 'intelligibility'.

meaning is repudiated. Secondly, if you do what cannot rightly be done, and sever (repudiate) orientation or openness to procreation (procreative meaning) from your would-be marital act, that act *cannot* really have the unitive meaning you doubtless were hoping for, either. After all, the unitive meaning is union *in marriage*.[16] For their love to be conjugal, and their act of love be an act of marital commitment—of the marital *fides* that as Aquinas shows is central to the human and Christian ethic of sex and marriage—it must express, actualize, and enable them to experience their marriage, which is defined by the conjunction of its *two* aspects, its *dual* point. Otherwise the spouses' mutual affectionate feelings may remain, may be vivid, may be expressed in their sex acts, but will no longer be truly conjugal (marital). That is the line of thought that John Paul II made prominent in his Apostolic Exhortation *Familiaris Consortio* (1981) when, after adopting and ratifying the 1980 Synod of Bishops' reaffirmation of *HV* 9, 11, and 12, he says that

the innate language that expresses the total reciprocal self-giving of husband and wife is overlaid, through contraception, by an objectively contradictory language, namely that of not giving oneself totally to the other. This leads not only to a positive refusal to be open to life but also to a falsification of the inner truth of conjugal love…[17]

That seems right. But it is not the central line of thought in *Humanae Vitae*, which is closer to the central tradition about the *marital* precondition for a sex act to be morally sound, marriage being a fundamental human good,[18] its desirability being picked out in one of practical reason's primary

---

[16]   Thus, when Anscombe comes to explain why unitive and procreative significance *cannot* be separated (or: are inseparable), her explanation in each instance rests on the fact that the relevant unitive meaning is the unitive meaning which 'deriv[es] from the significance of married life', from 'the actual profound union of the married state': *Faith in a Hard Ground*, 197. Again (*ibid.*): '…we need to think very hard about this "unitive significance" of which *Humanae Vitae* treated. That the unitiveness *has to do with marriage, gets its character from marriage*, is clear'. There is, she is saying, no mileage to be had by thinking of the reciprocal relationship between unitive and procreative without understanding each of those terms in their bearing on the single intelligible and basic human good and institution, marriage. The 'programme for thought' that she rightly says is necessary is one that I am sketching here and have elaborated elsewhere: essay III.20 and essay III.22, sec. III. Also, and fundamentally, *LCL* ch. 9. For Anscombe (as for Peter Geach) this programme had to remain only a possibility, since she (and Geach) never developed a theory of principles of practical reason, fundamental goods, or their moral implications, as Grisez and I and others have sought to do.

[17]   *Familiaris Consortio*, 32.

[18]   John-Paul II, *Veritatis Splendor* (1993), sec. 48.3: '…respect for certain fundamental goods, without which [respect] one would fall into relativism and arbitrariness'; sec. 79.2 (*immediately* after the document's first formal condemnation of proportionalism—the condemnation towards which the whole document is oriented) teaches that the exceptionless negative moral norms protect

that ordered complex of 'personal goods' which serve the 'good of the person': the good which is the person himself and his perfection. These are the goods safeguarded by the commandments, which, according to Saint Thomas, contain the whole natural law.

principles,[19] and its point and worth being intrinsically *dual*—union and procreation, the contours of the former being shaped by the characteristics of the latter.

<h1 style="text-align:center">VI</h1>

The encyclical twice offers an account of the difference between contraception and a policy of periodic abstinence. Neither the sentence in sec. 11 nor the paragraph in sec. 16 makes the matter very clear. I would put it like this.

The policy of periodic abstinence involves three kinds of want or desire. First: in abstaining periodically, that is at those times when they judge that conception would or might well follow from the act or acts of intercourse forgone (abstained from), the spouses have a desire that contracepting couples share, the desire not to incur the burdens (for themselves or others) that would result from having, anytime soon, a baby, as they think they might have if they engaged in marital acts at probably fertile times, acts which they therefore forgo (abstain from) but contracepting couples do not. *HV* 16 says this desire is reasonable and morally right 'when a couple have sound reasons…arising from their physical or psychological condition or from external circumstances'. Such circumstances could be of many, many kinds: sec. 10 speaks of 'serious reasons' derived from 'physical, economic, psychological and social conditions' which can make it responsible to 'decide not to have another child whether for a definite or an indefinite length of time' even though, as sec. 9 had recalled in the words of the Council,

> marriage and marital love are by their nature directed toward the procreation and education of children [and] children are truly the supreme gift of marriage and contribute in the highest degree to the good of their parents.[20]

Secondly: their reason for this policy of abstaining rather than contracepting is that they want each of their sexual choices and acts to be of the kind that is truly marital because, in each act, there is retained each of the two aspects of marriage. For they understand more or less clearly that what is at stake is their adherence to the Christian and reasonable (natural law) thesis that sex acts (acts seeking sexual satisfaction) cannot be rightly chosen unless they are marital in kind—acts of husband with

---

See also sec. 52.2. One of the commandments forbids adultery. It is undeniable (though not asserted explicitly in *VS*) that the relevant fundamental personal good at stake in adultery and all other wrongful kinds of sex act is marriage. That marriage is indeed a fundamental human good, the object of a first principle of practical reason, is taught by Aquinas in *ST* I–II q.94 a.2c; see *Aquinas* 82; for the moral implications, see 143–54.

[19] See preceding note.   [20] *HV* sec. 9 quoting GS 50.

wife, wife with husband, expressive of both aspects of marriage, mutual love, and procreativeness.

Thirdly: their abstinence is only periodic, for they desire and from time to time intend and choose to experience, express, and actualize their marriage and their marital love for each other in such marital acts. Each marital act the couple engage in during infertile periods retains its orientation or openness to procreation, because in it they do together exactly what they do when they are fertile and wish or are willing to generate (conceive a child). Unless it is contracepted in any of the ways outlined in sec. 14, any act of genital union (of uniting by their organs of generation so that the male genitally emits and the female genitally accepts his seed of generation) is biologically a mating and humanly an act of the generative/procreative type, 'oriented in itself to the procreation of new life', even though in the vast majority of cases no generation can follow since her seed of generation, the ovum, is not present. As I say in the note to sec. 11 in my translation, it doesn't matter whether one uses the words 'oriented to' or 'open to' or 'ordered to'[21]—in each case the meaning (I should have said, the meaning here in the context of considering contraception) is established by the definition of contraception in sec. 14: in any instance of genital union, *orientation* or *openness* or *orderedness* to procreation is what is annulled, or not preserved, when something is done with intent to impede the procreativity of that union because it is thought that the union might otherwise result in procreation.

Couples willing to contracept share, as I said, the first of these wants involved in the policy of periodic abstention, the desire not to incur the burdens they foresee from having a baby anytime soon. But these couples lack or set aside or override the second, the desire to keep their intimacy fully marital by retaining in it each of 'the two inherent meanings of marital intercourse: unitive and procreative'; instead they choose to do precisely what the abstaining couples choose not to do. And insofar as the contracepting couple have the third desire—to experience, actualize, and express their *marriage* sexually—what they do in choosing to contracept entails that that desire remains really unfulfilled, because their act cannot express, actualize, or enable them truly to experience marriage's procreative aspect, since their contracepting means precisely this, that they are trying to eliminate from their would-be marital act the procreation they fear it would have resulted in had they not taken steps to prevent it doing so.

---

[21] Sec. 12 uses *ordo ad*, which I translate by 'orientation to'; in sec. 11, 'oriented' translates *ad...procreandam...destinatus*.

Of course, couples who abstain periodically will usually be taking steps in line with their policy, steps which make the policy not merely a set of wants but also an intention. But the steps in question are simply to discover the times when procreation is significantly likely to result from marital acts, so as to know when to abstain. The couple do nothing to impede the procreativeness of any act, nothing to prevent or impede the coming to be of any baby they envisage might come to be if they engaged in a marital act. Instead they forgo such acts, thus fulfilling both (1) their responsibility to serve the marital good and/or communal goods in which their marital good is integrated, by avoiding the burdens that having a baby anytime soon would create, and (2) their responsibility, shared with married and unmarried persons alike, to respect and serve the good of marriage by abstaining from non-marital sex acts.

There was of course no need for *Humanae Vitae* to be as elaborate as I have just been. But it might have crisply said that the difference between the choice of periodic abstinence and the choice of contraception and contracepted intercourse is this: in the former kind of choice the spouses honour their present responsibility not to conceive, and their desire to express their marital love sexually, and the responsibility of everyone at all times not to seek sexual satisfaction in a non-marital way, whereas in the latter, contraceptive kind of choice the spouses repudiate that universal responsibility and thereby fail to express sexually a truly marital love.[22]

---

[22] Or it might have stated the distinction along the lines that Anscombe articulates:

> The question is: Is the action one is performing of such-and-such a kind?—in the case in hand, of the generative kind [a necessary condition of it being of the marital kind]—and my answer [is]: no, not *qua* intentional action, if one has taken steps to render it infertile; yes, *qua* intentional action, if one has merely chosen to do it at a time when it won't be fertile....Is the point not particularly clear when someone resolutely refuses to do anything to make his [or her] acts of intercourse infertile?...[The difference is between bringing it about that they have intercourse when she is infertile and having intercourse when, on purpose with a view to intercourse, they have brought it about that she is infertile]. (Anscombe, 'Reply' [to Winch, Tanner, and Williams] at 161.)

Working in 1972–5 with the then standard English translation of *HV* 16 (which by 1978 she realized was 'bad': *Faith in a Hard Ground*, 194), according to which couples periodically abstaining and contracepting couples are each 'perfectly clear in their intention to avoid children and mean to secure that none will be born' (*ibid.*, 182), she called this [supposed] intention the 'further intention' of each of the two kinds of couple, and then pointed out that the difference is in the *intentional actions* of the two kinds of couple, in pursuit of their shared *further intention*. In contraceptive intercourse,

> the action is not left by you as the kind of act by which life is transmitted, but is purposely rendered infertile, and so changed to another sort of act altogether....[T]o intend such an act is not to intend a marriage act at all, whether or not we're married. An act of ordinary intercourse in marriage at an infertile time, though, is a perfectly ordinary act of marital intercourse...(*Faith in a Hard Ground*, 183.)

Calling periodic abstinence the rhythm method, she says:

> ...you use the rhythm method not just by having intercourse now, but by not having it next week, say; and not having it next week isn't something that does something to today's intercourse to turn it into an infertile act; today's intercourse *is* an ordinary act of intercourse, an ordinary marriage act. It's only if, in getting married, you proposed (like the Manicheans) to

VII

In my last note in the pamphlet, to sec. 16, I summed all this up by saying, in relation to various aspects of the encyclical's terminology that I've not mentioned here:

These differences of formulation do not affect the moral position developed in the encyclical. For as secs. 11, 12 and 13 have explained (presuposing secs. 8, 9 and 10, and following *Gaudium et Spes* 51), the moral point is not that natural processes should never be impeded; nor, as sec. 15 has made clear, is it that the processes of a human reproductive system should never be deliberately altered or subjected to techniques or 'artificial' methods. The moral point is rather that such an intervention is wrong when choosing to make it is choosing to deprive an act of intercourse (foreseen, present or past) of its expressiveness of marriage's and marital love's procreativeness—that is, is choosing to deprive that act of intercourse of its orientation or openness to procreation, its 'procreative meaning' [one of the two meanings that, if intercourse is to be truly marital— enabling the spouses to express, experience, and actualize their marriage—must each be preserved and never separated]. There is inevitably such a deliberate deprivation of procreative meaning or expressiveness whenever husband or wife do something to impede an act of intercourse from having the generative outcome to which (they believe) *that act* would or might otherwise have led by natural processes. Willingness to do this is indeed an approach to birth regulation quite different in moral character from the approach of those who, though similarly having good reason not to procreate, are unwilling to deprive any of their acts of intercourse of procreative meaning or expressiveness, and so instead abstain from intercourse when they think its natural outcome would or might be conception.

confine intercourse to infertile periods, that you'd be falsifying marriage and entering into a mere concubinage....(*Ibid.*, 184.)

On the next page she articulates the decisive reason why intending an act 'of the generative kind', 'the kind of act by which life is transmitted', is so important:

Humanly speaking, the good and the point of a sexual act is marriage. Sexual acts that are not true marriage acts either are mere lasciviousness, or an Ersatz, an attempt to achieve that special unitedness which only a real commitment, marriage, can promise....This—that the good and point of a sexual act is marriage—is why only what is capable of being a marriage act is natural sex...(*Ibid.*, 185.)

Though she does not explicitly say so, this link between the defining close-in intention in contraception (and contracepted intercourse) and marriage is what gives that close-in intention its exceptionless moral significance, as compared with the variable (*ibid.*, 185) moral significance of the act of sabotage which she contrasts with working to rule in order to illustrate the difference (*ibid.*, 184–5) between contracepting and periodic abstinence ('the rhythm method'). Sabotage is exceptionlessly opposed to, or at least, not an instance of, *doing one's job*; but unlike marriage (see n. 16 above) one's job and doing it is not a matter of a fundamental human good or the object of a divine commandment.

As to the proper translation of *HV* 16 on the state of mind that contracepting couples may share with couples avoiding conception by periodic abstinence, my translation has it that they are agreed 'in wanting [*velle*]...to avoid children and to make sure that none are likely to come'; the translation Anscombe offered when condemning the then current CTS translation of the sentence, in 1978, was: 'the couples are alike in meaning to avoid children' (*ibid.*, 194).

I should add this. Many aspects of the formulation of *Humanae Vitae*, and the elements of obscurity there undoubtedly are in that formulation, seem to me to result from a desire which I believe Paul VI must have had, and reasonably so, to avoid tying the Church's teaching to any philosophical or even theological (as distinct from doctrinal) theories or forms of explanation. During the middle and later phases of his Commission's work, a highly influential figure was the Jesuit theologian Josef Fuchs, whose course *De Castitate* (on chastity) at the great Roman university, the Gregorianum, had for some years been the state-of-the-art treatment of the Catholic understanding of sex and marriage.[23] The book of the course gives a fine account of the two fundamental aspects of the good and institution of marriage, and of those two aspects' significance as the two meanings of the marital act, decisive for the wrongness of contraception. But the ethical theory or form of explanation of right and wrong employed in the course book was little more than this: that natural functions ought not to be frustrated or perverted.[24] Precisely that fragile principle—which had grown up among seventeenth-century theologians on the back of a misunderstanding of an argument of Aquinas about lying—was what Germain Grisez comprehensively critiqued and refuted in his book *Contraception and the Natural Law* in 1964; and so Fuchs's abandonment of his own moral argument against contraception occurred during his time on the Commission and greatly affected it.[25] In fact, however, Grisez's book also replaced the perverted-faculty theory with a much sounder account of practical reason's first principles and their moral implication, and of contraception's incompatibility with them. But Paul VI was entirely correct in regarding the Christian doctrine on marriage as something that has deeper roots in revelation (including revelation's teachings about natural reason) than in any theology or philosophical theory. Grisez's own 1964 argumentation on contraception and natural law has changed and greatly developed in its account of first principles and their moral implications, and his account of the wrongness of contraception has bifurcated into two distinct though complementary accounts, one pointing to the contra-life meaning of contraception and the other to its contra-marriage aspect, the latter being closer to *Gaudium et Spes* and *Humanae Vitae* than to Grisez's own 1964 account.[26] Anyway, Paul VI steers pretty clear of all theories,

---

[23] Fuchs, *De Castitate et Ordine Sexuali.*   [24] *Ibid.*, e.g. 53, 80, 84.

[25] And of course affected former students of his such as Fr Richard McCormick SJ, who recounts his change of view as occurring in tandem with Fuchs's: 'Self-Assessment and Self-Indictment' at 38.

[26] My own thinking on the matter has changed significantly since 1968 and 1980, by getting clear that the relevant first principle bearing on sex acts directs us to the good not precisely of pro-creation but of marriage. Getting clear about that in relation to contraception and contracepted sex

lightly indicating here and there the possible links between the moral norm about contraception and wider theoretical principles such as first principles of practical reason (in the citation in sec. 10 to Aquinas, *ST* I–II q.94 a.2), or the rightful limits to one's powers over one's own body, and the reverence due to 'the whole human organism and its natural functions' (mentioned in secs 13.2 and 17.2). So the terminology floats a bit, and articulations of the position are longer on exposition than on illuminating arguments—which are, however, available. The argumentative core, partly left implicit, is what I have identified and laid out a bit in earlier parts of this essay.

VIII

Paul VI's exposition of doctrinal principles contains an additional, free-standing element, a review in sec. 17 of some likely bad consequences of widespread use of contraception. He mentions four: (i) facilitating marital infidelity and 'a general decay of morals', (ii) offering an easy way round the moral law, I suppose on fornication and adultery, (iii) replacement of respect for women with willingness to use women in the service of self-centred male desire, and (iv) willingness to surrender to governments the power to make contraception, sterilization, and/or abortion more or less compulsory. Now supposing that consequences such as these were likely and/or have actually ensued, in what sense can they be said to be relevant to doctrinal principles? The encyclical is not constructing a consequentialist, proportionalist, or any other utilitarian-style argument that directs you to maximize good consequences, minimize bad consequences, and try to work out the quantities or proportions of good and bad so as to net them off against each other and identify the best (or least bad) and thereby the right choice or the right moral rule of thumb. So what is this talk of consequences doing, here in the part on doctrinal principles, or at least what should it have been doing? I think the point was, or should have been, to help us (in the words of sec. 21 about what spouses need) 'profoundly appreciate the true goods of life and family', that is, I add, appreciate the place of those goods in the human community of families, neighbourhoods, countries, and succeeding generations, and their dependence on virtuous stable dispositions of character which are shaped by choices and the like-it-or-not logic of choices, choices that like all choices *last*—subsist—in

is made complex by the fact that the choice to contracept is always a choice distinct from the choice to have (contracepted) sex, and precisely as the choice to prevent the coming-to-be of the new person whose coming-to-be is envisaged as a real possibility in relation to a specific sex act (or series of them) is a choice not directly against the good of marriage but directly against the good of human life (in its inception/procreation): see 1988e and n. 31 below.

the character of individuals and groups unless and until, if ever, they are repudiated and repented of.

Looking at Paul VI's list, one can see more truth in it than has often been recognized. But it is scarcely the measure, or even an outline or broad hint, of what the last forty years' developments have made clear about the impact of contraception's being widely adopted as a morally acceptable kind of choice. The third item, about women being used by men, was incautiously worded and widely mocked, not altogether justly, for overlooking (it was said) women's own desire for sex. And certainly it underplayed the scale of the revolution. Anscombe's *Contraception and Chastity* opens by asking us to 'contemplate a familiar point: the *fantastic change* that has come about in people's situation in respect of having children because of the invention of efficient contraceptives'.[27] She goes on to describe the contrast there has always been between heathen morality and Christian morality, and then adds:

> But the quarrel is far greater between Christianity and the present-day heathen, post-Christian, morality that has sprung up as a result of contraception. In one word: Christianity taught that men ought to be as chaste as pagans thought honest women ought to be; the contraceptive morality teaches that women need be as little chaste as pagans thought men need be.[28]

It was in this post-encyclical essay that Anscombe first reached an insight she had not yet reached when, in the years before the encyclical, she demonstrated the inter-connectedness of the teaching against contraception with the teachings against other kinds of sexual immorality. The new insight was one you've already heard me quote, that 'the good and the point of a sexual act is marriage'.[29] Since marriage as an institution or form of life makes sense only because of its appropriateness as the framework for procreation and education of children, the severing of procreative meaning from sex between married as well as unmarried people makes it impossible for clear-headed persons choosing this severance to regard the good and the point of a sexual act as marriage, or to regard sex acts within marriage as expressing, actualizing, and enabling the parties to experience precisely this marriage itself. Instead, as the logic of contraceptive choosing becomes clear-headedly understood and embraced, marriage becomes just one convenient (but sometimes inconvenient) framework within which to pursue what has come to be regarded as the relevant real good (and everyone's right), the good of (and right to) more or less regular sexual satisfaction, the enjoyment of which is rather impeded by children both

---

[27] *Faith in a Hard Ground*, 170.   [28] *Ibid.*, 171, amending 'need to be as little'.
[29] *Ibid.*, 185.

in their prospect and their equally inconvenient presence. So the loss of understanding of marriage goes hand in hand with loss of understanding of sex.

Change of practical principles entails change of character. Of course the changes of character may be muted, softened, obscured in many ways by people's inconsistency, their lack of clear-headedness, and their partially remaining good character. But since we are intelligent beings, the principles we adopt tend, in our holding of them, to work themselves towards consistency. So more or less radical consequences of big changes of principle start to make themselves apparent, more or less radically, in observable phenomena. Thus, we find very widespread and early fornication, that is, pre-marital or extra-marital sex, running over into bisexual and same-sex sex that may in some cases imitate aspects of marriage by introducing children into the relationship but that characteristically insists more or less overtly on the relationship's openness, the freedom of the partners (not necessarily a *couple*) to have sex with others at will— thus defacing still further the image of marriage in the imitation. These changes overwhelm whole widespread and historic ecclesial bodies like the Anglican communion, whose presiding bishop not unreasonably takes his communion's acceptance of contraception to be the rationally necessitating ground for its acceptance of gay sex. Whole societies are subjected to a vast social revolution, as great as any in human history: same-sex 'marriage', whose impact on our children and our future can hardly fail to be more profound and far-reaching than anyone can clearly imagine.

Again, the severance of sex from procreation smoothes the way for generation of children without sex, by in vitro fertilization or other reproductive technologies that, like IVF, are more a matter of *production* of children than of assisting intercourse to its natural destination, and so are involved in other moral evils in the nature of enslavement: radical inequality between producer and product, manifested but not exhaustively by willingness to cull, freeze, experiment destructively on, farm for parts, and finally to flush away embryos who are each unquestionably a little male or female human individual. Men become virtually irrelevant to the generation of children: one or a very few anonymous men could supply all the male seed needed for countries-full of artificially generated children, only whose mothers need ever be known. Some men respond to this incipient redundancy with a kind of androgynization, one light manifestation of which is 'metrosexuality' as a cultural style.

Again, the countries that have most enthusiastically adopted contraception face depopulation of a historically unprecedented kind and scale. And this phenomenon is not, of course, the result simply of the availability of contraceptives or even of people's willingness in principle to use them, but of profound changes in people's understanding of the point and good of marriage and family. One of Anscombe's four fine essays on contraception in *Faith in a Hard Ground*, the second volume of her posthumously published collected essays, urges priests, back in 1978 when the over-population scare was at its height:

I believe that the message ought to be 'Get to having babies—you are going to ruin your country and often your personal future by regarding, say, two as quite enough, when you have no great excuse.... There is already a ghastly dearth of children in the West because of the present fashion.[30]

But neither priests, nor anyone else much, thought of, put out, or responded to any such message. Indeed, today's European societies, seemingly hollowed out and as if androgynized and in any case scarcely half reproducing themselves, seem to be resigning themselves to surrendering their territories and culture to more fertile peoples, many of them with a religion of domination and submission and little care for reason's refinements.

These are speculative thoughts which, even if Paul VI had been able to anticipate them, would scarcely have been fitting, perhaps, for the encyclical. Less speculative are the implications and consequences traced out in 1995 in sec. 13 of John Paul II's encyclical *Evangelium Vitae*. There he traces out an inner connection between contraception and abortion. He neither endorses nor denies the thesis that contraception is opposed not only to chastity and the marital good but also to life (not the life of an actual baby but the life of the baby specifically envisaged by contraceptors as liable to result from their intercourse and therefore made the object of steps taken precisely to prevent him or her coming to be)—the line of thought developed by Grisez and me and others[31] as continuous with a strand in the Church's historic teaching against contraception, a strand not taken up in *Gaudium et Spes* or *Humanae Vitae*. But having recalled that the Church, in its critics' eyes, 'obstinately continues to teach the moral unlawfulness of contraception', the 1995 encyclical states that 'the negative values inherent in the "contraceptive mentality"...are such that they...strengthen [the] temptation [to abortion in the case of failed contraception] when an unwanted life is conceived', because in that mentality 'the life which could result from a sexual encounter...becomes an enemy to be avoided at all costs, and abortion becomes the only possible decisive response to

---

[30] *Ibid.*, 204.
[31] 1988e; *LCL* 506–19; modifications in detail in Grisez and Boyle, 'Reply to Our Critics and Collaborators' at 231–2.

failed contraception'. So, John Paul II observes, 'the pro-abortion culture is especially strong precisely where the Church's teaching on contraception is rejected'.[32] For, to make again my point about principles, where a sound principle of action is set aside in favour of an unsound, the consequences may in practice extend far beyond the application of either principle, since principles are linked in principle with other principles, and the implications of abandoning one may involve several others, as often emerges in practice and its palpable effects.

One word about the consequences within the Church. I'm not thinking of the consequences of the issuing of the encyclical, though the effects of clerical and to some extent episcopal resistance to it were very severe indeed. I'm thinking of the effect of accepting contraception. One kind of effect can be indicated by recalling that Fr Josef Fuchs, who in 1966 argued that changing the teaching on contraception would change nothing else in core Catholic moral doctrine, and in particular would leave intact the teaching about homosexual acts, since these acts are against human dignity, had within a few years become a central figure in the proportionalist school of moral theology. That theology left standing none of the core Christian moral teachings on specific kinds of act and on the decisive moral importance of kinds of close-in intention—and so was judged utterly misguided in the encyclical *Veritatis Splendor* secs 79 and 81, in 1993.[33] Meanwhile, gay sex took 'dignity' not as a defeater but an all-justifying slogan.

But among married couples the effect of accepting contraception was a considerable relief from hardship. If you look on the lawn to the north of the Hesburgh Library tower [on the campus of the University of Notre Dame] you will see a bronze plaque saying 'This area was the site of "Vetville" married student housing 1945–1962. Many were the trials—thanks to the Holy Family for the many blessings needed to persevere.' We can be sure that some and perhaps many of the many trials had to do with the difficulties of periodic abstinence, especially with uncertain ovulatory cycles, and of children coming when not expected. The swathes of young Catholics who chose to contracept with some kind of licence from complaisant confessors, or on their own licence, as the clergy in the late 1950s or early 1960s fell silent about the historic teaching, could in a sense *relax*. Those Vetville dates again: 1945–1962. Elizabeth Anscombe describes the fading of spirituality, the wateriness of faith, the settling down into worldliness, that accompanied the adoption of contraception by many married Catholics and

---

[32] *EV* 13.

[33] See *MA* at 84–101 on the significance of contraception in the emergence of the proportionalism later analysed and condemned in *Veritatis Splendor*. On Fuchs, see *ibid.*, 4n, 14n, 46n, 76n, 94–5, 97n, 99n, 100, 195n.

its more or less silent approval by many of their pastors, and gives us a date: 'It was in 1963, late I am sure, that I became aware of the peculiar dreadful miasma of the present day that was spreading over the Church...'[34] As she said in my home country in 1978, 'Among the contraceptive Catholic populations there is an awful spiritual deadness, which will last until they are weaned from their vices'—she means *these* vices.[35] Those who like me can scarcely summon up such frankness can nonetheless acknowledge the justice of her assessment. The trials involved in living a Christian marriage without contraception are very real, and much greater for some than others in ways whose disparity God alone comprehends and draws out good from in his providence. But the strength and other spiritual goods which *Humanae Vitae* describes at some length in sec. 21 as fruits of the practice of 'morally right and proper birth regulation' are real, too, most visibly to the spiritual eye of faith. These fruits build up the Kingdom which we have to *seek first* (Matthew 6: 33), and unless despaired of they will be found to have lasted into the completed Kingdom in which, as GS 39 teaches in its sublime re-expression of Gospel faith, we will find again all the good fruits of our nature and effort, but cleansed of all dirt, lit up, and transformed in the eternal and universal kingdom of truth and life, holiness and grace, justice, love, and peace.

IX

Still, consequences are not what is morally decisive, even when they result from a network of principles that are related to each other intrinsically and not merely by cause and effect, and that work out as virtues or, when unsound, as vices in the character and soul of those who adopt them, and as practices with palpable consequences when acted upon. What is morally decisive is the *object* of chosen acts, the close-in intention that is defined by the set of means and ends articulated in the proposal which a deliberating person adopts when he or she makes a choice,[36] and carries out in acting

---

[34] *Faith in a Hard Ground*, 209.   [35] *Ibid.*, 203 (in an address to clergy in Melbourne).
[36] See *Veritatis Splendor* 78:

> In order to be able to grasp the object of an act which specifies that act morally, it is therefore necessary to place oneself *in the perspective of the acting person*. The object of the act of willing is in fact a freely chosen kind of behaviour... By the object of a given moral act, then, one cannot mean a process or an event of the merely physical order, to be assessed on the basis of its ability to bring about a given state of affairs in the outside world. Rather, that object is the proximate end of a deliberate decision which determines the act of willing on the part of the acting person.

The encyclical follows tradition in distinguishing object, intention, and circumstances. In this traditional idiom, 'intention' means what I (and Anscombe) call the 'further' or 'further-out' intention. (For the particular act to be *rightful*, both its object *and* its intention must be right (not-wrong); a good object—giving to the poor—will not justify a bad intention, such as deceiving bystanders about one's character; the circumstances, moreover, must not be inappropriate (giving to poor bystanders

on it. There is the object of a genuine marital act: expressing, experiencing, and actualizing our commitment to each other and our *marriage* (as a communion of life, and a vocation, entered upon with exclusiveness and permanence for the sake of procreating and educating children) *in* the sexual uniting that culminates in the one-flesh giving and accepting of the husband's seed emitted in the wife's organ of generation. There is the object of an act of contraception, which—whatever the method—will be to prevent or make less likely the procreation which is envisaged as liable to result from an act of intercourse. And there is the object of such an act of intercourse, chosen with the contraceptive impact in mind and in such reliance upon that impact that procreative meaning is excluded from the act, and with it a defining aspect of marriage—with the entailment that it becomes non-marital and in its own way like the other kinds of non-marital act which Christians and other reasonable people exclude from their deliberations in order to respect and keep intelligible the good and institution of marriage. That, I believe, is the teaching of *Humanae Vitae*, which I have been commending to you.

what one owes as wages to one's poor employees makes the charitable giving wrongful).) But in the tradition, as in Aquinas, e.g. *ST* II–II q.64 a.7 on self-defence, the term 'object' is sometimes replaced by the word 'intention', meaning the close-in (proximate) intention.

24

HELL AND HOPE[*]

I

The dreadful mystery of hell, about which Jesus of Nazareth and his apostles and their successors down to modern times insistently warn us, was no less grim and disconcerting to cultured people in the cities of the late fourth century or the early sixteenth century than in the late twentieth century: grim, disconcerting and, as we loosely say, 'intolerable'. This we can see in the writings of the saints, Thomas More[1] for the early sixteenth century, Augustine for the late fourth and early fifth. In reflecting on this element in the divine revelation accomplished in Jesus Christ, More and Augustine show their full sympathy with the sentiments of those Christians who felt that the prospect for sinners could not be as really bad as Jesus's warnings suggest. Augustine keeps the promise he makes at the beginning of c.17 of book 19 of *The City of God*, to dispute *pacifice* (without rancour) with *misericordibus nostris*, compassionate fellow Christians who refuse to believe that the punishment of hell will be without end, with those—he has met and has talked with them—who, though apparently venerating the Scriptures, lead reprehensible lives and argue that God's mercy and compassion must prevail over their deserts, if only because God could not refuse the prayers of the saints in heaven who will intercede for them…, and with many others whose more or less compassionate though incompatible arguments Augustine sets out for us. Indeed, in the writings of the theologians who today freely reject the beliefs about hell held by Augustine and More in common with the entire Catholic tradition, it is hard to find any argument not canvassed and, in most cases, rather cogently disposed of in Chapters 17 to 27 (the end) of book 21 of *The City of God*. One sign of the decay widespread in Catholic theology today is that

---

[*] Unpublished paper, read to Catholic student societies in Oxford in 1990 and, with revisions, in 1998.
[1] *Dialogue of Comfort against Tribulation*, xxvi, 249.

those chapters are not attended to, and that Augustine's often definitive refutations of views today promoted by theologians are simply ignored by those whom they most concern.

II

Still, Augustine is also part of the problem, just to this extent: his philosophical theology, for reasons which I cannot even try to sketch here, contributed rather strongly to a theological account of the point of human existence which became classical and dominant until very recently, though never definitively proposed by the Church itself—a theology in which the point of human existence is the vision of God in heaven, to which contemplative vision all other human goods, all other aspects of human fulfilment in this world, and all human choices and actions promoting and/or respecting those goods, could be no more than instrumental, mere means used. In this classical theology and in the piety it inspired, the relation between respecting and promoting human goods such as bodily life, excellence in work, or comradeship and attaining what gives human life its point, the vision of God, remains quite unclear. There seems to be a gap between the 'means' and the end. The gap is filled with the concepts of law and merit, *law* conceived not so much in terms of an articulation of the necessity of suitable means to an appropriate end but rather in terms of a set of conditions laid down by God as the terms on which he undertakes to fulfil his offer to make possible and actual what for us would otherwise be impossible, the vision of his divine being; and *merit* conceived as the satisfying of those conditions by the free choices of a human subject. And as God administers the reward for conformity to his laws, a reward which has no intrinsic connection with the content of those laws, so he administers the punishments for violating them, penalties which in the more serious cases of defiance or contempt for his limitless goodness and authority extend to punishment if not without limit at least without end. There is much in Augustine's great corpus of work which goes beyond, even far beyond this legalistic conception of the human destiny revealed by Christ; but it is a conception encouraged by much that is central to his thought. And the contemporary revolt against hell is inspired and fuelled by disgust at and revolt against the implications of such legalism—a revolt which, however, presupposes and in no way escapes from the legalistic premises themselves.

Those theologians who reject what I shall simply call the Catholic teaching on hell (but who intend to remain Catholic theologians and not mere secular humanists) sometimes give prominence to an important truth often obscured by the legalistic model of the judge administering rewards and punishments. There is a fundamental asymmetry between our relationship to the possibility of heaven and our relationship to the possibility of hell. But they do not grasp the full grounds for or implications of this asymmetry. A great contemporary theologian who accepts the Catholic teaching on hell but not the legalistic theology and piety in which it was often embedded has explained the grounds and implications of the asymmetry in a way which I may paraphrase thus.

Heaven is possible only by God's absolutely free and gratuitous decision to enable his bodily, intelligent, and free creature to be also a participant in the divine family, in the divine life, and so far forth in the divine nature—a possibility made actual by divine grace. No human choice, action, work could have brought about any such partaking in the divine communion of persons; indeed, no human choice, action, or work could by itself have merited it, for meriting it is nothing other than, in response to and on the strength of God's gifts, doing one's part within that friendship with God which he has freely promised, a friendship which he makes actual by his constant mercy in both inspiring and responding to every human effort to enter and re-enter it. But the loss and misery of hell is something one brings about by one's free choices, without the need for any further response on God's part, if one wilfully rejects or abuses God's gifts, not least the human goods made available to us by his action as Creator. Hell is not an extrinsic penalty selected by some special divine decree as human penalties are selected by human legislators and judges. Hell is a self-made judgment, the inherent outcome of a sin by which one refuses to remain and grow in friendship with God. Its central misery is separation from God and exclusion from communion in heavenly fulfilment; when the Church, echoing Jesus, says that those in hell suffer from fire she teaches nothing more nor less than that the essential misery of permanent unfulfilment will have natural and painful consequences at the level of experience, 'a repercussion on the whole being of the sinner' as the Congregation of the Doctrine of the Faith's Letter on Eschatology said in 1979; and this need involve nothing especially created for or imposed upon those involved.

Now, while there is thus a fundamental asymmetry between heaven and hell in relation to God's action, there is also a fundamental parallelism between them in relation to human action. For, given God's promises and gifts, human actions have an intrinsic relationship to heavenly fulfilment. This relationship eluded the classic legalistic theology, and eludes the revisionist legalistic theology which dominates Catholic seminaries and universities today. It is the relationship affirmed in the great teaching of Vatican II, in *Gaudium et Spes*, paras 38–9, that human choices and acts which, in an upright way, promote and respect human goods thereby 'prepare the material of the heavenly kingdom', for if we obey the Lord and in his Spirit nurture on earth any and all of the goods of our nature and our work, we will find these goods and their good fruits again, but freed of stain, and burnished and transfigured, in the completed kingdom of truth and life, holiness and grace, justice, love, and peace.

I should interject here, to avoid misunderstanding, that this 'obedience to the Lord in his Spirit' may be quite implicit. For, as Paul VI's Credo of the People of God teaches in the words of the Second Vatican Council and in full continuity with the Catholic tradition:

We believe that the Church is necessary for salvation, for the sole mediator and way of salvation is Christ, who becomes present to us in his Body which is the Church. But the divine design embraces all men: and indeed those who, though ignorant of the Gospel of Christ and of his Church through no fault of their own, still seek God with a sincere heart and who, under the influence of grace, struggle by their works to fulfil his will, known through the dictate of conscience, they also, in a number known only to God, are able to achieve salvation.

To return to the main thread of the Council's teaching on the relation between human choices and actions and the eternal kingdom: heavenly fulfilment, in short, is no extrinsic reward but a 'finding again' of the goods which one had cultivated in one's morally significant choices in this life, the very same goods though now fitted for the divine family, a realm without imperfection and without end. And these goods constitutive of heaven are not just the good of contemplative vision (now unimaginably extended by God's gift) but include, constitutively, all the basic goods intrinsic to our bodily, intelligent, active, free, and companionable nature. And this teaching has its fullest intelligibility in the context of the truth known to a sound philosophy of action: free choices last, beyond the time of the action which carries them out; they last in and as constitutive of the character of the chooser, until, if ever, they are repented of, reversed by some incompatible free choice. Free choice is self-determination. And hell, too, is the lasting of a free choice or choices made and not repented of before the death which, in removing the present complexity and variability of our nature, removes (we must assume) the possibility of changing one's mind. Hell is the lasting of the impenitent sinner's refusal to remain and grow in friendship with God, together with the intrinsic implications of that persisting refusal.

III

What one might call a liberalized Christianity, which seeks a compromise with the Enlightenment's moral and historical critique of Christian faith, rejects the implications of classic legalism but is unable to replace its premises. Liberalized Christianity quite reasonably refuses to accept that this life with its human goods is a mere expendable booster rocket to get us into heavenly orbit, a mere test with rewards for those who jump the hurdles and punishment for those who don't. And it distinguishes itself from secular humanism by accepting the idea of heaven. But instead of superseding legalism by an attentive understanding of the Council's reformulation of the constant Christian teaching, liberal Christianity simply evades the issue of legalism by postulating, in effect, that heaven is inevitable. Hell is at best ignored, and at worst its real possibility is denied.

In the forefront of the denial is often some appeal to the supposed sophistication of contemporary biblical studies, or the alleged '"linguistic turn" of modern consciousness with its unprecedented concern for the way that the means we use to express ourselves cannot be separated from the question of what we are expressing'.[2] '...[N]ow through the slow process of biblical education, certain conclusions seem quite firm: the eschatological statements of the New Testament are seen to demand a symbolic interpretation. There is no question of material fire.'[3] The short-sightedness and complacency of such statements is evident enough. There is no awareness that the tradition represented by Augustine was very well aware that Scripture includes a good measure of symbolic, metaphoric 'means of expression' which do not assert as propositions what they 'literally' state in words.

Nor is there any serious attempt to explain the limits of the symbolic interpretation. If nothing 'material' corresponds to what the Lord spoke of as 'fire', is there any bodily resurrection corresponding to what the Lord only speaks of indirectly (though Paul and the Church's creeds affirm it directly)? How are these modern critics to respond to Augustine's ancient argument (*City of God* xxi, 23) that if one part of Christ's saying is symbolic, the parallel part of the same saying should be assumed to be symbolic, too; if it is mere symbolism when Jesus says 'they will go away into eternal punishment', how could it fail to be mere symbolism when he finishes the sentence: 'but the righteous into eternal life'? So this critique of hell generates unease about heaven—perhaps talk of heaven is likewise no more than a way of interpreting the 'existential significance' of

---

[2] Duffy, 'Hell' at 364.   [3] Dalton, *Salvation and Damnation*, 80.

life in this world? And so there emerges an effective silence about heaven, a silence with which all Catholic churchgoers of the past two decades are quite familiar, and whose debilitating effect on Christian hope and life is felt by all.

What grounds the 'demand' that scripture's eschatological statements be interpreted non-literally? Karl Rahner offers this argument:

> what Scripture says about hell is to be interpreted in keeping with its literary character as 'threat-discourse' and hence not to be read as a preview of something which will exist some day.[4]

But if a threat gives no preview of what might well happen some day, it is a bluff; and bluffing by one who has some foreknowledge of what will and will not happen is lying. And in fact there is no need to place what Scripture says about hell in the category of threats (*comminationes, Drohungen*). It belongs properly in the category of warnings (*admonitiones, Verwarnungen*): if you run across the road without looking you'll finish up like that dead squirrel. Rahner's categorization—taken over from some modern scripture scholars—manifests the very legalism he tried to subvert.

The real arguments against the Catholic teaching on hell are moral arguments; the appeals to literary typologies are by themselves too feeble to be taken seriously. But the moral arguments themselves are vulnerable to a devastating moral counter-argument, of which we have just had an intimation (and Augustine had already alluded to it[5]): if such appeals do not attribute to the Church and its sacred writers the most abject misunderstanding or fabrication of God's revelation, they attribute to God, to Jesus himself, the will to stage a mendacious bluff.

IV

Strangely, a rather full bag of arguments against the Catholic teaching on hell is the little book *Dare We Hope? with A Short Discourse on Hell*, one of the very late writings of Hans Urs von Balthasar, who died in 1988 shortly before being installed as cardinal. In the vast corpus of this Swiss theologian there is much to admire; many faithful Catholics look to his Christocentric theological reflections for an intelligent, profound, and faithful resistance to the liberalized, semi-secular Christianity flowing from the later Karl Rahner into the Church's seminaries and schools; and no one should wish lightly and unadvisedly to contradict this altogether exceptionally learned, sensitive and reflective Christian.

---

[4] 'Hell' in Rahner, *Encyclopedia of Theology*, 603.   [5] *De Civitate Dei* xxi, 18(ii).

The full title of the main book in this composite volume is *Dare We Hope 'That All Men Be Saved'?*. Things start and, I'm afraid, end badly because von Balthasar, without pausing for serious analysis and reflection, scornfully rejects as paradoxical (20) an elementary and fundamental clarification of the logically ambiguous phrase 'hope that all will be saved'. Is there any human person of whom we can say 'We have no basis for hope that he or she will be, or will have been, saved—there is no hope that he or she will be found, at the end, within God's friendship in Christ's kingdom'? No, there is no human being of whom we can say that. As Catholic faith and piety have held from the beginning, we as yet know nothing of the final destiny of any individual human being. So there is no particular human person for whose final salvation we cannot rightly pray; presented with a list of names of all who have ever lived, there is no one on the list whom one can identify as ineligible to be prayed for.[6] In that sense of 'that all will', then, the tradition teaches that we not only dare to but must hope that all will be saved. But: 'Is there any theological reason to hope that everyone will be, or will have been, saved?' No, there is no such theological reason. While there is no logical necessity that anyone should be lost, and no knowledge that any have been lost, the facts of human freedom and human sin give us reason to expect that at the end of human history, some will be found to have been lost to God's friendship and the Kingdom of Jesus. How many? Of that we do not have the faintest idea and should not speculate; for on this matter there are no sufficient data to warrant any conclusion.

Von Balthasar engages in much irony at the expense of the theological and pious tradition which fears that *many* are lost. But in the end (rather too late) he rightly admits that 'At bottom it makes no difference whether they are many or few' (192)—that is, makes no difference to the bone he has to pick with Catholic tradition. I fear, however, that von Balthasar does not clearly realize just why it makes no difference. It makes no difference because, willy-nilly, all his arguments for hoping (in the second sense) that all men are saved are in fact arguments that it is inconsistent with God's nature, and therefore impossible, for *any* human creature to be lost.

---

[6] *Ibid.*, xxi, 24; Suarez, *De Oratione* tr. 4, lib 1, c. 15, quoted by von Balthasar at 37–8n. Augustine, loc. cit., lucidly explains why we pray for the salvation of all the living, but not for people under a description such as 'those who died infidel and as enemies of the people of God'; the Church's prayer for the living is that all may be saved and for the dead that the faithful departed may be saved (remembering always that faith can be very implicit). To pray for those (we do not know who and how many) who, having died without any saving faith, have already been lost makes no more sense than praying for the Devil and his angels. Even Gerard Manley Hopkins did not believe that there is sense in praying for people already in hell. For the reasons why we should reject Hopkins's view that we should pray for people not to have gone to hell, see Peter Geach, *God and the Soul*, 89–94. In short, the Church both does and does not pray for the salvation of all, according as the reference of 'all people' shifts its temporal focus. [This page ignores the canonized saints.]

Now this is not something von Balthasar wishes to admit (even, I think, to himself) about the character of his argument. He wants to be a faithful Catholic theologian, not a semi-secular theologian of the ordinary sort who willingly write off as symbol and myth anything and everything in Scripture and Tradition which they find too much for 'modern men and women'. He knows that to deny the possibility, the real possibility, of hell is to make nonsense of the revelation in Jesus and to evacuate human existence of that whole depth and seriousness which the words and life of Jesus so plainly communicate. So he offers a fundamental distinction: we each should acknowledge that, for me myself, being lost in hell is a real possibility; but at the same time we should hold that for any human person to be lost in hell is inconsistent with God's saving will and power and with the efficacy of Christ's saving sacrifice.

I am afraid that this is self-contradictory. It is not a mystery like the nature of the Trinity, defying human explanation. It is not a mere fruitful 'paradox'. It is a self-contradiction in relation to something well within the experience and understanding of each of us: our membership of the human race, of the logical class, human being. If there is no real possibility that anyone will be lost, there is no real possibility that I will be. If there is a real possibility that I will be lost, there is a real possibility that some human being will be lost. Moreover, since neither I nor von Balthasar know anything relevant to distinguish my case from that of others, there must then be a real possibility that others, even very many others, will likewise be lost. To invite each reader or listener to judge that there is a real possibility that he or she will be lost while telling all of them that there is no real possibility that any of them will be is, alas, not profound. It is well-meaning. But to accept the invitation would be simply foolish. The Christian revelation and faith has incomprehensible depths; it is 'folly to the Greeks'; but it is not stupid.

I am sorry to say that hereabouts the eminent theologian covers over his incoherence with ironies at the expense of the 'theological Monsignore' who populates hell with sinners but always somehow, 'consciously or unconsciously', exempts himself. Indeed, von Balthasar here permits himself to suggest that St Augustine himself never worried, after his conversion, about his own salvation. This insinuation is decorated with texts which have not the slightest tendency to support it, and passes over in silence—a silence which to me makes von Balthasar's book ring hollow—what we know about that great saint. As Augustine says in a last sermon (no. 382):

Whoever does not want to fear, let him probe into his inmost self. Do not just touch the surface; go down into yourself; reach into the inmost corner of your heart. Examine it then with care: see there, whether a poisoned vein of the wasting love of the world still does not pulse,…whether you are not caught in some law of the senses; whether you are never elated with empty boasting, never depressed by some vain anxiety…

Whoever does not want to fear for his salvation needs to repent of his most secret sins, and to put away all complacency about them. As his friend and biographer Possidius reports:

this holy man…was always in the habit of telling us, when we talked as intimates, that even praiseworthy Christians and bishops…should not leave this life without having performed due and exacting penance. This is what he did in his own last illness [in the high summer of 430]: for he ordered the four psalms of David that deal with penance to be copied out. From his sickbed he could see these sheets of paper every day, hanging on his walls, and would read them, crying constantly and deeply. And lest his attention be distracted from this in any way, almost ten days before his death, he asked that none of us should come in to see him, except at those hours when the doctors would come to examine him or his meals were brought. This was duly observed: and so he had all that stretch of time to pray.[7]

Let us hear the beginning of one of those four psalms on the walls of Augustine's bedroom, Psalm 50/51:

Miserere mei, Deus, secundum magnam misericordiam tuam;
et secundum multitudinem miserationum tuarum, dele iniquitatem meam.
Amplius lava me ab iniquitate mea,
et a peccato meo munda me.
Quoniam iniquitatem meam ego cognosco, et peccatum meum contra me est
    semper.
Have mercy on me O God, as thou art ever rich in mercy;
In the abundance of thy compassion, blot out the record of my wrong;
Wash me clean, cleaner yet of my wrong, and purge me of my sin.
For I know indeed my own wrongfulness, and my sin stands ever before me…

Cor mundum crea in me, Deus,
et spiritum rectum innova in visceribus meis…
A clean heart create in me O God
and put a right spirit within me…

Benigne fac, Domine, in bona voluntate tua Sion,
ut aedificentur muri Jerusalem.
By your good will, O Lord, give prosperity to Sion,
So that the walls may be built of Jerusalem…

---

[7] Possidius, *Life of Saint Augustine*, c. xxxi; Brown, *Augustine of Hippo*, 436.

of that holy city for which Augustine lived and taught and prayed and hoped, the holy city which is being built up here, in mystery, by human choices and actions made and done in the spirit of the Lord (GS 39).

We cannot *hope* to reach in the end what we *know* we will reach in the end. Twist and turn as he may, von Balthasar's universalism cuts off Christian *hope* for *eternal life* at its root by replacing it with a certainty. If everyone goes to heaven no matter what they do, nobody can do anything with the intention of sharing, or helping others to share, in heavenly glory, in *fulfilment* in the cooperative relationship with God. Balthasar calls his perspective 'practical-prescriptive...not theoretical-cognitive' (211), but the whole thrust of Christian revelation is to draw practical 'prescription' from the 'theoretical' truths of God's plan, of the human predicament and the means of redemption from it. To set the two perspectives in opposition, as von Balthasar does, is to fall back into legalism.

And, as I said, for the 'practical certainty' offered by von Balthasar with many disclaimers and much reluctance (and by liberalized Christians with little hesitation and no real reluctance) we have grounds neither in revelation nor, of course, in experience.

Von Balthasar tries to make out, to be sure, that the revelation of God's love gives ground for denying that any human person will eternally refuse it. He suggests that to accept that even one person will be lost is to deny 'the effective truth of Christ's statement that, on the Cross, he will draw all men to himself'.[8]

...along with the words of threat [NB!], Holy Scripture also contains many words of hope for all, and...to transform the former into objective facts would mean that the latter would lose all sense and force.[9]

Now von Balthasar knows how Catholic theology has always understood such statements about God's will that all men be saved, not indeed as devoid of all sense and force, but as references to God's conditional, antecedent will, as distinct from what God wills *consequenter* in view of the meritorious or guilty choices of men and angels. But von Balthasar mocks such distinctions and explanations (183–4), and labels them 'frightful speculations' (23), 'strange distinctions' (208). He does not stay to ask how God is to be exculpated from willing human sin itself if such distinctions are not drawn. He declares at the outset that it is 'neither permissible nor achievable' to make any synthesis between those statements in the New Testament which speak of God's will and ability to save all men and

---

[8] von Balthasar, *Dare We Hope?*, 26; the context is *massa damnata*, but von Balthasar elsewhere acknowledges that numbers do not make a difference.

[9] *Ibid.*, 166 (from *A Short Discourse on Hell*).

those many statements which speak of being lost for all eternity. Such an outlawing of the attempt at synthesis seems to me to cut off the very roots of Catholic theology, of faith's search for understanding all the central givens of revelation with all the resources of human reflection.

The arguments of von Balthasar, and of course of the less sensitive liberalized Christians who would think his efforts too cautious and tortuous, all seem to me to imply this premise: that if all people are not saved, God will have been shown to be not all-powerful or not truly a God of salvation, not boundlessly generous and merciful. But that premise is disastrous, for two reasons. The first, perhaps less important, is that, as von Balthasar admits, it is a truth of the Catholic faith, infallibly defined by the Creed of the Fourth Lateran Council in 1215 in keeping with the Lord's words in Matthew 25: 41, that the *reprobi* in their resurrected bodies will undergo perpetual punishment *cum diabolo*—with the Devil (D-S 802). In other words, there is (though liberalized Christians scornfully deny it) at least one free willing and intelligent creature, Satan (whose reality is affirmed by the Second Vatican Council in eight different places), who is in hell for ever; and that is consistent with God's salvific generosity. To Augustine, that seemed decisive against most of the arguments which he listed; and von Balthasar offers against this cogent logic nothing but ironies and evasive rhetoric.

The second reason, perhaps more important, for rejecting his major premise is this (I have already intimated it). Willy-nilly but with strict necessity, that premise entails that Jesus Christ, in warning us of hell, both portrayed God as not all-powerful or not truly a boundlessly generous God of salvation, and did so falsely, treating his hearers for 2,000 years as puppets to be drawn to virtue by a bluff. Thus, von Balthasar's argument about hell inserts into the very centre of a theology intended to be Christocentric a catastrophic deformation of the very image and character of Christ. The thesis with which von Balthasar wants to sum up his position is this: 'Whoever reckons with the possibility of even only one person's being lost besides himself is hardly able to love unreservedly...'. But then Christ is 'hardly able to love unreservedly', or else merely pretended, time and again pretended, to 'reckon with the possibility of some being lost'.

I return to the position of the Tradition. It is not the same as von Balthasar's pervasive caricature (which of course had some basis in a certain rhetoric and piety): that we know that hell is 'populated' with human persons or, in his equally odious phrase, is 'full'. The Catholic faith has never taught that we know anything about the numbers of human beings 'in Hell', whether the number be zero or some very large number. What the Catholic faith, I believe, claims to know, in reliance on the Lord, is that any who by their free choice, maintained until death, have refused to enter into or remain within God's friendship will undergo that perpetual loss and misery. The claim against which von Balthasar's arguments are directed is not, properly stated, a claim to knowledge of what will happen; it is a claim that if any, or even many, turn out to have made that refusal and to undergo that natural penalty of it, that will not be inconsistent in even the smallest degree with God's boundlessly generous love, but will be simply the consequence of God's respect for human freedom; and so, while we may and must maintain a hope for each and every human person that he or she will be saved, we are not entitled to expect—we have no theological ground to expect—that all will be.

How much more could be said! But I shall finish with two remarks by two of von Balthasar's critics. The first is Fr James O'Connor, in the middle of a powerful critique of von Balthasar's book:

One pauses again and again to ask oneself: do we really have any nearly sufficient appreciation of how much the Lord loves us and gives himself for our benefit? The answer, of course, must be that we do not. It is an appreciation which has to be constantly deepened....[10]

And the other remark is simply the closing words of book 21 of the *City of God*:

These observations may suffice for a reply to those who, while not slighting the authority of the Sacred Scriptures which we have as our common possession, nonetheless interpret them wrongly and suppose that what is going to happen is not what the Scriptures speak of, but what they themselves would like to happen ... *quod ipsi volunt* ...

or, one might say (without retreating from or watering down Augustine's sober judgment), *quod nos omnes volumus*, what we all would like to happen.

---

[10] O'Connor, 'Von Balthasar and Salvation' at 19.

BIBLIOGRAPHY OF THE WORKS OF
JOHN FINNIS

1962	a		'Developments in Judicial Jurisprudence', Adelaide L Rev 1: 317–37
	b		'The Immorality of the Deterrent', Adelaide Univ Mag: 47–61
1963			'Doves and Serpents', The Old Palace 38: 438–41
1967	a	I.17	'Reason and Passion: The Constitutional Dialectic of Free Speech and Obscenity', University of Pennyslvania L Rev 116: 222–43
	b	IV.8	'Blackstone's Theoretical Intentions', Natural L Forum 12: 63–83
	c		'Punishment and Pedagogy', The Oxford Review 5: 83–93
	d		'Review of Zelman Cowen, *Sir John Latham and Other Papers*', LQR 83: 289–90
1968	a	III.10	'Old and New in Hart's Philosophy of Punishment', The Oxford Review 8: 73–80
	b		'Constitutional Law', *Annual Survey of Commonwealth Law 1967* (Butterworth), 20–33, 71–98
	c		'Separation of Powers in the Australian Constitution', Adelaide L Rev 3: 159–77
	d		Review of Neville March Hunnings, *Film Censors and the Law*, LQR 84: 430–2
	e		'Natural Law in *Humanae vitae*', LQR 84: 467–71
	f		Review of H. Phillip Levy, *The Press Council*, LQR 84: 582
	g		'Law, Morality and Mind Control', Zenith (University Museum, Oxford) 6: 7–8
1969	a		'Constitutional Law', *Annual Survey of Commonwealth Law 1968* (Butterworth), 2–15, 32–49, 53–75, 98–114
	b		Review of Herbert L. Packer, *The Limits of the Criminal Sanction*, Oxford Magazine 86 no. 1 (new series), 10–11
1970	a	I.6	'Reason, Authority and Friendship in Law and Morals', in Khanbai, Katz, and Pineau (eds), *Jowett Papers 1968–1969* (Oxford: Blackwell), 101–24
	b		'Natural Law and Unnatural Acts', Heythrop J 11: 365–87
	c		i. 'Abortion and Legal Rationality', Adelaide L Rev 3: 431–67 ii. 'Three Schemes of Regulation', in Noonan (ed.), *The Morality of Abortion: Legal and Historical Perspectives* (HUP)
	d		'Constitutional Law', *Annual Survey of Commonwealth Law 1969* (Butterworth), 2–4, 27–34, 37–50, 65–81
	e		Review of H.B. Acton, *The Philosophy of Punishment*, Oxford Magazine 87 (new series) (13 April)
	f		Review of Colin Howard, *Australian Constitutional Law*, LQR 86: 416–18

1971   a   IV.21   'Revolutions and Continuity of Law', in A.W.B. Simpson (ed.), *Oxford Essays in Jurisprudence: Second Series* (OUP), 44–76

     b   'The Abortion Act: What Has Changed?', Criminal L Rev: 3–12

     c   'Constitutional Law', *Annual Survey of Commonwealth Law 1970* (Butterworth), 2–4, 17–31, 33–42, 51–60

1972   a   III.11   'The Restoration of Retribution', Analysis 32: 131–5

     b   IV.18   'Some Professorial Fallacies about Rights', Adelaide L Rev 4: 377–88

     c   'The Value of the Human Person', Twentieth Century [Australia] 27: 126–37

     d   'Bentham et le droit naturel classique', Archives de Philosophie du Droit 17: 423–7

     e   'Constitutional Law', *Annual Survey of Commonwealth Law 1971* (Butterworth), 2–5, 11–25, 28–41

     f   'Meaning and Ambiguity in Punishment (and Penology)', Osgoode Hall LJ 10: 264–8

1973   a   III.3   Review of John Rawls, *A Theory of Justice* (1972), Oxford Magazine 90 no. 1 (new series) (26 January)

     b   III.18   'The Rights and Wrongs of Abortion: A Reply to Judith Jarvis Thomson', Philosophy & Public Affairs 2: 117–45

     c   'Constitutional Law', *Annual Survey of Commonwealth Law 1972* (Butterworth), 2–8, 23–56, 62–6

1974   a   'Constitutional Law', *Annual Survey of Commonwealth Law 1973* (Butterworth), 1–66

     b   'Commonwealth and Dependencies', in *Halsbury's Laws of England*, vol. 6 (4th edn, Butterworth), 315–601

     c   'Rights and Wrongs in Legal Responses to Population Growth', in J.N. Santamaria (ed.), *Man—How Will He Survive?* (Adelaide), 91–100

     d   Review of R.S. Gae, *The Bank Nationalisation Case and the Constitution*, Modern L Rev 37: 120

1975   'Constitutional Law', *Annual Survey of Commonwealth Law 1974* (Butterworth), 1–61

1976   a   'Constitutional Law', *Annual Survey of Commonwealth Law 1975* (Butterworth), 1–56

     b   Chapters 18–21 (with Germain Grisez), in R. Lawler, D.W. Wuerl, and T.C. Lawler (eds), *The Teaching of Christ* (Huntingdon, IN: OSV), 275–354

1977   a   I.3   'Scepticism, Self-refutation and the Good of Truth', in P.M. Hacker and J. Raz (eds), *Law, Morality and Society: Essays in Honour of H.L.A. Hart* (OUP), 247–67

     b   'Some Formal Remarks about "Custom"', in International Law Association, Report of the First Meeting [April 1977] on the Theory and Methodology of International Law, 14–21

1978   a   'Catholic Social Teaching: *Populorum Progressio* and After', Church Alert (SODEPAX Newsletter) 19: 2–9; also in James V. Schall (ed.), *Liberation Theology in Latin America* (San Francisco: Ignatius Press, 1982)

	b		'Conscience, Infallibility and Contraception', The Month 239: 410–17
	c		'Abortion: Legal Aspects of', in Warren T. Reich (ed.), *Encyclopedia of Bioethics* (New York: Free Press), 26–32
1979	a	V.18	'Catholic Faith and the World Order: Reflections on E.R. Norman', Clergy Rev 64: 309–18
			'The Foundations of Human Rights', Cooperation in Education 26: 19–28
1980	a		*Natural Law and Natural Rights* (OUP) (425 pp)

        Legge Naturali e Diritti Naturali (trans. F. Di Blasi) (Milan: Giappichelli, 1996)

        Ley Natural y Derechos Naturales (trans. C. Orrego) (Buenos Aires: Abeledo-Perrot, 2000)

        Prawo naturalne i uprawnienia naturalne (trans. Karolina Lossman) Klasycy Filozofii Prawa (Warsaw: Dom Wydawniczy ABC, 2001)

        自然法与自然权利 ([Mandarin] trans. Jiaojiao Dong, Yi Yang, Xiaohui Liang) (Beijing: 2004)

        Lei Natural e Direitos Naturais (trans. Leila Mendes) (Sao Leopoldo, Brazil: Editora Unisinos, 2007)

    b   'Reflections on an Essay in Christian Ethics: Part I: Authority in Morals', Clergy Rev 65: 51–7; 'Part II: Morals and Method', 87–93

    c   V.19 'The Natural Law, Objective Morality, and Vatican II', in William E. May (ed.), *Principles of Catholic Moral Life* (Chicago: Franciscan Herald Press), 113–49

1981	a		[*British North America Acts: The Role of Parliament*: Report from the Foreign Affairs Committee, House of Commons Paper 1980–81 HC 42 (21 January) (87 pp)]
	b		'Observations de M J.M. Finnis' [on Georges Kalinowski's review of *Natural Law and Natural Rights*], Archives de Philosophie du Droit 26: 425–7
	c		[Foreign Affairs Committee, *Supplementary Report on the British North America Acts: The Role of Parliament*, House of Commons Paper 1980–81 HC 295 (15 April) (23 pp)]
	d		[Foreign Affairs Committee, *Third Report on the British North America Acts: The Role of Parliament*, House of Commons Paper 1981–82 HC 128 (22 December) (17 pp)]
	e		'Natural Law and the "Is"-"Ought" Question: An Invitation to Professor Veatch', Cath Lawyer 26: 266–77
1982	a		(with Germain Grisez) 'The Basic Principles of Natural Law: A Reply to Ralph McInerny', AJJ 26: 21–31
	b		Review of Anthony Battaglia, *Towards a Reformulation of Natural Law*, Scottish J Theol 35: 555–6
1983	a		'The Responsibilities of the United Kingdom Parliament and Government under the Australian Constitution', Adelaide L Rev 9: 91–107
	b		*Fundamentals of Ethics* (OUP; Washington, DC: Georgetown University Press) (163 pp)
	c		'Power to Enforce Treaties in Australia—The High Court goes Centralist?', Oxford J Legal St 3: 126–30

	d		'The Fundamental Themes of *Laborem Exercens*', in Paul L. Williams (ed.), *Catholic Social Thought and the Social Teaching of John Paul II* (Scranton: Northeast Books), 19–31
	e		['In Vitro Fertilisation: Morality and Public Policy', Evidence submitted by the Catholic Bishops' Joint Committee on Bio-ethical Issues to the [Warnock] Committee of Inquiry into Human Fertilisation and Embryology, May, 5–18]
1984	a	I.10	i. 'Practical Reasoning, Human Goods and the End of Man', Proc Am Cath Phil Ass 58: 23–36; also in ii. New Blackfriars 66 (1985) 438–51
	b	IV.2	'The Authority of Law in the Predicament of Contemporary Social Theory', J Law, Ethics & Pub Policy 1: 115–37
	c		['Response to the Warnock Report', submission to Secretary of State for Social Services by the Catholic Bishops' Joint Committee on Bio-ethical Issues, December, 3–17]
	d		'IVF and the Catholic Tradition', The Month 246: 55–8
	e		'Reforming the Expanded External Affairs Power', in Report of the External Affairs Subcommittee to the Standing Committee of the Australian Constitutional Convention (September), 43–51
1985	a	III.1	'A Bill of Rights for Britain? The Moral of Contemporary Jurisprudence' (Maccabaean Lecture in Jurisprudence), Proc Brit Acad 71: 303–31
	b	IV.9	'On "Positivism" and "Legal-Rational Authority"', Oxford J Leg St 3: 74–90
	c	IV.13	'On "The Critical Legal Studies Movement"', AJJ 30: 21–42; also in J. Bell and J. Eekelaar (eds), *Oxford Essays in Jurisprudence: Third Series* (OUP, 1987), 145–65
	d		'Morality and the Ministry of Defence' (review), The Tablet, 3 August, 804–5
	e		'Personal Integrity, Sexual Morality and Responsible Parenthood', Anthropos [now Anthropotes] 1: 43–55
1986	a		'The "Natural Law Tradition"', J Legal Ed 36: 492–5
	b		'The Laws of God, the Laws of Man and Reverence for Human Life', in R. Hittinger (ed.), *Linking the Human Life Issues* (Chicago: Regnery Books), 59–98
1987	a	I.9	'Natural Inclinations and Natural Rights: Deriving "Ought" from "Is" according to Aquinas', in L. Elders and K. Hedwig (eds), *Lex et Libertas: Freedom and Law according to St Thomas Aquinas* (Studi Tomistici 30, Libreria Editrice Vaticana), 43–55
	b	II.8	'The Act of the Person' *Persona Verità e Morale*, atti del Congresso Internazionale di Teologia Morale, Rome 1986 (Rome: Città Nuova Editrice), 159–75
	c	III.2	'Legal Enforcement of Duties to Oneself: Kant v. Neo-Kantians', Columbia L Rev 87: 433–56
	d	IV.4	'On Positivism and the Foundations of Legal Authority: Comment', in Ruth Gavison (ed.), *Issues in Legal Philosophy: the Influence of H.L.A. Hart* (OUP), 62–75

	e	IV.12	'On Reason and Authority in Law's Empire', Law and Philosophy 6: 357–80
	f		Germain Grisez, Joseph Boyle, and John Finnis, 'Practical Principles, Moral Truth, and Ultimate Ends', AJJ 32: 99–151 (also, with original table of contents restored, in 1991d)
	g		*Nuclear Deterrence, Morality and Realism* (with Joseph Boyle and Germain Grisez) (OUP) (429 pp)
	h		'Answers [to questions about nuclear and non-nuclear defence options]', in Oliver Ramsbottom (ed.), *Choices: Nuclear and Non-Nuclear Defence Options* (London: Brasseys' Defence Publishers), 219–34
	i		'The Claim of Absolutes', The Tablet 241: 364–6
	j		['On Human Infertility Services and Bioethical Research', response by the Catholic Bishops' Joint Committee on Bio-ethical Issues to the Department of Health and Social Security, June, 3–12]
1988	a	V.21	'The Consistent Ethic: A Philosophical Critique', in Thomas G. Fuechtmann (ed.), *Consistent Ethic of Life* (Kansas: Sheed & Ward), 140–81
	b	V.20	'Nuclear Deterrence, Christian Conscience, and the End of Christendom', New Oxford Rev [Berkeley, CA] July–August: 6–16
	c		'Goods are Meant for Everyone: Reflection on Encyclical *Sollicitudo Rei Socialis*', L'Osservatore Romano, weekly edn, 21 March, 21
	d		' "Faith and Morals": A Note', The Month 21/2: 563–7
	e		Germain Grisez, Joseph Boyle, John Finnis, and William E. May, ' "Every Marital Act Ought to be Open to New Life": Toward a Clearer Understanding', The Thomist 52: 365–426, also in Grisez, Boyle, Finnis, and May, *The Teaching of Humanae Vitae: A Defense* (San Francisco: Ignatius Press); Italian trans. in Anthropotes 1: 73–122
	f		'Absolute Moral Norms: Their Ground, Force and Permanence', Anthropotes 2: 287–303
1989	a	II.5	'Persons and their Associations', Proc Aristotelian Soc Supp vol. 63: 267–74
	b	IV.3	'Law as Coordination', Ratio Juris 2: 97–104
	c	V.11	'On Creation and Ethics', Anthropotes 2: 197–206
	d		'La morale chrétienne et la guerre: entretien avec John Finnis', Catholica 13: 15–23
	e		'Russell Hittinger's Straw Man', Fellowship of Catholic Scholars Newsletter 12/2: 6–8 (corrigenda in following issue)
	f		'Nuclear Deterrence and Christian Vocation', New Blackfriars 70: 380–7
1990	a	I.12	'Aristotle, Aquinas, and Moral Absolutes', Catholica: International Quarterly Selection 12: 7–15; Spanish trans. by Carlos I. Massini Correas in Persona y Derecho 28 (1993), and in A.G. Marques

			and J. Garcia-Huidobro (eds), *Razon y Praxis* (Valparaiso: Edeval, 1994), 319–36
	b	IV.16	'Allocating Risks and Suffering: Some Hidden Traps', Cleveland State L Rev 38: 193–207
	c		'Natural Law and Legal Reasoning', Cleveland State L Rev 38: 1–13
	d	IV.17	'Concluding Reflections', Cleveland State L Rev 38: 231–50
	e	V.16	'Conscience in the Letter to the Duke of Norfolk', in Ian Ker and Alan G. Hill (eds), *Newman after a Hundred Years* (OUP), 401–18
	f		Joseph Boyle, Germain Grisez, and John Finnis, 'Incoherence and Consequentialism (or Proportionalism)—A Rejoinder', American Cath Phil Q 64: 271–7
	g		'The Natural Moral Law and Faith', in Russell E. Smith (ed.), *The Twenty-Fifth Anniversary of Vatican II: A Look Back and a Look Ahead* (Braintree, MA: Pope John Center), 223–38; discussion (with Alasdair MacIntyre), 250–62
1991	a	II.9	'Object and Intention in Moral Judgments according to St Thomas Aquinas', The Thomist 55: 1–27; rev. version in J. Follon and J. McEvoy (eds), *Finalité et Intentionnalité: Doctrine Thomiste et Perspectives Modernes*, Bibliothèque Philosophique de Louvain No. 35 (Paris: J. Vrin, 1992), 127–48
	b	II.10	'Intention and Side-effects', in R.G. Frey and Christopher W. Morris (eds), *Liability and Responsibility: Essays in Law and Morals* (CUP), 32–64
	c		*Moral Absolutes: Tradition, Revision and Truth* (Washington, DC: Catholic University of America Press) (115 pp); *Absolutos Morales: Tradición, Revisión y Verdad* (trans. Juan José García Norro) (Barcelona: Ediciones Internacionales Universitarias, EUNSA SA); *Gli assoluti morali: Tradizione, revisione & verità* (trans. Andrea Maria Maccarini) (Milan: Edizioni Ares, 1993)
	d		'Introduction', in John Finnis (ed.), *Natural Law*, vol. I (International Library of Essays in Law and Legal Theory, Schools 1.1) (Dartmouth: New York University Press), xi–xxiii
	e		'Introduction', in John Finnis (ed.), *Natural Law*, vol. II (International Library of Essays in Law and Legal Theory, Schools 1.2) (Dartmouth: Aldershot, Sydney), xi–xvi
	f		'A propos de la "valeur intrinsèque de la vie humaine"', Catholica 28: 15–21
	g		'Commonwealth and Dependencies', in *Halsbury's Laws of England*, vol. 6 re-issue (4th edn, London: Butterworth), 345–559
1992	a	I.14	'Natural Law and Legal Reasoning', in Robert P. George (ed.), *Natural Law Theory: Contemporary Essays* (OUP), 134–57; Spanish trans. By Carlos I. Massini Correas in Persona y Derecho 33 (1995)
	b	III.7	'Commentary on Dummett and Weithman', in Brian Barry and Robert E. Goodin (eds), *Free Movement: Ethical Issues in the Transnational Migration of People and of Money* (University Park, Pennsylvania: University of Pennsylvania Press), 203–10

c   III.15   'Economics, Justice and the Value of Life: Concluding Remarks',
             in Luke Gormally (ed.), *Economics and the Dependent Elderly:*
             Autonomy, Justice and Quality of Care (CUP), 189–98

d   V.9   *'Historical Consciousness' and Theological Foundations,* Etienne
             Gilson Lecture No. 15 (Toronto: Pontifical Institute of
             Mediaeval Studies) (32 pp)

e   V.17   'On the Grace of Humility: A New Theological Reflection', The
             Allen Review 7: 4–7

1993   a   II.16/   'Abortion and Health Care Ethics', in Raanan Gillon (ed.),
           III.19   *Principles of Health Care Ethics* (Chichester: John Wiley), 547–57

       b   'The Legal Status of the Unborn Baby', Catholic Medical Quarterly
                    43: 5–11

       c   II.19   *'Bland*: Crossing the Rubicon?', LQR 109: 329–37

       d   'Theology and the Four Principles: A Roman Catholic View I'
                    (with Anthony Fisher OP), in Raanon Gillon (ed.), *Principles of*
                    Health Care Ethics (Chichester: John Wiley), 31–44

       e   'The "Value of Human Life" and "The Right to Death": Some
                    Reflections on *Cruzan* and Ronald Dworkin', Southern Illinois
                    University LJ 17: 559–71

1994   a   II.12   'On Conditional Intentions and Preparatory Intentions', in Luke
                    Gormally (ed.), *Moral Truth and Moral Tradition: Essays in Honour*
                    of Peter Geach and Elizabeth Anscombe (Dublin: Four Courts
                    Press), 163–76

       b   'Law, Morality, and "Sexual Orientation"', Notre Dame L Rev
                    69: 1049–76; also, with additions, Notre Dame J Law, Ethics &
                    Public Policy 9 (1995) 11–39

       c   'Liberalism and Natural Law Theory', Mercer L Rev 45: 687–704

       d   '"Shameless Acts" in Colorado: Abuse of Scholarship in
                    Constitutional Cases', Academic Questions 7/4: 10–41

       e   Germain Grisez and John Finnis, 'Negative Moral Precepts
                    Protect the Dignity of the Human Person', L'Osservatore
                    Romano, English edn, 23 February

       f   'Beyond the Encyclical', The Tablet, 8 January, reprinted in John
                    Wilkins (ed.), *Understanding* Veritatis Splendor (London: SPCK),
                    69–76

       g   Germain Grisez, John Finnis, and William E. May,
                    'Indissolubility, Divorce and Holy Communion', New Blackfriars
                    75 (June), 321–30

       h   '"Living Will" Legislation', in Luke Gormally (ed.), *Euthanasia,*
                    Clinical Practice and the Law (London: Linacre Centre), 167–76

       i   'Unjust Laws in a Democratic Society: Some Philosophical and
                    Theological Reflections', in Joseph Joblin and Réal Tremblay
                    (eds), *I cattolici e la società pluralista: il caso delle leggi imperfette:*
                    atti del I Colloquio sui cattolici nella società pluralista: Roma, 9–12
                    Novembre 1994 (Bologna: ESP), 99–114

1995   a   II.11   'Intention in Tort Law', in David Owen (ed.), *Philosophical*
                    Foundations of Tort Law (OUP), 229–48

b   III.14 'A Philosophical Case against Euthanasia', 'The Fragile Case for Euthanasia: A Reply to John Harris', and 'Misunderstanding the Case against Euthanasia: Response to Harris's First Reply', in John Keown (ed.), *Euthanasia: Ethical, Legal and Clinical Perspectives* (CUP), 23–35, 46–55, 62–71

c   'History of Philosophy of Law' (465–8), 'Problems in the Philosophy of Law' (468–72), 'Austin' (67), 'Defeasible' (181), 'Dworkin' (209–10), 'Grotius' (328), 'Hart' (334), 'Legal Positivism' (476–7), 'Legal Realism' (477), 'Natural Law' (606–7), 'Natural Rights' (607), in Ted Honderich (ed.), *Oxford Companion to Philosophy* (OUP)

1996 a   III.5 'Is Natural Law Theory Compatible with Limited Government?', in Robert P. George (ed.), *Natural Law, Liberalism, and Morality* (OUP), 1–26

b   III.13 'The Ethics of War and Peace in the Catholic Natural Law Tradition', in Terry Nardin (ed.), *The Ethics of War and Peace* (Princeton University Press), 15–39

c   IV.7 'The Truth in Legal Positivism', in Robert P. George (ed.), *The Autonomy of Law: Essays on Legal Positivism* (OUP), 195–214

d   'Unjust Laws in a Democratic Society: Some Philosophical and Theological Reflections', Notre Dame L Rev 71: 595–604 (a revised version of 1994i)

e   I.13 'Loi naturelle', in Monique Canto-Sperber (ed.), *Dictionnaire de Philosophie Morale* (Paris: Presses Universitaires de France), 862–8

1997 a   'Natural Law—Positive Law', in A. Lopez Trujillo, I. Herranz, and E. Sgreccia (eds), *'Evangelium Vitae' and Law* (Rome: Libreria Editrice Vaticana), 199–209

b   I.15 'Commensuration and Public Reason', in Ruth Chang (ed.), *Incommensurability, Comparability and Practical Reasoning* (HUP), 215–33, 285–9

c   III.21 'Law, Morality and "Sexual Orientation"', in John Corvino (ed.), *Same Sex: Debating the Ethics, Science, and Culture of Homosexuality* (Lanham: Rowman & Littlefield), 31–43

d   III.22 'The Good of Marriage and the Morality of Sexual Relations: Some Philosophical and Historical Observations', AJJ 42: 97–134

1998 a   I.16 'Public Reason, Abortion and Cloning', Valparaiso Univ LR 32: 361–82

b   III.16 'Euthanasia, Morality and Law', Loyola of Los Angeles L Rev 31: 1123–45

c   V.3 'On the Practical Meaning of Secularism', Notre Dame L Rev 73: 491–515

d   *Aquinas: Moral, Political, and Legal Theory* (OUP) (xxi + 385 pp)

e   'Public Good: The Specifically Political Common Good in Aquinas', in Robert P. George (ed.), *Natural Law and Moral Inquiry* (Washington, DC: Georgetown University Press), 174–209

	f		'Natural Law', in Edward Craig (ed.), *Routledge Encyclopaedia of Philosophy*, vol. 6 (London: Routledge), 685–90
1999	a	I.2	'Natural Law and the Ethics of Discourse', AJJ 43: 53–73; also in Ratio Juris 12: 354–73
	b	III.12	'Retribution: Punishment's Formative Aim', AJJ 44: 91–103
	c	IV.20	'The Fairy Tale's Moral', LQR 115: 170–5
	d	V.6	'The Catholic Church and Public Policy Debates in Western Liberal Societies: The Basis and Limits of Intellectual Engagement', in Luke Gormally (ed.), *Issues for a Catholic Bioethic* (London: Linacre Centre), 261–73
	e		'What is the Common Good, and Why does it Concern the Client's Lawyer?', South Texas L Rev 40: 41–53
2000	a	II.1	'The Priority of Persons', in Jeremy Horder (ed.), *Oxford Essays in Jurisprudence, Fourth Series* (OUP), 1–15
	b	II.17	'Some Fundamental Evils of Generating Human Embryos by Cloning', in Cosimo Marco Mazzoni (ed.), *Etica della Ricerca Biologica* (Florence: Leo S. Olschki Editore), 115–23; also in C.M. Mazzoni (ed.), *Ethics and Law in Biological Research* (The Hague, London: Martinus Nijhoff; Boston: Kluwer, 2002), 99–106
	c		'Abortion, Natural Law and Public Reason', in Robert P. George and Christopher Wolfe (eds), *Natural Law and Public Reason* (Washington, DC: Georgetown University Press), 71–105
	d		'On the Incoherence of Legal Positivism', Notre Dame L Rev 75: 1597–611
	e		'God the Father', in Peter Newby (ed.), *Occasional Papers from the Millennium Conferences at the Oxford University Catholic Chaplaincy* No. 1 (Oxford), 24–6
2001	a	II.13	'"Direct" and "Indirect": A Reply to Critics of Our Action Theory' (with Germain Grisez and Joseph Boyle), The Thomist 65: 1–44
	b	III.6	'Virtue and the Constitution of the United States', Fordham L Rev 69: 1595–602
	c		'Reason, Faith and Homosexual Acts', Catholic Social Science Review 6: 61–9
2002	a	IV.5	'Natural Law: The Classical Tradition', in Jules Coleman and Scott Shapiro (eds), *The Oxford Handbook of Jurisprudence and Philosophy of Law* (OUP), 1–60
	b	V.22	'Secularism, the Root of the Culture of Death', in Luke Gormally (ed.), *Culture of Life—Culture of Death* (London: Linacre Centre)
	c		'Aquinas on *jus* and Hart on Rights: A Response', Rev of Politics 64: 407–10
	d		Patrick H. Martin and John Finnis, 'The Identity of "Anthony Rivers"', Recusant History 26: 39–74
	e		—— and —— 'Tyrwhitt of Kettleby, Part I: Goddard Tyrwhitt, Martyr, 1580', Recusant History 26: 301–13
2003	a	III.8	'Natural Law & the Re-making of Boundaries', in Allen Buchanan and Margaret Moore (eds), *States, Nations, and Boundaries: The Ethics of Making Boundaries* (CUP), 171–8

b	IV.1	'Law and What I Truly Should Decide', AJJ 48: 107–30
c	V.10	'Saint Thomas More and the Crisis in Faith and Morals', The Priest 7/1: 10–15, 29–30
d		'Secularism, Morality and Politics', L'Osservatore Romano, English edn, 29 January, 9
e		'Shakespeare's Intercession for *Love's Martyr*' (with Patrick Martin), Times Literary Supplement, no. 5220, 18 April, 12–14
f		'An Intrinsically Disordered Attraction', in John F. Harvey and Gerard V. Bradley (eds), *Same-Sex Attraction: A Parents' Guide* (South Bend: St Augustine's Press), 89–99
g		'Nature and Natural Law in Contemporary Philosophical and Theological Debates: Some Observations', in Juan Correa and Elio Sgreccia (eds), *The Nature & Dignity of the Human Person as the Foundation of the Right to Life: The Challenges of Contemporary Culture* (Rome: Libreria Editrice Vaticana), 81–109
h		Patrick H. Martin and John Finnis, 'Tyrwhitt of Kettleby, Part II: Robert Tyrwhitt, a Main Benefactor of John Gerard SJ, 1599–1605', Recusant History 27: 556–69
i		—— and —— 'Thomas Thorpe, "W.S." and the Catholic Intelligencers', Elizabethan Literary Renaissance, 1–43
j		—— and —— '*Caesar*, Succession, and the Chastisement of Rulers', Notre Dame L Rev 78: 1045–74
k		'Commonwealth and Dependencies', in *Halsbury's Laws of England*, vol. 6 re-issue (4th edn, London: Butterworth), 409–518
l		'Abortion for Cleft Palate: The Human Fertilisation and Embryology Act 1990', Sunday Telegraph, 7 December
m		'An Oxford Play Festival in 1582' (with Patrick Martin), Notes & Queries 50: 391–4
2004 a	II.18	'Per un'etica dell'eguaglianza nel diritto alla vita: Un commento a Peter Singer', in Rosangela Barcaro and Paolo Becchi (eds), *Questioni Mortali: L'Attuale Dibattito sulla Morte Cerebrale e il Problema dei Trapianti* (Naples: Edizioni Scientifiche Italiane), 127–39
b	IV.22	'Helping Enact Unjust Laws without Complicity in Injustice', AJJ 49: 11–42
2005 a	I.1	'Foundations of Practical Reason Revisited', AJJ 50: 109–32
b	I.4	'Self-referential (or Performative) Inconsistency: Its Significance for Truth', Proceedings of the Catholic Philosophical Association 78: 13–21
c	II.2	'"The Thing I Am": Personal Identity in Aquinas and Shakespeare', Social Philosophy & Policy 22: 250–82; also in Ellen Frankel Paul, Fred D. Miller, and Jeffrey Paul (eds), *Personal Identity* (CUP), 250–82
d	IV.6	'Philosophy of Law' (Chinese trans.), in Ouyang Kang (ed.), *The Map of Contemporary British and American Philosophy* (Beijing: Dangdai Yingmei Zhexue Ditu), 388–413

	e		'On "Public Reason"', in *O Racji Pulicznej* (Warsaw: Ius et Lex), 7–30 (Polish trans.), 33–56 (English original); <http://ssrn.com/abstract=955815>
	f		'Restricting Legalised Abortion is not Intrinsically Unjust', in Helen Watt (ed.), *Cooperation, Complicity & Conscience* (London: Linacre Centre), 209–45
	g		'A Vote Decisive for … a More Restrictive Law', in Helen Watt (ed.), *Cooperation, Complicity & Conscience* (London: Linacre Centre), 269–95
	h		'Aquinas' Moral, Political, and Legal Philosophy', Stanford Encyclopedia of Philosophy; <http://plato.stanford.edu/entries/aquinas-moral-political/>
	i		Patrick H. Martin and John Finnis, 'Benedicam Dominum: Ben Jonson's Strange 1605 Inscription', Times Literary Supplement, 4 November, 12–13
	j		—— and —— 'The Secret Sharers: "Anthony Rivers" and the Appellant Controversy, 1601–2', Huntingdon Library Q 69/2: 195–238
2006	a	V.4	'Religion and State: Some Main Issues and Sources', AJJ 51: 107–30
	b		'Observations for the Austral Conference to mark the 25th Anniversary of *Natural Law and Natural Rights*', Cuadernos de Extensión Jurídica (Universidad de los Andes) no. 13: 27–30
2007	a	III.9	'Nationality, Alienage and Constitutional Principle', LQR 123: 417–45
	b	IV.10	'On Hart's Ways: Law as Reason and as Fact', AJJ 52: 25–53; also in Matthew Kramer and Claire Grant (eds), *The Legacy of H.L.A. Hart: Legal, Political & Moral Philosophy* (OUP, 2009), 1–27
	c		'Natural Law Theories', Stanford Encyclopedia of Philosophy; <http://plato.stanford.edu/entries/natural-law-theories/>
2008	a	I.5/ II.7/V.8	'Reason, Revelation, Universality and Particularity in Ethics', AJJ 53: 23–48
	b	II.6	'Universality, Personal and Social Identity, and Law', address, Congresso Sul-Americano de Filosofia do Direito, Porto Alegre, Brazil, 4 October 2007; Oxford Legal Studies Research Paper 5; <http://ssrn.com/abstract=1094277>
	c	III.20	'Marriage: A Basic and Exigent Good', The Monist 91: 396–414
	d	[V.13]	'Grounds of Law & Legal Theory: A Response', Legal Theory 13: 315–44
	e		'Common Law Constraints: Whose Common Good Counts?', Oxford Legal Studies Research Paper 10; <http://ssrn.com/abstract_id=1100628>
	f		*Humanae Vitae*: A New Translation with Notes (London: Catholic Truth Society) (31 pp)
2009	a	II.3	'Anscombe's Essays', National Catholic Bioethics Q 9/1: 199–207
	b	IV.11	'H.L.A. Hart: A Twentieth Century Oxford Political Philosopher', AJJ 54: 161–85

c   V.1   'Does Free Exercise of Religion Deserve Constitutional Mention?',
            AJJ 54: 41–66

d   V.2   'Telling the Truth about God and Man in a Pluralist Society:
            Economy or Explication?', in Christopher Wolfe (ed.), *The Naked
            Public Square Revisited: Religion & Politics in the Twenty-First
            Century* (Wilmington: ISI Books), 111–25, 204–9

e   'Endorsing Discrimination between Faiths: A Case of Extreme
            Speech?', in Ivan Hare and James Weinstein (eds), *Extreme Speech
            and Democracy* (OUP), 430–41

f   'Discrimination between Religions: Some Thoughts on Reading
            Greenawalt's *Religion and the Constitution*', Constitutional
            Commentary 25: 265–71

g   'Commonwealth', in *Halsbury's Laws of England*, vol. 13 (5th edn,
            London: LexisNexis), 471–589

h   'Why Religious Liberty is a Special, Important and Limited Right',
            Notre Dame Legal Studies Paper 09–11; <http://ssrn.com/
            abstract=1392278>

i   'The Lords' Eerie Swansong: A Note on *R. (Purdy) v Director of
            Public Prosecutions*', Oxford Legal Studies Research Paper 31;
            <http://ssrn.com/abstract=1477281>

j   'The Mental Capacity Act 2005: Some Ethical and Legal Issues',
            in Helen Watt (ed.), *Incapacity & Care: Controversies in Healthcare
            and Research* (London: Linacre Centre), 95–105

k   'Debate over the Interpretation of *Dignitas personae*'s Teaching on
            Embryo Adoption', National Catholic Bioethics Q 9: 475–8

2010   a   II.14   'Directly Discriminatory Decisions: A Missed Opportunity', LQR
                      126: 491–6

        b   'Law as Idea, Ideal and Duty: A Comment on Simmonds, *Law as a
                    Moral Idea*', Jurisprudence 1: 247–53

OTHER WORKS CITED

Abbott, Walter M. SJ (ed.) (1966), *The Documents of Vatican II* (London and New York: Herder)

Anscombe, Elizabeth ([1961] 1981), 'War and Murder', in her *Collected Philosophical Papers*, vol. 3 (Oxford: Blackwell), 51–61

——(1972), 'Reply' [to Peter Winch, Michael Tanner, and Bernard Williams, in The Human World 9: 48–51, as revised and abridged] in M.D. Bayles (ed.), *Ethics and Population* (Cambridge, Mass.: Schenkman Publishing, 1976), 160–1

Arber, Edward (ed.) (1895), *A Harmony of the Essays etc. of Francis Bacon* (Westminster: Constable)

Aubert, Jean Marie (1964), *Loi de Dieu: Lois des Hommes* (Tournai: Desclée)

Ayer, A.J. (1973), 'The Claims of Theology', The Listener (9 August) 90/2315: 167–8 (also in Ayer, *The Central Questions of Philosophy* (London: Weidenfeld & Nicolson; New York: Morrow, 1974), 211–35)

Balthasar, Hans Urs von (1987), *Kleiner Diskurs über die Hölle* (Einsiedeln: Johannes)

——(1988), *Dare We Hope 'That All Men Be Saved'? with a Short Treatise on Hell* (San Francisco: Ignatius Press) (*Was dürfen wir hoffen?* (Einsiedeln: Johannes, 1986))

Becker, Carl (1932), *The Heavenly City of the Eighteenth-Century Philosophers* (New Haven: Yale University Press)

Bouyer, Louis (1982), *The Church of God: Body of Christ and Temple of the Spirit*, (trans. Charles Quinn) (Quincy: Franciscan Press)

Boyle, Joseph M. (1972), 'Self-Referential Inconsistency, Inevitable Falsity and Metaphysical Argumentation', Metaphilosophy 3: 25–42

——, Grisez, Germain, and Tollefsen, Olaf (1976), *Free Choice: A Self-Referential Argument* (Notre Dame: University of Notre Dame Press)

——(1978), '*Praeter Intentionem* in Aquinas', The Thomist 42: 649–65

——(1984), 'The Principle of Double Effect: Good Actions Entangled in Evil', in Donald G. McCarthy (ed.), *Moral Theology Today: Certitudes and Doubts* (Saint Louis: Pope John Center)

——(1998), 'The Place of Religion in the Practical Reasoning of Individuals and Groups', AJJ 43: 1–24

——(1999), 'Collaboration and Integrity: How to Think Clearly about Moral Problems of Co-operation', in Luke Gormally (ed.), *Issues for a Catholic Bioethic* (London: Linacre Centre), 187–99

Bradley, Gerard V. (2007), *Religious Liberty in the American Republic* (Washington, DC: The Heritage Foundation)

Braine, David (1994), *The Human Person: Animal and Spirit* (Notre Dame: University of Notre Dame Press)

Brown, Peter R.L. ([1967] 1990), *Augustine of Hippo: A Biography* (Berkeley: University of California Press)

Campbell, W.E. (1949), *Erasmus, Tyndale, and More* (London: Eyre & Spottiswoode; Milwaukee: Bruce Publishing)

Castelli, Jim (1983), *The Bishops and the Bomb* (New York: Doubleday)

Chadwick, Owen (1975), *The Secularization of the European Mind in the Nineteenth Century* (CUP)

Charlton, William (1988), *Philosophy and Christian Belief* (London: Sheed & Ward)

Congregation for the Doctrine of the Faith (1974), *Quaestio de Abortu. Declaration on Procured Abortion*, 18 November: AAS 66: 730–47

—— (1979), *Letter on Certain Questions regarding Eschatology*, 17 May: AAS 71: 939–43

—— (1987), *Donum Vitae. Instruction on Respect for Human Life in its Origin and on the Dignity of Procreation*, 22 February: AAS 80: 70–102

Conzemius, V. (1978), 'Acton, Döllinger and Gladstone: A Strange Variety of Anti-Infallibilists', in J.D. Bastable (ed.), *Newman and Gladstone: Centennial Essays* (Dublin: Veritas), 27–55

Crowe, Frederick E. (ed.) (1985), *A Third Collection: Papers by Bernard J.F. Lonergan, S.J.* (New York: Paulist Press)

Curran, Charles E. (1974), *New Perspectives in Moral Theology* (Notre Dame: Fides)

Dalton, William J. (1977), *Salvation and Damnation* (Butler, Wisc.: Clergy Book Service)

D'Arcy, Eric (1981), 'Conscience and Meta-Ethics Newman vis-à-vis Anglo-American Philosophy Today', in *John Henry Newman: Theologian and Cardinal* (Brescia and Rome: Studia Urbaniana), 173–213

Darwin, Charles ([1882] 1982), *The Autobiography of Charles Darwin, 1809–1882: with original omissions restored* (ed. Nora Barlow) (London: Collins)

Dawkins, Richard (2006), *The God Delusion* (London: Bantam Books)

—— (2009), 'Dawkins on Darwin', Times Literary Supplement, 11 February

Delhaye, Philippe OP (1964), *La Conscience Morale du Chrétien* (Tournai: Desclée), (trans. C. Underhill Quinn as *The Christian Conscience* (New York: Desclée, 1968))

Dewey, John (1929), *The Quest for Certainty: A Study of the Relation of Knowledge and Action* (New York: Minton, Balch)

Donagan, Alan (1977), *The Theory of Morality* (Chicago and London: University of Chicago Press)

Dorr, Donal J. (1969), 'Karl Rahner's "Formal Existential Ethics"', Irish Theol Q 36: 211–29

Duffy, Kevin (1984), 'Hell', Australasian Catholic Record 61: 358–68

Dummett, Michael (1979), *Catholicism and World Order: Some Reflections on the 1978 Reith Lectures* (London: Catholic Institute for International Relations)

Dworkin, Ronald et al. (1997), 'Assisted Suicide: The Philosophers' Brief', New York Review of Books, 27 March

—— (2006), *Justice in Robes* (HUP)

Eisgruber, Christopher L. and Sager, Lawrence G. (1994), 'The Vulnerability of Consciences: The Constitutional Basis for Protecting Religious Conduct', U Chicago L Rev 61: 1245–315

—— and —— (2007), *Religious Freedom and the Constitution* (HUP)

Fletcher, Joseph (1960), *Morals and Medicine* (Boston: Beacon)

Flew, Anthony (2007), *There is a God: How the World's Most Notorious Atheist Changed his Mind* (New York: HarperOne)

Ford, John C. SJ and Grisez, Germain (1978), 'Contraception and the Infallibility of the Ordinary Magisterium', Theological Studies 39: 258–312; also in Ford, John C. SJ, Grisez, Germain, Boyle, Joseph, Finnis, John, et al. (1988), *The Teaching of Humanae Vitae: A Defense* (San Francisco: Ignatius Press), 129–55

Fuchs, Joseph (1960), *Theologia Moralis Generalis, pars prima* (Rome: Editrice Università Gregoriana)

—— (1963), *De Castitate et Ordine Sexuali* (3rd edn, Rome: Editrice Università Gregoriana)

—— (1965), *Natural Law: A Theological Investigation* (Dublin: Gill)

—— (1984), *Christian Ethics in a Secular Arena* (Washington, DC: Georgetown University Press)

—— (1985), 'Christian Faith and the Disposing of Human Life', Theological Studies 46: 664

Gadamer, H.-G. (1965), *Wahrheit und Methode* (2nd edn, Tubingen: J.C.B. Mohr)

Gardeil, Antoine (1911), 'De la "certitude probable"', Revue des sciences philosophiques et théologiques 5: 237–66, 441–85

Garrow, David J. (1994), *Liberty and Sexuality: The Right to Privacy and the Making of Roe v Wade* (Oxford: Macmillan Maxwell International)

Geach, Mary and Gormally, Luke (eds) (2008), *Faith in a Hard Ground: Essays on Religion, Philosophy and Ethics by G.E.M. Anscombe* (Exeter and Charlottesville: Imprint Academic)

Geach, Peter T. (1969), *God and the Soul* (London: Routledge and Kegan Paul)

George, Robert P. (1997), 'Public Reason and Political Conflict: Abortion and Homosexuality', Yale LJ 106: 2475–504

Gessert, Robert and Hehir, J. Bryan (1976), *The New Nuclear Debate* (New York: Council on Religion and International Affairs)

Gilson, Etienne (1936), *The Spirit of Mediaeval Philosophy*, Gifford Lectures 1931–1932 (London: Sheed & Ward)

Glover, Jonathan (1977), *Causing Deaths and Saving Lives* (Harmondsworth: Penguin)

Greenawalt, Kent (1995), *Private Consciences and Public Reasons* (OUP)

Grisez, Germain (1970), 'Toward a Consistent Natural-Law Ethics of Killing', AJJ 15: 64

—— (1975), *Beyond the New Theism: A Philosophy of Religion* (Notre Dame: University of Notre Dame Press); reprinted with a new preface: *God: A Philosophical Preface to Faith* (South Bend: St Augustine's Press, 2005)

—— (1978) 'Against Consequentialism', AJJ 23: 21–72

—— (1985), 'Public Funding of Abortion: A Reply to Richard A. McCormick, SJ', Homiletic and Pastoral Rev 85.9 (June 1985): 32

—— (1989), 'When Do People Begin?', Proc Am Cath Phil Ass 63: 27–47

—— (1997), *The Way of the Lord Jesus*, vol. 3, *Difficult Moral Problems* (Quincy: Franciscan Press)

—— (1999), 'Healthcare as Part of a Christian's Vocation', in Luke Gormally (ed.), *Issues for a Catholic Bioethic* (London: Linacre Centre), 151–8

—— ([1975] 2004), *God? Philosophical Preface to Faith* (South Bend: St Augustine's Press) (first published by University of Notre Dame Press as *Beyond the New Theism*)

—— (2006), *Is Democracy Possible Here? Principles for a New Political Debate* (Princeton and Oxford: Princeton University Press)

—— and Boyle, Joseph M. (1979), *Life and Death with Liberty and Justice: A Contribution to the Euthanasia Debate* (Notre Dame and London: University of Notre Dame Press)

—— and —— (1998), 'Response to Our Critics and Our Collaborators', in Robert P. George (ed.), *Natural Law and Moral Inquiry: Ethics, Metaphysics, and Politics in the Work of Germain Grisez* (Washington, DC: Catholic University of America Press)

—— and Ford, John C. SJ (1978), 'Contraception and the Infallibility of the Ordinary Magisterium', Theological Studies 39: 258–312; also in Ford, John C. SJ, Grisez, Germain, Boyle, Joseph, Finnis, John et al. (1988), *The Teaching of Humanae Vitae: A Defense* (San Francisco: Ignatius Press), 129–55

—— and —— (1991), *Fulfilment in Christ: A Summary of Christian Moral Principles* (Notre Dame and London: University of Notre Dame Press)

Gula, Richard M. (1989), *Reason Informed by Faith: Foundations of Catholic Morality* (New York: Paulist Press)

Habermas, Jürgen (2008), *Between Naturalism and Religion: Philosophical Essays* (Cambridge, UK and Malden, Mass.: Polity Press)

Haldane, John and Smart, J.J.C. (1996), *Atheism & Theism* (Oxford: Blackwell)

Hamel, Edouard SJ (1975), 'La Théologie morale entre l'Ecriture et la raison', Gregorianum 56: 273–319

Hamel, Ronald P. and Himes, Kenneth R. O.F.M. (eds) (1989), *Introduction to Christian Ethics* (New York: Paulist Press)

Hampton, Jean (1993), 'The Moral Commitments of Liberalism', in David Copp, Jean Hampton, and John E. Roemer, *The Idea of Democracy* (CUP)

Harris, John (1985), *The Value of Life: An Introduction to Medical Ethics* (London and Boston: Routledge and Kegan Paul)

Harrison, Brian (1988), *Religious Liberty and Contraception* (Melbourne: John XXIII Fellowship Co-operative)

Hart, H.L.A. (1983), *Essays in Jurisprudence and Philosophy* (OUP)

Hemer, Colin J. (1989), *The Book of Acts in the Setting of Hellenistic History* (Tubingen: J.C.B. Mohr)

Hengel, Martin (1979), *Acts and the History of Earliest Christianity* [*Zur urchristlichen Geschichtsschreibung*] (London: SCM)

Himes, Michael J. (1983), 'The Human Person in Contemporary Theology: From Human Nature to Authentic Subjectivity', excerpted in Hamel and Himes (eds), *Introduction to Christian Ethics*

Hughes, Gerard J. SJ (1978), *Authority in Morals: An Essay in Christian Ethics* (London: Sheed & Ward)

—— (2004), 'Newman and the Particularity of Conscience', in Ian Ker and Terrence Merrigan (eds), *Newman and Faith* (Louvain Theological & Pastoral Monographs n. 31) (Louvain: Peeters Press), 53–74

Hurley, Susan (1989), *Natural Reasons: Personality and Polity* (OUP)

Jensen, Joseph (1978), 'Does *porneia* mean Fornication? A Critique of Bruce Malina', Novum Testamentum 20: 161–84

Jonsen, A.R. SJ et al. (1975), 'Critical Issues in Newborn Intensive Care: A Conference Report and Policy Proposal', Pediatrics 55: 756

Kant, Immanuel ([1785] 1969), *Foundations of the Metaphysics of Morals* (trans. Lewis White Beck) (Indianapolis: Bobbs-Merrill)

—— ([1790] 1960), *Religion Within the Limits of Reason Alone* (trans. Theodore M. Greene and Hoyt H. Hudson) (New York: Harper and Row)

Kenny, Anthony (1983), *Thomas More* (OUP)

Kiely, Bartholomew SJ (1985), 'The Impracticability of Proportionalism', Gregorianum 66: 655–86

Kittel, Gerhard (1964), *A Theological Dictionary of the New Testament* (trans. and ed. Geoffrey W. Bromiley) (Grand Rapids: Eerdmans)

Knauer (1979), 'The Hermeneutic Function of the Principle of Double Effect', in Charles E. Curran and Richard A. McCormick (eds), *Readings in Moral Theology No 1* (New York: Paulist Press), 1–39

Koppelman, Andrew (2002), 'Secular Purpose', Virginia L Rev 88: 87

—— (2006), 'Is it Fair to Give Religion Special Treatment?', U Ill L Rev: 571–603

Lacey, Nicola (2004), *A Life of H.L.A. Hart: The Nightmare and the Noble Dream* (OUP)

Lagrange, J.M. [Marie-Joseph] (1905), *Historical Criticism and the Old Testament* (London: Catholic Truth Society)

Langholm, Odd (1984), *The Aristotelian Analysis of Usury* (Bergen and Oslo: Universitetsforlaget AS)

Latourelle, René (1988), *The Miracles of Jesus and the Theology of Miracles* (Mahwah: Paulist Press)

Lee, Patrick (1981), 'Permanence of the Ten Commandments: St Thomas and His Modern Commentators', Theological Studies 42: 422–43

Linacre Centre (1982), *Euthanasia and Clinical Practice: Trends, Principles and Alternatives* (London: Linacre Centre)

Lonergan, Bernard (1958), *Insight: A Study of Human Understanding* (London: Longmans)

—— (1968), *Verbum* (London: Darton, Longman & Todd)

—— (1972), *Method in Theology* (London: Darton, Longman & Todd)

—— (1974), *A Second Collection* (London: Darton, Longman & Todd)

—— (1985), *A Third Collection: Papers by Bernard J.F. Lonergan, S.J.* (ed. Frederick E. Crowe) (New York: Paulist Press)

Macedo, Stephen (1990), *Liberal Virtues* (OUP)

Maritain, Jacques (1957), *On the Philosophy of History* (ed. Joseph W. Evans) (New York: Scribner)

Matthews, Steven (2008), *Theology and Science in the Thought of Francis Bacon* (Aldershot and Burlington: Ashgate)

McBrien, Richard P. (1980), *Catholicism* (Oak Green: Winston Press)

McCormick, Richard A. SJ (1964), 'Self-Assessment and Self-Indictment', in his *Contraception and the Natural Law* (Milwaukee: Bruce Publishing)

—— (1974), 'To Save or Let Die: The Dilemma of Modern Medicine', J Am Med Assoc 229: 172

—— (1975), 'A Proposal of "Quality of Life" Criteria for Sustaining Life', Hospital Progress 56: 79

—— (1975), 'Notes on Moral Theology', Theological Studies 36: 77–128

—— (1978), 'Notes on Moral Theology', Theological Studies 39: 76–138

—— (1981), *Notes on Moral Theology 1965 through 1980* (Washington, DC: University Press of America)

—— (1984), 'Medicaid and Abortion', Theological Studies 45: 715–21

—— (1985), *Health and Medicine in the Catholic Tradition: Tradition in Transition* (New York: Crossroad Pub Co.)

—— (1985), 'Notes on Moral Theology: 1984', Theological Studies 46: 715–21

—— (1988), 'The consistent ethic of life: is there an historical soft underbelly?', in Thomas G. Fuechtmann (ed.), *Consistent Ethic of Life* (Kansas: Sheed & Ward), 96–122

—— and Ramsey, Paul (eds) (1978), *Doing Evil to Achieve Good* (Chicago: Loyola University Press)

McInerny, Ralph (1995), *Aquinas Against the Averroists: On There Being Only One Intellect* (Lafayette: Purdue University Press)

Medeiros, Archbishop (1971), 'A Call to a Consistent Ethic of Life and the Law', *Pilot*, 10 July 1971, 7

Meyer, Ben F. (1979), *The Aims of Jesus* (London: SCM Press)

More, Thomas ([1532] 1973), *The Confutation of Tyndale's Answer*, vol. 9 of *The Complete Works of Thomas More* (ed. Louis A. Schuster) (New Haven: Yale University Press, 1963–97)

—— ([1534] 1951), *Dialogue of Comfort against Tribulation* (ed. Monica Stevens) (London: Sheed & Ward)

—— ([1535] 1969), *Thomas More's Prayer Book* (ed. Louis B. Martz and Richard Sylvester) (New Haven: Yale University Press)

—— ([1535] 1976), *De Tristitia Christi*, vol. 14 of *The Complete Works of St Thomas More* (ed. Clarence H. Miller) (Newhaven and London: Yale University Press)

Murphy, Mark C. (2008), 'Finnis on Nature, Reason, God', Legal Theory 13: 187–209

Nagel, Thomas (1987), 'Moral Conflict and Political Legitimacy', Philosophy and Public Affairs 16: 215–40

Newman, John Henry ([1833], 3rd edn 1871), *The Arians of the Fourth Century* (London: Lumley)

—— ([1843], [3rd edn 1871], 1909), *Fifteen Sermons Preached before the University of Oxford* (London: Longmans, Green)

—— ([1845] 1888), *An Essay on the Development of Christian Doctrine* (Notre Dame: University of Notre Dame Press, 1989)

—— ([1852, 1858], 1976), *The Idea of a University* (ed. Ian Ker) (OUP)

—— ([1864, 1865], 1913), *Apologia Pro Vita Sua: The Two Versions of 1864 and 1865* (ed. Wilfrid Ward) (OUP)

—— ([1864, 1865] 1967), *Apologia pro Vita Sua: Being a History of His Religious Opinions* (ed. Martin J. Svaglic) (OUP)

—— ([1870] 1985), *An Essay in Aid of a Grammar of Assent* (ed. Ian Ker) (OUP)

—— (1891), *Certain Difficulties Felt by Anglicans in Catholic Teaching Considered* (London and New York: Longmans, Green)

—— (1976), *The Theological Papers of John Henry Newman on Faith and Certainty* (ed. H.M. de Achaval and J.D. Holmes) (OUP)

Nicolau, Michael and Salaverri, Joachim (1962), *Sacrae Theologiae Summa* (Madrid: Biblioteca de Autores Cristianos)

Nietzsche, Friedrich ([1887] 1996), *On the Genealogy of Morals* (trans. Douglas Smith) (OUP)

Noonan, John T. (1965), *Contraception: A History of its Treatment by the Catholic Theologians and Canonists* (HUP)

Norman, Edward R. (1976), *Church and Society in England 1770–1970* (OUP)

—— (1978), 'Christianity and Politics', in Maurice Cowling (ed.), *Conservative Essays* (London: Cassell), 69–81

—— (1979), *Christianity and the World Order* (The BBC Reith Lectures, 1978) (OUP)

O'Connell, Timothy E. (1978), *Principles for a Catholic Morality* (New York: Seabury Press)

O'Connor, James (1989), 'Von Balthasar and Salvation', Homiletic and Pastoral Rev 89: 10–21

Parfit, Derek (1984), *Reasons and Persons* (OUP)

Perry, Michael J. (2008), 'Morality and Normativity', Legal Theory 13: 211–55

Peschke, Karl-Heinz SVD (1988), 'Tragfähigkeit und Grenzen des Prinzips der Doppelwirkung', Studia Moralia 26: 101

Porter, Jean (1996), '"Direct" and "Indirect" in Grisez's Moral Theory', Theological Studies 57: 611–32

Posner, Richard (1998), 'The Problematics of Moral and Legal Theory', Harv L Rev 111: 1637–717

—— (2003), *Law, Pragmatism, and Democracy* (HUP)

Price, Anthony (1989), *Love and Friendship in Plato and Aristotle* (OUP)

Quinlan, Michael (2009), *Thinking about Nuclear Weapons* (OUP)

Rahner, Karl (1964) 'Dangers in Catholicism Today: The Appeal to Conscience', in his *Nature and Grace: Dilemmas in the Modern Church* (New York: Sheed & Ward)

—— (1965), 'Natural Moral Law', in Karl Rahner and Herbert Vorgrimler, *Concise Theological Dictionary* (Freiburg: Herder)

—— (1972), 'The Historicity of Theology', in his *Theological Investigations*, IX (New York: Crossroad Pub Co., 1973)

—— (1973), *Theological Investigations*, IX (New York: Crossroad Pub Co.)

—— (1975), *Encyclopedia of Theology: A Conscise 'Sacramentum Mundi'* (London: Burns Oates)

—— (1976), 'Basic Observations on the Subject of Changeable and Unchangeable Factors in the Church', in his *Theological Investigations*, XIV (New York: Crossroad Pub Co.), 15

Ratzinger, Joseph (1985), *The Ratzinger Report: An Exclusive Interview on the State of the Church* (ed. Vittorio Messori) (Leominster: Fowler Wright)

Rawls, John (1971), *A Theory of Justice* (HUP)

—— ([1993] 1996), *Political Liberalism* (New York: Columbia University Press)

—— (1999), *The Law of Peoples* (HUP)

Raz, Joseph (1986), *The Morality of Freedom* (OUP)

—— (1990), 'Facing Diversity', Philosophy and Public Affairs 19: 3–46

—— ([1994] 1995), *Ethics in the Public Domain* (OUP)

—— (1998), 'Multiculturalism', Ratio Juris 11: 193–205

Regan, Augustine CSsR (1968), 'The Worth of Human Life', Studia Moralia 6: 207–77

—— (1979), *Thou Shall Not Kill* (Dublin: Mercier)

Reiman, Jeffrey H. (1997), *Critical Moral Liberalism: Theory and Practice* (Lanham, Md.; London: Rowman & Littlefield)

Richardson, Alan (1964), *History, Sacred and Profane* (London: SCM Press)

Rickman, H.P. (ed.) (1976), *Wilhelm Dilthey: Selected Writings* (CUP)

Rhonheimer, Martin (1987), *Natur als Grundlage der Moral* (Innsbruck: Tyrolia)

Robinson, John A.T. (1973), *Redating the New Testament* (London: SCM Press)

Saeed, Abdullay and Saeed, Hassan (2004), *Freedom of religion, Apostasy and Islam* (Aldershot: Ashgate)

Scheffler, Samuel (1982), *The Rejection of Consequentialism* (OUP)

Schmitt, Charles B. (1983), *John Case and Aristotelianism in Renaissance England* (Kingston, Ont.: McGill-Queen's University Press)

Schnackenburg, R. (1965), *The Moral Teaching of the New Testament* (New York: Herder)

Schüller, Bruno SJ (1980), 'La Moralité de moyens: la relation de moyen à fin dans une éthique normative de caractère téléologique', Recherches de Science Religieuse 68: 205

Searle, John R. (1992), *The Rediscovery of the Mind* (Cambridge, Mass.; London: MIT Press)

Sidgwick, Henry ([1874] 1907), *The Methods of Ethics* (7th edn, London: Macmillan)

Singer, Peter (1979), *Practical Ethics* (CUP)

Smart, J.J.C. and Haldane, John (1996), *Atheism & Theism* (Oxford: Blackwell)

—— and Williams, Bernard (1973), *Utilitarianism: For and Against* (CUP)

Spicq, Ceslau (1961), *Dieu et l'Homme selon le Nouveau Testament* (Paris: Ed. du Cerf)

—— (1970), *Théologie morale du Nouveau Testament* (Paris: Gabalda)

Staudinger, Hugo (1981), 'Die Zerstörung Jerusalems bei Flavius Josephus und im Evangelium des Lukas', Informationsdienst Deutsches Institut für Bildung und Wissen (Paderborn)

Tooley, Michael (1983), *Abortion and Infanticide* (OUP)

United States Catholic Bishops (1983), *The Challenge of Peace: God's Promise and Our Response: a Pastoral Letter on War and Peace* (Washington, DC: US Catholic Conference)

—— (1988), 'Building Peace: A Pastoral Reflection on the Response to "The Challenge of Peace"', 21 July 1988, Origins 18/9: 129–33

—— 'Report [by Ad Hoc Committee on the Moral Evaluation of Deterrence] on "The Challenge of Peace" and Policy Developments 1983–1988', 21 July 1988, Origins 18/9: 133

Van Riet, Simone (1976), 'La *Somme contre les Gentils* et la polémique Islamo-Chrétienne', in G. Verbeke and D. Verhelst, *Aquinas and Problems of His Time* (Leuven University Press; The Hague: Martinus Nijhoff), 150–60

Voegelin, Eric (1944), 'Nietzsche, the Crisis and the War', J of Politics 6: 177–212

—— (1957), *Plato and Aristotle* (Baton Rouge: Louisiana State University Press)

—— (1968), *Science, Politics, and Gnosticism: Two Essays* (South Bend, Ind.: Gateway Editions)

—— ([1958] 2000), 'Science, Politics, and Gnosticism', in *The Collected Works of Eric Voegelin*, vol. 5, *Modernity Without Restraint* (ed. Manfred Henningsen) (Columbia, Missouri: University of Missouri Press)

—— (1975), *From Enlightenment to Revolution* (ed. John Hallowell) (Durham, NC: Duke University Press)

Walter, James J. (1988), 'Response to John Finnis: A Theological Critique' in Thomas G. Fuechtmann (ed.), *Consistent Ethic of Life* (Kansas: Sheed & Ward), 182–95

Wegemer, Gerard B. and Smith, Stephen W. (2004), *A Thomas More Source Book* (Washington, DC: Catholic University of America Press)

Wenham, John W. (1991), *Redating Matthew, Mark and Luke: A Fresh Assault on the Synoptic Problem* (London: Hodder & Stoughton)

Williams, Bernard (1981), *Moral Luck* (CUP)

—— and Smart, J.J.C. (1973), *Utilitarianism: For and Against* (CUP)

Wojtyla, Karol (1979), *The Acting Person* (trans. Andrej Potocki) (Dordrecht: Reidel)

Wright, N. Thomas (1998), 'The Resurrection as a Historical Problem', 'Early Traditions and the Origins of Christianity', and 'The Resurrection and the Postmodern Dilemma', Sewanee Theological Review 41

—— (2002), 'Jesus' Resurrection and Christian Origins', Gregorianum 83: 615–35

—— (2003), *The Resurrection of the Son of God* (London: SPCK)

—— (2003), 'What Happened at the Resurrection?', The Church Times, 17 April

—— (2005), 'Resurrecting Old Arguments: Responding to Four Essays', J for the Study of the Historical Jesus 3: 209–32

ACKNOWLEDGEMENTS

The following essays were originally published as indicated:

Essay 1: 'Does Free Exercise of Religion Deserve Constitutional Mention?', American Journal of Jurisprudence 54: 41–66

Essay 2: 'Telling the Truth about God and Man in a Pluralist Society: Economy or Explication?', in Christopher Wolfe (ed.), *The Naked Public Square Revisited: Religion & Politics in the Twenty-First Century* (ISI Books, 2009), 111–25, 204–9

Essay 3: 'On the Practical Meaning of Secularism', Notre Dame Law Review 73: 491–515

Essay 4: 'Religion and State: Some Main Issues and Sources', American Journal of Jurisprudence 51: 107–30

Essay 6: 'The Catholic Church and Public Policy Debates in Western Liberal Societies: The Basis and Limits of Intellectual Engagement', in Luke Gormally (ed.), *Issues for a Catholic Bioethic* (Linacre Centre, 1999), 261–73

Essay 8: 'Reason, Revelation, Universality and Particularity in Ethics', American Journal of Jurisprudence 53: 23–48

Essay 9: *'Historical Consciousness' and Theological Foundations*, Etienne Gilson Lecture No. 15 (Toronto: Pontifical Institute of Mediaeval Studies)

Essay 10: 'Saint Thomas More and the Crisis in Faith and Morals', The Priest 7/1: 10–15, 29–30

Essay 11: 'On Creation and Ethics', Anthropotes 2: 197–206

Essay 13: 'Grounds of Law & Legal Theory: A Response', Legal Theory 13: 315–44

Essay 16: 'Conscience in the Letter to the Duke of Norfolk', in Ian Ker and Alan G. Hill (eds), *Newman after a Hundred Years* (OUP, 1990), 401–18

Essay 17: 'On the Grace of Humility: A New Theological Reflection', The Allen Review 7: 4–7

Essay 18: 'Catholic Faith and the World Order: Reflections on E.R. Norman', Clergy Review 64: 309–18

Essay 19: 'The Natural Law, Objective Morality, and Vatican II', in William E. May (ed.), *Principles of Catholic Moral Life* (Franciscan Herald Press, 1980), 113–49

Essay 20: 'Nuclear Deterrence, Christian Conscience, and the End of Christendom', New Oxford Review [Berkeley, CA] July–August: 6–16

Essay 21: 'The Consistent Ethic: A Philosophical Critique', in Thomas G. Fuechtmann (ed.), *Consistent Ethic of Life* (Sheed & Ward), 140–81

INDEX

Abbott, Chief Justice (Charles) II: 200, 204; IV: 341–2

Abbott, Thomas Kingsmill III: 55n, 64n

Abbott, Walter M IV: 52n; V: 173, 215n, 266

abduction I: 45n; IV: 11, 394
  explained IV: 1214

Abelard, Peter II: 245, 247; IV: 187n, 328n

abortion III: 15, 279, 282–312; V: 167, 172, 213, 221, 224, 266, 292, 296–7, 306–7, 340, 346–7, 352; and slavery I: 56–8; funding of II: 147, 171; V: 322–3; involvement in II: 170; III: 312–3; legalization of I: 56–8, 209, 256–7, 263–4, 267–74, 276; II: 27, 301; IV: 267n, 436–66; V: 70–2, 110, 121–3, 126, 315, 330–1; partial birth a.ˈ II: 250, 252, 268

Abraham V: 86n, 240, 272n, 298

action, act-analysis II.8–14; includes investigating and reflecting I: 19, 127, 135, 203, 303; includes deliberating I: 1, 5; includes discussing I: 41, 50; *see also* epistemological principle; intransitivity; marriage; natures; object

absolutes, moral, see affirmative, Aquinas, Aristotle, exceptionless, moral, rights

Acton, John V: 209n

Adair, Douglas I: 282n

Admiraal, Peter III: 266

affirmative [v negative] moral rules and responsibilities I: 101–2, 189; III: 7, 119; IV: 15, 128, 141, 143, 366, 368, 370, 373; V: 7, 221–2, 267, 285, 293–4, 311–4, 317–22, 324–7
  cannot be absolute I: 226

aggregative theories of right and wrong I: 205, 209–11, 225, 229, 234, 242, 245, 254; III: 32, 196, 242–4, 248, 250; IV: 53–5, 61, 121–2, 356, 368, 371; V: 77

Albert, St. V: 150

Alcibiades IV: 159

Alexander of Hales III: 187, 359–60n

Alexy, Robert I: 85n

Alkire, Sabina I: 10–11, 28

Allen, R.E. I: 41n, 49n, 51n, 186n; III: 100–1, 378n

Alphonsus Liguori, St. V: 216n, 219, 221n

Altman, Denis III: 59n

altruism II: 110; III: 69; IV: 57–61, 68, 75
  not friendship I: 47n

Ames, J.B. I: 228n; II: 209n, 211

Amin, Idi II: 84

analogical reasoning IV.19

analogy, analogical terms IV: 395–6; V: 131

Anderson, Elizabeth S. I: 235n, 253n

Ando, T. I: 160n

Andrews, J.A. III: 30

Angas, George Fife II: xii

Angas, George French II: xi

analogia fidei V: 159

analogical reasoning IV.19 and 129–30

analogy, analogical terms IV: 395–6; V: 131; defined I: 5, IV: 395–6; also I: 35, 97, 109, 254; II: 117, 215; III: 4, 24, 178, 326; IV: 109, 120, 160–1, 186, 312, 351, 438n; V: 32, 144, 205

anima mea non est ego I: 166; II: 40, 42; V: 330

Anscombe, G.E.M. (Elizabeth) embryonic life II: 291–2; friendship between strangers II: 129n; 'I' 93n; intention and double effect: 13–14, 76–7, 159, 189–93, 225n, 268n; III: 235, 296; IV: 236n; V: 366n; marriage and contraception V: 352, 355n, 358–9n, 362, 364–5; mystical value of human being I: 36; moral ought II: 74–5; proposal 3n; spirit 5–6, 8–9, 69–74; III: 4; state authority IV: 85–7; voting paradox III: 22n; IV: 54; *also* V: 116, 162

Anselm of Canterbury, St. V: 179n, 182

Aquinas, Thomas I: 14n; 'a liberal' V: 113 (*see also* affirmative v negative norms, central-case analysis, *ut in pluribus*)
  on 'act of generative kind' III: 326n, 382–3; IV: 135n; adjudication IV: 127–9; basic good of life I: 34; *beatitudo* and *beatitudo imperfecta* I: 162–72, 185; *bonum ex integra causa malum ex quocumque defectu* II: 172; connaturality I: 205; II: 73; conscience V: 10, 169, 171, 216, 218–20, 222; *consensus* II: 155–7, 231–2; created beings I: 96–7; deliberation as first *de seipso* I: 183; II: 50, 103; IV: 25; *determinatio* needed between reasonable options I: 230; IV: 149, 179, 181–2, 324; V: 318n; discourse opponents I: 44n;

Aquinas, Thomas (*cont.*)
  divine judgment II: 66; embryonic life II: 39n, 288; V: 307; epistemological